RACE AND NATIONALISM IN
TRINIDAD AND TOBAGO

SELWYN D. RYAN

Race and Nationalism in Trinidad and Tobago: a study of decolonization in a multiracial society

UNIVERSITY OF TORONTO PRESS

© University of Toronto Press 1972
  Toronto and Buffalo
  Printed in Canada
  ISBN 0-8020-5256-8
  ISBN Microfiche 0-8020-0095-9
  LC 70-185735

To Joy, Michele, and Kwamena

Contents

TABLES

MAPS

Acknowledgments

In the preparation of this book, I have been helped in many ways by such a variety of people that it would be difficult to name them all. The major financial support for the study came from a fellowship given by the Center for International Studies of Cornell University in 1963, and I wish to thank the then Director, Steven Muller, not only for arranging the fellowship, but for his encouragement and interest, and for his many helpful suggestions about the manuscript. Continuing financial assistance for additional field research and secretarial help came from York University, to which I also owe a great deal of gratitude. The book was published with the help of a grant from the Social Science Research Council of Canada, using funds provided by the Canada Council, and a grant from the Publications Fund of the University of Toronto Press.

I wish to record my appreciation to Professors Douglas Verney, Ivar Oxaal, Roy Thomas, and Frances Henry, who were kind enough to read parts of the manuscript and offer editorial suggestions. Thanks are also due to Wilfrid Alexander, Adrian Cola Rienzi, the late Rudranath Capildeo, Winston Mahabir, I.K. Merrit, and E.C. Richardson from whose conversations I benefited much. I also wish to thank the staff of Balisier House (PNM headquarters) and the Trinidad Public Library for the many courtesies extended me during my research trips to Trinidad. Of the various authors who have guided me through the labyrinths of Caribbean history, none has been more influential than Eric Williams, on whose pioneering studies I have relied heavily.

I am especially indebted to my wife, who not only collaborated in data collection and in typing and editing crude drafts of the manuscript, but stoically endured the many deprivations of time and companionship that my attachment to this project entailed.

The bulk of this work was written in 1967, though revisions have been made to take account of more recent events. Trinidad and the Caribbean in general are in a state of flux, and it is certain that parts of this analysis will be outdated by the time it appears in print. But this is a fate that all books which deal with contemporary politics have to suffer, and the problem is compounded with books that deal with the 'third world'.

SR
Port of Spain, July 1971

Abbreviations

ACDC *Action Committee of Democratic Citizens*
ANC *African National Congress*
BEWRU *British Empire Workers and Rate-payers Union*
BEHRP *British Empire Home Rule Party*
CNLP *Caribbean National Labour Party*
CLC *Caribbean Labour Congress*
CSA *Civil Service Association*
DLP *Democratic Labour Party*
EIC *East Indian Congress*
FLP *Federal Labour Party*
FWTU *Federated Workers Trade Union*
ILP *Independent Labour Party*
LP *Liberal Party*
LRC *Legislative Reform Committee*
NJAC *National Joint Action Committee*
OWTU *Oilfield Workers Trade Union*
POPPG *Party of Political Progress Groups*
PDP *People's Democratic Party*
PNM *People's National Movement*
PEM *People's Education Movement*
SWTU *Seamen and Waterfront Trade Union*
TECA *Teachers Economic and Cultural Association*
TLC *Trinidad Citizens League*
TLP *Trinidad Labour Party*
TSEFWTU *Trinidad Sugar Estates and Factory Workers Trade Union*

TUC *Trades Union Congress*
TWA *Trinidad Workingmen's Association*
UF *United Front*
UNIP *United National Independence Party*
URO *United Revolutionary Organization*
WFP *Workers and Farmers Party*
WINP *West Indian National Party*
WIIP *West Indian Independence Party*
YIP *Young Indian Party*

One Trinidad and Tobago dollar – $1 (TT) – is equal approximately to 50 cents US.

Leading newspapers of Trinidad and Tobago

The *Bomb* w
The *Clarion* w, *d*
The *Daily Mirror* D, *d*
The *East Indian Weekly* w, *d*
The *Express* D
The *Labour Leader* w, *d*
Moko o
The *Nation* w
The *People* w, *d*
The PNM *Weekly* w, *d*
The *Port of Spain Gazette* D, *d*

The *Statesman* w, *d*
The *Sunday Guardian* w
Tapia o
The *Trinidad Chronicle* (TC) D, *d*
The *Trinidad Guardian* (TG) D
The *Vanguard* w

w – weekly
D – daily
d – defunct
o – occasional

RACE AND NATIONALISM IN
TRINIDAD AND TOBAGO

We cannot get away from the critic's tempers, his impatiences, his sorenesses, his friendships, his spite, his enthusiasms, nay, his very politics and religion if they are touched by what he criticizes. They are all hard at work.

GEORGE BERNARD SHAW

Introduction

Trinidad is a small nation of about 1,980 square miles situated off the north-eastern coast of South America. Its population of approximately one million represents a microcosm of the world's peoples and is perhaps one of the most exciting laboratories for the study of race relations. Within its small compass are to be found people of African, Indian, European, and Chinese extraction, most of whom are descendants of those who came or were brought to the island to cultivate or manage the sugar plantations which were the mainstay of its economy up to the turn of the century. According to the 1960 census, which gave the population as 827,957, Negroes constitute roughly 43.5 per cent of the population, Indians (both Hindu and Moslem) approximately 36.5 per cent, Europeans 2 per cent, and Chinese 1 per cent. Mixtures – the combinations are numerous – account for about 17 per cent of the population. This latter figure would be much larger if it were possible to detect readily all those who are in fact racially mixed. Many who are classified as Negro or white can trace a European or African ancestor in their family history. Trinidad's religious diversity is even more bewildering than its racial complexity. Catholics (36 per cent), Presbyterians (4), Anglicans (21), Hindus (24), Moslems (6), Baptists (2), and a host of other Christian (6) and non-Christian sects (1 per cent) mingle in this dense little island state.

The present study attempts to analyse the transition to nationhood of this former British sugar-producing colony, and to examine some of the problems with which it has been confronted since it gained Independence. The principal aim has been to explore the influence which the island's cultural and ethnic diversity has had on the struggle for political and social reform and to suggest explanations for the failure of the programme of radical decolonization which nationalists had confidently assumed would follow upon political independence.

It is always difficult to determine where one phase of a country's history ends and another begins. Yet for heuristic purposes it is often necessary to invent epochal divisions where, properly speaking, none exist. Almost invariably, however, there occur in the life of a people decisive events which serve to call attention to groups, tendencies, and values which, up to that time, had not yet come into focus. The history of Trinidad and Tobago can be conveniently divided into six major periods. The first dates from 1498 when the island was discovered by Columbus for the King of Spain to 1797 when it was captured and integrated into the British Empire. The three centuries of Spanish rule did not result in much that was of great significance for the island's future development. The Spaniards had neither the will nor the resources to colonize the society effectively and until 1783 were never interested in large-scale settlement. Their main interest was in creating a mining economy based on precious metals. The failure to find gold or the famed El Dorado accounts in large part for Spanish negligence of Trinidad.

Perhaps the most significant contribution of Spanish rule in Trinidad was the decimation of the aboriginal Indians. The natives were enslaved and sold to other colonies, forced to convert to Catholicism and to engage in strenuous and unfamiliar economic activities. Many were tortured and put to death for resisting the *conquistadores*. The Indians proved incapable of adapting to the new socio-economic order, and by the time the British arrived on the island there were only about one thousand of them left. Spanish missionaries like Bartolomé de las Casas waged long and arduous struggles to alleviate the plight of the Indians, and though some success was eventually achieved, it came too late to prevent their progressive extinction. It was in this context that African slave labour was first imported into the island. Las Casas himself had argued that the African would make a better slave than the Indian since he was stronger, less primitive, and more adaptable.

In the latter years of Spanish rule there was an incursion of large numbers of aristocratic French *emigrés* and their slaves – victims of the Jacobin terror in France and in her Caribbean colonies – who were attracted by the liberal land grants offered in 1783 by the King of Spain to settlers of Catholic persuasion. Prior to this, Spain had tried to exclude all but Spaniards from settling or trading with Trinidad, and it is for this reason that the effective settlement and development of the colony came so much later than in other Caribbean colonies.

The second major period in Trinidad's history, which may be termed the old colonial order, dates from the British conquest in 1797 to the end of the First World War in 1918. It witnessed the consolidation of British rule and the plantation system, the emancipation of African slaves in 1834, the importation of Indian indentured labourers in 1845, and the first stages of the struggle for representative government. For most of this period the struggle was waged by the European community and mixed professional elements, though by the end of the nineteenth century a Negro working class had begun to develop political consciousness and to make demands of its own.

The third stage spans most of the inter-war years – 1919 to 1936. It was in this period that the reform movement became dominated by the Negro working class which, curiously enough, chose as its leader a radical European planter of Corsican extraction, Captain Arthur Cipriani. The period also witnessed the introduction of elected representatives into the Governor's Legislative Council for the first time in 1925. Whereas older British colonies had popularly elected assemblies, this system never became part of British constitutional practice in Trinidad. The Legislative and Executive Councils were progressively democratized by the addition of elected members, but the basic system remained unchanged until 1961 when bicameralism and responsible government were first introduced.

The year 1937 was perhaps the most decisive watershed in the colony's history. It was a year that witnessed the seizure of political leadership and initiative by Negroes and Indians following a dramatic general strike which heralded the beginning of fundamental changes in British colonial policy. The strike, which enveloped other West Indian colonies, seemed destructive and abortive at the time, but it had the effect of accelerating the pace of constitutional and socio-economic changes in the West Indies as a whole. It made the survival of the old colonial system virtually impossible. The strike was followed by the Second World War and the temporary cessation of open political agitation. The period 1937 to 1946 can be considered as the fourth stage in Trinidad's political development.

The year 1946 marked the beginning of the fifth and what might be called the modern period in Trinidad's history. The postwar years saw the introduction of universal suffrage, the maturation of the trade-union movement, the transfer of a considerable degree of executive authority to elected officials (1950), and the intensification of the movement for self-government and federation. The period, dominated by an ebullient Portuguese creole, Albert Gomes, came to an end in 1955 with the appearance of the first genuinely successful mass-nationalist movement under the leadership of Dr Eric Williams, one of the West Indies' most distinguished scholars. It was the People's National Movement under his leadership which took Trinidad to Independence in 1962. The Williams era, the sixth and most fascinating in Trinidad's chequered history, is now in its terminal phase. The massive street demonstrations in support of Black Power in February, March, and April of 1970, the imposition of a state of emergency, and the arrest and trial of large numbers of people for sedition and treason, in a very dramatic way signalled the passing of a phase of Trinidad's historical development and began what appears to be a period that will be marked by dictatorship, political instability, and economic collapse.

The main focus of this study concerns the periods from 1919 to 1971. The history of Trinidad in the years before 1919 has been dealt with by others, and only a brief analysis of that period has been attempted.[1] The post-1970 Williams era will have to be the subject of another study. Most of the work done on Trinidad after 1919 has been sociological and anthropological. Little of the political history of the island has been written and it is hoped that this pioneering effort, with all its limitations, will fill a gap in Caribbean historiography and stimulate further efforts to explore more deeply the experiences of this fascinating Caribbean country. It is also hoped that the study will be of some significance to people concerned with the general problem of decolonization in small and racially fragmented societies. Much of the literature and political discussion on political development has ignored the critical factor of size, and, as this study attempts to illustrate, options that may be possible in the large new states are not genuinely open to the smaller ones, especially those situated in the Atlantic crossroads.

In Trinidad and throughout the Caribbean debate on the meaning and reality of decolonization has been lively and acrimonious. Radical intellectuals and trade-union leaders in the area contend, quite rightly, that decolonization means something more than formal independence. They see independence as merely the framework on which the social, economic, and political structures of the old plantation society may be reorganized. Prior to Independence it was assumed that a programme designed to promote these goals would appeal to all ethnic elements in the society and that 'exogenously induced' sectional cleavages would be rendered marginal as the whole society mobilized itself to achieve genuine nationhood. Few believed that revolutionary violence would have been necessary to achieve significant structural changes. But in the English-speaking Caribbean today, the call for the violent overthrow of existing regimes is heard frequently among radical trade unionists and intellectuals. The radicals have now come to believe that the middle-class movements which led these territories to Independence have failed to

---

1   Eric Williams, *History of the People of Trinidad and Tobago*, New York, 1964; Gertrude Carmichael, *History of the West Indian Islands of Trinidad and Tobago, 1498–1900*, London, 1961; Carlton Ottley, *An Account of Life in Spanish Trinidad, 1498–1953*, Port of Spain, 1955; Donald Wood, *Trinidad in Transition*, Oxford, 1968; Hewan Craig, *The Legislative Council of Trinidad and Tobago*, London, 1951; James Millette, *The Genesis of Crown Colony Government: Trinidad 1783–1840*, Port of Spain, 1970.

come to grips with the plantation system and the racial and socially stratified society which it cradles, and they are convinced that the Cuban economic model is more relevant to the real problems of Caribbean society than the Puerto Rican, which relies heavily on subsidized private capital from the American mainland. The experiences of Guyana and Santo Domingo have also confirmed them in their belief that the electoral road is closed to any movement which is determined to challenge American imperialism in the hemisphere.[2]

Radicals complain that the dominant political movements of the region have remained sectional and that instead of narrowing the gaps between classes and ethnic groups, reformist politics have widened them. They do not accept the thesis of Furnivall and others that 'nationalism within a plural society is a disruptive force tending to shatter and not consolidate its social order.'[3] They believe that the problem is to be found in the character of the movements which parade as nationalist. Caribbean leaders, it is claimed, have done no more than create sectional blocs to maintain their political power.[4] They have not created genuinely national symbols relevant to the needs of Caribbean societies, nor have they given these symbols meaningful social content.[5] Instead they have moved into the positions once occupied by the former colonial élite without really deepening the basis of social and economic power.

Like the late Franz Fanon, a native of Martinique, they complain that the national élites of the 'third world' have lost touch with the people. According to Fanon, these privileged mandarins have pursued policies that create swollen and parasitic capitals which drain rural hinterlands of talent, resources, and

2 The Guyanese constitution was suspended in 1953 and the British and American Governments have worked very closely since to contain the Marxist leader Cheddi Jagan. Cf. Arthur Schlesinger, *A Thousand Days*, Boston, 1965, pp. 773–7. In the 1968 elections, a combination of electoral fraud and American intervention helped to defeat Jagan and the People's Progressive Party and to entrench Forbes Burnham's more accommodationist People's National Congress.
Santo Domingo was invaded by American troops in 1965 to head off what was feared to be a possible threat to the Monroe Doctrine. Chileans were however able to elect and install a Marxist régime in 1970 despite attempts by powerful corporate interests to get the American Government to intervene.
3 J.S. Furnivall, *Netherlands India: A Study of Plural Economy*, Cambridge, 1939, p. 468. For an analysis of some of the theoretical issues involved in the concept of pluralism, see M.G. Smith, *The Plural Society in the British West Indies*, Berkeley, 1965; Leo Despres, *Cultural Pluralism and Nationalist Politics in British Guyana*, New York, 1967.
4 For a perceptive analysis of the social basis of the People's National Movement in Trinidad, see Ivar Oxaal, *Black Intellectuals Come to Power*, Cambridge, Mass., 1968, esp. chap. 8.
5 Fred Riggs refers to the pseudo-nationalism of these movements as 'nostrification'. *Administration in Developing Countries*, Boston, 1964, p. 160.

energy. The parties they lead have ceased to be dynamic organisms expressing the needs of the masses. The result has been anarchy and the resurgence of tribal and racialist politics. Dissolving this class and communal tension required, at a minimum, 'an economic programme ... a doctrine concerning the division of wealth and social relations ... an idea of man and an idea of humanity. ... No demagogic formula and no collusion with the former occupying power can take the place of this programme.'[6] While Fanon did not rule out the possibility that these goals could be achieved by non-violent means, the odds were against it. 'Decolonization ... will not only come to pass after a murderous and decisive struggle. ... You do not turn any society ... upside down ... if you are not ... ready for violence at all times.'[7] Caribbean radicals believe that Fanon's diagnosis well defines the Caribbean situation, and they have echoed his call for violence.

While agreeing basically with the claims of the Caribbean left, the argument of this book (see Part Four) is that revolutionary violence in the Caribbean context is neither a meaningful nor a desirable alternative. The Algerian case on which many of Fanon's hypotheses are based offers no reason for optimism, and the evidence of the Cuban case is ambiguous. In any event, the peculiar combination of internal and international circumstances which allowed the Cuban revolution to succeed is not likely to reappear in the immediate future. As Regis Debray quite aptly remarked, 'The Revolution has revolutionized the counter-revolution.'[8] Whatever the truth about Cuba might be, it is clear that a Cuban-style revolution is not an option for Caribbean societies at the moment.

In Trinidad and Tobago, the overriding factors to be considered are size, population density, and the racial mixture. One finds several racially and culturally exclusive groups struggling for power and jobs within an extraordinarily small area. Rather than unite oppressed blacks and Indians in a class struggle to dislodge the present ruling-coalition, violence, whatever the original intention, may well turn into a fatal racial confrontation between the two groups.[9] As Max Weber warned and experience has shown, 'There are

6 *The Wretched of the Earth*, New York, 1966, p. 162.
7 *Ibid.*, p. 31.
8 *Revolution in the Revolution?*, New York, 1968. See Leo Huberman and Paul Sweezy, 'Socialism in Cuba,' *Monthly Review*, 1969, for a balanced account of the Cuban revolution. See also Arslan Humbaraci, *Algeria: A Revolution That Failed*, New York, 1966; David and Marina Ottaway, *Algeria: The Politics of a Socialist Revolution*, Berkeley, 1970.
9 In March and April 1970 Black Power militants attempted to link up with Indian sugar workers by making the symbolic gesture of helping them to cut cane. But during the massive street demonstrations that took place, several Indian-owned establishments were burned down or damaged. This was not the intention of serious

diabolical forces lurking in all violence ... and the final result of political action often, no, even regularly stands in completely inadequate and often paradoxical relation to its original meaning.'[10] It is not clear that the benefits of pursuing this strategy will outweigh the likely costs, both internally and externally, nor has it been demonstrated that it is the only available alternative, as it appears to be in Haiti and most of Latin America.

The smallness of Trinidadian society has helped to create a situation where social relationships within the dominant creole culture are remarkably fluid. There is not that latifundia-based class rigidity that one finds in many Latin American societies, nor that impersonal detachment one finds in larger societies which emerges and nurtures blinding attachments to violence.[11] Hate is not a characteristic of the political culture, though group tensions exist at several levels of the society.

As far as the Indian cultural fragment is concerned, a desire for social integration as a part of an oppressed *class* is not the dominating impulse. Status elevation and legitimacy as a group seems to be a considerably more relevant goal than the obscuring of all racial differences and peculiarities.[12]

militants, but the incidents allowed conservative elements in the Indian community to suggest that the triumph of Black Power would not be in the best interests of the Indian community. Indians in Trinidad could not have missed the remark made by Stokely Carmichael in Guyana that Black Power did not include Indians as such, and that blacks and Indians had to form separate political organizations. Radical Guyanese were visibly annoyed and Cheddi Jagan chided Carmichael: 'If the struggle is economic and ideological and is against imperialism, there is no necessity for expressing it in racial terminology. This is emotional and unscientific and causes confusion.' Indian racialists were, however, delighted to have their view confirmed by Carmichael. *Trinidad Guardian*, May 10, 1970 (hereafter cited as TG).

10 H. Gerth and C.W. Mills, *From Max Weber*, Oxford, 1959, p. 117. As Gordon Lewis also notes, 'There is a tendency in Debray, as in Fanon, to speak in semi-mystical terms of revolutionary violence as a cathartic agent ... and his argument comes perilously close to the grim error that Marx identified as "playing with revolution". There is a comparable tendency, then, to underestimate the legacy of hate and conflict that civil war leaves behind in any society.' 'Theory and Practice of Insurrection', in Huberman and Sweezy (eds.), *Regis Debray and the Latin American Revolution*, New York, 1968, p. 117. For a good analysis of the role of violence in Fanon's writings, see Peter Worsley, 'Revolutionary Theories', *Monthly Review*, vol. 1, no. 21, May, 1969, pp. 30–49.

11 As Douglas Hall remarks, 'In Jamaica, people live closely together, and the divisions of social class are not now so clear as they used to be. Familiarity need not bring contempt, but it will certainly wash away mystery, awe and majesty. The judge looks less formidable in his wig and gown if we have often seen him in his shorts.' 'The Colonial Legacy in Jamaica', *New World*, vol. 4, no. 3, 1968, pp. 20–1.

12 Ramdath Jagessar notes, 'Urban Indians are unrepresentative of their people. ... Indians are largely a rural people, quiet, conservative and attached to the land. They live in the Western hemisphere, but they are Eastern peoples. If Negroes look to

Caribbean radicals have committed themselves to a programme based on the premise of the 'innate goodness of the people'. The ultimate aim of this strategy is total assimilation of all ethnic elements into a culturally neutral creole culture, a goal that is an expression of the universalistic liberal ideology which rejects race as a relevant variable in the behaviour of people and which has until recently been optimistic about the prospects of creating integrated societies. That ideology had rejected the separate-but-equal philosophy that prevailed in the United States after 1896 as being repugnant morally and unworkable in practice.

But radical American blacks are today returning to the separate-but-equal position and are now demanding that both aspects of the doctrine be implemented. What they want is justice for blacks rather than cultural integration into white society. They are now concerned with asserting the validity of their own cultural and group experience and are seeking to give it political expression. Elsewhere the phenomenon is the same. Instead of subcultures dissolving, one finds a growing activation of cultural consciousness, a rejection of the view that subcultures must give way to dominant ones, a reassertion of the validity of primordial attachments, and the search for a geopolitical base to nourish and sustain these attachments. The French and the Indians in Canada, the Ibos in Nigeria, non-Arabs in the Sudan, the Slovaks in Czechoslovakia, the Walloons in Belgium, the Ras Tafarians in Jamaica are only a few of the many cases that abound. Social scientists are also beginning to move away from the dichotomous poles of integration and segregation and to recognize that in the contemporary context controlled pluralism is the only real alternative to internal war. As one recent study of the problem concludes, 'Some polities now visibly plural will no doubt succeed in rendering the national component of citizen identity paramount. But in many ... stable coexistence is the best outcome that can reasonably be expected. ... The twin progeny of modernization – cultural pluralism and nationalism – must find reconciliation because the world offers no other choice.'[13]

the Americans and Europeans and wish to be bourgeois, Christian, materialistic and intellectual, Indians do not. They hold to traditions and behaviour from India, despising all else as inferior. They are not and do not care to be part of Trinidad's cultural callaloo.' 'Indian Iceberg', *Tapia*, Nov. 16, 1969. See also Ramdath Jagessar, 'East Indians and Integration', *Moko*, Jan. 17, 1969, and the contrary view of Syl Lowhar, *Tapia*, Dec. 21, 1969.

13   Fred von de Mehden, C.W. Anderson, and Crawford Young (eds.), *Issues in Political Development*, New York, 1967, p. 82. C. Geertz also notes, 'The alternative to a civil politics of primordial compromise would seem to be either Balkanization, Herrenvolk fanaticism or the forcible suppression of ethnic assertion by a leviathan state.' C. Geertz (ed.), *Old Societies, New States*, Chicago, 1963, p. 157.

Some Caribbean radicals accept this thesis but insist that group tension can only be contained by a faster rate of economic growth and a more equitable distribution of the social product. They also believe that the structural changes which are required for this cannot be implemented piecemeal. Frustrated by the painfully slow pace of change, they ascribe a kind of magical power to revolution without bothering (in fact refusing) to attempt any rigorous analysis of what options are open to the revolution assuming it is 'made'. What we are told by some is that the role of the revolutionary intellectual is to 'define the problem' and educate and activate the people who will then 'peacefully choose their own weapons'.[14] Others either take refuge in the formula that in a crisis 'on s'engage et puis on voit' or assume that an international coalition of radicals in the West and the 'third world' will before long shift the balance of world power away from the U.S.-dominated imperialist alliance. Some radicals are aware, however, that a U.S. retreat from Asia and Africa might not apply to the Latin American and Caribbean areas and that one should expect greater vigilance and concentration of counter-insurgency resources in this hemisphere.[15]

An element of escapism is clearly apparent in the posture of the revolutionary who believes that everything has to change before any improvement at all can be achieved. As Albert Hirschman has noted, this attitude stems from impatience and an inability to 'see' small but significant changes. The revolutionary is anxious to 'dispense with the need to visualize the process of change in its intricate and perhaps unpleasant details by telescoping it into an undivided whole'.[16] The reformer, on the other hand 'fights on though objectively he has already lost – and occasionally goes on to win. ... Since he *acts*, he learns from his mistakes and from resistance he encounters, and frequently ends up as a wily individual from whom the revolutionary may well learn a trick or two'.[17] The latter, believing violent revolution to be a prerequisite for structural change, takes to pamphleteering, coffee-shop plotting, and inter-

14 As Lloyd Best writes, 'Our first duty and our most radical contribution is to describe the facts as they are. This is what will arm the community with one of the vital resources it needs to handle governments.' See 'The Intellectual Tradition and Social Change in the Caribbean', *New World Fortnightly*, nos. 27 and 28, 1965.

15 Amando Hart expressed a more optimistic view to the Fourth Latin American Student Congress in Havana in August 1966. As Hart notes, 'Twenty million men would be needed to withstand the onslaught of the masses of [Latin America], and even assuming the absurd idea that imperialism could mobilize so many men ... how many powerful forces would not explode within the U.S. in the face of this extraordinary event?' 'The Latin American Revolution: A New Phase', *Monthly Review*, vol. 18, no. 9, 1967, p. 10.

16 *Journeys towards Progress*, New York, 1963, pp. 251–3.

17 *Ibid.*, p. 271.

national talkfests, often in the safety of exile. He waits until the situation has been ripened by the activities of the reformer and then moves in to ridicule the latter's naiveté.[18]

In Trinidad and the English-speaking Caribbean, a greater measure of decolonization can be achieved without violent revolution. The social systems of these communities are flexible enough to make meaningful incremental changes possible. It is true that the ruling élites are succumbing to the temptation to use 'legal' and even arbitrary violence to contain growing protest.[19] It is also true that they are excessively preoccupied with old metropolitan symbols and relationships and too ready to bend backwards to accommodate the forces of international capitalism. Caribbean governments can indeed be accused of having drawn the lines on what is 'pragmatic' somewhat too narrowly; but the advocates of 'structural' change have also done little to convince them that the alternatives which they propose are economically *and* politically feasible. Other than calling for state ownership of the major productive forces of the economy and urging 'people-oriented' policies, or pointing to the example of Cuba, they have not yet defined with any clarity what the inner and outer limits of decolonization in the contemporary Caribbean are, or what strategies and minimum conditions are necessary to achieve the twin goals of genuine economic development and an egalitarian society. This is the task to which Caribbean intellectuals must dedicate their energies.[20] The past has

18   Hannah Arendt, *On Revolution*, New York, 1965, pp. 262–3.
19   As Dr James Millette complains, 'Since the onset of independence, the governments of the Commonwealth Caribbean have been consistently demonstrating an attitude of greater and greater barbarism to the people of the region ... they are selecting intimidation and outright violence as instruments of social repression ... and are beginning to concert their efforts in this regard.' 'The Caribbean Free Trade Association', *New World*, vol. 4, no. 4, 1968, p. 47.
20   Dr Norman Girvan makes a similar plea: 'Czechoslovakia must be a sobering pointer to the political costs of a programme which relies on Soviet support to rescue any Caribbean parish from the dislocation which would follow the immediate and wholesale expropriation of United States interests. Cuba, which to many represents the ideal for the rest of the Caribbean, is already bearing these costs. ... The substitution of Tweedledum for Tweedledee, it appears, even within the context of a genuinely popular revolution, sets up mechanisms of political response which make the governmental apparatus more sensitive to the needs of metropolitan policy than to the opinions of the local population, at least in some areas.
     This makes it all the more imperative for Caribbean people to discover the possibilities for social equality, economic welfare and cultural freedom for the region without metropolitan suffocation by the West or East. In this discovery Caribbean people with training in whatever skill, whether in architecture or economics, physics or political science, have an indispensable part to play. For whereas only the population as a whole can make a revolution, the concrete and permanent forms of the new

been disscected and the contemporary problem defined but we still do not know enough about what has to be done or whether what is 'historically necessary is historically possible'.

Some readers will note that despite the current demand that persons of African descent be referred to as 'blacks' rather than 'Negroes' (the latter term being a creation of Europeans and heavily burdened with racist and colonial assumptions), the words 'Negro', 'African', and 'black' have been used interchangeably in this work. It does not seem to me that a change of name, symbolic though such change might be, will substantially affect the way in which peoples of African descent will regard themselves or are looked upon by others. For many, the change will mean no more than a substitution of black masks for the white masks about which Fanon wrote.[21] More important than a change of name is the need for people of African descent to rediscover and identify positively with selective aspects of their African heritage. It is worth noting here that in the Caribbean the all-embracing use of the word 'black' would pose problems which are less relevant in North America, where the term can be used meaningfully to categorize Afro-Americans of all hues. In the Caribbean, differences in shade continue to be of significance. But more important is the difficulty presented by the Indian population, most of whom do not consider themselves 'black', though in an epidermal sense many of them are. The terms 'Afro-Trinidadian' and 'Indo-Trinidadian' are more accurate, but extremely cumbersome, and the most convenient procedure would seem to be to retain the existing classifications. The word 'Negro' must indeed be purged of its cultural impediments, but this can only be achieved by the development of a new consciousness and by radically different modes of behaviour on the part of black peoples. Redefining a term by giving it new content is a more legitimate exercise than using new ones which simply create new sets of problems without solving old ones.

society are to a large extent devised by trained persons, in architecture, economics, engineering, education, drama and political organization. And if we do not do our own thinking in these fields, others will continue to do it for us, as they have done for three centuries.' *New World*, vol. 4, no. 3, 1968, p. 2.
21 *Black Skins, White Masks*, New York, 1967.

Part One

The five chapters in Part One deal essentially with the early years of the reform movement. Even so, they cover a rather extended period, beginning with the British conquest in 1797 and ending in 1955 when the movement came under the disciplined leadership of Dr Eric Williams. Some of the key events in this period were the founding of the Trinidad Labour Party, an island-wide strike in 1919, the reconstitution of the TLP under the leadership of A.A. Cipriani in the same year, and the introduction of elected members into the Governor's Legislative Council, which up to that time had been dominated by planter and merchant interests.

Of importance too was the rise of a more radical working-class movement led by T. Uriah Butler and a major island-wide strike in 1936 which Butler's activities precipitated. This strike altered the orientation of British colonial policy in the Caribbean and in other parts of the Empire and focused British parliamentary opinion on the colonies as perhaps nothing before it had done. As Arthur Creech Jones noted during the parliamentary debate on the crisis, 'It is a tragedy of human folly that it takes a great upheaval to remind us of our obligations and responsibilities.'*

The stimulation of the trade-union movement and the visit of a royal commission under the chairmanship of Lord Moyne were the most direct results of the workers' rebellion. The recommendations of the Commission paved the way for a greater devolution of power to native elements and a more concerted movement towards the unification of the West Indies on a federal basis. These developments were strongly opposed by the Indian population, which feared

---

* Great Britain, House of Commons, *Parliamentary Debates, 1937–8*, vol. 332, p. 788.

that it would suffer if the protection of the Crown, such as it was, were withdrawn.

The basic conclusion of this part of the study is that while, in the period before 1946, British governments were not very eager to concede self-rule to Trinidad and the West Indies in general, in the postwar years the obstacles to independence were largely internal. Divisions between and within racial groups and among the islands considerably weakened the nationalist movement and made it only too easy for white-settler groups and the Colonial Office to find excuses for continuing their domination of the community. This view is not accepted by radical nationalists, who place the blame for the weakness and fragmentation of the nationalist forces on the Colonial Office. However, there is good reason to believe that if the Trinidadian élite had presented the Colonial Office with a disciplined mass movement which knew its own mind, full internal self-rule might have been conceded in 1950. Arthur Creech Jones had in fact made this promise as Colonial Secretary in 1946, and it is quite likely that it would have been honoured as it was in the Gold Coast in 1951. In any event, it is not apparent that what took place in Ghana between 1951 and 1957 was in any way markedly in advance of what was achieved in Trinidad between 1950 and 1955 under the quasi-cabinet regime that was established in 1950. The argument of chapter 5 is that more was achieved during this period than is commonly conceded by latter-day nationalists.

1

The old colonial order
1797-1919

The dominant institution of the old colonial order in Trinidad and Tobago was the sugar plantation. It was the plantation and the relations of production which developed on and around it which determined in large part the colony's basic value system and its social and political organization. The origins of the peoples of the colony, their geographic and hierarchical distribution, and the code of etiquette which governed relationships among them can only be fully understood in the context of the plantation economy.

ECONOMIC STRUCTURE

For most of the eighteenth and nineteenth centuries, sugar was by far the most important commodity on which the island depended for its livelihood. After the emancipation of the slaves in 1834, there was some doubt whether the plantation system, which relied heavily on cheap and disciplined labour, would survive at all; and it was only after the British government agreed to the importation of Indian indentured labourers at public expense to replace Negroes, who for a variety of reasons refused to work on the plantations, that the sugar industry managed to avoid the extinction with which it seemed faced in the 1840s.[1] Sugar manufacture, largely though not exclusively controlled by ab-

1 Attempts to recruit European yeomen, Portuguese from Madeira, and Chinese had proven relatively unsuccessful. Those who did come remained for a short while on the plantations, and were soon to be found in the quickly developing service sector of the economy. For an authoritative discussion of the post-emancipation labour crisis see Eric Williams, *History of the People of Trinidad and Tobago*, New York 1964, chap. 8.

sentee British interests, continued to generate most of the economy's income until 1911. Then it was superseded by cocoa farming, which had been developing quite rapidly in the last decades of the nineteenth century. The successful development of the cocoa industry also represented the triumph of an Indian and Negro peasantry which the sugar plantocracy had long tried to stifle in the interests of maintaining its hegemony over the labour force. Requiring little overhead capital or labour, cocoa was ideally suited to peasant cultivation.

Mercantile families also played a key role in the early development of the colony. For the most part they were exporters of agricultural staples, especially cocoa and coffee, and importers of basic commodities. As in other underdeveloped societies, merchants also invested in numerous other profit-making undertakings. Many had substantial holdings in sugar and cocoa, but merchant capital also found outlets in the developing oil industry, which began to show commercial possibilities around the turn of the twentieth century, in the manufacture of ice, leather, soap, and matches, as well as in rolling stock, banking, and publishing houses.

It was this merchant-plantocracy which, together with the Colonial Office and its officials, ruled Trinidad. There were occasions when the interests of the British government and/or British absentee capital were fundamentally opposed to that of the white élite, and at such times the inner logic of the Crown colony system was given full expression.[2] But these cleavages, important as they were, do not obscure the basic unity which existed throughout the period between the white creole élite and the Colonial Office.[3] The Governor and his officials were quite frequently their captives, and they governed largely, though by no means exclusively, in their interest.

2   Williams observes, 'The island's economy duplicated that fundamental cleavage between local and British interests which characterized its political life. The principal function of British political domination was to protect British economic interests at the expense of the local. ... It did this either positively, as in the vigorous support of the sugar and oil industry, or negatively, as in its subordination of the cocoa industry or its passive indifference or active hostility to the small farmer.' 'Education of a Young Colonial', PNM *Weekly*, June 8, 1956.

3   There were notable economic cleavages within the white creole class itself, especially between the French creole plantocracy and the British creole merchant class which exported its produce. The Cocoa Planters Association, a co-operative marketing agency, was founded in 1916 by French creole cocoa-producers who felt that they were being exploited by the British mercantile community. The merchants fought the CPA bitterly and went so far as to claim that it was inspired by pro-German interests. These claims were given credence by the British authorities for some time, but were later proven to be false. For a discussion of this see Arthur da Silva, CPA *Brochure 1905–1958*, Port of Spain, 1958.

SOCIAL STRUCTURE

At the top of the social pyramid were to be found those persons who had substantial holdings in real estate, owners of commercial enterprises, the salaried professional, managerial, and overseer class, and British officials. These people and their families constituted not merely an upper class, but a caste apart, the common denominator of which was 'whiteness'. Regardless of cultural or educational status, provided one was white, entry was permitted.[4]

The white caste was not socially or nationally homogeneous, however. In addition to French, Scottish, and English settlers, who together with British officials, constituted the cream of the society, there were also small clusters of people of Spanish and German descent.[5] Though somewhat lower in rank, they nevertheless formed an acceptable part of the white society. A distinction should also be made between those whites who were natives or creoles and those who were recent immigrants. Relations between these groups, while mostly cordial, were often strained. Culturally they were very different, the creoles being West Indian rather than European. They were more aristocratic and status-conscious and considerably more opposed to social reform than were the Europeans. Some creoles who claimed racial purity were in fact racially mixed. A distinction should also be made between 'principal whites', i.e. the wealthy planters and merchants, and the 'secondary whites' who were their salaried employees. The behaviour patterns of these two groups were quite different.[6] The only 'whites' who were not accepted into the caste were the Portuguese,[7] Jews, Syrians, and Lebanese, most of whom were to be found in the petty trades – retail stores, groceries, rum shops, itinerant huckstering – which did not rate inclusion among those associated with 'whiteness'.

Next in the social hierarchy were the mulattoes (coloured) of various shades, by-products of contact between black slave and white slavemaster.[8]

4   Unlike some of the other islands, for example, Barbados, Trinidad does not have unintegrated rural enclaves of 'poor-white' descendants of European indentured farmers.

5   For most of the nineteenth century the French creoles dominated the social life of the community, even though it was a British possession. Many of them were full-blooded aristocrats who had emigrated from France, Haiti, and other French colonies during the Jacobin terror. Cf. Donald Wood, *Trinidad in Transition,* Oxford, 1968, chap. 9.

6   For an analysis of the cultural differences in West Indian society see M.G. Smith, *The Plural Society in the British West Indies,* Los Angeles, 1965.

7   The Portuguese were brought to Trinidad as a possible replacement for the Negroes after emancipation. The experiment proved abortive.

8   In the Caribbean context 'coloured' refers to people of mixed racial ancestry and not to full Negroes.

While every coloured person did not belong to the middle class, it was generally true that the middle class was predominantly coloured. As a class, they possessed all the psychodynamic characteristics of middle classes everywhere, though their problem was complicated by factors of race, the legacy of a slave past, and the nature of the West Indian economy. Generally, the aim of the coloured strata was to penetrate as far as possible into white society. They disparaged their ancestral past and strove to eliminate or conceal all evidence of their negroid origin. They accepted and internalized all the myths about black inferiority, and imitated with exaggerated fidelity the cultural patterns of the Europeans. The coloured middle class has been bitterly attacked and cruelly portrayed by black radicals, and while these strictures are at times deserved, the fact remains that members of this class made a very critical contribution to the modernizing of the Caribbean. They took advantage of every opportunity that was open to them for self-improvement.

At the bottom of the social pyramid were slaves and ex-slaves and the Indian and Chinese indentured labourers who cultivated the plantations and performed other menial roles. Much has already been written about the character traits of lower-class Negroes, and about the deplorable conditions in which they lived under the old colonial order.[9] Suffice it to say here that many of the characteristics of the brown middle class – its deculturation, its lack of pride in its *négritude*, in Africa, and in any aspect of the slave past – were also true of the lower-class Negro, though the intensity of the latter's reaction was considerably less marked. The few African survivals which persist in religious expression and in modes of dress are to be found mainly, though not exclusively, among this group.

The condition of the Indians was not very different from that of the Negro lower class.[10] Both groups suffered in much the same way at the hands of white employers, though it may be wondered whether either was worse off *materially* than they had been in the areas from which they came. Unlike the Negroes, the Indians had come as indentured freemen, and some attempt was made to ensure that their treatment was humane and that their traditional institutions were not destroyed as they had been with the Africans. In the early years some success was achieved in this regard, but as the influence of abolitionist sentiment declined in England, the British government grew less and

9   Lloyd Braithwaithe, 'Social Stratification in Trinidad', *Social and Economic Studies*, ISER, vol. 2, nos. 2 and 3, October 1953, pp. 122–57; Eric Williams, *The Negro in the Caribbean*, Washington DC, 1942; *idem, Capitalism and Slavery*, London, 1965. For a description of the social structure of the plantation around 1820, see Smith, *The Plural Society*, chap. 5.

10   Cf. Williams, *History*, chap. 9.

less concerned about the social condition of the servile elements in the colonies. Like the emancipated Negroes, the Indians were left to the mercy of the plantocracy.[11] The Protector of the Immigrants – an official appointed by the Crown to look after the interests of the Indians – had neither the resources nor the official support which he needed if he was to prevail against the plantocracy. The post was abolished in 1917, the year in which the indenture system itself was finally abolished.

Despite some harassment and proselytizing by creole elements, the Indians were able to retain a great deal of their religious and other traditional customs, and for this reason they have never been fully integrated into the cultural mainstream of the society as were people of African and European ancestry.[12] As Indians moved into the urban areas and the retail service trades, they began to participate in the creole culture, but the fact remains that they were and still are an essentially agricultural people. As sugar declined in importance, they moved into rice- and cocoa-growing and into market-gardening. Whereas for the Negro the land brought back memories of the slave past, for the Indian the ownership of land was a mark of status as well as a form of economic security.

Relations between Negroes and Indians on and around the plantations were never quite cordial. The arrival of the Indians generated a conflict situation. The Africans, influenced by abolitionists and opponents of the plantation system, were quite hostile to the newcomers, whom they regarded as 'pagan' and 'heathen'.[13] They felt themselves more 'native' and more civilized than the Hindus, who now constituted a distinct threat to their newly won freedom. This hostile attitude was reciprocated by the Indians, who found the Africans 'awkward, vulgar in manners and savage'.[14] It appears that the colour of the Africans led Indians to identify them with the followers of Rawana, the demon king of the Hindu Ramayana epic, and they feared that contact with the Africans would be polluting.[15] The newcomers were decidedly rigid in their deter-

11 Cf. Edgar Erickson, 'The Introduction of East Indian Coolies into the British West Indies', *Journal of Modern History*, vol. 6, no. 2, June 1934, pp. 127–46.

12 Cf. Morton Klass, *East Indians in Trinidad*, New York, 1961; A. and J. Niehoff, *East Indians in the West Indies*, Milwaukee, 1960; Barton Schwartz, *The Dissolution of Caste in Trinidad and Tobago*, Ann Arbor, University Microfilms, n.d.

13 Africans arrived on the island more than a generation before the Indians, and thus had more time to be influenced by Western values. Many of the slaves were in fact slave 'immigrants' from other islands and the United States, and were thus even more exposed to Western influences. In 1871 there were only 4,250 persons of African provenance in the colony.

14 Charles Kingsley, *At Last: A Christmas in the West Indies*, New York, 1871, p. 148.

15 'The colour line not only divides Indian from Indian – but cuts off Indians from other

mination to preserve the 'purity of the Indian race'. Their minority status, plus their fear of pollution, encouraged vigilance and orthodoxy. The fact that the Indians believed they were in Trinidad as transients also encouraged feelings of allegiance to India and alienated them from the mainstream of West Indian society. As the Trinidadian novelist V. S. Naípaul observes,

Everything which made the Indian alien in the society gave him strength. His alienness insulated him from the black-white struggle. He was taboo-ridden as no other person on the island; he had complicated rules about food and about what was unclean. His religion gave him values which were not the white values of the rest of the community, and preserved him from self-contempt; he never lost pride in his origins. More important than religion was his family organization, an enclosing self-sufficient world absorbed with its quarrels and jealousies, as difficult for the outsider to penetrate as for one of its members to escape. It protected and imprisoned, a static world, awaiting decay. ...

Living by themselves in villages, the Indians were able to have a complete community life. It was a world eaten up with jealousies and family feuds and village feuds; but it was a world of its own, a community within the colonial society, without responsibility, with authority doubly and trebly removed. Loyalties were narrow: to the family, the village. This has been responsible for the village-headman type of politician the Indian favours, and explains why Indian leadership has been so deplorable, so unfitted to handle the mechanics of party and policy.

A peasant-minded, money-minded community, spiritually static because cut off from its roots, its religion reduced to rites without philosophy, set in a materialist colonial society: a combination of historical accidents and national temperament has turned the Trinidad Indian into the complete colonial, even more philistine than the white.[16]

It was not, of course, possible for Indians to maintain a completely separate social existence. Work and some of the routines of life brought them into con-

coloured people. The fact that a pyramid of colour snobbery stands in the midst of the Hindu social structure inevitably complicates Hindu relations with Negroid races. ... The Hindu posture towards Negroes has often been explained by a strict caste-outcaste analogy in which the Negro is a dark-skinned equal of the untouchable and therefore instinctively shunned. But the problem is not that simple'. Selig Harrison, *India: The Most Dangerous Decades*, Princeton, 1960, pp. 125–6. For a similar observation with regard to Indians in East Africa, see T.O. Elias, *Government and Politics in Africa*, New York, 1963.

16   V.S. Naipaul, *Middle Passage*, London, 1962, pp. 81–2.

tact with Negroes, and there is enough evidence to indicate that miscegenation was not uncommon, especially between Negro men and East Indian women.[17] In most cases, however, these contacts generated conflict and hostility rather than greater understanding. Indians resented miscegenation and the fact that the Negro was given precedence in supervisory jobs on the plantation and elsewhere in society.[18] So far as can be discerned, however, there were never any serious clashes between Negroes and Indians, though eruptions on an individual or small group basis there certainly were. Most of the struggles between the two communities have been political and economic; there has been little organized co-operation between them, though on occasion temporary alliances have been formed for one purpose or another.

Life on the plantations and in the villages also led to a considerable flattening out of Indian culture and the decline of some of the caste exclusivism that was characteristic of traditional life in India. As Schwartz, Clarke, Crowley, and Niehoff all agree, the historical factors associated with the indenture system and the broader economic and political structure of Trinidad made it difficult for the ideas and concepts introduced by the Indians to take firm root.[19] But while there is general agreement that caste as an organizational system has broken down in most parts of the community due to lack of postive reinforcement, it is also evident that in religious, family, and individual contexts it continues to have relevance. Some correlation remains between class and caste, and high-caste Hindus dominate leadership roles among Indians, especially in areas such as religion and politics.

The Chinese, once a marginal part of the lower strata, were one of the most upwardly mobile communities in the society. On leaving the plantation they moved into market-gardening and retail and service trades, where they competed with urban Indians. Unlike the Indians, however, they did not maintain the same intense desire to return to their motherland, and they readily adopted the norms of the creole society. As Daniel Hart wrote of them, 'On becoming Christians, they enter readily to the manner of dress of the generality of the inhabitants; they freely marry creole women and are careful in selecting those who are handsome. ... As labourers they are steady and hard-

17 Cf. Barton Schwartz, 'Caste and Endogomy in Trinidad', *South Western Journal of Anthropology*, vol. 20, no. 1, 1964, pp. 58–66.
18 A fairly popular view in Trinidad is that Negro field supervisors lightened the work loads of East Indian women for financial or sexual bribes. The writer has not been able to ascertain the validity of this report; it is claimed that the Indian male resented this, but bore his indignity with fortitude.
19 Cf. essays by Colin Clarke, Arthur Niehoff, and Barton Schwartz, *Caste in Overseas Communities*, M. Schwartz (ed.), San Francisco, 1967.

working, seldom ever seen drunk, excellent gardeners, and in business sharp and attentive.'[20]

The fact that their pigmentation approximated that of the whites was a lever which the Chinese were able to use to good advantage. As the whites came under siege they came to regard the Chinese as a sort of buffer against the tide of black radicalism. It was the Chinese and not the Negro or Indian who first benefited from the demands for West Indianization.

To say that the Chinese rapidly became acculturated does not mean that they had no subculture of their own. They did and still do retain a significant degree of exclusivism in their family and business life. But there is no evidence that there was at any time a 'Chinatown' in Trinidad or that any attempt was made to found separate schools or churches, though language-training programmes were occasionally organized. Perhaps the critical factor was size. The Chinese never exceeded 1 per cent of the total Trinidad population.

POLITICAL STRUCTURE

The decision of the British government to administer Trinidad as a pure Crown colony without any elected institutions must be seen in the context of the traumatic emancipation crisis through which the plantation system was put in the 1830s and 40s. All pleas by the merchants and the plantocracy for a 'British type of constitution' were rejected by the metropolitan government on the ground that the British population, and indeed the white population as a whole, was vastly outnumbered by non-whites.[21] It was argued that elective government, if introduced, would mean domination by the small white community, if they alone were given the right to vote, or by the free coloured, if they were included, as the British Government felt they had to be; the British wanted

---

20   Daniel Hart, *Trinidad: Historical and Statistical View*, Port of Spain, 1866, p. 100. Few Chinese women came to the island in the early years.

Year	Total	White	Coloured	Native Indians	Chinese	Slaves
1783	2,763	126	295	2,032		310
1797	17,712	2,151	4,474	1,078		10,009
1800	22,850	2,359	4,408	1,071		15,012
1805	30,076	2,434	5,801	1,733		20,108
1810	31,143	2,487	6,269	1,659		20,728
1815	38,348	3,219	9,563	1,147		24,329
1820	41,348	3,707	13,965	910	29	22,738
1828	42,262	3,310	14,980	727	12	23,230
1831	41,675	3,319	16,285	672	7	21,032

21   Estimated population of Trinidad 1783–1831, *West Indian Census*, 1941, p. ix, cited in Braithwaithe, 'Social Stratification', p. 92.

neither. But the decisive factor which influenced the thinking of the British government related to the abolition of the slave trade and, later on, to the emancipation of the slaves. As Lord Liverpool wrote, 'It is essential for this purpose, that in a new colony the Crown should not divest itself of its power of legislation, and that neither the Crown nor Parliament should be subject to the embarrassments which, on such an occasion, might perhaps arise from the conflicting views of the Imperial Parliament and of a subordinate legislature.'[22] The British government, while agreeing in principle with the arguments for representative government, also contended that it was not advisable in a society constituted as was Trinidad. Representative government, properly understood, required an identity of interest between rulers and ruled which did not obtain in the colony. As Lord Goderich, the Secretary of State for the Colonies, declared in 1832, 'Society in Trinidad is divided into castes as strongly marked as those of Hinduism, nor can any man who has but an ordinary knowledge of the history and general character of mankind, doubt what must be the effect of such distinctions when in addition to their other privileges, the superior races are entrusted with a legislative authority over the inferior.'[23]

The British government did, however, make important concessions later on. In 1831 a Legislative Council consisting of appointed officials only was established. With minor changes, the system created then was to last for ninety-four years. The principal changes which were later introduced had the effect of giving to the Governor more on-the-spot authority, and to the Council a greater say in the finances of the colony. But the changes did not affect the basic theory of the system, namely, that if pressed to the limit, the Governor was to have the final authority, subject only to modification by the Crown.

EARLY REFORM MOVEMENTS

The demand for political reform continued unabated, however, despite Britain's adamance. The principal driving-force (though by no means the only one) behind the reform movement in the early nineteenth century was the French creole element, which bitterly opposed the anglicizing policies of the British government. The French and English both agreed on the need for greater independence from the Colonial Office, but were often divided on other basic issues. One of the earliest organized protest movements against Colonial Office control was the Legislative Reform Committee, which functioned from about 1856 to the outbreak of the First World War. It was largely

22 Liverpool to the Governor of Trinidad, Nov. 27, 1810, cited by Hewan Craig, *The Legislative Council of Trinidad and Tobago*, London, 1951, p. 17.
23 *Ibid.*, p. 19.

an alliance of coloured professionals, French creole cocoa interests, and English merchants. The principal issue that agitated them was state-sponsored East Indian immigration. The reformists, who considered themselves every whit as competent to run the affairs of the colony as were 'carpet-bagging' British officials, complained that creoles were being deprived of the political power rightfully theirs. They objected strongly to the strangle-hold which British officialdom had over the colony's revenues and economic programming, and to the fact that the entire political and legal structure of the colony seemed geared to service the needs of absentee sugar interests rather than the interests of the colony as a whole.

The Legislative Reform Committee was essentially a classical liberal organization and it did not enjoy mass appeal. The first genuine working-class movement which emerged in the colony was the Trinidad Workingmen's Association.[24] Founded in 1897, the TWA played a pioneering role in radicalizing the urban masses of the colony. Although the Association and the Committee agreed generally on the need for constitutional reform, a great deal of class and organizational jeolousy existed between the two groups. The latter was characterized as an opportunistic and bourgeois organization which was willing to fight to defend its own class interests but was nevertheless opposed to extending any benefits to the working class. To the TWA the issues in conflict involved not only the question of home rule, but the equally vital question of 'who should rule at home'. The reformists were also accused of seeking to displace the TWA as the Trinidad 'affiliate' of the British Labour party.[25]

The Association, under the leadership of Alfred Richards, a mulatto apothecary, campaigned, among other things, for the restoration of elective municipal government in the capital city of Port of Spain where it had been suspended in 1898 following a clash with the Colonial Office over matters of finance, for the ending of Indian indentured labour which it claimed depressed the living conditions of Negro workers, for the nativization of the Trinidad electricity company, and for the elimination of health hazards in the capital city.

In terms of legislation for which its pressures were responsible, the success of the TWA was quite limited. It suffered serious setbacks in a disastrous waterfront strike in 1902, and an equally disastrous 'water riot' in 1903.[26] By 1906 its membership had dwindled to a mere 223 from the thousand members

---

24 A Trinidad Working Men's Club was founded by Claude Phillips in 1877, but it did not last any length of time.
25 There was no formal linkage between the TWA and the Labour Party, but relationships were quite cordial between a few MPs and the leaders of the Association.
26 The riots were a result of a decision taken to meter water usage.

ascribed to it in 1900. The outbreak of war in 1914 and the enlistment of some of its leaders in the British West India Regiment also contributed to the decline of the Association. By the end of the war it was only a memory, but one that was powerful enough to appeal to those who had been deeply influenced by wartime experiences and the democratic vistas which Wilsonian idealism had opened up before the subject peoples of the world.

The historical role of the TWA cannot be measured purely in terms of its legislative gains, which were negligible. Though never rigorously organized, the Association played a crucial role in recruiting the black masses into the national political process and in socializing them into the norms of collective action. The activities of the TWA also marked the beginning of the effort to forge an effective alliance between coloured middle-class professionals and manual workers. This effort was later to form one of the dominant themes of reform politics in the area.

2
The crisis of the old colonial order 1919-36

The years between the First and Second World War witnessed a radical shift in the structure of politics in the colony. By 1919 most of the upper- and middle-class elements had abandoned the field of reform politics, and were being openly grateful to the Colonial Office for having had the foresight to reject their earlier demands for constitutional reform. There were some exceptions who continued to voice demands for modest reforms through the Reform Committee, but the reform movement of the twenties was almost completely dominated by black working-class elements.

Although the Trinidad Workingmen's Association did not survive the dislocation of the war years, the idea of working-class co-operation lingered on. Some members of the working class had served in Europe with the British West India Regiment in the First World War and had been deeply affected by radical ideas. Indeed, it is difficult to overemphasize the war's effect in generating revolutionary ideas among West Indian workers. Captain Cipriani, the Commander of the British West India Regiment, observed that workers who had gone abroad had come back emancipated from old prejudices and superstitions which hitherto had posed stumbling blocks to effective social action.

The economic crisis that followed the end of hostilities gave added urgency to the activities of the veterans, as did the rise of revolutionary movements around the world. Prices of food and clothing had risen considerably during the war, and were beyond the reach of most of the lower class. Servicemen grumbled that while they had risked their lives to 'make the world safe for democracy', stay-at-home capitalists who had fattened on war profits showed no willingness to share them with returned workers and others similarly placed. They also felt that not enough had been done to re-integrate them into the work force.

Unrest expressed itself in a rash of strikes which began on the waterfront in December 1919 and spread to all parts of the island, including the ward of Tobago. In the nearest thing to a general strike the colony had yet seen, mobs marched up and down the city streets forcing merchants to close. With an admixture of coercion and genuine support, the entire city was held to ransom by the demonstrators. Even domestic labourers were called out in what was generally regarded as a crusade against the white aristocracy. Over a thousand men, including recent immigrants from other colonies, were involved in the demonstrations. So too were previously passive Indian labourers. As one commentator observed, 'The humble worker, whose unmurmuring utility has long been recognized in the life of our city – the coolie carrier – has taken to the prevailing idea, and has made known his intention to ask for more.'[1]

Not long before the disturbances began, a decision had been taken to recreate the Workingmen's Association. Though it had little to do with the launching of the strike, the reconstituted TWA came to play a vital role in organizing it and in presenting the worker's grievances. During the fourteen days of the strike, three thousand workers joined the TWA; it boasted six thousand members by the end of 1919. Whites were horrified by these events. Some businessmen were frankly opposed to having any dealings with the TWA. 'The mob has tasted blood; its leaders have envisaged the delights of power and are threatening more to come.' 'The rioters are anarchists, myrmidons of a gang of scallywags from the other islands who had hoodwinked the Trinidad masses.' These were some of the comments heard. In a defensive gesture the whites quickly established a vigilante platoon consisting of about 270 planters and merchants.

But there were others who did not believe that the TWA should be smashed. Some merchants felt that the thrust could be taken out of the movement if timely concessions were made. The *Trinidad Guardian*, a newspaper owned by native businessmen, condemned the leaders of the demonstrations for what was viewed as a 'deliberate and unashamed attempt to set class against class, to provoke labour against capital, to persuade an uneducated and credulous proletariat that preposterous demands can be enforced by terrorist methods'; but the paper nevertheless welcomed the appearance of the TWA, which it hoped would moderate and constitutionalize the demands of the burgeoning labour movement.[2]

The labour movement gained a significant boost when it came under the leadership of that knight-errant of Trinidad politics, A.A. Cipriani. He had gained the confidence and respect of black servicemen during and after the

---

1 The workers involved were cartermen who brought fodder into the city. The Indian sugar workers did not join the protest movement in large numbers.
2 *Trinidad Guardian* (TG), Dec. 1 and 4, 1919.

war and was immensely popular with urban lower-class elements.[3] Until the rise of Marcus Garvey's Black Pride and Back to Africa Movement, no serious objection was raised to having a white planter lead a predominantly black lower-class social protest movement, certainly an event unique in the world-wide anti-colonial struggle of coloured peoples. Between 1919 and 1934 the TWA, under the presidency of Cipriani, was undisputably the dominant left-wing political force in the British Caribbean. As C.L.R. James recalls, once Cipriani entered politics, 'he put himself forward as the champion of the common people ... the barefooted man. Before long this white man was acknowledged as leader by hundreds and thousands of black people and East Indians.'[4]

THE WOOD COMMISSION AND THE INDIANS

The visit in 1921 of a Colonial Office investigatory commission under Major Wood helped to crystallize a new development in the politics of the country. The ending of indentured immigration in 1917 had forced the Indians to make some attempt to come to terms with the society which they had chosen to adopt. For the first time we find them becoming articulate and taking a stand on public issues in an instrumental fashion. Two groups testified before Major Wood, the East Indian National Congress and a representation from the established communal élite. The East Indian National Congress, which claimed to represent the younger and more 'progressive' elements in the community, agreed to constitutional changes that would democratize politics in the colony, but insisted that such changes be on the basis of communal representation. They claimed that they would be swamped under a system of open electoral politics. They also insisted that the Indian community should be considered a single political unit. As they told Major Wood, 'Religious differences in the East Indian population did not create any political issue between the Christian [Indian], Hindu and Mohammedan, and could not fairly be adduced as a reason for refusing [Indians] separate representation as a race.'[5] The Congress also opposed any educational or literacy test on the ground that all taxpayers had a stake in the society and should therefore be allowed to vote without dis-

---

3   Cipriani had in fact suggested to the servicemen that they put their trust in him during peacetime as they had during the war. In 1919 he was elected President of the Soldiers and Sailors Union. The workers also wanted to nominate him as their spokesman on the City Council. C.L.R. James disagrees that Cipriani actively sought the sponsorship of the workers. 'It was only after much persuasion that ... already a man over forty, he entered politics.' *The Black Jacobins*, New York, 1963, p. 403.
4   *Ibid.*
5   *Report by the Hon. E.F.L. Wood, MP, on His Visit to the West Indies and British Guiana, December 1921 to February 1922*, Cmd. 1679, London 1922, p. 24.

crimination. If a literacy test were to be imposed, however, they insisted that competence in one of their own languages be regarded as adequate.

The second Indian group opposed change altogether. They felt that the old system of nomination by the Governor to the Legislative Council was the only one in which Indians would be guaranteed representation in proportion to their numbers and influence. They claimed that the Indian community had been denied the benefits of education and could not maximize the possibilities of the democratic political method. The fact that they were illiterate in English and spoke not one but five Indian languages was also seen as an obstacle to effective political combination. As Major Wood himself agreed, 'The East Indians, the backbone of the agricultural industry ... are the "underdogs" politically when compared to the Negroes, owing to the superior educational advantages of the latter.'[6]

A third group, the Young Indian Party, which at the time of Wood's visit was not yet fully organized, but which was to become vocal as the decade advanced, rejected the positions taken by their elders.[7] The Party opposed both communal representation and the nominated system on the grounds that Indians had no unique interest to protect. While a few members agreed that Indian culture and identity were worth preserving, though not by political means, the majority did not regard as 'unfortunate' the tendency of a growing number of Indians to adopt Western modes of dress and behaviour and to become 'creolized'.[8] They believed that the established Indian leadership was mistaken in its attempt to ritualize 'the dead past' and in its unwillingness to identify with the other have-not groups in the society. Essentially the Indian radicals sought to mobilize the Indian masses for what they viewed as a class struggle which cut across racial and creedal lines.[9]

This point of view never became dominant within the Indian community, which looked askance at this detraditionalized element. Radical though they were on economic issues, the Indian masses did not respond readily to the argument that their welfare was intimately linked with the struggle of other

---

6 *Ibid.*, p. 25.
7 As the *East Indian Weekly* noted (April 27, 1929), 'It was a case of the particularity of age against the audacity of youth.'
8 'The process of nationalization is undermining the people, and unless something is done to check its progress, the race will be a standing disgrace to the Indian nation.' Bharat Ashram to *ibid.*, Aug. 11, 1928.
9 The editor of the *East Indian Weekly*, C.B. Mathura, announced on March 7, 1928 that the policy of the paper 'will be to represent the views of the masses and classes irrespective of colour or creed'. The *Weekly* consistently supported the TWA and Cipriani, and sought to encourage a pro-Federation attitude on the part of its readers.

blacks for democratic constitutional reforms and for federation. They were in fact deeply fearful that these developments would undermine their growing economic and political strength and their cultural integrity. From the moment of their entry into the community's political life their aim was to slow down for as long as possible the movement for radical constitutional change.

Major Wood saw no reason why a modicum of political reform should not be granted to the colony. He noted that there was a considerable driving-force behind the reform movement, and felt that it would be impossible in the long run to withhold from Trinidad concessions which had recently been granted to Grenada, however much conditions differed in the two colonies. Wood was also sensitive to the peculiar dilemma of the black man in the West Indies, completely detribalized, his perspectives entirely dominated by the British super-ordinate system: 'The whole history of the African population in the West Indies inevitably drives them towards representative institutions fashioned after the British model. They look for growth to the only source and pattern that they know, and aspire to share in what has been the peculiarly British gift of representative institutions.'[10] Wood was aware that Trinidad, more than any other island in the West Indies, lacked 'any homogeneous public opinion', that it was 'socially divided into all kinds of groups which have few relations with each other'; but he was convinced that a skilfully designed constitutional system could circumvent the problems that seemed endemic to a polyethnic society.

Given the nature of the society, Wood refused to endorse the demand for an immediate grant of responsible government, which he viewed as a will-o'-the-wisp, something not likely to come on the political agenda 'within measurable distance of time'. He argued that 'The only effect of granting responsible government might be to entrench in power a financial oligarchy which would entirely dominate the colony and use its power for the purpose of benefiting one class instead of the community as a whole.'[11] Wood also advanced the

---

10   *Wood Report*, p. 25. Wood argued that concessions were inevitable, and that delay would rob them of 'usefulness and grace'. 'Several reasons combine to make it likely that the common demand for a measure of representative government will in the long run prove irresistible. The wave of democratic sentiment has been powerfully stimulated by the war. Education is rapidly spreading, and tending to produce a coloured and black intelligentsia, of which the members are quick to absorb elements of knowledge requisite for entry into the learned professions. They return from travel abroad with minds emancipated and enlarged, ready to devote time and energy to propaganda among their own people. Local traditions of representative institutions reinforce these tendencies.' *Ibid.*, p. 5. Even though admitting that the masses were not as committed to the idea of reform as their middle-class spokesmen contended, he recognized that 'the educated and intelligent minority of today is powerful enough to mould the thought of the majority of tomorrow.' *Ibid.*, p. 6.

11   *Ibid.*, p. 6.

classical argument that responsible government was not meaningful in a society in which there was no leisure class independent of constituency ties which could aggregate the interests of all communities impartially. For a long time to come, this function would have to be performed by British official cadres. The argument of the radicals that the official class was controlled by the sugar interests did not appear to impress him.

Wood seemed mainly concerned that 'no action should be taken which would disturb the confidence felt by capital in the stability of the local government'.[12] He also argued that the size and the isolation of the colony would make the experiment in responsible government difficult if not impracticable. Given its limited physical resources, economic viability was also not a real possibility. Wood also opposed communal representation on the ground that it would be a bad precedent and impossible to apply in practice:

If a concession of this kind were granted to the East Indians, there would be no logical reason for withholding it from persons of French, Spanish or Chinese descent, a situation which would become impossible. Moreover, it would be a retrograde step from the point of view of the future development of the colony to accentuate and perpetuate differences which, in order to produce a homogeneous community, it should be the object of statesmanship to remove. The East Indians are an important element in the community, and it would be a great misfortune if they were encouraged to stand aside from the main current of political life instead of sharing in it, and assisting to guide its course.[13]

The constitutional reforms which followed upon Major Wood's Report were extremely modest.[14] The Legislative Council was now to consist of twenty-six members, twelve of whom were to be officials; there were to be thirteen unofficial members, seven of whom were to be elected. The remaining six were to be nominated by the Governor. It was felt that nominations could be used to redress any imbalance in the system caused by the use of direct elections. The twenty-sixth member of the Council, and the linchpin of the whole system, was, as before, the Governor, who retained both his original and casting votes. The Governor was *de facto* Prime Minister, and with the routine support of his 'official party' he could always count on a majority of one; in practice the majority was always larger, since the unofficial members rarely operated as a single unit.

The franchise was also extremely limited. The right to vote was confined to those who had substantial property or high incomes. Candidates for election were required to have even more substantial holdings in real and movable

12   *Ibid.*, p. 7.   13   *Ibid.*, p. 27.
14   Some of its key draughtsmen were members of the Legislative Reform Committee.

estate.[15] Members of the Legislative Council were not to be paid, a provision which also served to close its doors to all but the well-to-do. In effect, constitutional reform served to place political power in the hands of the very oligarchy which Major Wood had feared would be the principal beneficiaries of responsible government.

THE ELECTIONS OF 1925

The first general election held in Trinidad took place on February 7, 1925, ninety-four years after the British had taken formal possession of the island. Generally speaking, it was an unexciting election. In the rural areas, it was clear that the population had not yet become politicized. Personalities and the issue of race loomed large in the calculations of the voter. Only in the city of Port of Spain where a wealthy businessman, Major Randolph Rust, fought the TWA President, Captain Cipriani, was there any enthusiasm and concentration on issues. Rust and his supporters took the view that politics was a business and that it should be run by businessmen and others who had a stake in the society. Trinidad had no room for class parties or ideologies of the left or right. 'We are not organizing to oppose the Government. We aspire to have truly representative men as unofficials on the Legislative Council to be advisers of the Government ... especially with regard to the raising and expenditure of funds.'[16] Labour and capital were complementary and both had a responsibility to the community. Cipriani's 'bolshevist' politics, they feared, were setting class against class and race against race.

Cipriani, who claimed to speak for the 'unwashed and unsoaped barefooted men', agreed that, as constituted, the Legislative Council would in fact be dominated by business interests, and that no revolutionary legislation would ever be sanctioned by it. The system had to be altered fundamentally by adult suffrage and by abolishing the nominated element which perpetuated the rule of a family clique.[17] Trinidad must be administered on behalf of Trinidadians, not in the interest of men who still considered England 'home'.

Of the registered voting population of 21,794, only 6,832 or roughly 29 per cent voted, though it must be observed that 6,100 voters in two uncontested constituencies were deprived of their franchise. Approximately 46 per cent of those who had an opportunity to exercise the franchise did so. In Port of Spain, Cipriani received about 57 per cent of the votes which were validly

---

15   For details see Eric Williams, *History of the People of Trinidad and Tobago*, New York, 1964, pp. 220–1.

16   TG, Jan. 8, 1925.

17   'I will never stop shouting and if you [elect] me ... I will see that the bastard Legislative Council is abolished.' *Ibid.*

cast. Despite the hostility of the established press and the limited nature of the franchise, Cipriani had undoubtedly proven to be the favourite of the Trinidad masses. Those who did not have the vote supported him in other ways. But it is also clear that he had the support of the bulk of the non-white middle class as well.

In the Council, Cipriani was supported intermittently by three legislators who identified with the TWA, but for the most part it was 'Cipriani against the system'. Day after day, and in and out of the Council, he hurled himself heroically against the arraigned forces of capital and privilege. He fought for workmen's compensation, old age pensions, the eight-hour day, minimum wages, and compulsory education; against the Habitual Idlers Ordinance which the planter-dominated Legislative Council had enacted to curb vagrancy on the part of the East Indians; and against the continuation of child labour on the plantations. Like Alfred Richards, the leader of the old TWA, he also campaigned vigorously for the nativization of the electricity company.[18] 'An utterly fearless man, he never left the colonial government in any doubt as to what it was up against.'[19] He often reminded the Government that if he raised his little finger the masses might not be easy to control.

THE CIPRIANI MOVEMENT AND THE TRINIDAD LABOUR PARTY

Although a radical socialist, Cipriani was no Marxist. He did not believe in the inevitability of class struggle and the eventual collapse of the capitalist order. His was not apocalyptic politics. There is no evidence that he ever relied for guidance on any closely reasoned body of economic thought. He had a strong dislike for the West India Committee (an organization which represented absentee interests in London), the Chamber of Commerce, and British officials – 'their wire-pullers at the Colonial Office'. For him, the Crown colony system was a grand conspiracy of local and alien capitalists, a system under which the 'colony was being bled white and the worker defrauded, pilloried and exploited'.

A staunch advocate of West Indianization, he refused to believe that West Indians could not manage their own affairs. West Indians, unlike tribalized Africans, did not need British tutelage, he argued. They were 'gentlemen, a highly civilized, cultured and educated people ... having the same aspirations as the white man. They were the equals of any Englishman.' It was an insult for them to have to accept 'the uncouth, rude and in many cases, uneducated

---

18   The battle against the establishment was also carried on by Howard Bishop, editor of the *Labour Leader*, the organ of the TWA.
19   James, *Black Jacobins*, p. 403.

domination of the favourites and spoilt children of Downing Street or to be forced to put up with the big-stick autocracy of the official from Africa'.[20]

The white community fought a desperate rearguard action against Cipriani, whom they accused of being either a bolshevik or demented. For his Robin-Hood economics, they had nothing but contempt, and they professed complete unawareness of any discontent among the working classes, whom they regarded as a happy and contented lot. All the dusty old Victorian arguments about freedom of contract and the right to alienate one's own labour were unashamedly trotted out to blunt the demand for social and political reform. Capitalism was riding high, at least until the depression of the thirties shook its very foundations.

Numerous examples of the stolid, unsympathetic attitude of the ruling élite could be found in the pages of the report of the commission which was appointed to enquire into the question of child labour on the plantations. The testimony of E.A. Robinson, one of the colony's wealthiest and most influential creole sugar-planters, might be taken as a representative example. Robinson, who was opposed to compulsory education for the children of labourers, declared: 'This is an agricultural country. Unless you put the children on to working in the fields when they are young, you will never get them to do so later. If you want to turn all these people into a lot of clerks, caneweighers, and people of that sort, all you have to do is to prevent them from working in the fields until they are 16 years old; then I guarantee you will have but very few labourers in the Colony.'[21] Robinson's aim, and that of the plantocracy in general, was to deny educational opportunity to Negroes and Indians 'lest you ruin the country'. One might 'give them some education in the way of reading and writing, but no more. Even then I would say educate only the bright ones; not the whole mass.'[22]

Cipriani, on the other hand, never ceased to remind the lower classes that education was their greatest asset, their principal lever of mobility, and he urged them to make every sacrifice to see that their children got the best possible education. The plantocracy opposed compulsory general public education until they were literally coerced into accepting it by the British government in 1935. The Indians were the principal victims of their negligence.

White employers similarly opposed the introduction of legislation to legalize combinations among working-class elements. Cipriani took the view that if the government was really sincere about the contract theory of industrial relations, it should remove the obstacles that prevented labour from strengthening

20 Anonymous, *His Best Orations*, Port of Spain, 1949, p. 70.
21 Williams, *History*, p. 212.
22 *Ibid.*, p. 213.

its countervailing power. Rather, the government seemed to be surreptitiously encouraging the white employer class to arm itself against coloured labour. In 1930, when the military vote came up for consideration, Cipriani opposed it on the ground that: 'The Light Infantry Volunteers [also known as the Vigilantes] is a battalion of employers ... prominent cocoa and sugar planters ... [who] have formed themselves into a band for the purpose of quelling attempts at industrial unrest ... [or] collective bargaining of labour.'[23]

The case for the introduction of trade-union legislation in the colonies was taken by Cipriani to the British Labour party's Commonwealth Conference in 1930. The Labour party was challenged to square its refusal to promote the trade-union movement in the colonies with its own fundamental principles.[24] The Labour government under Ramsay MacDonald ultimately responded to this and similar appeals, and in September 1930 Sidney Webb circularized colonial governments urging them to introduce trade-union ordinances. But the government of Trinidad and Tobago ignored the despatch until 1932, when legislation was finally enacted. The new ordinance was nevertheless a meaningless instrument as far as the workers were concerned, since it omitted all provisions which would safeguard the right of unions to picket peacefully. Further, it gave them no immunity against action in tort along the lines of the 1906 Trade Disputes Act in the United Kingdom. Cipriani and the TWA protested, but to no avail.

The new ordinance posed a serious problem for Cipriani and the TWA. Should the Association now function as a pure trade union without legal protection, or should it operate on both the political and labour fronts as it had done before? The question was debated in left-wing circles, with a minority taking the view that the TWA should continue to function as a 'twin-movement'. Cipriani, on the other hand, preferred to take the advice of the British Trades Union Congress, and refused to register the TWA under the new ordinance. Its two union affiliates, the Stevedores Union and the Railway Union, also declined to register.

To underline the significance of the choice, the name Trinidad Workingmen's Association was dropped in 1934 and was replaced by Trinidad Labour Party. Cipriani believed that political agitation had to be given primacy at that stage of the country's development. Fundamental reforms had to be secured at the political level before the working class could successfully demand improvement in living standards which it so badly needed. As Kwame Nkrumah, ex-President of Ghana, was to say later on, 'Seek ye first the political king-

23 Hansard, May 23, 1930, pp. 250–2.
24 Cf. C.L.R. James, *The Life of Captain Cipriani: An Account of British Government in the West Indies*, Nelson, Lancs., 1932, p. 105.

dom, and all else will be added unto you.' Cipriani did not wish to run the risk of having the labour movement destroyed in the courts for illegal industrial activities.

THE GROWTH OF NATIONAL CONSCIOUSNESS

Captain Cipriani was the first genuinely 'national' political leader to emerge in Trinidad and Tobago. He was loved and admired by thousands of people all over the country who looked to him for leadership and guidance. Honesty of purpose, sincerity, and generosity were his hallmarks. A good orator and phrase-maker, he had that gift without which, as Carlyle suggested, no man can become a great leader; he was a proven 'chief of talkers'. Cipriani was an impassioned man with an ability to incite the passions of others. By means of his attention-attracting antics, his 'extravaganzas' as they were referred to then, he succeeded in awakening the 'barefooted man' to the relevance of national politics to his daily routine. He was the instrument by which large numbers of individuals who had previously experienced no basic attraction towards one another came to develop feelings of national kinship and identification. Through him the Legislative Council also began to acquire popular legitimation.

The fact that Cipriani was white did not detract in any way from his political acceptability. His whiteness was in fact a positive asset. Given the context of politics at that time, it would have been very difficult for an individual of either Indian or African extraction to bridge the gaps that separated the two major communities. The situation demanded a neutral ethnic type. Moreover, for colonials, whiteness was still a highly valued attribute, and Cipriani's charisma owed as much to his whiteness as it did to his other leadership qualities. To be white was to be blessed, to have the gift of grace. The masses, especially the urban blacks, were flattered by Cipriani's championship of their cause. They likewise believed that as an interceding agent he would be more useful than one of their own – someone not so blessed.

Cipriani was much less successful in his dealings with Indians, who still remained relatively isolated figures on and around the plantations, than he was with the more mobilized Negro population. The evidence suggests that Cipriani made no systematic attempt to reach the Indian masses on a person-to-person level. For the most part he relied on his radical Indian followers, some of whom were once members of the Young Indian Party, to mobilize them for the Trinidad Labour Party. Dr Williams' view that 'with these Indian colleagues Cipriani brought into the working-class movement a substantial section of the Indian working class, giving to the Trinidad movement for self-government an inter-racial solidarity which augured well for the future'[25] is not borne out by the available evidence. The bulk of the Indian population, working-class or otherwise, did not identify with the nationalist movement. The rural Indian in particular was not yet able, or in fact willing, to identify with abstract institutions like 'council' or 'party'; nor did such symbols as 'national self-determination' and 'socialism' mean much to him. He thought mainly in terms of persons who could understand his language and his problems, and who would safeguard and promote his ethnic interests. For him, it was still very much a case of *apan jāt* – Indian for Indian. This is not to say that the Indians did not admire Cipriani for the stands he took on their behalf, and for his struggle to improve the working conditions of the masses; but they were decidedly aloof to his fight for self-government and federation.

As a political leader Captain Cipriani had serious limitations. As one of Trinidad's noted polemicists observed, 'Only up to a point was Cipriani a leader. He taught his adherents how to organize constitutionally and press demands, but he was not a political thinker. ... He was a sturdy patriot with a blazing sense of injustice who could initiate mass movements but not control or develop them.'[26]

Although in 1934 the TWA/TLP boasted a membership of 130,000 people from all classes, creeds, and races, it is more correct to regard these as followers rather than as members in the true sense of the term. It had few of the hallmarks of the modern mass political party. Not even in the Legislative Council did the three-man TLP team function as a coherent unit. Each MLC operated more or less as an independent, voting as his conscience or interest dictated. It should be noted, however, that the nature of the franchise and the constitutional system did not encourage party loyalty or cohesion. The constitution did not lend itself readily to machine-type politics. There was little patronage to disburse, since the Governor and his principal officials still held a monopoly over the distribution of perquisites.[27]

Cipriani deliberately tried to maintain the TLP as a loose coalition. He was not anxious to have a closely articulated organization which would limit his ability to manoeuvre. He often said that all he wanted from his barefooted followers was 'the strength of their numbers'. He continuously entreated for sacrificial struggle but never succeeded in mobilizing his followers on a sustained basis for the attainment of identified goals. Many of his lieutenants attempted to impress upon him the need for middle- and lower-level political

25 Williams, *History*, p. 224.
26 Max Farquhar, 'Absence of Leadership Deplored', TG, July 31, 1956.
27 The era of machine politics dates from the introduction of universal suffrage in 1946.

and trade-union activity, but without much success. Cipriani failed to appreciate the developing needs of those for whom he spoke. As Max Farquhar noted, 'His leadership did not survive the evolution of the barefoot man ... into the working class proletariat protected by trade unions. ... His rugged individualism was soon overrun ... and he was left stranded, a lonely monument of defiance, forgotten.'[28]

By 1935 the Cipriani movement showed obvious signs of disintegration, though it was not before the general strike of 1937 that the *coup de grâce* was finally administered. Fifteen years of undisputed leadership seemed to have sapped Cipriani's will to fight the establishment, which, by the mid-thirties, had already begun to regard him as a 'statesman and patriot'. It is true that in 1934–5 the movement seems to have expanded considerably as determined attempts were made to reinvigorate and enlarge its membership and to familiarize members with reasons for the change of name, but by the end of 1935 the TLP had lost much of its hold on the masses, especially in the oil-bearing areas in the south of the island. Even as new branches were being formed, stalwarts admitted a fall in membership.

A number of events contributed to the declining influence of the TLP in this period. The primary factor was growing unemployment and spiraling prices consequent upon the world economic depression. In March of 1935, following an abortive strike at one of the oil fields, a group of eighty workers led by Tubal Uriah Butler started out on a sixty-mile hunger march to the capital city, an event that marked the first major open challenge to Cipriani's leadership. Butler himself was a member of the TLP, as were some of the men who followed him. Cipriani successfully headed off the demonstration before it erupted into violence, and urged the workers to continue using constitutional procedures to air their grievances.[29] But it is clear that the workers were grow-

---

28   TG, Feb. 9, 1956.
29   Cipriani, together with the police, stopped the march with the promise that he would arrange for a delegation to see the Governor about their grievances. Though the promise was kept, no redress was forthcoming. On May 19, 1933 Cipriani told a restless gathering of workers that while he did not dispute their constitutional rights to organize a hunger march, it had to be recognized that such a gesture involved real dangers. 'If, however, you are insistent upon this form of demonstration, then I advise not a huge, but a small one, well controlled and led by men who are sound and level-headed and who will not forget that violence in any form ... will hinder ... your legitimate demands.' There must be no repetition of the fiasco of 1903. 'Violence was the way of the communists and not of socialists.' Violence as a strategy for the gaining of power had lost its legitimacy, he believed. *People*, May 20, 1933. 'As far as the West Indies are concerned, our method must be peaceful because we have neither means, money nor arms. ... Our path must be one of peaceful evolution because we cannot fight, because the violence that West Indians might

ing more and more impatient with Cipriani's Fabianism, and were eager to take to the streets to dramatize their plight. The rise of direct-action movements around the world was beginning to influence them. Despite the limitations on trade-union activity, there were strikes in the oil and sugar industries in 1935, as well as in the public sector.

The struggle for minimum wages also served to heighten dissatisfaction with Cipriani's leadership. Together with the Negro Welfare and Cultural League, the TWA/TLP had been in the vanguard of the fight for minimum-wage legislation. When this was finally introduced in 1935 it was a crude disappointment to the workers in that it gave them no concrete hope that they would receive a living wage. The bill was in fact only an enabling ordinance which permitted the government to act if it determined that an enterprise was paying substandard wages.

What further infuriated workers was that Cipriani signed the report of the Wages Board, which had been appointed to draw up a cost-of-living index.[30] The report itself, by using questionable indices for assessing the real needs of the population, gave the impression that few workers were being paid substandard wages. No minimum-wage legislation followed. The failure of the minimum-wage movement marked the end of an era wherein workers were prepared to accept arguments in favour of political moderation. They were becoming more predisposed to listen to the militant voices which were calling for the organization of trade unions to take care of the day-to-day needs of the worker regardless of the risks involved.

It is worth noting that in 1936 two of Cipriani's lieutenants struck out on their own, taking a substantial number of the party members with them. Both Adrian Cola Rienzi and Uriah Butler had come to feel that they could no longer function within the TLP and founded organizations designed to promote the workers' cause more aggressively. In the case of Rienzi, who founded the Trinidad Citizens League in 1936, Cipriani made it quite clear that he considered him a communist as well as a threat to his leadership.[31] Cipriani's main weakness was his congenital inability to share leadership, and his unwillingness to listen to the younger voices in the Party:

There [was] nothing savouring of democracy in the operation of the organization. ... Many a member who attempted to exercise rigorously his God-given right of

use is a kind of violence that has never convinced anybody, and frequently has recoiled on the heads of those who practised it.' At the West Indian Conference, Dominica, in 1933, *His Best Orations*, p. 101.
30 Council Paper no. 88, Port of Spain, 1936.
31 Cipriani had always opposed the tendency of southern sections of the TWA under Rienzi's leadership to caucus and function as a bloc at island-wide meetings.

doing a little thinking for himself was forced to quit. Anything the Captain said or did, whether right or wrong, reasonable or foolish, if questioned, angered his idolators. Honest differences of opinion were regarded by his satellites as manifestations of disloyalty. ... Only those who could submit their minds and personalities to domination, and perceive wisdom in every whim and caprice of the gallant Captain, could remain in his movement; and the others went out and started to spread their ideas and doctrines.[32]

The TLP was further weakened because of the *ad hoc* nature of its operations and its failure to evolve any coherent ideology relevant to the needs of the time.[33] As with other Trinidadian political formations which succeeded it, the TLP was essentially a one-man affair, destined to fade into oblivion when its leader ceased to command magic enough to bind followers to his person. Cipriani never succeeded in projecting his undoubted charismatic influence unto the organization itself. And when in the strike crisis of 1936–7 his popularity suffered a sharp decline, the TLP, despite efforts to revive it, ceased to have any real influence. Cipriani failed the colony's labour movement at the most critical stage of its development.[34] C.L.R. James believes, 'If in 1937 Cipriani had been the man he had been ten years earlier, self-government, federation and economic integration ... could have been initiated then. But the old warrior was nearly seventy. He flinched at the mass upheavals which he, more than anyone else had prepared, and the opportunity was lost.'[35] After 1936 the torch of leadership had passed to others. The blue-shirted proletariat had seized the initiative from the barefooted 'khaki brigade'.

In spite of his limitations as a party leader, Cipriani contributed more than any other figure of his time towards the building of a national consciousness among Trinidadians. He constantly urged them and other West Indians to

32 E.R. Blades, 'The Wailing of Vivian Henry', *People*, Feb. 19, 1938. F.W. Dalley also wrote that 'The new Party was ... largely a one-man affair despite its island-wide character and its numerous branches. It seems to have lacked a political philosophy or even a considered programme adapted to the needs of the situation.' *Trade Union Organization and Industrial Relations in Trinidad*, Port of Spain, 1947, p. 5.

33 'The Party was not built upon the foundation of any particular political or social ideology, but around the personalities of its President General. The Party minus Captain Cipriani does not exist. The moment the gallant captain ceased to exert a magic influence upon the rank and file ... his society began to crumble.' Blades, 'Vivian Henry'.

34 Conservatives as well as radicals regretted that Cipriani had failed the labour movement in its time of troubles. As the *Guardian* noted, 'It is a matter for regret that he failed to keep in touch with the new trends in the movement, thus depriving it of the steadying influence of his mature experience.' TG, April 23, 1945.

35 *Black Jacobins*, p. 404.

cultivate pride in themselves and in their country. The solution to the problems of the area was their responsibility. As he told the 1933 West Indian Conference: 'We shall not be sold to the United States of America. We are not going to become a Canadian province; we will not continue under Crown rule. We are going to enjoy rights of citizenship such as every other part of the Empire enjoys; we claim it on the grounds that the scale upon which we are to be judged must be the scale of merit, and upon this, we claim the right to administer the government of our country.'[36] It is worth noting, however, that Cipriani was a great lover of the monarchy and the Empire, and that he was always loyalist in his politics. At no time did he come out for full independence from Britain. All demands for social and political reforms were made within the imperial framework.

Cipriani died in 1945. One year later, the colony held its first elections under universal suffrage. In those years too the first positive steps were being taken to make federation a reality. Cipriani had seriously undermined the legitimacy of the old colonial system. But it was Butler who brought it down.

36   Speech at West Indian Conference, Dominica, *His Best Orations*, p. 102.

3

The collapse of the old political order
1936-45

The depression of the 1930s showed up only too well the precarious nature of the colonial economy. The entire agricultural sector on which the bulk of the population relied for a livelihood was brought to a state of near-collapse. Since most of its currency earnings came from the export of agricultural staples, the colony found itself unable to maintain its living standards.[1] The depression struck just when asphalt and oil were beginning to make a noticeable impact on the colony's economy.[2] But despite its buoyancy the mineral industry did not absorb the slack in the economy occasioned by the decline in agriculture.[3] The industry's contribution to the colony's revenues was minimal. A commission which investigated the oil industry in 1927 noted that, 'Compared with the terms granted in most countries, there is no doubt about the leniency of the royalty rates hitherto demanded by the Government in Trinidad.'[4] There

1 Whereas the average yearly earnings of the agricultural sector between 1926 and 1928 amounted to £2,902,645, in 1935 it had dropped to £1,696,423. Great Britain, Colonial Office, *Report of Commission on Trinidad and Tobago Disturbances, 1937*, Cmd. 5641, London, 1938; hereafter *Forster Report*.
2 Between 1920 and 1927 oil production expanded by 250 per cent, the 1927 output being in the vicinity of 5,380,178 barrels. By 1936 it had reached 13,237,030 barrels, an increase of 150 per cent. The production of asphalt, however, suffered a decline during the depression years. In the 1932–6 period, production averaged 82,763 tons compared with 187,142 tons in the 1927–31 period, a decline of 44 per cent. Trinidad had become the foremost producer of oil in the British Empire, accounting for 62.8 per cent of the total output. This, however, was only about .92 per cent of the world's total production in 1936. *Ibid.*, p. 23.
3 The oil and asphalt industries employed only 9,000 people directly with an estimated 27,000 persons dependent upon them for a livelihood.
4 *Oil Industry of Trinidad*, report of Sir Thomas Holland, 1928, cited in Williams, *History of the People of Trinidad and Tobago*, New York, 1964, p. 225.

was a loud cry that, as a wasting asset, oil should contribute more to the social development of the colony.[5] The wages in the industry, although higher than in the agricultural sector, were extremely low, partly as a result of the demands of the plantocracy that oil should not be permitted to dislocate the wage structure. The rapid development of the oil industry had a very unsettling effect on the entire society, especially in the southern region where its principal operations were located, and it was no surprise that the historic general strike of 1937 was nurtured in this area.

BUTLER AND THE 1937 STRIKE

The crisis produced a different style of leadership from the one which Cipriani typified. A new political figure, the sweaty demagogue, had made his appearance, not only in Trinidad, but throughout most of the West Indian islands. In Trinidad and Tobago, the new leader was Tubal Uriah Butler, and the political style he represented came to be known as 'Butlerism'.

Butler was born in Grenada around 1891. During the First World War he joined the West India Regiment and, like many of the radicals of his time, hero-worshipped Cipriani. He was attracted to Trinidad by the 'oil boom' of the early twenties, and, being a compulsive agitator, very quickly became involved in left-wing politics. Butler possessed many of the attributes of the typical political agitator. A magnificent and fiery orator, he had, much more than did Cipriani, the ability to inflame the masses. He not only knew the crowds to whom he spoke more intimately than did the Captain but had the additional advantage of being able to speak to them in their own idiom. He was of the masses in every sense of the word. He was also a man obsessed with a sense of mission. He believed that God had appointed him to lead the people of the West Indies from the wilderness of colonialism. Uriah Butler, with the help of God, was, in his view, the 'saviour' of the enslaved masses of the West Indies.[6] All the energy and conviction which he had formerly displayed as an evangelizing Moravian Baptist were now applied to the cause of political

5 Opponents of increased taxation of oil stressed the need to maintain a steady inflow of risk-taking capital for investments in new fields.

6 'After years and years of weepings and groanings, untold miseries and complainings, prayers and petitioning ... the toiling masses of the colony prayed to the God of Justice and Fairplay, Freedom and Liberty, the God of their ancient and incomparably glorious African forefathers, to send them a leader. He came in the name of the Spiritual Lion of the Tribe of Judah, the Great King Jesus ... in a new political organization known as the British Empire Workers and Citizens Home Rule Party of Trinidad where he took evidence of the sufferings of his people. I look to Jesus Christ. ... Let us hope that God in his mercy will not desert his suffering black children in South Trinidad, and that justice will in the end prevail.' People, June 26, 1937.

emancipation. Convinced that Cipriani's 'back-pedalling and somersaulting tactics' were restraining the progress of the workers, Butler founded his first political party, the British Empire Workers and Citizens Home Rule Party, in 1936. Together with those whom he called his 'working-class warriors', he argued that Cipriani's methods had been given fair trial, and had proven ineffectual. As a 'white liberal' Cipriani hesitated just when a final 'big push' was vitally necessary; he was too reliant on his white friends in the British Labour party.

The plight of the worker was indeed becoming more and more desperate, and desperate strategies were called for. Between 1935 and 1937, Butler went up and down the oil belt rallying people to his banner. His prophetic and expressive language attracted many persons who had now ceased to see in shades of grey.[7] For them depression and unemployment were not the result of the workings of the world forces beyond the control of Trinidad, but rather the machinations of the 'blue-eyed devils' who disposed of the colony's economic and political fortunes. The oil magnates were the arch-offenders in this regard. Butler's strategy was to wage a frontal attack on the colonial order. He and other radicals believed that no advances could be achieved for the working class unless they themselves were willing to make real sacrifices. One must not only rail against the old order; one must be willing to take direct action to overthrow it, if necessary. The rise of militant mass movements in Europe and America which were preaching the gospel of direct action had begun to embolden the Trinidadian masses. The notion of the general strike and its magical potency had come to dominate their counsels.

But the decision to go on strike was taken only after every other alternative had been tried and had failed. Butler had even gone down on his knees to beg the Governor to intervene on behalf of his suffering followers. Approaches were also made to the employers by way of letters and open appeals. Both parties were informed that the workers would have to strike in order to dramatize their plight if redress was not forthcoming.[8] According to Butler, the attitude of the employers was: 'Ignore the nigger; these blacks only bark, they cannot bite.' It was only after he had become firmly convinced that British justice and fair play were not available to loyal British blacks under the colonial system that he yielded to demands for a general strike. 'The prayers,

7   In 1937, before his 'martyrdom', Butler claimed that his Party had one thousand members. He confessed, however, that not all of these were hard-core 'working-class warriors'. The militants numbered only about one hundred.

8   'I never intended to hide from the Government, but bravely and at every turn, and in my own peculiar impressive and fiery manner, warned them of the course such unrest was liable to take.' *People*, July 3, 1937. The Governor had promised to visit the depressed areas, but did not keep his promise.

petitions and bootlicking tactics of a suffering class' having failed, there was no choice but to accept the challenge of the employers. Butler insists that no violence was ever intended. 'The strike was carefully planned to eliminate or minimize the use of armed violence.'[9] It was thought that a sit-down strike would be enough to dramatize the worker's determination. In Butler's view it was the heavy-handed blundering of the police and the employer class which transformed what began as a constitutional withdrawal of labour into a savage expression of racial and class violence that took the lives of fourteen people, caused injury to fifty-nine, and did substantial damage to property. The strike released all the pent-up emotions of the blacks. Sabotage, which had always been a latent characteristic of the slave system, now became legitimate as the masses looted, burned, and destroyed. The underlying causes of the strike were fivefold: they involved economic problems, racial tension, poor labour relations, constitutional difficulties, and the role of Butler himself.

Economic causes
The economic crisis through which the colony was going was in large part responsible for the climate which precipitated the disturbances. Rising prices, reduced wages, and widespread unemployment and underemployment lay at the bottom of it all. During the extraordinary session of the Legislative Council summoned on July 9 to discuss the riots, the Governor, Sir Murchison Fletcher, revealed that prices had risen approximately 17 per cent over the 1935 figures.[10] It was also known that despite the depression the oil companies had had an extremely prosperous year.[11]

The same was true in sugar. By dint of rigid economies, rationalization, increased acreages, and the stabilization of prices and quotas following upon the International Sugar Conference of 1937, the sugar companies were actually able to declare dividends of 5½ to 7½ per cent in 1937. These dividends were declared, however, at the expense of wage increases for sugar workers. As the Forster Commission observed, 'During this period of rational-

9 Butler, like Cipriani, was always loyal to the Crown and British ideals. He referred to his followers as 'a band of *Empire Patriots* sworn to rid Trinidad and the Empire of evil employer policies and unconstitutional governmental policies everywhere under the good old Union Jack'. *People*, June 26, 1937.
10 *Hansard*, July 9, 1937, pp. 256–8. Figures put out by the Central Statistical Office indicate that this figure was an exaggeration. Using 1935 as a base year (100), the cso estimated that the cost of living index had risen to 111 by January of 1938. *Annual Statistical Digest*, Government of Trinidad and Tobago, 1935–52.
11 Balance sheets published in London showed that oil profits had jumped from £669,128 in 1935–6 to £1,090,949 in 1936–7. Dividends paid amounted to 30 per cent, a 5 per cent increase over 1935–6. *People*, Jan. 29, 1938.

ization, labour contributed its share by continuing to accept a standard of wage and living conditions far below that which is desirable.'[12]

The Governor himself was convinced that the colony's income-distribution system was iniquitous, and he took the unprecedented step of calling upon industries, especially sugar, to 'examine their position and see whether they cannot spare something more for labour than they now pay ... perhaps they might either declare no dividend until labour conditions are better, or declare a minimum dividend and apply the balance to the improvement of those conditions'.[13]

Another source of industrial unrest was the gap in wages between skilled and unskilled workers. The Governor put his finger on the problem when he declared:

In Trinidad we have a surplus of unskilled labour, the supply being greater than the demand. On the other hand, there is a comparative scarcity of skilled and semi-skilled workers, the result being that, while unskilled labour is depressed, the skilled man gets a considerably higher proportionate wage. In England the difference between unskilled labour and the skilled artisan, skilled in the full sense of the word, is roughly 33⅓ %. In Trinidad the difference between unskilled and skilled workers is 150%.[14]

Unskilled workers complained that they were being forced to work for as many as ninety hours per week at 70 or 80 cents per hour, and that they were living in subhuman conditions. In addition to a 50 per cent increase to bring them up to what was considered a living-wage, they demanded free medical attention, improved working conditions, and double pay for overtime work. The oil companies offered a 2-cent-per-hour increase with no fringe benefits. As far as they knew, 'the workers were happy, contented people who had been misled by extremist mountebanks.'

12 *Forster Report*, p. 14.
13 *Hansard*, July 9, 1937, p. 257. The Governor showed an extreme sensitivity to the plight of the peasants and other unskilled workers when he declared: 'The agriculture industry ... is at the base of our troubles. Things move there in a vicious circle. Agriculture has been depressed, the unskilled labour market has been overstocked, wages have been pressed down. When a man has not got a living wage, he cannot possibly be efficient; he is worried, there are debts, rent unpaid, wife ill, a number of hungry children to be fed and he cannot put in a proper full day's work. Nobody can, under such conditions.' To underline his sincerity, and to give a lead to other concerns, the Governor raised the wages of government workers and introduced the eight-hour day, 'which is the utmost that people of enfeebled physique should be called upon to work'. *Ibid.*, p. 258.
14 *Ibid.*, p. 254.

The racial factor

Race was the second underlying cause of the disturbances. The fact that those who suffered most during the depression years were Negro and Indian did not go unnoticed. This was something that Butler and the Negro Welfare and Cultural League repeatedly stressed. The oil workers were also bitterly opposed to the oil companies' policy of employing South African whites in top technical and managerial positions. The workers complained that the South Africans treated them as though they were tribalized Bantus.[15] Another vexing problem concerned that of promotion. Blacks objected strongly to the practice of appointing young white men to senior posts over the heads of qualified black men. The fact that segregated recreational and hospital facilities were maintained also provoked the ire of the workers, as did the belief that managers were recruiting Indians to replace militant Negro workers.[16]

While for the most part these tensions and grievances were latent, the inflammatory speeches of Butler, and the rape of Abyssinia by Italy served to bring them to the surface. The pleas of Haile Selassie to the League of Nations and the do-nothing attitude of the white democracies had left a searing imprint on the minds of the West Indian masses.[17] Curiously enough, the Forster Commission relegated to insignificance the contention that racial animosity was a key factor during the disturbance:

Despite the cosmopolitan character of its population, the Colony is singularly free from religious or racial animosities, and consequently no disturbances other than that of industrial character could at any time have been anticipated; nor indeed outside the comparatively small hooligan element was racial agitation a feature of the disturbances. The evidence shows that racial feeling when, and to the extent which, it arises is a secondary symptom of some primary form of discontent. We are satisfied that if disturbances arise in the future it will be out of a failure to

15 One of the larger oil companies, Trinidad Leaseholds, had close institutional connections with the Central Mining and Investment Corporation of South Africa. 'South African bosses do not seem to appreciate that the methods and conditions that obtain in the land of Oom Paul cannot be conducive to peace in a place like Trinidad. Black men here have been brought up to believe in British Justice. ... You cannot treat an intelligent people whose civilization is European in the same way you deal with a backward community without causing trouble.' 'Our Labour Troubles'. *People*, June 26, 1937.

16 The East Indian worker was very late in moving into the oil industry. Negroes had by then come to regard oil as their own preserve.

17 'The betrayal of Abyssinia is nearly as much to blame for the riots in Trinidad and Tobago as is the high cost of living.' Calder Marshall, *Glory Dead*, London, 1939, p. 254.

appreciate and meet industrial problems in a Colony with an awakening industrial consciousness.[18]

The commissioners, like other commissioners before them, were completely blinded by the superficial harmony which governed racial relations in the Caribbean. In point of fact, the 'hooligan element' was merely giving open expression to feelings of aggression covertly held by others. The remarks of the commission are perhaps true in so far as they refer to the agricultural population; for outside of the industrial sector anti-white hostility does not seem to have loomed very large. The industrial population was much more aware of the social and economic gap which divided it from the ruling élite. The demonstrative effect of radio, cinema, and the press had had a much greater impact on the urban dweller than on his rural counterpart. The feelings of normlessness and ethnic rivalry which enervated urban folk in a rapidly changing society were muted in the countryside by the influence of family, church, and other primary relationships. The slower rate of economic change did not produce the type of discontinuities that one found in the oil-producing regions of the colony. Closer ethnic juxtaposition in the towns also served to sharpen inter-group hostility.

Inadequate labour relations
The third factor underlying the disturbances, and perhaps the most immediate, was the almost total absence of institutional arrangements for the articulation of the grievances of the working class. At the time of the disturbances, apart from Butler's organization, there were only two weak and rather ineffective trade unions in existence. As a result of this lack, there was a continuous accumulation of grievances which, in more mature economies, would have been dealt with in the normal course of management-labour relations. Without a union to intercede for him and cushion the effect of his new relationship to large-scale machinery, the worker was left completely isolated, a victim of the frustrations and uncertainties typical of such situations.

It is important to observe here that it was the local and not the British government which was principally to blame for the total absence of any conciliating machinery in the colony. Permission to establish an industrial court had been granted as far back as 1920. Although the enabling legislation had

18   *Forster Report*, p. 79. During the strike, workers looted bungalows, called domestic servants off the job, forced whites to frog-march out of their homes, etc. In the course of my discussions with old workers, I found them very eager to tell of these incidents. The Governor himself reported to the Legislature that the reports he had from the fields indicated that the strike was becoming racial.

been passed by the Legislature, and the court's first president appointed, the court itself was never established. Similarly, though the establishment of minimum wage-fixing machinery was recommended to the colonial Legislature by the home government, and an enabling ordinance passed in the colony to that effect in 1935, nothing concrete was achieved. The colonial government further demonstrated its insensitivity to the welfare of the working class by failing to act on the recommendation put forward by the Secretary of State for the Colonies that labour departments be created to help bridge the gap between manager and worker.

So deficient was the communication between employers and employees that the former could claim there was no general demand for wage increases among the working population. The employers' contentions lacked credibility, however, since the representative of the oil industry on the Legislative Council was aware of price movements, and had in fact proposed a small wage increase to the Petroleum Association. It would appear that the crisis was hastened by the belief that the oil companies had refused the recommended wage increases and were considering other methods for dealing with the problem.[19] The absence of proper channels of communication must thus be identified as one of the essential causes of this state of affairs. As the Forster Report rightly observed, 'Where no organized machinery existed for collective representations and joint discussions, what the work-people were thinking could only find expression by individual complaints, and as these were not likely to be too sympathetically received, the number in fact put forward cannot be regarded as a safe indication of the measure of discontent.'[20]

Worker-management relationships in the sugar industry were no better than they were in the oil industry. The Indians who made up the bulk of the work force in the sugar belt lived and worker in conditions that were even more

19 The Association had actually agreed to raising the wages of the lowest wage brackets by a penny an hour but was still exercised over the problem of a general wage increase.
20 *Forster Report*, pp. 80–1. The observations of Mr Nankivell, the Acting Colonial Secretary for Trinidad, in this context are also worth repeating: 'We also were given to understand by the men that they were not encouraged to make any complaints: further than that, they were afraid to! There was no proper channel through which such complaints could be made. We know from personal experience that if juniors in a large firm or a large government department make complaints they are likely to be branded as discontented workers, or as so many people like to call them, agitators and communists. It is a very easy way to deal with difficulties when anyone complains to dub him communist and agitator. As soon as one has done that, he is finished: nobody else wants to hear what he has to say; whether he be right or wrong, he must be wrong because he is a communist and an agitator.' *Hansard*, July 19, 1937, p. 264.

primitive than their Negro counterparts in the oil industry. With the ending of the indenture system in 1917, the Indians were deprived of whatever little assistance they were afforded by the Protector of Immigrants, to whom they had the right to protest in case of injustice or neglect arising out of their terms of contract. Following 1917, the employer was relieved of any legal responsibility for his employees, who were now at the mercy of the plantation overseer. As the commissioners noted,

Employers engaged in the sugar industry appear to have displayed a lack of regard for the well-being of their labour. ... In no direction is this lack of regard more apparent then in the deplorable conditions in which a large number of the labourers and their families are housed. ... The consequent undercurrent of discontent could not fail to find expression among a large section of the work-people when the outbreak of the disturbances on 19th June awakened in them a more or less conscious sense of common interest in the removal of common disabilities.[21]

There is some uncertainty regarding the extent to which the Indian community was spontaneously involved in the riots of 1937. According to the planters, the Indians were unwilling participants in strike activity. They were said to be 'perfectly happy in their conditions'. The Governor did not accept this contention however. Theirs was a case of lethargy induced by disease and hunger, a lethargy that was 'broken only on festive occasions or in times of disorder'.[22]

In contrast to workers in the sugar industry, those in the cocoa and coffee industries were not affected in any noticeable way by the disturbances. The Forster Commission speculated that the closer and more enlightened relations between labour and management which characterized plantation operations in these two industries were largely responsible for the failure of the protest movement there. The commissioners seemed convinced that the communication gap between management and labour was the principal reason for the explosion of 1937: 'Had there existed in the oilfields and elsewhere organized means of collective bargaining through which the claims or grievances of the work-people would have found ample means of expression, there can be little doubt but that the disturbances which subsequently arose might have been avoided. As it was, the road was open to any irresponsible leadership that might appear upon the scene.'[23] In short, they did not believe that political issues were important ingredients of the crisis.

21 *Forster Report*, pp 75–6.
22 *Hansard*, July 19, 1937, p. 252. The Indians were among the most diseased elements of the population. As a result of the poor sewerage facilities of the barracks in which they were made to live, there was a heavy incidence of ankylostomiasis (hookworm). In some Indian districts approximately 80 per cent of the population was infected.
23 *Forster Report*, p. 81.

The constitutional factor

It is evident, however, that the unrepresentative nature of the political system was a major underlying cause of the eruptions. One of the things that became clear in 1937 was that Trinidad had no native spokesman who could intervene authoritatively in a crisis of this magnitude. Of the seven elected members of the Legislature, only Cipriani could have made any claim to popular legitimacy; and, as noted above, Cipriani (who was out of the colony when the crisis broke) no longer commanded the respect which he once enjoyed. Cipriani had so completely overshadowed the other members of the Trinidad Labour Party that there was no one within its ranks who could speak with any authority. The crisis merely served to illustrate the extent to which the Legislative Council was unresponsive to the needs of the native population. As Dr Tito Achong observed, 'The Council was a three-cornered device for the maintenance of unmitigated lordship over the so-called native population. ... The Government has not yielded one wee bit of the prerogative it enjoyed prior to the Wood "Reform". It and the elected block have no common ground for collaboration in the interest of the socio-economic progress of the people as a whole. Their points of difference are marked, fundamental ... and seemingly irreconcilable.'[24]

The elected representatives themselves did not reflect the opinions of the masses. At no time did they concert their efforts to pressure the Government for the implementation of a programme to meet the problems facing the community. It is no exaggeration to claim that the non-officials were invariably the Governor's 'yes-men', who were more concerned about their standing with the establishment than about the workers, who pointedly ignored them during the crisis. Given the limited nature of the franchise, this was not surprising. For the most part, the elected representatives were satisfied with being appointed to powerless committees, with assurances and explanations of government policy, and with the occasional snipe at the citadels of power.

24 *People*, Jan. 8, 1938. Achong, who was one of the few professionals to identify and assist the workers, lamented the fact that the professional middle class did not come forward to provide leadership. 'Education and leadership in Trinidad appear to be incompatible things. From the coterie of educated natives, no leadership has yet sprung, and none appears within sight. Persons with some sort of education, especially those schooled in the professions at the expense of public funds, are dexterous only in angling for subordinate jobs, where they are satisfied to live a vegetative life. They show no interest in public movements and seem not at all prone to adjusting themselves for disinterested service ... whatever leadership there is, is in the hands of ... proletarians. ... Psychologically, the so-called educated class are beaten. Their personality is seriously traumatized. The disease however is not an inherent one; its etiology is purely environmental, due mainly to the absence of local bodies within which leadership could be nurtured as was the case in Jamaica.' *Ibid.*, Jan. 22, 1938.

With the working-class leadership undergoing a major transition, and with Butler in detention, it fell to the Governor of the colony, Sir Murchison Fletcher, and the Acting Colonial Secretary, N. Nankivell, to assume the national leadership.[25] From one point of view it may be said that during the crisis of 1937 the Crown colony system in Trinidad and Tobago enjoyed its finest hour. Normally colonial governors were expected to function in a variety of roles which in practice were not always consistent. They were expected to represent the Crown in all its dignity and imperial majesty; they were also expected to function as prime ministers and leaders of the official 'party'. It was also understood that, as the embodiment of the trusteeship idea, the Governor would assume the role of defender of and spokesman for the welfare of the natives under his tutelage.

Generally speaking, governors and their officials tended to neglect the last-mentioned responsibility which, theoretically speaking, was the most important, and were over-protective of the interests of metropolitan and local capital. As Calder Marshall wrote,

If Trinidad is a true example of Crown Colony government, the theory is a myth, covering a history of savage exploitation. Trinidad has never been a poor island. Since the English seizure of it, wealth has constantly been drained from the island, a toll taken from the various peoples imported there to be exploited. ... It is a rich island, with 90% of the population impoverished. ... The benevolent tyranny which is supposed to be superior to the interests of exploiting capital, has in fact legislated throughout in the interests of that class. It has been the political side of capitalism, with a different personnel but to a common aim. ... The benevolent tyranny, close to the demands of big business but distant from the workers, has blundered on, deaf to the cries of distress because it has not tried to listen.[26]

The fundamental difficulty, of course, was that the trusteeship concept had been born in the era of laissez-faire capitalism; the ideas involved in the two concepts of protection and capitalism were quite inconsistent, and, except for fitful moments, the inconsistencies were resolved in favour of the latter. Hewan Craig puts the matter a little differently, but his conclusion is the same:

The doctrine of trusteeship on which the system was based was suited to conditions in the West Indies of the nineteenth century, but in the present century it became increasingly difficult to apply. In the time of slavery and after, the government could intervene effectively to prevent exploitation of the negroes in its more brutal

---

25   The principal intermediary between the workers and the authorities during Butler's enforced absence from the political scene was Rienzi.

26   *Glory Dead*, pp. 284–5. Marshall, an English journalist, was in Trinidad during the disturbances and assisted workers in their efforts to organize themselves.

and obvious forms. It was not equipped, either ideologically or technically, to combat the more subtle forms of exploitation which are liable to occur in a modern economy. The Home government, although the Secretary of State accepted personal responsibility for the shortcomings of the Trinidad government, relied for its knowledge of local conditions chiefly on the governor and could not be expected to function with full effectiveness as guardian of the interests of the working class.[27]

The type of educational social service state which was implicit in the trusteeship idea never became a part of British colonial policy until 1938–9.

But in 1937 the Governor, no doubt in the face of serious opposition, took his trusteeship role seriously and emerged, if only for a short while, as the champion of the interests of the worker. Fletcher tried to build a sadly needed bridge between the white ruling class and the black working force. He felt that the white man, by his attitudes and actions, was encouraging fear and hostility rather than respect, and suggested to the white community that its members could not realistically expect to safeguard their lives and property by the use of force. Legitimacy and social control did not normally ensue from the use of naked force. 'The white employer class in Trinidad will find in tact and sympathy a shield far more sure than any forest of bayonets to be planted here.'[28]

Fletcher in fact seemed to welcome the riots. He felt that they provided the opportunity for the introduction of a number of social and political changes which were necessary for the well-being of the colony. 'We needed a cataclysm in order to act', he declared. The disturbances had provided the colony with a 'salutary purge which, given good will on all sides, should render the body social more healthy and more happy. If this lesson which has been taught, is learned, and if its meaning is taken to heart – if there is inculcated thereby more generosity, more sympathy, more patience, then our travail will not have been in vain and a new Trinidad will come to birth.'[29]

Uriah Butler and the crisis
The activity of Butler was another major factor in the disturbances. Butler's role in introducing the element of 'positive action' into the politics of the country has already been mentioned. What needs to be examined further is

27 *The Legislative Council of Trinidad and Tobago*, London, 1951, p. 138.
28 *Hansard*, July 19, 1937, p. 258.
29 *Hansard*, July 19, 1937, p. 259. Fletcher maintained that it was the white settlers who thwarted attempts on the part of the administration to improve the living standards of the people. 'Captain Cipriani had for years moved this Council to fix a minimum wage. We have found many obstacles which we have not been able to surmount, but now the opportunity has come, and it has been taken by the Government in order to fix definitely a minimum wage, not a large one, but a wage which will give a reasonable livelihood to the people.'

Butler's historical 'responsibility' for the events of 1937. Was Butler a great leader of the masses, or was he the unwitting instrument of larger forces over which he had little control? The Forster Commission, which was quite unsympathetic to Butler, whom it described as a 'fanatical negro', inclined towards the latter view. While agreeing that the 'immediate cause of the outbreak was the activities of Butler and the unruly element of which his following was mainly composed',[30] the commissioners felt that Butler's power over the workers had been greatly exaggerated. Indeed they believed that had the Governor acted sooner to detain Butler, rather than first attempting to negotiate with him, the crisis would have been considerably shortened.[31]

But the fact is that there was no other spokesman acceptable to the workers to whom the Governor could turn. Butler was extremely popular with them, and, as events showed, the attempt to effect his arrest merely served to sharpen the crisis.[32] By moving against Butler, the authorities had in fact co-operated in his 'martyrdom'.[33] Butler's historical role was thus to provide the catalyst, to crystallize and articulate the grievances that people had long nursed, and to offer them an 'acceptable' outlet for aggressive dispositions which Cipriani had held in check. But it is not correct to claim, as some do, that Butler was a great national hero, one of the liberators of the West Indian people. Calder Marshall's estimate is nearer the mark:

Butler was in fact neither a fanatic nor a great leader. He was an agitator. But it is necessary to clarify the meaning of the word 'agitator'. No agitator is capable of putting into people's heads ideas that are not there already. His function is to put the ideas that are already in people's heads into words. His superiority lies in articulation. He is capable in his speeches and on rarer occasions in his actions to give expression to the thoughts and the desires of the people. It is when the fate of one man becomes identified with the fate of the group that trouble is liable to start.

30 *Forster Report*, p. 82. Butler's first strike call to the workers on June 7 was abortive.
31 For this point of view, they claimed the support of Cipriani and the TLP, who had also contended that the Butlerites were stirring up racial ill-will and inciting violence, and that the Governor should deal harshly and quickly with these 'false heroes'.
32 'We solemnly vote not to resume work unless we are fully assured by our leader ... that the Oil Companies have arrived at an adequate settlement wtih him. ... We want no other leader and we demand no arrest of him.' Resolution of the Strike Action Committee, *People*, June 26, 1937.
33 'Uriah Butler remains a figure around whom is grouped a feeling of reverence. He is the inspiration of the movement, almost the patron saint. The imprisonment ... provided the island with a popular martyr.' Marshall, *Glory Dead*, p. 235. Butler was tried and sentenced to two years for sedition. He was released in 1939 before completing his sentence.

... The police succeeded in producing this identification. Butler had been saying what people thought for a long while. ... [He] had suddenly become the leader of the coloured workers.[34]

Sir Murchison Fletcher also shared the view that Butler's principal function was as a sort of political midwife at the *accouchement* of the new social order. 'Butler is an agitator ... a person who stirs things up. I have tried to stir things up; and Butler has done it so much more effectively then I have been able to.'[35]

Cipriani's behaviour during the crisis, and that of the TLP, indicate that they had lost touch with the aspirations of the worker.[36] Butler was accused of using the element of race to overthrow Cipriani as the idol of the masses. Cipriani himself was deeply chagrined that after so many years of sacrifice on the workers' behalf, they had deserted him for 'false gods'. But as Hewan Craig observes,

Cipriani's decline and Butler's rise in working-class favour were ... to some degree symptomatic of the changing attitude of the Trinidad negro towards the white man. ... The fact that Cipriani was a white man may have been to his advantage when he assumed the leadership of the labour movement in the 1920s. Cipriani's shortcomings as a labour leader may have contributed to the subsequent decline in white prestige, but it is possible that this was brought about also by his success in other respects – in articulating the workers' grievances, in teaching them to organize for political action, in awakening them to a realization of their power. It was probably inevitable in the natural course of development of the labour movement that negro leaders of working-class origin should arise, but to some extent it was also perhaps the very attitude which Cipriani had aroused among the workers which caused them to transfer their allegiance to Butler in 1937.[37]

34 *Ibid.*, p. 227.
35 *Hansard*, July 19, 1937, p. 276. Fletcher felt that though Butler tended to be 'extravagant and deficient in judgment, there runs through all his speeches and more particularly his letters, an undercurrent of earnest appeal made in all sincerity, to which a deaf ear has been turned'.
36 The TLP in fact supported the Government during the crisis. Cipriani told the workers that their demand for a 50 per cent increase was unreasonable and that it would not meet with the support of 'friends in London'. The companies could not afford it, he insisted. The workers, on the other hand, felt that a 100 per cent increase was much more reasonable. Cipriani also bitterly denounced the strategy of 'direct action' as being dangerous and irresponsible. 'The policy of the TLP has always been to set its face against such methods ... [it] is deadly opposed to anything savouring of violence and red riot ... those within its ranks who feel dissatisfied ... have only one thing to do, and that is to get out and that too, quickly. We will not ... be any party to a regime of holdups.' TG, June 26, 1937.
37 Craig, *Legislative Council*, pp. 123–4. When in June of 1939 Rienzi introduced a

CONSEQUENCES OF THE DISTURBANCES

The riots of 1937 produced two important consequences for the future development of the colony. There was a noticeable intensification of class-consciousness on the part of the workers. Equally important, the riots had served to advertise the plight of the West Indian masses in a way that no single spokesman had been able to do in the past, with the result that the British Government found itself forced to intervene more directly in the affairs of the colony in order to fulfil its trusteeship responsibility.

The growth of the trade-union movement
The need for trade unions became evident to the workers during the crisis.[38] Failure had taught them to realize that unless they organized, they would remain forever at the mercy of employers who were themselves organized and co-ordinated. The change in attitude required for this development was immense. As Marshall observed, 'The attitude of many workers prior to the strike was that they were not planning their lives on more than a two or three day basis. They were not used to thinking in more distant terms. Undercutting was a common thing – each man for himself.'[39]

Even before the crisis was over, meetings were being held by workers all over the country to lay plans for the organization of unions. One of the fundamental problems that bedevilled these efforts was that of leadership, the need to find a core of skilled organizers and negotiators from among their own rank who could devote full-time attention to the cause of working-class solidarity and advancement. The problem was only temporarily shelved by the seemingly unanimous feeling that there was only one man who, in Butler's absence, could be entrusted with the leadership of the movement: that man was Adrian Cola Rienzi who had been the workers' principal negotiator during the disturbances.

The fact that Negro oil workers approached Rienzi, an Indian, and asked him to be their leader was significant. Racial considerations were not allowed

proposal into the Legislative Council that June 19 should be made a public holiday 'as a day which in the minds of the workers in Trinidad marks a landmark in the history of the working-class movement in this colony', Cipriani vehemently opposed it. He rejoined, 'I think that every right-minded person in this colony would like to forget June 19. The birth of trade unionism does not date from June 19. It dates from very much further back, and all those who think rightly and have the best interest of the working class at heart in this colony would like to forget forever June 19 and are not asking for the making of a day for the adulation of false heroes.' Both Roodal and Teelucksingh, old members of the TLP applauded Cipriani's statement. Craig, *Legislative Council*, p. 90.

38   There were a few unions prior to 1937, but none of any great significance.
39   *Glory Dead*, p. 218.

to stand in the way of class needs. But Calder Marshall is correct in his view that 'had there been two men who could help them equally, one a Negro and the other an East Indian, the Negro would have been chosen. But here, the issue was clear cut. There was only one man and he was of a different race. The race question became insignificant.'[40]

Rienzi presided over the formation of two of the most powerful trade unions in the colony's history, the Oilfield Workers Trade Union, which was founded with the Governor's encouragement one month after the strike, and the All Trinidad Sugar Estates and Factory Workers Trade Union. He also assisted significantly in the formation of a third, the Federated Workers Trade Union. The fact that 7,000 of the 9,000 oil workers joined the OWTU is perhaps the best indication of the growing sophistication and collectivity-consciousness of the industrial workers. The comparative figures in the Sugar Union were also indicative of a fundamental problem with which it is still struggling – the seeming incapacity of the Indian worker for effective combination. Of the 34,000 workers, mainly Indian, in the sugar industry, only 2,000 joined the ATSE&FWTU, and it is quite possible that most of these were Negro factory workers rather than Indian plantation hands.

The formation of the unions was only part of the problem however. To get them functioning responsibly and effectively was a much more difficult operation. This was especially important, since nothing was done until 1943 to modify the trades union ordinance in a way that would safeguard the right of peaceful picketing or give the unions immunity against action in tort. The Forster Commission did recognize the problems with which the new unions would be faced, and urged that 'some means be found to protect unions from the errors of inexperience during the transition stage between their inception and the time when they are fully capable of negotiating unaided directly with employers'.[41]

The Forster Commission recommended that a department of labour be created which would be responsible, *inter alia*, for promoting the conciliation of disputes between management and labour, for providing statistical and other information on wage and price movements, job opportunities or the lack of them, and other such resource data which neither management nor labour was at the time equipped to provide.[42] It likewise proposed the establishment of an industrial court with an outsider as president, but both management and labour were irreconcilably opposed to this point, labour especially, since it

---

40 *Ibid.*, pp. 232–3.
41 *Forster Report*, p. 87.
42 The Department of Labour was in fact created in 1938, by which time there were seventeen unions in existence.

feared that such a court would prove inimical to its institutional and other interests.

Despite these recommendations, the new Governor, Sir Hubert Young (1937–1942), did very little to encourage the new movement until pressures were applied by the Colonial Office.[43] The employers did their best to frustrate the solidarity of the 'blue shirts', as the workers called themselves. Victimization, threats, the introduction of 'house' unions, and a cleverly manipulated reward system were all tried, but without avail. Very few workers broke ranks. The Petroleum Association finally recognized the Oilfield Workers Trade Union in April 1938.[44] The 'check off' and the 'closed shop' were conceded in 1948.[45] The Sugar Manufacturers did not recognize the Sugar Union (which had to be reinforced by support from the OWTU) until 1945.

The growing solidarity of the workers was fully demonstrated in the elections of 1938 when for the first time in the history of the colony a trade-union leader was returned to the Legislature.[46] Rienzi's performance at the polls indicated that he had the support of some middle-class elements as well. The workers were divided as to whether or not the union should become involved in politics, but the majority believed that it was necessary to have a

43   The appointment of Young was bitterly resented by workers and left-wing opinion in London. Young had crushed a strike in the copper mines of Northern Rhodesia in 1935 and it was believed that his choice was dictated by absentee interests in London.

44   The oil and sugar disputes were submitted to arbitration in 1938, the first industrial dispute to be settled by such a procedure in the Empire. The arbitration procedure adopted in 1938 and which allowed the authorities to intervene in the case of an apprehended dispute, was in fact circulated as a model to other colonial governments by the Colonial Office. B.C. Roberts, *Labour in the Tropical Territories of the Commonwealth*, Durham, NC, 1964, p. 185. The workers themselves believed that they were fairly treated. Wages in some cases went up by almost 50 per cent (in the case of those who were lowest paid). War bonuses were also conceded. *Facts You Ought To Know*, OWTU pamphlet, San Fernando, 1938. It would appear that pressure from the Colonial Office encouraged sugar interests to announce plans for a £50,000 housing project. The oil companies also announced the establishment of a provident fund for its employees.

45   This decision was taken following a strike, called by Butler in 1946, aimed at destroying the OWTU, whose leadership Butler was trying to recover. George Bowrin, 'Thirty Years of Progress', *Vanguard*, July 25, 1967. The oil employers had come to the conclusion that the OWTU was a stabilizing force in the industry. It is worth noting that it was not until 1958 that the OWTU called out its workers on strike.

46   Rienzi won the San Fernando constituency by 2,003 to 547 votes. Cipriani maintained his position in the capital city and was returned unopposed. But in the minds of at least the southern workers, Rienzi was the new 'tribune of the people'. The workers' paper declared editorially, 'Captain Cipriani is no longer the acknowledged leader of the labour movement in the island. He is only a labour politician with a diminished following.' *People*, Jan. 29, 1939.

spokesman in the Legislature to replace Cipriani, in whom they had lost confidence. Militant political action in the Legislature must reinforce activity by the unions if victories were to be obtained. As John Rojas, a leading militant and Rienzi's successor as President, expressed it:

The struggle against capitalist exploitation is necessarily a political struggle. The working class cannot develop its economic organization and wage its economic battles without political rights, and without first coming into political power. In securing a seat in the Legislative Council, we have secured a strategic position in our class struggle. But we need to reinforce this by action to convince empolyers of our willingness to fight. No weeping, beseeching, or kneeling at the feet of capitalists or any commission of inquiry can bring about our salvation.[47]

British reaction to the crisis

The disturbances in the Caribbean, and particularly those in Trinidad, shook the British Empire. The crisis helped to focus attention on the problems of governing the Empire as nothing before had done since the struggle over emancipation in the nineteenth century. During the parliamentary debate on the Report of the Forster Commission, Mr W. Lunn, MP (Labour), noted that the crisis had caused such a sensation in British political circles that it was impossible to get a copy of the Report. Another Labour MP, Mr J. Maxton, also noted that this was no 'ordinary colonial debate', and expressed his thanks to Sir Murchison Fletcher and Uriah Butler who had 'performed a service ... to this House of Commons in bringing the condition of these people prominently to our attention'. Butler, he noted, had 'performed a great service to coloured workers in every part of the British Empire. It is only when there is a Butler to speak out ... that the world begins to hear.'[48]

Similar statements came from Colonial Office officials as well. The Secretary of State for the Colonies, Mr Malcom MacDonald, agreed that the events in the West Indies were not the result of a 'passing whim of this or that individual ... movements simply on the surface ... which we can dismiss lightly. ... These outbreaks express a sense of unrest which is fairly widespread and which will remain a source of further trouble unless we can do something effective ... to meet the legitimate grievances of our fellow subjects in the West Indies.'[49]

Labour MPs were especially critical of what they viewed as the predatory behaviour of the investing community in Trinidad and the Caribbean. Com-

---

47   *Ibid.*, March 5, 1938.
48   Great Britain, House of Commons, *Parliamentary Debates, 1937–8*, vol. 332, pp. 766, 817.
49   *Parliamentary Debates, 1938*, vol. 377, p. 86.

plaints were levelled at their 'fearful neglect' of employees' welfare, the 'indescribable' housing, working, and sanitation conditions which they tolerated in and around their establishments, their insensitivity to the need for collective bargaining machinery, the huge profits which were being made in oil and sugar, and the huge dividends which were being paid to shareholders. It was observed that while wages stagnated at a low level, Apex Oil Company and Trinidad Leaseholds Limited had paid dividends of 45 per cent and 30 per cent respectively in 1937. The Duke of Montrose, one of the leading oil shareholders, was criticized for suggesting that the disturbances were due to 'insidious communist propaganda on anti-racial lines' even though the leading spokesman for the industry in Trinidad, Colonel Hickling, had admitted that it was the rising cost of living that was mainly responsible for the crisis.[50] Critics also pointed to the tremendous influence which large investors had over Crown officials not only in the colony but in Britain as well. As Aneuran Bevan (who called the Trinidad story 'an astonishing one') remarked, 'There ... exist in this island formidable financial groups having the gifts of employment in their power with enormous political influence here.'[51]

The Colonial Office was seen as the unwitting and often the conscious ally of the investing community. Mr Ormsby-Gore, who was in charge of the Office when the crisis broke, was accused of failing to support the Governor, of taking the side of investors during the crisis, and of giving too narrow a definition to subversion. It was agreed that the Colonial Office had been taking a more liberal stand since 1930, but it was observed that no follow-up action was being taken to ensure that liberal dispatches were given effect in the colonies. As Arthur Creech Jones lamented,

Too often the policies of the Colonial Secretary are determined by certain principles of imperialism. Big interests have had to be satisfied and ministers have been afraid to offend. It is true that declarations of great liberal principles have been made ... but the Colonial Office has tended to wait on events. It has issued many circulars, with which few of us could quarrel. [But] there has been little energy in following them up and seeing in what degree ... the various colonial governments

---

50 The petroleum lobby denied these charges, claiming that the workers had ample opportunities to present grievances, and that there was no general dissatisfaction with the wage rates paid in the oil industry. They admitted, however, that prices had climbed steeply in 1937 and that wages had not been adjusted expeditiously. It was also claimed that working and housing conditions in the industry were not as bad as suggested and that they were often better than those in England. It was argued that it was the responsibility of the Colonial Government to look after social welfare, not business which was not yet certain of the long-run promise of the industry. *Ibid.*, vol. 332, p. 790. Speech of Arthur Creech Jones.

51 *Ibid.*, p. 841.

are putting them into operation. We have a right to ask why it is that the good intentions of the Colonial Office are so frequently balked.[52]

Creech Jones also suggested that part of the blame had to be shared by colonial agents in the colonies who 'tend to get a little out of touch with the main currents of opinions in the territories. ... Continuous social meetings with the well to do ... made officials a little detached from ... the people for whom they are responsible.'[53] Others noted that Parliament was also to be blamed for not exercising any supervisory responsibility over the activity of the Colonial Office. But, as Bevan complained, 'The House of Commons is incompetent to govern the island ... we in this House are not doing our job; [but] it is impossible to have information about the situation in so many parts of the world. Whatever the reason ... this House ... is not to be trusted with the stewardship of these areas. ... Had it not been for an inspired Negro genius in Trinidad, we should be ignorant in regard to the miseries of these people.'[54]

Some parliamentarians noted that the root problem lay in the inadequacies of the staffing and functioning of the Colonial Office. It was suggested that, while the Colonial Office might have been able to protect colonials from the cruder forms of slave exploitation in the early nineteenth century, it was now unable to safeguard them from wage exploitation by large industrial interests with powerful friends in the Conservative Party and inside the Colonial Office itself. Other problems related to the inability to recruit able officials, the rapid turnover in personnel in the colonies, unwillingness of the Treasury to make funds available for colonial administration, communication gaps between colonies and headquarters, and the frequency of crises and the absence of any professional planning machinery in the Colonial Office. The result was government by 'jerks and spasms' following crises.

The Colonial Secretary accepted responsibility for the crisis in the Caribbean. He agreed that, 'In Trinidad, there is still an official majority which I have to instruct the Governor to use. I therefore am fully responsible for their legislation and their administration.'[55] Ormsby-Gore noted, however, that while he was formally responsible, the Governor must 'take full responsibility for the action or inaction of everyone of his subordinates in ... Trinidad and Tobago'. He denied that he was responsible for the inaction of the government

---

52 Ormsby-Gore denied that he was partial to capital or that profits and dividends were as high as many believed. He noted that of the twenty-two oil companies operating in Trinidad only two were successful. The sugar companies paid no dividends between 1929 and 1931, and between 1935 and 1937 dividends did not exceed 6 per cent, which, in his view, was not 'excessively unreasonable'. *Ibid.*, pp. 788–98.

53 *Ibid.*, vol. 337, p. 155.

54 *Ibid.*, vol. 332, p. 842.   55 *Ibid.*, p. 822.

of Trinidad, which had a budgetary surplus of £100,000 which could have been used for welfare purposes. 'I am quite clear in my own mind that I never restrained the Government ... from putting into force any of the statutory powers which they already possessed. Not only that, but I never turned down a single request that they made, and I would go further and say that I told [the Governor] about the Labour Party's and of my view that there was need for social reform in Trinidad ... and he must have known that ... in anything he proposed for action he would have my most active support.'[56]

Ormsby-Gore denied that Fletcher was recalled for his presumed progressive views and that his successors would therefore hesitate to take similar stances. According to the Colonial Secretary, Fletcher was asked to resign because of his ill-timed speeches in the Legislature, his lack of tact in inviting one of the leading oilmen to be his weekend guest during the crisis, his open declaration that he was an agitator, his open praise of Butler's activities, his inability to decide whether troops were necessary, and his remark to Cipriani that there was no privilege of free speech in the Legislature. Ormsby-Gore claimed that Fletcher had compromised himself with both labour and capital and that he was not sufficient to the tasks that had to be carried out in the colony. What was needed was 'a physically more robust and quite frankly a more determined Governor to put through the Report and the reforms'.[57] Ormsby-Gore and his successor, Malcom MacDonald, assured the House that the Colonial Office would be reorganized to make it more competent to deal with colonial problems, especially those relating to labour. As Ormsby-Gore noted, 'The question of labour is likely to become more prominent throughout the Colonial Empire. ... I am quite sure that good will in this case [can] come out of evil. ... I am tired of speeches. I want action.'[58] The Colonial Secretary, however, did not agree with the view that self-government was the

---

56   *Ibid.*, pp. 828–9.
57   *Ibid.*, p. 834. Fletcher first opposed the idea of relying on troops to quell the riots, and then cabled for them. He declared that the confidence of the business community had been badly shaken and that the presence of troops would restore needed confidence. When Cipriani rose in the Legislature on October 22 and opposed the purchasing of rifles for the largely white volunteer force on the grounds that the employer class should not be allowed to use the Treasury to arm itself against the workers, the Governor accused him of using subversive propaganda calculated to set class against class and, in fact threatened to prosecute him for sedition. A week later he warned the country that the Government would use all its resources to 'crush out' any further disorder, and withdrew arms from the general population. Cf. *Hansard*, October 29, 1937.
58   *Parliamentary Debates, 1938*, vol. 332, p. 836. According to B.C. Roberts, major changes were in fact made in the Colonial Office. 'From this time onward labour matters were the subject of continuous attention within the Colonial Office instead of

only answer to the problem. What was needed was greater imperial responsibility: 'In Trinidad the problem is intensely complicated ... and the state has to take its part in preventing clashes and in assuring progressive conditions. Apart ... from the danger of clashes between capital and labour, there is this extraordinary racial mixture. In those circumstances, there is a great responsibility upon whomsoever is in my job, and upon whomsoever under me is charged with the local responsibility of governing that country.'[59] As a prelude to basic change in the orientation of policy which was being planned for the Caribbean area, a West India Royal Commission under the Chairmanship of Lord Moyne was appointed in 1938. The Commission was to tour the whole English-speaking Caribbean area, since the rebellion had not been confined to Trinidad alone. It visited the islands in 1938–9 and submitted its reports in 1939. So serious were its findings that the British government withheld publication of the report lest its contents give gratuitous propaganda to its wartime enemies. The major recommendations were nevertheless released and a few put into effect before the end of the war.[60] Among the many recommendations made by the Moyne Commission, only those which deal with the question of constitutional reform in Trinidad will concern us. The commissioners were extremely cautious and ambivalent about the constitutional problem. While they were aware of the weakness of the colonial political system, they were unwilling to recommend full responsible government, which in the view of many was the only possible corrective. They believed that the colony needed a more 'representative' government, not 'responsible' government. To make the system more representative the Commission proposed that elected members be permitted to participate in government, though only in an advisory capacity. Membership on official committees and on the Governor's Executive Council would allow them to gain valuable insights into the problems of

being considered *ad hoc* as issues arose in each territory. This change was part of a broader revision in Colonial Office thinking which affected a great many other spheres of activity besides labour; for example, general economic development, education, health, agriculture and scientific research. All began to receive systematic consideration and were made the subject of general policy.' Roberts, *Labour in the Tropical Territories of the Commonwealth*, p. 184. In 1938 Major Orde Brown was appointed Labour Advisor to the Secretary of State; shortly after, he visited the West Indies to report on conditions there. Cf. *Labour Conditions in the West Indies,* Cmd. 6070, London, 1939. In 1939 a new Social Services Department was also established in the Colonial Office to watch over the execution of policy and to provide technical help where necessary. Cf. Roberts, *Labour in the Tropical Commonwealth,* p. 184.

59 *Parliamentary Debates 1938*, vol. 332, pp. 824–5.
60 *West India* Royal Commission 1938–9, *Statement of Action Taken on the Recommendations,* Cmd. 6656, London, 1939.

government. Both government and governed would benefit from this experiment, it was believed. The government would be much better informed about the needs and demands of the population as well as its possible reactions to government policy. By the same token, the government would now be able to rely on the close co-operation of the elected members on the Executive Council.

To ensure that the new elected represenatives did not remain just another ineffective appendage to the colonial chariot, the Commission recommended 'the object of policy should be the introduction of universal adult suffrage'. The commissioners were, however, undecided about the speed with which this new experiment should be introduced. Some felt it should be done immediately; others urged gradualism. They seemingly compromised by recommending the appointment of a fully representative committee which would go into the question, keeping in mind the issue of Federation and the need to have some sort of uniformity in franchise arrangements throughout the area. The Commission further advised that the margin between the qualifications for voting and those for membership in the Legislative Council should be considerably reduced.

The recommendations met with satisfaction of neither left- nor right-wing forces in the colony. They were anathema to the conservatives, who felt that the disturbances had sufficiently undermined the existing social structure and believed that 'any steps which might accelerate the pace of that social process should at least be postponed until the West Indian peoples had had time to adjust themselves to the new circumstances brought about those changes'.[61] The 'Bourbons', shaken by the uprisings of the 1930s and frightened by the emergence of labour militancy which had an unmistakable anti-white bias, were understandably unwilling to concede a constitutional system which would have facilitated the development of political parties associated with the new trade unions; this was already occurring in Jamaica. Universal suffrage in their view could only serve to return irresponsible agitators to the Legislative Council. That this type of politician should also be in the Governor's Executive Council was to them even more unthinkable.

Rather than adjust themselves to the new social movement, the whites sought to throttle it completely. The only security in which they appeared to have confidence was the bayonet and an autocratic Governor who saw things their way. Albert Gomes described their attitude very well: 'Some people think that if we granted so much freedom to the masses of the island at the present time ... it would be tantamount to releasing a sort of tidal wave that would sweep everything in its path, and in short lead to chaos. ... I do not agree with

---

61   *Report of the West India Royal Commission*, Cmd. 6174, London, 1939 (hereafter referred to as the *Moyne Commission*), p. 380.

that conception. I feel that the granting of adult suffrage will pour oil on troubled waters.'[62] Gomes was attempting to tell the whites that, unless they were prepared to make enlightened concessions, the ruin they prophesied might indeed be self-fulfilled.

Left-wing elements were chagrined by the Commission's lack of boldness. They dismissed as sheer casuistry the commissioners' argument that if they gave the elected members majority status, they would also have to strengthen the power of the Governor. The commissioners had reasoned that the colony had to avoid a constitutional system which would lead inevitably to systematic clashes between the Legislature and an Executive Council responsible to it, on the one hand, and the Governor, on the other. This was especially important because of the proposed plan to have the British government expend considerable sums on welfare projects. The commissioners were of the firm opinion that the British taxpayer must be given some sort of guarantee that the voted funds would be used for the stated purposes. As they declared, 'The claim for independence is irreconcilable with that financial control which, though not necessary in its present form, must continue to be exercised in the interest of the home taxpayer.'[63] At that time it was generally assumed that no country could aspire to independence unless it was in a position to sustain itself economically without the assistance of foreign governments. It was against this generally accepted point of view that the radicals of the prewar period stumbled hopelessly.[64]

THE STRUGGLE FOR ADULT SUFFRAGE

In 1941 the struggle between left and right shifted to the deliberations of the Franchise Committee.[65] The lines of battle were drawn around three main

62 *Report of the Franchise Committee of Trinidad and Tobago,* Council Paper no. 35, Port of Spain, 1944, pp. 110–11.
63 In 1940 the Colonial Development and Welfare Act, designed to make funds available for approved schemes of economic and social development, was passed. The act made grants conditional upon the colony's attitude towards trade unions, fair wages, and child labour. 'The inclusion of these conditions in the act gave the Colonial Office almost its first real power to coerce colonial governments into carrying out the policies it was recommending.' Roberts, *Labour in the Tropical Commonwealth,* p. 188.
64 In 1945 the Secretary of State for the Colonies modified the position of the British government somewhat when he observed that 'It will no doubt be generally appreciated that financial stability (*which is of course very different from economic self-sufficiency*) is an essential accompaniment of full self-government, and that the latter cannot be a reality without the former.' 'Secretary of State for the Colonies Despatch,' *Hansard,* July 13, 1945, p. 255 (italics supplied).
65 Though appointed in May 1941, the Committee never reported until 1944.

issues: adult suffrage, the question of a literacy test, and the qualifications necessary for membership in the Legislative Council. The Committee's Majority Report, which recommended that the franchise be made available to all who were twenty-one years of age, not legally incapacitated, and able to understand spoken English, was signed by thirty of its thirty-three members. Of the thirty, sixteen nevertheless supported a rider opposing universal suffrage. Some of these were even anxious to retain the *status quo*, and were only barely persuaded to accept a 50 per cent reduction of the property qualification which the rider proposed. One member of this group, Dr Lawrence, advanced the view that 'in a mixed community like ours, one where opinions differ so, where the outlook of life varies so, we are justified in saying that we should go slowly when we are putting into the hands of all and sundry a power so fertile of the highest result when highly exercised'.[66] Similarly, Sir Lennox O'Reilly, the main spokesman of the gradualist school, though admitting that he was not happy about the income or property qualifications *per se*, nevertheless wanted to be assured that 'the persons who are going to exercise their votes are persons who are thinking about the interests of the community, and whose personal interests are bound up with the interests of the community'.[67]

The opposition to the conservatives came from two directions – from the moderates and from the radicals. The centre group contended that universal suffrage was not a critical innovation, since it was not being accompanied by the grant of self-government. T.M. Kelshall was typical of this point of view: 'If we were going to legislate for self-government in Trinidad, I would most unhesitatingly object to adult franchise. [However], there is no prospect of that in this generation or even perhaps in the generation to succeed.'[68]

The principal spokesmen for the left, Albert Gomes, Adrian Cola Rienzi, Ralph Mentor, and Quintin O'Connor, based their general argument in favour of universal suffrage on the premise that it was those persons who did not have a stake in the colony, the nomads, the squatters, and the poor who needed the vote most. O'Connor, in a memorandum submitted on behalf of the Trinidad and Tobago Union of Shop Assistants and Clerks and the Federated Workers Trade Union, prophesied that there would be more '1937s' if the workers were denied the vote. He maintained that property qualifications for membership in the Legislative Council 'restricted the selection of Legislators to persons, who, because of their affluence, were inclined to be aloof from the people whose interests were different from theirs'.[69]

The only issue on which the radicals were seriously divided was the

---

66 *Report of the Franchise Committee*, p. 111.
67 *Hansard*, Oct. 6, 1944, pp. 377–99.
68 *Report of the Franchise Committee*, p. 108.
69 *Ibid.*, pp. 138–40.

literacy question. Gomes, O'Connor, and Mentor supported the proposal that only those persons who understood spoken English should be allowed to vote. On the surface this appeared to be a perfectly reasonable condition. The Indian community, however, regarded it as being directed mainly at them. As Rienzi contended, 'To insist that a voter should understand the English language when spoken would lead to the irresistible conclusion that this qualification has been introduced to deprive a large proportion of the Indian community of the right to vote. ... This is quite naturally resented as an unfair discrimination against an important section of the population which has made a valuable contribution to the prosperity of the Colony.'[70] Rienzi noted that English was not required of Indians when they went to war. Moreover, Indians owned extensive properties and should not be denied the instruments with which to safeguard their interests. The Indian community, led by Rienzi and officials of the India Club, mounted a powerful opposition to the provision, and in the end it had to be withdrawn. The Secretary of State for the Colonies instructed the Governor to use the official vote to overrule the majority decision on the literacy question and made it abundantly clear that he wished to have suffrage placed on the widest possible basis. The acute group-consciousness and seeming cohesiveness of the Indian community, in relation to other elements in the society in the postwar years, received a great deal of its driving force from this event, perhaps just as much as it did from the independence movement in India itself.

It should be noted, however, that Rienzi was not expressing the sentiments of the whole Indian community when he came out in support of universal suffrage.[71] Other Indians vigorously opposed it as being inimical to the best interests of their community. As one declared, 'The mass of East Indians in the colony are definitely opposed to adult suffrage for another fifty years because an election by adult suffrage would endanger the aims and aspirations of the Indian masses.'[72] The dominant reaction was fear and apprehension that they would be overrun by an intolerant Negro majority. Because of this fear, and perhaps for no other reason, the role of the Indian in Trinidad and Tobago was that of a counter-revolutionary political force, the aim of which was to delay as long as possible the transfer of power to native elements. With the growing feeling of nationalism that developed among Negro elements in the postwar era, this opposition to political change was to become even more vehement.

70   *Ibid.*, p.10.
71   Roodal declared that he endorsed it because his political enemy, Adrian Rienzi, had been its principal opponent. (Told to the writer by Rienzi.)
72   Paul Blanshard, *Democracy and Empire in the Caribbean: A Contemporary Review,* New York, 1947, p. 227.

4

Postwar nationalism
1946-50

The end of the war saw the return to the West Indies of a large number of professionals and veterans, many of whom had become involved in one way or another with progressive movements in metropolitan capitals. These men had taken seriously the promise that the war had been fought to make the world safe for democracy and the common man, and it was no surprise that they were invariably to be found in the vanguard of national movements throughout the islands. Blocked opportunities and anxiety for status had driven hundreds of West Indians into a search for higher education at universities abroad, where they came into contact with whites who were not nearly as hostile to their ambitions as those at home. Many of them were rudely shocked to see whites performing menial roles which hitherto they had associated only with blacks. All around them they found evidence that undermined the myths they had come to accept about white superiority. They also found that, intellectually, they were no worse off than the average European with whom they came in contact.

As students, and in other arenas of activity, West Indians strove hard to prove to themselves, and to whites, that they were not inferior beings. This anxiety to prove and to convince impelled many to achievements that would not have been forthcoming otherwise. In this they were no different from the thousands of other colonial 'Calibans' who flocked into metropolitan halls of learning in the 1930s and 40s. Today the proving instinct, the feeling that upon one's performance depends the transvaluation of self and group, is no longer as great a motivating force as it used to be. But it served to give powerful momentum to the developing nationalist movement in the colonies.

The visit to the colonies of thousands of American and British servicemen, who, like soldiers everywhere, behaved in a very ungentlemanly manner, also contributed to the undermining of the racial ideology that supported the colonial power structure. Once Caribbean society ceased to be an isolated unit, the structure of race relations began to crumble.[1] The success of the Labour party in England and the struggles for independence in India, Burma, Indonesia, the Gold Coast, and the Philippines were also closely followed in the colonies, and the feeling grew, slowly but perceptibly, that West Indians too should have their 'brave new world'. The idea of Empire had begun to lose some of its legitimacy.

One of the more important expressions of this sentiment was the formation in Trinidad of the West Indian National Party. The founders of the Party strongly believed that 'The time is ripe for the West Indian peoples themselves to make a constructive contribution towards the solution of the economic, social and political problems of these islands instead of waiting for action by the Colonial Governments. There is need for an organized body to express the West Indies' viewpoint and to assist in the re-organization of the economic and political structure of these islands which will come at the end of the war.'[2] It was felt that such an organization would help to give the people the confidence, which they so sadly lacked, to govern themselves.

The leaders of the Party were fully aware of the phenomenon that bedevilled nationalist movements in the West Indies, namely the feeling of impotence that enervates the mind and stultifies the will to act. This is not a uniquely West Indian phenomenon. Unless the oppressed believe that they are capable of altering the conditions which affect them, the tendency is to escape into apathy, or to await the benign intervention of some outside agent. Party leaders believed that there was need for a systematic programme of indocrination and political education to embolden the masses. To effect this, they planned to establish a network of branches and study groups, as well as statistical and fact-finding agencies which would provide intellectual resources for these units. The Party also hoped to work with and through the rapidly maturing trade-union movement.

The Party programme emphasized that its aim was to develop '*a West Indian national consciousness* based not on racial origins but on the community of interests of all West Indians'.[3] Some party leaders consciously

1 The importance of 'isolation' in generating the personality and social types that are incident to the plantation has been noted by Edgar T. Thompson. 'The Plantation: The Physical Basis of Traditional Race Relations', *Race Relations and the Race Problem*, Durham, NC, 1939.
2 *Statement of Policy. Programme and Constitution of the West Indian National Party*. Port of Spain, 1942. The Party was founded in 1942.
3 *Ibid.*

strove to bring Indians into the fold. These attempts met with little success however. Paul Blanshard was correct when he observed that

East Indian jealousy of coloured leadership is still an important factor in Trinidad labour and politics, and the two groups tend to form their own instruments of power. This national racial division explains why a small British official group at the top of Trinidad society was able to hold control of the colony for so long without any semblance of democratic institutions. Protest movements have tended to be either Negro and mulatto, or East Indian, with the East Indian movements showing consistent weakness. One reason for this weakness is a sharp political division within the East Indian community itself.[4]

The WINP blueprint for postwar reconstruction was a bold and wide-ranging document which had strong overtones of socialist utopianism. The economic problems with which the country had to grapple were enormous. The war and the presence of an American naval base on the island had seriously disrupted the colony's agriculture which was just beginning to recover from the depression.[5] Although there was an increased demand for the colony's agricultural products, mass migration of labour from the countryside in search of the 'yankee dollar' had made it extremely difficult for agricultural concerns, especially sugar and cocoa, to obtain an adequate labour supply.

The postwar problem was compounded by the refusal of retrenched base employees to return to the land; instead they further complicated the already serious unemployment problem in the cities and the oil belt. The wave of industrial unrest which erupted in 1946–8 was due mainly to the absence of adequate economic opportunity for the swollen labour force. Increased life expectancy, the absence of fertility controls, and the secular trend towards mechanization also contributed to the problems that faced the postwar generation of would-be reformers.

To cope with these problems, the WINP called for 'redistribution of the land, so that the landless may, by means of planned land settlement schemes, acquire holdings adequate to the maintenance of the settler and his family'.[6] The creation of a sturdy, contented, and economically viable peasantry was the ultimate goal. The Party also went on record as being totally opposed to the old plantation system. The sugar estates as well as the grinding and refining processes were to be taken over by the state and put into the hands of state-sponsored co-operatives.

---

4   Blanshard, *Democracy and Empire in the Caribbean*, p. 114.
5   The naval base was established in 1941 at Chaguaramas on the north-west peninsula of the island as part of the Anglo-American lend-lease agreement.
6   *Programme and Constitution of the* WINP.

The Party also promised to nationalize oil and other extracting industries such as asphalt. It was argued that too much of the country's wealth was being exported abroad in the form of profits which should have been used to finance much-needed social welfare schemes. Oil's direct contribution to the revenues in 1947 amounted to $9,700,000 (TT) or 20 per cent of the total, but spokesmen for the industry insisted that its indirect contributions were even larger, somewhere in the vicinity of 33⅓ per cent.[7] It was also claimed that while the industry employed an average of 14,000 directly out of a total work force of 141,000, many more were employed in subsidiary operations. The industry estimated that its total contribution to the economy in 1947 in terms of wages, salaries, taxes, royalties, local purchases, etc. was approximately $33 million.[8] The WINP insisted, however, that the industry's direct contributions to the Treasury and the total wage bill were inadequate. Oil was a temporary 'windfall', and the colony should maximize the benefits which it offered. Nationalization was the one sure way to guarantee that all profits were retained to be used on behalf of the inhabitants of the island.

The rest of the programme called for industrial and agricultural diversification, state control of public utilities and communication media, West Indianization of the managerial work force and of the school curriculum 'to bring it more in tune with the environment', free education at both primary and secondary levels, school health programmes, free medical and hospital services for all, protective insurance programmes, and improved working conditions for all. In short the WINP was promising, quite unrealistically, to introduce a comprehensive welfare-state programme based on that which the British Labour party was advocating for the more fully developed economy of the United Kingdom.

THE ELECTIONS OF 1946

The elections of 1946, the first to be held under universal suffrage, provided the first opportunity for the new nationalist forces to test their strength. The WINP did not contest the elections as an independent party. The Party's leaders agreed to enter a coalition with other progressive groups in the hope that such a front would capture all nine elective seats in the Council. The driving force behind the United Front was Jack Kelshall, a white creole veteran. Kelshall, who was familiar with the popular-front strategy that was in vogue among left-wing groups in Europe, believed that radicals in the colony must unite their forces if they hoped to defeat the forces of reaction. He was also anxious

---

7 *Report of the Economics Committee*, Port of Spain, 1949, p. 18.
8 *Ibid.*

to put an end to the continuous rivalry that had characterized politics on the left. Given the limitations of the constitution, it was felt that unity on the left was the only strategy by which progressivism could triumph.

The Manifesto of the United Front pointed out that Cipriani and the other elected members of the old Legislative Council were ineffective principally because they functioned as independents, even though most belonged to the TLP. The Front reminded the electorate of the odds under which Cipriani had laboured as an individual. 'Remember the Good Captain; alone he was helpless. Cipriani as an individual could only obtain for his followers the crumbs from the table of the Old Colonial System. Only in unity could we obtain the whole loaf.'[9] The programme of the Front contained two principal planks, socialism and responsible government.

'Our Front is a Socialist Front ... primarily a working-class little man's front,' declared the group's Manifesto. The nationalization programme of the WINP was endorsed and taken over by the Front in its entirety. The Front's leaders did not believe that socialism and nationalization were utopian pipe-dreams. The success of the British Labour party and the confident hope that assistance could be expected from that quarter buoyed their enthusiasm. The problem of finding the capital to pay compensation to the expropriated concerns did not appear at all insuperable. Their answer to the problem was 'borrow and pay out of profits'; they would 'borrow at 3 per cent and invest at 10 per cent'.

Opposition to the Front's plan for nationalization was strong and came from two sources, orthodox trade unionists and conservative businessmen. The unionists did not agree with the Front's Manifesto contending that 'the economic basis of trade unionism is socialism, and that any man who, as a trade unionist, tells you that our industries cannot be nationalized is either a knave or a fool'. One could just as logically contend that trade unionism was a logical extension of capitalism. The fate of trade unions in the Soviet Union was often cited by this element in the Party.

While the ideological clash between the socialists and the orthodox trade unionists should not be exaggerated, the cleavage was there. Differences of opinion between the 'Moscow-philes' and those who followed the lead of pro-Western federations hardened into an open split in 1948–9 when Western trade unions withdrew from the communist-dominated WCFTU. Leadership rivalries also divided unionists. The leaders of the Federated Workers Trade Union, the Southern Workers Trade Union, and the Oilfield Workers Trade Union accepted the socialist principles of the Front, but broke with it over the question of allocating seats. They contested the election under the banner of the Trades Union Council and Socialist Party.

9 *United Front Manifesto*, Port of Spain, 1946.

The second attack came from conservative forces who pointed out that oil was a highly speculative industry, the continued prosperity of which depended upon the availability of risk capital in large amounts. It was noted that during the war exploratory drilling had almost come to a halt. Proven fields had been extensively used and were nearly exhausted. Unless risk capital was forthcoming, it was feared that the industry would not survive. Conservatives also contended that the highly technical skills and the marketing arrangements needed by such an industry would not be available if the industry were nationalized. It was claimed that a government-owned oil industry would be at the mercy of international combines, only able to sell its oil abroad at prices fixed by those combines. It was also feared that a small industry such as Trinidad's could not survive at all unless additional supplies of crude oil and more markets and shipping facilities were made available by the giant international combines and the governments to which they had access.

The other key issue in the 1946 election was responsible government. Perhaps the word 'issue' is inadvisable, since all candidates agreed (if only vaguely) on its desirability, if not on the timing of its introduction. Responsible government was nevertheless one of the main talking points of the campaign. The United Front's Manifesto declared: 'The most important aim ... is responsible government. It is most important because before the Front can even begin to legislate in the interests of our island's half million people, responsible government must be achieved.' It was also argued that although the British Labour government was committed to granting responsible government, it would not concede it unless it could be demonstrated that the people of Trinidad had satisfactorily served their apprenticeship and that they really wanted it. Only by returning a party such as the United Front, which could make responsible government work, would this maturity be demonstrated. Independent candidates opposed this view, and stressed that maturity could only be shown if experienced candidates were returned. Unity *per se* was no substitute for experience, honesty, and integrity.

Another consistent variation on the dominant theme of responsible government was the nominated system. For 160 years of the colony's political history, the question of the nominated system had been a vital issue.[10] To the progressives, the system was a glorified 'class dictatorship' which now had to make way for a genuine 'people's government'. Conservatives and moderates nevertheless viewed it as the only method that guaranteed the inclusion of responsible and qualified people in the Legislative Council.

The election campaign of 1946 differed from anything that had been witnessed in the colony before. It was the first time, for instance, that all con-

---

10   From 1801, when the Governor's first Council of Advice was appointed, to the colony's Independence in 1961.

stituencies had been contested.[11] Campaigning was vigorous, heated, and confused, as candidates battled for the nine available seats. As one commentator remarked, 'It was a bitter and confused campaign in which party labels and purposes were inextricably tangled with racial animosities and personal ambitions.'[12] It would seem that election candidates had come to feel that only two strategies would mobilize the previously inert masses of the population: bribes and race. All accounts agree that these were the principal weapons in the contest. Every party and candidate accused the other of using them to gain electoral advantage.

Of the parties which contested the election, only three returned candidates. The Butler Party and the United Front returned three each, though Butler himself was defeated by Albert Gomes. Butler and Gomes were generally regarded as rivals for the leadership of the working class, and it was Butler's mistake to move out of his stronghold in the oil belt to challenge Gomes in Port of Spain. The Trades Union Council and Socialist Party returned two candidates. The other successful candidate was an Independent.[13] The Front was very disappointed with its showing. It had in fact picked up only one additional seat, since two of its successful candidates were already members of the Council. It had represented itself to the public as a genuine multiracial unit consisting not only the WINP, the Federated Workers Trade Union, and the Negro Welfare, Cultural and Social Association, but the Indian National Council as well. Its team had included one Chinese creole, two European creoles, one Syrian creole, two Indians, and three Negroes, all of whom insisted that their politics were based on class rather than on the ethnic factor. But despite its efforts to project a multiracial appeal, the Front had become identified with Negro progressivism, and was completely shut out in predominantly Indian constituencies.

The Front could have improved its position only if Butler and other trade-union leaders had joined the coalition, but there were too few seats to parcel out among all parties. Each candidate wanted to be assigned a seat where he had a chance of success, and too few were willing to stand down in favour of others. Unhappily there was no leader who could allocate seats authoritatively. Butler, who was by far the most popular leader, refused to join the Front unless he was recognized as the 'chief servant'.

There are a number of differing evaluations on the performance of the

11   In 1925, five of the seven constituencies were contested. In 1928, 1935, and 1938, only three, four, and two, respectively, were contested.
12   Blanshard, *Democracy and Empire*, p. 160.
13   Albert Gomes, Roy Joseph, and Patrick Solomon were the Front's successful candidates. A.P.T. James, Chanka Maraj, and Timothy Roodal were the successful Butlerites. Victor Bryan and C.C. Abidh were the TUC's successes. The Independent was a Hindu, Ranjit Kumar.

electorate. Detractors pointed to the rowdyism and heckling that have since come to characterize elections on the island. The smallness of the turnout was also taken to indicate indifference on the part of the masses. Of the 259,512 eligible voters, 137,281 cast their ballots (approximately 53 per cent). But if one takes into account the fact that rain and slow voting due to the novelty of the whole procedure kept many from exercising their suffrage, it could be argued that the performance of the electorate was creditable. The press was divided in its opinions about the election. The *Port of Spain Gazette* suggested that 'people will not go to a great deal of trouble either as candidates or as voters to secure representation in a House which can more appropriately be described as advisory or consultative as anything else'.[14] The *Trinidad Guardian*, on the other hand, complained about the gross irresponsibility which characterized the campaign. Too many candidates made 'empty promises ... to overthrow the established order, nationalize industry, introduce sweeping social changes and bring Israel out of Egypt with signs and wonders even if it bankrupted the exchequer'.[15] The *Guardian* in fact felt it necessary to remind its readers that 'The Legislature's constitution remained unchanged in spite of adult suffrage. The Governor continues as President.'[16] There were other commentators who felt that the election merely provided an occasion for the venting of the latest primitivism in the society. In their view, the campaign was a vast exercise in 'obeah', 'voodoo', and other forms of religious magic.

Many people lamented the fact that race had played such a decisive role in the election. It was feared that adult suffrage had merely served to politicize and harden the cleavages in the society.[17] Albert Gomes felt compelled to warn that further instalments of constitutional reform might have to be postponed indefinitely:

We have not yet reached the stage where political impulse is guided by cognate considerations. As a people, we have not yet crystallised into that hard mould of objective opinion which guarantees stable development to a country. The pattern of our population in terms of loyalty to fundamental patriotic motifs is confused and chaotic. ... Unless we can produce in the next five years a fusion of the disparate and extraneous loyalties that now bedevil us, then the progress of Trinidad as a cohesive organism is a mere fantastic notion of the idealists in our midst. Our position, as revealed by the election, is not a happy one.[18]

14   July 3, 1946.
15   July 30, 1946.
16   *Ibid.*
17   It is wrong, however, to say that 1946 marked the *beginning* of racial politics in Trinidad. As I have tried to show, race was a continuing factor in the political life of the community. Cf. my article 'The Struggle for Afro-Indian Solidarity in Trinidad and Tobago', *Index*, vol. 1, no. 4, September 1966.
18   *Sunday Guardian*, July 7, 1946.

Gomes was not satisfied that the men returned to the Council were of a sufficiently high calibre to be entrusted with greater political responsibility: 'Our political talent as displayed in the election seems much too fluid and unstable to earn us the right to more ample political opportunities. We have not yet begun to think politically.'[19] Gomes argued that Trinidad and Tobago needed two things most of all before self-government could be demanded: education and economic development. Illiteracy and superstition had to be eradicated if the people were to be made to appreciate the significance of the democratic experiment. Education and widened economic opportunities were seen as the only possible solvents of the tensions which were threatening to envelop the society. 'The national groups in Trinidad will continue to hark back to former loyalties so long as Trinidad offers them no more than the day-to-day agony of eking out an existence.'[20] Democratic institutions without a viable economic substructure were a meaningless farce. It is perhaps for this reason that Gomes abandoned his flaming radicalism after 1946, and progressively shifted into the camp of the moderates.

THE STRUGGLE FOR RESPONSIBLE GOVERNMENT

Whatever the intentions of the Moyne Commission, the new eighteen-member Legislature did not function as a team. In practice the Legislature divided itself into two blocs. The three Crown officials, the six nominated members, and the four elected members who were placed on the Executive Council functioned as one unit, and the remaining five elected members constituted an 'opposition bloc'. The divisions were never firmly drawn, but in a majority of cases the members of the Governor's coalition were found on the same side of the line. There was more movement from 'out' to 'in' than there was from 'in' to 'out'. One of the major consequences of this was a further weakening of the already fragile radical coalition.

The United Front had gone to the polls with a pledge to demand immediate responsible government. Members had also promised to work as a team to achieve this goal. Whatever the pre-electoral understanding, the Front did not function as a unit in the Legislative Council. It collapsed from both internal cleavages and external pressures. The first crisis that it encountered was the calling of two of its members, Albert Gomes and Roy Joseph, to the Executive Council. This had the immediate effect of thrusting the third member, Patrick

19   *Ibid.*
20   *Ibid.* Ironically, Gomes did admit that democracy might be the *prerequisite* to a programme of mass education. He did not feel that a colonial government would introduce it. *Hansard*, Nov. 22, 1946, pp. 41–5.

Solomon, into the camp of the 'outs'.[21] The second crisis came over the question of strategy to be used for promoting the issue of responsible government. The 'out'-wing felt that an immediate demand should be made for it. Those on the Executive Council believed that a committee should be appointed to consider the feasibility of the proposed reform and, to the consternation of their colleagues, introduced a successful motion to that effect.[22]

THE CONSTITUTIONAL REFORM COMMITTEE

The Committee, which consisted of elected and nominated legislators and public figures selected by the Governor, submitted its report on February 17, 1946. It was not unanimous in its recommendations. In addition to the majority report written by the chairman, Sir Lennox O'Reilly, there were two minority opinions submitted by two newly elected MLCs, Dr Patrick Solomon and the Hon Ranjit Kumar. The majority report recommended six constitutional changes:

a   that an Executive Council consisting of 12 persons shall be the chief instrument of policy and that it shall be responsible to the Legislature;
b   that 6 of the 12 members shall be *elected* by the entire Legislative Council (excluding the 3 officials who shall also be ex-officio members of the Council);
c   that a leader of the Executive Council shall be chosen from among the 9 unofficial members of that body;
d   that the Governor shall no longer be a member of the Legislative Council but that he shall continue to preside over the Executive Council with a casting vote only;
e   that a Speaker from outside the Council shall be nominated by the Governor and shall have a casting vote only;

21   It is reported that Solomon was also invited to the Council but was persuaded that such a move would prejudice his standing in the eyes of the masses.
22   Roy Joseph, who introduced the motion, claims that there was no debate in the Front or the WINP on the matter before he introduced his motion. Joseph in fact objected to the attempt made by Party colleagues to have him withdraw the motion. As he said, 'We are different beings and we cannot all unite on every point; we have to act as we see things and not as any individual would like us to see them. It is expected that on minor issues, elected members will disagree in the same way as nominated or official members.' For Debate on the motion cf. *Hansard*, Dec. 6, 1946, pp. 147–86. The WINP was never able to function well as a unit and broke up over personal rivalries and jealousies. Its major weakness was being essentially a party of prima donnas without grass-roots support. It also suffered from lack of an authoritative leader who could unify it and arouse the masses as Dr Williams was to do a decade later.

f   that the Legislative Council shall consist of 27 members, 18 of whom shall be elected, 6 nominated and 3 officials.[23]

The majority report opposed the creation of an upper chamber on the grounds that it would lead to friction and crises between the two houses. It preferred instead to mix the differently chosen elements in both the Executive and the Legislative Councils. This arrangement it was felt would permit closer union between the nominated official and elected elements. It 'would enable the elected members ... to appreciate and respect even more than they do now the views of the nominated members ... and conversely, the nominated element, which some think are inarticulate, would be drawn more closely to the elected side'.[24]

Dr Solomon's Minority Report made two principal objections:

a   the Committee was not sufficiently representative;
b   the proposed new constitution was retrograde and not in keeping with the wishes of the people.

Solomon contended, with some plausibility, that the Governor had adopted a simple but unprogressive method of selecting the members of the Committee. He had merely appointed the unofficial members of the Legislative Council, 'some diehards from the old Franchise Committee, and a few people chosen at random from among those whose names appear occasionally in the press'. Such a method of selection was bound to under-represent progressive opinion.[25]

Solomon also took strong objection to the retention of the Governor as head of the Executive Council and the presence of the official and nominated element on that body. To Dr Solomon, this was not responsible government at all. That institution assumes that the executive will consist of elected members who are responsible to a legislature elected by the people. Apart from the question of numbers, the proposed system was not essentially different from the old one. Not only was the nominated element being strengthened in the Executive Council, but the Council itself and its proposed new leader had little new power.[26] The Governor held all the 'trumping' power. The proposed leader could neither choose nor dismiss his 'cabinet' colleagues, and had no

---

23 *Report of the Constitutional Reform Committee, February 17, 1946,* Port of Spain, 1946, pp. 2–9.
24 *Ibid.,* p. 5.
25 *Ibid.,* p. 9.
26 Whereas in the existing Executive Council there was only one nominated member to four elected, in the proposed plan the ratio would be three to six, a 25 per cent increase.

levers to encourage true collegiality. Dismissing an elected member of the Executive Council required the approval of two-thirds of the membership of the Legislative Council. There was not even a guarantee that the leader would be an *elected* member. Such a system was bound to produce conflict and fragmentation and was a clear attempt to frustrate the development of political parties.

Solomon pointed out that while on the surface it appeared that the elected element was in a majority of nine (excluding the Speaker's casting vote), the mechanics of the system would serve to put it in a virtual 'minority' position. He feared that the six elected representatives on the Executive Council would form a bloc with the other six members of that body. This governing bloc could also count on the three remaining nominated members in the Legislature to out-vote the other twelve elected members.

The arguments against the Solomon thesis came principally from Albert Gomes, who campaigned in the Legislature for a continuation of the policy of graduated political change which would avoid 'dislocation, recantation and remorse'. One should not make a 'fetish of democracy', he chided.[27] Gomes did, however, attempt to meet some of the criticisms by proposing that the number of elected members on the Executive Council be increased to seven, thereby giving this element a normal majority of one on that body, though this would have had the secondary effect of reducing to eleven the number of elected 'backbenchers' in the Legislative Council. Gomes brushed aside other objections with the claim that the new constitutional proposals were quite revolutionary. They meant 'an almost complete transference of power from the hands of the Governor whose role and position are pivotal in the Crown Colony system, to the people through their elected representatives'.[28] True, the Governor had reserve powers, but they could not be exercised arbitrarily. He had to consult the Executive Council first, and he had to refer the matter as soon as possible to the Secretary of State for the Colonies. Whatever the legal niceties, power had in fact passed to the representatives of the people.

There was also the valuable provision that five members of the Executive Council could now summon a meeting of that body, whereas previously only the Governor had had the power to do so. The decision to reject the proposal for an upper chamber was also regarded as a victory for the people. Vested interests which would have been in a strategic position in such a body to block change were now in a 'slender minority' in the unicameral chamber. Gomes'

27 Gomes noted that there were many who felt that no further political reforms should be introduced, in view of the wave of industrial unrest which gripped the country in those years (the waterfront and sugar strikes and the growing strength of Butlerism).
28 Debate on the Constitutional Reform Proposals, *Hansard*, Nov. 22, 1946, pp. 41–3.

position was that there were circumstances peculiar to Trinidad which rendered it extremely difficut for the bicameral system to function as it functioned in England.

In his attack on the radical progressives, Gomes was joined by conservative elements of the coloured middle class, who feared that responsible government on a fully elective basis would rob them of the legacy of political power which they felt it was their turn to enjoy. The elective process, they argued, could not guarantee the election of men of calibre, and nomination had to be retained as a compensatory precaution.

The Kumar minority report objected to the majority report on roughly the same grounds as did Solomon's, but it did not support the idea of immediate responsible government. Kumar contended that the presence of the Crown in the politics of the colony was still needed, since Trinidad was not economically viable and could not do without economic support from Britain. The Crown also had to be given the opportunity to protect, if necessary, the rights of British capital. Kumar argued as well that the West Indies were too important to British strategic interests and that no British government would agree to abandon control of its colonies in the region. Kumar's principal concern was to defend the rights of the minority element for which he claimed to speak. The retention of the Crown colony system, however modified, was the only true safeguard for minorities. Kumar did not believe that a Negro-dominated majority party would deal fairly with the Indian community, which he felt was not yet sophisticated enough to take full advantage of a transfer of political power. 'In Trinidad we have a minority problem, and it is the duty of the majority to gain the confidence of the minorities by showing them that in any proposal for self-government, the minorities would have equal rights. I am afraid that in this colony, the majority community has not yet done that. It has made no effort to try and instil confidence in the hearts of the minorities. In fact, there have been leaders whose actions and utterances have given minorities suspicion of the very opposite.'[29]

Kumar struck closer to the core of the problem when he suggested that the colony's constitutional system should be devised in such a way as to allow nominated members to hold a balance of power between the two ethnic groups. When there was unity among the elected members, they should prevail. But on issues which threatened to divide the community, there was need for the restraining hand of the Crown and its nominees. As he pointedly declared, 'I do not think we should invite the possibilities of a political party which might gain a slight majority at an election, controlling the whole colony and entirely over-riding the interests of the other portion that might find itself with a small

29   *Hansard*, Dec. 6, 1946, p. 178.

minority ... *We have to make provision to see that Government is not controlled by a dictator and his party.*[30] Kumar's efforts to impede the granting of responsible government were buttressed by action outside the Legislature. During the 1940s, Hindu pundits went up and down the country warning their flock that they would be politically and culturally swamped by the Negro majority if self-government was granted. Thousands flocked to the temples to hear the movement for self-government opposed as the work of irresponsible creole demagogues who, in pursuit of power, were willing to trample on minority groups. The East Indian National Congress, of which Ranjit Kumar was President, also sent a memorandum to the Colonial Office to clarify the attitude of the Indians to self-government and Federation. A delegation was also sent to London to support the majority report of the Constitutional Committee.

Kumar, who was a radical on economic issues, was not completely opposed to all reform proposals. As an alternative to the nominated system, he renewed the old demand for communal representation. He wanted half the seats in the Legislature and one-third of the positions in the civil service reserved for Indians. But the more radically oriented leaders in the Indian community refused to support any demands for communal representation. Some of them charged that Indian leaders who opposed self-government were tools of the plantocracy, which they accused of encouraging and subsidizing Indian reaction. As one of them noted, 'The issues involved are whether [Indians] should join the call for separate representation, whether they should align themselves with vested interests, or whether they should join the progressives in the demand for responsible government. There is no problem of race at present, and if race is encouraged by any means whatsoever, it would cause a rift between these people with disastrous consequences to both.'[31] The Indian radicals felt that Indians had to choose between India and Trinidad. If they chose to stay in Trinidad, they must support progressive forces or be crushed. Though aware of the ugly forces gathering about them, they nevertheless agreed that the cleavages would only be sharpened if communal representation were to be introduced, as had been the case in Ceylon. They believed that Negroes would continue to vote for responsible Indians, as they had done in previous elections. For this reason they also rejected the suggestion that Trinidad Indians should push for a political union with British Guiana.

The Colonial Office accepted the majority report in principle, but objected

---

30   *Ibid.* Kumar's true views on responsible government are very difficult to define with precision. At one juncture he claimed that West Indians did not have the same claim to independence as Africans and Asians, who were sovereign people before the colonizers came. The West Indian people were recent immigrants to this area; they had been created by colonialism.

31   Simbhoonath Capildeo, *Clarion*, April 17, 1948.

to the size of the Executive Council membership, which was reduced from twelve to nine. There were now to be five elected members chosen by the entire Council, one member without portfolio nominated by the Governor, and three Crown officials – the Colonial Secretary, the Financial Secretary, and the Attorney General. The elected element thus held a slight majority of one if they were united on any issue. The proposal to create a leader of government business was also dropped. The Secretary of State for the Colonies, Arthur Creech Jones, stated that his aim under the proposed constitution was 'to give the people of Trinidad and Tobago a dominant voice in the control of their own affairs', though he admitted that 'there is indeed no conclusive answer to the argument that a system of nomination is contrary to accepted democratic principle'. He felt, however, that there were 'special considerations' which had to be taken into account in Trinidad and promised that 'as soon as it can be brought about by orderly process, in the particular circumstances of each territory, the legislature [would] become fully elective'.[32] To give substance to this promise, he recommended that the numerical strength of the nominated element be reduced from six to five, and further ordered that nominees should be chosen not to represent vested interests, as was the case in the past, but to serve the interests of the colony as a whole.[33] Creech Jones made one other observation that deserves attention, since it was one of the key arguments advanced by the Colonial Office whenever demands for responsible government were rejected:

Experience has shown that the success of parliamentary government depends largely on the existence of responsible parties with coherent and definite programmes. It cannot be said ... that in Trinidad and Tobago this condition is as yet fulfilled. *No doubt the limitations of the existing constitution in part account for this failure.* It is clear, however, that until there has been a further opportunity under more favourable circumstances for political parties to develop and work out definite programmes, the grant of responsible government would be unlikely to succeed.[34]

32 The Secretary of State opposed the view that the nominated member should be elected to the Council in the same way as the other MLC's. It would be 'obviously anomalous to give an elective character in the Executive Council to a member who owes his position in the Legislative Council to nomination'. It is clear, however, that the Colonial Office was not yet convinced, as it was in 1956, that it was 'safe' to transfer real power to elected officials. *The New Constitution – Full Text of Secretary of State's Despatch*, Port of Spain, 1949, p. 4.
33 By reducing the nominated element to five, a 13-to-13 balance now existed between the 'out' elected members and the nominated executive bloc.
34 *Secretary of State's Despatch*, p. 3, italics supplied.

Creech Jones' assumption was that, in the absence of coherent parties, 'a wholly elected Executive Council ... would tend to reproduce the dissensions in the Legislature from which it had been chosen. ... Policy would be dictated by the caprices of individual politicians rather than by the consensus of genuinely representative opinion.'[35] The three officials and the nominated member on the Executive Council were thus expected to provide the sobriety, responsibility, and administrative skills which that body needed.

Creech Jones was well aware that parties were just as much a consequence of certain types of constitutional systems as they were 'prerequisites' for their proper functioning. The dynamics of Trinidad's constitutional system contributed as much to slow the growth of political parties as did the plural nature of the society. The one served to reinforce and exacerbate the other. The constitution offered no premium to representatives who might otherwise have been encouraged to combine. It also offered few instrumentalities for maintaining these combinations once they were attempted. On the contrary, every encouragement was given to the anarchic individualism that characterized Trinidad's political class. It is clear, however, that it was not the Colonial Office that was primarily responsible for devising the constitutional arrangements under which Trinidad was governed. Had the Colonial Office been faced with a clear and consistent demand for a more advanced constitution, there is every reason to believe that it would have granted one, at least in the years after the Second World War. It was the divisions within the political élite itself and the community in general that made it necessary or at least provided the excuse, for the British Government to continue in its role as referee of group conflict in Trinidad.

35 *Ibid.*

5
Apprenticeship to freedom
1950-5

The new constitution which was to be introduced following the general election of 1950 was the first major attempt to modify the colonial political system since the rebellion of 1937. That constitution fell far short of what radicals had hoped for in the postwar period. Some advance was made in that five popularly elected officials were to be put in charge of key ministries. But the constitutional instrument was still essentially a colonial one since it was the Governor, acting alone, who assigned the portfolios to these elected officials. The power of the ministers also had to be shared with Crown-appointed civil servants both within their own departments and in others headed by Crown officials. Moreover, ultimate power still rested with the Crown.

It was hoped by people on the left that a united progressive coalition would emerge during the elections to force the British government to redeem the pledge of the Colonial Office, but no such coalition was forthcoming. The election of 1950 again demonstrated the fragmentation of Trinidad's politics. One hundred and forty-one candidates vied for the eighteen elective seats on the Legislative Council. Of these, ninety were Independents and fifty-one carried some kind of party label. Instead of one or two major parties, no fewer than five contested the election. Only one of these, the Political Progress Group, was genuinely new. The others, the British Empire Workers and Ratepayers Union (the Butler party), the Trinidad Labour Party, the Caribbean Socialist Party, and the Trades Union Council, consisted of elements which shared the same basic ideological position but found it as difficult to work together as they had in 1946.

The Political Progress Group
The Political Progress Group consisted mainly of white and mixed elements

who shared a moderate point of view on constitutional and economic reform. It was the concrete expression of a conclusion which was beginning to permeate the upper- and middle-class sectors of the society, namely, that it would soon be no longer possible for them to depend on the device of nomination for adequate representation. If they were to maintain some influence on the society, they had to be prepared to take part in its political life on an equal basis with other political formations.

The Trinidad Labour Party

During the months prior to the election, an attempt was made to revitalize the old TLP which had almost disappeared from the political scene after the death of its founder-leader, Captain Cipriani. The main figure behind the effort was Raymond Hamel-Smith who, like Cipriani, was white creole. The TLP's new manifesto was a hard-hitting radical programme calling for 'responsible government with socialism'. The Party, which came out in favour of 'public control and ownership of lands, mines, minerals and of the means of production, distribution, communication and exchange', regarded nationalization as the only means by which the economy could be West Indianized. Nationalization was a prerequisite to economic democracy: 'We do not work for the abolition of capitalism so that bureaucracy can be enthroned. ... We desire fundamental socialism where the workers, producers and the organized consumers become the direct owners of the machinery of wealth, production and distribution within the framework of a West Indian economy. The workers and technicians must control the nationalized economy.'[1]

The Labour Party also made it clear that the economic problems which faced Trinidad and Tobago could not be solved in isolation, and urged the calling of 'an economic conference [to make plans] for the socialistic reconstruction of the British West Indies, closely linked with the other liberated colonial peoples in the area'.[2] Although the new leaders made a genuine attempt to transform it into a properly organized, dues-paying, multiethnic organization, nothing much came of their attempts. Party meetings never attracted more than two or three hundred persons, and the attempt of the new president to invest himself in the mantle of Cipriani was a clear failure.

The Caribbean Socialist Party

The Caribbean Socialist Party, founded by Patrick Solomon after the collapse of the West Indian National Party and the United Front, never really functioned as an effective election machine. Many of the individuals who had identified with it deserted to fight as independents or to work with other parties.

1   *Clarion*, March 13, 1945.
2   *Ibid.*, July 13, 1948.

During the election campaign Solomon was in effect a 'general without an army, a leader without a party'.[3]

The Trades Union Council

The Trades Union Council was not officially a political party, but an association. Some of its leaders believed that the workers needed to have direct representation on the Legislative Council, since experience had shown that they could not rely on middle-class intellectuals and professionals to maintain working-class sympathies once they were successful at the polls. It is also clear that labour leaders regarded political careers as being more glamorous and secure than careers in the trade-union movement.

Several abortive attempts were made to fuse these three left-wing groups into a unified coalition. Party leaders realized the consequences of left-wing fragmentation, but seemed unable to arrive at any pre-electoral arrangements that would satisfy everyone. It was 1946 all over again. As the TLP journal the *Clarion* declared editorially, 'It is tragic that the leaders of the various left-wing movements, particularly the TLP, the TUC, and the CSP, cannot see their way to arrive at some *modus vivendi*. To continue this senseless internecine warfare is to make certain that the Government of this country remains for some considerable period out of the hands of the working class.'[4] The *Clarion* also complained that, 'The strength of the workers is being frittered away by dissension among groups closely similar in their political outlook. The great millstones of Trinidad politics – personal loyalties and clashes of personalities – are preventing the weight of reasoned and progressive thinking from making itself felt. The similarity of the ideological approach is ignored.'[5]

The Butler Party

The only successful electoral alliance formed during the election was that between Butler and a group of Indian politicians. After his release from detention in 1940 Butler had struggled to regain the leadership of the working-class movement and the Oilfield Workers Trade Union. Butler claimed that the OWTU leadership was denying him the power and the glory that were justifiably his, and in retaliation he tried to engineer a strike which would destroy the OWTU, activities for which he was again detained by the colonial authorities in 1941.[6] In 1946 Butler again called a general strike that almost brought the economy to a standstill. His supreme goal, like that of Cipriani

---

3 'CSP Rats Desert Sinking Ship', the *Clarion*, July 29, 1950. People like Jack Kelshall, Simbhoonath Capildeo, A.P.T. James and C. Alexander deserted the Party.
4 *Clarion*, Nov. 4, 1950.
5 *Ibid.*, Oct. 21, 1950.
6 Butler was given a well-paying, responsible position with the Union, but he wanted nothing less than the leadership and refused to be bound by the decisions of the

and Rienzi before him, was to 'mix sugar and oil', to rally a coalition of Negro oil workers and Indian sugar workers behind a 'people's government' which would revolutionize the distribution of political and economic power in Trinidad and Tobago. The orthodox trade-union movement was only tinkering with the system, he argued. The Sugar Workers Union in particular was a 'capitalist stooge'. It was in these circumstances that Butler's Negro-Indian alliance was forged in 1950.

Butler's attack on the orthodox trade-union movement appealed to Indian political aspirants who were interested in destroying the power of their rivals who controlled trade union 'vote banks'.[7] It should be recalled, however, that the nexus between Butler and the Indians was forged as early as 1937. They had given Butler considerable legal and financial help during his time of troubles, and in the 1946 election he had shown his gratitude by endorsing Indian candidates, two of whom were successful. Butler's popularity was immense, and many aspirants for legislative honours felt that their political futures depended on him.[8]

RESULTS OF THE 1950 ELECTION AND THE FORMATION OF THE NEW GOVERNMENT

The elections were keenly contested, with the Butler Party winning six seats on the new Council; of these, four were won by Indians. The CSP, the TLP, and

organization. After his expulsion from the OWTU he organized the British Empire Workers and Ratepayers Union, which was duly registered and recognized by the Trinidad Asphalt Company. In the view or orthodox unionists, the BEWRU was not a trade union at all but a fascist paramilitary organization.

F.W. Dalley also noted that Butlerism was more akin to seventeenth-century 'fifth monarchism' than to twentieth-century trade unionism. According to Dalley, Butler was a 'curious phenomenon' who had a 'peculiar influence on the masses.' 'This Butler atmosphere has to be experienced to be fully appreciated ... it is partly superstitious, but partly also due to fear of physical violence ... and not without cause.' *Trade Union Organization and Industrial Relations in Trinidad*, Port of Spain, 1947, p. 21.

Butler's claim that his second internment during the war was engineered by the OWTU leadership is without foundation. The authorities feared that activities in the oil belt were endangering a vital sinew of the British war effort and detained him until 1945. This only added to Butler's popularity. In 1946 he and his followers stormed the Red House, the seat of political power in Trinidad. Many feared it was 1937 all over again. The authorities moved to head him off any such eventuality by banning Butler from the oil belt under the Emergency Powers Ordinance.

7 Ranjit Kumar, for example, was opposing C.C. Abidh, President of the Sugar Workers Union in central Trinidad.

8 'It would appear that candidates who sought the support of Uriah Butler have paid, and will continue to pay, in meal and malt for that support.' Dalley, *Trade Union*,

the PPG each won two seats.[9] Of the ninety Independents, six were returned. The results posed a tremendous problem for radical forces in the colony; it was quite obvious that some sort of alliance was necessary if they were going to capture the government. But radicals found it just as difficult to forge a post-electoral alliance as to form a pre-electoral front. The *Clarion* put its finger on the problem when it declared: 'There is little likelihood of a coalition of elected members in an effort to decide the composition of the Executive. Such a coalition will have to be led by Butler. It is doubtful whether other members would agree to that. It is also certain that the nominated members would not consider such a move to be in the best interests of the colony and would use their not inconsiderable strength to prevent it. The distribution of real power in our society, in our new Legislature, might very well remain what it was before.'[10]

The election of members to the Executive Council showed only too well the accuracy of this observation. Only one representative of the left gained election, and he was generally regarded as being on the right of this group. No Butlerite was elected, although the original bloc of six was increased to eight by the decision of two other elected members to attach themselves to the party. Although they constituted the largest single group in the Legislative Council, the Butlerites were not given even a token seat on the Executive Council. The aim of the nominated-official bloc was to deny Butler the legitimacy which ministerial office would have afforded him. Other politicians also felt that their chances for office would have been enhanced considerably if the Butlerites were shut out of the Executive Council. It was widely agreed that Butler did not have the administrative and intellectual skills that were needed for the leadership role to which he aspired.

The right and centre elements in the country were enthusiastic about the manner in which their constitutional engineering had thwarted the Butler menace. Gomes declared, 'I am glad that some of us insisted in the face of opposition that without the nominated system, this country would have been consigned to persons lacking in experience, balance and perspective; and indeed our plight might have been extremely desperate at this moment.'[11]

p. 27. Dalley lamented, 'It was not creditable to the leaders of public opinion in Trinidad that Uriah Butler holds the position he does among the unlettered population. ... Legislators feel that they are bound to his chariot-wheels.' *Ibid.*, p. 35.

9   The Presidents of both the CSP and the TLP (Patrick Solomon and Raymond Hamel-Smith, respectively) were defeated at the polls. Solomon retired from politics and the CSP disappeared from the political scene. The TLP re-emerged in 1956 for the last time.

10   Sept. 23, 1950.

11   'The PPG and the Political Future', *Trinidad Guardian*, Oct. 19,1950.

Gomes also contended, with much justification, that the election was not fought on the basis of conflicting ideologies: 'It had been for a long time a straight fight between those who believed that human affairs are assisted by the application of violent methods and those who believed in peaceful and gradual change.'[12]

Butler felt quite differently about the elections. To him the struggle was between the forces of evil and the children of God, and his exclusion from office was nothing short of 'political blasphemy', 'a spectacle ... never surpassed even in the most distasteful era of British Crown colony government in the West Indies'. The whole constitutional framework and the election of ministers was the work of a 'capitalist conspiracy', and 'imperialist-fascist coalition'. Butler warned that he and his Party would form the greatest opposition bloc ever to be recorded in the history of the land.[13] He also promised 'agitation inside the Legislature far surpassing anything in the history of ... a Council which has blighted the growth of this country for so many years'.[14]

The new session of the Council opened in a state of tension, and it was widely feared that the colony was poised for a new wave of unrest. These fears never materialized, however, as Butlerism rapidly became a spent force. The alliance between Indian politicians and Butler quickly fell apart as it became apparent that Butler was an obstacle to their political advancement. Without power and patronage to dispense, Butler had nothing with which to hold his extremely individualistic following. Moreover, he was a difficult leader to work with. He had a magnificent contempt for organization and consequently was never able to harness the fierce loyalty which he generated in his followers. His leadership was always personal. As one observer declared, 'Butlerism remains a set-up with a positive hostility towards co-operation.'[15] Another commentator regarded Butler as 'a revivalist gone wrong, a shouter who was diverted from the lanes to the Legislature, a missionary who missed his way. The Bible is his handbook and the minor prophets his model. Not in all his twenty years of buccaneering in West Indian politics has "Buzz" put forward anything closer to a political programme than a thundering declaration of war on the object of his dislike at the moment, or an equally noisy and vague promise to lead his followers to the new Jerusalem.'[16]

12   TG, Oct. 1, 1950.
13   TG, Oct. 25, 1950. Butler promised to come to Woodford Square (Trinidad's Hyde Park) after every sitting of the Legislative Council and report to the people what was transacted in that body. He promised to make the administration of Sir Hubert Rence, the new Governor, as 'rancid as ever'.
14   TG, Sept. 23, 1950.
15   Dennis Mahabir, 'Can Butlerism Survive?' Clarion, Nov. 4, 1950.
16   K.T. Mills, 'Political Personalities', TG, Sept. 2, 1956.

Butler's weaknesses as a leader go a long way towards explaining the failure of the nationalist movement to develop more fully and powerfully in the early fifties. Some of the conditions requisite for success were there. Butler's 'martyrdom' had won him the support of a substantial Negro following, and through his alliance with Indian professionals a large number of Indians were available for mobilization. But Butler, who probably had a more substantial direct following among Indians than did Cipriani, was just as incapable of directing this popular enthusiasm into stable and durable channels.[17] He was a mesmerizer *par excellence*, but his leadership abilities ended there. Like Cipriani, he suspected everyone of wanting to be the 'chief servant', of wanting to challenge him for the leadership of the working class, a position which he felt was legitimately his. It was Butler and no one else who had dared to twist the lion's tail. Now the 'spoilsmen' were trying to capture the movement. Butler also complained that insular jealousy frustrated his leadership role. His colleagues, he claimed, suffered from 'great island chauvinism', and would not recognize him, a Grenadian, as the 'chief servant', the only person who could 'win Jerusalem and cross into Egypt with glory'.[18] There is little evidence to substantiate this charge, however.

Eric Williams, the man who finally succeeded in hammering out a durable nationalist coalition, had this to say about Butler:

Butler had become a national hero, and Trinidad and Tobago had received a new political leader. ... The real problem, however, was that Butler proved inadequate to the task either of forming a political party or of organizing the oilfield workers; and whilst his popularity was undoubted and was fully deserved, and whilst he never swerved in his demand for self-government for Trinidad and Tobago, he proved as inadequate as Cipriani had proved before him in the sense of mobilizing the mass movement that he had helped to develop and guiding it along the inevitable organizational channels for the capture of political power and for the use of that power when it had been captured.[19]

17 Dalley is largely correct when he claims that Butler's popularity among Indians was not direct. 'Mr Butler's influence with the East Indians has hitherto not been at all commensurate with that of Mr Kumar, himself an Indian speaking their language and understanding their way of life. Had not he, Mr Kumar, personally visited the Caroni estates and fanned the flames, the [1947 sugar] strike would, notwithstanding Mr Butler's efforts and those of his followers, have remained insignificant.' *Trade Union*, p. 21.

18 Butler was incredibly vain. In London in 1948 to 'present the case for the Indian and Negro Workers', Butler wrote home to say: 'In London, I am being lionized by the British Press. I am looked upon as the Man of the Hour from the Colonies. I am immediately recognized wherever I go, recognized as the man greater than Bustamante.' *Port of Spain Gazette*, July 21, 1948.

19 Eric Williams, *History of the People of Trinidad and Tobago*, New York, 1964, p. 235.

The quasi-ministerial system, 1950–6
How well the 'Knox Street Quintette' (as the five ministers were popularly called) succeeded in fulfilling the responsibilities entrusted to them in 1950 is still one of the more controversial issues in Trinidad's political history. Despite the bitter attacks which were mounted on the quasi-ministerial régime by later nationalists, in retrospect it can be said that it performed moderately well. The system suffered from obvious disadvantages – handicaps which some of the ministers themselves had helped to create. The men who formed the ministry were all professional politicians of the most individualistic and anarchic sort, and no one in 1950 could have anticipated that they would have held together, given the enormous pressures towards fragmentation. The members of the ministerial team had little in common save political ambition; some of them had in fact been fierce political enemies at one time or another. Yet they maintained for the most part some semblance of collegiality. Until the last months of the régime, the institution of collective responsibility was generally maintained. 'At no time did the Government come close to foundering. On the contrary, ministerial responsibility ... sharpened personal initiative and thus provided the administration with a liveliness which it previously lacked.'[20]

The ministers functioned within very narrow political and constitutional limits and had to pursue policies which would meet with the approval of the Colonial Office and powerful vested interests in the society. Certainly this is what the Secretary of State implied when he declared that further constitutional advance would depend on how 'responsibly' the elected ministers exercised their trust, and on how much they were able to allay the 'misgivings ... of those directly concerned'. At any time, provided they had the backing of the Colonial Office and the Governor, vested interests represented in the Legislature could have utilized the immense power which they had at their disposal to hamstring the efforts of the ministers.[21]

The ministers thus made no effort to draw up programmes or pursue policies that would change the social structure of the colony in any radical way. They sought to operate within the existing framework, making concessions to each social class or ethnic group as expediency suggested. It probably never

20 Max Farquhar, TG, May 20, 1956.
21 Two ministers have agreed that while the Governor and his officials had vast powers and influence, majority decisions were accepted in the Executive Council only when a majority of the elected element formed part of the winning combination. While it could be argued that if the elected element had worked as a team, they would have been able to push through a radical programme were they minded to do so, it must be admitted that the constitutional framework could have proven to be a serious inhibiting factor. The finances of the colony were still under the control of a Crown-appointed official.

even occurred to any of them that they should attempt to mobilize mass support behind a programme aimed at a radical social, economic, or cultural reconstruction of the society. For the most part, they were, and behaved like, machine politicians. Theirs was not the politics of purpose or of vision. None of them, except perhaps Albert Gomes, had the stuff of which national leaders were made, and Gomes had destroyed his popular legitimacy by the cautious attitudes which he adopted towards the trade-union movement and constitutional reform. Unfortunately for the ministerial régime – at least from the point of view of its popularity – it was Gomes who dominated the political stage during the five-year period.[22]

Albert Gomes is indeed one of the more colourful and controversial figures in Trinidad's political history. But did he betray the workers who had put him in power, as many have come to believe, or was he indeed a real statesman who served his country well without fear of popular disapprobation? Was he a pure opportunist who cared for nothing else than the maintenance of his own political career, or was there some inner logic which explains his many tergiversations?

Gomes came into politics in the 1930s as a radical who functioned considerably to the left of Cipriani. He had been quite active in the trade-union movement and had held leadership positions in the Federated Workers Trade Union. He represented himself before the workers as the logical successor to Cipriani, and indeed won the seat that became vacant after Cipriani's death. But once in power he systematically jettisoned most of his old radical comrades and principles, and moved closer and closer to the establishment. By 1948 he had virtually become its most effective spokesman. His elevation to the key ministry of Industry, Labour and Commerce in 1950 was eloquent testimony to the regard in which he was held by these forces.[23]

To people on the left, Gomes' career after 1946 represented a betrayal of the workers, to whom he now appeared as a willing collaborator and tool of the 'capitalist clique'. Most trade-union leaders are quite convinced that he was the instrument by which the employer class sought to destroy the trade-union movement. Gomes is even credited with having destroyed the effectiveness of the very union which helped to launch him into power, in order to bury, once and for all, the memory of his 'red' past and to fulfil a personal vendetta.[24]

22 The politics of the period has been sneeringly referred to as 'Gomesocracy'. Gomes, in fact, once boasted, 'I am the Government of Trinidad and Tobago.'
23 The combination of these three vital policy areas into one ministry was a clever manoeuvre on the part of the establishment. Had Gomes been Minister of Labour alone, his entire political career might have been very different.
24 While trade-union leaders agree that Gomes did very little to encourage the development of trade unionism, a few are nevertheless of the opinion that Gomes has been

While there is no doubt that Gomes did very little to encourage the development of the trade-union movement, there is, at the same time, no real evidence to support the conventional opinion that he and the entire ministerial régime were consistently hostile and insensitive to the plight of the 'little man'. The five ministers seem to have taken the position that what the colony needed most of all was stability and a healthy climate in order to attract the foreign capital which they regarded as a *sine qua non* of its economic development. Their general policy, though never clearly articulated, seems to have been designed to keep social overhead expenditure down to well defined if narrow limits, to keep taxation rates low, and to give as many incentives to foreign private enterprise as were needed to attract it to the colony. The Pioneer Industries Ordinance of 1952, which operated on the principle of giving enormous tax exemptions to prospective developers, was the cornerstone of this programme. Gomes also laboured successfully to maintain the system of imperial protection for the colony's agricultural staples. Although he was harshly criticized for what appeared then to be colonial thinking, no radical alternatives have since been substituted. Gomes has in fact claimed it was the efforts of the 1950–6 régime in the area of industrial diversification that laid the foundation for the expansionist social programmes of its successor.[25]

To complement their economic policy, the régime maintained a tight rein over the strike activity of the working force, though strikes were never outlawed. Gomes' strategy was to function as an active mediator between capital and labour, to pre-empt strikes by forcing both parties to make concessions before the issue came to a head. The comparably small number of man-hours lost between 1951 and 1955 testifies to the success of this strategy.[26] It is perhaps true, as unionists claim, that the ministerial régime and Gomes in particular tended to discriminate in favour of capital, but there is hard evidence to show that on occasion Gomes did come down on the side of labour when he felt management was in the wrong, or when he felt it politically necessary to rule in favour of the workers.[27]

unfairly portrayed as an enemy of the worker. Gomes, they claim, deserted the FWTU because of personality differences with Quintin O'Connor, and Gomes himself saw the break with O'Connor as stemming mainly from the differences in the roles which they were called upon to perform: 'Our political and personal relations cooled when, as a member of the Government sharing collective responsibility, I was involved in decisions to which he did not react favourably, but he never lost my affection and respect.' *West Indian Economist*, vol. 1, no. 8, Feb. 1959, p. 11.

25 The *Times Supplement on Trinidad and Tobago*, London, Jan. 15, 1966.
26 From the beginning of 1951 to the end of 1955, only 3,209 man-hours were lost in strike activity. In the election year of 1956, 11,028 man-hours were lost. *Annual Statistical Digest*, Port of Spain, 1966, p. 53.
27 Gomes fought the commercial interests over the question of increased wages for

Similarly, though the Minister of Agriculture, Victor Bryan, was accused of being unduly partial to the interests of the plantocracy and the merchant shippers of the colony's agricultural staples, there is no evidence to indicate that he had abandoned the small farmer. The 'cocoa pool', as the marketing arrangement which he sponsored came to be known, was really aimed at cushioning the small farmer against the impact of seasonal fluctuations in the price of his product. Many of the policies adopted by the Nationalist Government in both the industrial and agricultural sectors of the economy after 1956 were really initiated in the 1950–6 period.

The greatest weakness of the ministerial régime was its inability to project an image of moral integrity, unity, cohesiveness, rationality, and reforming zeal. Despite what was in fact an impressive record of real co-operation on many fronts, to the public it appeared that the administration was guided solely by an ethic of *chacun pour soi*. Too often decisions seemed to be made capriciously and without any long-term planning or interdepartmental consultation. Max Farquhar is correct when he ascribes this weakness to the absence of an undisputed and legitimate national leader who could provide the sort of spiritual guidance and the illusion of unity and harmony which the mass mind needs. The administration spoke in a babble of unorchestrated voices.

The fatal flaw in the previous Constitution was that while in great advance of what had formerly obtained, in that through the provision of Ministers, some semblance of responsible government was thereby enjoined, it lacked the guiding hand of an accredited leader. Greatly handicapped by this defect, each Minister, determined on the success of the system particularly in so far as it applied to his own Ministry, became more and more individualistic. The Government meant his own Ministry. Thus, despite many notable and impressive achievements, the Government collectively had to bear the full brunt of responsibility for many grave personal errors, which would never have occurred had they been a team working loyally together under a fully responsible head. They laboured earnestly on occasion to offer the illusion of a team, but could not conceal their long suffering ill-assortment. They were veritably a patch-work Government of queer odds and ends. They knew it themselves, but accommodated themselves too readily to the fact.[28]

clerks and of retrenchment in 1955, and allowed clerical unions to protest without interference from the authorities. The Seamen and Waterfront Workers Trade Union also obtained one of its best labour contracts under Gomes' administration. Gomes was also responsible for establishing a number of wage councils in areas not adequately served by unions.

28 Max Farquhar, 'Voters Said No Confidence in Previous Government', the *Sunday Guardian*, Sept. 30, 1956. Gomes himself said very much the same thing in 1964:

THE CONSTITUTIONAL DEBATE, 1955–6

When the constitutional issue was re-opened in 1955, the ministerial system was the most debated issue. Had it worked satisfactorily enough to allow removal of the restraints with which it was hedged, or was there need for a further transitional period? The Sinanan Committee, which had been appointed to advise on the feasibility of further constitutional reform, recommended that, although the system had worked reasonably well, conditions in the country had not changed sufficiently to permit it to recommend any radical departures. As the majority report stated,

With the multiplicity of parties and the unlikelihood of a few strong parties emerging, and with the difficulty of welding a people together of such varied racial compositions, a certain amount of caution should be observed. The imminence of a West Indian Federation also influenced some members to advocate the continuance of the unicameral system as they considered that the existence of the Federal Parliament would make a more complicated system undesirable on grounds both of the extra expense involved and the reduction in legislative jurisdiction of the island legislature ... it was too early to depart entirely from the framework of the old constitution which had proved to be a workable one and one suited to the country in its present state of development.[29]

The Committee did, however, make a few far-reaching suggestions. It recommended the creation of an Executive Council consisting of ten elected ministers, one of whom was to be designated chief minister. But the latter's powers were to be limited. He was to have no say in the choice or removal of his ministerial colleagues, though he might be consulted about the allocation of portfolios. The Governor was still to remain chairman of the Executive Council. These provisions met with the same objections that were raised in 1948. It was felt by some that it would have been more useful, from the point of view of cabinet collegiality, to employ the French device of having a chief minister chosen by the Legislature, who would in turn select a cabinet which would then be submitted to the Legislature for approval or disapproval. Alter-

'The five ministers were held together by no single party or political obligation. The result was a sort of bastard coalition which appeared to work well, but could not present a uniform image to the electorate. To a large extent each minister pursued his own inclinations undisturbed by the others without discipline from the centre; normal tensions and rivalries were aggravated.' Albert Gomes, 'A Politician Recalls', TG, Jan. 22, 1964.

29 *Report of the Constitutional Committee*, Council Paper no. 16, Port of Spain, 1956, p. 5.

natively, the choice of chief minister could have been first made by the Governor from among those most likely to command support.

There was also some opposition to the very idea of appointing of a chief minister, on the ground that his position would be untenable given the absence of parties. Objections were also raised by others against the way in which the ministers were to be selected, that is, by the whole Legislature consisting of twenty-four elected members, five nominated members, and two officials. It was possible, for instance, that a party which returned fourteen or fifteen candidates to the Legislature could be excluded from office. A radical party would have to win as many as sixteen or seventeen of the twenty-four seats to form an effective government, since they could not expect to obtain support from the nominated-official bloc.

The recommendation that an elected minister of finance should replace the appointed Financial Secretary was vigorously opposed by business elements in the society, who feared that such a minister would indulge in reckless spending. But those who had had experience with the old system felt that it was no longer workable. The Financial Secretary had too often found himself in situations where he had to adjudicate the demands of five elected ministers. Given the constitutional advances already conceded, this was an embarrassing role for any official. The Governor himself, Sir Edward Beetham, did not believe that there was any risk of financial unorthodoxy, since the new minister was 'unlikely to expose himself to criticism, or to risk his good repute primarily for the sake of enabling his colleagues to enhance theirs'. The Governor also believed that critics of the proposal underestimated the influence of the permanent staffs of the ministries, 'where the real strength of the ministry lies'.[30]

The Governor endorsed the majority report of the Committee, though he recommended certain modifications relating to the size of the Executive Council. He felt that there should be eight rather than ten elected ministers; an Executive Council of twelve (ten elected plus two officials) would be top heavy he maintained. He also accepted the contention that such a council could govern with the support of the five nominated members. With the smaller ministry, elected backbenchers would have a majority of one. Beetham did not agree with the argument of the radicals that the constitutional framework inhibited the development of political parties. The case of the Gold Coast was cited to illustrate his view that if there was a homogeneous political opinion in the colony, it would express itself in a well-organized political party that could come to power: 'The constitution would then operate in accordance with many

---

30 'Governor's Despatch to the Secretary of State', appended to *Report of the Constitutional Committee, Ibid.,* p. 49.

of the conventions usually applying in a parliamentary system.'[31] Constitutions may help to shape parties, but it is equally true that parties shape constitutions.

On the question of the chief minister, Beetham admitted that there were some difficulties in this experiment; but he felt that there was an overriding need for an elected head of government to speak for Trinidad in the Caribbean and abroad (especially with Federation in the offing), someone who would concern himself with the over-all working of the ministerial team. On the question of how the Executive Council was to be chosen, Beetham felt that the constitution allowed for all sorts of possibilities. If no party achieved a majority, then the method of electing and dismissing ministers would assume a greater amount of give-and-take among elements forming the government coalition. 'If, however, a majority party or a coalition group came to power, their leader could select his own team and secure approval for it by the use of their majority ...'[32]

Beetham also favoured the retention of the nominated system within the unicameral framework, though he recognized that a second chamber might be needed at a later stage. As he noted, 'The drawback of an Upper House is that when it exercises its functions of bringing to bear other experience and judgement on a problem, too often its comments appear to be, or are represented to be, a criticism of the decisions of the people's representatives. It is criticism after the event which often leads to frustration. Under the single chamber system, the final decision represents the amalgam of the different points of view.'[33]

The Governor felt that the genius of the proposed constitution lay in its flexibility. It could work with or without a viable party system. If a majority opinion were to crystallize, and if such a majority were 'undoubted and persistent', it could break through all the existing restraints of the constitutional system. But the pluralism of the society and the absence of an undisputed popular leader made such a majority difficult to mobilize. The odds were against it in Trinidad and Tobago. The view that the nominated element held the balance of power appeared unshakable. Events were to vindicate Beetham.

FEDERATION, THE INDIANS, AND THE POSTPONEMENT CRISIS

In April of 1955, a motion to postpone the general elections due for September of that year was pushed through the Legislative Council. It was claimed that more time was necessary for debating the Report of the Constitutional Committee, for getting the necessary approval of the Colonial Office, and for

31   *Ibid.*, p. 54.   32   *Ibid.*, p. 53.   33   *Ibid.*, p. 52.

making preparations for holding elections under the new statutory instruments. Several possible reasons have been advanced to explain this decision, which was greeted with a tremendous outburst of protest from the press, local councils and other associations, and a substantial section of the public. No one really took the official reasons very seriously. One of the most popular explanations was that the members of the Legislature were so conscious of their failures that they decided that extra time was needed to put their houses in order.

The uncertain fate of the proposed Federation was also seen as a probable reason for the postponement. It was certainly the one which motivated the British government, which was quite anxious to make absolutely sure that the federal pact was concluded and elections held before there was any change of personnel in the Trinidad Legislature.[34] There was a real fear that an anti-federationist coalition based on the Indian community might emerge victorious and destroy the prospect of West Indian federalism. The question of the Indians' position in the Federation had come to a head during the debate in the Legislative Council on the proposed federal plan agreed to in London in 1953. There were extremely heated charges and counter-charges that the Indians were attempting to wreck the aspirations of the West Indian community. Indians were reminded that many of their leaders had strongly opposed the federal idea in the past and that their MLCs had sent a memorandum to the Secretary of State protesting against Federation on the ground that 'they [Indians] had worked hard to build this country, and that Federation, if it came, would mean that Negroes would be able to get the better of Indians'. It was also claimed that one Indian MLC was 'parading up and down the country' telling Indians that Negroes from the smaller islands 'will come and mix with the Indian race and pollute it'.[35]

Indian MLCs, however, denied that they were against Federation; they were merely opposed to the idea of unrestricted immigration. As the Hon. Mitra Sinanan put it, 'The plain, simple and unvarnished truth is that we are all committed to the question of Federation. But what we say is that whilst we agree on the principle of Federation, we want to make sure that the structure and form are good for the political climate and ambitions of the people of the colony. ... We can say without fear of contradiction that the country does not

34   The next federal conference was scheduled for February 7, 1956.
35   Albert Gomes, *Hansard*, Dec. 10, 1954, p. 690. The Indian opinion on Federation was at no time homogeneous or consistent, but up to the end of 1955 at least, majority sentiment was against it. Cf. my article 'The Struggle for Afro-Indian Solidarity', *Index*, vol. 1, no. 4, Sept. 1966, pp. 34 ff., and Jesse Proctor's 'East Indians and the Federation of the West Indies', *India Quarterly*, vol. 17, no. 4, Oct.–Dec. 1961, pp. 370–95.

want any unrestricted immigration.'[36] But non-Indian politicians refused to accept these protestations at face value. They felt that Indians were firmly opposed to Federation, but were afraid to say so openly. Instead, they were trying to establish road blocks in the hope that delay would result in the scrapping of the project. Whether or not this was a fair characterization of the position of the Indians is difficult to say. It would appear that up to 1956 most Indians were hostile to Federation, but that the attempts which were made in this year to give them greater constitutional protection in the federal system went a long way towards relieving some of their fears. By 1958 their scepticism towards Federation had completely evaporated.

Another possible explanation for the postponement was the widespread belief that the Hindu-based People's Democratic Party was likely to return the largest bloc of candidates to the Legislature if the elections were held in 1955. The Hindus were the only well-organized group in the country, and non-Indians considered the prospect of a Hindu-controlled government intolerable. Postponement may thus have appeared to fulfil two crucial functions. It would save both the Federation and the non-Indian population by giving other forces time to organize. Whatever the reason, postponement was a serious tactical blunder on the part of the old legislature, since it gave Dr Williams and the new nationalist forces the time and the issues around which to organize. Before the postponement, these groups were thinking in terms of placing one man in the Legislature who would express their views. By the end of 1955 they could even dare to think of capturing all the urban constituencies. As one of the ministers put it, 'We ran from the PDP frying-pan into the PNM fire.'

36 *Hansard*, Dec. 10, 1954, p. 557–8.

Part Two

Part Two traces the rise of the People's National Movement in 1955–6, its organizational and ideological structure, and its reception in the community. These two years were perhaps the most exciting and hopeful in Trinidad's political development. The nationalist movement, which for over two generations had meandered sluggishly and seemingly without direction, in 1955 became a rushing torrent enveloping large numbers of people who had hitherto remained aloof and apolitical.

The dynamism and revolutionary idealism of the PNM was as challenging to those who were hungry for change and meaningful leadership as it was frightening to established elements in the society. Politically conservative Hindus, white settlers and businessmen, the Catholic Church, the old-line trade unions, and political leaders all feared its powerful hold over the Negro masses and did their utmost to undermine its influence. The elections of 1956, seen by many as a conflict of two worlds – the old world of colonialism, racial snobbery, and corruption, and the new with its promise of integral decolonization – were the most critical that the country had yet witnessed. The victory of the PNM brought to fruition the work of those who had struggled to create meaningful party politics in Trinidad and Tobago, and it appeared that the country had finally rid itself of its reputation in the Caribbean for political immaturity. The appearance was not to last.

6
The rally of the progressives

The year 1955 saw the emergence of an entirely new brand of political leadership in the colony, a leadership which finally succeeded in stimulating a fuller measure of political commitment on the part of the middle classes. The political alienation of the middle class had been partly due to a crisis of confidence. They did not believe that the West Indies could long survive without the moral and physical presence of the imperial power.[1] The more conservative elements also feared that if political power were fully transferred, the *hoi polloi* and the demagogues who appealed to them would be the main beneficiaries. They were thus opposed to any exclusive reliance on the ballot box, and clung just as tenaciously to the nominated system as did Indians and white creoles. The fundamental problem, of course, was their unwillingness to compete on equal terms with 'demagogues' for the suffrage of the masses. Politics was too sweaty, to ridden with graft and corruption for their taste.

To engage in politics successfully one had to have funds to pay professional canvassers, opinion leaders of the various ethnic groups, and enumerators to pad voting lists and ferret out the 'dead vote'. One had to be able to

---

1 'The West Indies can never stand alone nationally, economically, culturally or otherwise without the protection of a great power. Let British capitalism take flight from Trinidad tomorrow, and we face disaster; let British law and order and the much criticized British administration depart, and the West Indies would revert to barbarism within a year. Our plain duty, even self-interest and self-preservation, dictates that we continue to be part of the British Empire. We do ourselves a great injustice if we feel we can do without Britain and that we should not share the little we have with her sons and daughters, in return for the manifold blessing we receive.' Henry Hudson-Phillips, QC, *Port of Spain Gazette*, Aug. 8, 1948.

employ all the attention-getting artifices of the demagogue, and make lavish promises to provide those little conveniences which meant a lot to the man in the street but which, to the middle class, were not objects of national concern. Politics in Trinidad was essentially parish-pump politics, *praja* politics, as it was known in the Indian community. Universal issues did not excite the masses in any fundamental way. They were concerned, in the main, with the immediate fulfilment of their deeply felt material deprivations. Their perspectives were short in range and quite parochial. In such an atmosphere, honest men had of necessity 'to sacrifice reason to popular mass opinion'.[2] However well-intentioned, inevitably and inexorably they became enveloped by the quagmire of Trinidad politics.

While most of the middle class remained aloof from politics, there was always a small element which was prepared to work actively for political change and social reform. Between 1950 and 1956 some of them met quite frequently to discuss the political ills of Trinidad and of the West Indies as a whole. Two groups which later contributed significantly to the development of the nationalist movement in the colony were the Teachers Economic and Cultural Association and the Political Education Group. The Teachers Economic and Cultural Association, a co-operative formed in 1935 by a group of radical urban Negroes, was one expression of the widespread anger over the discriminatory manner in which the avenues of economic and social advancement were kept closed to Negroes. Frustration stemmed not only from the treatment meted out to teachers by the religious and state educational offices, which were largely staffed by whites, but from the attitude of the established Teachers Union, which they believed had become too accommodationist. TECA was conceived with two goals in mind. It was primarily organized to cater to the economic, cultural, and professional well-being of its members. In this role it functioned both as a co-operative and as a ginger group around the Teachers Union. Its second goal was the 'uplift of the people'. The members saw themselves as a sort of yeast group which would later form the nucleus of a mass cultural movement. This aspect of TECA's purpose was looked after by one of its subcommittees which was established around 1950 and which later became known as the People's Education Movement.[3]

---

2   Only from the white creole district, north Port of Spain, was it possible to win without an effective political machine.

3   The leading members of this group were J. Sheldon Donaldson, F.G. Maynard, A.A. Alexander, and De Wilton Rogers, all of whom (except Maynard) were to play crucial roles in the nationalist movement that mushroomed in 1956. It is also interesting to note that all of these men, with the exception of Maynard, were 'renegade' Roman Catholics. According to De Wilton Rogers, its Director General, TECA's aims were: (*a*) to co-ordinate and synthesize all movements for the economic

The Political Education Group was an extremely high-powered cluster of professionals representing some of the best minds in the colony. The membership of the PEG was predominantly Negro but it included at least four Indians among its eighteen or so members.[4] Every aspect of the country's political, economic, and social life was systematically discussed at their meetings. By the middle of 1955 the group agreed that there was need for a new party which would emphasize mass political education and not the mere pursuit of power.[5] Dr Eric Williams, who had emerged as the accepted opinion leader in the group, was their unanimous choice to take the programme to the people. Williams was much more politically sophisticated than his colleagues. He had taught political science at Howard University, and his research position at the Anglo-American Caribbean Economic Commission had also provided him with the type of authoritative information which was not available to the rest of the group. His leadership capabilities, his drive and capacity for sustained concentration, and his organizational genius were clearly apparent to all.[6]

and cultural advance of the teacher, including literary, artistic and dramatic activities; (b) the establishment of an Institute of Cultural Studies; (c) to bring to the notice of the proper authorities such matters as concern its members; (d) reformation of the educational system in the West Indies as a whole; (e) to make the people aware of the legacies of slavery and the role of the Negro in the contemporary world; (f) to put an end to the philosophy of acceptance and passivity which affected the rank and file. 'Out of this Womb Came PNM', *Nation*, Jan. 21, 1966.

4   'The formation of the Political Education Group itself was neither deliberately conceived nor planned. The Group rather grew out of the stimulation of private discussions in the aftermath of informal gatherings, and was, to some extent, inspired by the series of public lectures and talks delivered about this time by Dr Eric Williams. Basically, its creation was at once a manifest symptom and an inevitable result of the reaction to the current social and political situation. Its true inspiration was the need to find an avenue for expression, and to canalise thinking by the development of a new formula for the remedies for the prevalent social, political, and economic ills of the country. The Political Education Group was not a group of intellectuals or for intellectuals, though it was stimulated by a certain intellectualism. It was a heterogeneous group whose members were shocked with concern by their vivid realization of the social and political evils of the time.' W.J. Alexander, 'Birth of the PNM and Its Descent into the Political Arena', *Nation*, Jan. 21, 1966.

5   According to Alexander, 'There was a sharp division on a contrary view that the situation could be met by the infusion of new life into one or other of the existing political parties.' The Butler Party and the People's Democratic Party were given consideration, but the idea was later rejected. 'There was ... a conscious apprehension that ideas which had been precisely hammered out in a small cohesive group may become swamped in the complexities which large membership brings with it.' *Ibid.*

6   Members of the group have confessed that they always suspected Williams of a tendency towards megalomania even in this early period, though he strove valiantly to conceal this.

Dr Williams hesitated a long time before finally deciding to enter upon a career of political activism. His indecision angered some of his colleagues, who felt that for all his expressed concern for the people of Trinidad and Tobago, he preferred the cushions of his lucrative post at the Caribbean Commission.[7] His dismissal from the Commission, however, brought to a dramatic end his reluctance to plunge into the uncertainties of politics. He had been handed a ready-made issue with which to build a political career.

The events relating to Dr Williams' dismissal form an essential link in the chain of events leading up to the launching of the nationalist movement in 1956. By the terms of his contract with the Caribbean Commission, Williams had been forbidden to engage in any open political discussion or writing about West Indian politics unless advance notice and copies of his statements were submitted to the colonial authorities of the areas concerned. It would appear that freedom to write and speak on sensitive issues had always been a central issue in Williams' relations with the Directorate of the Commission, which took objection to his radical anti-colonialist interpretation of Caribbean history and politics. Personality conflicts no doubt aggravated the difficulties. Williams had an undisguised contempt for the 'academic incompetence' of his metropolitan colleagues, and he believed the Commission was out of step with the aspirations of progressive forces in the Caribbean.

If Williams had come to the conclusion that the Commission was a *fainéant* imperialist agency, it might have been wondered why he continued to associate with it, and why he had sought to be promoted to the vacant position of Secretary General. Anticipating suspicions, Williams explained:

I tolerated those conditions for over twelve years [because] I represented ... the cause of the West Indian people. I also had more personal reasons. My connection with the Commission brought me into close contact with present problems in territories, the study of whose history has been the principal purpose of my adult life, while my association with representatives of the metropolitan governments enabled me to understand, as I could not otherwise have understood, the mess in which the West Indies find themselves today.[8]

From the point of view of the effect which Williams wished to create, it was a brilliant apologia. He had cast himself in the role of the providential messiah who had been preparing himself in the wilderness of the Commission so that

7 Quite a few of Williams' friends, including Norman Manley, sought to discourage him from entering political life on the grounds that the masses were ungrateful and would reject him as they had rejected Cipriani.
8 *My Relations with the Caribbean Commission, 1943–1955*, Port of Spain, 1955.

he might with greater effectiveness 'set his people free'. His main strategy was to get the masses to regard his personal struggle as *their* struggle – the struggle of the qualified black West Indian for recognition and advancement. As he told them, 'The issues are not personal, but political; they involve not a single individual, but the West Indian people ... mine was not an individual case. ... I stand before you tonight, ... the representative of a principle, a cause, and a defeat. The principle is the principle of intellectual freedom. The cause is the cause of the West Indian people. The defeat is the defeat of the policy of appointing local men to high office.'[9] Williams also told his listeners that he had turned down many job offers which would have taken him out of the West Indies. 'I have decided to let down my bucket where I am, now, right here with you in the West Indies.'[10]

The enthusiasm with which Williams' speech was received made it quite apparent that the people had found a new hero. Williams' cocky boastfulness and pugnacity elicited a ready response in the Trinidadian masses. The fact that he was a brilliant academician, accepted and recognized as a scholar in Britain and the United States, added to his legitimacy in their eyes, for to them, as to most colonials, the winning of recognition in status-defining metropolitan cultures, was and still is a prerequisite for acceptance.

It is worth noting that the organization which sponsored Williams' historic lecture was the People's Education Movement. The PEM had come to believe that Williams was the leader they had been seeking, the man best equipped to uplift the people. They had also come to believe that the audiences Williams had been addressing prior to his dismissal from the Commission were too

9 *Ibid.*, pp. 1 and 47. Williams also claimed that he did not wish to 'flee the imperialist enemy', or give in to the pressures of the West Indian plantocracy, which was demanding his removal. He made it known that it was the Trinidad government, especially Albert Gomes, who had engineered his dismissal because they feared the explosive impact of his role in the adult education movement. The circumstances leading to Williams' decision to go to the people are not always clear. No doubt it was greatly influenced by the concerted attempt of the Government, especially the Minister of Labour, Albert Gomes, and the Minister of Education, Roy Joseph, to deny Williams the use of government buildings for his adult education programme. Pressure from his colleagues also provided him with the courage which he seemed to have lacked in those early months of 1955. It is certain, however, that had it not been for his dismissal from the Commission, Williams would not have entered active political life in 1955, much as he might have nursed secret ambitions to follow in the footsteps of Manley and Muñoz Marin. Williams has argued that he was certain he would one day enter West Indian politics, and his dismissal from the Commission merely affected the timing. His claim that he was immensely relieved to hear of his dismissal does not seem to square with the available evidence. It was an awkward attempt at *post facto* rationalization.

10 *Ibid.*, p. 51.

professional and middle class, and they had urged him to come out into the open and take the message to the people.[11]

WILLIAMS AND THE CONSTITUTION

Williams objected to the proposal of the 1955 Constitution Reform Committee for the retention of the single chamber system and the maintenance of the Governor's nominees in this body, claiming that it maintained the old colonial framework intact. He noted that Trinidad had never had a democratic lower house as did many of the other West Indian islands, and that the Legislative Council was, in essence, the upper house, which had merely been expanded to include elected members. The quasi-ministerial system was also seen as a travesty of what a proper cabinet system should be. Williams put the blame for the persistent failure of the nationalist movement in Trinidad and Tobago mainly on the inadequacies of the institutional framework. Unless Trinidad and Tobago were conceded British parliamentary institutions, political chaos and backwardness would continue to prevail.[12] What was needed was the creation of a purely elective lower chamber, leaving the existing chamber to the nominated element. Here Williams turned his back on the whole radical tradition in Trinidad and Tobago, a tradition which was virtually unanimous in opposing a second chamber. His argument was that in the context of Trinidad politics, vested economic and religious interests must be given some say in the running of the country. 'The nominated system is so essential that if it did not exist, it would be necessary to invent it.'[13]

Williams listed three defects of the system as it existed. In the first place, the nominated element had too decisive an influence in the system. 'One should take the nominated members out of the single chamber legislature where they can *determine* what we do, either by being in a majority, or by assisting ministers to get a majority, and put them in a second chamber, in a position ...

11 Williams became a consultant to the PEM in 1950. 'I have always held the view that the work of organizations such as the Caribbean Commission can very easily degenerate into a mere collection of papers and documents unless vitality is injected into it by the people whom it is designed to serve. In addition, as you know, I am constantly fighting against that West Indian complacency which is prepared to sit down and await official pontification, to applaud publicly and grumble privately. I feel that wherever possible, the people, the ordinary people should be encouraged and stimulated to look themselves into the problems of the area, discuss them and develop their own point of view.' Williams to De Wilton Rogers, *Nation*, Jan. 21, 1966.
12 Eric Williams, *Constitution Reform in Trinidad and Tobago*, Public Affairs Pamphlet no. 2, Port of Spain, 1955, p. 28.
13 *Ibid.*, p. 31.

to warn and comfort, but not to command.'[14] Williams also observed that the nominated system was not being used as extensively as it should be. If the two-chamber system were to be introduced, it would then be possible to give representation to a greater variety of special interests. The third defect concerned the manner in which special interests were appointed. The fact that these appointments were made by the Governor with the approval of the Colonial Office detracted from the legitimacy of such nominees. Inevitably, they had come to be regarded as the Governor's stooges. Special interests must in future choose their own representatives. 'The second chamber must not be dominated by the Governor, by the Secretary of State for the Colonies, or *by the party in power*.'[15]

Williams' constitutional proposals were a model of moderation. What was striking about them was the enormous concessions which were made to the vested interests in the society, interests which on the surface Williams appeared to be attacking. Williams in fact conceded to the proposed upper chamber a greater delaying power than that enjoyed by the House of Lords after 1910. On non-financial matters the upper chamber was to be permitted to delay legislation for as long as twenty-four months! He defended this provision on the grounds that checks and balances were necessary in a society as politically inexperienced as Trinidad and Tobago:

Checks and balances [are] necessary in a democratic society. Such checks and balances are doubly necessary when, as is always possible, one party might sweep the polls and find itself without effective opposition in the elected house, as has happened with Bradshaw in St Kitts, Bird in Antigua, Gairy in Grenada, Nkrumah in the Gold Coast and Muñoz Marin in Puerto Rico. To make assurance doubly sure, the delaying power of twelve months enjoyed by the House of Lords in Britain should be extended to twenty-four months in Trinidad as the system is new and as we have only a limited experience of democratic process. That experience dates back only thirty-two years, a short time in the life of man and an insignificant period in the life of a country.[16]

Two possible explanations might be advanced for Williams' constitutional moderation. It could be argued that the provisions demonstrated how conservative he really was despite his revolutionary rhetoric. The entire set of proposals was considerably to the right of those proposed by radicals in the 1940s. Williams appeared to be just as suspicious of dominant parties based on mass support as were the conformist middle classes. Indeed, he seemed to place himself in the republican rather than in the populist democratic tradition. It was to Alexander Hamilton, for example, that he turned for arguments to

14 *Ibid.*, p. 32.   15 *Ibid.*, p. 33.   16 *Ibid.*, p. 35.

justify his proposals for a constitution that would include checks on the popular assembly. The appeal to vested interests might be viewed as a genuine attempt to offer them the opportunity to play a responsible and constructive role in the development of the region. These forces 'can help run the country', he advised his followers. But it is also possible to argue that Williams, though a committed radical, was deliberately casting himself in the role of the aggregator who, if given a chance, would unite all the disparate elements in the society. As such, he quite calculatingly designed a constitution which would appeal to all classes and all ethnic and creedal groups. Bouquets were thrown at every important sector of the society. As he confessed, 'The proposals were designed to reconcile all conflicting points of view ... to provide common ground for the widest possible measure of co-operation between all classes, races, colours and religions for the constructive work ahead of us in the field of economic and social development.'[17]

What Trinidad needed most of all, he argued, was a genuine multiracial party. Earlier attempts had been made to create a party that would cut across the vertical and horizontal interests of the society. Their weakness stemmed in part from the failure of those who led them to inspire the necessary confidence in the genuineness of their multiracial idealism. Cipriani, Solomon, Butler, Hamel-Smith, and others never offered the minorities any constitutional safeguards with which they could defend themselves in time of need. This was Williams' unique contribution to the constitutional debate. He felt that with these constitutional safeguards, people of varying ethnic backgrounds would feel free to join a mass nationalist party. By implication, however, Williams was putting the blame for the failure of the attempts at multiracial unity on the political class in Trinidad and not on the Colonial Office. As he said later on, 'The last apology or excuse for colonization will have been removed when Caribbean democracy can prove that minority rights are quite safe in its hands.'[18]

Williams' constitutional proposal, which was embodied in a petition to the Secretary of State for the Colonies, was signed by 27,811 people from all over the country. Support came from all religious, ethnic, and class groups, though the non-Indian community was heavily over-represented.[19] This opera-

---

17 *Ibid.*, p. 36.
18 Eric Williams, 'Race Relations in Caribbean Society', in Vera Rubin (ed.),
    Caribbean Studies: A Symposium, Kingston, Jamaica, 1957, p. 60.
19 Of the 27,811 signatures there were:

Roman Catholics	11,850	Anglicans	10,041
Hindus	1,115	Methodists	1,108
Moslems	717	Spiritual Baptists	499
Presbyterians	471	Adventists	392
Moravians	222	Unclassified	1,356

tion, the marshalling of signatures to convince the Colonial Office that Trinidad was ripe for constitutional change, provided the nucleus for the large volunteer network that was to take the nationalists to electoral victory in 1956.

'THE NEW PROFESSOR OF THE NEW ECONOMICS'

'The important thing in the history of the Negro in the Caribbean is not the political flag that floats over him, but the economy that strangles him.' Eric Williams, *The Negro in the Caribbean*.

Prior to 1955 it was assumed that once self-government was achieved, reorganization of the economy would follow as a matter of course. Given this Micawber-like optimism, none of the earlier nationalists ever bothered to give any serious systematic thought to the problems involved in the transformation of the West Indian economy. Socialism and nationalism were seen as the magical keys that would solve all West Indian problems. West Indian reformers imbibed very deeply, and quite uncritically, the socialist utopianism of the British Labour Movement. Eric Williams was the first would-be reformer in Trinidad to break openly with the socialist tradition. Whether his open disapproval stemmed from inner conviction or from sheer political opportunism is a controversial question about which we shall speculate later. But his treatise *The Economic Problems of Trinidad and Tobago* did show that he had a clear understanding of the inherent weakness of any socialist solution to the fundamental West Indian problem.

The core problem which faces any reformer in the Caribbean centres on the need to provide meaningful employment for a rapidly increasing population in an area which is considerably underendowed in economic resources. Williams' key criticism of the ministerial régime was that it had made no real effort to reduce the colony's dangerous dependence on oil and sugar.[20] His argument was that these industries could not expand fast enough to absorb the vast numbers who were seeking employment. Indeed, the critical fact was that the continued expansion of these two industries, especially sugar, could be achieved only if they became more fully mechanized.[21]

---

20 The extent to which oil dominated the economy can be gleaned from the following figures: Oil was responsible for 72 per cent of the colony's export trade in 1946 and for 75 per cent from 1950 to 1954. In the period 1947–54, sugar contributed a steady 10 per cent. Cited in Eric Williams, *The Economic Problems of Trinidad and Tobago*, Public Affairs Pamphlet no. 1, Port of Spain, July 1955.

21 Williams saw this tendency in the sugar industry as being both inevitable and desirable: 'This reduction of employment in the sugar industry is not an accident and is not due to malice. It is long overdue. The British West Indies have depended for too long on manpower in agriculture; the excessive and indiscriminate importa-

Even though the old régime had acknowledged the need to diversify the economy, its policies had reinforced the existing economic pattern by discouraging (even if unwittingly) agricultural rationalization. Instead of making bold and imaginative attempts to industrialize the society, the ministers had directed most of their attention to securing permanent protection for the colony's agriculural staples – especially sugar and citrus. Permanent protection depended on prolongation of the colonial relationships. It was 'exactly the policy that has been pursued by the British West Indies sugar industry for the past two-and-a-half centuries. It is the philosophy of colonialism. ... Further protection should be asked for a specific period, twenty-five years, to set us on our feet in the early days of self-government.'[22] Those who argued that the West Indies should expand sugar as a crop with which to earn the desired wealth to pay for its imports from abroad were reminded that a monocultural economy is a precarious economy, always subject to the whims of world markets and the forces of nature. Similar arguments would be made by the Cuban reformers a few years later.

If one could not rely on sugar, one still could not leave the industry as it was. Williams agreed with Dr Arthur Lewis that 'new forms must be created which will take the West Indian sugar industry "out of politics" in the sense of earning general acceptance, or the West Indian community will sooner or later simply tear itself in pieces, and destroy the sugar industry in the process'.[23] He believed that 'the Negro must be given a more equitable share of the wealth he produces. The sugar industry and the land that goes with it can no longer continue to be the monopoly of a few absentee companies.' Williams was aware, however, that fragmentation of the land into two- and five-acre plots might be a political but not an economic solution. As he declared, 'We must not harbour the mistaken notion that the alternative to the plantation system with its army of landless blacks is a system of peasant proprietorship, the division of the large estate into small farms. The small-scale production of subsistence farming would be reactionary.'[24]

Subsistence peasant-farming increased the numbers on the land, but was

tion of labour, Negro slaves and Indian indentured immigrants, has been the principal cause of the technological backwardness of British West Indian agriculture. The reduction of labour going on today in the sugar industry in Trinidad and Tobago is a continuation of a process that had been going on for the past sixty years in British West Indian agriculture.' *Ibid.*, p. 6.

22   *Ibid.*, p. 5.   23   *Ibid.*, p. 7.
24   Eric Williams, *The Negro in the Caribbean*, Washington DC, 1942, p. 45. Williams was concerned with the tendency on the part of the sugar-planters to gobble up all the land that they could put their hands on. As we have noted earlier, the growth of an independent peasant class had been bitterly opposed by the plantocracy on the grounds that such a development would reduce the availability of labour and increase its cost.

not the key to the emancipation of the peasantry. The small farm was not a viable economic unit. It would also be difficult for a family based on such a unit to make any dignified and meaningful contribution to the cultural and civic life of the community. As far as land reform was concerned, then, there seemed to be two alternatives. One might either create a twenty- to fifty-acre peasant class which the state would have to subsidize heavily in terms of know-how and capital, or, if public capital could not be found, leave agriculture to large-scale operation by agencies that had the capital.

Williams preferred the former.[25] He believed that a sensible programme of peasant proprietorship would have significant political, social, and economic advantages. Politically, it was seen as contributing to the weakening of the power of the sugar barons over the masses. At the same time, it might very well help to ameliorate the potentially explosive relationship between Indian and Negro on the plantation. It was also felt that a viable peasantry would help to clear up some of the social evils of the plantation system: the barrack system with all its attendant dangers to the health of the entire community, the servile mentality of the peasant with his lack of drive and enthusiasm, and his dependence on the godfather figure. Williams believed that the acquisition of a piece of land would give the small farmer a sign of his ascent into a higher social class and engender in him the civic and personal pride he lacked. Economically, the intention of the programme was to transform Negro and Indian wage-earners into petty bourgeois farmers who would be encouraged to plant food crops. The country needed to import fewer of the basic food commodities which, with some effort and initiative, it could easily produce.

Whether or not one chose to maintain the plantation system intact, the question of rural unemployment still posed enormous difficulties. But to Williams the answer was simple. One had to embark on a bold and dynamic programme of industrial diversification. Not only would diversification absorb labour surpluses from the land and the new entrants into the labour market, it was also seen as a prerequisite to a meaningful existence for those who remained on the land. The agricultural and industrial revolutions were to reinforce each other.

Williams acknowledged that the old régime had begun a policy of encouraging potential investors by dangling the bait of tax exemptions.[26] He felt,

---

25   *Ibid.*, pp. 46–51. Williams advocated that legal restrictions should be placed on the size of plantations. The upper ceiling should be 500 acres.

26   Gomes, who told Trinidadians that they must 'industrialize or die', later despaired of the prospect of an industrialized Trinidad. 'There was a school of wishful thinking economists who set up a picture of an ideal world and proposed that a diversification of the economics of countries dependent on plantation products would solve all problems. This policy had been tried in Trinidad but had not produced this miracle.' Cited in PNM *Weekly*, Sept. 13, 1956.

however, that its failure was due to lack of effort on related fronts. One needed to erect tariff walls, where necessary, to allow embryonic industries an opportunity to get on their feet. The state, too, might well take an initiative in establishing industries that did not seem sufficiently profitable to private investors. Williams was aware of the formidable costs involved in establishing new industries, and it does not appear that he was very sanguine about state-sponsored industrialization. In his view the solution to Trinidad's economic problem was a high-powered industrial development corporation with a dynamic programme aimed at attracting private capital.[27] Williams seemed immensely confident that an energetic, scientifically-oriented, and puritanically austere regime could successfully mobilize the energies of the community. He knew that the task would not be easy, and he noted the possibility that, with a rapidly expanding population, economic development in Trinidad and Tobago might be a sisyphean undertaking; but such doubts were not allowed to stand in the way of purposeful effort.[28]

Williams was aware of the political implications of an economic programme of the type he outlined. Any other strategy would have been explosive in a community as ethnically mixed as Trinidad. As Arthur Lewis had warned, 'A community which is mixed racially needs, even more than other communities, to create for itself social and economic institutions which are broadly accepted.'[29] It is in this context that Williams' rejection of socialism must be considered. In his ability to perceive that socialism would divide rather than unite the community he demonstrated a tactical superiority over those reformers who had preceded him. If one were seriously interested in mobilizing not only have-not Negroes, but Indians, Chinese, and Europeans as well, one really could not make an appeal on the basis of class. The only people in the West Indies who responded positively to the socialist creed were lower-class Negroes and a sprinkling of intellectuals. The Indian masses, still largely a rural people with a passionate desire to acquire land and to succeed in the retail trades, would surely have been alienated by an economic strategy which, so they feared, would have taken from them everything for which they were

27   The responsibility of the corporation included much more than simply advising investors about the possible advantage of locating plants in Trinidad. 'The corporation will have to assist investors to the greatest extent possible by preparing the sites for factories, even building the factories, training workers, and doing the necessary market and other research. It should make that active search for new markets which the Government has criminally failed to make.' Williams, *Economic Problems*, p. 18.

28   Williams seemed to feel that with Federation the population crisis might be postponed for a long while. British Guiana, British Honduras, and Dominica were seen as natural outlets for the surplus population of the other units.

29   Williams, *Economic Problems*, p. 7.

struggling. It is true that no West Indian socialist had ever thought of col-
lectivizing all forms of agricultural production or retail distribution, but the
fear was there. The same held true for the small but economically powerful
Chinese community, most of whom were anti-Peking, even though some took
pride in China's emergence as a world power.[30] Needless to say, the European
business community and the established press were fiercely opposed to
socialism, and, unless one were really prepared to resort to violence, it was
pointless to attempt to 'convert' them to it.

Despite what many thought at the time, Williams was not really a socialist.
It is true that he had written a study of the abolition of slavery from a rather
Marxist point of view, and that he occasionally used the language common to
people of that persuasion. This led many to believe that he was a crypto-
communist who had changed his strategy though not his goals. It was argued
that Williams, who was at one time suspected by the United States authorities
of communist affiliations, was behaving like a trimmer in order to mobilize a
mass following with which to strike later on. Others felt that his seeming
orthodoxy was an overdone attempt to give the lie once and for all to the
whisperings that he was a doctrinaire Marxist. Such arguments showed a
genuine misunderstanding of his real motivations in those years. There is little
doubt that the driving impetus was his belief that he could, if given the chance,
clear up the 'mess' which the British had left in the West Indies, and do the
job better than any imperialist bureaucrat. He was confident that he knew
more about the West Indies than any colonial administrator, or any other
West Indian for that matter. If any one could cure the West Indian cancer, it
was he, 'Mr Caribbean'. Williams was quite familiar with the abortive socialist
experiment in Puerto Rico, and was not prepared to have it repeated in
Trinidad. He was aware too that Trinidad, like British Guiana and Guatemala,
would have had to face British hostility and the full fury of the United States
if any such experiments were tried.

All these factors, however, merely served to reinforce Williams' own
reformist tendencies. He was interested in nationalist and not class politics.
'Operation Jobs' was a rallying cry behind which such a national coalition
could best be mobilized. As he himself phrased it,

It is not a question of race, religion or colour; it is not a question of labour or
capital. It is a question of jobs, schools, houses, water. It calls for the united effort
of the entire population. ... Puerto Rico has found the key to the door of this
development programme. This is not only an economic question. It is also political.

30 No study has been made of the Chinese in Trinidad, but the available evidence indicates that the bulk of them identify with pre-communist China or with the Kuomin-
tang regime in Taiwan.

... Trinidad too must find that key which would open the door behind which the dynamic energies of our people are at present confined, to unleash the drive and enthusiasm which warm the heart in Puerto Rico and inspire confidence in the future.[31]

That key was to be found in a new mass political movement which he aspired to lead.

THE POLITICS OF PURPOSE

The behaviour of the parties in the past had generated a great amount of cynicism in the community. As far as the public was concerned, parties were creations that appeared around election time only to fade into oblivion on the morrow of the election. The United Front, the Trinidad Labour Party, and the Butler Party were only a few, though perhaps the most notorious, of these electoral combinations. Williams and his colleagues were aware at the outset that the success of their new movement would depend on how well they managed to overcome this widespread anti-party feeling, and their awareness inspired them to go to the people with *The Case for Party Politics in Trinidad and Tobago*.[32]

In this pamphlet Williams reminded Trinidadians that no individual politician, no matter how well intentioned, could successfully implement the glittering promises made before election day. He might, of course, be instrumental in obtaining a 'standpipe' here, a school there, and so on. But the problems which confronted the island could not be solved by parish-pump politics. What was needed was a *national party* with a *national programme* designed to cope with issues that were *national* in scope. Parties in the past had failed for essentially two reasons. The first was the basic deficiency in the constitution, which worked in ways that discouraged party cohesion. The second was related to the nature of the parties which had been formed in the past. Strictly speaking, they were not parties at all, but 'conglomerations of individuals around a certain man', with no programme that was collectively thought out and drafted.

Williams' approach to parties was somewhat Burkean, but where Burke could assume that there was an already existing opinion which individuals should unite to project, in Trinidad, national opinion had to be created. 'One of the fundamental deficiencies in the political life of Trinidad and Tobago is [its] low level of political intelligence.' What Trinidad needed was a good

---

31   Williams, *Economic Problems*, pp. 34–5.
32   Public Affairs Pamphlet no. 4, Port of Spain, 1955.

democratic but highly disciplined political party which would dedicate itself
to the satisfaction 'of the principal need of today – the political education of
the people. All its activities must be subordinate to this, must draw sustenance
from this, and must find their meaning in this.'[33] The Periclean ideal of a
participant democracy was also held out to the people. A party must not
attempt to guide the people simply by lecturing to them. Political education,
if it is to be effective, must entail much more: 'Every step taken by the party
must be a step calculated not only to do something in the interest of the people
or for the good of the people, but rather designed to get the people to do things
for themselves and to think for themselves. ... The party is conceived of as a
vast educational agency.'[34]

On the question of party democracy, Williams promised that, in contra-
distinction to the old 'cadre' parties which previously sought the people's vote,
the party membership itself, in its various groups and divisions, would select
the candidates for public office. Candidates would not be permitted to foist
themselves upon the voters. The party must be a mass-based, dues-paying
structure, organized from the bottom up. The regular payment of dues was the
best guarantee that members had against the domination of the party by
wealthy pressure groups. The public officers of the party would also be called
upon to give an account of their stewardship to the membership at fixed intervals. These, then, were to be the basic organizational principles upon which
the People's National Movement would be based.

33   *Ibid.*, p. 11.
34   Williams also promised that if the new party won power it would explain to the
     people the meaning and scope of legislation 'long before they are debated and
     passed, so that public opinion can express itself on them'. *Ibid.*, p. 13.

7

A movement is born

The inaugural conference of the People's National Movement was held on January 15, 1956, with about two hundred and fifty members present. Before the historic conference assembled, however, a substantial amount of planning and organization had already taken place, which in fact had done more to determine the nature of the Movement than the decisions taken at the conference.[1] One basic decision made in advance related to the naming of the organization. It was felt that the term 'party' was too limiting and suggested a mere electioneering machine. The term 'movement' better described the aim of the group – the creation of an organization which was dedicated to radical social transformation. As the Charter later declared:

We are not another of the transitory and artificial combinations to which you have grown accustomed in election years, or another bandwagon of dissident and disappointed politicians each out merely to get a seat in the Legislature. ... Nor are we an ordinary party in the accepted narrow sense of the word. We are rather a rally, a convention of all and for all, a mobilization of all the forces in the com-

---

1 According to W.J. Alexander, 'The decision to form a new political party ... was approached with tremendous hesitation. ... The political atmosphere was murky, the social conditions were forbidding, the initial reaction ... expected to be chilling. ... There were setbacks and defections, disillusionment and disappointments, but no lack of enthusiasm.' However, by the end of 1955 the response to Williams had convinced all that to hesitate would be to 'disappoint the legitimate expectations of the people'. W.J. Alexander, 'Birth of the PNM and Its Descent into the Political Arena', *Nation*, Jan. 21, 1966.

munity, cutting across race and religion, class and colour, with emphasis on united action by all the people in the common cause.[2]

The inaugural conference met in an atmosphere of enthusiasm, optimism, collegiality, and camaraderie. The event was as historic as it was revolutionary. No other movement in the history of Trinidad and Tobago had ever succeeded in mobilizing such a varied collection of influential and dedicated people for such a specifically political purpose. The main business to be settled was the discussion and adoption of a People's Charter and a constitution, and the election of officers. All the evidence indicates that these vital matters were settled without rancour or acrimony. Floor and platform were in basic harmony throughout most of the proceedings, a circumstance that disillusioned founding members would soon look back upon wistfully. This harmony was possible largely because the fundamental clashes over organization and ideology had already taken place within the drafting committees. Here, as one of the founding members, Wilfrid Alexander, recalled, 'The clash of ideas and ideals, of isms and ideologies, of doctrines and philosophies ... that went into the making of these documents ... the fight over these things ended in creation of a nationalist party in which doctrinaire ideology [was] subordinated to practical philosophy.'[3] The adoption of the People's Charter was among the first decisions taken by the Movement. The Charter, now a largely forgotten document, was conceived as a statement of fundamental principles.

THE CHARTER

Political fundamentals
Under the category of things political, the Charter came out with the demand for immediate self-government in internal affairs on the basis of the Williams proposals for constitutional reform outlined in the petition.[4] In addition, reform of the system of local government was proposed, with emphasis on the rationalization of fiscal relationships between the central government and the local councils. Expansion of the power of these councils, which were seen as vital training grounds for the exercise of civic responsibilities, was also advocated. Morality in public affairs was given special prominence. To the essentially middle-class conference, the decline in public morality seemed the most

2 'The People's Charter: A Statement of Fundamental Principles', in PNM – *Major Party Documents*, vol. 1, Port of Spain, 1966, p. 21.
3 Alexander, 'Birth of the PNM'.
4 'People's Charter', pp. 23–6.

serious problem the country faced. Hitherto, as Williams had chided, 'The middle class had for the most part been content to leave the corruption alone, to try to pass on the other side, rather than fight actively against it as the workers have done.'[5] Now they were willing to heed his warning that unless they made an effort to eliminate nepotism, favouritism, and graft from the social system, they themselves would be engulfed by it.

The Charter also stressed the need to promote an enlightened and self-confident public opinion, West Indianization, and inter-racial solidarity. De-colonization had to be integral, but it was not to be allowed to lead to the creation of a new cultural and political dominance by the Negro majority. Respect must be had for all cultural contributions to the West Indian mélange. Since the ethnic configuration of Trinidad and Tobago made it 'a microcosm of the new political grouping which emerged at Bandung', the Movement, whose aim it was to mirror that microcosm, pledged itself to the 'promotion ... and to the cultivation of the spirit of Bandung on the sugar plantations of Trinidad'.[6]

Economic fundamentals

The Charter's statement of fundamental economic principles varied little from the ideas articulated in Williams' *Economic Problems of Trinidad and Tobago*, but it did give official endorsement to Williams' view that a socialist ideology must be eschewed in the economic sphere even if the Movement was to consist of people of 'broadly socialist views'. What sense did nationalization make in a community which lacked the basic skills to run a large enterprise? As one founding member reflected later on,

The PNM avoided this common error and pitfall of West Indian parties. It refused to preach socialism in an island where there is no great accumulation of capital wealth and where poverty and ignorance alone abound. By not doing this, it is free to attract to its fold a wider following. More important than all this, however, is the fact that the mental horizon is left free from political labels and encumbrances which do not apply to the West Indian scene, and which only serve to clutter the mental faculties in its attempts to find solutions to the pressing political problems.[7]

The general economic statement projected the image of an intensely concerned, scientifically oriented, efficient and puritanical organization equal to the task of clearing away the baneful effects of centuries of imperialist neglect.

---

5   The Case for Party Politics, p. 23.   6   'People's Charter', p. 23.
7   E.C. Richardson, 'Significance of History in West Indian Affairs', PNM *Weekly*, March 4, 1957.

Intelligence, assiduity, and a rational utilization of all the country's natural resources were its means. The Charter confidently declared that 'no difficulty in raising the necessary capital [for investment] was anticipated'. Investors and loan agencies would be readily attracted by a 'powerful political organization, a careful plan, an energetic people and a contented and well-trained labour force'. No gloomy forebodings beclouded the pages of the Charter. There was, however, a clearly nativist streak about the economic statement. Efforts were to be made to de-emphasize those areas of the economy which were dominated by the interests of external capital.

Social fundamentals

The creation of a welfare state was the basic promise of the Charter. The aim was to provide a 'well-housed, well-educated, well-fed, healthy population. The provision of social services as a matter of right and not of grace is a fundamental feature of progress in the modern world'. The problem of reconciling this consumptionist programme with the imperatives of economic development were postponed for later consideration.

Under the heading of 'labour policy', the Charter pledged to accelerate the development of democratic trade unionism which the Crown colony system had frustrated. But workers were told that once they were given the right to choose their own representatives and to bargain as equals, 'capital was nothing to be afraid of'. By the same token, capital must be responsive to the legitimate democratic and nationalistic aspirations of the worker. As Williams had put it earlier:

Capital must understand that the day when West Indians were content merely to hew wood and draw water for private investors is gone forever. The worker today requires inducements, incentives and guarantees, just as much as the investor does. The Party must be the defender of the workers, the political arm of the labour movement, providing particularly the information and data so urgently needed by the workers in their organizations. ... It must not, however, actively intervene in the formation of management of trade unions; the people of Trinidad and Tobago are sick and tired of scheming politicians riding on the backs of the workers to gain the confidence of the Colonial Office and the Chamber of Commerce.[8]

In its statement on education, the Movement sought to assuage some of the fears that had developed about its plans for education because of Dr Williams' uncompromising hostility to the denominational school; it tried to do so without sacrificing any of its convictions as to what was needed to rationalize the general educational system. The Charter made it clear that sepa-

8 *Case for Party Politics*, p. 10.

rate schools would not be abolished. It specifically declared that the 'right of the parent to send his child to a school of his own choice' should not be prejudiced. But it was evident that the Movement intended the state to have a much wider authority over private schools than was previously the case. According to the Charter, the present educational system had the following principal characteristics:

I the uncritical imposition of alien standards and curricula unrelated to local needs, developed in a different climate for people with a different history and different traditions, and, as an inevitable consequence of this, the disparagement of the local culture, standards and traditions;

II concentration on the small group needed to fill the positions opened to them in the imperialist structure and subordination of the needs of the masses;

III the abdication by the state of its educational responsibilities to the point where, had it not been for the Christian Churches, the Christian population would have been neglected as the non-Christian population has, until recently been.[9]

The educational programme sought to alter this pattern. Educational opportunities must be widened to satisfy the legitimate demand of the people for education according to their capabilities, and not their social or economic class. As far as possible, education was to be free up to secondary school level. The emphasis on classical education also had to be altered; economic development required concentration on technical, vocational, and business training rather than on the grammar school mystique.

Like nationalist parties in other newly developing countries, the PNM pledged to eliminate illiteracy. It also declared itself anxious to foster the development of Caribbean art, literature, and culture in order to correct the tendency in West Indians, encouraged by the old colonial system of which the churches were an essential part, to denigrate anything un-European as being primitive. As Williams had said earlier, 'The West Indian school of tomorrow must make a positive fetish of the West Indian environment.'[10]

The constitution of the Movement
The basic unit of the Movement was to be the party group, and membership was open to persons who agreed to be governed by the decisions and discipline of the Movement, provided such a person was 'not a member of any other political party or organization whose principles ... are inconsistent with those of the Movement.' Membership was also declared open to organizations such as trade unions and friendly societies which accepted the principles of the

9 'People's Charter', pp. 29–32.
10 *Port of Spain Gazette*, Dec. 5, 1954.

Movement, 'provided [they] were not affiliated to any other political party or organization, or were not committed to the political support of an individual whose policy or programme was incompatible with those of the Movement ...'.

One of the key questions that had to be settled was the manner in which these affiliate organizations, especially the trade unions, would relate to the Movement. A few individuals proposed that the Movement should be the political arm of the trade-union movement, just like the British Labour party. This would mean that affiliate unions would subscribe heavily to the Movement and enjoy substantial voting rights and privileges in the naming of candidates.[11] The majority opposed this view, however. It was agreed that in the case of trade unions, membership would be calculated only on the basis of those who agreed to identify with the Movement, and to pay a political fee. The unions would then pay an affiliation fee ranging from $5.00 (TT) to a maximum of $20.00 (TT) depending on the number of persons who 'contracted in'.

The 'contracting in' stipulation was not relevant for other organizations. As far as voting at annual conventions was concerned, functional interests affiliated to the Party were given one vote only. The conference felt that if the Movement became too closely identified in the public mind with the predominantly Negro proletariat, the prospect of rallying the rest of the community would be impaired. Most of the trade-unionist foundation members endorsed this arrangement. They were also aware that it would have been unwise for any union to become organically linked with the Movement. For one thing, there was no certainty that the PNM would form the next government; and even if this were the case, no labour leader wanted to be placed in a position where he had to accept directives from the Movement. There was also the additional danger that the unity of unions with politically differentiated memberships would be compromised. The PNM quite deliberately turned its back on the pattern of union-nationalist party fusion that had developed in the rest of the Caribbean after 1937. The different ethnic compo-

---

11   Some trade-union officials (the names frequently mentioned include John Rojas, then boss of the powerful Oilfield Workers Trade Union, Quintin O'Connor, and Simeon Alexander of the Federated Workers Trade Union) sought to colonize the Movement before it was officially launched by attempting to seek guarantees of candidacies in return for the voting support of their union membership. This was vigorously opposed on the ground that the Movement should make no deals, nor should it admit people whose political pasts constituted electoral and ideological liabilities. Moreover, the business of naming candidates was the primary responsibility of the party group, subject, however, to the approval of the central executive. The provision which gave the party group the power to nominate candidates was specifically inserted to frustrate the attempts of notables to capture the Party.

sition of the island was no doubt one of the most significant considerations. The fact that the unions were already well developed by 1955, with strong and ambitious leaders, also made it unlikely that the PNM would have agreed to pursue 'united front from above' agreements with them.

Authority in the Movement

As with most mass democratic parties, the annual convention was recognized as the supreme authority in the Movement. Its members were determined to reverse the normal pattern of party behaviour in Trinidad whereby political parties, such as they were, were dominated by those members who had succeeded electorally. Indeed, no party so far had ever really succeeded in maintaining for any length of time a fully autonomous party bureaucracy. The PNM sought to correct this by providing in its constitution that the legislative group of the Movement would be responsible to the general council and ultimately to the annual convention. The convention was to have final authority over all policy issues and matters involving discipline, though the day-to-day business of running the Movement was to be left in the hands of the central executive and the general council, which was to be the governing body of the Movement between conventions.

The democratic aspirations of the founders of the Movement were somewhat tempered by their keen understanding of the harsh realities of Trinidadian society. While they essayed to create a democratic party, they were also determined to have a highly disciplined organization. To guarantee this, they took the far-reaching decision that members elected by the inaugural conference should be retained for the length of a legislative term. This provision was intensely debated among the inner core of the Political Education Group and was at one time strongly opposed by Dr Williams, who felt it would compromise the Movement's democratic ideals. Was it not possible that this rule might perpetuate in the top hierarchy a hand-picked leadership whose enthusiasms might have been keen in the early years, but who no longer served the Movement with zeal and distinction? Might this not deny the Movement the opportunity to recruit badly needed talent at the top level? Those who argued for the provision insisted that it was important to keep the founding group together at the top so that the Charter ideals of the Movement might be zealously preserved.[12] They felt that it would probably take about five years

12 Most of the early foundation members were elected to the general council and central executive of the Movement. Many of the later pre-conference recruits who felt that they should have been rewarded for their courage were later given positions on standing committees. Generally speaking, ambitions for office were not too openly revealed in the early period of the Movement's history. It took a while for feelings of jealousy and pique to emerge in the open.

for these ideals to penetrate deeply enough among the rank and file; until such time, the founders should retain control of the Movement.

The democratic ideal was important, but it was equally necessary to prevent the Movement from destroying itself because of yearly fights over leadership positions. West Indian history was replete with the skeletons of political parties which fell victim to the bitter struggles of the spoilsmen. It was quite a normal thing for defeated 'bosses' and their followings to stalk out of parties – parties which they helped to create – amidst the glare of newspaper publicity. These were powerful arguments to which Dr Williams eventually gave in, though he succeeded in having the phrase, 'for a legislative term' substituted for the five-year provision.

The conference also sought to protect the Movement from being undermined by the ill-discipline of its members. The constitution stipulated that anyone who sought political office at any level outside of the party framework, or in defiance of the Movement, would automatically forfeit his membership for a period of at least five years. Similar punishment was to be meted out to any one who 'publicly makes any pronouncement which in the opinion of the general council is contradictory to the principles, policy and programme of the Movement, or who enters into public controversy with any other member of the Movement thereon', unless that member could explain his conduct to the satisfaction of the general council.[13]

Members of the Movement serving on public bodies were also required to vote in accordance with the directives of the Movement, although it was not made clear who had the power to issue such directives. Any member who voted otherwise, or failed to vote, or who conducted himself in a manner contradictory to the principles and programme of the Movement, was also subject to this 'sudden death' provision in the constitution. These rules, stern though they were, were wise precautions, having regard to the buccaneering manner in which the Trinidad political class conducted itself. Indeed, the real question was whether or not the medicine was powerful enough to cure the cancer.

13 'Constitution of the People's National Movement', in PNM – *Major Party Documents*, vol. 1, Port of Spain, 1966, p. 14.

8
The elections of 1956:
the parties

The elections of 1956, the first the newly constituted Movement had to face, were beyond doubt the most exciting Trinidad and Tobago had yet witnessed. It was a conflict between two worlds: between the bright, brave, revolutionary new world of the People's National Movement and the forces which had come to regard it as a threat to the privileged position they enjoyed in the society. Eight parties and thirty-nine independents contested the election. What follows is an attempt to identify some of the more important parties and the attitudes which they took towards the PNM.

THE PARTY OF POLITICAL PROGRESS GROUPS

The circumstances under which the POPPG was formed in 1947 have already been described.[1] Despite sporadic attempts over the years to expand and broaden its base, the POPPG remained essentially what it was in the late forties – a relaxed and loosely articulated collection of squirely businessmen, professionals, and members of the managerial and executive élite. The centre of gravity in the Party was decidedly in the white or fair-skinned upper and middle class. Whatever success the Party enjoyed in the past stemmed from the fact that its members, as individuals, were in a position to pay 'influentials' to canvass for them among the basically uninformed electorate. Apart from Albert Gomes, the Party did not have any leader who had the mass appeal of Eric Williams, nor did it include in its ranks anyone with his organizing competence. It did make an attempt to liberalize its image by bringing Negro

1 See chap. 5.

professionals into its ranks, and by endeavouring to establish party groups and branches throughout the country; but it was congenitally incapable of any real expansion or democratization. The few branches that were formed in urban centres outside the capital city invariably came under the control of the same commercial and managerial types. The Party remained a prisoner of its origins.

The difficulties which confronted the POPPG stemmed largely from its identification in the public mind with the Chamber of Commerce, the Roman Catholic hierarchy, and the French creole element in the society. Many of the Party's leaders were members of the Chamber and pillars of the Catholic Church – 'canopy boys' or *portes de l'eglise* as they were popularly known.[2] The POPPG was thus constantly being accused of supporting only those people who could be expected to safeguard the interests of the Church and the merchant community. The President of the Party, a Negro professional, insisted with much justification that the Party was really liberal and not conservative. The POPPG was not even dogmatic in its liberalism. On the question of private and public ownership it took a very pragmatic position. As one of its leading members put it, 'The POPPG believes in private enterprise [but] subscribes to ... nationalization, where taking all things into consideration, this is in the best interests of the community. ... Where private enterprise has failed, or where it lacks the necessary resources, it is the duty of the state to step in. The Party is [however] against the nationalization of all means of production, distribution and exchange, as this stultifies individual enterprise and initiative and allows government too great a control over the lives of individuals.'[3]

It was exactly the position taken by the PNM and almost all other political parties in the country. The POPPG admitted that many of its leaders were members of the Chamber of Commerce, but denied that the Party was captive to it. The contributions which came into the Party's coffers were said to have come from individuals rather than from corporate associations. It is very likely, however, that these 'individual' contributions were, in effect, disguised company donations. The same position was taken on the Catholic Church. The President of the Party agreed that many of its members were prominent Catholics, but repeatedly denied that the Party was ever the marionette of the hierarchy, as was popularly believed. Whatever the truth of the matter, it was quite clear that the POPPG could not free itself from the conservative corner into which it had been pushed by its enemies. Regardless of the liberal intentions of some of its officials, the Party attracted many to its fold who were

2   A former president of the Chamber of Commerce, Sir Gerald Wight was also chairman of the POPPG between 1947 and 1950.
3   Henry Hudson-Phillips, QC, *Trinidad Guardian* (TG), July 22, 1956.

diehard conservatives, people who saw it as the only remaining bulwark against the 'subversive' forces at work in the society.

What the white creoles, especially those of Roman Catholic persuasion, feared most of all was the PNM's approach to the school and birth-control issues. They refused to accept at face value the PNM's assurance that it had no plans to nationalize all schools or impose birth control. They were also extremely angry with Williams for 'not letting slave history rest', for projecting onto them the blame for all the evils of the plantation system. It was strongly felt that he was using the guise of multiracialism to appeal subtly to latent Negro hostilities against whites.[4]

The POPPG's Manifesto condemned ideas of class struggle, class oligarchy, dictatorship of the masses, and racial or religious intolerance, evils of which the Party accused the PNM. Members boasted that their Party was truly democratic, unlike the PNM, which they could not help viewing as a 'one-man dictatorship'. The PNM's five-year rule seemed a clear 'sign-post to totalitarianism'. But there were many people, both inside and outside the POPPG, who argued that despite surface appearances there were no fundamental differences between it and the PNM. Differences of style, tempo, and rhetoric there certainly were, but on issues of policy there was no basic cleavage. Indeed, each party accused the other of copying its manifesto. One leading member of the POPPG's more liberal wing even went so far as to propose that the parties should enter into a coalition to ward off 'the greater danger facing the country' – the Hindu People's Democratic Party. It was feared that, given the fragmentation of the colony's party system, a weak and unstable government would emerge, and that in such a situation, the PDP might very well come to hold the balance of power.[5]

The coalition manoeuvre was a disastrous failure, as neither party was prepared to entertain it. The POPPG maintained that though the two parties might share the same economic philosophies, they differed diametrically on basic principles. 'The POPPG stands strongly for fundamental human rights and for the fostering of religion and spiritual principles. The Party fails to find these attributes at present in the PNM, and a merger is therefore out of the question.'[6]

The proponents of the alliance, who, like many others, had split loyalties,

4 By condemning the social and economic monopoly which white creoles had on the society, and by advocating multiracialism, Williams was indirectly playing on hostile sentiments latent in the Negro population, who understood his message very well. Multiracialism for them meant a better deal for Negroes – a status reversal *vis-à-vis* whites.

5 Hudson-Phillips, QC, 'Open Letter', TG, July 3, 1956.

6 TG, July 5, 1956.

urged quite sensibly that a coalition was not a merger. The POPPG could easily refuse to go along with such policies as were inimical to its principles. The POPPG executive remained firmly opposed, however, though its decision angered many who felt that the 'national interest' was being sacrificed to parochial prejudices. There was widespread speculation that the coalition was indeed vetoed by the Roman Catholic hierarchy. Canon Max Farquhar complained that 'The POPPG has become the cat's-paw of influential religious direction, and thus become adamant in prejudiced hostility to the PNM. Thus, the politics of the colony must be sacrificed in favour of certain religious inhibitions which are not shared by the majority of the community. And so, any possibility of a coalition would be abstractly precluded, not only on the ground of political impracticability, but in deference to certain vested religious interests.'[7]

In any event the PNM expressed no interest in a 'united front from above' coalition with the POPPG. Its leaders saw quite clearly that the POPPG was on the defensive, and that it was losing its supporters and paid canvassers, who, so it was rumoured, were accepting POPPG money while campaigning secretly for the PNM. Why should the PNM share leadership when the evidence indicated that it would sweep the urban areas where the POPPG might have been expected to gain its greatest support? The POPPG was thus left with the alternative of facing the polls alone or merging with the five outgoing ministers. Many believed that the latter course was strategically necessary if the PNM was to be stopped. Others argued that any attempt to bring the ex-ministers into the Party would contribute even more to the Party's annihilation, since the PNM's fire was concentrated mainly on the members of the old ministerial régime.

The POPPG's dilemma was that it could not make up its mind just what its policy should be towards the outgoing ministers. It was quite aware that it had become associated in the public mind with the old régime, yet it could do nothing to alter this image. Despite pressure from some of its members, the leadership could not agree to disavow Gomes, whom everyone expected to retain his seat in the Legislature. In the end, the Party adopted an attitude of passive support for the ex-ministers.

As the campaign advanced, it was clear that the POPPG had failed to get its message over to the electorate. The Party's campaigning lacked spirit and

7   *Ibid.*, July 15, 1956. In a letter to the *Trinidad Chronicle*, another angry observer put it this way: 'The PNM and the POPPG, too ignorant to recognize this danger [the Indians], treat coalition like a dread disease and will have nothing to do with one another. I suppose as the election approaches, both parties will unleash all the fires of hate at one another, allow Maraj to walk into power and then weep on one another's shoulder or blame each other.' TC, July 11, 1956.

organization, and it found itself on the defensive, unable to match the positive dynamism of Dr Williams and the PNM. Part of the failure was due to the absence of an authoritative and legitimate leader. But essentially the problem was one of origins. The Party was never able to shake itself free of the influences of the Chamber of Commerce and the Roman Catholic Church, however informal these influences might have been. It found itself completely out of step with the revolutionary temper of the masses. On paper there were few basic differences between the PNM and the POPPG, but there was one inarticulate premise which the masses sensed quite readily. The PNM was subtly seeking to shift the class and ethnic basis of political and social power in the colony.

THE TRINIDAD LABOUR PARTY

Following the 1950 elections, the old Trinidad Labour Party had become dormant. Most of those who had fought under its banner had left for newer groupings. But as the oldest political party in the colony, the TLP was bound to appeal to politicians. The 1956 version of the TLP consisted mainly of 'old world' politicians who had already achieved electoral success under other party banners at both the national and local levels. The new leaders of the Party claimed that, as the party of Cipriani, the TLP and not the PNM was the true heir to working-class leadership. The President, Minister of Agriculture Victor Bryan, declared that the TLP was not socialist but labour, and that its policy was to hold the balance between the demands of both capital and labour.

The TLP's main talking-point was that the PNM represented the middle classes. All of Williams' strictures against the middle class in *The Negro in the Caribbean* were trotted out and used against the PNM in the campaign. The TLP proclaimed itself emphatically anti-intellectual, and warned the masses that they were deluding themselves if they thought that scholarship winners who had been living with books all their lives could cure their ills. The PNM's emphasis on the need for scientific skill in politics forced every other party to preach the virtues of political instinct. The PNM's subtle anti-clericalism also forced the TLP to join forces with others to preach the 'virtues of Godliness'. 'Because of these men', thundered Bryan, 'priests in the pulpit are going down in sackcloth and ashes to save Trinidad from the disaster which befell British Guiana.'[8]

The TLP tried to forge a solid labour front to stop the PNM, but nothing came of the proposal, though an alliance was later concluded with a small

---

8   The decision of the Guianese government to nationalize denominational schools in 1953 was partly responsible for the events which led to the suspension of the constitution.

splinter group from the POPPG which called itself the National Democratic Party. It had become clear since 1936 that the party of Cipriani had lost the support of the urban worker. Only among the rural proletariat in the eastern regions of the island and in Tobago did the party show any strength. But here it was not the TLP, but the candidates themselves who really mattered to the voters.[9] For reasons which will be explored later on, the rural voter in 1956 remained relatively immune to the attraction of Dr Williams.

THE CARIBBEAN NATIONAL LABOUR PARTY

The CNLP was born out of the failure of some of the colony's key trade union bosses to come to any mutually satisfactory working agreement with the leadership of the PNM. The CNLP leaders restated the view that political power was a fundamental prerequisite to the economic emancipation of the worker. Middle-class politicians in the past had affected to represent the workers as they were doing now, but there was no reason to believe that the present group would prove any more solicitous of the needs of the working class than their predecessors.

The CNLP's main attack was directed not against the POPPG but against the PNM. Both Williams and John Rojas, the president of the CNLP, seemed determined to destroy each other politically. Part of the hostility was no doubt due to personal animosities, but policy differences were also involved. The main differences related to the place of American capital in the economy of the country and the use of union funds for political purposes. The CNLP and the PNM clashed over the attempt on the part of Texaco Oil Company to purchase British oil interests in Trinidad. The PNM endorsed the move on the grounds that the Americans had vitally needed capital for the expansion of the country's oil production. Williams in fact argued that the take-over was inevitable and symbolized the decline of British financial supremacy and the fulfilment of America's 'manifest destiny'.

The CNLP, on the other hand, maintained that oil workers would be worse off under American management, and quite irresponsibly accused the PNM – which was now translated as 'Petroleum National Movement' – of having come under the domination of American oil interests.[10] Rojas argued that if the oil

---

9   Bryan, whether consciously or not, described very well the essentially feudal relationship which existed between himself and his followers in the eastern counties. He was the patron of a fiefdom that belonged to him by right. As he put it, 'The seat belongs to me. Many are trying to take it from me but I am going to defend my rights.' TC, Sept. 21, 1956.

10   The chairman of the PNM, Learie Constantine, was at the time assistant legal adviser to one of the largest oil companies on the island.

companies wished to sell their holdings, the Trinidad government should 'buy 51% or even 40% of the shares so that we can have a say on the Board of Directors. If we are working towards Federation with the hope of dominion status, it is necessary to be economically self-sufficient. But how can we be so when the mineral resources are being traded away.'[11] The CNLP president did not, however, advocate complete nationalization as he had done during the 1946 election.

The second issue that embittered relations between the two leaders was the charge by Williams that Rojas was using union funds, equipment, and vehicles without authorization on behalf of the CNLP, and that generally the funds of the OWTU were being misappropriated. The CNLP/OWTU boss angrily accused Williams of seeking to discredit and subvert the OWTU leadership so that the PNM could later control it. It was also observed that the leaders of a 'rebel movement' within the OWTU were prominent PNM members. There is no clear evidence, however, that Williams was deliberately using the 'rebels' to capture the OWTU, though he was quite anxious to destroy Rojas and the CNLP by capturing the votes of the oilfield workers. The 'rebels' themselves denied that they were taking orders from the PNM; they opposed the OWTU leadership as a matter of principle. The union had no authority to endorse the CNLP, or to use union funds to support candidates who were not members of the OWTU. They pointed to the fact that the CNLP included middle-class politicians even though it was masquerading as a workers' party. They also declared that Rojas was risking the disruption of the union to satisfy his own lust for personal power.[12]

The CNLP never really succeeded in convincing the workers that it had much to offer by way of a programme. Although most of the Party's leaders were known to be socialist in orientation, the Party's offerings were paler versions of the PNM's. Apart from the oil issue, there were no real differences of policy separating the two parties.[13] The CNLP thus chose to wage a defensive campaign on the issue of the style of the PNM. The PNM was seen as a fascist organization dedicated to smashing the labour movement once it achieved power. Parallels were drawn between the ideology, organization, and symbolism of the People's National Movement and the Nazis in Germany. The PNM's opposition to mergers, for instance, was seen as a typical Nazi device.

11   TG, Jan. 14, 1955.
12   Some of the old socialist professionals helped to found the CNLP. Among these were Raymond Hamel-Smith, former president of the TLP, Adrian Cola Rienzi, P.T. Georges, and Quintin O'Connor.
13   Of course, the CNLP did not see it this way. To them the PNM and the POPPG were both capitalist parties which represented big business and the Chamber of Commerce.

The PNM was also accused of intolerance and vandalism and of breaking up the meetings of its opponents. This, it was said, was part of the strategy of fascism, which assumes that to win over the lower strata of the people there must be a visible show of strength.

It is true that PNM supporters were extremely intolerant during the campaign. They disrupted meetings by loud heckling and other familiar tactics; but there is no reason to believe that *at this time* rowdyism was encouraged by the party hierarchy. The fact is that the masses did not want to hear anyone whose campaign lacked the intellectual stimulation of the PNM. They had found their messiah and their minds were closed to any other prophet.

THE WEST INDIAN INDEPENDENCE PARTY

The West Indian Independence Party was the only political party in Trinidad that was ever avowedly Marxist. Not very much was known about it. There was, as one observer remarked, 'a conspiracy of silence surrounding the Party. It was unmentionable by tacit agreement of polite society.' It does not appear that the Party was extra-territorially inspired, though this was the prevailing feeling at the time. One of its leaders, Lennox Pierre, always denied that it was, but the intensification of the cold war and the events in British Guiana and Guatemala had made the government and public opinion wary of any suspected communist influence in their midst.

Whether or not the WIIP was externally manipulated, the fact remains that at one time its leaders were decidedly Moscow-phile. Nevertheless, the fundamental programme of the Party did not include any specific detail that was not espoused by other parties, though its tone was more fiercely anti-imperialistic. What was distinctive about the WIIP, according to the report of a Commission which was appointed in 1954 to investigate the causes of industrial unrest in the colony, was that 'most of the speeches made in support of the programme from public platforms, especially from the Communist element which has become more and more predominant, were, and still are calculated to lead to violence and disorder.'[14]

Trinidadians and Anglo–West Indians in general have been curiously immune to communist appeals even though there are objective and deeply felt needs that might predispose them to respond positively. This is in part due to their belief that the United States would destroy any Soviet beach-head in its sphere of influence. But the overriding factor which explains the lack of interest in an 'alien' ideology is the widespread tendency among the inhabitants of the

14   F. W. Dalley, *Report into General Industrial Conditions and Labour Relations in Trinidad*, Port of Spain, 1954, p. 39.

area to accept British and American value systems uncritically. Trinidadians have never looked beyond Britain for their political ideology. The rules of cricket are expected to carry over into the political sphere.

It was against this entrenched value configuration that the WIIP had to struggle. And unfortunately for the Party, it had neither the human nor the instrumental resources to prevail against these forces. None of its leaders had the ability to project themselves or their ideology to the masses. That they were patriots genuinely concerned with the plight of the West Indian masses is beyond question. But revolutionary parties are never successfully forged out of sincerity alone. Without funds and organization, the Party was able to contest only one constituency in the 1956 election, and very little was heard about its campaign. The communications media made no reference to its activities, except to publish its views, together with that of other parties, on the private enterprise and public control controversy that flickered briefly during the campaign. Few people outside of the capital city seem to have known of the Party's existence in 1956.[15]

THE BUTLER PARTY

When the Party of Uriah Butler emerged as the largest political unit in the Legislative Council following the elections of 1950, Butler had expected to be called upon to form the Government. This honour being denied him, he had promised 'agitation far surpassing anything in the history of this Council'. But instead of remaining to do battle with the new administration as he had pledged, Butler spent most of the legislative term in the United Kingdom 'putting the case for the people of Trinidad and Tobago to the Colonial Office'. There is no evidence that Butler ever had much opportunity to discuss anything with Colonial Office officials or that he made any consistent efforts to do so.[16] Nevertheless, he felt that he could do in 1956 what he had done in 1950 – return home triumphantly on the eve of elections and defeat his rivals. He was quite sure that his 'ancient power' was enough to steal the thunder of the PNM. Butler was thus completely unprepared for the PNM phenomenon and stub-

---

15   The Party as a public force disappeared from the political scene after 1956, though its key members continued to meet privately.

16   Butler's peregrinations in the United Kingdom are still a mystery to all but his fiercest supporters, who believed that he spent most of his time advocating the liberation of the West Indian peoples. It appears that Butler did manage to obtain one half-hour audience with the Secretary of State for the Colonies, whom he said had promised him home rule. According to Butler, he was told by the Colonial Office to: 'Go to the people, preach unity as you did [in 1950] and return to the Colonial Office [victorious] and we will give you self-government, full and complete.'

bornly refused to acknowledge that the messianic mantle had passed to Eric Williams. He created a bit of a stir by declaring that he would challenge Dr Williams himself as he had challenged Albert Gomes in 1946. He bragged that he was the only Trinidadian politician who had successfully bridged the gap between Indians and Negroes, and that it was he, not Dr Williams, who was the architect of Negro-Indian unity. Reflecting on the fact that two of his former Indian colleagues had bolted the Party following the events of 1950, he added that 'two traitors do not make a nation'. He was not prepared, as he would be in 1958, to blame the Indians as a group for the treachery of a few ambitious politicians who had used him cavalierly in their quest for political power. Of the twenty candidates sponsored by the Butler Party, six were Indians.

Butler's failure in 1956 stemmed in part from his inability to perceive that his old 'fire and brimstone' style of haranguing the masses was no longer legitimate.[17] The cold, brittle, and unemotional style of Dr Williams had captivated the country, and it was extremely difficult for people of the old oratorical school to get a hearing. Butler, at one time the undisputed 'king of Woodford Square', could no longer hold court there without being subjected to vociferous heckling. Williams, now regarded as the logical successor to Butler, was not particularly happy about the humiliation to which Butler was being subjected. Butler had to be seen in proper historical perspective, he urged. The progress made in Trinidad and Tobago since 1937 stemmed from his opposition to the old colonial regime:

Some day in the future, when the people come to understand their history, they may even erect a monument to him, as the man who, whilst the middle and professional class Cipriani always excepted had abdicated their role as the natural leaders of the people for the mess of pottage handed out to colonials by the Colonial Office in the form of the nominated system, was the only one who dared publicly to challenge that system and protest, notwithstanding privations, against the oppression inherent in that system. That is Uriah Butler in historical perspective. Had he died during his internment or from a bullet from the Marines, he would have gone down in history as one of the martyrs in the cause of the Caribbean people.[18]

17 The hymn singing and chanting that typified Butler's meetings were completely absent from PNM meetings. The favourite party chant of the Butlerites was:
"A happy band of Butlerites we are, Oh we are,
We never went to college,
But Butler gave us knowledge,
What a happy band of Butlerites we are."
18 Eric Williams, *Federation: Two Lectures*, Port of Spain, 1956, p. 35. Reportedly, Williams was not entirely committed to the idea of opposing Butler.

Butler had 'outlived his usefulness', however. Political power could now be won without recourse to the barricades:

The days of street fighting are over. Those of the parliamentary majorities have arrived. We are now on the road to self-government, and Mr Butler underlines the Caribbean tragedy, of which Jamaica's Bustamante is another example. Beginning as trade union leaders they found themselves catapulted into politics before they could even understand what a programme is. It is only now, after some twenty years that ... Trinidad and ... Jamaica ... have begun to understand that agitation, militancy and graduation from jail do not equip a man for the tasks of government, legislation and planning. The problem of Trinidad and Jamaica today is to provide the political leadership in which both Butler and Bustamante, when tried in the balance, have been found wanting.[19]

Williams, always sensitive to the charge that he was a middle-class politician who did not really have the interest of the worker at heart, drew widely on his knowledge of the national revolutionary movement in the colonial world to reinforce his argument that it was no longer true that only a worker could represent the workers. Manley, Nehru, Nkrumah, Marin, Gaitskell, and Azikiwe were all intellectuals in politics. 'All over the world a new type of leader has been arising, especially in the former colonial areas, disproving the idea that only a man sprung from the working class can be trusted to do justice to the workers. ... Mr Butler is unsuited to the needs of our times and belongs to a pattern of activity from which the world outside has moved away.'[20]

Butler later conceded that Williams might emerge triumphant from the elections; in fact he admitted defeat by deciding against contesting the constituency chosen by Williams. He warned, however, that should Williams win a majority and then turn traitor to the people, 'so help me God, I will kill [him] with my own hands.'[21] It was clear that Butlerism was a spent force, even though Butler himself was still extremely popular in the oil belt.

THE PEOPLE'S DEMOCRATIC PARTY

Though it is not quite clear what the immediate circumstances were which led to the formation of the People's Democratic Party, there is little doubt that

19 *Ibid.*, p. 36.   20   *Ibid.*

21 TC, Aug. 12, 1956. Butler threatened Williams on more than one occasion. Obviously put out by the rough treatment he was encountering in the PNM strongholds, Butler warned, in an allusion to the burning of a Negro policeman during the riots of 1936, that if any of Dr Williams' 'stooges throw a stone at Butler, he [Dr Williams] will end like Charlie King, burning like a lantern in the presence of all men'. TG, Sept. 20, 1956.

soon after its foundation it became widely recognized as the political arm of the orthodox Hindu community, the vehicle of an Indian 'nationalist' movement which paralleled the Negro-dominated People's National Movement.[22] For the Hindu masses, though not for the intellectuals and the middle class, the leader of the PDP, Bhadase Maraj, filled the same role that Eric Williams filled for the Negroes. Maraj was the man who had done most to lift the masses up as a group, both through his own achievements – many Indians believe Maraj to be the wealthiest man on the island – and through his activities on behalf of the flock. By his efforts to establish schools and temples and by his carefully cultivated generosity (he contributed personally to school- and temple-building programmes and to funds for striking workers), he quickly gained a reputation as the foremost benefactor in the Hindu community.[23] To the masses, he was the 'Nehru of Trinidad' – a singularly inept comparison – or, variously, the 'chief', the 'rajah', 'babujii', or 'baba'. When he visited schools, children bowed and chanted as to a revered leader.

The People's Democratic Party encountered extremely rough treatment during the election campaign. The fear that the PDP would control the country in 1956 was real to many people, and Maraj's statements did very little to calm them. Maraj had called on all Indians to vote *en masse* to vindicate their forefathers who did not have the opportunity to vote. He openly boasted that the PDP would run the country after the election, a threat which the PNM took quite seriously. Having successfully crowded the POPPG and the former minis-ters out of the urban areas, it was now strategically necessary to isolate the PDP. The leader of the PDP had recently won a by-election on the election postponement issue,[24] and had also successfully claimed credit for sustaining and negotiating a critical industrial dispute involving recognition for sugar workers. Both events had combined to give his reputation a tremendous boost in the sugar belt and in the country as a whole.

The PNM's strategy was immaculately conceived and cleverly executed. The Movement, it will be recalled, had come forward as the embodiment of the Bandung spirit in Trinidad. Williams himself had done much to focus the atten-tion of the Indians on their social and economic plight by exposing the squalor

22 Cf. the discussion of the Hindu revivalist movement in my article 'The Struggle for Afro-Indian Solidarity in Trinidad and Tobago', *Index*, vol. 1, no. 4, Sept. 1966.
23 Maraj's home became a popular rallying centre for Hindus. All who had problems sought out his advice, financial help, arbitration, or intercession. He was generally recognized as one of the foremost 'brokers', acting not only within the Indian com-munity, but between it and other sections of society as well.
24 Maraj had resigned in protest against the Council's decision to postpone the 1955 elections. He won the by-election handsomely and the vote demonstrated his power-ful hold on the Hindu voter.

of plantation life in the nineteenth and early twentieth centuries. In a speech on India's Republic Day in 1954, Williams had endorsed the struggle of the Indian community to educate and improve itself:

Every struggle by Indians or by Africans for the improvement of labour relations and for embracing the dignity of labour in the British West Indies is a step in the direction of the modernisation of Caribbean society. Every step in the education of Indians is a step in the production of that well-informed body of citizens on which British West Indian democracy depends; every Indian admitted to the professions and the Civil Service is a further victory in the cause of that full participation of local men in the administration of the British West Indies without which self-government is a delusion.[25]

Williams understood quite well why the Indian masses should want to elevate people of their group to positions of leadership. If the orthodox Hindu masses could not be attracted to the PNM, even though a few Indian professionals were identified with it, the Indian community as a whole had to be prevented from rallying behind the PDP. The strategy, then, was to drive a wedge between orthodox Hindus on the one hand and the reformist Hindus, Moslems, and Christianized Indians on the other by portraying the PDP as an obscurantist communal organization. Williams' argument was two-fold. First, he irresponsibly suggested that there was a link between the Maha Sabha of Trinidad (which ostensibly was a purely religious organization representing orthodox Hindus) and the intolerant and fanatic Hindu Maha Sabha in India which both Gandhi and Nehru had vigorously denounced. Williams cleverly called in Nehru and Gandhi to fight his domestic battles. He quoted approvingly Nehru's statement that the Maha Sabha was 'aggressively communal, but that it covers up its extreme narrowness of outlook by using nationalist terminology. It represents small upper class reactionary groups taking advantage of the religious passions of the masses for their own ends. Every effort is made to avoid and suppress the consideration of economic issues.'[26]

The PDP was similarly represented as an economically conservative brahmin party, having nothing in common with the modern Indian secular nationalism of Tagore and Nehru, whom the masses in Trinidad admired: 'The Maha Sabha is unrepresentative of Indian culture. The real Indian democrats and internationalists are something quite different. Its representatives are Gandhi in religion, Nehru in politics and Tagore in literature. When we look to India it must be to the India of Bandung. And here at home it is to the Indians whose blood and sweat and tears have helped to build up our country – Indians who

25   TG, Jan. 28, 1955.
26   Jawaharlal Nehru, *Discovery of India*, cited in *ibid.*, Aug. 1, 1956.

are Moslems and Christians as well as Hindu, Indians who are democrats and not racialists.'[27] It was a clever broadside aimed at stirring up cross-pressures in the minds of reformist and progressive Hindus who identified with Nehru and Gandhi; he had made it extremely difficult for Christianized Indians and Moslems to endorse the PDP. As far as the Moslems were concerned, this would have been even more difficult since the Maha Sabha in India was a sworn enemy of Pakistan and the Moslem League.[28] The complementary part of this strategy was to place Moslems and Christian Indians in prominent positions within the People's National Movement.

The second prong of the PNM attack on the PDP was the suggestion that the PDP was nothing more than the political voice of the Maha Sabha. The PDP in fact had never really functioned as an autonomous political party with a constitution and a grass-roots organization. It felt no real need to organize since the branches of the Maha Sabha and the priesthood were easily convertible into political instrumentalities.[29] Apart from the role which the Hindu priesthood played in keeping the flock together, it has always been the source to which politicians turned for help in their political careers. Pundits were among the principal opinion leaders within the Hindu community, and a few of them used this advantage to seek political office.

There is considerable evidence to support the charge that many religious meetings in temples and in homes ultimately became political meetings, and that Hindus were enjoined to support their religion by ensuring that Hindus were elected to public bodies. Pundits were known to make individuals swear on the *lotah* (a holy Hindu vessel) to support candidates, and would threaten religious sanctions for broken pledges. Some Hindus were alarmed at the use to which religion was being put and appealed to Maraj in his capacity as President General of the Maha Sabha to call a halt to the prostitution of reli-

27   TG, Aug. 2, 1956.
28   Islam, like Hinduism, was undergoing a revival. The creation of Pakistan had served to sharpen Moslem cultural pride and feelings of separateness from Hindus. The revival movement came to the notice of the public during the celebrated 'Ohrini' affair. The issue at stake was whether or not Islamic school boards could insist that teachers wear traditional dress if they did not wish to do so. The Islamic associations and leagues representing the various sects were also involved in a substantial school-building and cultural programme. Moslem mosques everywhere became centres for a vigorous campaign of self- and group-improvement. In Moslem and Hindu communities, mosques and temples functioned both as places of worship and as schools, so urgent was the need for education.
29   The PNM had no such ready-made *gemeinschaft* sentiment and no élite on which to rely, and was thus compelled to build up associational grass-roots structures. As a party of radical change, the PNM also had to concentrate more on organization and discipline.

gion for political purposes: 'This candidate is making the Maha Sabha the mainstay of his campaign and with a paid pundit is pushing the Ramayana in the homes of the Hindus night after night. After every *Ramayan Sat Sang*, which is just an excuse to get Hindus together, the wicked job begins. The pundit then begins to sow the seed of discord. Then it is that he tells the Hindus gathered that unless they vote in a certain way, the Ramayan is in danger. He begins a merciless attack on the *Arya Samajists, the Moslems and the Negroes.*'[30]

PNM candidates of Indian extraction were also not above using race and caste for political benefit. One candidate tried to appeal to the lower-caste Hindus by branding the PDP as a 'brahmin party, a maharaj party': 'I have a secret to reveal to my Indian brothers and sisters. ... If you examine the religious sect of every Indian in the PDP, you will observe that only Brahmins and other privileged Hindus have been nominated. Any Indian who belonged to the lower class was neglected.'[31] The candidate also taunted Maraj by saying that while he himself was the son of 'a real Hindu who came from India', Maraj's father was a 'Christian named Matthew'. Maraj promptly dubbed his antagonist, as well as all other Indian supporters of the PNM, stooges, people whose anxiety for 'society' prevented them from defending the religion of their ancestors.

The PDP reacted angrily to the charges made against it. Williams, they felt, was 'a sawdust Caesar' who in his lust for power was willing to poison racial relations in the colony. First he had attacked whites, now Indians. Although loudly proclaiming its multiracial ideology, was not the PNM appealing to Negro pride and feelings of animosity?[32] The Maha Sabha denied that it was a political body like the Hindu Maha Sabha in India or the Moslem League in Pakistan. There was no connection between the movements, even though the term 'Maha Sabha' was common to both. The words merely meant 'great society' or 'council'.

It was noted that there was a Sanatan Dharma Maha Sabha in India composed of High Sanatanist priests, which had the full recognition of the Indian Government. Was it a mistake that Williams chose to associate the Maha Sabha in Trinidad with the Hindu Maha Sabha and not with the purely religious society in India? Officials acknowledged that the Maha Sabha in Trinidad

---

30 TC, Aug. 5, 1956.
31 *Ibid.*, Aug. 31, 1956. The fact that two Christian Indians had been endorsed by the PDP, confused the issue for some people.
32 It was pointed out that two Maha Sabha vice-presidents were members of the PNM. These two persons were subsequently thrown out of the PNM for suspected espionage. One of them fought the election on a PDP ticket.

was a militant organization, but argued that there were reasons for this. The Hindu community had a substantial problem to face. According to the 1946 census the Sanatanists in Trinidad were declining in number. Their ranks were being thinned out by the proselytizing activities of non-Sanatanists. The Maha Sabha was dedicated to recovering lost ground. Moreover, according to the 1946 Statistical Report 50.6 per cent of the Indian population was illiterate. The Maha Sabha was merely trying to remove that blot by building schools, and using whatever facilities were available for educational purposes.

The PNM insisted that it was in perfect sympathy with most of the goals and objectives of the Maha Sabha, but that it could not make light of the fact that the President General of the Sanatan Dharma Maha Sabha was also the leader of the People's Democratic Party.[33] Williams also attacked the idea that Hindi should be recognized as a medium of instruction in Hindu schools:

How can any responsible person argue that in 1955, the second, third generation offspring of people brought here 100 or even 40 years ago, *who do not speak Hindi in their homes*, have a right to demand their 'Mother tongue' in the schools? By what stretch of imagination can it be considered their mother tongue? ... The education system of this community of ours is dominated by one ponderous fact, disunity stemming from religious diversity. This diversity has only been aggravated by the recognition of non-Christian denominations which adds a racial difference ... to religious difference. ... I do not condemn the recognition of non-Christian denominations, but it would be suicidal to aggravate this religious diversity and religious difference by a linguistic differentiation.[34]

The linguistic controversy was extremely heated, and elicited widespread public comment. Some Indians felt that 'if Latin, Spanish, and French are expected to be learnt by our children in the schools and the expenditure for

33   PNM *Weekly*, Aug. 23, 1956. Williams' reply to the Maha Sabha on his supposed error was as interesting as it was politically devastating: 'The Maha Sabha now tries to draw the distinction between the Hindu Maha Sabha and the Sanatan Dharma Maha Sabha. I accept the distinction. But it is only a change of name involved. If the Maha Sabha insists on hearing what Mr Nehru had to say specifically about the Sanatan Dharma Maha Sabha, then here it is. ... "Today the firmest champions of British rule in India are the extreme communalists and the religious reactionaries and obscurantists. ... The Hindu Maha Sabha ... is left far behind in this backward moving race by the Sanatanists, who combine religious obscurantism of an extreme type with fervent, or at any rate, loudly expressed, loyalty to British rule. ... There is no more reactionary group in India both politically and socially." The Sanatanists in Trinidad, therefore, must attack Nehru, not me; unless of course, they wish to attack me because I know Nehru's works.'
34   Eric Williams, 'Education for Democratic Citizenship in the Caribbean', TG, May 20, 1955 (*italics supplied*).

teaching them is met from the general revenue, then why should not the Indian, who forms 37% of the colony's population, be given the facilities to learn Hindi?'[35] One Indian who was Christian, and a member of the PNM, argued that many Indians *do* consider Hindi their 'mother tongue', and quoted Milton Konvitz to the effect that 'language, as the carrier and preserver of a people's culture, may be of primary importance in sustaining living ties between the alien and the country from which he emigrated.'[36]

Some members of the creole community were sympathetic to the plight of the Indians, but opposed state sponsorship of Hindi teaching on the ground of impracticability: where would one draw the line? But just as many were implacably hostile to what was viewed as an 'upsurge of non-Christian religions linked to a vigorous and clamant insistence on indigenous culture and nationalism.'[37] The argument could be made, however, that in the case of the Indians, language and religion were closely identified, whereas this was not the case with African and Chinese languages. Very few Africans or Chinese in the West Indies professed religions other than Christianity. While the goal of national integration was an admirable one, the fundamental question being asked was 'integration on the basis of what?' There was in fact no valid reason why the state could not provide facilities for the teaching of Hindi at all levels of the school system for those who wished it.

Another area of dispute between the PDP and other parties was the PDP's supposed economic conservatism. Agricultural workers were warned that the leaders of the PDP were linked in an unholy alliance with the sugar plantocracy. The PDP élite denied this accusation and even made the ridiculous claim that they were socialists who favoured nationalization of some industries, though not oil and sugar. The Party came out in opposition to the Chamber of Commerce, 'the handmaiden of concentrated economic power', and to 'the old order in which a handful of economic aristocrats were allowed to place other interests above the community at large'.[38] It was observed that, although a few Hindus were landowners of some note, the community was largely a 'have not' one, struggling to make inroads in agriculture, business, and industry against the bitter hostility of Europeans, Chinese, and Middle-Easterners.[39]

35   *Ibid.*
36   Dennis Mahabir, TG, June 7, 1955. The cited passage is from Konvitz, *Alien and the Asiatic in American Law*, Ithaca, 1946.
37   TG, Jan. 16, 1955.
38   PDP Programme, *ibid.*, July 29, 1956.
39   The Indians, who in the past were mainly agriculturalists and petty traders in the villages, were gradually moving into the cities and con-urban areas where they established themselves in the retail trades, import-export commission houses, jewel crafts, tailoring, poultry and dairy processing and distribution, textile manufacture,

Party leaders reminded the electorate of their sacrifices on behalf of the workers, their contributions to trade-union development, and the fact that some of them were formerly associated with radical movements like the Butler Party, the United Front, and the Caribbean Socialist Party.[40] On the issue of multiracialism the Party's official position was that Indians were aiming not at domination but at co-operation. Co-operation with Negroes was vitally necessary, since they controlled the police and other public services. Maraj even reversed himself by declaring that 'East Indians will never gain power in Trinidad, nor do they have that ambition.' The Indian community was much too fragmented. The PDP also observed that it had sponsored three Negro candidates, a gesture which the Negro community dismissed as sheer opportunism. On the question of Federation, the Party insisted that it was a falsehood to accuse Indians in Trinidad and British Guiana of opposing Federation because they felt they were about to attain political dominance in the two areas on a communal basis.

The PDP was thus successfully isolated during the 1956 election campaign, though it made several attempts to escape the ghetto by seeking alliances with the TLP and the Butler Party.[41] Negro votes were crucial in a number of marginal constituencies, and the PDP wished to calm the fears of many Negroes that Maraj might be the country's first chief minister. It was openly bruited that in the event of a PDP victory, Maraj would not 'seek the crown', but would give the leadership to someone more acceptable to the entire community. The PDP was unsuccessful in its attempt to find allies in the urban areas and was forced to write off areas where Indians were not in commanding or near-commanding positions, except where Negroes could be found who

pottery, drug merchandising, motion picture exhibition, and mechanical transport. They have a virtual monopoly of the latter two areas. Many recent immigrants have gone directly into business, and Indians can truly boast that 'our people have permeated every cell of business life in this colony.' *Indian Centenary Review, 1845–1945*, Port of Spain, 1945, p. 97. Indians have also been doing extremely well in the professions, especially in law, medicine, and dentistry, and have established firm toeholds in the civil service, which is dominated by Negro and mixed elements. The competition between Indians and other retail-oriented ethnic groups such as Syrians, Chinese, Portuguese, and Europeans is extremely fierce in the main urban areas.

40 Three PDP candidates were former Butlerites. Another was once a member of the Caribbean Socialist Party and admitted to this writer that he was able to gain political success only after identifying with communalist activity. He claims to have regretted very much that politics in Trinidad at the time did not permit candidates to form alliances of their own choosing.

41 Maraj declared that Butler should not be forced to contest legislative honours but should be given a legislator's salary as an honourable pension. The PDP did not contest Butler's constituency.

'dared' to run on a PDP ticket in these areas.[42] The Party was able to contest only fourteen of the twenty-four constituencies.

THE INDEPENDENTS

More than any other West Indian territory, Trinidad – until recently – was the land of the independent professional politician. Perhaps in no other colony of its size have there been so many independents vying for so few seats. In the elections of 1946 there were over ninety such candidates, in 1950 one hundred and forty-one, and in 1956 thirty-nine. To many of these individuals politics provided the fastest way out of obscurity. In a claustrophobic society which offered to non-whites few opportunities for social and economic advancement, politics became the principal instrument for the achievement of status and wealth. In his quest for electoral success the independent professional had no scruples concerning the sources of his political support. Alliances were made and abandoned as the exigencies of electoral politics determined. The following remark of a Negro professional politician who was accused of accepting the help of Bhadase Maraj is typical of the picaroon mentality of this class: 'I joined with Maraj because you have to fight Indian with Indian. ... When I am fighting an election, if I have to jump on the devil's back to get the votes, I will do it. ... I want to win the election at all costs even if I have to make the Indians fight among themselves.'[43]

The typical independent politician in Trinidad operated along the lines of bosses everywhere. One of his main strategies was to attract to his machine as many influential people as possible, who for a consideration would contract to deliver a bloc of votes to him or to a candidate of his designation. Programmes were irrelevant to this type of political strategy. Face-to-face contacts and bribes were the main implements. In a multiethnic community it was also necessary to ensure that one's opinion leaders were representative of a cross-section of the population; one had to ensure that each ethnic group was left with the impression that one's success depended mainly on its patronage. This was especially true in the urban areas where the population was mixed.

One of the dangers of this sort of ethnic coalition-building, however, is that sooner or later the candidate runs afoul of one or other of the ethnic groups. Such was the case with one of the colony's most successful professionals, who controlled one of the most effective political machines that ever

42   Negro candidates ran on a PDP ticket in Port of Spain North-East, Laventille, and St Andrew–St David. One of these candidates had Indian familial and business connections.

43   TG, Aug. 21, 1956.

functioned in the underworld of Trinidad politics. For more than a decade the 'eighth army', as it was known by its enemies, and later by its friends, had the reputation of being able to secure the election of any candidate in the municipality of San Fernando. The proud boast of the 'eighth army' boss, the Minister of Education Roy Joseph, was that he was the 'product' of seven races. As a 'creole' Syrian, he was 'neutral' ethnically and therefore available to both Negro and Indian voters. Joseph also had close links with San Fernando's substantial Moslem community into which he had married. As a Catholic, he spared himself no effort to ingratiate himself with the Catholic authorities.

His solicitude for religion was not limited to Christian churches. As Minister of Education and Social Services in the 1950–6 régime, he endeavoured to see that religious grants were extended to non-Christian bodies as well. Joseph indeed put himself in the vanguard of the Hindu revivalist movement and gave the Hindus as much help as he could in their crash school-building programme. One of his key weaknesses in 1956 was that he allowed himself to become too closely identified with the Maha Sabha, thereby compromising his ethnic neutrality. His plight was compounded by a report that he had declared on a public platform that he had a mandate from the Archbishop to tell Catholics in his constituency to support him. Accused of running with the Catholics and hunting with the Hindus, Joseph found himself repudiated at the polls by Moslems, Christian Indians, and by a substantial number of Catholic voters. The ethnic tangle destroyed once and for all his carefully cultivated reputation of being San Fernando's most beneficient patron.

Since the independent politician had no party with whose policy he could identify, he had to devise ways of attracting attention to himself. The most familiar technique was to become socially ubiquitous as the campaign season approached. One had to attend rum shops, baptisms, funerals, weddings and similar functions, and in this way extend one's network of influence.[44] Candidates vied with each other in sending gifts and flowers to the sick and to those celebrating special occasions. In Indian communities rival candidates competed with each other to finance funerals and to provide cars, public address systems, alcohol, or drummers for religious or festive occasions. By such acts of 'benevolence' were loyalties traded. One minister of government owed his political popularity mainly to his widespread reputation as a successful 'mystic masseur'.

44 In most communities, the corner rum shop was the principal place where votes were bought and sold. Rum-shop owners were among the more important influential groups in the society. Tailors, money-lenders, butchers, school teachers, and pundits were also key influences in the Indian community. Each community was linked by opinion leaders of differing occupational callings. Butchers would hardly be among the influential group in the Negro community.

The professional politician also had to be very approachable. Indeed, one of their main criticisms against the PNM was that its brand of politics put it beyond the people; everything was too cold, distant, and planned. Most successful professionals held open house for at least an hour every day before going to the office, during which time scores of postulants came to seek help in 'fixing' one problem or another. In a society where ascriptive and lineage considerations were so important, a testimonial or a well-placed phone call opened doors that were normally closed to all but a few. One 'fix' was usually calculated to win the support not only of the individual recipient but of his family and friends as well. The main danger, of course, was that by helping an individual, one alienated others who secretly hoped for assistance, or who felt that success would have been possible for them if achievement criteria alone were employed.

The case of Joseph was a good example of the self-destructive character of boss rule in a society which is small and restricted in its career outlets. Since his successful entry into politics in 1939, Joseph's home had become, quite literally, the principal employment agency in San Fernando.[45] With people who owed their positions to him distributed widely and strategically over the community, Joseph was frequently able to place his friends and supporters in jobs. Fierce loyalty and electoral fidelity were expected from the recipients of his favours.

It was this type of essentially feudal relationship that kept the 'eighth army' and other such machines together. But over the years such patrons had accumulated innumerable foes – mainly among people whom they had destroyed or failed to assist – many of whom now turned to the PNM as the instrument of their vengeance. Fear had hitherto prevented many from coming out into the open, and even in 1956 there were still persons – mainly teachers, municipal clerks, and politicians – who dared not embrace the PNM too openly.

45   Joseph made no secret of his availability. He told his followers, 'I want to assure everyone that you must never hesitate to call upon me if ever you feel that I can be of assistance to you; for I want you to remember that in me you have one who has dedicated his life to the service of the people whom he loves so much and the country he feels is his.' 'The Political Reporter: Political Personalities No. 2', TG, Aug. 1, 1956.

9
The elections of 1956: campaign issues

During the elections of 1956 the major issues which had been at the centre of political debate for almost a century were given exhaustive airing. Of major importance was the question of secularizing the educational system, the question of family planning, the role of the press in the struggle for political reform, morality in public life, and, of critical importance, the position of the various racial groups in the society.

THE DENOMINATIONAL SCHOOLS ISSUE

Although the PNM had conceded the right of parents to educate their offspring as they saw fit, loyal Catholics insisted on regarding Williams' academic views as those of the Party. It was difficult for many Trinidadians to understand that a political leader might hold and maintain views which are at variance with those of his party. This was especially the case with the PNM, since for most people Williams was the PNM. Thus a statement made by Williams in May of 1955 ('I see in the denominational school the breeding ground of disunity') was viewed as being representative of the Party's thinking. His insistence that the state school provided 'the opportunity for cultivating a spirit of nationalism among the West Indian people and eradicating the racial suspicions and antagonisms growing in our midst' was also seen as a clear threat that he would nationalize the educational system given the chance. Nor could Catholics accept his view that 'denominational schools should be allowed to continue, subject to the cessation of state subsidies, certification of teachers and inspection of schools by the State.'[1]

1   TG, May 18, 1955.

The possibility of a state-controlled curriculum alarmed the Catholic Church. To the Church the content of education in church schools was not a negotiable matter. The principles of Catholic education sprang from verities that were 'supernatural and supranational'. Nationalistic and utilitarian imperatives could not be allowed to subvert such principles. The hierarchy acknowledged that national integration was a legitimate ideal, and agreed that the Church must 'carefully avoid any action which would seem to encourage cleavages along racial lines or in any other way be divisive of the social unity of our emergent community'.[2] But the answer was not to be found in the national take-over of all schools, or in an imposed uniformity.

It was an open secret, however, that Catholic schools were prone to discriminate against children who did not have the 'proper' social or ethnic qualifications. Indians and Negroes were the ones who suffered most from these invidious selection practices. The emphasis on religious instruction to the detriment of subjects which would provide the sort of technical skills needed for a newly developing community was also lamented by the more secularly minded. In an attempt to arrive at a sort of 'concordat' with the Church, Dr Williams proposed five points as an irreducible 'recipe for national education':

1   respect for the law of the land which provides for denominational participation in education with state aid;
2   enforcement of that law with respect to state control of buildings and building standards, curriculum and text books, the conditions of employment of teachers, and proper use of state funds;
3   the working out of a curriculum suited to the needs of the expanding economy which PNM will make possible;
4   integration of the various sections of the community;
5   raising of standards, especially academic, in all schools.[3]

It was a package which was clearly unacceptable to the Catholic Church.

It must be noted that the Catholic Church was not the only religious group to oppose state control; Hindus and Moslems were also against it. While the Catholics were accused of using the denominational school to advance whites and near-whites, Hindus and Moslems were accused of using theirs as cells for the inculcation of a creedal nationalism that was inimical to the broader interests of the society. Williams tried to rally the Hindus by noting that Gandhi had been fundamentally opposed to state support of religious instruction; but the Hindus remained unconvinced.[4] Only the Protestant churches, mainly Anglican and Presbyterian, rallied to the defence of the PNM.

2   *Ibid.*, Jan. 22, 1956.   3   *Ibid.*
4   *Ibid.*, May 18, 1955.

THE BIRTH-CONTROL ISSUE

The question of the state's role in birth-control programmes was also a source of great conflict during the campaign. Williams' view that without family planning the economic goals of the country might never be fulfilled was widely shared among middle-class intellectuals. Williams also insisted that the problem of illegitimacy could best be solved by the diffusion of birth-control information throughout the population. As he wrote in a passage seemingly directed at the Catholic Church: 'Anyone ... and I say it with utmost deliberation ... who opposes the provision of birth-control facilities in Trinidad today is in fact condoning ... illegitimacy, is sacrificing the moral welfare of the entire community to group prejudices.'[5] To the Church this was a frank invitation to sexual 'promiscuity'. There could be no compromise on this issue.

The PNM had declared, however, that it considered the question of birth control a private and religious matter, and it was 'absolutely false to say that the Movement has ever advocated birth control'.[6] PNM stalwarts explained that out of sheer self-interest it was impossible for a party with so many Catholics in its ranks to endorse birth control as part of its official policy. The Catholic hierarchy nevertheless insisted, as it did on the question of denominational education, that Dr Williams' private views would sooner or later be adopted by the Party. In vain did party militants explain that the decision-making process in the Party was collegial. Events were to prove that the suspicions of the Church were not completely groundless.

The 1956 election thus found the Church in a poignant dilemma. Should it assume a *'non-expedit'* position and urge its flock to boycott the elections? Should it openly recommend that Catholics withhold their suffrage from the PNM? There was the danger that if the Church openly rejected the PNM it might later become the target of the policies of a revengeful government. It was also possible that the internal position of the Church would be seriously undermined if it made such a recommendation.

The policy eventually decided upon was that Catholics as citizens had a duty to vote, but such a responsibility should be exercised only after careful personal deliberation, and not at the dictate of any organized body. The Archbishop of Port of Spain enjoined that 'At this *crucial* moment of our history, when for *weal or woe* we inaugurate a new era, every person, man or woman, who has a vote must use it with a sense of responsibility, *not at the mere dictate of any party or junta.*'[7] The meaning of this statement was clear. The Arch-

---

5   Eric Williams, 'Educational Problems of the Caribbean in Historical Perspective', *ibid.*, Sept. 18, 1956.
6   PNM Manifesto in PNM – *Major Party Documents*, Port of Spain, 1956, p. 52.
7   The Official Statement of His Grace, the Archbishop of Port of Spain, TG, July 8, 1956 (italics supplied).

bishop was suggesting to Catholics that they should not be persuaded by the argument that party government was the prime goal for which Trinidadians should aim, though he was careful to add that he had no objection to any particular party. He did insist, however: 'Any candidate or party that will not make a *clear and unequivocal* statement in regard to the recognition and defense of these rights [the basic rights conferred by God on every human person] is by the very fact, according to the law of the Catholic Church, "suspect" and therefore unworthy of support by Catholic voters.'[8] The Archbishop was hostile to the concept of party wherein members are expected to accept uncritically the directives of the party élite. Catholics could not support such a party or movement: 'It is the duty of political parties and groups who seek to attract Catholics to their ranks to ensure that their programmes and policy agree with that of the Church, that they assure their members' complete freedom of action in matters of faith and morals as declared by the Church; and that they do not try to interfere with the members' right to vote according to their conscience. Catholics may not join or remain in any party that does not respect these principles.'[9]

The Church's anxiety stemmed from its fear that Williams' ultimate aim was to orient the PNM along totalitarian lines; that his insistence on discipline, organization, and intensive social mobilization, his intolerance and declamatory rhetoric were part of a clearly recognizable totalitarian syndrome. There was also a basic conflict between the Aristotelian metaphysics of the Church and the secular rationalism and nationalism of the PNM. In the Church's view, the PNM was making the 'error' of which the nineteenth-century progressive had been guilty, that is, of giving the state a purely rational purpose and seeking to make all men uniform in their view of what the ideal state was to be. Unity and national integration need not be obtained at the expense of destroying idiosyncratic structures and values in the society. Nor should morality be made subject to the imperatives of class struggle.

Rather than openly name the PNM as the enemy to be destroyed, the Church chose to wage its war by innuendo from the pulpit, a strategy that aroused tremendous hostility in the minds of many Catholics and non-Catho-

8   *Ibid.*, Sept. 2, 1956 (italics supplied). The Archbishop's view was that unless the PNM categorically stated that it was opposed *in principle* to birth control and state control of the school system, it could not expect to get the Church's blessing. To the Church it appeared that the PNM was temporizing for electoral reasons just as other totalitarian movements had done.
9   *Catholic News*, July 1956. Canon Farquhar felt that the Roman Catholics were full of cant and hypocrisy. He observed that, despite the fact that Catholics were in a majority in the last administration, contraceptives entered the colony freely, and were sold in the shops of Roman loyalists. TG, Sept. 23, 1956.

lics. One outraged Catholic declared, 'Every Sunday, instead of the long customary sermons, one has to listen to nothing short of a political meeting. ... we should not thrash out a political issue under the skirts of divine ceremonies. ... Anti-PNMism is forced into the heads of our unsuspecting school children in Catholic schools, colleges, and even convents. Why must the Church, in which I have lived for over 35 years, calumniate the PNM?'[10] Parish priests were also accused of telling the faithful that it was a mortal sin to vote PNM, and of using the young to reach the old.

There were a few radical 'actionist' Catholics who felt that the Church should make a bolder effort to fight the PNM. If victory was to be won, nothing short of an officially sponsored Catholic party would be adequate. As one of them wrote, 'His Grace should form a party strictly comprised of the Catholic clergy, and officially campaign for the forthcoming elections. ... This ... is necessary since there is no party in Trinidad which is wholly Catholic enough – not even the POPPG. ... We have a majority in the colony, and the time is ripe now, while we still have the nominated system with us. I see this as the only way to build a sound Catholic community.'[11] It was this type of creedal exclusivism that stimulated the frenzied anti-Catholicism that prevailed during the election campaign.

The Catholic community was split right down the middle. Catholic organizations were openly divided in their reactions to the PNM. A few members of the clergy and nunnery were also partial to the PNM. There were not many, however, who shared the view that the Church should sponsor its own political party. Never before had the Church in Trinidad been so publicly flagellated by its own followers. Outraged, the Archbishop declared, 'Nothing can be more rash and scandalous than for Catholics to resist, attack or hold up to ridicule the authority of the Church voiced by the Pope, or the Bishops in their dioceses. ... Such scandal must be corrected by every means possible.[12] Many interpreted this as a clear threat of sanctions which might include interdiction or even excommunication.

As election day drew nearer it was evident that the forces of nationalism had considerably undermined the Church's hold on its membership. The crowd had found a new messiah and a new political religion.[13] Human agency having proved unavailing, the Church turned to prayer. A few days before the

10 Letter to the Editor, TG, July 13, 1956.
11 Letter to the Editor, *ibid.*, July 25, 1956.
12 *Catholic News*, July 1956.
13 Williams' embellishment of Nkrumah's commandment bears repeating: 'We call on all those of little faith – seek ye first the kingdom of self-government and all other things shall be added unto you, for there shall be joy before the angels of Heaven for every nation that attaineth its independence.'

election, the *Catholic News* called editorially for prayer against the 'threat of slavery'. With an air of defeatism and despair, it declared, 'The diabolical forces aligned against us are *too powerful* to be vanquished by any merely human means of attack or defence. The struggle finally will be won or lost, in so far as we use or neglect to use the irresistible force of the spiritual weapons at our command.'[14]

It should be re-emphasized that the rabid anti-clericalism that prevailed in the urban areas antedated the 1956 election.[15] The creedal cleavages in the society were reinforced by class and ethnic considerations. Although many dark-skinned Negroes and Indians are Roman Catholics, a substantial number of urban Catholics are white or light-skinned. Many of them hold status-giving jobs in the civil service and the commercial sector, and the feeling existed, however latently, that Catholics enjoyed occupational and social privileges which other creedal groups did not.[16] It is for this reason that many felt that national integration could not possibly be achieved unless all schools were required to recruit on the basis of universal competitive examinations.

The Anglican and Presbyterian clergy tended to resent the position of dominance which Catholics claimed for their creed. Some of this hostility

14 *Catholic News*, Sept. 1956. The Archbishop proclaimed a *novena* ten days before the election. Catholics were called upon to pray that 'our elections may result in establishing ... in our country the kingdom of Jesus Christ.' Catholics were enjoined to repeat a special election prayer for the gift of true counsel. Part of the prayer read: 'Show me how I ought to vote in the coming elections, so as to promote the true welfare of our country and the welfare of ourselves, our family and our children.' TG, Sept. 14, 1956.

15 Albert Gomes once complained that the Roman Catholic clergy was too powerfully entrenched in municipal politics: 'The Roman Catholic Church wields a great deal of influence in the affairs of the municipality of Port of Spain. ... There was a time when it was said that unless a man was a Roman Catholic he could not be a mayor of Port of Spain. ... You know that not one year would pass by without a request coming from the Church for a spot for a church or a school or a gift from the Council at a nominal rental, and they pull their strings. They are very interested to know that they have sympathisers in these bodies. ... Many an important matter that has been decided by the Council was decided by certain caucuses in this particular organization.' *Report of the Franchise Committee of Trinidad and Tobago*, Council Paper no. 35, Port of Spain, 1944, p. 79.

16 It was also maintained that Catholics were opposed to Federation on almost the same grounds as Indians. 'In certain denominational quarters, Federation will always be anathema, since it poses for them a Trinidad merged into a larger West Indies, where certain entrenched rights and vested privileges now in being as a matter of course, may no longer remain acceptable without question of examination. Thus, whatever the species of objection raised, they were really a meretricious facade behind which lurked and flourished doubts and fears which it would not have been politic to stress publicly.' Max Farquhar, *Port of Spain Gazette*, Dec. 21, 1954.

exploded when one of the leading dailies, then dominated by Catholic interests, carried an unsigned feature article which declared: 'According to Catholic doctrine ... a state must accept the Catholic Church as the one and only true Church founded by God for the salvation of all men, and it must establish the Catholic religion as the official religion of the state. It can therefore allow non-Catholics to practise their religion only privately, not publicly; and it cannot give them freedom to propagate their erroneous doctrines and false practices. ... The State must accept us as the official religion.'[17] The fact that this statement appeared in bold black type led many to feel that powerful interests were behind it. The fact that it appeared during the heat of the campaign, and that no official disavowal was forthcoming, gave additional cause for suspicion.

In 1956 the Church found itself in the unenviable role of defender of the old order, the major obstacle to social reform. Apart from a few intermittent references to the responsibilities of 'employers to give a living wage to his employees', and to the 'rights of individuals without distinction of race, colour, creed or social condition', the Church had clearly ranged itself along with those forces which wanted to maintain the *status quo*. This was its major weakness.

THE ESTABLISHED PRESS

No treatment of that historic campaign can be complete without some mention of the role of the 'established' press, especially the powerful *Trinidad Guardian*. The *Guardian* and the leader of the PNM were virtually at war from 1955 onwards. The *Guardian*'s stand was one of almost continuous opposition to the Movement. Its hostility to the PNM was in fact a continuation of the hostility which it had levelled at Cipriani, Butler, Solomon, and Gomes (during his 'red' period). Having regard to the ownership of the newspaper, this attitude was not surprising. Its major shareholders were a group of native white and near-white business men who had a vested interest in the *status quo*.

Williams' hyperdemocratic political style did not appeal to the aristocratic-minded press barons. Woodford Square, which to Williams and his followers was both Parliament and University, was to the *Guardian* nothing more than a 'jungle ... the stalking ground of an aspirant for political honours'.[18] The *Guardian* feared Williams even more than it did Butler. Williams had the ability, which Butler did not, to go beyond the simple mass emotional-appeal. He had shown that he could organize and discipline a mass movement.

17   TG, Sept. 17, 1956. Williams attributed the article to a Catholic priest who was known to be hostile to the Party.
18   Cited in Williams, *Federation: Two Lectures*, p. 32.

The *Guardian*'s attack on the 'University and Parliament of Woodford Square' was bitterly resented by the PNM. Woodford Square was no jungle, Williams insisted; it was one of the finest experiments in mass political education anywhere in the world. The type of persons who attended 'lectures' was viewed as evidence enough. Williams was not exaggerating when he declared, 'Thousands have passed through its gates since my lectures began; those who dare not face the possible displeasure of their boss stay in their cars or on the adjoining sidewalks. People from all walks of life have come. ... It is only at carnival or at some great international sport event that one can see a larger or more representative cross-section of our community.'[19]

Before the arrival of Williams' 'discordant voice' on the political stage, the *Guardian* was the major influence moulding public opinion.[20] The masses, who were by and large politically illiterate, took their cues mainly from the *Guardian*. If the masses were to be mobilized successfully into the nationalist movement, if the decolonizing revolution was to be integral, the legitimacy of the *Guardian* as a source of opinion on domestic issues had to be completely destroyed. Williams grasped this fact clearly and obsessively, and unrelentingly attacked the daily. Ridicule, 'picong',[21] and a vigorous party organ, the PNM *Weekly* were his main weapons.

But as conservative as the *Guardian* was, it cannot fairly be said that it was pro-imperialist or 'feudal'. It was prepared to tolerate constitutional and social change that would limit the control of imperial interests without at the same time transferring power to the masses. The *Guardian* opposed British mercantilism and fought strenuously against metropolitan attempts to dissuade the country from pursuing a policy of industrialization.[22] It was in fact a national paper, though it certainly opposed the PNM's brand of messianic nationalism and did nothing to encourage the development of disciplined party politics. The paper openly urged its readers to ignore party labels and choose men of experience and integrity.

The *Guardian* placed such a premium on experience that it urged the public to 'return without hesitation ... the members of the last Council including Ministers who achieved an excellent record of progress'.[23] It was particu-

---

19   *Ibid.*, pp. 33–4.
20   It is true that there were small opinion newspapers like the TWA's *Labour Leader*, Cipriani's *Socialist*, the OWTU's *Vanguard*, Butler's *People*, and Hamel-Smith's *Clarion*, which had all been hammering away at the *Guardian*, but their circulation was very limited and confined to the urban areas.
21   'Picong' is the dialect version of the French 'piquant', and describes a cutting, pungent, and nettling remark.
22   'Statement of Policy', TG, May 17, 1956.
23   *Ibid.*, Sept. 9, 1956.

larly partial to Albert Gomes, whom it regarded as having provided Trinidad with the ideal type of political leadership which it needed at the time. By contrast, the *Guardian* attacked Williams as a dictator, and carried a portrait of him (entitled 'Heil Williams') next to that of Adolf Hitler! It nevertheless endorsed him along with two of his colleagues. Williams, it advised, should be made 'to win his spurs in opposition or in a ministry where his ability could be turned to good account'.

Much of what has been said of the *Guardian* is also relevant to the *Trinidad Chronicle*. The *Chronicle*, formerly the *Port of Spain Gazette*, was also locally owned. But whereas the bulk of the *Guardian*'s directorate came from the English creole community, French and Portuguese creoles dominated the *Chronicle*. A distinctly Catholic bias could be detected in its reporting, though the paper studiously refrained from commenting editorially on the school and birth-control issues. Its strategy was to open its 'Letters to the Editor' columns mainly to anti-PNM Catholics.

THE POLITICS OF INTEGRITY

Professor Gordon Lewis of the University of Puerto Rico once described Trinidad as the 'Sodom and Gomorrah of West Indian politics'. Similarly, the commission which was appointed in 1956 to choose a capital site for the Federation rejected Trinidad mainly on the ground of the corruptibility of its political life, which it feared might permeate the region as a whole. The cynicism of the politician whose premise was that 'in politics anything goes', had penetrated deeply into the psychology of the masses. The alienation of the public from political life was graphically expressed in the widespread tendency to refrain from voting, especially in the major urban areas. The prevailing norm was one of civic incompetence; purposeful change seemed impossible. There was no such thing as a national purpose; the individual learned to manipulate the system as best he could, *chacun pour soi*. As V. S. Naipaul observes,

Nationalism was impossible in Trinidad. In the colonial society every man had to be for himself; every man had to grasp whatever dignity and power he was allowed; he owed no loyalty to the island and scarcely any to his group. To understand this is to understand the squalor of the politics that came to Trinidad in 1946 when, after no popular agitation, universal adult suffrage was declared. ... The new politics were reserved for the enterprising, who had seen their prodigious commercial possibilities. There were no parties, only individuals. Corruption, not unexpected, aroused only amusement and even mild approval: Trinidad has always admired the 'sharp character' who, like the sixteenth-century picaroon of Spanish literature, survives and triumphs by his wits in a place where it is felt that all eminence is arrived at by crookedness.[24]

But those who were struggling to forge a new national movement were not prepared to accept the argument that there was something inherently base about the Trinidadian personality which made it unsuitable for clean and disciplined political organization. To dramatize the fact that it stood for a 'new deal', the PNM assumed a posture of uncompromising and puritanical electoral chastity. PNM was making no deals, no alliances; it would be 'PNM against the rest'. To importuning parasitic parties, Williams had this to say: 'If you really believe that there are too many parties and would like to reduce the number, then you must decide which of the existing parties have laid foundations worth building on. If you decide that our party is one of these, and you wish to join forces with us, then disband your own party, and join our party as individuals and take your chances on being nominated for elections and office on the same basis as all other members. ... Too many people were too eager to change principles for the sake of party and not *vice versa*.'[25]

It was clever strategy, and did much to reinforce the image of integrity and honesty which the Party sought to create from its inception. Williams felt sure that it was precisely this image that attracted people to the Party and drove its opponents to despair. Alliances were unwise for another reason. By including in its ranks old machines and professionals, the Party would be virtually committing suicide. Discipline and unity would become impossible. As Williams asserted, 'Our policy on this matter has been simple and honest. We cannot agree to inheriting the prejudices and antagonisms of others. Arrangements of alliances with other parties, we have every reason to believe from the past history of this colony, are as dangerous as shifting sands, and will sink below our feet and possibly engulf us after the elections.'[26] Williams underscored heavily the sad experiences of the Parliamentary Opposition Group,[27] the United Front, and the Butler Party to illustrate his point that mergers of progressive forces were inherently unstable. To bring so many notables under the umbrella of a single party would create immense difficulties for the Party when the time came for distributing the spoils of office. The coalition would splinter on the morrow of the election, causing the Party to collapse from within and undermining the confidence of the masses.

---

24   V.S. Naipaul, *Middle Passage*, London, 1962, p. 72.
25   TC, Aug. 12, 1956.   26   *Ibid.*, Aug. 1, 1956.
27   An ephemeral opposition had been formed in the Legislative Council by legislators who had not been included in the Governor's Executive Council, which had been enlarged to include four elected representatives in 1941.

Williams did not even want old political notables in the PNM as individuals. While he clearly hoped that the PNM would emerge from the election in a position of dominance, this was to be achieved without posing needless problems for the leadership. If notables came into the Party with their followings, leadership would have to be shared; bases of factionalism would be institutionalized.[28] To a man of Williams' temperament, this was intolerable. He wanted a united front policy, but it had to be a policy of united front from *below*, with the memberships of other parties *over* the heads of their leaders. And since the parties were already losing their followings to the PNM in the urban areas, alliances were not only undesirable but unnecessary.

Williams denied, as he had to, that there were no differences between the PNM and the other parties. The differences were not only stylistic but fundamental and spiritual. The PNM could not ally itself with the very forces it had been created to destroy. But to many people, including some in the Party, it seemed very unlikely that any party would emerge with a clear majority. Gomes chortled, 'The only Government will be a coalition Government.' But to the PNM, post-election deals were just as objectionable as pre-electoral alliances. Anxiety for power must not be allowed to corrupt the Movement which could fulfil its goals without achieving power. In any case, it was only a matter of time before the people would give the Party the opportunity to govern. As Williams advised, 'If not now, then in five years' time; if not then, ten years' time. The PNM has time and youth on its side. It can wait. The PNM's ... goal is the organization of one proper party in Trinidad and Tobago; it will arrive at this goal by political education of the people. There is no immediate hurry.'[29] As one political commentator wittily declared, 'PNM will have the whole hog or be violently anti-pork.'[30]

MULTIRACIALISM AND CANDIDATE CHOICE

In its choice of candidates, the PNM strove valiantly to be true to its multiracial ideal. But such a strategy, though commendable, went directly against the grain of the Party's principles on race and elections, which implied that there should

28 The PNM had dramatically underlined its seriousness by dismissing several of its members, including a founding member, for fraternizing with the 'enemy' or for campaigning as independents after failing to get party backing. As Patrick Solomon declared, 'Party discipline in the PNM is no joke as some have already found to their cost. In all matters it is to be made crystal clear that the Party is bigger than the member whatever his status, record or individual value. No one is more insistent on this than Dr Williams himself.' 'Why I joined the PNM,' PNM *Weekly*, July 16, 1956.
29 'A Disunited Front', *ibid*., July 2, 1956.
30 'Janus,' TC, Aug. 31, 1956.

be no attempt to choose candidates on the basis of their acceptability to particular ethnic constituencies. There were cases, however, where the Party chose Negro candidates to run in overwhelmingly Indian constituencies, and an Indian candidate to run in an urban constituency where Negroes and non-Indian mixes were numerically ascendant. The Party also chose a European to contest one of the suburban areas of the capital city, and a Chinese creole to do battle against Albert Gomes in the European creole fortress of Port of Spain North. The PNM had tried to get a prominent white creole to carry its banner in the latter constituency, but failed.

The Party did, nevertheless, obtain the public backing of some of the country's more powerful white creole families, much to the consternation of opposition circles. Party members welcomed these recruits enthusiastically, since they helped to give the Movement additional respectability. The fact that a few people of social and economic prominence were prepared to risk loss of standing within their community to identify with the PNM helped to crystallize the opinions of many who were still wavering. One creole of German extraction took the rather perceptive view that 'if a Movement such as the PNM fails to obtain a generous measure of active support from the type of persons referred to [white creoles], the possibility arises that the Movement will deviate from the path it now sets itself.'[31]

The breakdown of PNM candidates in terms of ethnic affiliation is shown in Table I, and in terms of vocational identification in Table II. The centre of gravity in the PNM was in the Negro professional class, though only seven of the twenty-four candidates were graduates of universities or inns of court. Only one candidate could be seriously considered a worker in the sense in which that term is commonly understood.

The uniqueness of the PNM's campaign stemmed partly from the fact that it relied mainly on a corps of volunteer workers. Only in a limited number of cases did the PNM pay small sums to unemployed people to conduct door-to-door campaigns. The Party and constituency groups were given the responsibility for raising money to pay for the election expenses of their representatives, the money to be sent directly to Party headquarters, whence it was disbursed to responsible committees. Candidates were made to sign bonds to pay a fixed percentage of their salaries to the Party treasury if elected. Both of these arrangements were substantial innovations to political life in Trinidad.

It is not clear just how much financial support the PNM got from the business community. Stalwarts insist that despite the impecuniousness of the Party, it accepted no money from businessmen. But there are a few known cases where substantial contributions were made, though it was made clear that

31   Jeffrey Stollmeyer, 'Why I Joined the PNM,' PNM *Weekly*, June 18, 1956.

TABLE I
PNM candidates 1956, by race

Negroes	15	
Chinese creole	1	(mixed)
Indian	6	(3 Moslem, 2 Hindus, 1 Presbyterian)
European	1	
Spanish creole	1	(mixed)

TABLE II
PNM candidates 1956, by vocation

Pharmacists	2	Teachers (incl. retired)	2
Doctors	2	Author	1
Accountants	2	Lawyers	2
Dentists	2	Clerk/storekeepers	2
Party organizer	1	Businessmen	7
Trade-union official	1		

donors should not consider themselves specially privileged if the PNM came to power.

For the first time in Trinidad, party candidates were presented to the people *en masse*, and required to repeat publicly pledges of dedication and fealty. The dramatic effect of these presentations can hardly be overestimated. The use of the American technique of the whistle-stop campaign excursion was an innovation that paid off heavily by giving confidence to the masses. The efficiency, modernity, and pervasiveness of the PNM's campaign had convinced many of its invincibility. The Party also successfully maintained its pledge to wage a clean campaign. Platform speakers were debarred from personal and family abuse; the public and not the private lives of opponents were attacked. When rebuked for the way in which its supporters heckled the meetings of its rivals, the Party replied that the heckling occurred because the PNM had so raised the level of campaign rhetoric that the masses had now come to expect more than abuse and mud-slinging from political platforms. The intolerance of the masses was not inspired by the Party élite. It was their own way of demonstrating that old-world politics had come to an end.

Of the three elections which had been held in the colony under universal suffrage, the 1956 election was unquestionably the most exciting. Wherever the PNM pitched its tents, it attracted crowds of people who were obviously aware that they were caught in the grip of a fundamental revolution. And though enthusiasm bordered on frenzy and hysteria, PNM open-air meetings were quiet and orderly. The magic of Williams' monotones hypnotized the urban masses. But there were several ugly features in the campaign. Racial violence always seemed imminent. 'Never before has race been watching race as it is watching race now', moaned Gomes. Threats of kidnapping and assassination, of impositions of religious and economic sanctions, were a standard feature of the campaign.[32] As one reporter declared, 'Never before was an election campaign so saddled with a mood of ugly savagery. Even to voice an opinion contrary to the man next to you was to invite a flood of threats and to incur deep-seated hostility. And in the rural areas, any candidate who runs into enemy territory must be prepared to vault walls and drains in order to decamp.'[33]

As the campaign drew to a close, it was clearly PNM against the rest. The Party had been the instrument of a *de facto* united front of established interests which would solidify soon after the election. The press, the Catholic hierarchy, big business, the old government and Legislature, and reportedly American agents all came out in opposition to the PNM. But the Movement could not be stopped. By singling out Williams for persecution, slander, and threats, the opposition had merely served to enhance the growing tendency to hero-worship him. They had completely misunderstood the phenomenon that was the People's National Movement.

32 One rice planter complained, 'This is trouble business. We are made to swear by *lotah* and lamp to support a certain candidate, otherwise some of the drivers and overseers would not give us work.' Threats were sent to Gomes as well as to the mother and daughter of Dr Williams.
33 TC, Sept. 21, 1956.

10
Victory and compromise

The results of the election on September 24 surprised the country and the Caribbean. For the first time in the history of Trinidad and Tobago a political party captured a majority of the elective seats in the Legislative Council. The People's National Movement won thirteen of the twenty-four seats, a feat which all West Indians agreed was something of a political miracle. Even though the Movement had won only 39 per cent of the popular vote, as far as its supporters were concerned the 'people' had given the PNM a mandate to govern.

Of the other parties, the PDP won five seats with 20.3 per cent of the total vote; the TLP-NDP and the Butler Party won two each. Of the thirty-nine Independents who contested, two were returned.

One of the biggest surprises of the elections was the complete failure of the POPPG to gain a seat in the Legislature. Also puzzling to most people was the defeat of veteran politician Albert Gomes. To some, Gomes' defeat was a disappointment, since it would have been exciting and politically enriching to have both Gomes and Williams in the same Legislature. But majority sentiment regarded Gomes' downfall as 'Trinidad redeeming itself'.

The defeat of Gomes in Port of Spain North did not, however, mean that the upper- and upper-middle-class elements of that constituency had supported the PNM wholeheartedly. Gomes won all the polling stations in those districts where such elements were concentrated. But the fact that the PNM was able to win a little less than 50 per cent of the total votes in the five stations indicates that the Party did manage to win the confidence of some members of the European creole community.[1]

---

1 Gomes won at only six out of thirty polling stations in Port of Spain North. One of

TABLE III
Election results 1956

Parties	Number of seats contested	Number of seats secured	Total votes polled	Percentage of electorate (electorate-339,028)	Percentage of votes cast
PNM	24	13	105,153	31	39
PDP	14	5	55,148	16	20
Butler Party	20	2	31,071	9	11
TLP-NDP	11	2	13,692	4	5
POPPG	9	—	14,019	4	5
WIIP	1	—	446	<1	<1
CPDP	1	—	627	<1	<1
CNLP	9	—	3,864	1	1.5
Independents	39	2	40,523	12	15
Sub-total			264,543	78	97.5
Rejected ballots			6,991	2	2.5
Grand total	128	24	271,534	80	100

SOURCE: *Report of the Legislative Council General Elections 1956*, Table 4, GPO, Port of Spain, 1958.

A closer look at the geographical distribution of the Party's support indicates that it triumphed mainly in the urban and suburban areas where nationalist feeling was more fully developed. In the rural areas the complex of old loyalties to the Church, family, and political father images proved resilient enough to withstand the charisma of Williams. The results also reflect the fact that although the PNM's campaign was island-wide, it was more intensely concentrated in urban areas and in the market centres of the countryside. The heartlands of the Hindu community were given only token stimulation. Then, too, the type of symbols which the PNM manipulated in 1955–6 – nationalism, public morality, secularism, Federation, and administrative rationality – were marginal issues in the rural areas. Gomes' explanation of the weak receptivity of rural voters to PNM slogans was quite perceptive:

They have very little of the sullenness of the urban types and certainly none of their truculence. Their psychology has been less complicated and corrupted by the teachings of their more learned compatriots whose frustrations they do not share.
The racial chauvinism we have been experiencing in recent years in this country is almost entirely a product of urban middle-class life and conditioning. And the same

these crossed class boundaries. In the five stations in the high-status residential areas, the total vote was 850 for Gomes to 402 for the PNM candidates.

may be said of our pseudo-nationalism which is so redolent of the inferiority complex. The rural type is not a disoriented type.[2]

Predictably, the PNM also failed to gain any seats in the sugar and water-crop belts where the Indians were concentrated. Butlerism also proved strong enough to prevent the PNM from winning any seats in the oil belt.

To most people it seemed obvious that Dr Williams would be called upon to form the government, but for a while there was considerable uncertainty. The PNM had indeed won a majority of the elected seats, but the Legislative Council consisted of thirty-one members altogether – twenty-four elected, five nominated, and two appointed officials. To have a working-majority, PNM needed to control at least sixteen seats. Left-wing forces reopened their demand for the united front coalition which the PNM had earlier rejected. The PNM, they argued, should invite the two Independents into their ranks. Alternatively, they were urged to work with the Butlerites and/or with the TLP.

No one felt bold enough to propose a parliamentary coalition between the PNM and the PDP. Such a coalition, despite its inherent difficulties, might have done more than any other gesture to dramatize the multiracial purpose of the PNM. The failure to conclude an alliance of this sort was to involve the PNM in immense and perhaps unnecessary difficulties in the months ahead. What no one said aloud in these days of uncertainty was that a left-wing coalition of the type proposed would have been, quite literally, an anti-Hindu coalition. Christian Indians and Moslems would have been included in any of these combinations, but no Hindus, who were all in the PDP.[3] The fact that a few Indians were included in the coalition would have meant little to the Hindus, who regarded such Indians as 'discontented' Moslems, or spoils- and society-seeking stooges.

None of the proposals for a left-wing coalition materialized. The PNM insisted that it would govern alone or go into Opposition. Declared Williams, 'Time is on our side.' The PNM was speculating that no effective government could be formed without it, unless PNM members broke ranks at the invitation of the Governor or the temptation of some other coalition manoeuvre. Many indeed believed that the lures of ministerial office might have tempted some PNM members to leave the Party, thereby disrupting it just as the United Front

2 TG, July 13, 1958. It should be noted, however, that the PNM only narrowly lost rural Tobago and ran fairly well in the rural counties in the east and north-east of the island. The Party even succeeded in gaining a plurality victory in the south-eastern counties of the country.
3 There were Hindus in the PNM, but none in its élite strata. By the time the elections were held, no more than three hundred Indians *of all creeds* had become card-holding members of the Party, a fraction of the Party's total membership.

and the Caribbean Socialist Party were disrupted. But to suggest this was to misunderstand the mood of the public in 1956. Such a breach of principle would have been unthinkable in PNM circles, and the public effectiveness of a renegade would have been nil.

The liberal Governor Sir Edward Beetham, and, after some hesitation, the Colonial Office, eventually decided that the interests and the stability of the country would be best served if the PNM were asked to govern. The escape clause in the constitution to which Beetham had referred earlier was brought into play.[4] To allow the PNM to form an effective Government, the Secretary of State, on the recommendation of the Governor, agreed to vary the instructions relating to the neutrality of the five nominated members by allowing the PNM to name two of them.[5]

It was agreed also that not only would the two nominees be subject to party discipline – i.e., their status as nominated members would depend on their continued acceptability to the government – but the other three nominations would not be given to people who were known to be openly hostile to the PNM. As an additional gesture of good faith, the Governor declared that the votes of the two appointed officials would 'normally' be available to the government as they had been to the colonial government in the past. The PNM was thus able to count on seventeen votes in normal circumstances. It was a brilliant coup, which showed that the Colonial Office was willing to redeem the pledge it had made in 1946 that it would respond positively to the development of effective party politics in Trinidad and Tobago.[6] The irony of the PNM manoeuvre was

4   Cf. chap. 5, p. 98–9.
5   This proposal was apparently opposed at first by the Governor on the grounds that such a specific concession was not necessary, since nominated members normally voted with the government. Williams noted, however, that nominated members on occasion did vote against the government on matters of principle. It was a surprising acknowledgment to make, but a necessary one if he was to gain agreement to his proposal that, unless the PNM could be assured a working majority, it would go into opposition.
6   Cf. chap. 4, p. 84. It might of course be argued that the Colonial Office had little choice unless it was prepared to risk the possibility of throwing Trinidad into chaos. The events in Trinidad were not unlike those in the Gold Coast in 1951 when the Colonial Office was confronted with a triumphant CPP. As Arden Clarke, the Governor, said on that occasion: 'Nkrumah and his party had the mass of the people behind them and there was no other party with appreciable public support to which one could turn. Without Nkrumah, the [Coussey] Constitution would be stillborn and nothing come of all the hopes, aspirations and concrete proposals for a greater measure of self-government. There would be no longer any faith in the good intentions of the British Government, and the Gold Coast would be plunged into disorders, violence and bloodshed.' Charles Arden Clarke, 'Eight Years of Transition in Ghana', African Affairs, vol. 57, Jan. 1958, p. 33.

not lost on many observers. The nominated *cum* official system which Dr Williams had so vehemently attacked as being the 'symbol of the island's arrested development' had now come to the rescue of the democratic movement.

The POPPG and the PDP vigorously opposed the concessions. It was argued that the Governor's action was unconstitutional, since it was the Legislature and not the Governor who had the power to choose the government. The Governor merely allotted portfolios; he had no knowledge of what the party configuration of the Legislature would be. Moreover, was he not manipulating a majority for the PNM which the country had refused to give it? The PDP was aware of the possibility that with the seven votes of the nominated-official bloc and those of the eleven non-PNM members, the PNM could have been prevented from holding office as the Butlerites were in 1950. The coalition might have been unstable, but it could have worked in the same way as had the Gomes régime.

The PDP also took the view that, by convention, nominated members should be free of party affiliation. By directing nominated members and officials to vote with the government, the Governor was making it impossible to overthrow the government. But the Governor had not really guaranteed the PNM an iron-clad majority; with only fifteen *assured* votes the PNM had only a 'conditional' majority. The additional two votes of the officials could easily have been withheld by the Governor if the PNM departed too far from the framework of expectations. The constitution, in the Governor's understanding, was thus a much more flexible instrument than the opposition imagined.

Interestingly enough, support for the Governor came from the *Trinidad Guardian*, which, in the traditional spirit of post-election honeymoons, declared editorially: 'A Party and leader, able to win 13 seats in a General Election, a feat never accomplished in Trinidad before, deserve an opportunity to show what they can do without petty spite or obstruction. If we have pointed to the Party's lack of experience, we do not intend to make it needlessly difficult for that same Party to acquire experience.'[7] Support also came from the Chamber of Commerce and the Catholic Church. In pledging its support to the government, the Chamber invited it to make use of the experience and knowledge of its members. 'All we ask is that we be given ample time to consider and comment on any matters, particularly those bits of legislation which might affect trade and commerce.' The Chamber of Commerce as a pressure group was very anxious to ensure its access to the new centres of decision-making.

The Catholic Church was anxious to heal the dangerous rift that had developed between itself and the PNM. The *Catholic News* observed, 'The

7   Sept. 30, 1956.

Catholic Church can live in peace and co-operation with any Government that will respect her own liberty in the sphere of faith and morals, and does not try to impose false ideas upon the people.'[8] The *News* noted strategically that His Grace the Archbishop 'never espoused or condemned any political party'. At the same time it called on all Catholics to pray for moderation on the part of their representatives, and urged them 'to co-operate loyally with the Government in all that was not opposed to the law of God'.[9]

Williams could not conceal his delight. 'The undue influence of certain shades of religious opinion bordering on intimidation in some cases has boomeranged. If prayers were said against the PNM, far more prayers were said for the PNM.'[10] Anglican clergymen also could not contain the glee they felt over the humiliation which the Catholic Church had suffered. The Moslem community was elated that Dr Williams had included a popular Moslem in the cabinet, since it was the first time a Moslem had been elevated to high governmental office. Moslems felt that their status in the community had been considerably uplifted.[11] The Moslem élite had calculated quite correctly that their chances of advancement were considerably better in the ranks of the PNM than in the Hindu PDP.

Left-wing forces were openly disappointed by the failure of the government to conclude an alliance with other elected members. It was felt that the PNM had concluded an alliance with POPPG types, if not with the POPPG itself. It was also noted that, of the two candidates whom Williams had recommended for nomination, one was a prominent white creole businessman.[12] The cabinet also included two substantial businessmen of European extraction. So 'respectable' did the cabinet look that Albert Gomes was forced to note: 'Within the Party itself, the middle-class elements are in the ascendancy. ... The choice of certain persons for ministerial positions and other plums indicate quite clearly that while the rump of the Party remains proletarian, its entire personality is being controlled by elements from higher social strata.'[13]

8   Sept. 30, 1956.   9   *Ibid.*   10   TG, Oct. 20, 1956.

11 'Ever since our forefathers came to these shores more than a hundred years ago, we have contributed with the other communities in no small measure to the economic development of our beloved island. Our political aspirations, however, did not meet with such salutary effects as it was only the late F.E.M. Hosein who succeeded in entering ... the Legislature. Since his death more than a quarter century ago, Muslims did not and could not gain a single seat in the Legislative Council.' 'The United Muslim Working League Congratulates Dr Williams', PNM *Weekly*, Nov. 1, 1956.

12 The nomination of Cyril Merry was seen by one POPPG official as a gesture 'rich in its social and political implications'. Merry was one of the white creoles who had joined the PNM. He was also a member of the Management Committee of the Chamber of Commerce.

13 'Right Turn Will Ensure Success', TG, Nov. 11, 1956.

The PNM had deliberately moved to the right to accommodate the very 'old world' forces to which it had just given battle. John Rojas, boss of the OWTU, noted that no genuine trade unionist was appointed to the cabinet or given a nomination. The PNM had selected a 'capitalist and a capitalist brief-holder as its nominees even though these types were already represented in the Cabinet'. But the workers themselves were in part to blame, since 'they had indicated their determination not to be represented by labour.' They had allowed Dr Williams to condition their minds against the idea of working-class political leadership. Under Williams the middle class had, in fact, seized power from the working class.[14] To the CNLP radicals the PNM victory was a counter-revolution, not revolution: 'Right-wing indoctrination plus anti-socialism had paid off to the extent where the oil companies and the commercialists no longer need to rely upon nomination to protect their interest.' The British Tory government was now very happy to relinquish power. 'The workers of Trinidad were now just where they were wanted.'[15]

What seemed to radical leftists like a complete capitulation to vested interests was to Williams and his colleagues a statesmanlike gesture in the cause of community integration. The PNM's first responsibility was to heal the wounds which the bitter election had opened. If an 'opening to the right' would achieve this goal, then they were prepared to give it a try. In his first victory speech following the opening of the Legislature, Williams declared that there would be 'no chopping of heads, no victimization'. The government would summon talent wherever it could be found regardless of race, class, or creed. Everyone was to be permitted to make a contribution to the development of the society. The right of others to differ from the government was to be scrupulously respected; no attempt was to be made to silence opposition. There were sceptics who doubted that these gestures demonstrated a genuine willingness to take advice, but the country at large applauded Williams for his surprising display of political 'maturity.'

14   TG, Sept. 28, 1956.
15   *Ibid.*

Part Three

Part Three covers the period from September 1956 to August 1962, a period
that witnessed the consolidation of power by the Negro-dominated People's
National Movement and the rally of opposition elements – mainly Hindu and
European – in the Democratic Labour Party. The conflict between the two
political groups was fierce and hysterical, and at times the community seemed
on the brink of racial war. This was especially true in 1960–1 when preparations were being made for the pre-Independence elections and the constitutional settlement upon which Independence was to be based. Last-minute
compromises by both parties in 1961 averted a racial crisis which many had
come to feel was inevitable.

The 'nationality' question muted the class issue considerably and effectively forestalled the emergence of a powerful working- and lower-class party
which would push the PNM to the left or expose the middle-class nature of its
leadership and policies. As Ivar Oxaal observes, the emergence of 'the East
Indian ... pseudo-party ... represented a gift from the gods' to the PNM.*

The period also witnessed the establishment of a West Indian Federation,
a bitter struggle between the PNM and the American government for the
return of territory which had been leased to the latter in 1941 for the establishment of a naval base and which was now required for the federal capital,
the withdrawal of Jamaica from the Federation in 1961, and the collapse of
the federal experiment.

Politics in these years dominated almost all aspects of life in the community. What was striking, however, was that despite enormous pressures the

* Ivar Oxaal, *Black Intellectuals Come to Power*, Cambridge, Mass., 1968, p. 155.

PNM maintained an image of solidarity and purposefulness which few had believed possible. The Democratic Labour Party, on the other hand, proved incapable of maintaining any unity, coherence, or stability, a circumstance that made any negotiation of political compromise enormously difficult.

11
The Nationalists in power
1956-8

The months following the assumption of power by the People's National Movement were almost barren of legislation, and many people were becoming sceptical and restive. Sensing the mood of rising frustration, the Party had to remind its followers that it had not promised a new heaven. What it had promised was that under its leadership, with hard work by all the people, and with the application of knowledge, some improvement would be effected in the standard of living.[1] The government had to be given time to plan its legislative schedule, since it had inherited from the last government a five-year development programme which was merely a collection of projects strung together without rhyme or reason. Before a rational development programme could be framed, committees had to be appointed to inquire into the state of the country. This was the scientific way to proceed. The committees were also seen by the new government as democratic workshops in which citizens could learn about the nuances of government, and as instruments through which persons initially hostile to the régime might be mobilized. They were seen as an essential part of the policy of national integration, though some Party stalwarts did feel that in its choice of committee personnel the government was rewarding its enemies and punishing its friends.

But opposition forces were determined to harass the government systematically. Motion after motion was introduced to embarrass the PNM, especially among its lower-class following. Proposals were introduced to increase old age pensions, to subsidize basic foodstuffs, to expand sugar welfare programmes, and so on. During 1956 and most of 1957 the opposition benches,

---

1 PNM *Weekly*, Nov. 8, 1956.

which included some of the most experienced parliamentarians, were clearly in the ascendancy. Opposition propaganda was extremely fierce. From the unforgiving pen of Albert Gomes, whose columns were carried in the *Guardian*, and from the *Guardian* itself, broadsides, most of them clearly excessive, were fired at the fledgling government. Interestingly, the irresponsibility of the attacks was perhaps the most important factor in neutralizing much of the constructive criticism that was legitimately being offered against the government.

One founding member of the Party sought to explain the PNM's performance in terms of the constitutional structure:

Because of the constitution, Government owes their existence and must depend for their week to week parliamentary survival on the guardians of vested interests; they are forced to respond to those very pressures which for 6 years prevented Mr Gomes from being a proper Minister of Labour and which dictated his policy as Minister of Commerce.

It is unfair to condemn Government's failure to launch a bold assault on the established bastions of vested interest when the guardians of vested interests in the Legislature, by virtue of being called upon to help Ministers get a majority, are in a position, not to 'warn' and 'comfort', but to 'determine' what the Government can and cannot do.[2]

It is possible to explain away the PNM's timidity in 1956 and 1957 on the basis of the inhibitions present in the constitutional framework, and to see its anxiety to change the constitution in this context. But the answer is really much simpler; the PNM was genuinely unprepared in those months to bring in the legislation which it was planning. The boldness of its first development budget was to startle everyone.

THE RALLY OF THE 'OUTS':
THE DEMOCRATIC LABOUR PARTY

The rally of the 'outs', which is so typical a feature of the politics of newly emergent countries, was not long in crystallizing. Trinidadians, who are in the main opposed to the idea of a one-party state, took it for granted that an opposition party would sooner or later be formed; the two-party system was considered to be an essential part of a mature democracy. But there was some question as to what elements would combine to form this opposition. Many feared that if the Hindu PDP were to emerge as the main opposition to the Negro-dominated PNM, the stability of the community would be seriously

2   David Nelson, *Trinidad Chronicle* (TC), April 2, 1957.

endangered. The Democratic Labour Party was, in a sense, 'invented' to prevent this.

The DLP consisted essentially of POPPG, PDP, and TLP elements. The initial difficulty in the unification exercise centred on the problem of fusing the predominantly Catholic white creoles with Hindu elements. There were POPPG cadres who did not wish to form any alliance with a 'pagan' element. They maintained that the POPPG should reorganize itself, perhaps under another name, and seek to improve its standing among the masses. The PNM had to be destroyed.

Another wing of the Party resisted this 'bitter-end' policy and warned that 'a continuance of the misguided attempt to break or discredit the PNM at all cost' would only lead to the intensification of racial and religious differences. Such a policy would also lead to a repetition of the recent electoral disaster. 'It was not the best way for a progressive conservative party to deal with the rising tide of West Indian nationalism.'[3] This wing of the Party preferred to accept the PNM's olive branch.

A third wing took the view that the Hindus provided the only alternative basis for a mass party. Whether one liked it or not, one had to accept the fact that if there was to be a two-party system, the second party must include the PDP. It would be unfortunate if Trinidad were to have an all-Indian opposition. The leading advocate of the PDP alliance was Gomes, who did not share the squeamishness of others about being in the same political bed with Bhadase Sagan Maraj.

The PDP itself, feeling its isolation in the Hindu ghetto, avidly welcomed the possibility of a merger. Unless its image were updated, power would forever escape it. The Moslems – at least the urban Moslems – and the Christian Indians would never identify with it; nor could it expect to obtain any significant Negro support. The PDP leaders at first insisted that they would keep their Party intact, and that, being the most powerful unit, they should lead the coalition. But this requirement was later abandoned.[4] The PDP seemed to have realized that the new party would be much more viable if all units were completely dissolved.

3 *Trinidad Guardian* (TG), Sept. 30, 1956.
4 The PDP itself was already having leadership difficulties. Maraj startled everyone in the early months of 1957 by declaring that he was no longer a member of the PDP. 'I want the public to hear that I do not enjoy the confidence of the four members [of the Parliamentary PDP] and I will like to be addressed in future, not as leader of the Party but as an individual.' TC, March 9, 1957. The struggle in the PDP arose over the attitude the Party should take on the federal issue. Maraj was willing to co-operate with the PNM, while his colleagues preferred to maintain their attitude of non-co-operation.

The imminent federal elections provided the catalyst for solidifying the opposition. The launching of the DLP had been continually deferred because no leader could be agreed upon; every notable felt that he had ample qualifications for leadership. It took the intervention of Jamaica's Alexander Bustamente to get the DLP to agree to be led provisionally by the TLP president, Victor Bryan. It was felt that the image of the DLP would suffer if Gomes or Maraj were given the leadership. It should also be pointed out that the DLP as constituted in 1957 was a *federal*, and not a territorial, party. The leadership issue in the territorial party was not to be settled for a long time.

With the Labour Party finally launched, the opposition intensified its policy of systematically opposing the PNM by introducing its first no-confidence motion on September 9, 1957. In terms of substantive policy, the Opposition criticized what it viewed as part of the government's plan to subject the public service to political control and partisanship, and there is indeed evidence to indicate that conflicts were beginning to arise between the newly elected government and senior civil servants appointed under the old régime. Many of these were persons whom the nationalists considered holdovers from the old order, persons of a different social class committed to values, policies, and ways of doing things quite at variance with those of the new political élite. Charges that civil servants were sabotaging the government's development plans, and counter-charges that politicians were muzzling or victimizing senior officials were frequent. The fact that many senior civil servants were white creoles only served to complicate some of the crucial issues involved. Quite a few resigned and went into business rather than work under a 'black' government. It seems that there was a general fear among white civil servants that they would be victimized sooner or later. Resignation was considered a more dignified course of action. As it turned out, very few were openly victimized in any way, much to the disappointment of party stalwarts.

The new government insisted that the civil service must recognize the new masters. The PNM must make laws and form and state government policy – not senior officials, as was the case in the colonial period. Party politics and a rationalized administration implied that the organs that executed the law should be subordinated to those that made it. As the party *Weekly* bluntly stated:

The PNM Government will, in its constitutional changes, see to it that ... matters pertaining to the Civil Service will be regularised. When this is done, there will be little doubt as to whom and in what direction the Civil Service will have to turn for direction and guidance. ... Many senior civil servants still think in terms of independence and an independent appeal to the Colonial Office. These officers cannot realize that full self-government is around the corner. ... the Civil Service should be there to serve any government the people elect. It is no longer possible to tolerate officials who can embarrass the Government and maintain their standing in that service.[5]

Efficiency and harmony of action demanded that all organs of the administration function as a united team with one public voice.

The opposition also accused the PNM of corruption. The fact that several ministers had borrowed public funds to purchase cars was seized upon as only the most celebrated instance of public immorality.[6] It was an irresponsible attack, and it drove the government to declare total war on the opposition. But nepotism and corruption were already beginning to re-appear in public life, if indeed they had ever disappeared.

The third major area of disagreement concerned the question of conditions under which foreign capital was to be allowed to come into the country. A definition of policy had been forced upon the government by the actions of an American firm assembling office equipment in Trinidad. Faced by a union demand for the right to organize workers in its employ, the management took the position that it was not prepared to tolerate 'outside interference' by any union, since its workers were well cared for and their wages were above the prevailing wage structure for persons in that classification. Factory conditions were also said to be optimum, and the extra-vocational welfare of workers was looked after by the company.

The government, which was particularly sensitive to the suspicion with which it was viewed by the trade-union movement, chose to support the demands of the union. The Minister of Labour advised that the government would not allow industrialists to come into the country, especially under the Pioneer Industries Ordinance which gave them exemption from certain forms of taxation, and do exactly as they pleased. The island was in need of foreign capital and welcomed it, but not at any price; self-respect and national pride would not permit it. Moreover, such a policy could only lead to industrial unrest. The Chief Minister took a much more belligerently nationalistic atti-

---

5 PNM *Weekly*, Sept. 2, 1957.
6 The bizarre 'Car loans' crisis is not important except in so far as it provided the issue around which the Opposition sought to rally its forces for an overthrow of the government. Briefly, it involved the question of whether or not a loan secured from the Accountant General by a minister violated the provision whereby officers holding emoluments under the Crown were debarred from entering into contracts with the Crown. The issue, which poisoned the country for over a year, was later thrown out by the Privy Council on the grounds that the Legislature was the only body which had the competence to determine its own membership. The opposition was at one time confident that the Colonial Office would help it to dislodge the government, using this as a pretext.

tude. 'Any industry coming in here and behaving decently will be given decent treatment. If they do not like our action, let them pull out.'[7] The company in its turn warned the government that if it continued in its policies, American companies would indeed 'bail out and go', to the ultimate detriment of the people of the country. While both sides were guilty of lack of good judgment and restraint, the government was right in condemning the paternalism which was so evident a feature of industrial relations in Trinidad. White employers believe that they understand and represent the interests of their employees much better than union leaders, some of whom it must be admitted are still extremely immature in their bargaining techniques. The composition of the society and its system of job allocation makes what is normally a class issue a racial one as well.

Trade unions, both in Trinidad and throughout the Caribbean, applauded the government's boldness. The incident in fact marked the beginning of that fundamental alliance between the trade-union movement and the PNM which was to bear such rich fruit in the 1961 elections but which was also to lead to some of the bitterest outbreaks of industrial unrest the country had witnessed thus far. As far as the trade unions were concerned, it was up to them to deepen the basis of the national revolution to make it meaningful to the worker.

The business community, it should be noted, had already begun to withdraw its confidence from the government. The commercial banks, bastions of the old order, had refused to make loans available to the government on the basis of promissory notes. The government was warned that its behaviour was damaging the country's reputation: 'The Chief Minister ought to be more guarded in his expression. ... He is preventing people from coming to invest money in Trinidad. ... the Colonial Office has refused to grant him assistance and we now have to pay the "cake" by way of higher taxation. It is not right for the Chief Minister to adopt this attitude in a small two-by-two colony like Trinidad. We cannot do that to our bosses in the Colonial Office, or act as we want with them.'[8]

The opposition also noted that although the PNM had pledged in its Manifesto that it would honour all international agreements, especially the one relating to the Bases Agreement of 1941, the government had allowed Jamaica and Barbados to force it into making a claim to the territory at Chaguaramas leased to the United States, on the ground that it was the only satisfactory site for the federal capital. Williams, insisted Maraj, had fallen for a trick that would lead to a re-opening of the capital site issue. 'The Americans will not stand for petty bullying even if it is true they occupy part of our terri-

7   TG, March 23, 1967.
8   Hon B. Maraj, *Hansard*, Sept. 9, 1957, p. 2301.

tory. You may speak to Woodford Square as you want, but you cannot speak to the Americans as you want. They partly control the entire Globe.'[9]

The final issue raised by the opposition was the question of the government's 'violation of our parliamentary institutions'. The Government, said the DLP, was emphasizing Whitehall and forgetting Westminster. It was by-passing standing committees, including the Finance Committee, suspending the business of the House to avoid private members' motions, by-passing the Tenders Board, and generally infringing on the rights of the minorities.

Alarm was expressed at the growing Caesarism and intolerance of Dr Williams and his followers. Williams was criticized for his statement that, given a chance, he would prevent other parties from using Woodford Square, for politically assassinating his enemies and rewarding friends of the PNM, for declaring 'war' on the Opposition, for regimenting his colleagues, for using committees to confront the opposition with *faits accomplis*, and for discriminating against rural areas which had not supported the PNM.[10] The attacks were devastating, and the Chief Minister himself was forced to admit that 'some of the points were really good', even if twisted.

The leader of the House, Dr Patrick Solomon, reassured the opposition that the government would not oppose its right to bring such motions, but warned that the PNM could not be expected to say 'thank you' for harassment. 'Mere self-defence demands that we use a reasonable degree of force ourselves.'[11] The honeymoon was clearly over and Trinidad was being readied for a period of bitter party warfare in which racial tension would mount beyond the limits previously considered tolerable.

The consolidation of the DLP was a development that the PNM had not envisaged. As the PNM organ observed, 'Bustamante's unification of the fragmentary groups in Trinidad was a fortuitous circumstance we never realised.'[12] At the second annual convention of the PNM in September 1957, its leader told assembled delegates that 'The Party runs this great danger – that as the strongest Party ever organized in Trinidad, it has brought together some of the worst characteristics of the political life of the old world which it was pledged to destroy.' Though recognizing the danger, few people in nationalist circles believed that the DLP would survive for any length of time. To the PNM, the DLP was not an opposition in the parliamentary sense of the word. 'It had no programme or philosophy but was merely a collection of individuals with

9 *Ibid.*, p. 2303.
10 The PNM had expelled two of its members on local councils for breaking Party discipline. Williams declared in public, 'We help to make these people, and by God, if they play the fool, we will break them.' TC, Oct. 3, 1957.
11 *Hansard*, Sept. 9, 1957, p. 2363.
12 PNM *Weekly*, Aug. 18, 1958.

some personal following.' There was also a great deal of confidence that the PNM could not be beaten in twenty-five years. Dr Williams himself maintained that the PNM faced no real threat except from within its own ranks – from the ill-discipline, ambition, intrigue, and inertia which were already manifest.

Despite the PNM's conviction that opposition was desirable and necessary in the democratic society to which it was committed, nationalists were extremely intolerant of such opposition whenever it presented itself. After 1957 the PNM practically declared war on the DLP, the press, the Chamber of Commerce, and the European community. As the Chief Minister had announced, 'From now on we shall attack "black is white" all who take PNM's name in vain.' Williams' solicitude for opposition was intellectual and abstract. His intolerance of actual opposition forces was rendered all the more acute because he and his colleagues were convinced of the righteousness of their cause, and of the treasonableness and irresponsibility of their opponents.

THE FIRST DEVELOPMENT PROGRAMME

By the end of 1957 the government was ready to introduce its first five-year development programme. It is difficult to describe the programme as scientific or far-reaching, since it was little more than a collection of desirable infrastructural projects which the PNM had pledged to introduce in 1956. These projects included subsidies to cane-farmers, peasants and fishermen, hospital and housing construction, better access roads for agricultural areas, rural electrification, harbour improvement, increased expenditures on education with the ultimate prospect of free education. Many of the projects had in fact been begun by the old régime.

In order to finance this programme, which was expected to cost $191 million (TT) funds had to be obtained from somewhere. The government had already failed in its bid to raise loans locally and on the United States and London markets, and the only alternative source was public revenue. Increased taxes were thus imposed on commodities such as rum, tobacco, gasoline, automobile licences, legal transactions, and the like. But the major anticipated source of new revenue was oil. The government declared that it would renegotiate its tax arrangements with the oil companies so as to secure a 50–50 split in oil profits. The Chief Minister, who was also Minister of Finance, noted that Venezuela had such an arrangement, and that in some middle-eastern areas the arrangement was 75–25.[13]

13 It might be instructive to note the views of the investigating commission appointed by
    the government in 1959 to study the oil industry. The report of Mr Walter Levy in
    fact endorsed several of the criticisms which the opposition had raised during the

Williams also did a complete somersault on the question of depletion allowances for the industry – the same allowances which he had earlier criticized the Gomes régime for not conceding. 'The case for the special concessions in marine drilling to Trinidad was simply overdone,' he maintained. 'It is not possible to see how anyone could have taken seriously in 1954 the old claim of probable exhaustion of reserves in a few years.' He now saw the subsequent decision to grant them as 'the worst example of political irresponsibility, the greatest sell-out in the history of Trinidad. It was the legacy of a Government which during the extension of its life beyond its legal term, gave away for 25 years, the birth-right of the people ... it was a ghastly illustration of colonialism and the lack of respect for colonials.'[14]

Trinidad's tax structure was the lowest in the Caribbean, the Chief Minister revealed. More people paid taxes on a percentage basis in both Jamaica and Barbados, islands that were not as well off as Trinidad.[15] If the

debate. Levy noted that Trinidad's position in the oil market combined elements of real strength with certain competitive disadvantages. Trinidad's geographic location and her inclusion in the sterling area were perhaps the most important of these advantages. The fact that its 'legal and institutional environment was conducive to private investment and development' was also a valuable consideration. Levy noted that Texaco had decided to base its South American refining operations in Trinidad. Major disadvantages included the narrow margin of profitability on local operations, high production costs, low productivity and wide spacing of wells, low ratio of proved reserves to current production, and competition from former consuming countries, mainly in South America. Companies in Trinidad also claimed that they had to dig seven times as many wells in Trinidad to get the volume yielded by one in Venezuela. To those who might have been contemplating nationalization, Levy warned that the marketing of Trinidad's oil depended heavily on the marketing operations of large established firms. 'Trinidad's oil may move through their distributing channels where it might not otherwise be strictly competitive on the basis of price considerations alone.' Another crucial aspect of the report related to the 50-50 issue. Levy noted that on the basis of the 1957 returns, royalties, revenues collected from rents, and income and company taxes, the Government took almost 52 per cent of the companies' pre-tax earnings. 'In other recent years, the Government's share has been less, but apparently not significantly different from the 50-50 sharing of the industry's earnings.' *Report into the Oil Industry in Trinidad & Tobago*, TG, Oct. 10, 1959.

14 Williams qualified his rejection of the allowances by saying that the concessions given were too wide. The government had not followed the advice of those who had warned that the concessions should await further geological study, and that they should not be given for operations that had not yet commenced. Provisions permitting review of the agreement in cases where prolific wells were struck should also have been inserted. Williams noted that such allowances were not given for operations in Lake Maracaibo or in the Persian Gulf. *Hansard*, Sept. 9, 1957, p. 556.

15 Williams cited the following statistics: The number of taxpayers in Trinidad was one-third the number in Jamaica, which had only twice the size of Trinidad's

country wanted improvements in social amenities, it had to pay for them. Moreover, it was better for Trinidad to pay for its development programme out of its own revenues, since high interest on loans from abroad would only add to the cost of the total programme. Virtue was being made out of necessity.

The opposition strongly criticized the government for planning to exhaust the colony's reserves on projects which, they argued, were aimed mainly at helping the urban population. Indian legislators were especially angry about the new taxes on licences, fuel, and alcohol, which, they maintained (quite unjustifiably), were directed specifically at the Indian community. They even declared that the Government was mobilizing support for the new tax structure by claiming that it was directed mainly against Indians. Butler's hostile anti-Indian outburst that the traitorous Indians should be taxed 'more and more' also served as an irritant to the Indians.[16]

The Negro urban community took the tax increases stoically. The fact that the protests of the Indian and European communities were so extravagant probably did much to rally them behind the PNM banner. But the budget, together with the issues described above, had helped to solidify the DLP, which had already begun its campaign for the first federal elections, to be held early in 1958.

> population, and less than twice the number in Barbados, whose population was only one-fifth that of Trinidad. Only 2 per cent of the population paid taxes in Trinidad, in comparison with 2½ per cent in British Honduras, 4 per cent in Jamaica, and 25 per cent in the United States. The scale of taxation was also lower. An income of $5,040 (TT) would be taxed $412 in Trinidad, whereas in Barbados and Jamaica it would be taxed $681 and $560 respectively.

16 TC, Dec. 17, 1957. Butler, stung by the defection to the DLP of one of the Indian MLCs from his Party, declared that he was finally convinced that all Indians were traitors, and that he would never again sponsor another Indian candidate. He even warned Dr Williams that very soon he would be 'deserted by all those Indians whom he is now putting into power – they are all traitors – one and all of them.'

12
The federal elections of 1958

The first stage of the protracted struggle to achieve political unity among the English-speaking Caribbean peoples came to an end in July 1957 when the British Parliament approved an Order-in-Council establishing the Federation of the West Indies. The Federation has now been dissolved, and only those aspects of its history which are germane to Trinidad's political development will be discussed in this study.

The elections to the first Parliament of the West Indies, which were scheduled for April 1958, provided the first opportunity for a country-wide electoral confrontation between the DLP and the PNM. Since its formation in 1957, the DLP had shown elements of strength as well as weakness. The weakness stemmed mainly from the excessive individualism of its members. Alexander Bustamante, who had been made life leader of the Federal Party, urged Trinidad DLP politicians to discipline themselves, to put party above self as a condition of effectiveness. 'No member must believe that because he has some following he is greater than the organisation. The organisation always comes first, the country and the members after.'[1] But unlike their Jamaican counterparts, Trinidad DLP chieftains were congenitally incapable of organizational fidelity. There were resignations and threats of resignations within weeks of the Party's founding. Maraj himself, conscious of his power as the Party's main vote-getter, was always threatening to resign and form a new party whenever he did not get his way. The fight over the selection of candidates for the federal elections almost split the Party wide open.

Younger elements were disgruntled about the Party's electoral preference

1   TG, Jan. 1, 1958.

for established notables and its seeming inability to present a positive image to the public. Even the *Trinidad Guardian*, the *de facto* organ of the DLP, found it necessary to criticize the DLP's political immaturity: 'An opposition, to be effective, should not concern itself merely with the strategy of keeping the Government extended on all fronts, useful as this might be. It should offer the electorate a positive programme which will carry conviction of its readiness to take over the administration of the country should the logic of events some day put it in a winning position.'[2] But try as it did, the DLP was never able to take advantage of this advice. It remained imprisoned by its origins.

The PNM contested the 1958 election as part of a coalition of what were then considered to be the progressive forces of West Indian politics: the People's National Party of Jamaica, the Barbados Labour Party, and other labour parties which were in power in the smaller units of the Federation. The fact that the West Indian Federal Labour Party (as the coalition was called) was conceived as a socialist united front posed ideological difficulties for the PNM. Some members felt that the Party must continue to 'fight shy of "isms" '. Dr Williams himself refused to entertain suggestions that PNM should 'go socialist':

The PNM should be chary of 18th century political labels and categories, especially those with an emotive appeal that have no relevance for a 20th century world, let alone a West Indian environment. In every case, the test must be which [economic strategy] is best designed to improve the living conditions and promote development of the people of the country as a whole. Placed against this background, nationalisation and private enterprise, public and private capitalism, become mere techniques to be used at one time or another for a larger end, and not merely as ends in themselves. PNM's sole aim is the removal of the political and economic barriers to the full development of the West Indian personality.[3]

But the fact that WIFLP was socialist did not deter the PNM from joining it. Williams observed that in spite of the socialist label, Jamaica and Barbados were pragmatic in their development strategy – no nationalization, no expropriation, no revolution. What is more, the WIFLP had agreed to create a separate category of 'associate members' for the parties which were not socialist, but which were nationalist and progressive. The Manifesto of the WIFLP itself said nothing that gave one the impression that it was a revolutionary socialist party. The economic strategy which it endorsed for the Federation was no different from that which was being followed by the PNM in Trinidad, and the PNP in Jamaica.

2   *Ibid.*, Nov. 11, 1958.
3   PNM *Weekly*, May 27, 1957.

The campaign in Trinidad, though on the whole not as fierce as in 1956, was much more racially tinged. Every issue was twisted to fit the racial cleavages in the society. Each party nevertheless strove to buttress its claim of being genuinely multiracial by wooing as candidates notables whose ethnic identification differed from the dominant one in the Party, even if this meant sacrificing the claims of some dedicated workers. The results were quite satisfactory. Of the ten candidates sponsored by the DLP, seven were non-Indian; four of the PNM's were non-Negro. But the value of such ticket-balancing strategies was severely compromised by the tendency of both parties to 'type' the other in racial terms. PNM followers promptly re-baptized non-Indian candidates in the DLP with Hindu or Moslem names. Such candidates who appeared on DLP platforms were invited to 'show us your capra'.[4] PNM followers also tended to view Negroes on the DLP ticket as 'enemies' and 'traitors', persons who could not see that a vote for the DLP was in effect an anti-Negro vote.[5] The Indian element in the DLP leadership also contributed to this unfortunate circumstance. One of their main talking-points in the campaign, especially in the rural areas, was that a victory for the DLP would mean that the first prime minister of the West Indies would be Indian.[6]

No party was blameless; there was instead a balance of blame. As the nationalist movement became more fully developed, the irresistible tendency was for race and nationhood to become interrelated. Both ethnic groups interpreted nationhood and emancipation in terms of their own communities and symbols. Even the party leaders, committed though they were to universalistic norms, could not resist the temptation to manipulate sectional symbols, sometimes subtly, sometimes quite unashamedly, in their pursuit of political advantage.

THE ISSUES

To the DLP the election presented an opportunity to use a federal base of power to neutralize the PNM at the territorial level. Many of the issues raised during the campaign were hang-overs from the 1956 election. The criticisms which were levelled at the ruling party during the debate on the 1957 no-

4   It was a PNM candidate, a Hindu, who unwittingly started the mischief of 're-baptism.' Accused of being in a Negro party, he replied, 'If anyone talks race, I am going to ask him if Gomes is a Maharaj, Bryan a Singh, and James a Pundit.' 'Capra' is an item of Indian dress worn by males around the loin.
5   These charges were made most frequently in the Tobago constituency which was almost 100 per cent Negro.
6   The DLP had designated Ashford Sinanan, its deputy leader, as its candidate for the prime ministership.

confidence motion were also given further airing. As far as Chaguaramas was concerned, it was obvious that Williams had seized upon it as *the* issue with which to mould an emotional nationalism. It should be noted that Williams had also used the controversy as a lever with which to negotiate a *rapprochement* with the Indian community following the 1956 election. The British commissioners who had been retained in 1956 to recommend sites for the location of the capital had rejected Trinidad because of the 'disruptive' influence which the Indian community was said to have had on its political life. Williams' vigorous condemnation of this slur on the Indian community had won him the support of many Indians whom he had alienated by his Maha Sabha address in 1956. This gain was reinforced by his clever decision to invite the leader of the PDP to join the government's delegation to the Federal Conference held in Jamaica in 1957, at which the capital site issue was to be settled.[7]

The decision of the PNM to go back on its pledge to respect the agreement between Britain and the United States concerning the terms under which a naval base was to be established in Trinidad neutralized all the advantages that had accrued as a result of Maraj's participation in the conference. Maraj's revelation that the government had earlier decided on an alternative capital site outside the base area further hardened the differences between him and the PNM. The charge of 'treasonable betrayal of confidential secrets' was frequently thrown about during the campaign. As far as the PNM was concerned, the Indian élite was putting a knife in the back of the new West Indian nation, something nationalists could not tolerate. There had to be a 'fight to the finish' between the two parties. 'One or the other party had to go to the wall because we can no longer tolerate this odd conglomeration of people who call themselves the DLP.'[8]

The DLP were similarly convinced that they were the true West Indian patriots. The question at stake was not whether the West Indies could lay claim to Chaguaramas, but whether they should. The true interests of the West Indies, they charged, were being sacrificed to satisfy the vendetta of one man.[9] The Party felt it was idle and unrealistic to talk about a neutral West Indies joining the Bandung bloc, since the hard facts of geography and economic dependence ruled out all prospects of neutrality being practised by the West Indies. The DLP felt that the bases agreement should be re-negotiated in such a way that United States funds would be forthcoming to assist the

7   Maraj viewed his decision to accept the invitation as the final reproof to those who maintained he was anti-Federation. But his PDP colleagues were quite annoyed that he had agreed to work with the government.
8   Dr P.V.J. Solomon, TG, March 4, 1958.
9   The allusion is to the unsettled relations between Williams and the United States authorities over responsibilities to his divorced wife.

Federation in solving its economic problems. Welfare issues should be placed before status issues. The DLP also claimed that talk about socialism, capital gains, and other punitive taxation measures, and insistence on the rights of trade unions, would scare away foreign capital. As the Deputy Leader of the Party warned, 'A socialist government dealing with taxation cannot win the full confidence of external or local capital and therefore must resort to increased taxation to maintain normal services. A policy of high taxation now in the West Indies would defeat its own aim because of its deterrent effect on investment. ... We are inflexible in our advocacy at all times that the only hope of the entire West Indies is the belief in private enterprise.'[10]

The DLP also underscored their contention that the PNM had a distinctly urban and middle-class bias, and that its development programme was prejudiced in favour of the urban bourgeoisie. It was noted that, while increased cost-of-living allowances were given to civil servants, no basic foodstuffs were subsidized; nor were pensions for the aged increased. And there were indeed protests from lower-class elements that the PNM had not relieved them from the yoke which they had had to endure under the Gomes régime. They were still the forgotten pariahs from 'behind the bridge'. This accusation was not entirely just. While it is true that there was an urban middle-class bias in the PNM, the government had not completely ignored the rural citizen. Its first provisional budget in 1957 had assigned funds to relieve the hardships of seasonable workers in the sugar industry, and had provided funds to create supplementary jobs for intermittent workers in both the rural and urban areas. Money was also provided to construct outdoor privies in the rural areas to combat the incidence of hookworm, and contributions were made to the Sugar Industry Welfare Fund for the servicing of lands made available for worker-housing by the sugar estates. In the development budget, modest sums had been allocated to help the farmer, fisherman, and other small proprietors. The Chief Minister had also declared that his government was anxious to stimulate a 'back to the land' movement and to ensure that the countryside was not subordinated to the urban areas as far as the normal amenities of civilization were concerned. The stated aim of the development programme was to lay the foundations of the national community. But the effects of the modest programme had not yet begun to be felt, and the DLP had proven to be a much more effective propaganda machine than the PNM had given it credit for.

THE RESULTS

The results of the elections came as a complete surprise to the PNM. The Party had become so used to easy victories in municipal areas that it had anticipated no difficulties in the federal elections. It had in fact ruled that no member already elected to public office might become a candidate for the election on the grounds that this would dislocate the development programme. It was also explained that by-elections to vacated positions would again involve the country in disruptive political strife. Moreover, the Party had decided that for the next five years its role would be to concentrate, not on federal politics, but on its development programme as a prerequisite to a more effective participation at the federal level in the years ahead. As Williams declared, 'If there is one party in the West Indies which cannot be expected to accept any excessive responsibility for the operation of the federal machine in the early years, it is the PNM.'[11] The PNM needed time to consolidate itself. The Party was still too young and too unformed to risk losing the concentrated attention of its best talent.

Despite its unwillingness to participate actively in federal politics, the PNM was stunned with disbelief when it was revealed that the DLP had won six of the ten seats allocated to Trinidad. Everyone agreed that it was a tremendous triumph, not so much for the DLP, but for Bhadase Maraj, who proved to be his Party's principal vote-getter. His supreme achievement was the 'political resurrection' of two ministers of the 'old order' who had been buried under the PNM landslide in 1956.[12] DLP supporters regarded the results as a welcome rebuff to the PNM, whose 'goose-stepping' and intolerant exclusivism had driven many to anger and frustration. Gomes, who had a genius for exaggerating the 'crimes' of the PNM, was not unfair when he observed that 'the attitude of the cohorts of the new cult was insufferable. ... Decent citizens were the victims of vulgar abuse on the streets, for no other reason than that they did not *look* like the sort of people who would be PNM supporters. A section of the community interpreted the victory [in 1956] as establishing their right to dominate the country even to the extent of subscribing to the belief that other elements were trespassers.'[13] Gomes saw the victory as 'a welcome Thermidorean reaction, a successful rally of decent people against a dictatorship of hooligans'.[14] The age of persecution hopefully was over. The DLP also claimed

---

11   *Ibid.*, March 3, 1958.
12   *Ibid.*, March 24, 1958. Both Roy Joseph and Albert Gomes had fought in constituencies with a substantial Hindu population.
13   'Behind the Curtain', TG, April 13, 1958.
14   The DLP taunted the PNM by asking whether hookworm disease had now affected non-Indian areas as well. The reference was to the statement of the Minister of Health, a Christian Indian, that 'the indirect cost [of hookworm] is very difficult to assess. One does not have to speculate on the effects of this type of anemia on productivity. But there is scope for speculation as to whether the fact that the PNM did not win a seat in the hookworm area could be correlated with the moral apathy that hookworm breeds.' It was an irresponsible piece of 'picong' which Hindus did not appreciate. *Hansard*, March 15, 1957, p. 1205.

that since Chaguaramas and government taxation policy were the main issues during the campaign, the PNM should, in fact, resign. The public had shown a lack of confidence in the Government.

Canon Farquhar spoke for many former PNM supporters who had become thoroughly disillusioned with the PNM when he declared that he hoped the defeat would have a sobering effect on 'fanatical nationalists whose minds had begun to lose touch with reality':

The defeat could, at the very worst, invoke only the spur of wholesome embarrassment, or else the timely corrective of humiliating disillusionment to a government whose chief besetting sin has been the familiar nemesis of being 'power drunk'. The most recent outburst of the Chief Minister, 'Don't get me blasted vex', follows in a sequence of hysterically unbalanced statements, which have too long pointed to flagrantly overweening conceit. Another favourite slogan, 'Heads will roll', used persistently in brandishing threats, is further indication of an attitude of mind dangerously out of hand.[15]

But the hoped for peace which the results had led DLP circles to expect was not forthcoming, since the PNM chose to interpret the election results not as a rebuff but as an impressive vote of confidence. The interpretation was based not on numbers of seats won – which they attributed to the mischance of electoral geography, but on the size and distribution of its popular vote. PNM psephologists, noted that although the total vote was about 20,000 less than it was in 1956, the Party had increased its take by over 12,000. By winning 117,432 of the 251,739 votes cast, they had in fact captured roughly 48 per cent of the electorate, compared to 38.9 per cent in 1956. This was especially significant in that the vote in the urban areas, where the PNM was entrenched, had declined, while that in the rural areas had increased. Sure of victory, PNM urban voters had stayed home. Nationalists were also proud of the fact that they had made substantial inroads into former 'enemy' territory. Not only had Negro-dominated Tobago fallen to the PNM,[16] the Party's performance in Indian-dominated areas had also improved over that of 1956; 950 additional votes were won in Caroni, 1,200 in Victoria, and 2,950 in St Patrick. This suggested to the PNM that, although they were not winning these areas outright, and probably never would, they were at least winning some adherents among the Indian community.

15 'Candid Comments', TG, March 16, 1958.
16 The PNM improved its position among rural Negroes considerably in 1958, especially in Tobago and the eastern counties. The Party had been giving substantial attention to Tobago, which they had narrowly lost – by 342 votes – in 1956. The DLP claimed that the PNM had used the Treasury to wage its campaign in the island ward. While the political significance of Tobago was not lost, the PNM was genuinely interested in correcting the neglect with which the island had been treated in the past.

But it did not follow that all the additional support which the PNM obtained in these areas came from Hindus. In 1958 there were many non-Indians who had switched to the PNM as racial polarization increased. Moreover, the PNM was represented by Indian candidates in two of these areas, and it is difficult to determine whether Indians who voted for the PNM gave their support to the Party itself or to these candidates. The overall increase of voting support for the PNM in 1958 could be easily explained as a displacement phenomenon. The withdrawal of independents and small parties from the electoral fray released a substantial number of voters, many of whom were not necessarily anti-PNM in 1956. Some who had been intensely cross-pressured in 1956 had resolved their indecision in favour of the Church. Now that the Church was no longer openly hostile to the PNM, many were available for mobilization by the Party.[17] Similarly, a substantial number who had supported patrons and parties which had since merged into the DLP had refused to follow their leaders, and had switched to the PNM.[18] The contention that the DLP's vote had decreased was invalid. The DLP did not exist in 1956, and it was sheer statistical chicanery to argue that all or most non-PNM votes in 1956 were 'potential' DLP votes. Only on the basis of such an assumption could Williams have maintained that the DLP vote had decreased by over 14,000.

THE APPEAL TO THE WEST INDIAN NATION

One of the more dramatic but unfortunate sequels to the election was the historic and far-reaching address delivered by Dr Williams on April 1, 1958. The address, entitled 'The Dangers Facing Trinidad and Tobago and the West Indian Nation' was an attempt to account for the defeat of the PNM in the federal election. The reason, declared Williams, was 'race, pure and unadulterated'. In certain areas where the PNM was literally decimated, the correlation between ethnicity and voting was almost total. A breakdown of

17   Catholic authorities had warmly approved Williams' move to squash the zeal of those who wished to erect a monument to him in commemmoration of his contribution to the political emancipation of the community. As the *Catholic Weekly* (March 23, 1957) declared editrially, 'His action comes as a virtual tonic to those who have been languishing for this sort of spirit among public leaders. ... It is a sign of true greatness when a leader does not lose sight of his mission, which is to strive for the welfare of those he leads and represents, even at the expense of self.'

18   While the non-PNM vote in the capital city was 18,851 in 1956, in 1958 it fell to 12,474 – a significant number nonetheless. The PNM's total vote in these areas also declined by about 2,000, but this can be explained by the lower voter turn-out in these constituencies, averaging 60 per cent in 1958, compared to 78 per cent in 1956. The unattractiveness of PNM candidates might also have affected the election voting figures.

TABLE IV
Ethnicity and voting in 1958 federal election:
selected electoral and polling divisions

Division	Number of Indians	DLP vote
Tunapuna	3,427	3,402
Curepe and St Augustine	3,140	4,284
Tacarigua	948	911
Arouca	1,567	1,454
D'Abadie	313	272
Piarco	277	300
Caroni	1,272	1,313
Total	10,944	11,936

TABLE V
Ethnicity and voting in 1958 federal
election: selected polling booths

Polling division	Indians	DLP votes
52	135	135
53	20	21
54	169	170
55	235	228
56	184	204
57	245	249
60	315	313
63	56	52
25	54	54
26	51	54
29	49	50
34	106	103
36	306	298
39	117	116
40	117	115
17	206	205
122	243	241

the vote in certain polling divisions 'chosen at random' by Williams revealed
the pattern shown in Tables IV and V.[19] The figures spoke for themselves
said Williams.[20] They showed the effects of the promises which were made to
the Indians that victory would mean an Indian prime minister and governing
general. Williams disclosed that during the campaign a letter addressed to 'My
dear Brother Indian', and signed, 'Yours truly Indian', had been circulated

19 PNM *Weekly*, April 21, 1958.
20 *Ibid*. He added, 'By hook or by crook, they brought out the Indian vote – the young
and old, the literate and illiterate, the lame, the halt and the blind.'

throughout the countryside. The letter accused Williams of 'favouring his own kind in the Cabinet', and of selecting 'a few Indians merely to mislead other Indians into supporting his movement in order to have a majority'. It concluded, 'If, my dear brother, you have realized these occurrences, and the shaky position in which our Indian people are placed, woe unto our Indian nation in the next ten years.'[21]

Williams saw this appeal to the Indian 'nation' as an insult to the people of the West Indies. 'The Indian nation is in India', he snapped, 'it is the India of socialism, of Afro-Asian unity, the India of Bandung.' Indians in Trinidad, far from being genuine Indians, were a 'recalcitrant and hostile minority masquerading as the Indian nation, and prostituting the name of India for its selfish, reactionary political ends.'[22] The growing tendency towards racial chauvinism, towards the exploitation of race as the basis of political power, was the great danger facing Trinidad and the West Indies.

Politicians like Victor Bryan and Albert Gomes also came in for their share of public excoriation. It was noted that while they had once bitterly attacked the Indians, they were now prepared to become 'Maraj's lick-spittles' in order to hold on to power. 'Thus do men sell their soul to gain their political world.' These men had talked loudly about Federation, and yet had forged an unholy alliance with a Party which was determined to destroy the Federation. Williams, in fact, now put himself on record as believing that a substantial sector of the Indian élite was still opposed to Federation: 'Many of them are opposed to Federation ... and who will forget the fanatical Indian stand against freedom of movement in Trinidad?'[23] No one who had heard Williams' speech could doubt that it would have significant political consequences.

But the fundamental question is, why did he, as Chief Minister of the country, make such an address? Was it merely the rash speech of a man motivated by anger and pique, a man and a Party who could not accept defeat gracefully?[24] Or was there some clever and calculating purpose to it all? Williams himself explained:

Tonight's analysis is not an attempt to juggle with election statistics. It is a factual, cold-blooded analysis of a situation which poses a dangerous threat to the stability and progress of our country and the new nation. As the party responsible for the initiation of an attempt to bring sanity, political morality, decency and self-respect

---

21 *Ibid.*   22 *Ibid.*   23 *Ibid.*
24 Many party members wept bitterly when the results were known. The DLP victory was a shocking affront to their pride. As the party organ admitted, 'Tears flowed freely that night, and the following day, there were thousands whose spirits were droopy. ... Since then, there has emerged the will and confidence that never again will a PNM victory be taken for granted.' *Ibid.*

to this country, it is our duty to warn the electorate and the people of this country of the situation which threatens to engulf the progress that has been achieved.[25]

Leading members of the Party still insist that their only purpose was to bring the racial issue out in the open so that the country might face it in a mature fashion. But it was clear that behind the glitter of cold statistics there were also hidden propaganda appeals to the Negro population, both in Trinidad and the West Indies. Williams betrayed his purpose openly when he declared:

We sympathize deeply with those misguided unfortunates who, *having ears to hear, heard not, having eyes to see, saw not*, who were complacent, for whom everything was in the bag, who had the DLP covered, who were too tired or busy to vote, who wanted a car to take them to the polling station around the corner. ... They will understand hereafter that he or she who stays home and does not come out to vote PNM, in effect votes DLP. They have learnt their lesson. Today they regret it bitterly, and they are *already swearing that it must never happen again*.[26]

It was a clever attempt to rouse the Negro population from their apathy and lethargy. They were fighting among themselves and treating the vote irresponsibly while the Indian community was mobilizing all its energies to capture power. Sympathy for the Movement was not enough. 'It is only the actual votes that matter in the long run! Nothing else!'[27]

Even if one were to be charitable and absolve the PNM élite from the charge of openly inciting racial counter-mobilization, one cannot condone the tactlessness of the address – especially when racial passions were already so inflamed. Williams spoke in his capacity as leader of the PNM, but he was also the country's Chief Minister. It would have been more prudent for an address of the sort to have been given by another official of the Party. It was one thing to be a psephologist in an academic treatise designed for a limited audience, but quite another to make that type of appeal in the public squares. The unsophisticated man in the street was bound to interpret it as a declaration of racial counter-exclusivism. When DLP parliamentarians in 1960 attempted to do the same thing – use sociology to make political appeals – Williams would accuse them of being 'stink with racialism'.

Indians in the Party élite were acutely and visibly embarrassed by the statement. It appears that they had not been consulted on the issue. A few of them in fact protested quite vigorously to Williams, and two Indian cabinet members threatened to resign, as did another non-Negro minister who was known to be dissatisfied with the outburst.[28] One of these ministers, Dr W.

25   *Ibid.*   26   *Ibid.* (Italics supplied).   27   *Ibid.*, editorial.
28   All three denied rumours of resignation, but it is well known that these ministers were

Mahabir, felt that the unfortunate effects of Williams' address had to be corrected, if possible, lest the community become enveloped by violent racial strife. He warned the PNM:

The challenge ... now is to stand firm ... against the temptations to fight racialism with racialism, because if we choose to fight racialism with racialism, the only possible result will be death, destruction and despair in this little country of ours, whose greatest boast to the outside world has always been the ability of our many races to dwell together in unity.

Let us all pledge jointly now, as a first step in the amelioration of an increasingly tense situation, that the two obscene and obsolete words 'nigger' and 'coolie' will be herewith banished from our vocabulary. ... Let us learn the lessons from our election experiences, but let us be forever mindful of the fact that PNM is something more than an election-winning machine, that it is, as I have said before, a way of life in which I firmly believe.[29]

Williams' address elicited frenzied outcries from the Indian community and the press. He was accused of using race to maintain his slipping power, of 'soiling other people's clothes while licking his wounds', of 'unleashing the mad dogs of racial strife'. Maraj declared that Williams would have to 'destroy every East Indian in Trinidad because we do not intend to sit with our arms folded and let him do what he wants'. What galled Maraj was the fact that the PNM had selected the Indians as the acceptable social target rather than the Europeans, who had rejected the PNM just as completely. Why not attack them?[30] It was argued that the statistics could also have been used to show that the DLP was defeated by a racial vote in the urban areas. Others agreed that the Indians were indeed clannish, but felt that their behaviour had to be viewed as a natural urge on the part of a minority to preserve its religion and culture, and to advance itself as a group.

The defeat of the PNM in the 1958 federal elections and in the two by-elections which followed could be ascribed to a number of factors apart from race. It is generally agreed that the Party began its campaign too late – approximately one month before the election. The fact that it ran a weak team also strained the loyalties of its followers somewhat. The PNM candidates

deeply chagrined by their exclusion from the inner circle of the cabinet. They were suspected of being either pro-American or partial to the DLP. The splits in the country were beginning to appear in the cabinet as well.

29   TG, April 23, 1958.
30   'The plain truth is that he is afraid to tread on the corns of the White people; but he is trying to sow the seeds of dissension between Indians and Negroes. We must not allow that day to come when we have to go into civil war because one man wants to keep at the height of his power.' *Ibid.*

proved unable to hold their own against the old chieftains whom they believed had been buried with the 'old order'. It is also clear that the government's 'tax like fire' budget just four months before the election was extremely injudicious, even if indicative of its honesty. The lower-class urban and rural voter especially was alienated by the new taxes, since he generally lacked the perspective to integrate his needs for social improvement with the corresponding necessity to pay increased taxation. Many who expected dramatic evidence that their aspirations were being fulfilled were already expressing disillusionment. The promised jobs, schools, and houses were still only being talked about. It also seems fair to say that the verbal and other excesses of the PNM alienated many who ordinarily would have identified with it rather than with the DLP.

But in the final analysis there is no escaping the fact that the DLP defeated the PNM principally because of the way in which the constituency boundaries were drawn. Anyone who had taken time to look would have seen that the PNM could not possibly have won more than five seats, unless they had assumed that the PNM's magic had exorcised the racial monster. A little less than half of its voting support was bottled up in the three urban and suburban areas of the capital city, and the remainder was so distributed that it could easily have been swamped by the Indian vote. It should also be recalled that the PNM had won four or five seats in 1956 because of splits within the Indian electorate. With many of these votes now largely solidified behind the DLP in enlarged constituencies, the results were predictable. The PNM vowed that never again would it leave the business of drawing electoral boundaries to a neutral electoral commission. The Party was also determined that the rural voter must in the future be more resolutely wooed.[31]

One further comment might be made: not only were independents and splinter parties completely routed, but the voters had implicitly rejected the one-party system, which many had feared in 1956. The two-party system seemed to have established itself at last.

31   C.L.R. James reasoned that if the rural voter were to be brought into the Movement much more had to be done to open channels of communication to the countryside. James was especially concerned that the Party newspaper did not have much circulation among rural readers: 'A political upheaval always creates new strata of readers and we believe that what took place in 1956 has created a new reading population which, so far, no attempts have been made to satisfy.' *Nation*, Dec. 6, 1958.

13
The constitutional imbroglio 1957-60

Given the intensity of racial feeling which the election had evoked among the population, it was to be expected that any attempt to alter the 1956 constitution would be fiercely opposed by those who stood to lose by the proposed changes. It will be recalled that the PNM had attacked the constitution as being 'bogus and fraudulent', but that they had promised to work with it until change became feasible. Within a year after they assumed power, proposals had been submitted to the Colonial Office for reform, the stated aim being to bring Trinidad's constitution into line with constitutions of other units of the Federation, mainly Jamaica and Barbados. By the middle of 1958, however, the Colonial Office had not stated publicly whether it approved or disapproved of the submitted proposals.

The PNM did not seem anxious to force the issue while its affairs at both governmental and party level were still disordered. But with the budget and the federal elections out of the way, the Party was ready to force the hand of the Colonial Office. In June of 1958 the government brought proposals before the Legislature aimed at eliminating the power of the Governor and the Crown to disallow laws passed by the people's representatives, in so far as these related to the internal affairs of the colony. Other major requests were for the creation of a Ministry of Home Affairs to control *inter alia* the police, and for the introduction of cabinet government based on the Westminster model.

These were far-reaching changes, and to the opponents of the PNM it appeared that the government was using its strategic advantages to consolidate itself as Nkrumah had done in Ghana. The government was accused of 'stampeding the country into constitutional change' when the Colonial Office had not made up its mind about the initial requests, and of employing 'salami tactics' to create a party-police state. Resentment was also aroused by the government's failure to ventilate the constitutional issue before it was brought before the House. It was maintained that the government had a responsibility to take the public and the opposition into its confidence. The DLP should not only have been consulted but invited to participate in discussions with the Colonial Office, since the issue was not purely a party matter.

The claim of the PNM that it had to keep abreast of constitutional changes in Jamaica was not acceptable to the Opposition. Jamaica, they argued, was not the proper yardstick to use. Jamaicans were a homogeneous people; the parties, though highly critical of each other, represented the same ethnic interests, and the constitutional issue could thus be debated without involving ethnic conflict. In a plural society it was not possible to apply bookish theories about what a democratic constitution ought to be.

The proposal to remove the police from under the control of an official representing the Colonial Office alarmed the opposition. When this request was conjoined with the demand for a politically appointed attorney general, suspicions were further aroused. The PNM denied that a politically appointed attorney general was part of any plan to establish a police state: 'We advocate this because we feel that the Government, as distinct from the Governor, is entitled to have official political advice, not merely legal advice – political advice in a legal sense or legal advice in a political sense. ... That advice should be available to the Party in power and to the Government through a legal man chosen by it, who represents the political views of the Party, and can advise on the political issues, or the legal issues involved in the political activities of the Government.'[1] The opposition feared, however, that with the power to initiate prosecutions in the hands of a politically appointed justice department, the predominantly Negro police force would be used against minority groups.

Some of the opposition's fiercest attacks were trained on the government's proposal to remove the Crown and its local representatives from the internal politics of the country. To the 'royalist-loyalist' element this was rank disloyalty and decidedly revolutionary. 'The Governor is the symbol of colonialism in this country. Remove him and you remove the first block. We do not want power taken from the hands of the representatives of the Queen and put in the hands of a modern Fuehrer in Trinidad and Tobago. We want to save this country from the fate of Haiti, and from what is happening in Ghana.'[2] If the power to disallow legislation were to be withdrawn, there was

1 Dr Patrick Solomon, *Nation*, Dec. 4, 1959.
2 Lionel Seukeran, *Hansard*, Nov. 21, 1958, p. 35. The same member declared quite frankly a few months earlier, 'We are trying to remain a colonial territory, and we do not intend to take the gates that would lead us to Moscow. We are heading for the gates of London to bring security to the West Indies.' TG, March 3, 1958.

nothing to stop the government from passing a punitive bill to deal with its political opponents.

The PNM's growing intransigence over Chaguaramas gave rise to additional fears that the PNM was 'eastward bound'. What would the government do if the United States and the Colonial Office refused to retreat on the bases issue? Would they proceed unilaterally and revoke the treaty, thereby confronting the Crown with open rebellion?[3] Was this not part of a plan to take Trinidad out of the Western defence system? Was the Chief Minister not being treasonable when he declared that his loyalties were to the people of Trinidad and Tobago, and not to the Crown? Had he not taken a loyalty oath to the Crown? What frightened this element most of all was the threat to the country's economic prosperity. 'We depend absolutely for our prosperity on the arrangements made with Great Britain in regard to sugar and citrus, and if these powers asking for the severance from the British Empire are obtained, then we would find ourselves in the most miserable position we have ever been in. You will not get any money from abroad.'[4]

The European business community was seething with unrest. The Chamber of Commerce complained that the PNM had given scant evidence of its willingness to tolerate opposing views, however well intentioned, and advised the government to pause and review the colony's situation before making further attempts to secure rapid constitutional advancement, lest investors be frightened away. In its haste to establish a 'modernized system of party government, the PNM appears to have put on blinkers, and [is] therefore missing or ignoring ... side issues of varying importance that cannot be and should not be ignored'.[5]

The government's reply to the Chamber of Commerce was that its views represented those of a minority; democracy implied that the government should represent the will of the majority. The Minister of Industry and Commerce (himself a successful white businessman) pointed out:

The members of this Chamber are perhaps one of the smallest minority groups in this country, and therefore it could hardly be expected that the Government should express the will of your minority. It may be that the feeling on the part of those

---

3　Williams had declared that the agreement was never ratified by the Legislative Council and never legally filed. It was also noted that leases of Crown land were only valid for thiry years. The present lease, made for ninety-nine years, was therefore illegal. Williams had insisted that he was not prepared to connive or tolerate such illegalities.

4　Neal Fahey, TG, June 14, 1958. Fahey himself was one of the colony's largest landowners and citrus producers.

5　TG, March 20, 1959.

members of your Chamber to which you have made reference, derives from a sense of disappointment over the fact that the majority view which the Government is constrained to follow, does not, in all cases, agree with the minority view of the members of your Chamber.[6]

It was this majoritarianism that minority communities in Trinidad found so frustrating; and, interestingly enough, it was on this very issue of democratic majoritarianism that the DLP tried to entrap the government.

Some members of the DLP were beginning to feel that it was politically unwise to make a blanket objection to constitutional reform: agree to change, they argued, but insist that new elections be held before the changes could be introduced. The issue on which they based this new stand was the nominated system. The PNM, they argued, was using 'undemocratic' methods to give it the majority position which it did not secure at the polls. As one opposition MLC put it, 'A prerequisite to Cabinet Government is to have a fully elected House. ... The first reform needed in this country is the removal of the nominated element from the single chamber legislature.'[7] It was a clever strategy. The DLP knew that the PNM would be embarrassed by this offer of co-operation to abandon the nominated system, as the PNM itself was pledged to do. The government was urged to go to the country and ask for a mandate to introduce full responsible government. The DLP, buoyed by their success in the federal elections, were confident that they would win a general election if one were called, and their strategy from 1958 onward was to try to get the Colonial Office to help them overthrow the PNM.

The government agreed that a change of the nominated system was a fundamental issue which would require electoral approval, since it necessarily involved the creation of a second chamber, but they refused to go to the polls until their promises to the electorate were fulfilled. Nevertheless they were clearly on the defensive. The changes they were proposing were substantial enough to take to the country. It is true that their Manifesto had pledged to introduce internal self-government, but they had also pledged to eliminate the nominated system and introduce a second chamber. What they were now proposing was that the Colonial Office institutionalize the precedent established in 1956 whereby the leader of the largest party in the House would have the right to choose a certain number of nominated representatives whom, technically, the Governor was still free to appoint in his own right. This was demanded as a safeguard against the possibility that the Colonial Office might reverse its instructions to the Governor, who could then nominate non-party

6   *Ibid.*
7   Lionel Seukeran, *Hansard*, Nov. 21, 1958, p. 31.

people. By the use of such a legalistic *coup* the Colonial Office could in fact have brought down the government.

While it is true that the Hindus, the Europeans, the established press, and the business community at times assumed an 'anti-nationalist' stand which Williams could legitimately describe as 'obscurantist, recalcitrant and reactionary', minority groups did have reason to be alienated from the PNM. The Party would certainly have had less difficulty in mobilizing the entire community behind it if its leaders had displayed a greater degree of patience and tolerance, provoked though they admittedly were. But by 1958 Dr Williams had become even more abusive and righteous. He attacked the white creole community when it stopped the PNM's winning streak in municipal elections, and warned them, 'We will be coming for you next time. ... PNM bulldozers will be digging into the hillsides and God help any minority groups that stand in the way.'[8] The DLP's victory, said Williams, posed a fundamental problem for the white community. Were they going to oppose to the bitter end the PNM's inter-racial progressive nationalism, or were they going to accept the invitation to come in as equal citizens?

Williams was deeply galled by the fact that the white upper class had now categorically turned against the PNM. Many of the younger members of the community who had earlier rebuked their elders for being so resolutely opposed to the PNM had by now gone over into hostile and sullen opposition. Polarization was becoming complete. Many, including PNM partisans, were fearful that if some real effort was not made to adjust group differences, the community would soon be engulfed in serious ethnic strife. Through the medium of the *Nation*, of which he was editor, C.L.R. James strove to woo the white community out of its hostility to the PNM. He urged them to view the Party in proper historical perspective:

The PNM is not some monstrous misfortune which has overtaken the unfortunate upper class in Trinidad and Tobago. Something like the PNM was due in Trinidad sooner or later. It is one of the features of modern society. ... It must be understood that political awakening and party politics came late to Trinidad after years of failure. Twenty years of nationalist and democratic development were accumulated underground in frustration and suppressed anger until it burst out in 1956. *It is in full tide*; it will not be halted nor diverted into frivolous or dead-end channels by the reckless and consciousless plots and manoeuvres of political desperadoes.[9]

James urged the white upper class to disestablish itself from DLP extremism

8   TG, Nov. 5, 1958. By November 1958 the PNM had control of thirty-two of the thirty-three municipal council seats. The winning DLP candidate, a prominent French creole, contested a constituency inhabited largely by European elements.

9   'Our Upper Classes', *Nation*, Feb. 28, 1959 (italics supplied). The PNM *Weekly* became the *Nation* in 1958 when James took over the editorship.

and participate in the political process in a constructive way. Instead of hoping in silence for a crash that would invite colonialist intervention, they should try to understand that the nationalist movement was going through a *necessary* phase which had to be accommodated. The upper class should try to provide a sobering influence on the community; instead, they 'pretend not to notice':

Frightened by the power of the PNM, and with an instinctive repulsion from its mass support, disappointed that the DLP has not developed into the conservative opposition that they hoped for, they think or behave as if they have no interest in politics. ... In the perpetual lies and scandals with which the opposition press bombards the PNM, your voice is silent. No elder statesman, no prominent industrialist, no distinguished social figure, no member of an old and well established family ... raises a single word in protest. ... Is all of Trinidad, which has what is called a stake in the country, so sunk in cynicism, in mean self-interest, in indifference to the public weal, in this stupid belief that 'anything goes' if the PNM is somehow defeated? Do they believe if this happens, the good old days will return?[10]

It is clear, however, that James understood the reason for the frustration and desperation which had overtaken the Indians and the white upper class. The activities of the Opposition were not all due to spite, obscurantism, maliciousness, and recalcitrance. Fear, mistrust, and reciprocal hostility were basic elements of the unfurling oppositionist drama.[11]

THE CABINET CRISIS

The Colonial Office went a long way towards meeting the PNM's demand for changes in the constitution. Cabinet government and most of the conventions relating to it were conceded. The Colonial Office had not, however, made up its mind about the transfer of the police, nor did it agree to take away altogether the power of the governor to withhold his assent to legislation. The governor was to be advised that henceforth this power was to be used only on advice from the Crown, whose power to legislate by Order-in-Council for the colony was left intact. The constitutional arrangements were scheduled to take effect in June of 1959. The PNM, however, at the very last minute decided that it would not accept cabinet government without control of the police.

10 'The New Desperadoes', *ibid.*, May 22, 1959.
11 After breaking with the PNM, James acknowledged that the Party provoked minority elements. He referred to the 'racial fanaticism of many in that party (chiefly some leaders and a portion of the rank and file, the lowest gangster types whom the gangster leaders ... miseducated)', *West Indians of East Indian Descent,* Ibis Pamphlet no. 1, San Fernando, Trinidad, 1965, p. 7.

It appears that the Colonial Office had given the DLP firm guarantees that it would not hand over the police. The PNM, however, took the view that there was no reason why the police should not be transferred. For the Colonial Office to withhold it was to say, in effect, that it had no confidence in the PNM. As Williams declared, 'The Colonial Office would not want to be in a position to say that it would give control of the police to Bustamante and the JLP and will deny it to Williams and the PNM. They could not say it. ... Trinidad is not British Guiana. Trinidad is not tainted with any dangerous ideology. ... Law and order are the last bastions of colonialism and it is necessary for the PNM to control it.'[12] In reply to the DLP observation that Trinidad was not Jamaica, he noted that control of the police had been handed over to elected ministers in multiracial Malaya and Singapore.

The extreme and uncompromising anti-colonialism of the PNM drove Gomes, who was at one time one of the stoutest opponents of colonialism, to assume the role of defender of imperialist intervention: 'There are times when the popular will can be so egregiously wrong as to justify redressive intervention by the extraneous authority. ... PNM has compromised itself and the popular movement in the West Indies. *It has established the need for continuing the presence of the British Government in the West Indies.* Opposition movements in particular have to thank their stars that they still have the parental shelter of the British authority to whom to look in their hour of travail.'[13]

But the Colonial Office soon found that it was in no position to resist the PNM on the police issue and decided to capitulate. Its hands were tied by the fact that the Governor, 'the man on the spot', had admitted that there was no reason why the police should not be transferred. With the Governor giving the PNM full support on most of the issues which arose during the period, the DLP had little hope of out-manoeuvring the PNM. The DLP, betrayed and outfoxed, could do no more than accept the assurances of the Colonial Office that there were still enough existing safeguards to prevent the PNM from misusing its newly gained prerogatives. The poor showing of the opposition during the crisis was due not only to the power of the PNM, which must have impressed the Colonial Office, but also to the weakness of the DLP, which never functioned as a cohesive unit. The DLP showed itself completely bankrupt once the Colonial Office decided to concede.[14]

The Colonial Office, it appears, had agreed in principle to transfer the police but had hoped to extract some concessions from the PNM on Chaguara-

---

12   *Nation*, July 10, 1959.
13   TG, April 1, 1959 (italics supplied).
14   By calling off the cabinet day celebrations, Williams had clearly forced the hand of

mas.[15] But the Chief Minister was not in a compromising mood. As he stated, 'I was not going to sacrifice my fundamental principles for a little power.' The fundamental purposes were to eliminate the influence of Downing Street from the politics of the country and to get the Americans out of Chaguaramas. Williams made it clear that full independence was now the goal of the PNM. 'Cabinet Government and the Premiership are ... but additional instruments for the constitutional but relentless achievement of this aim.' He deliberately threw down the gauntlet to the DLP. The central issue was treasonable colonialism or independence with dignity: 'The only alternative to the road to Independence is the road back to colonialism ... *the issue ... has nothing to do with race at all*, though race might complicate the objective social, political, and economic issues that are involved.'[16] And the road to Independence lay through Chaguaramas!

Chaguaramas had now become the central issue in the political struggle between the parties. To the PNM the reluctance of the Americans and the British to sit down and renegotiate the bases agreement was symbolic of an unwillingness to recognize that Trinidad in 1959 was vastly different from Trinidad in 1941. 'What hangs in the balance is whether this territory must submit to a new colonialism just at the time when it is making every effort to free itself from the old.'[17] The struggle was being waged not only on behalf of

the Colonial Office, which was becoming aware of the massive popular backing which the PNM could mobilize on almost any issue. DLP members were encouraged to endorse the police transfer in return for a firm promise that the Colonial Office would insist on an independent boundary commission before the next general election.

15 In his 'Reflections on the Caribbean Economic Community', written six years later, Williams had this to say about the incident: 'Mr Amery came and began all sorts of private discussions with the Governor and senior civil servants before he saw the Ministers. When he eventually condescended to see me, I made it plain to him ... that I saw no constitutional problem involved, and that I read into his mission an attempt to use a bogus ... constitutional issue in order to extract a concession from us on Chaguaramas. ... I would not discuss Chaguaramas on any terms while the constitutional issue ... remained unsettled. When he settled the issue, ... I let him have my views.' *Nation*, Oct. 8, 1965.

16 TG, July 22, 1959. Italics supplied. As Williams said on another occasion: 'I want everybody to know that the Government of the PNM of which I have the honour to be the leader, is not at any time going to be bought for $766,000 or for that matter $760 million. I am afraid the issues involved are worth far more than a few thousand dollars.' *Nation*, July 8, 1959.

17 C.L.R. James, *Nation*, Aug. 8, 1959. James, who carried the burden of the anti-American attack, saying things which the Premier could not say, accused the American government of 'incredible thick-headedness and bovine obstinacy. A sense of power and the arrogance of dominion seems to shut off the functioning of certain parts of the brain.' *Ibid.*

Trinidad alone, but for the West Indies as a whole. 'Trinidad, as the "spinal cord" of the West Indian national movement, is going to lead in giving the West Indies some conception of dignity, some conception of importance, some conception of self-reliance as the PNM has given to Trinidad and Tobago.'[18]

The country was hardly given time to digest the constitutional changes that had recently been introduced. In keeping with its promise that proposals for future constitutional changes would first be subjected to public and bi-partisan parliamentary scrutiny, the government appointed a Select Commit-tee on Constitutional Reform in June of 1959 and invited the public to submit memoranda on the question of political reform.

The PNM's new proposals were far-reaching. The most controversial de-mands were for a bicameral system, for a redrawing of the electoral boun-daries to permit an increase of six seats in the Legislature, and the appoint-ment of a West Indian governor on the advice of the cabinet. The most crucial demand of all was that a two-thirds majority of the Lower House be given the power to amend the constitution.

The DLP, strangely enough, refused to submit a prepared memorandum, and it was difficult for the public to know what specific proposals (if any) they had on the question of reform. This irresponsibility was compounded by the decision of the Party to boycott the debate on the Committee's report because of the government's refusal to allow them the freedom to choose their own delegation to the Colonial Office.[19] It is indeed difficult to decide where justice lay in this case. The PNM took the view that if the DLP was not suf-ficiently alert to its proper role as a responsible opposition, it should not expect the government to treat it as such. The DLP had forfeited the right to name its delegates. The *Guardian* took the opposite view. A tutelary government had a responsibility not only to govern, but also to ensure that a responsible opposition was cultivated: 'However ineffective the present Legislative Op-position, the correct procedure should at all times be followed if the Govern-ment is sincere in its desire to encourage the development of a functioning two-party system. The very weakness of the present Opposition furnishes grounds for special care in observing all the conventions of parliamentary usage.'[20]

The position of the DLP became clear at the negotiations in London. They

18   *Ibid.*, July 8, 1959.
19   The government had chosen someone who was not in good standing with the DLP, having broken ranks on the police issue. According to the DLP, the government had disregarded all established parliamentary conventions in its effort to split its ranks. The purpose of the boycott was to dramatize the opposition's unwillingness to give its imprimatur to any further constitutional changes under a PNM government.
20   TG, Oct. 10, 1959.

strongly opposed the proposal to alter the electoral boundaries on the ground that it was a palpable attempt on the part of the ruling party to obtain a virtual one-party system by electoral gerrymander. The PNM, it was argued, had seen the voting trends in the 1958 federal and 1959 county council elections, and were seeking to carve out new constituencies that would entrench them indefinitely.[21] Maraj warned that any such manoeuvre would lead inevitably to 'national convulsions'. If the boundaries had to be redrawn, an independent commission, recruited from either the United Kingdom or the United Nations, must be assigned the task.

The demand for a locally appointed Governor was also bitterly opposed. The DLP had been extremely unhappy with Sir Edward Beetham, who, generally speaking, tended to sympathize with nationalist forces. Apart from his apprehensions about punitive taxation of the oil industry, and the PNM's 'extremism' on Chaguaramas, Beetham had few difficulties with his cabinet.[22] But to the DLP, Beetham was a nightmare. By refusing to intervene against the PNM, the Governor, they said, 'was out of harmony with the rights and prerogatives he enjoys by provision of the Constitution'. The Governor was not yet a 'constitutional monarch' as Beetham seemed to imagine. If a Crown-appointed Governor was so partial to the PNM, the situation could only worsen if the PNM were given the right to name the next Governor. But the PNM was determined to make the Governor a constitutional monarch who would act only on the advice of his ministers. The Party had no patience with legal niceties about the differences between the roles of the heads of state in dependent and independent territories. As far as nationalists were concerned, a Crown-appointed Governor no longer had the right or authority to speak on behalf of the West Indian people.

The request to allow the Legislature to amend the constitution by a simple two-thirds majority in the Lower House was greeted with a storm of objections from opposition elements who claimed that if this recommendation was accepted there was nothing to prevent a party commanding such a majority from amending the constitution as it wished. The proposed second chamber also provoked a great deal of controversy. The DLP denounced the second chamber idea as being 'reactionary and unprogressive', and as a 'departure

---

21   The county council elections of 1959 had again divided the country roughly along racial lines. The parties almost tied in terms of seats won. Though the PNM again improved its position in the countryside, most of its support came from the counties of St George and Tobago.

22   The farewell address made by the Premier to Beetham testifies to the warmth of the relations between them. Beetham was later to take up an ambassadorial position with the Trinidad government. He also became a director of one of the country's oil companies. TG, March 10, 1959.

from one of the avowed purposes for which the Federation was established – the reduction of the size and cost of the apparatus of Government in the territories'.[23] A senate nominated in the manner proposed by the PNM would 'almost certainly become a means whereby the ruling party will be able to endow certain of its supporters with the elegant trappings of high political office, while remaining mere puppets of its over-riding control and authority'.[24] This was a valid observation, since the PNM had altered its basic position on the manner in which senators were to be chosen. In Williams' 1955–6 constitutional proposals, senators were to be appointed by vested interests themselves.[25]

Interestingly enough, the Colonial Office came out in support of the DLP against the senate idea. The PNM was aghast. Williams let it be known that if vested interests, to whom the concession was principally directed, did not want the second chamber, he would not 'stick his neck out' to force the hand of the Colonial Office. He also expressed dissatisfaction with the fact that vested interests had retreated into silence even though the government had appealed to them to speak out on national issues. The *Guardian* was, however, quite just when it maintained that the 'silence and cringing aloofness of the Chamber and other responsible organizations and individuals' was due to fear.[26] The Premier had shown himself so intolerant of views which from his perspectives seemed 'anti-national' that many who would normally have voiced a critical opinion had retreated into fearful silence. As an economic interest group, the Chamber of Commerce was reluctant to go on record on any issue with which it was in fundamental disagreement with the PNM.

The constitutional issue dragged on for the remaining months of 1959 and into 1960. Neither party budged from its basic position. The leader of the DLP maintained that had it 'not been for the special curcumstances which exist in the country today, we ... would surely be further on the road to Independence':

The actions of the Government over the last three years ... could not possibly inspire confidence. We have witnessed the Government's high-handed dealings with statutory boards and local bodies; their infiltration of the Civil Service; their tampering with the trade unions; their litigation with the Telephone Company; their intemperate attacks on individuals and concerns whose only fault would seem

23   TG, Nov. 12, 1959.
24   *Ibid*. The senate of eighteen was to be nominated by the Governor on the advice of the Premier. Seven senators were to come from the economic and religious interests of the community.
25   Cf. chap. 6.
26   TG, Sept. 23, 1959.

to be in their own power and prestige which they now enjoy. It would seem that the Government does not like opposition whether from political parties or from individual persons, and that they are determined to destroy every possible centre of opposition and resistance. We have registered increasingly that there exists in all of this a sinister pattern from which there emerges only the desire for power and more power, irrespective of any other consideration, even of the strangling economy of the country; and we have reluctantly, for some time now, come to the sad and unavoidable conclusion that in all of this there is a dictatorship in the making, and conditions are coming about in which freedom will not flourish. We stand by our declaration that there must be a general election before effect is given to reforms.[27]

This was also the line adopted by the Colonial Office, which now urged both parties to accept a compromise. The DLP was persuaded to agree to the proposed increase of seats, the new boundaries to be determined by an independent boundary commission. The Colonial Secretary, Mr Iain Macleod, suggested to the PNM that it should be left to whichever party that formed the government after the election to determine whether to accept fully or partially, or indeed reject, the constitutional changes to which he had agreed in principle. This gambit was extremely clever. It seemed a perfectly democratic and fair issue on which to take a stand; 'no reforms before the people have spoken'. Macleod was either gambling that Williams would accept, and perhaps lose the election, or refuse, thereby making it possible to hold up further reforms indefinitely. The PNM appeared trapped, since it did not feel confident enough to call a snap election.[28]

The PNM leader despatched a strong letter to the Colonial Secretary, whom he accused of conspiring to bring down his government. He asserted:

Your proposition will only strengthen the prevailing impression, nurtured by the 'crisis' which attended the inauguration of the Cabinet system, that every effort is being made to force upon us at all costs an election at the earliest possible moment, to give the Opposition an election issue, and to set back the movement for self-government to the degree that it is associated with the PNM. The proposition can serve only to maintain the suzerainty of the Colonial Office with all the restrictions

27 TG, Dec. 2, 1959.
28 Williams maintained that the people did not want an election at this time. Given the tension in the country, elections would only lead to violence. The country had already witnessed too many elections in a short space of time. Moreover, elections would only disrupt the government's development programme. He denied, however, that the PNM was afraid of being rejected at the polls. But as we shall argue later on, the PNM was anticipating a very close battle with the DLP. TG, June 12, 1959.

therein entailed on colonial emancipation and colonial development. ... You will appreciate that this is a situation which cannot be allowed to continue.[29]

There was no need for an election to decide the issue of bicameralism, added Williams, since the electorate had endorsed it in 1956. This, nevertheless, was a rather weak claim to make, since Williams was prepared earlier to abandon the second chamber which he had insisted was a 'gratuitous concession' to the vested interests. Moreover, as noted above, the senate now being advocated, along with some of the other recommendations relating to the size of the chamber, were quite different from the proposals contained in the Williams petition on constitutional reform.

The Premier also flatly opposed the idea of an independent boundary commission, whether externally or internally recruited. This was a chance that the PNM could not afford to take. To accept this was to commit political suicide, though Williams could not phrase the issue in these terms. Instead he noted that it would be difficult to get independent men, and that deadlock might arise between principals on the acceptability of nominees. A crisis might also arise if one party refused to accept the decision of the commission. The government would accept nothing less than the method used in Jamaica – a select committee of the Legislature with the Speaker as chairman. For the Colonial Office to refuse this was to declare that it had no confidence in the government elected by the people. What the Colonial Office did not take into consideration was the inflexible determination of the PNM. Nor did it fully realize how feeble was the reed on which the Party had pinned its hopes.

29   Williams to the Secretary of State for the Colonies, *Nation*, Dec. 18, 1959.

14
The 'war' for West Indian independence

During the latter months of 1959 and the early part of 1960, the struggle for an independent West Indies and for the return of the base areas leased to the Americans in 1941 reached a new intensity. The two issues became the focus of an intense war of nerves between the PNM on one side, and the Federal, British, and American governments on the other. The positions which the latter took indicated to the PNM that they were not yet fully committed to a genuinely independent West Indian nation.

To put the Chaguaramas issue in perspective, it should be noted that the Americans had met with West Indian leaders at a conference held in London in 1957 to discuss their request for the release of Chaguaramas for the new federal capital. That conference had appointed a technical commission to review the continued need for the base and report on its findings. The understanding was that the commission, which consisted of United States and British military experts, was a subcommittee of the conference and that it would report back to it. The American and British governments claimed otherwise, however, and declared the issue closed when the commission advised against the removal of the base to the alternative site offered by the Trinidad government. The Federal government, to the consternation of the PNM, agreed with the American proposal to allow the matter to remain where it was 'for say ten years'.[1]

---

1 According to Williams, Adams gave him only a 'couple of hours notice that he had accepted the American assurance that it would review the matter in ten years time. ... I knew that it was only a question of time before the final nails were driven into the coffin of West Indian nationalism on a federal basis.' 'Reflections on the

The Premier of Trinidad never forgave the Federal Prime Minister for what he considered to be an abject betrayal, especially since it was at the request of Adams, Manley, and others that he had made his first demand for return of the base. Williams was angry that other West Indian governments had not raised their voices to support Trinidad in its fight for Chaguaramas, and accused them of bartering their national souls for a mess of American pottage.[2] The Federal government, he insisted, was nothing but a stooge of the Colonial Office. Instead of carving out a role for itself that would give it dignity, it had simply joined the State Department and the Colonial Office in harassing the Trinidad government.[3] This view was further strengthened when U.S. Congressman Walter revealed that conversations with Sir Grantley Adams and other Federal officials had let him to believe that the Federal government was opposed to Williams' stand on Chaguaramas. That the Federal government, moreover, did not deny the revelation further incensed the Trinidad Premier. Williams also complained about the way in which the British government represented West Indian interests wtih other countries, and about the way in which it had used the Federal government to embarrass the Trinidad government in its dealings with Venezuela and Curaçao on matters relating to Trinidad alone.[4]

Caribbean Economic Community', *Nation*, Oct. 8, 1965. The Federal government later denied that it had agreed to any such proposal. It is clear, nevertheless, that Adams did in fact agree to the ten-year moratorium, but later sought to escape the embarrassing corner in which he found himself. His new proposals were: (*a*) that the base be eventually handed over for use as the capital; (*b*) that *three-cornered* talks between the West Indian, United States, and British governments be called to decide on the timing of the transfer, with the West Indies having the final word. The West Indies, he declared, did not wish to jeopardise the defence systems of the Western world, but, as part of that world, it demanded that it be consulted. Adams also agreed that the report of the commission, which ruled out handing over Chaguaramas, was a subcommittee's report and was therefore not binding on the West Indies. Adams to United States Consul Orebaugh, TG, March 21, 1959.

2   'The support we received from West Indian governments ... was infinitesimal ... here and there they sought to bargain support for our stand on Chaguaramas in return for some other concession. ... Our stand on this matter, as on so many others, was *no deals*.' 'Reflections', *Nation*, Oct. 8, 1965.

3   *The Approach of Independence* (Address of the Political Leader to the Fourth Annual Convention of the PNM, Port of Spain, 1960, p. 13. 'If the Federal Government wants to establish rights, it seems to me that it has a lot of foreign governments that it could take a firm attitude to. I'm getting a little tired of all these arrows constantly pointed at the heart of Trinidad.' *Nation*, June 6, 1959.

4   Williams was especially angry that Britain had done nothing to pressure the Venezuelan government to remove the 30 per cent surtax which had been imposed on goods entering Venezuela from Trinidad, and he was annoyed at their failure to prevent the Americans from establishing a missile-tracking station at Chaguaramas.

It is clear that there was a fundamental difference of opinion between Williams and the Colonial Office as to what Trinidad was 'entitled' to claim constitutionally. The Colonial Office held fast to precedent and insisted that, as a colony, Trinidad had no international status and thus could participate in diplomatic negotiations with foreign powers only through British governmental channels or in the presence of British observers. The same held for the Federal government, which in Britain's view was not a sovereign power. Williams was impatient with these juridical niceties. Independence was imminent, and the West Indies should be treated with the equality and courtesies that befitted its status. 'The only conclusion ... that can be drawn from the attitude of the Colonial Office is that it does not envisage the early attainment of Independence by the Federation.'[5] Either that or it conceived of Independence as a juridical masquerade behind which influence would continue to be maintained.

Williams could not understand why the British government was so stubborn in its refusal to pressure the Americans into sitting down to renegotiate the Chaguaramas lease. Britain was either a 'pusillanimous third-rate power' completely under the American thumb, or she had in fact abandoned the West Indies to the American sphere of influence – except in so far as it could be used as a 'valuable pawn in British diplomatic moves in other parts of the world'.[6] Britain and the United States were so contemptuous of the West Indies that they believed they could ignore it at will. As Williams allowed, 'Bad habits die hard; and the long tradition of metropolitan equation of the West Indies with naval bases and military outposts sub-serving metropolitan interests dominates metropolitan attitudes today with respect to the Independence of the West Indies.'[7]

Williams admitted, however, that the American reluctance to reopen the Chaguaramas issue might have been due to its reluctance to endanger base arrangements in other parts of the world. He nevertheless believed that the strategic importance of the base was not as great in the context of changes in military technology and naval warfare as was being claimed. It was a case of malice toward the PNM and contempt for the general population. Even if the

The British government replied that by the terms of the 1941 lease, the Americans needed no permit to establish the station.
5 The British government had also raised the surtax issue, but Venezuela insisted that it must be linked with negotiations for a new commercial treaty between Britain and Venezuela. The surtax had been imposed in 1900 to prevent Britain from dumping goods on the Venezuelan market through British colonial outlets.
6 *The Approach of Independence*, pp. 7–8. It appears that Williams at one point was seriously considering a unilateral declaration of Independence.
7 'Reflections', *Nation*, Oct. 8, 1963.

base was really needed, the conditions under which it was to be occupied had
to be renegotiated with the Trinidad government, which had the right to determine what commitments it would assume in the global nuclear-struggle.
Capital site or not, Chaguaramas was 'the principal hydra-head of colonialism
... the crux of West Indian Nationalism, the symbol of West Indian Independence'.[8]

The 'war' for West Indian Independence thus had to be waged on three
fronts – against the State Department, the Colonial Office, and the Federal
government. The struggle between the Trinidad and Federal governments
reached a point where verbal communication between West Indian leaders
had literally broken down. Williams quite explicitly declared, 'We have now
reached a stage where we have to examine with utmost care and suspicion, any
action that the Federal Government takes or does not take on any issue ...
Trinidad and Tobago is not going to support any West Indian Federal Government which starts off by being the stooge of the Colonial Office.'[9] Williams
saw the Federal government as the weak link in the chain of West Indian
Independence, as the medium through which foreign influences would seek
to operate to keep the West Indies joined to Western economic, political, and
strategic interests. Such a situation endangered not only the West Indies as a
whole, but the PNM in Trinidad as well: 'The whole life of the Federal Government was [thus] a conflict between the nationalist West Indian forces, with
the PNM in the lead, and foreign influences which sought to control the Federal
Government in general, with the specific aim thereby of controlling the PNM.
... We in the PNM had to fight against this all-pervasive foreign influence.'[10]
Williams in fact still believes very strongly that outside interference was one
of the principal reasons for the break-up of the federal experiment.

Stung by Williams' public insults, the Prime Minister of the Federation
took to the airwaves to reply in kind to the Trinidad Premier, whom he accused of being a 'slanderer'.[11] It was inconceivable, declared Adams, that

---

8   *The Approach of Independence*, p. 4.   9   *Ibid.*, p. 5.
10 'Reflections', *Nation*, Oct. 8, 1965.
11 Adams denied that the Federal Government was selling out to United States and
    United Kingdom interests, and that it did not wish to have the Trinidad government
    participate in the discussions about the base. Adams maintained that the position
    of the Federal government was that the West Indies must go to the talks as a single
    delegation which would consist of representatives from all units. The Trinidad
    government would be free to pursue matters which affected Trinidad alone and
    would be supported by the Federal government. On all other issues, the Federal
    government had suggested that there should be co-operation between the two levels
    of government. Whatever the justice of this contention, it is clear that the Federal
    government was worried about the strong line that Williams was taking on
    Chaguaramas.

anyone who wished a strong Federation should deny the Federal government the sole right to deal with external affairs. Adams was on strong grounds here, and Williams was indeed caught on the horns of a dilemma. He wanted a strong Federal government, but was not convinced that the existing one had distinguished itself in the cause of West Indian nationalism. It had not defended the Trinidad government in its struggle for constitutional reform or for Chaguaramas. He thus refused to participate in any three-power conference as part of an all West Indian delegation until the Federal government had stated more unequivocally what its stand was on the burning issues of the day. He did not want to find himself saddled with a decision to which the Federal government agreed over Trinidad's objections.

In his fanatical hostility to Adams, Williams was thus driven to take stands that conflicted with his basic federalist orientation. He even put himself on record as believing that his government's 'procedure was perfectly normal': 'It may well have to be one of the principal features of the conduct of foreign relations by a Federal Government where you have an Island Federation stretched over a long expanse of sea, with one particular island having interests in foreign affairs that another island did not have.'[12]

What alienated the PNM still further was the reluctance of the Federal government to agree to set a date for the achievement of West Indian Independence. As early as November 1958 Williams had decided on a date himself: 'The PNM is working for a powerful, healthy, economically viable West Indies, with Independence for Trinidad and Tobago by April 22, 1960 [eleven o'clock in the morning]. We want to be represented, and we want to take our place in the councils of the world.'[13] Conservative forces in the Caribbean opposed this on the grounds that too many issues had to be settled *within* the West Indies before Independence talks could begin. The small units, for instance, were anxious to know what would be their fate if British subventions

12 Premier's press conference, June 6, 1959. Williams maintained that the Federal government knew nothing of Trinidad's problems, but he refused to permit the Federal government to see the relevant files. 'The land is our land, and the problem is ours.' But he nevertheless maintained that the action of the Trinidad government in the external sphere would always be subject to the approval of the Federal government. Still, Williams was not even sure whether the Federal government should attend the conference by right or out of courtesy. He seemed to lean to the view that the role of the Federal government should be to speak for other units, and to look for clauses in the agreement that might later tie its hands. At one point, however, he did propose tripartite talks, provided they were preceded by bilateral talks between the American and Trinidad governments; the substance of these talks was to form the basis of Trinidad's position at the last conference. The United States refused.

13 TG, Nov. 26, 1958.

to their economies were terminated. It was also felt that the money spent on financing the responsibilities of Independence 'could usefully be spent on improving the economic conditions of the West Indian people. [The demand] is traceable to over-weening political ambitions.'[14]

But nationalist forces in Trinidad took a different view. It was necessary to establish firm guideposts and direct one's energies towards their achievement. The terminal colonial period in Trinidad was too full of uncertainties, too open to conflict, too time-wasting. The sooner it was brought to a close, the better for all concerned. Only then could energies be directed towards the building of the 'national community'. 'London is still the capital of the West Indies, and, as long as West Indian politicians carry that millstone around their necks, they will never be able to mobilise the full power of the West Indies to meet the grave problems that they have to overcome.'[15]

If the Federal government was not prepared to seek Independence at an early date or back Trinidad's demand for Changuaramas, Trinidad would take matters into its own hands.[16] It would emancipate the West Indies against its will. This was the prevailing sentiment at the PNM convention which met in March of 1960 and made the historic decision to take to the streets to dramatize its demand for the return of Chaguaramas. The 'war-hawks' in the Party wanted to march on the United States base, or to assemble a fishing fleet which would 'invade' Chaguaramas and plant the Trinidad flag. But saner heads warned that the Party must avoid any accidents which might result if the march got out of hand. The convention eventually agreed that the proper thing to do would be to march on the u.s. Consulate, the legal representative of the American government in Trinidad. The date chosen for the march was April 22, 1960; Williams was thus about to make good his boast that 'the Trinidad flag will fly over Chaguaramas before many of us are many days older'. If the Americans refused to renegotiate the agreement, it would be repudiated after Independence was achieved.

14   TG, Sept. 4, 1959.
15   C.L.R. James, Nation, Sept. 16, 1959. Williams often referred to the Nation under James' editorship as 'the established spearhead of the party militant, the textbook of Independence'. See, e.g., The Approach of Independence, p. 19.
16   The Party strongly considered breaking with the West Indian Federal Labour Party, which had not supported it in its struggles. During its entire life, the WIFLP never functioned as an effective political party. The conflicts which were evident at the inter-governmental level were reflected in the occasional conferences which were summoned. According to Williams' version, 'If any trend did appear in the Conference, it was ... that Trinidad should bargain for support on the Chaguaramas issue. ... I say with the utmost truth that my principal responsibility was to ensure that releases or ... executive decisions were not so twisted as to compromise the position of the PNM.' 'Reflections', Nation, Oct. 15, 1965.

The 'war' for West Indian Independence was to be bloodless, however. Williams told his followers:

Ours has been a peaceful and bloodless revolution. Keep it so. But precisely for that reason, it is a revolution that is far more dynamic, far more significant than all the revolutions that have taken place and are taking place in the world today. ... We have no [physical] weapons, we can't fight any battles, [but] we have the most powerful weapons of all. ... Our weapons are intellectual and moral arguments, and we will not hesitate to use them.[17]

Our 'base' is the University of Woodford Square, our 'army' is the citizen body; their 'arms' are the banners proclaiming Independence and their placards denouncing colonialism. ... The world history of the last ten years is there to tell us the outcome of this struggle. ... What counts is power. ... The British Government has many divisions, but dares not use them.[18]

Williams was determined to show the DLP, the Colonial Office, and the State Department – and indeed the rest of the West Indies – that he was not a lonely embittered agitator who had gone too far out on a shaky limb to satisfy a personal and pathological grudge against imagined 'devils'.[19] The resounding success of the march, despite torrential downpours, established that once and for all. Crowds – estimates varied from fifteen to thirty-five thousand

17 'From Slavery to Chaguaramas', *Nation*, July 20, 1959.
18 *Tribune* (organ of the PNM legislative group), vol. 1 & 2, pp. 25, 9, 21.
19 Williams denied vigorously that his 'struggle' was a personal one. He was 'only the mouthpiece of the aspirations of the West Indian people', and in that role, he would fight for a dignified settlement, 'with the last ounce of strength in my body'.
    'I today have more power in Trinidad and Tobago than any Trinidadian has ever had – any! All of us [in the cabinet] derive our power, the power that we have for good or evil, from people like you here tonight. ... No power on earth can make a crowd, and a highly politicalized crowd, cheer and applaud unless it felt an inner compulsion to do so.' C.L.R. James argues that Williams was in fact restraining the Party. *Nation*, Aug. 14, 1959.
    The Minister of Health Dr Mahabir also testified to the support which Williams had from his ministerial colleagues: 'Do not for a moment believe that in this issue the Political Leader has been a lonely genius out on a fragile limb. In the matter of Chaguaramas, he has had the *constant and unanimous support* of his cabinet colleagues. It is true that we shall never be able fully to control his occasional wicked turn of phrase, or to curb his propensity for provocative *picong*. But on the basic principles relating to Chaguaramas, there can be no compromise, and our principles are neither for sale nor for barter. The presence of an American Base on Trinidad soil without Trinidad's consent in an age of independence is a callous anachronism. ... We are bound to emerge victorious, and victory will include a greater respect by the Americans for us, and a closer friendship than ever before.' *Nation*, April 1, 1960.

– marched in the rain to Woodford Square, where the Trinidad flag was raised and 'the seven deadly sins' ritualistically consigned to the flames by Dr Williams.[20] It was one of the largest political demonstrations ever witnessed in Trinidad. Williams had made his point; the ball was in the court of the Americans. James commented: 'If the Americans are not now able to come to terms with us as to the details of the eventual return of the Base, then you have made it clear that our Independence will restore our rights to do as we please with our territory. ... Independence is just around the corner. Everybody knows that now. So that one way or another, the eventual return of Chaguaramas is safe.'[21]

The success of the march was eminently satisfying to Williams, for whom it came as a tonic, a purge, a sort of catharsis. 'A demonstration such as this is not only a political leap forward, it is also a spiritual purification.' Trinidad had at last done something' revolutionary', and had matured under his stimulation. The national community was now in the process of taking shape.[22] So reinforced did Williams feel that he proclaimed Trinidad sovereign and independent, 'in fact if not in law'. A firm attitude was extended to the Federal government as well. When Chaguaramas is returned, Williams noted, if the Federal government is still interested in using it for the capital, 'they can come in and we will sit down with them and bargain about it.'[23] He even warned that Trinidad might have to go it alone to Independence against its own will.

Conservative forces were alarmed at the new turn of events. The *Guardian*, which again made a pictorial comparison between Williams and Hitler, declared that Williams was pushing at an open door. Williams was accused of caudilloism, of paranoia, of being so desperate for an election issue that he was ready to destroy the West Indies in the process. 'Williams is trying to keep the West Indian revolution alive. ... He is badly in need of something about which

20 The seven documents ritualistically burnt were the 1941 lease agreement, the 1956 Trinidad constitution, the DLP statement on British Guiana, the Mudie report on the capital site, the telephone ordinance of 1939, and, of course, a copy of the *Trinidad Guardian*. Memoranda were sent to the British as well as the American government requesting Independence, Federation, the return of Chaguaramas, and a conference on West Indian bases at which Trinidad was to be represented as an equal principal.

21 The *Nation*, June 6, 1960. Williams had made it quite clear that 'with Independence, if no new agreement is reached, the 1941 agreement lapses'. *The Approach of Independence*, p. 13.

22 The report of the PNM General Council to the fifth annual convention in September 1960 boasted: 'This demonstration, its magnitude, its orderliness and its tremendous success, both in itself and its purpose, will go down in the history of Trinidad and Tobago and the West Indies as the Great Divide between Colonialism and Independence.'

23 The *Nation*, April 29, 1960.

people can get excited. His is the dilemma of every loud-mouthed demagogue during this period of history.'[24] Since the West Indian economy did not permit him to take a radical stand on class issues, he had found it necessary to create devils by establishing historical lies against colonialism. Colonialism had to be portrayed as an unmixed evil.

Dr Rudranath Capildeo, who replaced Maraj as leader of the DLP in March 1960, also accused Williams of seeking an issue where none really existed:

Constitutional advance in Trinidad came largely as a result of the efforts of others. The advance of Trinidad's Independence came in the wake of struggles conducted in other colonial lands. Thus the colonial revolution as far as Trinidad is concerned was over without a single shot being fired in this Territory.

There have been indeed riots from time to time, the most recent of which was in 1937. But this was not as a result of an organised political movement, presenting a political philosophy and moving towards political independence. ... PNM patriots feel frustrated that they have missed the opportunity to show their mettle in a colonial war.[25]

Leaders of opinion in other parts of the Caribbean also reminded Williams that Cipriani, Marryshow, Adams, and Manley had been preaching nationalism long before he entered political life. Manley himself declared by way of rebuff to Williams, 'It is a fact that the West Indies can have Independence as a Federation as soon as the West Indies wishes it. There is no problem about Independence – except the working out of the sort of Federation we want when we get Independence. I do not think there is any point in fixing a date for Independence until we have settled the future of the Federation which is our business.'[26]

The presence of known Marxists on the PNM platform also worried con-

---

24   Albert Gomes, TG, May 19, 1960. During an extended fuel strike, Williams even sought to deny the Federal government supplies of petrol for the maintenance of its essential services.

25   TG, April 18, 1960. For an account of Dr Capildeo's emergence as leader of the DLP, cf. chap. 17, pp. 252–3.

26   *Sunday Guardian*, April 17, 1960. Williams quite incorrectly argues that it was 'we [the PNM] who first started the tradition of West Indian nationalism ... we who for the first time in West Indian society raised the question of federation meaning the integration of the isolated economies.' *Speech on Independence*, Port of Spain, 1962, p. 18. West Indian economic integration had been preached since the end of the First World War by several people including Cipriani. After the Second World War it was one of the key planks in the platform of the West Indian National Party and the Caribbean Congress of Labour. Williams' contribution to the West Indian national tradition, though substantial, is not unique, as he likes to believe.

servative forces, who had long been concerned about the presence of a self-confessed Trotskyite, C.L.R. James, in the PNM leadership circle. They claimed that crypto-communists were infiltrating the Party and some agencies of government. The influence of James on Williams was seriously deplored.[27]

The new political leader of the DLP, Dr Capildeo, protested angrily against the political adventurism of the PNM, which he claimed would only harden the position of the Americans, who had shown that they would not capitulate to bullying tactics. Trinidad was in no position to impose physical sanctions on the Americans. The PNM, he maintained, was putting party before country. Dr Capildeo noted that although the DLP had been invited to participate in the march, it could not possibly have agreed to do so:

We are [called] traitors because we refuse to follow blindly the lead of the PNM in what it is pleased to call a national question. We cannot and do not intend to speak with a united voice when the united voice is the PNM's voice only. No discussions have been held by the PNM with officials of the DLP concerning the problem of Chaguaramas. A march has been called unilaterally by one political party, and because it has done so, it expects the other party to follow, simply because it says the march is national.[28]

But the DLP leader nevertheless felt that the Opposition must shift from the rigid position into which it had been forced. Capildeo repeated the old thesis about hemispheric fatalism and the mutual indispensability of Trinidad and the United States in the Western defence system, but he added:

Trinidad's burden should not be so large that it is out of proportion when her national wealth, resources, and land area are considered. The DLP's stand is that Chaguaramas must be returned to Trinidad. It shall endeavour to see that this end

27 James did not conceal the fact that he was a Marxist but denied that he was pushing Williams further than he would normally go. James insisted that he was *following* Williams: 'I was aware of a certain tone in the recent speeches of the Doctor; I followed that tone. If the Doctor changes his tone, I shall change mine also.' *Nation*, Aug. 7, 1959. On another occasion James reminded his critics, 'I am not a member of the General Council. I am not a member of any committee. I read the government documents. I listen to the Political Leader and I guide the paper according to these. If I am in a difficulty or I am uncertain, I consult him.' *Nation*, April 8, 1960. But orthodox party cadres were worried. Cabinet ministers were known to be concerned about the pervasiveness of James's influence over Williams, which they believe threatened their own position. It is an established fact that Williams' revolutionary speech on the role of the Party – 'Perspectives for Our Party' – was largely ghost-written by James.

28 TG, April 17, 1960. There were elements in the PNM who felt that the DLP should have been consulted on the proposed march before it was announced. Williams would have none of this 'disgraceful behaviour', 'this domestic sabotage'. 'Reflections' Oct. 15, 1965.

is achieved constitutionally, legally and in a civilised manner and within the bounds of decent international obligations.[29]

Capildeo agreed that too much land and too many resources were tied up in the bases agreement, and proposed that negotiations should be initiated for their partial transfer. It was also suggested that the United States allow its facilities to be more fully utilized for the training and employment of local personnel, and that as far as possible the operation and maintenance of the base should be the joint responsibility of the United States and Trinidad governments. 'In this way, the Base will become the symbol of partnership between the American and West Indian peoples.'[30]

Capildeo also attempted to bring home to Trinidadians, who were being saturated with propaganda about the glories of Independence, that the national state system, with its assumptions about sovereignty and self-determination, was obsolete in the context of the cold war and the bloc system. To talk about 'Independence' for a small nation like Trinidad was sheer myth-making and humbug:

The DLP recognizes that complete independence is now an antiquated concept, and that the new world situation demands not independence but interdependence. When you press for independence and remove the foreign administrator, you invite his brother to come in – the foreign technical expert; and you have simply changed one colonialism for a stronger one. This is nonsense to which talk of independence in a small undeveloped place like Trinidad can lead.[31]

Some nationalists admitted this in private, but in public Capildeo's sober statement was given the standard contemptuous treatment with which all such attempts at moderation are greeted in revolutionary periods. The imperatives of national community-building required that 'noble lies' be propagated for the benefit of a too dependent mass-mind.

THE 'CAPITULATION'

But the DLP had little basis for further intransigence. Its own internal weaknesses, and Williams' demonstration that he had massive public support behind him, finally convinced the Colonial Office and the Americans that they had little alternative but to come to honourable terms with the PNM. The capitulation of the Colonial Office was as complete as it was swift. What was particularly flattering to the PNM was that the Colonial Secretary, on the recommendation of the Governor General of the Federation, created a precedent by coming to Trinidad, rather than have delegations visit him in London. Macleod's

29   TG, April 17, 1960.   30   *Ibid.*   31   *Ibid.*

visit reflected the fact that the Colonial Office was becoming more and more concerned with the crisis in the West Indies which was delaying the granting of Independence. It had now become clear that the constitutional and Chaguaramas issues had to be settled and that British intervention was necessary to help West Indian politicians compromise on the outstanding issues in the protracted federal negotiations. Macleod in fact disclosed that West Indian Independence had been conceded by Britain two years ago, and that provision in the parliamentary timetable had even been made for it. The West Indies were told to 'hurry up' and take the freedom which was there for the asking. Britain needed 'no lecturing on the issue'; she was prepared to admit the West Indies to the Commonwealth and to sponsor her in the councils of the world.

It was felt at the time that Macleod made this statement to save the face of the Colonial Office and steal the thunder of the PNM.[32] But there is no reason to believe that Britain was opposed to West Indian Independence, especially after 1958. Her entire support of the Federation was viewed as an essential prerequisite to Independence. The Premier of Jamaica, Norman Manley, in fact noted that it was only timidity that was preventing the West Indies from gaining its Independence. 'The British Government is not withholding self-government from the West Indies. We can have [it] whenever we ask for it.'[33] This was true, but Britain was anxious to ensure that, while rid of her Caribbean burden, her strategic and economic interests in the area were nevertheless well served. The British government certainly did not treat the Federal government as if it had already conceded Independence and, as far as Trinidad was concerned, Williams had to fight for every concession that was finally made, though the Colonial Office was not unaware of the basic orthodoxy of the PNM, which Macleod jokingly maintained was on the right-wing of British Toryism. The Colonial Office at this stage certainly behaved as though it preferred to entrust political power in Trinidad to forces which were easier to manipulate.

It is interesting to note, however, that Britain's offer of freedom was still

32   Williams was somewhat ambivalent in his explanation of the 'capitulation' of the Colonial Office. His first impulse was to credit Britain's new *démarche* to the April 22 demonstration. 'Our tremendous ... demonstration ... made it impossible to deny the PNM claims for renegotiation of the Treaty, and it laid the foundations for West Indian nationhood.' But he hastened to add that this was 'in theory, if not in practice, for by April 22, 1960 the British Government ... was more anxious than the federal politicians to give the West Indies Independence. They wanted to join the ECM, and one essential step ... was to rid themselves of the West Indian millstones. ... So Macleod ... came down to settle outstanding issues with the PNM, to concede full internal self-government, and to urge West Indian slackers: "Hurry on to Independence".' 'Reflections', *Nation*, Oct. 15, 1965.

33   Sir John Mordecai, *The West Indies: The Federal Negotiations*, London, 1968, p. 237.

conditional. Independence was to be granted subject to the provision that 'the essentials of sovereignty were satisfied'. This was interpreted by some to mean that an independent West Indies would have to cut its ties with the British Treasury as well. Macleod had earlier promised that Britain 'recognises that the West Indies may not be able to assume the whole weight of the financial burdens which would normally fall to an independent member', but he had also added, *'if this proves to be so,* HMG will ... consider ... ways in which help might be given over a transitional period.'[34]

For many, this assurance was not 'hard' enough. It left a way out for Britain to claim *after* Independence was granted that the West Indies was better equipped to deal with problems of Independence than many other independent countries. This argument was in fact made during subsequent negotiations.[35] Adams put his finger on the essential problem confronting the West Indian nationalist movement when he noted that the West Indies feared to seek Independence because in London political independence was interpreted to mean economic independence as well. This was the core of the difficulty between Trinidad and the West Indies. Reasonably well-off economically, Trinidad could afford to take a tough stand against diplomacy by bribery.[36]

Jamaica and the rest of the West Indies were not prepared to risk any cuts in aid.[37] The issue was not treason or colonialism at all, but a crisis of confidence. Chaguaramas was not worth the sacrifice to those who thought in terms of welfare rather than status. Williams, however, had the vision to see that the two things were not necessarily alternatives. The West Indies should struggle to obtain both dignity *and* economic aid out of the bases issue as other nations like the Philippines and Morocco were doing. And in the course of that struggle, he had made his, and Trinidad's, the strongest and most respected voice in the Caribbean area.

34   *Ibid.,* p. 236.   35   *Ibid.,* p. 238.
36   Many Trinidadians did not agree that Trinidad could afford to turn its back on financial bribes from the United States and United Kingdom governments. The plantocracy and the *Guardian* were especially sensitive to the vulnerability of the dependent Trinidad economy. But nationalist forces refused to accept any bribes. Williams noted that the Secretary of State had said to him, 'If you want independence, you must have economic independence, you must pay for it.' Williams' reply was, 'I said fine. We don't want a penny from you. We are not getting any grants from you. We'll pay for our development ourselves. ... We must be free to make mistakes. We may make mistakes in 1956 but we will not make them in 1960, and in the history of self-government 10 years is a very short time in the life of a country or nation.' 'From Slavery to Chaguaramas', *Nation,* July 20, 1959.
37   Jamaica up to 1959 had received about $45 million WI from colonial welfare and development grants, whereas Trinidad had received only $7 million. Williams sought to convince West Indian leaders that what they would lose in colonial subventions they would receive from the Commonwealth or from other developed countries when the West Indies became independent.

THE MACLEOD FORMULA

The Macleod formula for constitutional reform can be described very briefly. The new constitution, which was to come into effect after the elections of 1961, provided for a senate of twenty-one members of which twelve were to be appointed on the advice of the government, two on the advice of the opposition, and seven by the Governor in consultation with vested interests. The Senate was to be given the power to delay for a year all bills save those deemed to be money bills. A cabinet of twelve ministers, a politically appointed attorney general, and a solicitor general to advise the Governor were also conceded. The Colonial Secretary did not, however, agree that the new Legislature should be given full sovereignty. The power to amend the constitution was reserved to the Crown and its agents, as was the right to withhold assent to legislation which appeared to be inconsistent with the constitution, Her Majesty's international obligations, or royal prerogatives. The notion of an independent boundary commission was abandoned. But despite all constitutional niceties, the arrangement meant that for most purposes Trinidad would become internally self-governing in 1961.

It is clear, however, that Macleod's visit was only marginally connected with the constitutional issue. Of principal importance was the Chaguaramas issue and Trinidad's demand for full participation as an autonomous unit. To the relief of everyone except the Federal government, Trinidad's demands were conceded. There was speculation that Macleod had in some way tied the constitutional settlement to a 'deal' on the Chaguaramas and federation issues. But Macleod insisted: 'There was no bargaining; Chaguaramas in no way, directly or indirectly, came into these constitutional discussions.'[38] But it can be reasonably surmised that Macleod's concessions were designed to disarm Williams and to persuade him to refrain from publicly criticizing Jamaica's decision to hold a referendum to determine whether or not the Jamaican people wanted to continue in the Federation.[39] It is also evident that he wanted to induce Williams to take a moderate stand on Chaguaramas.

38   TG, June 19, 1960.
39   Williams was bitterly opposed to Jamaica's being allowed to hold a referendum to decide whether or not she would stay in the Federation. It was clearly unconstitutional, as British authorities have since admitted. Macleod had also blundered into making it known that no sanctions would be imposed on Jamaica if she left the Federation. He must have feared that, if Williams spoke out against the right of Jamaicans to vote on the issue, it would only serve to weaken Manley's chances at the polls. Williams confessed, 'I intended to attack the [referendum] decision, but was persuaded not to do so by the Secretary of State.' Mordecai, The West Indies, p. 236.

As Sir John Mordecai, former Deputy Governor General of the Federation, has noted, 'Macleod adroitly ordered his programme, making a virtue of necessity in his first move. ... Advanced securement of Williams' good graces [on the constitutional issue] served well the major purpose of Macleod's visit – to get agreement upon a means of settling the Chaguaramas issue.'[40] The DLP were the net losers in the negotiations, but short of threatening physical resistance, the DLP could do little to force the combined hands of the PNM and the Colonial Office.[41]

The PNM was ecstatic over its victory. In a speech full of messianic symbolism, Williams told his followers that they 'can now see the promised land, the political kingdom'. As far as he was concerned, Trinidad was free to pursue its own career in the international sphere. 'Regardless of British reserve powers, arrangements are going to be made in the field of external relations involving the full and direct participation of the representatives of Trinidad and Tobago.' To underline his determination, an office was established in London to 'promote the financial and economic independence of Trinidad and Tobago'.[42] The PNM also began negotiations with the World Bank for a loan for expansion of its island-wide electricity programme. The agreement when concluded was only formally endorsed by the British government. But Williams also sought to reassure those who were still watching apprehensively. He not only reassured his hearers that Trinidad would not seek independence alone, but also promised that independence, when it came, would not mean that Trinidad would follow the path chosen by some newly emergent areas. 'We have seen that the coming of Independence sometimes brings results in the weakening of democracy. I am confident that we can avoid that.'[43]

---

40   *Ibid.*, p. 277.
41   Capildeo insists that he had little choice in the settlement. It was obvious that the Colonial Office was prepared to dictate a solution. The PNM, he notes, had convinced the Colonial Office that the DLP was not a viable party to which power could be entrusted.
42   *Nation*, July 11, 1960.
43   Williams' statement on the question of independence alone is worth noting for its historical significance: 'The very fact that considerations of this sort [going it alone] could, in 1960, be allowed to become fundamental political issues is an indication of the heritage left behind by colonialism, the parochial outlook, the inadequate preparation for self-government, the ignorance of our historical past, the congenital inability to see beyond the confines of our own puny territories, the obsession with ancient traditions of West Indian glory and importance. Everywhere the movement is towards unity and away from division; everywhere save in the West Indies. We in Trinidad and Tobago will be reducing ourselves to this lower political West Indian level if we too should try to talk of going it alone.' *Nation*, July 1, 1960.

15
Thunder on the right

The last months of 1960 and the year 1961 were among the most important in the life of the People's Nationalist Movement. It was in these months that one began to detect the gradual shift away from the politics of principle towards a more Machiavellian emphasis on the principles of politics. The Thermidorian reaction had begun to set in. Having obtained most of what it had demanded from the U.S. State Department and from the Colonial Office, the PNM could now return to the basically accommodationist reform strategy to which it had committed itself in 1956. The two main events that mark the beginning of this tendency were the signing of the new Chaguaramas Agreement and the Concordat with the Church.

THE CHAGUARAMAS AGREEMENT

During the agitation over Chaguaramas, a number of extreme statements had been made by nationalist spokesmen which had led many to believe that the position of the PNM was that the Americans must withdraw from Trinidad completely.[1] But the substantive position of the Party as approved in convention was much more moderate. The proposals made to the Americans in 1959 included the following requests: (1) that they give up such portions of

---

1 'Every West Indian island has been a base at some time or another. The development of every West Indian island has been subordinated for four and a half centuries to the strategic and military considerations of Europe. It is time to finish up with that sort of thing and allow us to live our lives in peace.' Eric Williams, 'The Road to Independence', *Nation*, July 24, 1959.

the leased area as were not being utilized for defence purposes to permit the beginning of construction work on the federal capital; (2) that they indicate when they proposed to leave Chaguaramas – the departure date to be no later than 1967, ten years after the first request for Chaguaramas had been made; (3) that if a base were still needed in Trinidad, it should be built at Irois Bay, the Chaguaramas area being too vital to the economic and recreational needs of the community to permit its continued alienation;[2] (4) that the United States make 'reparations' for the contribution that Trinidad and Tobago had been forced to make towards American defence during the past eighteen years (suggested compensation included the construction of a college of arts and science at the university, with a suitably endowed library, the building of a jet runway at Piarco airport, and the training of local military and technical personnel on the base); (5) that the base should be operated jointly by the governments of Trinidad and the United States.

The Party élite had repeatedly stated that their stand was not based on anti-Americanism, but on principles. The continued presence of the United States in Trinidad was something that had to be negotiated between the two countries. For the PNM the fact that Trinidad was not legally independent was irrelevant. What was important was the right to have some say as to whether bases were to be on Trinidadian soil, what power or powers should possess them, their location, and the conditions relating to their establishment and operation. It appears that the Americans had indicated their willingness in 1959 to sit down and bargain on these terms; however, for reasons which are not quite clear, but which seem to do with conflicts between the Trinidad and Federal governments, with the internal political struggle, and with American uncertainty about what sort of deal could be extracted from the PNM, the plans for the conference collapsed.[3]

By the end of 1960 all parties had agreed on an acceptable compromise. Formally, the talks were still to be 'tripartite', that is, the United States, the United Kingdom, and the Federal government would be the principals at the final stage of the negotiations, but the Americans agreed to negotiate first with

2   Nationalists were quite concerned about the amount of arable land that was tied up in the agreement with the United States, land that was known to be suited to the growing of citrus, cocoa, beans, and tobacco. The agreement also tied up some of the island's best beaches and deep water harbours, harbours which were said to be necessary for the expansion of the present overused docking facilities. The contribution which the United States presence was making to the economy was not considered large enough to offset these handicaps, since most of the material consumed from the base was imported from the United States without reference to local customs authorities.

3   Eric Williams, *The Approach of Independence*, Port of Spain, 1960, p. 13.

the government of each territory on which there were installations. Indeed it was at this stage that the material decisions were taken. The United States set aside its earlier stand that it would not negotiate with a non-sovereign power. The leader of the United States delegation, John Hay Whitney, asserted, 'The United States Government was conscious of the aspirations of West Indians who were taking the road to freedom which Americans themselves took not long ago, and wished therefore to conclude agreements conforming and contributing to those aspirations and acceptable to the people and their political representatives.'[4] It was a rather belated recognition, encouraged by diplomatic assurances that the PNM was not in fact committed to neutralism or American withdrawal. Moreover, the Americans were obviously becoming more and more embarrassed at having to 'bear the ugly image of an unwelcome giant straddling the front garden of a small, poor country'.[5]

Only a broad description of the settlement can be attempted here. By the terms of the accord, the United States agreed to release unconditionally most of the unused land surrounding the base at Chaguaramas and other locations in the north-west peninsula, and to release all lands outside of that peninsula. Certain parts of the base area were to be used jointly by United States and local defence and security forces. Facilities were also to be made available for the training of local personnel in certain technical and military fields. The United States was, however, allowed to retain its facilities at Chaguaramas until 1977, though provision was made for review in 1968, and at five-year intervals thereafter, to determine whether modifications were necessary in the terms of the lease. Withdrawal in 1977 was, however, not automatic, but contingent upon the state of global tension.[6] This in fact meant that the demand for Chaguaramas as the site of the federal capital was to all intents and purposes dropped. In return for Trinidad's agreement to a partnership role in the defence of the hemisphere, the US delegation agreed to recommend American participation in the improvement of the country's port, road, airport, and railway facilities, and to participate in the construction of an arts and sciences faculty at the Trinidad branch of the University of the West Indies.[7] It was also agreed that the Trinidad flag would be flown at Chaguaramas.

4   TG, Dec. 6, 1960.
5   Mordecai, *The West Indies: The Federal Negotiations*, p. 190.
6   This is not to be interpreted as a defeat for Williams, who had in fact indicated as early as 1959 that 'the Government shall undertake to keep under constant review the state of world tension in the context of the date of final evacuation stipulated.' *The History of Chaguaramas*, Port of Spain, 1960, p. 16. Withdrawal was completed in 1971 except for a small crew which mans a missile tracking unit.
7   According to Williams, the conference almost broke down on the university issue. The head of the delegation agreed to the proposal, but the State Department's delegate objected. The latter was overruled from Washington. 'Reflections', *Nation*, Oct. 15, 1965.

Though the Premier later admitted that the British government forced him to compromise on 'important issues', he affected to be 'extremely pleased' with the settlement.[8] He had gone into the conference determined that any new agreement must recognize the fundamental political fact that the political situation in Trinidad and Tobago in 1960 was quite different from the one existing in 1941, and this he had forced both the United States and British governments to acknowledge. Both governments had, in fact, for practical purposes recognized the 'independence' of Trinidad and the West Indies. In the words of Ambassador Whitney:

Your period of transition has served its purpose. The mantle of Independence is justified by the progress which you have made. We have great expectations of the role which a politically stable independent West Indies can play in world affairs. We want that kind of neighbour on our doorstep, using its helpful influence also in affairs of this hemisphere. If there was any doubt of our interest in West Indian Independence, our presence here today should dispel it. We have concluded this venture in what has been called 'anticipatory diplomacy' dealing with a nation as though it were fully independent. We hope it is soon.[9]

Early in 1961 British Prime Minister Harold Macmillan visited Trinidad, which he referred to as the 'Athens of the Caribbean', and again urged West Indians to 'hurry to independence'. His remarks on Trinidad were especially flattering:

Though one of the youngest Legislatures in the Commonwealth, I feel at once the strength of your Parliamentary traditions. ... We in Britain recognize how deeply you treasure the traditions and safeguards which are of such vital importance in the world if democracy is to survive. ... The negotiation of this Agreement was an act of real statesmanship. By it you made solemn recognition of the responsibility which you will soon assume in international affairs. ... You are not without material resources. You have greater moral and intellectual resources than many countries already playing a role in world affairs. You have powerful friends. Now that your moment of decision [to enter Federation] is upon you, you must not fail the outside world.[10]

8   Williams was not entirely happy about the settlement. As he said much later: 'The arrangement is a reasonable one. I had certain reservations but [agreed to it] in the interest of a general settlement. ... By and large, however, it is quite satisfactory.' TG, Nov. 30, 1962. Williams later had reason to be chagrined when the United States began to hedge on its commitments by insisting that 'counterpart' funds be provided by Trinidad and Tobago.
9   TG, Feb. 11, 1961. With the permission of the British government, the West Indian government had signed its first international treaty on February 10, 1961.
10   *Nation*, March 31, 1961.

For Williams this was the aspect of the negotiations that were perhaps worth most, since he must have felt at the time that, in terms of material gain, the agreement was a virtual 'sell out'. Only about $30 million (US) were involved. The DLP noted that the settlement did not represent any considerable advance over offers which the Americans had made in 1954–6, and was much less than the PNM had led its followers to expect.[11] The DLP also claimed that the Premier had done exactly what they had suggested in 1957–8. He had made Chaguaramas pay for the economic development of Trinidad and Tobago. What was once attacked as neo-colonialism was now being accepted enthusiastically by anti-colonialist forces. DLP politicians in fact dismissed the whole settlement as nothing more than a desperate electioneering manoeuvre.

Most PNM supporters did not agree that the settlement was of the same nature as that urged by conservative forces. They noted that even though conservative elements might have been disposed to revision initially, they had given no support whatsoever to PNM demands after 1957. Either their national feeling had been slumbering after 1957, or it had been deliberately sacrificed for the 'greater good' of discrediting the PNM and its leader. And it is true that established elements behaved as though it was sheer impudence on the part of Dr Williams to demand that the Americans leave Chaguaramas once they had indicated their unwillingness to do so in 1957.[12]

PNM supporters also noted that it was only in 1960 that the DLP had shifted away from the stand that the Americans should be left alone. DLP politicians might have been predisposed to negotiation on Chaguaramas, but in their desire to break the PNM they had taken stands which, in effect, would have allowed the Americans to stay under the terms imposed in 1941. The difference between the two parties on the issue was essentially one of temper. The DLP was prepared to accept dictation from the State Department and the Colonial Office;[13] Williams was not – once he was satisfied that the arrange-

---

11   The United States had in 1951–2 offered to allow the Trinidad government to use the deactivated base areas and some hospital and other facilities on the base, but these were always subject to repossession after forty-eight hours' notice. The essential difference in the new agreement was that most of the land and facilities were now to be unconditionally released. It was really a substantial difference, since permanent structures could now be constructed.

12   Williams was quite fair when he accused the established press of being ready to 'hang' him 'for treason against the U.S. government'. 'Reflections', *Nation*, Oct. 15, 1965.

13   As one PNM journalist observed, 'It is a very easy thing for the DLP to say that matters could have been arranged with "sitting around a conference table in a democratic manner"; but what except extreme political needling would have persuaded the American Gulliver to "sit around" any table anywhere with Lilliputian Trinidad?' Lynn Beckles, 'As I See It', *Nation*, April 7, 1961.

ment was a dishonourable one which had been imposed over the protests of a colonial Governor and the Executive Council of the period.[14]

Although most people in the PNM seemed gratified with the agreement, a sizable number were vocally dissatisfied. They complained bitterly that the Premier had conceded more than the Party had agreed to in convention, that he had sacrificed the left in the Party at the virtual dictation of the State Department. Even more shocking to them were the statements concerning foreign policy commitments which Williams and Manley had made after the signing of the agreement. Both men had put themselves on record as being 'with the West'. Manley observed that Chaguaramas posed the question of 'what role would the West Indies play as an independent nation?' His personal conviction was that 'we have done wisely ... in deciding that neutrality serves no purpose.'[15] Williams was even more expressive:

Trinidad and Tobago are not immune from those subversive tactics, rooted in treachery and intrigue, which seek to duplicate in the West Indies situations that have developed elsewhere. ... We face a recrudescence, as exasperating as it is unnecessary, of that disruption of our lives by tensions imported from outside which have weighed on the entire Caribbean for over four and a half centuries. ... So long as I and my colleagues, both Government and Party, have any responsibility for the affairs of Trinidad and Tobago, and through it, of the Federation, we shall continue to work for the achievement and maintenance of a stable democratic society which, insofar as there is any curtain dividing the world, is, as I have more than once unequivocally stated, ... West of that curtain, and not East of it. ... I am for the West Indies taking their place in the Western Hemisphere and for membership in the Organization of American States, without any loosening of ties with the Commonwealth.[16]

14   As he himself declared: 'I could not possibly put myself in a position in 1957 of being less concerned and less vigilant in defence of the fundamental interests of Trinidad than a British Colonial Governor and the Executive Council of the period of 1941.' TG, Aug. 8, 1958. It had also been discovered that Churchill and other members of the British Government and Parliament were opposed to the terms of the bases agreement. Churchill himself complained, 'For the sake of the precise list of instrumentalities [50 destroyers] mentioned, which in our sore need we greatly desire, we are asked to pay undefined concessions in all the islands and places mentioned ... as may be defined in the judgment of the United States. Your commitment is limited, ours is unlimited.' On another occasion Churchill noted, 'Deep feelings were aroused in Parliament and the Government at the idea of leasing any part of these historic territories, and if the issue were presented to the British as a naked trading of British possessions for the sake of fifty Destroyers, it would certainly have encountered violent opposition.' E.C. Richardson, 'Churchill and the Destroyers', TG, June 29, 1958.

15   TG, Feb. 11, 1961.   16   Ibid.

Left-wing forces, most notably C.L.R. James and Dr Winston Mahabir, were very chagrined by the direction in which the Party was now moving. Mahabir publicly stated that Trinidad and the West Indies had compromised their independence by entering into such an agreement. What would the leaders of the West Indies tell Ghana, India, and the rest of the Afro-Asian neutralist bloc, he complained? Why should West Indian delegates agree to tie the hands of the future independent West Indian Government which might have different views on foreign policy? Moreover, the Party had never been given the opportunity to discuss the whole question of alliances. Williams was arrogating to himself the right to make Party policy in this field.[17] Radical West Indian intellectuals were also vocally annoyed at what they were convinced was a palpable 'sell out'. It was aid with strings.

It has not been ascertained what sort of in-fighting developed in the Party and Government, but there is every reason to believe that it was fierce. The intemperate language used in public by Williams to excoriate his critics was perhaps indicative of the private needling he was receiving. Williams apparently sought to whip up a public scare about communist infiltration to cover up his capitulation. Either that, or he was genuinely seeking to disabuse the population of the myth of British West Indian exceptionalism. He observed on one occasion: 'Let us above all not be deluded into the smug complacency that it cannot happen here. There are communist parties in Martinique and Guadeloupe, not far away from us. Communist sympathizers are associated with other West Indian territories. We have some in our midst, and like elsewhere, they seek to infiltrate our trade-union movement.'[18] Williams lashed out mercilessly at the 'comsymps', who he claimed were trying to lead him along the path that the Fidelistas had taken:

17   But by agreeing to respect the bases agreement in their Manifesto in 1956, the Party had in fact declared for the West. It was also not the first occasion on which Williams had declared Trinidad on the side of the West.

18   TG, Oct 1, 1961. At a Party convention in September 1961, Williams listed Communism as one of the five dangers facing the PNM, the others being racialism, reversion to colonialism, unemployment, and trimmers, and wagon-riders. Communism was singled out because of the disruptive effect it has on economic planning and development. He cited the case of Venezuela, 'where serious planning for the reorganization of the society has become virtually impossible because of the permanent uncertainty and constant disorder'. Williams, it should be noted, had at first welcomed Castro's take-over of Cuba and some of his nationalization measures. When he met Castro in 1959, he declared that he sensed that he was meeting 'in the flesh the centuries-old frustration of the Cuban people for autonomy and democracy. ... Castro's revolution brings one step nearer the realization of the old dream of a Caribbean Confederation and also the goal of the ownership of the West Indies by the West Indian people themselves.' Nation, May 8, 1959.

Chaguaramas is becoming involved in a mess of intrigue. Communists and fellow travellers wanted me to pull their chestnuts out of the fire. I am not going to do it. If anybody tries to mess up this Chaguaramas issue as they are trying to do now, God help them when I talk publicly. ... If anybody tries to interfere with the national interest for the sake of pursuing a vendetta against me, or his hostility to the PNM, I am going to be sorry for that man. Anything short of crucifixion, that is what I promise. And I am not making any joke about it. The nation's interest comes first.[19]

While there were a few Marxists in Trinidad, there was no real evidence to give rise to fears of a communist *coup*. The West Indian Independence Party was quiet, and, as its leader declared, the Party had no plans for building membership. 'We are waiting to see what develops. Independence will be the time for considering whether the territory wants a socialist party.'[20] But fears of communist infiltration were being vocally expressed in the months of 1961, and security forces were requested to search files and offices of trade unions and suspected individuals.

While Williams was deeply concerned about events in Cuba, the man he seemed most concerned about was his erstwhile friend and confidant, C.L.R. James. James later denied that he was plotting any *coup*, but it is well known that he was extremely chagrined about the rightward thrust of the PNM in 1960, and that he was trying to build up internal support to force Williams and the Party to 'go forward'. Williams was apprehensive that James might attempt to split the Party and also that he might expose many of the confidences which they shared.[21] Dr Mahabir, the Minister of Health, also believed

19 TG, Feb. 11, 1961. Williams was quite determined to avoid the entanglement of the West Indies in cold war disputes. He admits, however, that he tried without much success to get Nkrumah and Nehru to give him support. He feels that he achieved a 'decisive victory' by settling the Chaguaramas issue without bringing it into 'the entanglement of the cold wars in the outside world'. *Nation*, Jan. 28, 1966.
20 Lennox Pierre, TG, Oct. 1, 1961.
21 It is quite likely that James is the 'Mr X' who according to Williams opposed the compromise because he 'wanted to be Political Adviser to the West Indian Prime Minister'. 'Reflections', *Nation*, Oct. 15, 1965. There is a strong suspicion that the Americans demanded James's 'scalp' as part of the Chaguaramas settlement. It is quite certain that there were other understandings which were not made public at the time. It appears, for example, that the Americans agreed to help the government to obtain loan and investment capital for its island-wide sewerage and electrification projects, both of which were considered crucial for the winning of the 1961 elections. If James constituted an obstacle to the 'national interest' as it was now being defined, he had to go. For James's version of the crisis between himself and Williams, see his *Party Politics in the West Indies*, Port of Spain, 1962.

that Williams' remarks referred to him and warned the country that freedom to think and to voice contrary ideas has to be protected against those who believed that party unity was more important than anything else.

But such discontents and warnings were lost on the general population for whom there was no doubt that 'the courageous Doctor' had scored a smashing triumph over the *Guardian*, the DLP, and the American colossus, and had taught Trinidadians how to be independent in spirit and in fact, if not in law. He had brought them pottage, but without any loss of national dignity. As a leading Party spokesman phrased it, 'What made Trinidadians – and in fact all West Indians – so happy was the fact that the chief mover in this whole issue, could, with such skill, utilize local sentiments within the prescribed limits, and in a comparatively short space of time, steer the West Indies to a point so eminently satisfying to national pride.'[22]

THE POLITICS OF EDUCATION: THE CONCORDAT

A considerable amount of attention has already been given to the positions taken by nationalists and religious groups on the explosive subject of education in the 1955–6 period. The issue, which had disappeared from public notice following the 1956 election, was again brought to the political agenda in July 1960. An important event which formed the essential backdrop for the heated discussions of 1960 was the publication of the report of the Committee on General Education which made recommendations for overhauling the educational system, with a view to the 'integration of the diverse elements which comprise our cosmopolitan population'.[23]

The recommendations of this committee contain the essence of the spirit which agitated the minds of nationalists in 1955–6 in so far as they related to the creation of a national multiracial community. The committee included representatives of most religious groups, but nevertheless contained a majority of PNM stalwarts and sympathizers.[24] It gratefully acknowledged the contribution which the churches had made to the educational development of the community, but noted that the system had created a number of difficulties and problems which were never anticipated when education mushroomed in the nineteenth century. Observing that there were now fifteen denominational school boards in existence, the committee felt that this fragmentation had

22 Lynn Beckles, *Nation*, April 21, 1961.
23 *Education Report of the Committee on General Education*, Port of Spain, 1960, p. 32.
24 The representatives of the Anglican and Roman Catholic churches refused to endorse the report.

contributed a great deal towards the creation of 'an unfortunate division of plural and parallel societies in Trinidad and Tobago'.[25]

Analysis of the ethnic distribution of certain schools revealed the alarming fact that some of them, even those in racially mixed areas, had as much as 97 per cent of their school population belonging to one racial group. 'This', the committee observed, 'is not a healthy prospect in so mixed a racial population, and does not envisage the harmonious mixing of the society outside school. Nor should this harmony be taken for granted.'[26]

The committee felt that a system of state schools could combine the best elements of all the various systems, while at the same time permitting the elimination of the glaring drawbacks of the existing system.[27] A strong case was made for a system of localized school boards which would consist of both state and denominational authorities. This, it was suggested, would permit the development of a planned school system which would serve the needs of the community as a whole, omitting at the same time the jealousy and rivalry which obtained among religious groups in terms of building construction, personnel recruitment, and management. And most important, it would achieve the stated aim of having most of the school population pass through the crucible of a common school system with common curricula and examinations. Those who resolutely refused to be absorbed into the new system should, however, be left free to maintain private and independent schools. The committee did not recommend that all schools should be nationalized, or that further construction of such schools should be prohibited. It did recommend that, in order to qualify for state aid, both primary and secondary schools must agree to come under the jurisdiction of the local boards and ultimately the Ministry of Education.

The report, and the government's proposals which were based on it, had an extremely rough passage in the Legislative Council. One MLC, a Christian Indian, declared that the committee had interpreted its terms of reference to mean not integration but 'subordination and subjugation of the several denominational authorities to the will of the PNM'.[28] Opposition from Hindu and Catholic groups in the country was intense. Catholic authorities noted, by way of justification for particularistic recruitment policies, that Catholic schools depended very largely on endowments from Catholic benefactors. The Church schools had their own traditions and obligations to their own people. Many parents sent their offspring to Catholic schools because they wished them to have a religiously influenced education. All this seemed threatened by the new arrangements.

25 *Education Report*, pp. 48–9.   26 *Ibid.*, p. 51.   27 *Ibid.*, p. 54.
28 Lionel Seukeran, *Hansard*, July 27, 1960, pp. 2999–3049.

The announced aim of the Government to make education free was also opposed on the ground that 'Catholic social doctrine disapproves of the welfare state in which Government provides all social services free of charge to its citizens indiscriminately.'[29] It was nevertheless admitted that, until the community as a whole had sufficient means to pay for such services, the government had an obligation to provide for those unable to pay. But parents should not be coerced by the state because they did not have the economic means to sustain their private choice.

While the Protestant churches seemed prepared to back most if not all of the government's education proposals, the Catholic Church was prepared to fight the 'schoolmaster Government' that was seeking to invade the schools to purvey its 'abominable totalitarian ideology'. Through its press, forums, and pulpits, the clergy resolutely sought to incite Catholics to put pressure on the government.[30] Fears were aroused that Hindus and Moslems would be in charge of Catholic schools, and that party cells for indoctrination would be established in the schools. In a pastoral letter which was read and explained in every church and oratory in the community, the Archbishop contested the view that 'education is essentially a national affair'. This was a postulate which clashed with 'the law of nature as well as the positive law of God'. Responsibility for the education of children belonged primarily to the family:

Those who govern the State and administer its resources must not think, nor act, as though children belonged to it, before they belong to the family, and that, consequently, the State has an absolute right over education. The State and the teachers it employs exist to supplement the insufficiency of the family and the Church. It acts *in loco parentum*, and not on its own authority. ... Ministers of State are not the owners of the monies they administer; they are trustees. Catholics of this Territory contribute indirectly and/or directly, to the taxes; they have, consequently, a right to demand an equitable share of the monies set aside for education so that their teachers and their schools shall be able to function in conformity with Catholic principles; and without any 'strings' other than that they render an account of the use made of monies disbursed to them.[31]

The Church, it was maintained, had no objection to its followers being good citizens, and in fact encouraged it. It agreed that they should have a suitable knowledge of their civic and national duties, and applauded the state's attempts

29 TG, July 27, 1960.
30 The Catholic Church had opposed similar suggestions which were made in 1851 by Governor Harris, who had proposed a purely state school system, and similar recommendations made by the Moyne Commission in 1939.
31 Count Finbar Ryan, *Pastoral on the Roman Catholic Education of Youth*, Port of Spain, 1960, p. 8.

to 'mobilize all the people's human resources' for the development of national pride and nationhood. But man also had purposes which were not earthbound. Temporal ideals must not be sacrificed to eternal ideals. The Church would therefore 'never assent' to any arrangement which would subject the government of schools to the civil and political power, whose seeming aim was to encourage communal interdenominational worship and 'bowdlerized' religious education. The purpose of religion in the schools was not to give children 'a tremendous emotional experience of love and fellowship', but rather specific indoctrination. The Church also expressed itself sympathetic to the need for the racial integration of the community, but argued that this goal could best be achieved by 'the acceptance of the supra-national ideal given the Catholic Church by its founder Jesus Christ'.[32] Not a word was said about correcting the type of ethnic exclusivism for which some of its schools were known.

The Archbishop presented what he believed to be the 'irreducible minimum' which the Church was prepared to accept in its negotiations with the State:

(i) While prepared to cooperate as far as possible with the 'Proposed Machinery of Administration' ... the Catholic Church cannot cede its ownership nor the right of direct control and management of Her primary and secondary schools. The existing managerial system may be modified and its working clarified, but the authority of the Church ... must be retained and safeguarded.

(ii) In Catholic schools, no books, lessons, nor apparatus to which the competent Catholic Authority formally objects may be introduced and imposed; nor in non-Catholic schools may Catholic teachers or children be compelled to use them.

(iii) No teachers, including especially head-teachers, to whom the competent Catholic Authority objects on grounds of faith and/or morals, shall be appointed to Catholic schools. ...

(iv) The pluralist composition of the pupil-body in Catholic schools and colleges is a natural and largely inevitable consequence of the pluralist composition, national, racial, linguistic, and religious, of our Trinidad and Tobago society. But ... disproportionate mixing of Catholic and non-Catholic children, must as far as possible be avoided, and the clerical Manager's right to supervise the entry of non-Catholic pupils and their conduct after admission must be recognized, as well as his right to demand their withdrawal should their creedal or moral influence be injurious.[33]

Concluded the Archbishop:

We trust that a Government which professes to be democratic will modify the

---

32   *Ibid.*, p. 7.   33   *Ibid.*, pp. 12–13.

recommendations in a manner satisfactory to the Catholic Church and Catholic parents. ... The Church is not raising a question of party politics ... but all should note that Catholics are roughly one-third of the population and include representatives of every section of our cosmopolitan community. *Their suffrage is no small power*.[34]

As in 1956, the Church was again prepared to engage its authority on a fundamental issue. PNM stalwarts in their egalitarian zeal were also prepared, as they were in 1956, to take up the gauntlet thrown down by the hierarchy. But not so the cabinet. With an approaching key election, the cabinet was anxious to remove all issues around which anti-PNM groups could forge a united front. The Chaguaramas and constitutional issues were already out of the way, and only the church remained to be accommodated. On Christmas Day, 1960, it was announced that Church and State had reached 'complete accord' in their negotiations on the school issue.

By the terms of the Concordat, the churches were confirmed in their proprietary rights to their schools. The right of the Church to veto the introduction of books, apparatus, and changes in the curriculum in their schools was also conceded. The churches also retained the right to insist that their religions be the only one taught in their schools by teachers who belonged to their denomination, though pupils of other faiths were not to be compelled to take such instruction. Churches were to be allowed access to state schools at stated times to give instruction to children of their flock.

The rights of appointment, retention, promotion, transfer, and dismissal of teachers were to be vested in the Public Service Commission as was the case with other civil servants, but denominational boards were given the right to refuse to accept or retain a teacher whose moral or religious conduct did not meet with their approval. Any disciplinary matter short of expulsion was to remain solely with the boards, which were also allowed to maintain teacher-training schools subject to the provision that selection to them had to be approved by the state. On the question of recruitment of pupils, the Church made its biggest compromise. Eighty per cent of those who entered the first form of the secondary schools were to be determined by the state on the basis of a common entrance examination. The principals of church schools were left free to allocate the remaining twenty per cent '*as they saw fit*, provided that *normally*, the pass list of the common entrance examination serve to provide the pupils'.[35] Church schools remained eligible for state aid.

The Government had obviously capitulated to the Catholic Church. While some of the drawbacks of the old system were corrected, especially in regard

34   *Ibid.*, p. 15 (italics supplied).   35   TG, Dec. 25, 1960.

to teacher and pupil recruitment since the state could now use its control of the 80 per cent pupil quota to change the complexion of the schools, the churches were left relatively free to carry on as before, with only a minimum of government supervision or dictation.[36] Moreover, despite the assumption that the examination pass list would be used as the basis for the recruitment of the churches' quota, in fact it meant that the Churches were free to assign scarce school places at state expense to pupils who need not possess the achievement criteria for admission, while qualified pupils were allowed to go unplaced. With 25,000 pupils competing for 4,000 places, this was a substantial concession to make. The egalitarian purpose of the PNM was seriously compromised. Some party stalwarts were infuriated, especially since the Party had not been consulted on the issue. The author of the Report, Senator Hamilton Maurice, remained outspokenly convinced that 'in a society of competing ethnic groups, a society where religious dogma combines with racial differences, the existing educational system poses the greatest threat to national unity.' Only a unified state system could contain the strife potential of the community. 'No system that is the servant of any one particular class, race or creed can achieve this goal.'[37]

The Protestant churches were quite pleased with the settlement which the Catholic hierarchy had been able to force on the PNM, though they might very well have been chagrined by the fact that the government had bargained mainly with the Catholic Church. Between 1960 and 1965 when the issue was reopened, the Catholic Church gave open support to the PNM regime.[38] The 'opening to the right' strategy had been given additional thrust. With the Church, the Colonial Office, and the State Department neutralized, Williams could declare to the nation that the road was now cleared of all the obstacles which had inhibited the creation of the national community.

But the consolidation of the power of the PNM was a prime prerequisite for effecting this goal. The Party that had initiated the 'revolution' had to be allowed to complete it, even if this meant that some of these revolutionary goals had to be sacrificed in the short run. As Williams warned the Party, 'I for one intend to play politics. Let everybody understand that. I have been accused for four years of playing politics. Well by God, they are going to get politics now, and I hope they recognise it.'[39] The 'no deals' era had come to a close.

36 Placement in the schools, within this 80 per cent quota, was still to be determined by the parents, wherever possible.
37 *Nation,* Dec. 21, 1962.
38 The schools issue was reopened in 1965 when the PNM dramatically revoked some of the major provisions of the Concordat. Cf. p. 340.
39 Williams to the Sixth Annual Convention, January 1961.

16

The elections of 1961: preparing the ground

Having settled the Chaguaramas and education issues to the satisfaction of the greater part of the population, the People's National Movement now sought to put the results of the election beyond doubt. The basic elements of this strategy involved introducing a permanent voter-registration system, deciding to use voting machines, limiting transportation for voters, and drafting new constituency boundaries.

CHANGING THE ELECTORAL RULES

Rules and regulations for the conduct of elections are certain to divide political parties in newly emergent communities where electoral stakes are high and the results are dependent upon the fairness of the system. At no time in the history of electoral politics in Trinidad and Tobago did the question of electoral rules so divide the community as in 1961. The PNM had promised quite early in its history that it would rewrite the country's electoral laws. In 1956 Dr Williams had suggested that the country ought to employ voting machines and a system of permanent voter registration. It was felt that these provisions would help to reduce the corruption and impersonation that were so characteristic of Trinidad politics.[1] In keeping with its promise to the electorate, the government in November 1960 tabled legislation to provide for permanent voter registration. The new rules provoked one of the bitterest political debates the country had witnessed thus far.

---

1 Eric Williams, 'The Voter and the Vote', PNM *Weekly*, Aug. 16, 1956. The use of voting machines was not something thought up by Williams in 1960 following the results of the elections of 1958 and 1959.

To the Opposition the rules seemed a palpable attempt to regiment rather than represent the community. It was claimed that a system of permanent registration, whereby a citizen was required to carry an identification card which carried his photograph and recorded the colour of his skin and eyes, his height, ethnicity, religion, occupation, marital status, and so on, was not only too complicated for a population with such a high rate of illiteracy, but also too susceptible to exploitation by an inquisitive government. The government was accused of planning some sort of mischief based on colour and race. The DLP also complained that the proposed method of collecting the information was too secretive, and would afford partisan enumerators the opportunity to discriminate if they so wished.

On the basis of figures borrowed from studies of American elections, the opposition estimated that roughly 16 per cent of the voting population would stay away from the polls because of the new rules, and that most of these were likely to come from lower-class illiterates who, it was claimed, would be reluctant to reveal sensitive information, much of which they probably could not recall. The more complicated the rules of registration procedure, the greater the rate of abstention. As far as the DLP was concerned, the new provisions were a subtle attempt to disenfranchise or reduce the political power of the Indian population, amongst whom illiteracy was highest. 'A racial dictatorship was emerging under the trappings of a pseudo-democratic legislative process.' One MLC warned the Government that it could not hold or discipline Trinidad with 2,000 policemen: 'We are going to fight it out in this country. ... If they think we are not serious ... and that we intend to sit idly by and allow them to pass it with their majority, let them come to their senses. If you want peace and security in this country you must make this election fair. If 20 per cent of the country stand up against you, your Government cannot carry on. ... You cannot make this country a success by putting 51 or 52 per cent against 48 per cent. Remember what controls the country, what gives you the discipline in this country. It is the British Navy and the British Army.'[2]

Some of the charges raised by the Opposition were, in perspective, ex-

2 S. Maharaj, *Hansard*, Jan. 20, 1961, pp. 1253–5. Threats and counter-threats flew fast and thick in the Chamber when the bill was debated. Dr Solomon warned that 'When he [Maharaj] stands there and talks sedition, war and revolution, he is challenging me in my substantive capacity as Minister of Home Affairs. ... I am not afraid to die, but let me tell the Hon Member something: neither he nor 20,000 like him, and anybody else he wants to mobilize as a revolutionary army, will stop me from doing what I consider to be my duty. ... If 20 per cent of the people object, you must take it away! Who are the 20 per cent that object? People who are being misled by insidious, malicious propaganda whipped up by these people on the Front Bench of the Opposition here and others of their own kind outside for one purpose only, to get the Government to delay the Election.' *Ibid.*, pp. 1263–4.

tremely irresponsible and far-fetched, and the government had no difficulty in demonstrating to all but hardened partisans that there was no racial purpose to the bill. Drawing on statistics from other American voting studies, Williams showed that wherever permanent registration and machine-voting had been employed, voter turn-out increased by about 15 per cent. Permanent registration and machines helped to eliminate the phenomenon of 'voter fatigue', especially when the state assumed the responsibility for ensuring that voters registered. Under the system being proposed for Trinidad, the voter, unlike his American counterpart, would be registered in his home. Only the photographing would be done at central points. Williams was also able to show that the questions asked bore no specific relationship to the southern United States or to South Africa, as the opposition claimed.

In response to some of the criticisms that were being made, the government introduced twenty-seven amendments to the bill which went a long way towards allaying some of the fears of the opposition.[3] But the government resolutely refused to entertain any suggestion that the regulations regarding photographing and the identification card be scrapped entirely. The card was the only efficient way of determining the identity of voters at the polling booth. The Minister of Home Affairs quite reasonably insisted, 'If you want to have democracy you must be prepared as disciplined persons to undergo some little inconvenience. You cannot have a system where there are no laws, where people can do just as they please. People have to obey laws in a civilized community.'[4]

In the middle of 1961 another controversial piece of legislation called the Representation of the Peoples Ordinance was published for public comment.

3   The more significant of these included the provision that witnesses be allowed to accompany registration officers when illiterates were being questioned, the provision of penalties for unfair practices on the part of enumerators, allowances for the non-presentation of birth certificates except in very doubtful cases, optional answering of all but five of the twenty questions, legal remedy for complaints as far as the Supreme Court, allowances for cases where photographing was opposed for religious or other conscientious reasons, and automatic registration for all those who had completed the registration procedures but who, for administrative reasons, did not obtain their photographed cards. There was to be no penalty for refusing to answer questions, but the voter had to accept the risk of not being recognized at the polls. Paid party scrutineers who were to accompany enumerators were also conceded by the Government.

4   *Hansard*, Jan. 20, 1961, pp. 1068–9. The minister maintained that since there were so many persons who used a thumbprint as a signature, other means had to be devised to recognize them; the government did not have enough fingerprint experts to distribute to every polling station. In the event that the photographing process was not completed, the voter would have to identify himself by repeating answers previously given on the questionnaire.

Adrian Cola Rienzi (courtesy *Trinidad Guardian*)

Captain A.A. Cipriani
(courtesy *Trinidad Guardian*)

Dr Patrick Solomon
(courtesy *Trinidad Guardian*)

Tubal Uriah 'Buzz' Butler (courtesy *Express*)

Albert Gomes (courtesy *Express*)

Badhase Saganmaraj (courtesy *Express*)   A.N.R. Robinson (courtesy *Express*)

George Weakes
(courtesy *Trinidad Guardian*)

Dr Rudranath Capildeo
(courtesy *Express*)

Dr Eric Williams (courtesy *Express*)

Black Power demonstrators, April 1970 (courtesy *Express*)

Lloyd Best and James Millette (courtesy *Express*)

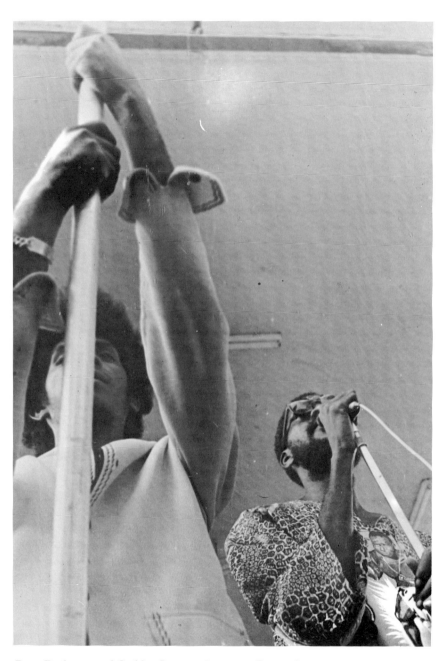

Dave Darbreau and Geddes Granger (courtesy *Express*)

Two of its provisions, the proposal to use voting machines instead of the ballot box, and the proposal that some limitation be put on the size of campaign chests and the use of hired vehicles for electoral purposes, were particularly novel and helped to intensify the hostility between the two parties.

Voting machines

The DLP put up an extremely strong stand against the voting machines on the grounds that they were unfamiliar to the population and would scare the unsophisticated rural voter. It was also argued that it was extremely easy for skilled technicians to tamper with the machines to produce a desired result. The DLP viewed the machines as a device to deprive it of the victory which it felt certain was within its grasp. The firm which supplied the machines denied that they could be rigged in any manner which would escape immediate detection.[5] The DLP argued, however, that it was not satisfied that the government was acting in good faith, and wanted an opportunity to examine the machines thoroughly. 'We are not against voting machines, *per se*. ... We are totally against the manner in which they have been introduced into the country. Voting machines do not remove voting-machine frauds. They only remove ballot-box frauds.'[6] Dr Capildeo suggested that the use of machines should be made an election issue. But the PNM was determined that the machines must be used and quite unreasonably opposed the suggestions that they be experimented with in local elections before being used at the national level. Presumably, the Government believed that voters would not have been sufficiently educated about their use by the beginning of November when municipal elections were normally held. The Opposition was convinced that there was some dark reason behind this refusal.

Transport limitation

Elections in Trinidad were usually characterized by the widespread use of motor vehicles to transport voters to the polls. Voters had come to expect and demand this service from candidates soliciting their franchise. The practice was frequently abused, especially in the rural areas where it was normal for

---

5   The representative of the firm (Shoup) was even prepared to bet the leader of the DLP $1,000 to $1 that no engineer he named could 'fix' the machines. Capildeo accepted the wager, but the gentleman in question left the country before arrangements for testing were completed. This only served to give further rise to suspicions. Capildeo took the view that anyone skilled in the mechanics of the machines would have no difficulty rigging them without detection. There is a strong suspicion in the Caribbean that Shoup is a front for the CIA and that the firm specializes in fixing elections.

6   TG, Sept. 4, 1961.

voters to be taken to more than one polling booth. Here candidates with limited access to motorized transport were at a distinct disadvantage. The PNM was quite determined to eliminate these practices, and introduced rather stringent limitations on the use of motor and animal-drawn vehicles on election day. Not only were the numbers rigidly limited, but careful measures were also taken to ensure that registered cars operated in one polling district only. Only one vehicle was allowed for every two thousand voters, and the police were given wide powers to impound cars suspected of violating the provisions.[7]

The DLP objected to these revolutionary provisions, which they again interpreted as a blow aimed specifically at the rural Indian. The argument was plausible in that Indians were known to have control of the bulk of the motor and animal-transport industry. The DLP was also correct in noting that one car to two thousand voters was hopelessly inadequate in rural, if not in urban, areas. It would make it difficult for many to vote, especially since employers were only required to give one hour off for voting purposes. Even the PNM (not the government) agreed that the limitations on the use of vehicles were too restrictive. The provision was later amended to allow one motor vehicle to every four hundred electors in rural areas, and two to every five hundred in constituencies where the population was more concentrated. It was a significant concession which helped to relieve some of the suspicions of the opposition.

The DLP also opposed the $2,400 (TT) ceiling put on election expenses. They wanted it replaced by a sliding-scale system which would allow higher ceilings in more difficult rural constituencies. It was also felt that party headquarters should be allowed to spend a general sum on behalf of candidates, as was the case in England. Both recommendations were rejected.

The debate on the ordinance strengthened objections which the DLP élite had earlier raised towards the whole idea of saddling the voter with identification cards. Dr Capildeo in fact called on his followers to destroy their identification cards:

The DLP leads the fight ... against the threat to civil liberty. I am going to tear up their identification card and throw it in their faces. I am appealing to you to stand with me. Your freedom is threatened. You are no longer in a position to say you are a free people unless you stand with me and destroy this Ordinance. ...

I have taken [an] irrevocable stand – the ballot box or boycott, and after the boycott, civil disobedience. We do not pay taxes, we do not co-operate because we have been cheated of our rights; we have been cheated of our inalienable right to select the Government of our own free choice.[8]

7   In the past no limitation was imposed on the numbers who might be carried in vehicles. The new ordinance now limited vehicles to five persons.
8   TG, Aug. 27, 1961.

Capildeo was not alone in making this demand. Louis Rostant, the French creole who had talked earlier about creating an underground resistance movement, called for the organization of a 'gigantic bonfire in Woodford Square' to destroy the cards. DLP parliamentarians promised full backing for whatever revolutionary measures their leader adopted to resist 'this nefarious act of Government', and threatened to filibuster the bill to convince the government, the public, and the British authorities that they were not prepared to accept the ordinance. The DLP was dismayed that such an important ordinance had not been hammered out in a bipartisan fashion.

While one must agree that a revolutionary ordinance of this sort ought to have been the subject of negotiation between government and opposition, there is little evidence to believe that there was any racial purpose to the legislation, which was an impressive and even puritanic attempt to correct, in so far as legislation and the threat of punishment could do so, some of the malpractices that typified elections in Trinidad. But as is so often the case, legislation which was desirable, well-meaning, and vitally necessary in modernizing a community was allowed to become the object of bitter hostility, alienation, suspicion, and threats to the social order. The government seemed congenitally incapable of neutralizing dissent, or more important, mobilizing bipartisan assent for its corrective legislation. Every act was made to seem an imposition on a recalcitrant or obscurantist minority. Williams' majoritarian thesis that 'when you win an election you are the boss with the responsibility to govern', was academically impeccable, but for one whose aim it was to build a 'national community', the strategy was extremely poor, myopic, and purpose-defeating.[9]

REDRAFTING THE ELECTORAL BOUNDARIES

It will be recalled that the Colonial Office had agreed to the creation of a boundaries commission which would be drawn largely from members of the Legislature instead of from among neutral persons from the West Indies or the United Kingdom as had been demanded by the DLP. The commission which was established under this ruling consisted of the Speaker of the Council as chairman, a judge, two members chosen by the government, and one member chosen by the opposition. The DLP, which lamented the fact that it had been betrayed by the Colonial Office, claimed that the commission was rigged by the PNM. With three party members on the commission, and a judge who was reputedly a party member, the one-member Opposition team did not have a chance.[10]

9 TG, May 19, 1962.
10 Investigations have strengthened my suspicion that the judge in question was either a member of the Party or a sympathizer.

The debate on the report of the commission provides extremely rich evidence in support of our fundamental thesis, *that ethnicity is the dominant variable in the political life of Trinidad and Tobago*. Whatever the issue, sooner or later the trails lead to the ethnic configuration of the community. The PNM insisted that the redrafting of the boundaries had nothing to do with race. It was a logical and scientific attempt to correct the cartographical indiscretions of the old regime. The DLP were, however, convinced that the PNM had counter-gerrymandered the community in an even more shameful way. The opposition member on the commission, who submitted a minority report, saw the majority report as a 'death blow to democracy'.[11]

The DLP complained that the commission had violated its terms of reference, which stated that constituencies should represent approximately 12,000 voters, and that any substantial departure from that figure was to be applicable only in the case of sparsely populated areas 'which, on account of size, isolation or inadequacy of communications', could not adequately be represented by a single member. The DLP member of the commission maintained that while he agreed that negroid Tobago should be given two seats on this basis, even though the total voting population of the island was around 13,500, the PNM delegation refused to do the same in other sparsely populated areas in Trinidad. Instead of overloading the urban areas, they did just the reverse. Most of the urban seats were 300 voters under the 12,000 pilot figure, while most of the rural areas exceeded it by 300, a discrepancy of some 600 voters. One seat in the capital city carried as few as 11,492 voters, while seats in the rural Indian belt carried as many as 12,735, 12,467, and 12,589, to give differences of over 1,000 voters. During the debate the PNM did more to point up the indiscretion of the former regime than to correct the impression that it had used the returns of previous elections to create majorities for itself. Six additional seats were given to the county of St George, which, admittedly, was the fastest growing in terms of population.[12] But it was precisely in this area that the PNM had shown itself strong. The county, if Port of Spain were to be included, now had thirteen of the thirty seats, all of which were expected to, and did in fact, go to the PNM.

The PNM took no chances even in Port of Spain, where the boundaries were redrafted to make sure that all potential DLP areas, i.e., the upper-class and upper-middle-class residential areas, were attached to heavily working-class areas where the PNM had been consistently strong. The DLP was not given an outside chance to gain a seat in the capital city as they had done in the 1958

---

11 *Hansard*, March 10, 1961, p. 1597.
12 Most of this growth was due to an influx from the countryside and from the smaller islands. The population of Port of Spain proper, which had four seats, was static.

and 1959 municipal elections. The PNM refused to accept the suggestion that they should have gone beyond the Port of Spain city limits, as they had done in San Fernando, to include part of the suburbs of St George, which might then have been given eight seats, all of which would have had a potential electorate closer to the 12,000 mark. In the countryside there was strong evidence to substantiate the DLP's claim that the PNM had herded as many Indian voters as was possible into constituencies which they could not possibly win, and had extracted from such areas large blocks of Negro voters who were then recombined into new constituencies.

Ten of the thirty constituencies contained populations which were more than 50 per cent Indian.[13] The DLP won them all. Whether or not there was any truth in the claim that one minister had boasted that the constituencies were 'scientifically gerrymandered' is difficult to say. But the evidence certainly suggests that the cartography was undertaken with the electoral returns of the previous elections in mind. The Government's delegation on the commission had been advised by a PNM constituency delimitation committee, which included some of the best surveyors in the country. As the report of the general secretary to the Special Party Convention, held in September 1961, declared, 'The committee carried out its assignment wonderfully, and advised the PNM members on the commission accordingly, the result of which is well known to all party members.'[14] The DLP, it was noted, had no comparable backroom boys.

The DLP was extremely incensed at what they considered to be political immorality on the part of a supposedly honest government. They claimed that it was now possible for the PNM to get a majority of seats with a minority of the popular vote. What is more, they could win the election without the support of the rural south and south-east. As the Honourable Stephen Maharaj warned, 'Importance must not only be attached to one portion or section of Trinidad. The people in the cities, the people in places like St George, are dependent on the people of the rural areas for their very life, and their very existence ... and so are the people of the rural areas dependent on the North. We cannot separate Trinidad. ... the action of this Government has certainly given a different status to different citizens.'[15] Maharaj introduced an amend-

13   Cf. chap. 18, tables VIII and IX.
14   Files of the PNM, PNM Headquarters, Port of Spain. One of these 'specialists' confessed to the writer that he was horrified that the secretary should have been guilty of the indiscretion of revealing such information in a report of this sort. There is no doubt whatsoever in the writer's mind that the constituencies were gerrymandered. The PNM had made only three miscalculations – Point-a-Pierre, Fyzabad, and perhaps Nariva. Cf. chap. 18, tables VIII and IX, and maps.
15   *Hansard*, March 10, 1961, p. 1650.

ment calling on the Colonial Office to disallow the majority report 'and to provide for a neutral boundaries commission comprising persons outside the membership of the House, and acceptable to both Government and Opposition by mutual agreement'.[16] Needless to say, the amendment was voted down. Completely alienated, the DLP felt driven to contemplate more forceful methods of protest.

16   *Ibid.*, p. 1660.

17
The elections of 1961:
parties and pressure groups

As an electoral machine, the PNM was in excellent condition on the eve of the 1961 election. The Party had 370 actively functioning party groups and a financial membership of approximately 16,395 which formed the nucleus of a slick and highly disciplined electoral unit.[1] From September 24, 1960, the fourth anniversary of its first victory at the polls, the Party busily began putting itself in shape for the coming 'cataclysmic' encounter.

Williams gave the Party a six-point code of responsibilities to guide it in the months ahead. The first was loyalty and discipline. Absenteeism and general delinquency in the execution of Party responsibilities at the pedestrian level, individualism, faction, intrigue, shoddy emotionalism in the selection of candidates – all had to be resolutely combatted. But discipline was not to be blind and unquestioning: 'Party democracy means the fullest opportunity for expression of your views on the policy when it is to be decided, and on the implementation and details of that policy, which, once a decision is arrived at by majority vote, must be supported and carried out by all.'[2]

The second responsibility was to the treasury of the Party. Williams complained that members were not disciplined in their financial responsibilities to the Party. Dues were paid intermittently, and insufficient support was being

---

1 There were about 431 groups on the books with over 45,000 members but many had ceased to be active.
2 Eric Williams, *Responsibilities of the Party Member*, Port of Spain, 1960, p. 3.

given to the press organs of the Movement.[3] It was noted, 'Donations from well wishers constitute by far the largest part of our revenue. There are times when we have had to solicit gifts to pay our debts, to pay wages and salaries, to meet rent, and light, and telephone bills. We are a poor Party.'[4] The Party, it was also noted, had support in business circles, and there were businessmen whom it owed and had not yet repaid. But if the PNM was to remain a mass party, unfettered by obligations to 'pressure groups' and individual lobbyists, if it was to continue to engage in successful political struggle, the membership had to do more to finance operations. 'The sinews of war is money. Our opponents have money to fight us. We must have money to fight them.'[5] The number of propaganda battles that the Party had waged during its period in power had put an enormous strain on its resources. Despite the massive propaganda output, the offices of the Movement were cramped, its officers underpaid, its printing press almost obsolete, and its files and finances in chaos and disorder. It was ironic, Williams noted, that a Party which had produced a government which had done so much to rationalize administration at the public level, was so undisciplined in the ordering of its own affairs.

The third responsibility urged on the Party rank and file was agitation and propaganda. Members were advised to take propaganda and agitation into every sphere of their daily rounds, 'in taxis and buses, at work, in clubs, friendly societies, and fraternal organizations, on and off the playing fields, at fêtes and functions of all sorts'.[6] The whole community must be politically socialized. The faithful had to be strengthened, and the uncommitted persuaded. The 'enemy' had to be attacked everywhere and put on the run. Members were advised to read Hansard and Party publications for the necessary ammunition for counter-propaganda. A research group was also established to feed information to Party cadres and to provide dossiers on the 'enemy'.

The fourth responsibility of the Party member was interracialism. The PNM, declared Williams, was not a mere electioneering machine, but something larger than itself, the function of which was the creation of a 'national community'. Members of the Party must be living exponents and symbols of

---

3   The *Nation*, the Party newspaper, had a circulation of about 11,000. The *Tribune*, organ of the Legislative Group, sold about 9,000 copies. The Party constantly lost money on these propaganda organs. Many businessmen refused to advertise lest their clientele suspect them of supporting the Party.

4   Williams, *Responsibilities*, pp. 3–4.

5   Williams, *Our Fourth Anniversary: The Last Lap*, Port of Spain, 1960, p. 13. The committee appointed to raise funds consisted of five businessmen of whom four were of European extraction. The appeal grossed approximately $180,000 (TT) a phenomenal achievement for a political party in Trinidad and Tobago.

6   Williams, *Responsibilities*, p. 5.

its multiracial and nationalist outlook. Williams warned Party members against the fallacy of assuming that all non-Negroes are anti-PNM, against the well-known tendency on the part of Negroes to make fun of Indians who accepted and displayed the symbols of nationalism. 'There are Hindus, Chinese and whites in the Movement.' Moslems, especially, 'are satisfied that they have equal stature in the Party'.[7] Party members must 'stop once and for all this infuriating nonsense that every Indian is anti-PNM. ... Some of the worst enemies of the PNM are as black as the ace of spades. Reaction knows no colour. ... A PNM Indian, trustworthy, loyal, devoted to the PNM, is a thousand times a better citizen than an anti-PNM African.'[8] No attempt must be made to impose cultural uniformity on minorities. What must be demanded, however, is that they accept certain fundamentals – the national community, West Indian Independence, and the return of Chaguaramas. Other groups had their legitimate cultural pride and affiliations. 'If we take pride in Ghana and Nigeria, we are strengthened as a new nation by being able to take pride also in India, Pakistan, China and Europe. Other groups too have their national pride. ... We ask these groups to accept the national community, that is all.'[9]

Williams admitted that the Party had not always lived up to its multiracial ideal: 'You cannot expect that you just proclaim interracial solidarity from the housetops, and, lo and behold! in four years, you break through all the tactics of divide and rule practised by imperialism for four centuries in our territories, you abolish the aristocracy of skin and colour which grew up within the imperialist framework. It takes time for some at least of the perspectives of the new society to be appreciated, and to become the conventions of the new day.'[10] The hope was that after Independence had been achieved, and the tension inherent in a period of rapid transition had been reduced, positive steps would be taken to fuse and solidify the constitutive elements of the society.

The fifth obligation enjoined upon Party members involved the selection of candidates who would carry the Movement's standard in public. The cavalier manner in which some candidates had been selected in the past, Williams complained, had saddled the Party with a number of incompetents who could not face up to the onerous responsibilities involved in office. The Party had to discipline too many persons for disloyalty, financial irregularities, failure to follow directives, and lobbying, all of which had served to reduce the prestige

---

7   *Ibid.*, p. 7.
8   *Ibid.*, pp. 7–9. Williams was surely suggesting that a Negro who did not identify with the PNM was something of a traitor.
9   *Ibid.*, p. 8.   10   *Ibid.*, p. 7.

of the PNM in the eyes of the public. In choosing candidates for 1961, party Groups were advised to 'think well whether you are enthroning factions, whether you are strengthening disloyalty, whether you are putting someone in power who will use the Party for his ends and move heaven and earth to evade his responsibilities, including financial, to the Party which takes him out of obscurity and puts him in the limelight of public acclaim.'[11]

The last appeal made to the Party related to the tremendous burdens which were devolving upon their political leader. This was perhaps one of the greatest problems which the Party had to face. Everything seemed to require the personal attention of Dr Williams. The Party held that view, as did members of the public. And although Williams made numerous appeals for mercy, it was difficult for Party members and citizens to appreciate that by by-passing other channels and demanding to see the 'boss' on every issue, they were contributing to the substantial administrative bottleneck which was already bedevilling the Party and the government. Williams himself was guilty, perhaps unwittingly, of encouraging this sort of dependence. He allowed himself to be appointed to the chairmanship of all the most important units of the Movement – the Legislative Group, the General Council, the Central Executive, the Policy Committee, the Editorial Board of the *Nation* and the *Tribune*, and the Candidate Screening Committee of the Central Executive. He was also a member of several standing and select committees appointed by the Party, to say nothing of his responsibilities at the national and federal levels, which were varied and crucially important at this time.

The entire system seemed to depend on the superhuman energies of one man who was expected to be chief job-getter, grievance officer, parliamentary debater, political strategist, economic planner (he was also Minister of Finance), Party architect, and inspirational force. Needless to say, the Party and the public also expected the 'Doc' to grace every public function and festivity with his charismatic presence. One would have difficulty locating many other national politicians in the developing areas who had assumed so successfully the many prodigious burdens that Williams heroically imposed upon himself. This dependence on the leader was an element of weakness, as it was of strength, and it was due mainly to the Party's rapid growth. The energies of all those who might have done much to build the Party, to train its cadres and educate the public, were too absorbed at the governmental level. No one but Williams had the ability, the stamina, or the determination to operate effectively at both party and state levels. Inevitably, he stole the entire show. There was no one in the Party with a following strong enough to challenge him, and he knew it.

11   *Ibid.*, p. 12.

During 1960–1, the Party's electoral machinery was drastically over-hauled. Operations committees and transport pools were established at all levels to ensure that supporters were registered and photographed. Speakers, party workers, and potential candidates were trained in the arts of campaign-ing in weekend schools which were established for this purpose. Instructions were given on the meaning and scope of party politics, the constitution, the elements of public speaking, the responsibilities of a good legislator, and the relationship between the central government and local and statutory bodies. It was a tremendous achievement which bore ample testimony to the organizing and inspiring genius of Dr Williams. It was by no means a one-man show, but the inspiration that galvanized the Party into such frenzied enthusiasm came from him as much as it did from fears of a DLP takeover. The machine was never allowed to relax until the last vote was counted. Despite its glaring imperfections, which had less to do with the framework itself than with the human element in that framework, there is no doubt that the Party was in superb shape as an electioneering machine in 1961. There had been no open splits or factional struggles of any major significance in the Party's five-year history, a remarkable performance under any circumstances, but one of revolutionary proportions in anarchic Trinidad.

THE DLP

Reference has already been made to the numerous splits and fissures that bedevilled the efforts of the DLP to forge a cohesive organization capable of coping with the PNM. The Party's basic need was for a leader who would command the type of loyalty and respect which PNM followers had for Dr Williams.[12] But it was also clear that the DLP was not attracting the younger and more progressive people in the community, the professionals, the white collar workers, and people who for one reason or another were alienated from the PNM and were looking for a home. To attract these people, the DLP would have to project a new image. There was need for a party which had a challeng-ing programme, one that was thinking seriously about the possibility of form-ing an alternative government, a party that was ready to get down to the time-consuming task of organizing a mass following into groups which would function with some degree of autonomy.

12   Part of the PNM's strength lay in the fact that the Party and the government spoke
       with one authoritative voice. As Dr W. Mahabir noted, 'The orchestra of Govern-
       ment enjoys the added advantage of a single conductor – an advantage which is in
       sharp contrast to the chaotic competition for leadership on the other side, with its
       ensuing confusion of themes and its irritating cacophony.' PNM's *New World*, Port
       of Spain, 1959, pp. 1–2.

The seeming imminence of a general election during 1959 and 1960 had given special urgency to the need for a new DLP leader. All efforts to form a third political force which would be truly 'non-racial' or 'all-racial' having failed, it was agreed that the only real hope for a viable, competitive two-party system in Trinidad lay in a reformed DLP.[13] Most people were convinced that Dr Rudranath Capildeo, a young mathematics lecturer at London University, was the man to do it. It was expected that he would lead the DLP out of its stubborn opposition to the People's Nationalist Movement. With the parties agreeing on the fundamentals of the national community, they could then compete on political rather than on racial issues.

After some hesitation, Capildeo succumbed to the pressures of Party and public and accepted the leadership. But the transfer of leadership generated a bitter power struggle that almost wrecked the Party. While most Party militants seemed willing to accept Capildeo, DLP chieftains were divided among themselves as to whether he was the right man for the job. Some felt that he had been away from the country for too long and was not sufficiently aware of the pitfalls of Trinidad politics. Others did not want to see Maraj pushed down if it meant a recurrence of the crisis of 1958–9 when a similar leadership dispute caused Maraj to walk out of the Party with the bulk of its Hindu membership. It is evident too that the Party professionals were anxious to retain Maraj because he was a proven vote winner and easier to manipulate. With Capildeo as the new leader, there were too many uncertainties about candidacies, policy, and authority in the Party.

A combination of circumstances nevertheless forced a reluctant Maraj to hand over the leadership. The transfer, which was effected amidst a show of unity and loyalty at a convention held in March 1960, seemed to augur well for the future.[14] But the crisis which many insiders had predicted was not long in coming. Capildeo's attempts to redefine party policy landed him in difficulty with those who had supported his candidacy as well as those who had opposed it. The disagreement was extremely fierce and affected both the Parliamentary Party and the Party in the country. The conflict, in fact, centred on the relationship of the Party in the country to the Party in the Legislature, a problem which the DLP had never been able to settle. The DLP could not even decide whom it wanted as its parliamentary leader.

13 It appears that attempts were made to lure two PNM ministers (who were known to be unhappy in the cabinet) into accepting the leadership role in a proposed third party to be based on the Chamber of Commerce.
14 Maraj gave up the leadership very reluctantly and only after a formula was arranged whereby it was made to appear that he had voluntarily agreed to the transfer of power. It has also been reported that some financial *quid pro quos* were negotiated, though this writer has not been able to ascertain the authenticity of the report.

The confusion alienated members of the non-Indian wing of the Party, which made an abortive attempt to dislodge Capildeo on the grounds that he had proven inadequate to the task of reforming the Party. Capildeo retaliated by dismissing the entire executive. The convention, he argued, had given him the sole authority to reorganize the Party.[15] The DLP leader was visibly shaken by the fiery baptism which he had received from DLP notables. As he observed later,

When I took over the leadership of the DLP, it was a great shock to me to realize that I was able to expend only 10 per cent of my energy in fighting the PNM. I had to spend 90 per cent in holding the Party together. ... Again and again, I realized that the greatest enemy of the Dems was not the PNM, but the membership. ... People who should have stood with me ... guiding my footsteps ... were engaged in intrigue after intrigue, which, if allowed to continue, would have destroyed the entire fabric of the Party and opened the road to dictatorship.[16]

The crisis took a serious toll on the health of Capildeo, who had to seek extended medical attention in England without having done much to rejuvenate the Party. He managed to return to Trinidad in May 1961 to lead the DLP into the 1961 elections, but he was still a sick man who felt it necessary to receive psychiatric help from an English spiritual healer.[17]

By the end of 1960 the leadership issue was thus thrown wide open all over again, with Maraj (who was recovering his health) trying to regain control. He based his claim for the leadership on what he felt was the spineless capitulation of Capildeo to the PNM and the Colonial Office on the boundaries commission. Maraj at one point was openly making plans to form a new party to smash the DLP, which was rapidly collapsing from within, while the PNM appeared on the verge of obtaining complete one-party dominance. The PNM had also done its share to harden the split by selecting two dissident opposition MLCs to participate in the conference on Chaguaramas. The whole show became 'curiouser and curiouser' when the Capildeo faction began accusing Maraj of having sold out to the PNM.[18] Maraj counter-charged that false

---

15   The attempt of the 'rebels' to recall the convention was a complete failure. Indian elements in the Party were angry at this treachery on the part of the POPPG-TLP element. As one noted, 'Not all who opposed the PNM did so for love or loyalty to the DLP. To what might be a surprising extent, support was given to the DLP only because it was the only straw to be clutched in waters made turbulent by PNM's totalitarian tendency.' TG, July 27, 1960.

16   *Ibid.*, May 3, 1961.

17   For an account of Capildeo's health problems, see Ivar Oxaal, *Black Intellectuals Come to Power*, Cambridge, Mass., 1968, chap. 9.

18   The government had paid one million dollars (TT) for some of Maraj's real estate,

rumours were being spread about him because he was a threat to the leadership. But, he warned, 'I am still the only man to beat Eric Williams and his Party. I did it twice in the past two years.'[19]

The need to keep Maraj out of the forefront of DLP politics grew out of the Party's valiant attempt to woo both the white creole element and the uncommitted voters whom it was believed Maraj would alienate. Maraj was successfully contained, and the Deputy Political Leader, Ashford Sinanan, began what turned out to be a highly competent job of building up the Party's electoral machine.[20] A fairly successful attempt was made to establish a women's auxiliary and a network of co-ordinated party groups in each of the polling districts to serve as the vanguard of the vote-getting effort. The drive to register Indian voters also provided useful activity around which the groups could be mobilized. The urgency of the electoral struggle stimulated a mass rally of minorities behind the Capildeo-Sinanan 'reform' faction of the DLP. Substantial numbers of prominent English, French, Syrian, and Chinese creoles decided to come off the fence to join the 'crusade of respectable people' against the PNM. Several established families publicly identified with the Party, and the handpicked executive was crowded with businessmen from the Chamber of Commerce.

The DLP was enthusiastic about the response to its appeal for a 'crusade' to stop the march of the PNM into a 'Castro-ite version of totalitarian dictatorship'. Members were especially delighted that Sir Gerald Wight, a white creole 'patrician', chose to return to politics under the DLP banner. This was perhaps one of the most significant events of the entire campaign, an event that helped to shape its entire tone. It was a significant coup for the DLP. Wight's decision to enlist helped legitimize the Party, and brought many of his type – 'the massas' as Williams promptly dubbed them – out in the open.

Despite these feverish efforts to reorganize the Party, no attempt was made to give it any permanent or autonomous foundation. There was always something temporary about the whole operation. The chronic unwillingness to create a firm and lasting base was in part due to the fact that DLP leaders did not want to be strait-jacketed. It was much easier to select executive members

ostensively for use as a housing estate. It was widely interpreted as a clever political bribe to keep Maraj in line, with the hope of splitting the DLP, or at least neutralizing him during the campaign. The land has remained unused so far as this author has been able to determine.

19   TG, Aug. 8, 1961.
20   Community pressure was brought to bear on Maraj to give up his leadership claim and his threat to smash the Party. It was noted that the PNM would be the main beneficiary if this threat were to be carried out. Maraj was later appointed to the recreated party executive.

and candidates when one had no recalcitrant party groups or conventions to contend with. The DLP preferred to remain as it was conceived, a collection of notables rather than a democratically structured mass party. But this is not entirely adequate as an explanation of the organizational weaknesses of the Party. Unimaginative leadership, lack of revolutionary zeal, and a general feeling that the Party could always count on the automatic loyalty of the Hindu masses also inhibited the urge towards organizational effort. It is worth noting that, in general, the persons who wished to give the Party genuine organization and coherence came from non-Indian groups whose main concern was not mass democracy but control of the volatile Hindu faction. DLP intra-party conflict was almost always at the élite level.

It should be observed that this restored alliance of the Hindus and the upper and upper-middle classes, at the expense of Maraj, caused grave misgivings among some orthodox Hindus who felt that the 'Chief' had been cruelly used by the old POPPG faction. There were also complaints that the new DLP executive was too heavily weighted against Indians. Of the twenty-nine members, only nine were Indians, and they were mainly from the parliamentary arm of the Party. Of the remaining twenty, nine were of European stock, five were Negro, four were of Chinese stock, and two were Syrians – all men of high professional or business standing in the community. Of the nine members of the inner 'cabinet' of the executive, only two were Indians. The remaining seven included four Negroes, two Europeans, and one Chinese. Of the thirty candidates chosen to contest the election, only eleven were Indians. The precise ethnic breakdown is shown in Table VI.[21] The élite was clearly a mixed bag. No less than 63 per cent of the Party's candidates were non-Indian, and among Indians, Moslems did as well as Hindus. While it is true that all the Hindu candidates were given safe rural constituencies, two such constituencies were given to Negroes and another to a Moslem. The DLP thus felt quite justified in its boast that it was 'a miniature United Nations, a rally of all creeds, races, and walks of life'. It had leaned over backwards to prove to all that it was not a mere Hindu faction.

It was clear to the DLP leadership that the Party could not defeat the PNM without the help of non-Indian elements. The Party needed the financial backing of the European business community as much as it needed the voting support of Moslems, anti-PNM Negroes, and others who were uncommitted. Dr Capildeo made it quite clear to the Hindus that alone they could win only thirteen seats. They needed Negro votes, especially those in the two Tobago

---

21   These are rough classifications. At times one has to place individuals quite arbitrarily into categories, especially when one is dealing with mixed elements. One commentator, a Hindu, classified fifteen candidates as being Negro.

TABLE VI
Ethnic affiliation of
DLP candidates 1961

Hindus	4
Moslems	4
Christian Indians	3
Negroes	8
Mixed	6
Syrians	1
Chinese creole	3
French creole	1

seats, and it was mainly for this reason that the Party endorsed the proposal that Tobago be given independent status in the Federation. The major premise that guided the reorganization of the Party and the selection of notables was that it would take nothing short of a grand coalition of all 'out' groups to overthrow the PNM. DLP faithfuls talked glibly of the new formation as a 'way of life', something that would last beyond the noise of election battle, but few were misled. It was a fragile house of cards, a rally of convenience, which almost disintegrated before election day.

THE TRADE UNION CONGRESS

The fundamental dilemma that confronted the Trade Union Congress in 1961 was to find a way to translate its strong sympathy for the PNM into political terms without endangering its tradition of official independence from political parties. Many union leaders felt that it would be dangerous for labour to become too closely identified with the PNM and warned their colleagues that, should the PNM lose the elections, labour could expect very unsympathetic treatment from the DLP. Moreover, the unity of the trade-union movement would be compromised since there were unions with large anti-PNM elements who would resent having the Trade Union Congress support the PNM just as others had resented the Oilfield Workers Trade Union leaders' support of the CNLP in 1956.

But majority sentiment in the TUC was clearly in favour of the labour movement endorsing the PNM. The event that helped to crystallize the pro-PNM labour manoeuvre in 1961 was the decision of the predominantly Negro Civil Service Association to take to the streets almost on the eve of the election in protest against the government's failure to settle a festering dispute with its own employees. PNM supporters were horrified at the CSA's 'indiscretion'. It was felt that they were trying to embarrass the government at a difficult time. The anger of party followers was intensified when it was reported that the CSA was in collusion with the DLP to force the hand of the government. This, they felt, was treason and racial suicide. The CSA, however, saw the matter quite differently: 'There have been suggestions that the Association should suspend its vigorous representation ... until after the elections, so as to avoid any possible embarrassment to Government. ... Because of the peculiar position in which [the Union] finds itself, it is convinced that this stand would be danger-ous, especially as it represents a Civil Service which is pledged to serve faith-fully and efficiently whatever Government is in power. The Association emphatically refutes any suggestion that it is playing politics.'[22] There is no doubt that the Government was annoyed by the CSA's decision, but it very wisely made no move to stop the demonstration. The march on Chaguaramas had legitimized street demonstrations for political advantage, and the PNM was being made the victim of its own education of the masses. But the march provided the excuse which pro-PNM labour elements were looking for in order to get the TUC to come out openly in support of the PNM. In an historic decision, the TUC not only decided to endorse the PNM, but also to counter-march on its behalf. Pro-PNM labour leaders now seized on all the numerous anti-labour statements which had been uttered by the press and the DLP to underscore their argument that labour must ensure that the DLP be smashed in 1961. This was a *sine qua non* of the continued advance of the trade-union movement. John Rojas, OWTU boss and a former hostile critic of the PNM, declared, 'Politics can make or break you. ... TUC leaders cannot sit idly by. ... The DLP carries a labour label, but it is quite obvious that it is strictly a conservative party, an instrument of big business.'[23] Big business had financial resources to lobby and to support the DLP; the unions had only their numbers to contribute.

The DLP leadership, it was noted, was calling for restrictive labour legis-lation while the PNM had pledged that it would introduce none, a promise it later felt compelled to break. The labour movement had found over the past five years that it had a sure and proven friend in the PNM. The TUC roundly condemned the DLP for disapproving of strikes, for its promise to hand back the nationalized telephone company to its former owners, and for its threats to the police and the Governor, whom it promised to 'fire' if it won the elec-tion. Other unionists outside the PNM camp noted, quite correctly, that Dr Williams had also condemned wildcat strikes.[24] The labour leadership was in

22 TG, Oct. 21, 1961.
23 TG, Nov. 28, 1961.
24 'A sudden stoppage of work, however justified, can affect total production and therefore the increase in the national income. Both collective and independent labour instability, whatever its cause, can jeopardize the investment climate by affecting our international reputation. An irresponsible trade union can set a bad

fact accused of playing politics in order to stake out claims for seats in the Senate.

The street marches in favour of the PNM were huge, noisy, and at times quite disorderly. The atmosphere of many were quite carnival-like, complete with steelbands. The *Guardian* and the DLP, which referred to the marchers as 'rabble parading under the banner of a trade union', called upon the government to ban the marches. Williams' only reply was that the *Guardian* had the freedom of the press, and the workers the right of assembly. To the Unionists he said, 'March where the hell you like.' Williams was openly grateful for the impressive display of support which the PNM had received from the workers. As he declared, 'If there is any group in the community which is going to defend democracy and self-government, that group is the workers. ... If any group is the repository of patriotism, that would be the workers of the country. No Government will survive without the point of view of the labour movement behind it ... and we have it. ... No one else could defend us you know. ... The workers are the force of the future. ... After the elections I recognise my *friends*.'[25] Although in 1955 Williams had opposed any representation for labour in the Senate, he now made it quite clear that he intended to nominate unionists to the upper chamber. He also promised to establish a labour college to teach unionists economics, sociology, and politics so that they might not be at a disadvantage at the bargaining table.[26] While there is little doubt that the PNM could have won without the marches, the margin of victory was substantially affected by the zeal with which labour's support was manifested. The workers had started a movement which caught on and spread to other groups as well.

The success with which the PNM had handled labour between 1956 and 1961 was quite unique in the history of the nationalist movement in the West Indies. The Party was able to mobilize and retain the support of the working class without having to organize it in affiliate unions. As C.L.R. James observed, 'Whereas it is the standard practice in the West Indies for political parties to create unions, or vice versa, here the TUC is independent. The fact that an independent body has endorsed the PNM was very significant. It testified to the confidence which the unions had in the PNM.'[27] The unions had

example to the younger generation coming behind us and can pose a threat to democratic procedures by substituting the methods of the conference table to the wielding of the big stick.' TG, Oct. 7, 1961.

25   *Ibid.*, Nov. 28, 1961 (italics supplied). Williams had been especially solicitous of the interests of the port workers, whom he provided with ambulances and other long-needed services.

26   This promise was fulfilled in 1966.

27   TG, Nov. 17, 1961. James had since been expelled from the PNM.

translated the 'massa day done' spirit into terms meaningful to them.[28] But they had also created tremendous problems for the PNM on the morrow of the elections.

THE CHAMBER OF COMMERCE

Unlike the Trade Union Congress, the Chamber of Commerce, as the major voice of the business community in the territory, preferred to retain its official position of political neutrality. The Chamber in fact took the view that, by its articles of association, it could not support any political party directly or indirectly. As an associational body which included individuals and firms which identified with both political parties, it could not take any partisan action.[29]

There were many who refused to take the Chamber's protestation seriously. As in 1956, PNM supporters were convinced that the Chamber was against them, and that it was giving financial and organizational support to the DLP. Williams himself complained that business, 'which never had it so good' was pouring enormous sums of money into the DLP war chest.[30] There were good enough reasons to suspect that business was partial to the DLP, since many prominent businessmen were on the DLP executive; but this is to simplify grossly what was in fact a much more complex issue.

The period since 1956 had been a rather difficult one for elements of the business community who were identified with the old order; they clearly missed the political, social, and economic privileges which they enjoyed under the protective umbrella of the earlier system. Despite the fact that the economy was extremely buoyant during this five-year period, the business élite nevertheless felt that its access to the arenas of public policy-making had been seriously restricted. Williams had proclaimed quite loudly that he would give no special treatment to the old lobbies, and publicly expressed contempt for the old privileged groups who were trying to use the medium of the cocktail party to influence decisions as they had been wont to do in the past. There was a shift of power, and the business community was keenly conscious of it. The victories of the labour movement in industrial disputes with the telephone, oil, and cement companies symbolized and documented this fact. Other legislation such as the new Workmen's Compensation Ordinance, the Hire-Purchase Bill, and the Agricultural Small-Holdings Act had provided additional glosses

28 Cf., chap. 18, pp. 272–5.
29 TG, Dec. 1, 1961.
30 Williams even threatened to reveal the names of the firms involved, and subtly encouraged his supporters to patronize selectively.

which underlined the fact that political power was being exercised on behalf of the small man.

But to say all this is not to agree with the view that business was over-whelmingly pro-TLP in 1961. The interest-group 'universe' was much more pluralized than many would concede. Williams himself knew this very well. As he said on one occasion:

What we have today is a large segment of the community-union of this, that or the other, Chamber of Commerce North and South, Manufacturers' Association, Busi-nessmen's Association, Agricultural Society of the island or of parts, each pulling this way or that way, each seeking to establish itself and promote its own interest, even at the expense of others, not caring about the others, each seeing an individual tree in the whole forest. This gets us nowhere, and the community, subjected to a barrage of propaganda from all sides, itself cannot see the wood for the trees.[31]

Many business groups had concluded that regardless of their personal dislike for the PNM, it was suicidal to oppose it frontally. A few of them in fact enter-tained positive feelings of allegiance towards the PNM. Whether out of love or opportunism, the fact remains that business gave as much money to the PNM in 1961 as it did to the DLP. DLP executives even contend that the PNM re-ceived more. All the firms interviewed in the course of this research reported that they divided their contributions equally between the two parties regard-less of what employees might have felt or done as individuals. This was true of both native and foreign firms. Chinese businessmen were quite emphatic that they gave equally to both groups, though there is a strong suspicion that they were more partial to the PNM. One prominent member of this group, in an unguarded remark, intimated that he did not really care which of the two major ethnic groups destroyed the other, just so long as he was left free to make his profits. The impression conveyed was that this was not an uncommon view in his and other business circles.

The business community had apprehensions about both political parties. Cross-pressures were intense for many, especially for native elements. Dr Capildeo's threats of violence sent business into a tailspin. The Chamber of Commerce was quite explicit about its fears:

The ripple of violence which has appeared on the scene and which threatens to develop into a wave, is deplored by the Chamber, not only for the death or injuries to persons and the destruction of properties, but also for the crippling effect which it will have on the economic development of the area.

This Territory, noted in the past for its stable and responsible Governments and for

31   TG, July 28, 1960.

its peaceful and tolerant people, is in danger of losing that reputation. Once lost, it will be many long years before investors from overseas can be convinced that it is safe to bring their capital and their technical skills here.[32]

The Chamber only hesitated at the last moment from openly naming Capildeo as the principal threat to social peace.

Another unspoken (at least in public) objection which the European business aristocracy held against Capildeo was his 'Indian-ness'. If it is clear that many of them did not want a 'black' prime minister, it was even clearer that they preferred that unhappy fate to the prospect of a 'coolie' prime minister whom they felt they could trust even less. This preference held as much for the social groups they represented. Capildeo was quite aware of this, and in fact bitterly denounced the Chamber for what he felt was its egregious failure to overcome ethnic prejudices and come to the rescue of democracy in Trinidad. This to him was the real issue. He warned them against the illusion that they were sufficiently entrenched in their hillside bivouacs and could stay out of the arena of politics. It was a phantasmagoria which they would soon come to regret.

But as alienated as big business was from the DLP, it was also afraid of the PNM. It was deeply concerned about the damage which Williams' massa day done' campaign strategy might do to the social order as they knew and preferred it. It was also concerned about the 'dangerous' alliance between labour and government which the elections had solidified; and it was for this reason that many businessmen who had no love for the PNM contributed so heavily to its appeal fund. It was the least they could do to weaken the feelings of dependence which nationalist forces were beginning to feel for labour. The dilemma of the business community in 1961 was real and poignant, and this should be borne in mind as the campaign strategy of the PNM is examined. One gets an entirely different impression from the loaded and inflammatory rhetoric of Dr Williams.

32   *Ibid.*, Dec. 1, 1961.

18

The elections of 1961:
issues and results

A comparison of the published policy statements of the two parties does not reveal many striking dissimilarities. The main issue that divided them was that of Federation. When the Jamaican electorate voted 'no' to Federation on September 19, 1961, the remaining nine units were faced with the problem of deciding whether to continue the union, to separate, or to create a new and different kind of federal or unitary framework.[1] As the largest and wealthiest of the units, Trinidad's attitude would be crucial to the outcome of any new negotiations. The DLP declared itself to be unequivocally in favour of a Federation of the southern and eastern Caribbean islands. The Party had come to realize, rather belatedly, that in Federation lay their only real chance to provide effective counteracting power to the PNM in Trinidad. Experience had shown that the fear of Negro solidarity against the Indian minority was largely misplaced. It had turned out to be sheer myth. Dr Capildeo had in fact argued very strongly that the powers of review and veto which the Colonial Office was about to relinquish in Trinidad should be given to the Federal government.[2] It was an extremely sound argument, and had it been pursued

---

1 For an analysis of these events, see chap. 19.
2 Capildeo had declared, 'The powers which now rest in the Colonial Office should rest in the Federation. But we do not want that power to be whittled down and its remnants given to the Federation. This will ensure the Federation with powers giving it control, but from the standpoint of veto. We cannot agree that the Trinidad Government, by precipitating talks on constitutional reform, should be allowed the opportunity to whittle down these powers to their barest minimum, if not destroy them in their entirety, thus enervating the Federal Government.' TG, May 30, 1960. It should be noted that Williams had no fundamental quarrel with this argument.

consistently the DLP might very well have escaped the dilemma in which it found itself. It could have opposed the PNM drive for constitutional reform without having to defend colonialism.

In a statement issued in October 1961, the Trinidad unit of the Federal DLP declared that the old reasons for Federation – economic necessity, international prestige, common defence, and national unity – remained, and were more likely to be achieved by the continued association of the remaining nine territories. The DLP also repeated its demand that Tobago should be separated from Trinidad and constituted as an independent unit in the Federation: 'Tobagonians must be encouraged to manage their own affairs. We support full independence for Tobago within the Federation, with economic assistance from Trinidad, in addition to the assistance given by the Federal Government, until Tobago becomes economically viable. If the Federal capital is to be moved at all, we advocate its removal to Tobago.'[3] This was a palpable attempt to weaken the power of the Negro vote in Trinidad. It was also hoped that this tactic might help to swing the two Tobago seats into the DLP column.

The parties also differed in the amount of emphasis which they gave to different sectors of the economy. The PNM continued to stress industrialization, while the DLP maintained that, important as industry was, agriculture remained the backbone of the economy. It was still the largest employer of labour: 'Agriculture is the oldest of our industries, and remains the most important, being the mainstay of the national economy. This will be the position for the foreseeable future, whatever the prospects of industrialization.'[4] On the question of trade unionism, the Party reiterated its warning that political unionism had no place in Trinidad. It deplored what it viewed as an obvious mutual partisanship on the part of the unions and the PNM.

The DLP made a number of lavish promises to expand the welfare state, to intensify technical education so that emigrants might be better trained, to build a full university in Trinidad rather than just a few faculties, and to modernize the country's transportation services, including a tunnel to the north coast that would encourage tourism. The Party also promised to lower taxation rates, to ensure that the public revenues were more productively spent and accounted for, to reform the civil service and rid it of political influence, to restore and extend the power of local government, and to safeguard the rule of law and the independence and efficiency of the judiciary.

He agreed that 'the overall responsibility for the preservation of law and order, constitutional guarantees, and the rights of minorities belongs to the Federal Government ... such reserve powers that are necessary belong to the Federal Government.' *The Approach of Independence*, Port of Spain, 1960, p. 6.

3 DLP *Guide to Policy*, Port of Spain, 1961, p. 5.
4 DLP *Plan for Agriculture*, Port of Spain, 1961, p. 4.

The DLP was quite persuaded that the rule of law was no longer a meaningful principle in Trinidad and Tobago. The PNM, or at least its spirit, was enthroned in the judiciary as well. Capildeo's thesis was that in the modern parliamentary state where power was held by the cabinet, the only real restraint was an alert public opinion. What the PNM had done, he argued, was to divide public opinion by manufacturing crises and subtly exploiting racial differences. In the process, critical opinion had become silenced; frustrations, which would normally be focused on the government in power, were directed to minority elements, who were made the acceptable targets of blame. By posing as the redeemer of the Negro, Williams had put himself beyond the pale of effective critical intelligence. To dissent was to split the ranks, to be treasonable. Whether the population was aware of it or not, Williams had used race and the symbols of democracy to establish a dictatorship, unchecked and unbalanced, and to camouflage a naked will to power and dominance.[5] Trinidad society had been 'murdered' by a revolution which had been carried through under the cloak of democratic and legal theory.[6]

But race was not the only tool used to silence dissent. Williams, the DLP argued, had destroyed the local press and had intimidated individuals who might have been disposed to criticize the performance of the regime.[7] There were indeed many people who were alienated by the Party, but who feared to come out in the open. Self-interest and cowardice reinforced each other. The DLP put the blame squarely on the middle classes for their 'spiritual flabbiness'. As one DLP candidate expressed it, 'The lack of a strong public opinion in Trinidad and Tobago is the chief cause of the political brinkmanship of our political leaders. If and when this country falls into full totalitarianism, the spinelessness of our middle-class society will be the sole cause.'[8]

On the question of public morality and financial integrity, the DLP had much to criticize. They claimed, with good justification, that the PNM was using the treasury to finance the election. They held that the government had used special warrants to hand out $6.5 million (TT) to daily paid workers in

---

5   Capildeo admitted that Indian leaders had also used the issue of race for political purposes; he even suggested that this was the reason why they have never produced an outstanding national leader. 'Dr Williams', he said, 'took a leaf from their book; that is the big disappointment about him. If people think I am going to be a racial leader, they have the wrong man.' TG, April 30, 1961. Capildeo disclosed that he had voted for the PNM in 1956.

6   R. Capildeo, 'The Rule of Law', TG, Aug. 3, 1961.

7   The DLP blamed the collapse of the *Trinidad Chronicle* and the takeover of the *Trinidad Guardian* by a foreign company on the systematic war which Williams had waged against them.

8   Robert Donaldson, 'A Strong Public Opinion a National Necessity', *Statesman*, Jan. 19, 1962.

TABLE VII
Revenue and expenditure 1956–61

Year	Revenue ($TT)	Expenditure ($TT)
1956	$ 88,468,000	$ 88,759,000
1957	101,610,000	84,798,000
1958	130,032,000	123,542,000
1959	137,060,000	163,749,000
1960	162,387,000	150,192,000
1961	147,943,000	194,645,000

retroactive pay, $4.5 million to the unemployed in an unco-ordinated 'boon-doggling' crash programme, the benefits of which went mainly to PNM areas and supporters, and $2.5 million for a job-evaluation scheme to hold civil servants in line. As in the old order, it was said, sections of the population were being extravagantly bribed. The DLP also complained that deficit financing had depleted the country's reserves. According to figures released by the Central Statistical Office, expenditure exceeded revenue in 1959 and 1961 (Table VII).[9]

The government's handling of the financing of the island-wide sewer programme also came in for a merciless muckraking. The sordid details of the 'sewerage scandal' cannot be told here. Suffice it to say that the series of circumstances surrounding the negotiations between the government, the Swiss-West-Indies Bank, and the Compagnie française de transactions internationales left many people wondering just how seriously they should take the PNM's claim to be the restorer of public morality. According to the evidence documented by the DLP press, evidence which included photographic copies of letters, notes, official communications, and ministerial bank accounts in Switzerland which were leaked out, international financiers had offered to provide a press for the PNM, shares to four or five ministers in a projected metal works company, huge overdrafts, and other privileges, in return for franchises to operate a number of concerns and, above all, to serve as the government's agents for financing the sewerage project. Because of indiscretions on the part of principals, news of the negotiations began to filter to the informed public, and before long mushroomed into one of the biggest public scandals the country had yet faced.

Williams, who was not personally named in any of the transactions, made a brilliant defence of the integrity of his administration, which seemed to satisfy most of his party followers and those who refused to believe that the PNM could ever be guilty of such shady practices. But a large bloc of opinion re-

9 *Annual Statistical Digest*, Port of Spain, 1962, p. 159.

mained suspicious. If the DLP had concentrated mainly on its published programme and on the record of the PNM administration, perhaps the 'sewerage
scandal' might have swayed more floating voters. The outcome might not have
been significantly different in terms of seats, but the popular vote might have
been considerably affected, especially in the urban areas. But the Party alienated and frightened away much of the support which might have been attracted
to it by introducing the spectre of armed violence into the campaign.

For a while the DLP was quite undecided whether or not it should contest
the election. Party officials complained that not only were they not properly
consulted on the decision to use the voting machines, but they were not even
given adequate opportunity to examine them. The veil of secrecy which sur-
rounded the machines made the DLP quite suspicious that the PNM was tampering with them in their place of storage. Members could not understand why
they were not allowed to import one privately so that they could satisfy themselves that it was tamper-proof.[10] So desperate had Capildeo become, in fact,
that he issued a clarion call for a thousand of his followers 'to come forward
on election day and smash up a thousand voting machines'.[11] He assured his
followers that if the PNM won the election, only a revolution could dislodge
them in the future.

But it was over the question of PNM 'hooliganism' and the partisanship of

10   The DLP organ the *Statesman* reported (Dec. 8, 1961) that the Minister of Home
  Affairs had told a DLP businessman, 'If you bring down voting machines and give
  them to the so-and-so DLP in order that they may teach their supporters how to vote,
  I shall break you socially, politically and economically.' The Party feared that
  many 'DLP voters' – an accepted euphemism for Indians – would not be able to
  complete all the procedures involved in casting votes on the machine, especially
  when, for lack of proper electrical facilities, the machine had to be manually
  operated. It was also feared that partisan machine attendants would give false
  guidance to such voters. They claimed that if the Representation of the Peoples
  Ordinance had not been debated *before* they saw the machines, they would have
  known that they would have needed two polling agents, one of whom would work
  with the machine attendant. The DLP was also dissatisfied with the type of instructions that 'their voters' had been given in the use of the machines.
11   Capildeo at San Fernando, Sept. 10, 1961. Capildeo always insisted that he had
  threatened violence against machines and never against persons. But in the same
  speech, we find him declaring, 'Today I have come, but I have come not to bring
  peace, but to bring a sword. We have brought peace long enough and they cannot
  understand.' Capildeo explained later that his threats of violence were meant to
  dramatize the plight of the opposition and force the community and the media to
  listen to it. He bitterly complained that the communications media were opposed to
  the DLP, and that the government had also refused to grant them time on the radio
  network to state their case.

the police that the temper of the DLP really exploded. The DLP complained that their 'people' had become the principal targets of Negro vandalism. Items on the catalogue of woes related by the DLP press included the stoning of mosques and temples, the looting of Indian homes and retail establishments, the beating of Indian vendors, the slashing of tires on the cars of Europeans, the pulling down of DLP streamers, the breaking-up of DLP election meetings, police brutality, and the use of insulting expressions, for example, 'We don't want no roti government', and 'Coolie must feed nigger'.

The DLP organ was replete with bold headlines: 'Dark Times Ahead', 'Floods of Strife', 'The PNM, the Police, and Violence', 'Rule By Force', 'Sleep No More', 'A Nightmare Reign of Terror Is Upon Us', 'Towards a Crisis', 'Congolese-Type National Guard'. There is no doubt that the Indians felt themselves a persecuted minority. They were convinced that the PNM élite was not really making more than a token effort to contain their followers. Williams' invitation to his followers to 'march where the hell you like' was seen as an open invitation to attack the Indian community. Woodford Square had become a shrine of hate where minorities were offered up for sacrifice, they complained. So tense had the situation become that Indians were ready to believe that a programme of inoculation in the countryside was the beginning of mass genocide. Wild but groundless rumours began circulating that six hundred Indian children had died following the inoculations. There were also similar reports that Indians planned to retaliate by attacking police stations and schools in Port of Spain.

In the last two months before the elections, DLP politicians were becoming increasingly desperate and seemed ready to plunge the community into open strife, which now seemed the only redressive measure at hand.[12] On October 8, Capildeo told his constituents, 'The day we are ready, we will take over this country and not a thing will stop us. ... If [the Governor] is so misguided as to tell us no, we are going to Macleod, and if he is stupid enough to tell us no, then we will come back and take over. It is as simple as that.'[13]

On October 10, the statements became even more extreme. 'The only remedy' to PNM persecution 'is to adopt the South American method of bloodshed and riot, revolution or civil disobedience, until you grind Government

---

12 The DLP appealed vainly to the Governor, who refused to overstep what he felt were his constitutional limitations. The DLP disagreed with this interpretation of the Governor's role. It argued that he was still the representative of Her Majesty the Queen, and should, therefore, grant an audience to the Party. It is in this context that the question of consultation must be viewed when we discuss the Independence Constitution.

13 Capildeo, TG, Oct. 8, 1961.

operations to a full stop, and then you get possession.'[14] The racial bloodbath which many were beginning to fear seemed more imminent on Sunday, October 15; one of the largest crowds to assemble for a political meeting began dispersing in alarm when they heard Capildeo tell his supporters to 'Arm yourselves with weapons in order to take over this country. ... get ready to march on Whitehall; get ready now. Get ready to march on Government House ... that is what I am asking you to do.'[15]

The meeting, which was held on Queen's Park Savannah, not far from the Governor's residence, was viewed by the DLP as a test case to determine whether they would be allowed to conduct their meetings in peace. They claimed that they had deliberately avoided Woodford Square for the serene atmosphere of the greens in front of the Governor General's home. Reports vary about how much heckling there was, but Capildeo felt it was more than enough. If the police and the government could not or would not restrain the crowd, there was no alternative but to turn crowd against crowd:

Wherever PNM holds a meeting, break it up; wherever PNM holds a meeting, destroy them. Do not give them a chance. Those are my instructions to you today.
Wherever Dr Williams goes, run him out of town; wherever Dr Solomon goes, run him out of town. From now on, the chips are down, and I expect you to stand with us, and free this country from this type of hooliganism once and for all.
I am asking you to arm yourselves with a weapon in order to take over this country. I have stood as much of this nonsense as I can stand.[16]

Trinidad seemed poised on the brink of racial war; security forces were immediately alerted. The *Guardian*, which appealed for an 'armistice' between the two 'warring' groups, warned the leader of the DLP that it would not support him or anyone else who threatened the flouting of the law. 'Force', declared the *Guardian*, 'was alien to our tradition. ... An Opposition is expected to con-

---

14 Capildeo, Oct. 10, Port of Spain, to a group of businessmen. Capildeo was well aware that this was an idle threat and that Caroni, a predominantly Indian county, was perhaps the only area where he could make a successful 'stand'. As he told a prayer-meeting in Caroni, 'We shall not rest until final victory is achieved ... even if Caroni alone is left. The fight will be carried on and we will make people outside feel the force of our arms, the strength of our intellect and the breadth and vision of our character.' April 17, 1960.
15 Capildeo at Queen's Park Savannah, Sunday, Oct. 15, 1961.
16 From a tape of the proceedings. The official police report maintained that there was no more heckling than is normally associated with meetings of that size. Apologists for Capildeo disclosed that he suffered from an illness, which, when aggravated, disturbed his balance. The fact that such remarks were frequently made leads us to discount this explanation.

duct itself with the restraint of an alternative Government' if it expects to enjoy public confidence.[17]

The PNM was quite convinced that the aim of the DLP leadership was to incite violence as a method of forcing the Colonial Office to intervene and postpone the elections. But the government itself was taking no chances. Minister of Home Affairs Dr Patrick Solomon, who was given the sobriquet 'Minister of War', warned Dr Capildeo that 'anyone who adores the guillotine must be equally ready to caress its cold steel.'[18] When Capildeo showed no willingness to recant, but in fact reprimanded his followers for their cowardice and irresolution, Solomon again warned: 'If Capildeo incites violence, I will slap him in gaol fast ... and he would not get out again. Nobody will be able to bail him out. ... No tuppeny ha-penny dictator [is] going to walk through this country and tell people to take up arms.'[19] Belatedly remembering that there was 'due process of law', Solomon added, 'I would take him before the Judge, and the Judge would impose the necessary sentence.'[20]

As a precautionary measure, a state of emergency was declared in a number of areas where fatal violence had occurred. The office of the DLP political leader was also raided for evidence of sedition. The DLP protested that emergencies were not declared in areas where violence directed at them had also erupted. They also complained that during the search for hidden arms, Indian women were indecently frisked by Negro policemen.[21] The precautionary measures served to harden the hostilities that embittered both sides, but they did have the effect of shocking the community out of its complacent feeling that 'it could never happen here'. It was to the credit of both parties

---

17 TG, Oct. 16, 1961. A content analysis of the *Guardian* during the period reveals a clear PNM bias. The daily played down many of the reports of hooliganism which are a rather normal part of tropical elections, but which reached rather alarming proportions in 1961. The new *Guardian* ownership, it appeared, had abandoned the oppositionist policy of its predecessors for television rights.

18 *Ibid.*, Sept. 16, 1961.

19 'I thought I was leading men, not women. I thought you had red blood in your veins. You don't have. Which of you would slap Dr Williams in his face? ... Not one of you.' Capildeo at Streatham Lodge, Nov. 19, 1961.

20 TG, Nov. 23, 1961.

21 It appears that in certain areas traditional gang rivalries had become politicized. The main purpose of the emergency, in addition to whatever arms nests might have been uncovered, was to give confidence to the terror-stricken population of the area. The government also requested the Federal government to release the Trinidad contingent of the West Indian Army, a request which was refused, much to the anger and dismay of the Trinidad government. The Federal government took the position, a correct one, that the Army was a federal unit, and as such no island had the right to request specific elements of it. It is in the context of this crisis that demands for a national guard begin to be heard.

that they chose to hesitate at the brink.[22] Had Capildeo been preventively detained, his 'martyrdom' would most certainly have been the signal for racial war. But Capildeo had clearly proven to be the DLP's greatest liability during the campaign, provoked though he most certainly was.

THE PNM PLATFORM

The major themes of the PNM's campaign in 1961 were national independence, equality, and interracial solidarity. These were to be the essential pillars of the 'new society'. On the question of Federation, the Party's view was that Trinidad's future role in the Caribbean should not be discussed during the campaign as the DLP had suggested. At a special election convention held in September, Dr Williams told the Party that the issue was still very 'unsubstantial', too filled with uncertainties, for a decision to be made at that time.[23]

The Party agreed quite enthusiastically to go along with this advice, and voted to leave the matter in the hands of the leader and his close advisers, who gave the assurance that, following the election, the country would be given the opportunity to make its views known on the subject. The PNM promised that before the Federation issue was negotiated it would 'educate and take the general feel of the population before it says anything'.[24] But it was also noted that, legally, the Federation no longer existed. There was no Federation to stay in: 'one from ten leaves zero' in constitutional law.

The reaction of the public to the decision to take Federation out of the campaign was mixed and did not necessarily follow party lines. The *Guardian*, which under its new management was basically pro-Government, endorsed the PNM's stand: 'The electorate should not be asked to pass judgment on issues, the full implications of which the politicians themselves have not yet been able to grasp.'[25] The DLP took a different view: parochial issues should not have precedence over a vital issue like Federation.[26]

22 Capildeo himself suspended all open air meetings temporarily in the hope of forestalling the spread of violence, and called upon the population to pray for racial peace. The Party also declined to contest the municipal elections in November 1961 on the grounds that it would only disturb the territory more than was necessary.
23 Files of the PNM's special convention, held on September 23, 1961.
24 Williams warned non-Trinidadian politicians against coming to campaign for Federation in Trinidad: 'If there is any interference from any outside quarter in the Trinidad and Tobago elections, I will call a meeting in 24 hours and blow up the whole damn scandal of the Federation.' TG, Oct. 6, 1961. The remarks may very well have been directed to the Colonial Office as well.
25 *Ibid.*, Sept. 27, 1961.
26 Williams was unreasonably contemptuous of the DLP's demand that the issue be debated. 'What business is it of the DLP if we are opposed to [discussing the idea] ...

The Manifesto of the PNM was in large part an attempt to make the public aware of what the Party had achieved during its term of office. The PNM took credit for the creation of approximately 40,000 new jobs, though it admitted that these gains were offset by a reduction of 8 per cent of the labour force in the oil and asphalt industries, 50 per cent in the sugar factories, and about 20 per cent on the sugar estates. Mechanization had eliminated as many jobs as had been created by new industries.[27] The PNM also took it as a vote of confidence that thirty-two new industries with an investment capital of $33 million (TT) had been attracted to the island since 1956, creating jobs for an additional 3,375 persons.[28] In 1961 alone, as many as fifty-three applications had been received for pioneer status. The Party Manifesto seemed quite optimistic that the job problem could be solved by the methods which had been pursued in the past.

The Party boasted too about its efforts to expand the supply of water and electricity to all areas of the community, though admitting needs continued to outrun facilities. Credit was also claimed for the construction of 33,000 outdoor privies, which had helped to eradicate the hookworm disease; for the new Workmen's Compensation Ordinance,[29] which had given increased and wider protection to the worker; for the Hire-Purchase Ordinance, which had made it more difficult for firms to repossess purchases after a fixed percentage of the amount owed was paid; for the Agricultural Small-Holdings Ordinance, designed to give peasants greater security of tenure; and for efforts in the field

of Federation? When we are ready to come and tell the population what they should do, [we will do so]. ... We know that we enjoy the confidence of the population to such an extent that we merely have to explain the issues, the pros and cons, argue this and argue that, and the whole population, when it sees the issues ... would go along as one united nation on this issue. ... They tell me that 99 per cent of the people in the country would follow blindly whatever I say on Federation. If that is so, then that only puts a greater responsibility on my shoulders not to play the fool and go leading the people up the garden path.' Williams at Fifth Street, Barataria (undated tape of speech).

27 DLP economist Peter Farquhar wondered why the PNM did not state baldly that employment had fallen since 1956 instead of equivocating as it did. The statistics of the Manifesto were described as a 'transparent trick and a singularly stupid attempt to deceive the electorate'. *Statesman*, Oct. 15, 1961.

28 The figure was a projection into the future. The new industries had only absorbed 1,540 persons by 1961.

29 The new compensation ordinance sought to give protection to domestics and peasants as well as industrial workers; the old ordinance had excluded peasants on plantations under thirty acres. The government now insisted that it was unlawful for any person to employ a workman unless there was in force a policy of insurance in regard to that worker. Business groups, especially small firms, argued that they were in no position to meet the financial implications of this policy.

of housing for people of all classes, including the Indian estate-worker, who no longer lived in barracks.

The reserves were indeed low, but they had gone into the creation of much-needed welfare services and social overhead capital. The government made no apologies for its crash programmes, which it claimed were designed to give the small man a job. Preoccupation with classical economics must not be permitted to obscure the needs of the 'forgotten man', who had to live in the meantime. As he surveyed the achievements of the past five years, Williams boasted that nothing had been accomplished in Puerto Rico under Muñoz Marin that had not been accomplished by the PNM in its first term.

But no one was more aware of the incompleteness of the PNM revolution than Williams himself. And as the PNM Manifesto reminded people, 'A national revolution cannot be expected, in a mere five years, to correct the neglect and deficiencies of centuries.' In terms of legislation introduced and passed, the PNM had indeed created a fundamental social revolution. But by 1961 much of the legislation was still on paper awaiting administrative machinery to give it significance. The PNM was demanding, then, a chance to finish the job which it had begun in 1956.

Williams chose to make the black-white issue the basis of most of his campaign speeches. In speech after speech he poured scorn on the European creole community and even accused them, rather unfairly, of supporting the DLP's call for violence. 'These vagabonds ... these people whose hands are at your throats, see your rising dignity and economic progress as something to be destroyed so that they may enter and rule.' He warned that he would use his knowledge of West Indian history to put their counter-revolutionary attempt in perspective:

They cuss me out because I know the history of Trinidad and Tobago. I didn't go into politics to forget what I used to teach in the University where I paid the price of my judgment. ... If I started to use history as the murderous ruthless weapon that it could become in my hands, boy I am sorry for them. After all, I did not write that history. They wrote it; I only analyse it.[30]

30 Williams told the masses that whatever history he knew, he had learned at their expense: 'Everything that I learned, I will pass on to you. By giving you information about your past, I am giving you the weapon which you can use to defend yourselves. The education of the people has been the popular rock on which I built the PNM, and the gates of the DLP hell will never prevail against it.' Williams at Woodford Square, Nov. 9, 1961. Referring to Capildeo's threats to use the sword, Williams replied, 'Anyone can come to you with the sword. I come to you with the pen. The pen is mightier than the sword. I bring to you the pen to analyse, the pen to write out the history of the past, the pen to shape the history of the future, the pen to organize society.' Williams, TG, Oct. 18, 1961.

He reminded the masses of the Water Riots of 1903 during which the upper class used the masses to fight their battles while they enjoyed all the benefits:

Violence is nothing new to the history of Trinidad and Tobago. History has shown that it is the traditional weapon, the traditional tool of the privileged. ... The call to arms is not merely the frothings of a mad scientist, but something familiar to West Indian history. This call to arms is the last dying attempt to strangle the national movement. It is up to you to decide what you do with the freedom given you by the PNM. You can cut their throats if you wish; the future is in your hands.[31]

Williams accused the whites of being opposed to him because he was black. PNM canvassers were being insulted in the 'European belt' as they were in 1956:

Hundreds of people are saying that they don't want any black Premier. ... Pure blasted prejudice, social prejudice is the issue in this election. They don't like the PNM because the PNM stands for equality, and because the PNM takes the humble person in this country and says 'hold your head high, damn you, don't hang it down any more'. This is the age of self-government. It is Massa whose head is knocked down, that's all. Ours is a very simple philosophy. You take from those who have had too much for too long, and distribute it among those who have had too little for too long.[32]

Williams accused the whites of rejecting the conciliatory hand which had been offered them after 1956. Numerous appeals had been made for their co-operation, for their understanding; yet they turned to the DLP. This was especially true of the creole Europeans:

The local business big-shot families, French creoles in particular, determined to control this country as they controlled it for several years, are going all about the place irritating PNM members, saying they don't want any black Premier. For five years we have tried to make a national community of this whole people ... it didn't matter who attacked us in 1956. We invited all and sundry to work for the benefit of the country as a whole, and after five years to have this offensive campaign, sparing no effort or money to destroy the PNM and push the country back into the slavery and domination that we of the PNM have brought it away from. ... We didn't cut anybody's head off. ... I would like to send some of them over to Cuba

31 *Nation*, Nov. 17, 1961. The bitter attacks on the police were also seen as an invitation to the Colonial Office to land troops and suspend the constitution as they had done in British Guiana.
32 Williams at St George County Council Hall (undated tape). This and other speeches referred to below were monitored on tapes made by the PNM Secretariat during the elections of 1961.

for Castro to do a little purging and see what happens when they come back. Ladies and Gentlemen, they have it good here.[33]

The 'massas' were also accused of being opposed to the government's decision to introduce free secondary education. All the old arguments against the ascriptive bias of the old school system were again aired. In spite of the new concordat, which was not yet operative, Williams still pointed the accusing finger at the Catholic school system. 'Even if you could afford to pay, they gave preference to the Venezuelan child.' The 'massas' were up in arms against the new education system because it made it more difficult for them to bribe their way into the island's best schools. 'But they can't do that any more. Nobody is getting in unless they pass the Common Qualifying Examination.' The Honourable John O'Halloran, himself a European, also declared that whites were opposed to the new system because they knew that their sons could not compete equally with the achievement-oriented sons of lower-class parents; nor did they want to send their children to school with coloured 'rabs'.[34]

The PNM's proudest boast during the campaign was that it had now freed the educational system of the virus of influence-peddling. Education was no longer open only to the privileged aristocracy of the skin; it was free.[35] Williams warned parents that they should avoid giving their ingrained prejudices to the young: 'Set the children free. Let them show their talent and make their contribution to the building of the national community.'

He also accused French creoles of seeking to mount an economic counter-revolution: 'They are trying to get their blasted hands back at your throats after we, the PNM, have moved them. The exporters wanted to be free again to defraud the cocoa farmers, to pay them unfair prices based on quantity rather than quality. They wanted the Telephone Company handed back to the old Company. They were also planning to restrain labour, to fix wages, and return to the old practices whereby troops and scabs were used to break strikes.'[36] This was the programme that the DLP – 'the shoe-shine boys for the planters and merchants in Port of Spain' – had endorsed. 'The DLP', Williams claimed, 'was waging a last-ditch fight because they knew that if they lost in 1961 they

---

33 Williams at La Brea and Barataria (undated tape).
34 There was much truth in this accusation. Some white creoles, and even the brown middle-classes, were opposed to an education system in which children of black lower-class families were permitted to socialize with their offspring.
35 Education was not yet entirely free, but this was promised in the budget of 1960. The programme for 1961 was to increase secondary school scholarships from one hundred to four hundred. We have already noted that there was a loophole in the Concordat which made it possible for children to be admitted on ascriptive grounds. See chap. 15.
36 Undated tape.

would be saddled with the PNM for another three decades.' They wanted to stop the revolution, and 'restore the old order with its social practices that have kept you and me where we have been with all our frustrations and inhibitions. But if there is one thing I am going to do in this election, it is to mobilize the whole force of national dignity and national decency to defeat once and for all the DLP and their reactionary tendencies.'[37]

It should be noted that Negroes were not the only ones to whom this type of appeal was made. Indian proletarians and cane-farmers were reminded that they too were the victims of the 'massa' system. 'Sahib day done', he told them. Williams informed the Indians that he had concerned himself with the history of their degradation as much as he had with that of the Negroes. 'I know the history of every one of you here better than anyone else in Trinidad', he boasted. 'I have made that my business, and knowing that history, I know the road we have to go. The only alternative to that road is the road we have come from, the road of the planters and the road of the merchants in Port of Spain.'[38] The Government's health programme in the sugar belt, the new bargaining status given to the independent cane-farmers, the tractor pools, and the new tenure arrangements were all designed to correct the neglect of the

37   The comments of Albert Gomes on the question of counter-revolution are worth repeating at some length. It is an assessment with which, for the most part, I agree. 'If counter-revolution it is, who is responsible for it? Did PNM scuttle its own so-called revolution, or is the Opposition, as Dr Williams now alleges, making the attempt to do this? The truth is that Dr Williams and his Party have been zig-zagging along the political road since 1956, alternately driving to the Left and to the Right – until 1960, a year that marks a definite turn to the Right with the ruthless unloading of Mr C.L.R. James and the *détente* with the Americans over Chaguaramas . ... any suggestion that the election is a battle between the forces of progress (PNM) and those of reaction (DLP) is a convenient fiction invented by Dr Williams. ... In an ideological sense, this is a battle between Tweedledum and Tweedledee, both of whom are driving hard on the Right. If Dr Williams sees capitalist ghosts in the Opposition camp, he has only to be reminded of the capitalist phantoms in his own camp. ... No doubt Dr. Williams has justifiable grounds for accusing many of his opponents of opposing him and his Party because they do not like to see persons like himself in prominent positions, nor are such persons at all willing to bend to the winds of change.
'But Dr Williams would be indulging in dangerous self-deception if he were to conclude that that is the entire story. The truth is that thousands of people in Trinidad and Tobago, who desire the same change that he does, disagree entirely with both the methods by which he has introduced such changes and the venomous character he has imparted to the actual changes. ... To them, the election is a fight not to re-establish the *status quo ante* but to retrieve some of the order and the goodwill and the ordinary decency without which, no matter the ostensible gains, progress is not worthwhile.' Albert Gomes, 'PNM Counter-Revolution', TG, Nov. 19, 1961.
38   Williams at Chaguanas (undated tape).

sahib era. Free education was for Indians too, he reminded them: 'We don't have any segregation in the PNM. You have to understand that this is a social revolution at work in Trinidad and Tobago that knows no colour, that knows no race, that distinguishes only between the depressed and the disinterested, and those who have always had too much. The election issues are social not racial. Race has only confused and complicated the issue. We can't work miracles, but our goal is racial integration.'[39]

Williams was trying to appeal to the Indians over the heads of their leaders, who he said had done nothing in the pre-1956 period to help the people's economic plight, but had merely ridden on their backs into power. They, the sons of the sahibs, had now joined the plantocracy to keep the masses where they were. The PNM's aim was to forge a revolutionary front of the 'have-nots' against the 'haves'.

Williams considered it strategically necessary to win at least one seat in the Indian strongholds.[40] It was the evidence which he needed to show that his Movement could cut through the inherited prejudices of the colonial past. In 1961, however, he was not too sanguine about the possibilities; nevertheless he felt sure that, if not in 1961, certainly in the near future 'DLP fathers would produce PNM sons' once the revolution had begun to have its full impact.

In response to the spate of criticism that his 'calibanistic anti-massa' raving was sheer racialism, the purpose of which was to turn blacks against whites, Williams repeated what he had often said before: 'Not all Massas were white, nor were all whites Massas', though the majority of them were. 'Massa is not a racial term', he corrected. 'Massa is the symbol of a bygone age. Massa Day is a social phenomenon; Massa Day Done connotes a political awakening and a social revolution.'[41] He drew attention to the number of whites, both in Europe and the West Indies, who had opposed the plantation system.

He also made reference to the West Indian *café-au-lait* society, which had constituted itself a new caste on the periphery of the white establishment.

39   Williams at Couva (undated tape).
40   In this context it should be noted that Williams was also anxious to win Butler's following in the oil belt. To do this, he found it necessary to play down Butler's role in the 1937 riots. He told the residents of Strikers' Village, 'When you the people had decided to fight for your emancipation, you did it, not Butler. He led you. You created your own traditions then. If you feel ashamed of what your erstwhile leader of yesterday is attempting to do today, move away from him, hang your head in shame. The old man led the movement, your movement. Today you must lift it higher than it was in 1937. ... We the PNM will continue what you started. Leaders have come and gone before. Any national movement will also throw up its own leaders. ... Mr Butler is a national figure and as such should have been left to glory in his past actions.' (Undated tape.)
41   Eric Williams, *Massa Day Done*, Port of Spain, 1961, p. 2.

These people were still opposed, as they had been in the past, to any social progress which threatened to displace them from their preferential positions. Williams never really trusted the mixed Trinidadian middle class, who he believed were identifying with the DLP. He reprimanded the 'so-called respectable people' for their lack of patriotism, for their abdication to the masses: 'You have today a curious picture in Trinidad and Tobago. Where one was forced once to associate political power and prestige with people who were considered respectable, today one has to go down to the mass movement ... for the expressions of patriotism, decency and self-respect.'[42] Middle-class blacks also came in for their share of abuse. They too were social climbers, 'anxious to get close to the massas', and unconcerned about the needs of the masses.

The hostile reaction to Williams' 'massa day done' electoral strategy did not come from whites and near-whites alone. Some of its most vocal critics were Negroes who insisted that it was either mischievous or misleading in terms of fact. One such critic expressed concern that Williams seemed unable to settle into the role of a national statesman. While applauding Williams for his 'rousing evangelism' which had hastened the coming of responsible government, he nevertheless felt that it was time for him to shift his image from that of the protest leader to that of a sober and responsible statesman.[43]

Criticism of Williams' analysis also came from the small African National Congress (ANC). John Broome, its founder and leader, noted that despite the PNM's proud boasts, the Negro population still did not have any significant economic or social status. The majority were still employed in menial occupations. Given this situation, it was surprising that there had been no open revolt against the system. Using idioms similar to those used by Black Muslims in America, Broome urged Africans (a term he preferred to 'Negroes') to begin doing business on a racial basis. Africans should 'buy black' and strive to build up an economic empire of their own.

Broome was aware of the dangers of this programme in a close society such as Trinidad's: 'The question lurks in one's mind as to how it is possible to achieve this aim without endangering racial relationships.' But he believed that with tolerance and understanding no problem need arise. He felt sure that everyone 'agrees and sees the necessity for collective security among Africans in the West Indies. Once it is conceded that this is necessary, and once it is agreed that the strategy is not anti-white or anti-Indian in its bias,

42 Williams at Cornelio St., Woodbrook (undated tape).
43 Canon Farquhar felt that Williams had not calculated accurately the latent impact that such sloganeering would have on social order and discipline. He was 'throwing out the baby with the bath water'.

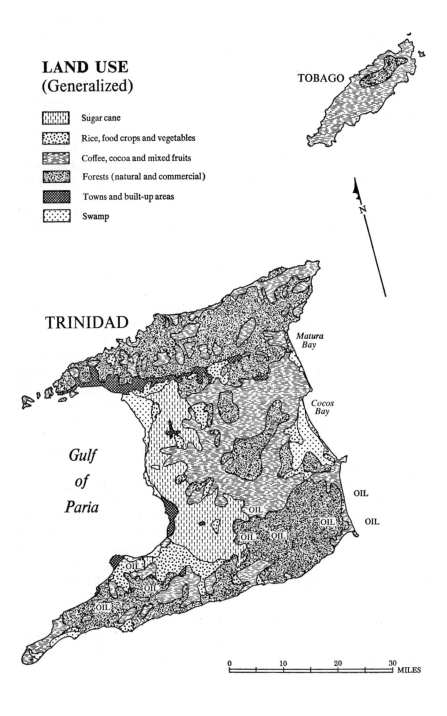

LAND USE
(Generalized)

▦	Sugar cane
▦	Rice, food crops and vegetables
▦	Coffee, cocoa and mixed fruits
▦	Forests (natural and commercial)
▦	Towns and built-up areas
▦	Swamp

TOBAGO

N

TRINIDAD

Matura Bay

Cocos Bay

Gulf of Paria

OIL

OIL

OIL

OIL

OIL

OIL

OIL

OIL

OIL

0	10	20	30

MILES

but rather pro-black, there should be no hostility.'[44] Broome's criticism was that Williams talked a lot about African dignity, but that he had done little to give it economic significance. Williams, in truth, had reminded the masses of the economic power which they held in their hands to punish anti-national merchants, but on no occasion had he ever publicly urged pro-black purchasing strategies. Given the ideology of the PNM, he simply could not, though he must have thought about it quite frequently.

Broome's criticisms about the failure of the PNM to do much by way of integral West-Indianization were correct, though they were somewhat unfair. Williams had always expressed himself determined that the West Indies must be run by West Indians. But at the same time he was not anxious to farm out strategic jobs to West Indians simply because they were West Indians. Nevertheless, over the five-year period, the top levels of the administration, both in the civil service and on statutory boards, had been almost fully West-Indianized, and the bulk of the appointees were mixed or fully negroid.

It was in the private sector that the problem presented real difficulties. Except for a limited number of cases, there were few dark Negroes or Indians in the senior offices of the industrial and commercial establishments of the community. Many of these firms still imported Europeans to fill positions which, with a little training, locals could have filled:

Looking around in several Port of Spain offices, there sit comfortably behind executive desks third raters from abroad, doing jobs from which Trinidadians have been kept out and which our people can do much better. And what is more, jobs are found for their wives. These people should never have been allowed to enter the country for the purposes for which they came and remained – doing jobs of no particular importance and requiring no particular skill, and what is more, depriving our Trinidadians of a job. Heed must be paid to our national aspirations, and our people must be allowed to grow to the full height of their stature in their own country. Gone must be the days when a linesman from Yorkshire can pose as an engineer in Port of Spain.[45]

Some firms had made efforts to promote to managerial positions locals who had long been stagnating in their employ, but these were essentially mixed *café-au-lait* people, not Indians or Negroes, who, to this day, have only marginal representation in the business-managerial élite. One journalist complained, 'The shade complex is the curse of Trinidad society. It makes a hollow mockery of the words "local man". How many "local men" of a certain colour and race make the progress in the sphere of private employment to

44   TG, Oct. 17, 1961.
45   *Ibid.*, Feb. 3, 1963.

which their ability, conscientiousness and integrity entitle them? The square deal and fair shares principle must be extended to private industry.'[46]

Some employers were anxious to bring in skilled persons of any colour to cope with the increased volume of business and to maintain their competitive positions, but resistance within firms, especially family establishments, proved too strong. Williams complained about these discriminatory practices, but not until 1963 did he attempt to impose curbs on the importation of alien personnel. Even this did not go very far in altering the complexion of offices in the private sector, which are still largely owned by European and North American capital. There are many radicals who wish that the PNM as a party, if not as a government, would do more to organize sanctions to force employers to give equal opportunity to talent, irrespective of its ethnic identification.

But such considerations were not very relevant to the campaign of 1961. If Negroes worried about them, the general feeling seems to have been that before long in Trinidad it would be 'Please Mr Nigger, Please!', to use the phrase of the calypso. Certainly this is what Williams seemed to have been promising when he advised the 'disinherited and the dispossessed' to hold their heads high since they were about to come into their kingdom. As he exhorted:

Hold up your heads high, all of you, the disinherited and dispossessed, brought here in the lowest states of degradation to work on a sugar plantation or a cocoa estate for Massa. All of you, don't hang your heads in shame. You are today taking over this country from the Massa's hand. ... In the last five years I have symbolised, as the head of the Government, the determination of PNM and the majority of the people of the country never to allow Massa to have the privileges that he has had in the fifty or a hundred years before.[47]

Borrowing another phrase from the calypso, he advised the masses to, 'clear the way, and let the people make their play'.

Williams warned the DLP against speculating on intervention from the Colonial Office to delay the movement to Independence. He unequivocally rejected the charge that he was pro-Castro and made it quite clear that he was not in sympathy with what he referred to as Castro's 'extravagance':

We will tolerate no interference from the United Kingdom in the electoral laws of Trinidad and Tobago. Trinidad wanted neither intervention from the right nor from the left; it merely wanted to be left free to build its own national community now that some of the major struggles against colonialism were behind. That revolu-

46   *Ibid.*, Nov. 24, 1957.
47   Williams at Nariva (undated tape).

RACIAL PATTERNS
By minor civil divisions

Over 50% Creole

Over 50% East Indian

Not over 50% of either

TOBAGO

Scarborough

N

ST. DAVID

U.S. LEASED
AREA

ST. GEORGE

•Arima

ST. ANDREWS

Port of Spain

CARONI

NARIVA

TRINIDAD

San Fernando

VICTORIA

MAYARO

ST. PATRICK

```
0        10        20        30
|‖‖‖‖‖|‖‖‖‖‖|‖‖‖‖‖|‖‖‖‖‖|  MILES
```

tion has been peaceful ... no blood flowed in Trinidad. ... Some people are opposing this. If they do not like it, they can go to Castro, or they can go to Jagan.[48]

The PNM campaign in 1961 was an enormous success and few objective analysts doubted that the Party would be returned with an increased majority. It was also clear that despite the extremely radical tone of Williams' campaign speeches, the Party was planning no radical swing to the left. Williams' supreme achievement in 1961 was to convince his followers that Independence would mean a new deal for the small man, while at the same time maintaining Anglo-American confidence in his Party's orthodoxy.

ELECTION RESULTS

Both the PNM and the DLP were confident of victory. Both parties were sure that they would win a minimum of ten seats and a fair share of those where the two major ethnic groups were relatively evenly balanced. Though the PNM 'ran scared', it nevertheless felt certain that it would win twenty of the thirty seats. The DLP, fooled by the large crowds which followed its meetings perhaps out of curiosity and the expectation of excitement, widely anticipated that it would win twenty-three to twenty-five seats. That the Party won only ten seats came as a shock to many. One DLP candidate, on the morrow of the election, declared: 'Surprise more than disappointment agitates me at the result of this election. All of us believed we had an excellent chance to form the Government. We worked ceaselessly as a team to achieve this aim. Now, in retrospect, I can visualize that we were not as well organized as we thought. Perhaps, too, we made tactless mistakes and underrated our opponents.'[49]

Other members of the DLP were not as graceful. They noted with chagrin that the PNM had won all six of the newly created seats, and were frankly puzzled by the showing which the PNM made in presumably Indian strongholds. The political leader of the DLP declared, 'We did not fight an election. We simply went through the motions of a monstrous farce. We were given certain seats by the PNM and we wrestled two from them – Point-a-Pierre and Fyzabad.' Far from providing a method which would ensure free elections as far as human ingenuity could guarantee, as Williams had claimed, 'the PNM has found a way to win elections without popular support.'[50]

The PNM was jubilant over its victory and the fact that by winning 58 per

---

48   Williams was referring to C.L.R. James, who was expelled from the Party in September 1961 on an absurd charge of embezzling Party funds; but it was an open secret that James wanted to push the revolution further to the left. TG, Oct. 6, 1961.

49   Hon L. Seukeran, *ibid.*, Dec. 5, 1961.

50   The *Statesman*, Dec. 8, 1961.

cent of the popular vote it could no longer be accused of being a minority government. The Party was also enthusiastic about the wide distribution of its support. It had won two of the three rural constituencies in the eastern counties and ran very well in the third. It had also won the two St Patrick constituencies that had given birth to the revolutionary nationalist movement in the 1930s and which, until then, had remained relatively faithful to Butler. Butler himself was decisively defeated, gaining only 617 votes or roughly 6 per cent of the votes in his constituency. Both Tobago constituencies, predictably, went to the PNM.[51] Victory in Port of Spain North was especially satisfying to the nationalists, though the white and near-white upper and middle classes of that constituency had again rejected the PNM.[52] In the three sugar seats of Caroni, the PNM ran fairly well, gaining an average of 33 per cent of the votes, with a 40 per cent share in Caroni East, which it had been accused of gerrymandering.

Tables VIII and IX show the extent to which party support coincided with the racial distribution of the population. A number of conclusions can be drawn from these figures. The PNM had improved its hold on the voters in the four Port of Spain constituencies. Whereas in 1956 the Party had received roughly 67 per cent of the votes, in 1961 this figure was increased to 74 per cent. But considering the assumed omnipotence of the Party in the urban areas, it is perhaps surprising that the DLP did so well. When the figures for the city as a whole are compared with the returns from the lower-class Negro constituency of Laventille, where the PNM gained 93.53 per cent, the only conclusion that can emerge is that the DLP vote in the city came mainly from the upper and middle classes. The 'Massa day done' slogan had achieved its desired effect. If one looks at Port of Spain North and West, where the middle- and upper-class elements represent a fair proportion of the population, the DLP performance appears decidedly better. Here the Party gained roughly 33 per cent of the vote. Given the extremely unimaginative campaign which the DLP waged, this percentage is even more surprising. The argument that the PNM was rejected by large sections of the middle class is given further support by the figures from San Fernando West, where the DLP won an impressive 42.59 per cent of that electorate. The PNM had only improved its position there by 3 per cent since 1956. Considering its boasts of impressive achievements, this was indeed puzzling.

One can conclude two things from the analysis of these selected urban constituencies. First of all, it appears that the PNM's style of governing had not appealed to a large number of people in urban Trinidad, especially those

51 Tobago's old feudal boss A.P.T. James died shortly after.
52 Williams was himself defeated in the middle-class areas of his largely lower-class constituency.

TABLE VIII
The ethnic geography of electoral districts 1961

	District	Total	Negro	White	East Indian	Chinese	Mixed	Others
Diego Martin	N	30,850	15,809	2,031	4,064	459	8,055	432
	%		51.24	6.58	13.17	1.49	26.11	1.40
Maraval	N	31,478	15,251	3,313	4,588	373	7,540	413
	%		48.45	10.52	14.57	1.18	23.95	1.31
San Juan	N	32,944	22,049	111	3,878	237	6,473	196
	%		66.93	0.34	11.77	0.72	19.65	0.59
Laventille	N	23,674	20,144	32	946	105	2,399	48
	%		85.09	0.14	3.99	0.44	10.13	0.20
Barataria	N	31,053	12,470	20	13,538	287	4,579	159
	%		40.16	0.06	43.60	0.92	14.74	0.51
St. Augustine	N	33,401	8,893	607	19,475	230	4,000	196
	%		26.62	1.82	58.31	0.69	11.97	0.59
St. Joseph	N	28,198	12,629	382	6,225	352	8,129	481
	%		44.79	1.35	22.08	1.25	28.83	1.71
Tunapuna	N	27,670	10,940	459	10,585	186	5,138	362
	%		39.54	1.66	38.25	0.67	18.57	1.31
Arima	N	27,133	8,783	176	6,448	322	10,716	688
	%		32.37	0.65	23.76	1.19	39.49	2.54
Toco-Manzanilla	N	22,337	11,226	69	5,032	123	5,676	211
	%		50.26	0.31	22.53	0.55	25.41	0.94
Nariva	N	28,732	7,845	85	15,226	113	5,110	353
	%		27.30	0.29	52.99	0.39	17.78	1.23
Ortoire-Mayaro	N	28,514	11,763	96	11,238	103	4,993	321
	%		41.25	0.34	39.41	0.36	17.51	1.12
Point Fortin	N	27,647	15,136	440	7,340	238	4,317	176
	%		54.75	1.59	26.55	0.86	15.61	0.64
La Brea	N	28,770	17,400	92	5,638	405	5,085	150
	%		60.48	0.32	19.60	1.41	17.67	0.52
Siparia	N	30,638	6,273	192	20,800	155	3,082	136
	%		20.47	0.63	67.89	0.50	10.06	0.44
Pointe-A-Pierre	N	30,069	9,492	1,227	16,876	96	2,301	77
	%		31.57	4.08	56.12	0.32	7.65	0.26
Couva	N	28,380	6,683	258	19,591	85	1,723	40
	%		23.55	0.91	69.03	0.30	6.07	0.14
Fyzabad	N	25,680	9,176	141	14,205	132	1,975	51
	%		35.73	0.55	55.31	0.51	7.69	0.20
Naparima	N	31,678	4,893	148	25,453	99	1,085	0
	%		15.45	0.47	80.35	0.31	3.42	0.00

TABLE VIII continued

	District	Total	Negro	White	East Indian	Chinese	Mixed	Others
Caroni East	N	32,113	6,528	54	21,019	150	4,129	233
	%		20.33	0.17	65.45	0.47	12.86	0.72
Chaguanas	N	29,987	5,624	69	22,617	179	1,409	89
	%		18.75	0.23	75.42	0.60	4.70	0.30
Princes Town	N	31,558	7,272	75	21,022	118	2,997	74
	%		23.04	0.24	66.61	0.37	9.50	0.23
San Fernando East	N	30,687	15,797	599	10,079	212	4,000	0
	%		51.48	1.95	32.84	0.69	13.03	0.00
San Fernando West	N	27,847	11,766	884	8,128	592	6,077	400
	%		42.25	3.17	29.19	2.12	21.82	1.44
Port of Spain North	N	30,884	18,601	2,094	1,299	975	6,338	1,577
	%		60.23	6.78	4.21	3.16	20.52	5.11
Port of Spain South	N	23,945	14,728	452	1,653	1,006	5,279	827
	%		61.51	1.89	6.90	4.20	22.05	3.45
Port of Spain East	N	23,270	17,129	86	1,229	323	4,363	140
	%		73.61	0.37	5.28	1.39	18.75	0.60
Port of Spain West	N	23,516	10,563	722	4,203	798	6,318	912
	%		44.92	3.07	17.87	3.39	26.87	3.88
Tobago East	N	14,030	13,300	42	182	6	449	51
	%		94.80	0.30	1.30	0.04	3.20	0.36
Tobago West	N	19,303	17,780	214	232	54	979	44
	%		92.13	1.10	1.20	0.27	5.10	0.20

TABLE IX
The results of the Trinidad and Tobago
general elections 1961

	Votes cast	Candidates' percentage of total votes cast
Diego Martin		
PNM	9,017	69.55
DLP	3,151	24.32
ANC	784	6.05
Maraval		
PNM	8,161	66.54
DLP	4,102	33.45
San Juan		
PNM	10,330	80.20
DLP	2,549	19.79

TABLE IX continued

	Votes cast	Candidates' percentage of total votes cast
Laventille		
PNM	10,494	93.53
DLP	725	6.46
Barataria		
PNM	7,513	56.28
DLP	5,835	43.71
St. Augustine		
DLP	8,256	64.23
PNM	4,596	35.76
St Joseph		
PNM	8,184	66.53
DLP	4,116	33.46
Tunapuna		
PNM	6,690	57.71
DLP	4,901	42.28
Arima		
PNM	6,719	60.86
DLP	4,320	39.13
Toco-Manzanilla		
PNM	6,033	66.74
DLP	3,006	33.25
Nariva		
DLP	6,938	60.84
PNM	4,464	39.15
Ortoire-Mayaro		
PNM	6,792	60.81
DLP	4,152	37.21
Butler	213	1.90
Point Fortin		
PNM	7,019	61.50
DLP	4,098	35.90
Butler	296	2.59
La Brea		
PNM	7,924	76.50
DLP	1,816	17.53
Butler	617	5.95
Siparia		
DLP	7,483	64.984
PNM	4,030	34.998
Pointe-a-Pierre		
DLP	6,705	57.18
PNM	5,021	42.81
Couva		
DLP	8,239	69.03
PNM	3,695	30.96

TABLE IX continued

	Votes cast	Candidates' percentage of total votes cast
Fyzabad		
DLP	6,624	49.35
PNM	6,498	48.40
Butler	210	1.56
Ind.	90	.69
Naparima		
DLP	8,815	77.54
PNM	2,553	22.45
Caroni East		
DLP	6,767	59.40
PNM	4,624	40.59
Chaguanas		
DLP	8,329	72.64
PNM	3,140	27.35
Princes Town		
DLP	7,986	65.79
PNM	4,151	3.42
San Fernando East		
PNM	9,061	71.87
DLP	3,546	28.12
San Fernando West		
PNM	6,441	57.40
DLP	4,779	42.59
Port of Spain North		
PNM	6,959	68.29
DLP	3,230	31.70
Port of Spain South		
PNM	7,809	80.24
DLP	1,922	19.75
Port of Spain East		
PNM	8,292	83.88
DLP	1,077	10.89
ANC	516	5.22
Port of Spain West		
PNM	5,853	60.81
DLP	3,438	34.38
ANC	334	3.47
Tobago East		
PNM	3,401	69.85
DLP	1,468	30.14
Tobago West		
PNM	4,807	67.90
Ind.	1,412	19.94
DLP	860	12.14

Source: *Report on the General Elections 1961.* Port of Spain, 1965, Table 4.

who did not identify with the Negro majority. The middle class is predominantly mixed racially. It can also be argued that, had the DLP not suffered as much in the past from leadership crises, and had Capildeo not frightened the population to such an extent by his call to arms, the results might very well have been different in terms of popular votes, if not in seats. There are informed people who believe that the DLP could have won the election had Capildeo proven equal to the expectations which many held in 1960. The thesis of this study – that ethnicity was more relevant than cognitive evaluations – leads me to reject this contention. The figures are quite eloquent in their support of this assumption: the DLP won only those areas where the total Indian population exceeded 50 per cent.

The DLP was convinced, however, that the election results were fraudulent, and that the voting machines had been manipulated to produce the desired percentages. It felt that the PNM's margin of victory was too nearly identical with its pre-election predictions to be accidental. The DLP claimed too that there was an evident pattern in the way in which the machines malfunctioned. Most of the mechanical breakdowns and delays had occurred in areas which were heavily Indian. Officials were late or else were unfamiliar with the apparatus, and nothing had been done to ensure that polling booths were properly equipped with the proper electrical outlets. This was regarded as part of a deliberate attempt to slow down the voting procedure so as to reduce the DLP's popular vote and, if possible, to deprive late-arriving rural field workers of the franchise.[53] It was also noted that there were frequent discrepancies between the figures recorded on the machines and those proclaimed by officials.

The DLP, in fact, claimed that it had won twenty-two seats, many of them in the northern part of the island. It was especially sure that it had won the Barataria constituency where the Indian population is large.[54] The Party

53 Officials say that the breakdowns were due to human errors, especially where the population was not literate. They noted that only 50 per cent of the population had availed itself of the government's voter education programme. Representatives of the manufacturers noted that only 2 per cent of the machines needed repairs during the election. It should also be noted that the government had extended the time for voting to allow all who were in the voting compound at 6.00 PM to register their vote. In reply to DLP charges that this was illegal and designed to permit the machines to register the planned percentages, the government held that the gesture was aimed at preventing social unrest and accusations of calculated disenfranchisement.

54 It appears that PNM officials were a bit surprised at their victory in this constituency. It is even reported that they hoped the candidate contesting that seat, a Moslem whom many considered a liability to the Party in terms of public morality and trustworthiness, would be defeated. According to this line of argument, the Party did not want to run the risk of losing its Moslem following by openly declaring that, of all of

claimed that it had run very well in the Negro sections of the constituency but had been surprisingly defeated where Indians predominated.[55] It was so convinced that it had been defrauded at the polls and that the results did not represent the true position of the country that it decided to boycott the Legislature and seek redress in the courts.[56] As Capildeo told his followers, 'The DLP will not offer themselves as any prisoners tied to the triumphant chariots of the PNM.'[57] At the same time, he rejected the claim of some DLP extremists that they should resign their seats and petition the British Government for partition. Capildeo was sensible enough to know that partition would never be conceded, even if it were a desirable solution to the problem; neither would

its past candidates, he was the only one who had to be rejected by the Party on morality charges.

55   The Indian population was larger than the Negro population but less than the combined total of Negro and mixed.

56   The DLP petitioned to have the results in six constituencies voided, but the Supreme Court ruled out the claim. The majority opinion was that the rule that 'every voting machine used for the recording of votes ... shall be so constructed as to register correctly', was quite different from the assumption of the petitioners that the machines *had* to register correctly. The minority view was that, in the absence of specific information as to why the machines malfunctioned, it must be assumed that they were constructed improperly. In the view of the dissenting justice, 'If a machine which is constructed to do certain things fails to do those things on its first using, the initial and logical inference is that it is not properly constructed.' It is rather difficult to understand why the Court refused to insist that a thorough examination of the machines be carried out to determine the cause of malfunction. As Corbin himself observed, 'It is not easy to understand the reluctance of the respondent to agree to this [examination of machines by experts], for it is quite conceivable that, had there been such an inspection of the machines, it would have been made clear that there was a simple explanation for the misrecording which did not seriously affect the overall accuracy of the machines, and that the final readings, even on the defective machines, could have been relied upon. Any such evidence would have obviated the necessity to draw inferences. If only a small inaccuracy is seen in one counter, this may nevertheless indicate a serious malfunctioning of the machine. ... I cannot presume that a machine which has been seen to be inaccurate in one material particular has nevertheless accurately performed in other respects.' The Chief Electoral Office disclosed that 80 to 90 of the 230 machines showed discrepancies in the figures recorded. He blamed the difficulties on human failures; voters did not follow instructions. A spokesman for the company also suggested that climatic factors might have been responsible for some errors. The humidity in the storage area was too high, he observed. Electrical failures also contributed to the difficulties. While one must reject the claim that the PNM rigged the machines, the decision to use them, however well-intentioned, turned out to be a grave mistake, needlessly compounded by the unnecessary atmosphere of secrecy and suspicion which the behaviour of the government generated.

57   TG, Dec. 14, 1961.

he resign: 'If we resigned, the PNM would get the *usual stooges* to come forward to fight the vacant seats. We have no intention of resigning to allow them to do what they like. We will seek to put into effect the DLP Manifesto as far as possible within the limitations imposed by the House. We will not let the PNM have everything to itself in a one-party State.'[58]

The DLP was still hoping to invite British intervention. As the party organ warned, now that the constitutional struggle was coming to a close, foreign policy would be used to create crises: 'Democracy will be struck on the head with a heavy hammer while the grass under our feet will be cut by a sickle. Let the Colonial Office play Pontius Pilate.'[59] But the Colonial Office was not disposed to listen to the entreaties of the DLP. As far as the Colonial Secretary was concerned, Trinidad was internally self-governing, and he had no intention of telling it how to run its affairs. His main hope was that the PNM would agree to remain with the rest of the southern Caribbean in a new federal unit. The Colonial Office had long concluded that the DLP was not a genuine alternative to the PNM government and that it had nothing to fear from the PNM.

FORMING THE GOVERNMENT

In staffing the ministries and the Senate, the PNM tried as far as possible to give expression to its multiracial philosophy. Of the twelve cabinet places, two went to Moslems, two to persons of European stock, and eight to Negroes, including one female. There were no Hindus among the PNM legislative team, and for the second time the Hindus remained unrepresented in the government. This deficiency was somewhat compensated for in the Senate by the appointment of a Hindu party member. One senate place each was given to Syrian and Chinese creoles. The remaining nine senate places which the government had at its disposal went to Negroes and mixed elements. Seven of these were predominantly negroid; one trade unionist was included among them.[60] The Governor's senate appointees (i.e., the independents) redressed the ethnic balance somewhat. There were three white creole businessmen, one trade unionist, one solicitor, one musical director, and one Hindu businessman. Three of the Governor's appointees were negroid. The DLP refused to make any nominations.

The composition of the Senate made it quite obvious that the government

---

58   *Ibid.*, Dec. 8, 1961 (italics supplied).
59   *Statesman*, Dec. 22, 1961.
60   The trade unionist selected was one of the most ardent Party supporters in the union movement, and had been instrumental in getting the TUC to march in favour of the PNM. John Rojas of OWTU was among the Governor's appointees.

would have no trouble there. The complexion of the new body also symbolized that a new type of man had come to inherit the seats of the once-mighty plantocracy. The Premier was quite frank about the significance of his selection of senators. From now on it was 'down with the big boys'. As he put it, 'You can't trust the people at the top. The small people are going to come up and forward: the lines are drawn. We want the people on Statutory Boards and other adjuncts of Government.'[61]

Whites and near-whites did not take kindly to their displacement.[62] Even Albert Gomes, who had once identified himself with the Negro proletariat, now complained that he had been displaced from political life because he belonged to neither of the two dominant ethnic groups. Gomes in fact elected to go into exile in the United Kingdom. Hindus and Moslems were equally dissatisfied with their representation in the Senate. Given that together they constituted roughly 37 per cent of the population, they felt they deserved far more than the token two places they received. This they claimed was a shocking denial of the vaunted multiracialism of the PNM regime. Demands for parity were already being heard in certain places.

61 TG, Dec. 7, 1961.
62 Although the Roman Catholic Church reaffirmed its pledge of loyalty to the Government it reminded the PNM that: 'The furtherance of the common welfare implied that the Government fosters the well being of all classes and sections of the people. Fidelity to this trust of safeguarding the rights of minorities is the test of high-mindedness and is the hallmark of true statesmanship.' *Catholic News*, Dec. 9, 1961.

19

Federation and the
Caribbean economic community

The federal constitution agreed upon in February of 1956 had been a temporary settlement. By the terms of article 118, provision had been made for a review of that document not later than the fifth anniversary of the date on which Federation officially came into effect (January 3, 1958). The key issues that had never been satisfactorily settled were the sources of revenue for the Federal government, freedom of movement of people and goods, and the question of the division of responsibility for the economic development of the units of Federation.

The review conference, which few believed would be scheduled before 1961 or 1962, was in fact summoned much earlier. The decision to accelerate the date for the meeting grew out of party and unit competition within the Federal Parliament during its very first session, and out of a general sense of frustration about the limitations of a constitution which had left a variety of discretionary powers to the Crown-appointed Governor General and which had provided for revenues which were grossly inadequate to meet the needs of the Federal government. This unexpected development met with the approval of the PNM, which had always complained that the Federal constitution was totally unrealistic in the light of the needs of the West Indies. The PNM's position was stated in a document put out by the Premier's office entitled *The Economics of Nationhood*:

The ... economics of nationhood ... in the West Indies demands a Government absolutely and completely independent. A Federal Government, in attempting the profoundly difficult task of laying the foundation of a national economy, must have complete command of all its material and other resources, including its perspective for the future. ...

These islands have a long history of insularity, even of isolation, rooted in the historical development of their economy and trade and the difficulties of communications for centuries. No amount of subjective, that is to say historical, cultural or other activity of the time can be expected to overcome this heritage. Only a powerful and centrally directed economic co-ordination and interdependence can create the true foundations of a nation. Barbados will not unify with St Kitts, or Trinidad with British Guiana, or Jamaica with Antigua. They will be knit together only through their common allegiance to a Central Government. Anything else will discredit the conception of Federation, and in the end leave the islands more divided than before.[1]

Trinidad's position was that a newly independent Federation needed above all an adequate and independent source of revenue if it was to fulfil the functions which independence would necessitate. The poor showing of the Federal Government was in part due to the strait-jacketed system of fixed grants from unit governments which the 1956 constitution had provided for. Trinidad proposed that the Federal Government must be given the sole power to raise external loans as well as extensive revenue-raising authority. 'An independent West Indies [Government] will be considered credit-worthy by foreign investors ... only if it has large independent sources of revenue.'[2] The Federal government must also be given the main responsibility for central banking and the manipulation of finances to counteract economic fluctuations. This power could not possibly be exercised properly unless the central government had flexible taxation powers. In fact, what Trinidad was proposing was that the central government be given the power to 'impose any kind of tax' in the interest of economic rationality and *equality*. *The Economics of Nationhood* declared quite bluntly:

[The] rationale of Federation [does not] lie in the opportunity it provides for the 'better off' members of the Federation to narrow the gap between themselves and the 'better off' countries *outside* the Federation.

To argue that the 'better off' territories within the Federation must be aided to get still 'better off' so that they will, eventually, be better able to assist their weaker brethren is to ignore the harsh fact that, meanwhile, the gap will be growing steadily wider; so that, the longer the delay, the greater the amount of assistance that will be needed.[3]

1 Port of Spain, 1959, p. 3.　　　2 *Ibid.*, p. 7.　　　3 *Ibid.*, p. 10.

Only by the equalizing principle could the Federal government inhibit excessive migration from the poorer to the better-off units, migration which would bleed the small units of their skilled and semi-skilled personnel, thereby rendering more difficult the cost and problems of future development. The absorption of migrants would also prove to be an expensive undertaking. 'In their own interests the "better off" territories would wish to do all in their power to ensure for their "poorer" brethren immediate and adequate assistance. One way of ensuring this would be to accept the principle of equalisation as the basis of distribution of development funds.'[4]

The Economics of Nationhood embodied a new and radical Hamiltonian approach to the question of West Indian nationhood. It broke decisively with the earlier tradition of federation as a mere instrument of administrative rationalization and co-operation in defence and external affairs which had been endorsed by the British and other West Indian governments. The PNM in fact placed the *people* of the West Indies at the core of its thinking. The West Indian people interacting with a dynamic central government would be the bedrock on which federation would succeed. It claimed that only a perspective such as that embodied in *The Economics of Nationhood* was adequate to stimulate the idealism and dynamism that would be needed to overcome the disunity and insularity inherited from colonialism:

We are confident that given a clear and elevated perspective, the people will guarantee the success of what is proposed here by their readiness to double their efforts, their willing patience under the inevitable difficulties of readjustment, and the sacrifices of immediate needs for ultimate aims which will periodically be needed. In this atmosphere, with the further stimulus created by freedom of movement, we can confidently expect an increase in social discipline, an outburst of creative activity directed to the improvement of the economy, and a general increase in the productivity of labour which will be one of the most powerful forces working towards the raising of the material standards and cultural levels of the new West Indies nation. The concept of nationhood and the national economy can do this. Nothing else can.[5]

The Economics of Nationhood was the most explosive document that had so far been injected into the federal debate. The Jamaicans reacted to it as if it were a red flag waved in front of a maddened bull. The Premier of Jamaica dismissed it as 'childish'; so too did the DLP and the British government, which feared that by demanding a 'classical' federation, Trinidad was destroying the chances for any kind of federation at all.

To understand the hostile reaction with which *The Economics of Nationhood* was created, it is necessary to state, very briefly, what had happened in

4   *Ibid.*, p. 11.   5   *Ibid.*, p. 6.

Jamaica since the Federation had come into effect. Before the crystallization of Federation, there was a fairly widespread belief throughout the West Indies that federalism was the only instrument through which independence and economic viability could be achieved. After the Federation was inaugurated, a number of factors led to the re-examination of this assumption and to the strengthening of the anti-federal sentiment which had always been latent in Jamaica. The fact that the federal capital was situated in Trinidad represented the first serious challenge to the ascendancy which Jamaicans had always assumed. Of even greater importance was the fact that the new Federal government was controlled not by Jamaicans, but by politicians from the eastern Caribbean.[6] Manley and Bustamante had both chosen to remain in Jamaica rather than go to far-off Port of Spain, with the inevitable consequence that as far as Jamaica was concerned, there was no transfer of loyalty to the Federal government, which always remained something alien and potentially mischievous.

These two factors alone would have been sufficient to generate tensions that could have endangered Federation. Jamaican pride and apprehensions were further provoked by the extremely ill-advised remark made by the Federal Prime Minister in mid-1958 that the Federal government needed the power to impose taxation on income and profits, and that it might do so in future with retroactive effect. In retrospect it is fair to say that this was the most damaging blow that had ever been delivered to the fledgling union. From then on the Federation was on the defensive in Jamaica.

A land-acquisition ordinance passed by the Federal government in 1958 also intensified fears about Federation, as did Trinidad's objection to the establishment of an oil refinery in Jamaica. 'The realization that the Federal Government was a separate entity which might do things that would affect Jamaica was a shocking experience for a large number of Jamaicans. ... Until the Federal Parliament was actually functioning, very few Jamaicans had paid any attention to the ... meaning of federation ... outside of the small circle of those involved directly or indirectly in the making of government policy. ... Until ... the reference to retroactive taxation ... the firm assumption [was] that nothing in Jamaica's position would be changed.'[7]

6   The Federal Prime Minister, Sir Grantley Adams, was a Barbadian. The fact that both the PNM and the People's National Party in Jamaica had been defeated in the federal elections led to a situation where the Federal Parliamentary Labour Party was controlled by politicians from the eastern Caribbean. Both Manley (who came to power in 1955) and Williams had felt that the exigencies of domestic politics made it unsafe for them to leave the governments which they had recently organized.
7   H.W. Springer, *Reflections on the Failure of the First West Indian Federation*, Cambridge, Mass., 1962, p. 20.

Keen political rivalry between two evenly matched political parties, and an imminent election, made it almost inevitable that politicians would compete fiercely to defend the 'Jamaican first' principle. (Had there been a dominant one-party system in Jamaica as there was in the other units, Federation would be a reality today.) It was the Jamaica Labour Party under Bustamante's leadership that seized the initiative and began a systematic policy of manipulating the insular nationalism that had been awakened in the 1930s. The JLP went on record as being in opposition to any revision of the constitution which would give the Federal government the power to impose retroactive taxation or interfere with the tax or tariff structure of the units without their consent. It also raised the demand for representation by population which so far had not been applied in the division of elective seats at the federal level. Bustamante also made it clear that he would never accept the principle that Jamaica should subsidize the poorer units as *The Economics of Nationhood* implied.

All this took place before the end of 1958, and it was into this atmosphere that the Trinidad document was thrown. Manley, who had always been an ardent federalist, found himself on the defensive both in the country and within his People's National Party, which had always harboured a powerful anti-federal wing. When the review conference assembled in 1959, it was clear to everyone that Jamaica had to be placated at all costs if she were to be persuaded to remain in Federation. Manley admitted that Jamaica had much to gain from Federation. Although Jamaica could become a dominion by itself, it would not enjoy the same international status as would a united West Indian nation. From an economic point of view, a united West Indies would also prove more attractive to investors and loan agencies, and would be able to bargain more effectively in the trade marts of the world. It would also be more economical to administer public services for a population of three million rather than one and a half million.

Manley, however, insisted that the West Indies should seek to enjoy these advantages within a confederal framework. Jamaica had certain unique economic problems which made it absolutely necessary that she retain maximum freedom to control the direction of her own economic development:

The beginning of Federation has coincided almost with the climax of the combination of activities which have been undertaken by Jamaica with a view to a transition to a higher level of economy. ... For this reason, the Federation must proceed more slowly than other Federations in the past. Jamaica has the highest percentage of unemployment of any country in the West Indies [18 per cent for males and 38 per cent for females in 1961]. ... Consequently, there is no part of the West Indies in which any disruption of the forward progress would be more damaging and disastrous ... to the whole future of Federation.[8]

Manley did not agree with Williams' argument that the poorer units should be developed industrially *pari passu* with Trinidad and Jamaica. He felt that these islands should concentrate on agriculture, since industrial development would yield only marginal returns. It was also clear that, unlike Trinidad, Jamaica believed she had less to gain from developing the economies of the eastern Caribbean, since Trinidad and not Jamaica had to bear the brunt of population movements from these islands.

The 1959 conference was a dismal failure; it settled nothing and had to be adjourned prematurely. Confusion and frustration developed over the formula for parliamentary representation, over the timing of independence, over the question of finance, and over the terms of reference of committees which were to report back to the conference at a later date.[9] 'Behind the turmoil ... lay the uncompromising assertion of Trinidad and Tobago of the two fundamental West Indian truths of economic integration and Dominion Status as against the position of Jamaica that [was] neither truly Federation nor truly Confederation.'[10]

Though hoping that some acceptable formula could be found to ensure Jamaica's continued participation in the Federation, Manley was clearly beginning to have doubts. In January 1960 he sought and was given the assurance of the Colonial Office that Jamaica could achieve independence on her own if she left the Federation. In June Manley made another move which finally proved fatal to the cause of West Indian political unity: he announced that the Jamaican people would have to decide by way of a referendum whether or not they would remain in Federation. Manley, who had earlier dismissed the referendum proposal as a 'betrayal of responsibility and leadership', insisted that the decision of the JLP to come out openly against Federa-

8 Cited by Springer, *ibid.*, pp. 25–6.
9 Jamaica insisted on being given 32 out of 65 seats or 34 out of 68. Trinidad insisted that contribution to federal revenues be considered as well, and offered 34 out of 73. 'While there was a general readiness to concede the principle enunciated by Jamaica, there was a general fear of the consequence of such a dominating position, and Jamaica's truculence did nothing to allay those fears.' Eric Williams, *Reports on the Inter-Governmental Conference*, Port of Spain, 1961, p. 10.
10 *Ibid.*, p. 12. In his 'Reflections' Williams, referring to the *Economics of Nationhood*, noted, 'We never for one moment expected that its acceptance would be a pushover. We anticipated difficulty, but were not by any means inflexible in our approach.' *Nation*, Oct. 1, 1965.

tion left him with no alternative. As he told his federal party colleagues, 'When the West Indies achieves independence, there should be no talk of any unit seceding. ... Neither Jamaica nor the Federation can proceed into the future on a basis of uncertainty.'[11]

When the conference resumed its deliberations in May 1961, the Jamaican delegation was in an extremely strong bargaining position and the conference had little alternative but to accept its version of the federal arrangement.[12] The only serious point of difference concerned the timing and the formula for transferring the vital issues of industrial development and income tax from the reserve list to which they had been assigned to the federal list where it was agreed they ought to be ultimately.[13] Jamaica wanted to make any transfer subject to approval by the unit governments and the Federal Parliament in which she would be in a commanding position. The Trinidad government conceded that Jamaica's economic position was precarious, but argued that a more flexible amendment procedure should be agreed upon. Jamaica should not make the mistake of confusing Federation, which she would inevitably lead, with the existing Federal government, which was everybody's nightmare:

We of the Trinidad and Tobago delegation urged the Conference to appreciate Jamaica's difficulties and understand, if even it did not accept, Jamaica's fear that these difficulties might be aggravated by Federal lack of experience. We stated publicly that it was because we recognized these difficulties that we would accept Jamaica's stand on representation, the Council of Ministers, the Reserve List, and phasing of Customs Union over nine years. But we indicated to Jamaica that, in our opinion, it did not sufficiently emphasize the advantages it would gain from Federation. ... We asked Jamaica, in return for our recognition of her present difficulties and our readiness to agree to a ten-year moratorium on the subjects on the Reserve List, not to subject the Federation after ten years to the veto of a single

11   Mordecai, *The West Indies: The Federal Negotiations*, p. 226.
12   The Trinidad government conceded reluctantly that Jamaica's position would prevail. 'If there was to be a Federation, there had to be an accommodation between ... Trinidad and Jamaica ... for Jamaica, referendum or no referendum, would walk out of the Federation if it failed to secure some of the safeguards which rightly or wrongly it demanded; ... we ... decided that Jamaica was not to be pushed to the wall ... and the growth of Federal power would be more gradual than in our hearts we had originally anticipated.' Williams, *Reports on the Inter-Governmental Conference*, p. 27.
13   The reserve list proposal was advanced by Manley and accepted by Trinidad. 'The Reserve List proposal represents not only a formula for saving our Federation, but also a great contribution to the ... practice of Federal systems of Government.' *Ibid.*, p. 22.

territory in circumstances that could conceivably be quite different and not as unfavourable to Jamaica as they are today.[14]

Trinidad made it clear that economic development also involved freedom of movement, and that Jamaica's demands could not be considered in isolation. Though the Trinidad delegation agreed to leave freedom of movement on the exclusive list, it insisted that the power of the Federal government in this area remain inactive 'until such time as it assumed jurisdiction over the subjects on the Reserve List'.[15] It was also noted that industrial development involved the raising of external loans and participation in the field of foreign affairs.[16]

The issue of transfers from the reserve list was not settled until the final conference on Federation, which was held in London at Lancaster House in June 1961. With the support of the British, Federal, and other unit governments, all of which were unwilling to see Manley lose the forthcoming referendum, Jamaica was able to gain acceptance for all of her demands. On September 19, 1961, the Jamaican people nevertheless stunned the West Indies by voting against Federation by a 54–46 per cent majority, finally putting an end to any immediate hopes for West Indian political unity.[17]

Dr Williams has argued that the Jamaican referendum was only the ostensible reason for the collapse of the Federation, which he in fact referred to as 'an absolute blessing in disguise':

I say it openly, to the Party, that if Jamaica had won the referendum I was going to come to the PNM and propose that they reject the Lancaster House Conference. I was going to propose to the Party that they should not join the Federation. ...
The Party would have had to decide. The Party would have been free to go into the Federation. They would have gone into Federation with another political leader. I would not have been false to my conscience. I would not have agreed to take on the responsibilities for putting that rope around the neck of the people of Trinidad and Tobago by accepting that bastard Federation that was created in Lancaster House.[18]

---

14 *Ibid.*, pp. 28–9.
15 *Ibid.*, p. 30.
16 'Our position is that a Unit Territory should have the right to negotiate on matters within its legislative competence with a foreign government, subject to keeping the Federal Government informed at all stages ... and subject to Federal ratification of any agreement reached.' *Ibid.*, p. 36.
17 The vote (256,261 to 217,319) was perhaps more indicative of the decline in popularity of Manley and the PNP in the rural areas than it was of a basic hostility to Federation. The urban voter remained faithful to the PNP by a four-to-one margin.
18 *Speech on Independence*, Port of Spain, 1962, pp. 19, 20, 24.

The Trinidad delegation had been extremely angry about the treatment it received, and had made it clear to the conference that it would not accept the results. It was defeated on every issue which it considered fundamental. In particular, it was defeated on the questions of freedom of movement, unit conduct of external affairs, and the formula for British Guiana's accession to the union.[19] The Lancaster House formula in their view was 'merely a concession to the smaller units [who wanted freedom of movement] and Jamaica at the expense of Trinidad. [It produced] a Federation that was merely an administrative superstructure. ... It had nothing to do with economic realities.'[20] Williams denies, with much justice, that Trinidad was responsible for breaking up the Federation, as many people in fact assert. Despite the seeming inflexibility in his demands for a strong union, he had gone a long way to conciliate Jamaica. In point of fact, it is fair to say that Trinidad was least responsible for the Federation's demise. The Federal and British governments must accept most of the blame, the former for provoking Jamaica and not inspiring her confidence in Federation, and the latter for making it easy for her to break the federal pact. Had Manley come to the centre, of course, the crisis might never have developed, though it is arguable that if he had done so and the PNP had lost power to the JLP in 1959, the JLP might still have wrecked Federation. It is genuinely difficult to apportion blame in this unfortunate affair.

W. Arthur Lewis ascribes blame for the collapse of the Federation to the 'awful' leadership of the West Indian politicians. Among the costly errors Lewis cites was the politicians' tendency to rely on 'open diplomacy' rather than on informal negotiations. As Lewis complains:

Their ... big failure was ... [that] they adopted a standard pattern for communicating with each other ... based on 'open diplomacy', which in practice meant shouting at each other by press or radio, or by issuing Ministry Papers or obtaining binding resolutions in their legislative assemblies before setting off to meet each other. ... This neglect of the elementary rules of diplomacy soon poisoned the personal relationships among the three men, and between them and the federal leaders on the other islands, with the result that by the middle of 1961 the chief champions of the Federation were hardly on speaking terms with each other.[21]

19 Jamaica was opposed to any formula that would upset her numerical predominance in the Federal Parliament. *Ibid.*, p. 18.
20 *Ibid.*, p. 19.
21 See Lewis's 'Epilogue' in Mordecai, *The West Indies*, pp. 455–62. For fuller discussions cf. Neville H. Cooper, 'The Federal Theme in the British Caribbean with Special Reference to Jamaica and Trinidad', unpublished MA thesis, University of Toronto, 1966.

Lewis in fact believes 'the Federation was destroyed by poor leadership rather than by the intractability of its own internal problems', though he is not confident that 'wise leadership could put it together again'.

THE DECISION TO 'GO IT ALONE'

The anti-Federation vote in Jamaica posed a crucial dilemma for the PNM. Decisions concerning the fate of the Federation were left almost entirely in its hands. Although the PNM had decided that Federation should not be made an issue in the general election, Williams had made numerous statements during the campaign which provided clues to his thinking on the issue. On one occasion, he declared:

We of the PNM don't know if we should go along in any association at all; and if we are to go in an association, we don't know if it is to be a Federation. ... I for one, and I am sure the PNM, will not go in for any Federation at the sacrifice of the people of Trinidad and Tobago just for the sake of supporting British or American policy, whatever it might be. You and I have not fought for West Indian nationhood ... merely to find ourselves a little pocket on a string held by Britain ... or America which might want another banana republic in this part of the world. We are going to have Independence by ourselves without their help. Let us have something that everybody can respect and understand, especially ... when it costs a lot of money.[22]

On another occasion he seemed less uncertain, and warned:

People will come here to take up land we don't have, possibly to take up jobs at rates of wages lower than the workers of Trinidad and Tobago would work, come in here perhaps to be strike breakers, ... come in here looking for houses that don't exist and create shanty towns, while we are at present and at an enormous expense cleaning the shanty town on the outskirts of Port of Spain. *That is the type of argument the* DLP *brings.*[23]

Williams did admit that he was 'sorry' for the smaller units and promised that Trinidad would help fight to get Britain to acknowledge her responsibility to them, 'but not at our expense'.[24]

22 Williams at the Arima Race Stand, undated tape.
23 Williams at San Fernando, undated tape italics supplied. The decision of the PNM to appoint two of its Federal MLC's to the Trinidad Senate and another to the cabinet was also evidence of the direction in which it was going.
24 Williams at Cornelio Street, Woodbrook, undated tape. On May 24, 1961, before the referendum, Williams had declared, 'We ... were not imperialists, we had not exploited other territories, and whilst we were willing to help our smaller neighbours

Williams was clearly hinting what his own decision would be, or at least was sounding for response. He openly rejected the DLP's suggestion that Trinidad should go into a new Federation which Britain and the United States would help to finance. He noted that neither country had ever given any indication that it would offer substantial aid to the West Indies, certainly not in terms that bore any relationship to the economic realities of the situation. As far as he was concerned, the DLP, vested interests, and outside forces were supporting the Federation only because they saw in it an opportunity to break the PNM's hegemony in Trinidad. Williams had nightmares about a Federal government controlled by a coalition of the DLP and other Caribbean politicians. 'Imagine what will happen if this vindictive and ferocious Opposition that we have ... could, with some backward politicians, get control of the *PNM's treasury*. All of them want to get control of Trinidad's revenue from oil.'[25]

During the negotiations on Federation, Williams and other Caribbean politicians had come to dislike each other intensely, and verbal communication between them had often broken down. The 'mendicant mentality' of the politicians from the eastern Caribbean, born of necessity rather than predisposition, infuriated Williams. Dr Arthur Lewis, who tried to persuade Williams to continue in some form of Federation with the Leeward and Windward Islands, found him implacably opposed to working with the eastern Caribbean politicians. 'He would have nothing to do with a Federation run by Sir Grantley Adams and his company. The existing Federation must be wound up.'[26] Lewis also found that, while Williams was inclined towards a unitary state arrangement rather than a federal one, other PNM politicians were not anxious to continue in any form of association with the other units and were encouraging Williams to take Trinidad to Independence alone.

In an attempt to get a consensus on the federation issue, the PNM executive established a committee to study the problem and report back to a special convention to be held on January 27, 1962. Whether by design or not, the committee contained several persons who were known to favour a federal solution. Before the convention met, however, it was announced that the Secretary of State for the Colonies, Mr. Maudling, would be paying a visit to the West Indies. Williams, it appears, suspected that Maudling's aim was to force Trinidad to continue in the Federation. To forestall this, the committee procedure was abandoned and a meeting of the Party's General Council was

achieve nationhood if only because we did not want colonialism perpetuated next to us, we could not undertake that at the cost of our own economic stability. ... If Jamaica left [,] Trinidad and Tobago ... would not undertake to carry the rest of the Federation.' *Reports on the Inter-Governmental Conference*, pp. 19, 30.

25 Williams at the St George County Council, undated tape (italics supplied).
26 *The Agony of the Eight*, Barbados, 1965, cited in Mordecai, *West Indies*, p. 416.

summoned to decide the issue. Under Williams' leadership the Council recommended that Trinidad should go to Independence alone, but that any other island which wished to join it in a unitary state would be welcome to do so. The pro-federalists were decisively out-manoeuvred. According to Mordecai, this new arrangement allowed Williams to 'marry his own inclinations towards association in a unitary state with his colleagues' yearnings for Independence now. ... This dilemma resolved, the proposed elaborate consultation of public opinion so repeatedly announced, was no longer considered necessary, and was simply set aside.'[27]

When the PNM convention met to settle the issue, the prevailing mood was clearly against Federation. The party élite argued that Trinidad had wasted too much time and money on Federation ($20 million (TT) in four years) and could not afford such waste any longer. Important decisions which were affecting Trinidad's economic position were being taken in the councils of the European Economic Community, and it was felt that Britain was not to be trusted to negotiate the best agreements for Trinidad. No one knew how long it would take for a new Federation to come to fruition, and PNM politicians were not anxious to go through the exasperating and interminable rounds of discussions that the establishment of a new structure would involve.[28] Decisions in the context of the modern world had to be made fast, and efficiency could not be expected from the ministries of the 'smaller islands'. It was no surprise that the convention overwhelmingly approved (subject to a few changes in phrasing) the resolution of the General Council that 'Trinidad and Tobago reject unequivocally any participation in a Federation of the Eastern Caribbean, and proceed forthwith to National Independence, without prejudice to the future incorporation in the unitary state of Trinidad and Tobago of any Territory of the Eastern Caribbean whose people may so desire, on terms to be mutually agreed, or to the future establishment of a Common Economic Community embracing the entire Caribbean Area.'[29]

The basic arguments made on behalf of the General Council's proposals fell under two main categories, economic and political. The economic case

27 *Ibid.*, p. 440.
28 'If you have to continue [negotiating Federation], for God's sake leave me out of it. These negotiations that have been going on for three years! To sit down again! Must we negotiate thirteen years more to end up with another fiasco? ... I never want to attend another conference of Governments to discuss the question of a Federation ... to go through the ordeal ... beat your head against a concrete wall ... to have people tell you absolutely cavalierly, man we ain't interested in ... principles, all we want to know and talk about is economic aid and freedom of movement.' *Speech on Independence*, pp. 20, 39.
29 *Nation*, Jan. 15, 1962.

was very convincingly made. It was noted that in an Eastern Caribbean Federation, Trinidad would have as much as 55 per cent of the population and contribute 75 per cent of the total revenue. It was also noted that Trinidad's trade with the eight other units was minimal – $16 million (TT) of a total external trade of $897 million. These units also had a net public debt of $46 million which it was felt Trinidad would have to absorb. For an additional market of 670,000 persons, these burdens were not considered economically worth while. There was some question as to how valuable this limited market would continue to be, since the 'Little Eight' were still maintaining 'a proud insistence on new industries which constitute half of our exports to them'. The 'injudicious duplication of industries such as cement, beer and oil-refining'[30] threatened to reduce even more the value of these units as markets for the Trinidad economy.

The cost of sustaining the elaborate administrative structures of the eight units, once grants-in-aid from the British Treasury were cut off, was also cited as reason for pause.[31] The problem of migration to Trinidad was starkly documented. In 1958 and 1959, 10,000 migrants from these islands came to Trinidad, while 37,000 went to the United Kingdom. With the closing of the United Kingdom 'border', Trinidad was expected to be the prime focus of population movements in the southern and eastern Caribbean. The social services of the community were considered inadequate to sustain such pressure. Problems were also expected to arise from the disparities in the levels of economic development in the various units. The gross domestic product at factor cost per capita (in TT dollars) was $822 in Trinidad, $443 in Barbados, $259 in the Leewards, and $240 in the Windwards.

To combat the anticipated charges that Trinidad was too small and too weak economically to sustain Independence, a battery of comparative statistics were adduced to show that Trinidad was much better positioned to do so than most of the independent Afro-Asian states. With a per capita income in 1960 of $500 (US), Trinidad was, next to Cuba and Puerto Rico, the wealthiest of the underdeveloped states.[32]

---

30 *Ibid.*
31 Excluding Barbados, roughly 20 per cent of the recurrent budgets of the Leeward and Windward Islands came from the United Kingdom.
32 A report of the World Bank was also cited. The report had noted, 'With a per capita income of about $500 U.S. (about $850 WI in 1960) the people of Trinidad enjoy one of the highest standards of living in any Afro-Asian community. Trinidad is one of the most prosperous areas in Central and South America.' The report also noted that there was as yet no pressing land shortage, that the country had a high rate of literacy, a substantial middle class which included independent business and professional men, good social services, low public debt, a growth rate of 10%, and a stable political climate. *Nation*, Jan. 15, 1962.

The case was powerfully argued, and most doubters – at least within the Party – seemed convinced, especially when it was shown that the cost of Independence in terms of new commitments would not exceed the costs (to Trinidad) of the federal agreement worked out at Lancaster House in 1960. But the case for Independence in political terms was much more difficult to make. The General Council's resolution made no mention of political considerations at all, except to say that the Federation afforded too many opportunities for 'foreign intrigues in West Indian affairs'. The political justifications were left to the speeches of the party élite. Williams' arguments were quite familiar. He complained of the time lost on bargaining which involved a sacrifice of the April 22, 1960, deadline for Independence which he had set, and 'the narrowness of vision and unwillingness to change old patterns' that characterized the politicians of the eastern Caribbean. Williams argued, however, that the General Council's proposals – a unitary state with those who wished to join Trinidad, and a Caribbean Economic Community – were revolutionary initiatives, which, in the long run, would provide the solution to the West Indian dilemma: 'What the General Council ... proposes to you ... is nothing short of a revolution in Caribbean society with its history of disunity and separation, metropolitan domination and outward looking. ... The temporary partial disappointment itself contains the seed, itself lays the foundation for the larger permanent hopes of the West Indian area in the world.'[33]

For Williams a Caribbean Economic Community had now become the method whereby the whole of the Caribbean would be reunited. The failure of the political federation of the British Caribbean was not to mean the end of the pan-Caribbeanism which he confessed had always been his ultimate goal. Economic integration and co-operation in the use of certain vital common services should now be viewed as the principal means to break down the linguistic, cultural, and historical barriers that divided the West Indies. It was time for the Caribbean to look inward and depend on its own resources. The Papal Donation of 1493 was dead, but there was no reason to continue accepting as permanent the divisions that were the result of four-and-a-half centuries of European rivalry and domination.[34]

It was a bright dream which West Indians before Williams had entertained. But one wonders whether Williams seriously believed in the possibility of bringing the viciously competing sugar economies of the Caribbean into any sort of common market. With Cuba excluded for ideological and practical

33 *Speech on Independence*, pp. 22, 30.
34 'If ... somebody in Africa can talk about Pan-Africa ... somebody in the West Indies has to raise the call for some larger unity, something that makes sense, something that can represent a certain amount of intellectual dignity and economic perspective for the people of these frustrated areas who don't know where to go.' *Ibid.*, p. 23.

reasons, Williams' proposals seemed even more visionary. If it could be argued that the uneven economic development in the West Indies was one of the main obstacles to Federation, then it seemed all the more difficult to visualize any meaningful Caribbean economic unit, however much one might agree on its desirability and necessity. Williams was certainly aware of the difficulties that his proposal involved, but seemed to view it as an ideal to which all West Indians should bend their energies in the future.[35] It was the only medium through which the economic viability of the area could be achieved. And political unity might indeed grow out of successful economic co-operation.

There seemed one fundamental flaw in the unitary state thesis which the General Council had proposed for the immediate future. The very arguments that were made against the idea of an Eastern Caribbean federation were even more powerful when applied to the idea of an expanding unitary state, and it would appear that some of the isolationists in the cabinet accepted the latter because they knew it would never be realized. Williams was not that certain, however, and argued that the unitary state would be more rational and more efficient from the point of view of administrative organization and social and economic planning. If the Philippines and Hawaii could make a unitary system work, so could the West Indies. Distance was no longer the problem it used to be.

As true as this might be, the decision still meant that Trinidad had to jeopardize its economic development by diverting time, energy, and resources for the development of the eastern Caribbean. And if the suggestion that the British and American governments should help finance the Federation was to be rejected as being unrealistic and beggarly, the same held for arguments that Britain should underwrite the costs of developing the 'depressed areas' of the unitary state which Williams insisted was still Britain's responsibility. It was Britain that had 'sucked the orange dry ... and we would never allow Trinidad and Tobago's stability and economic progress to be endangered by pulling Britain's chestnuts out of her own fire'.[36] The British nevertheless made it quite clear that Trinidad would have to foot the bill for developing those islands that chose to join it.[37]

35 Williams did not believe that his proposal was a mere abstraction. 'If Europe could overcome its division, so could the West Indies. If the Caribbean gets together, there might not be any great scope for interchange. But are we sure there would not be? Isn't the economy of Belgium to a large extent competitive with the economy of Germany? The Europeans have been able to work out some sort of rational division of the market. ... Why should we assume that ... we couldn't get together and work out some sort of common policy as producers interested in markets ...?' *Ibid.*, p. 28.
36 Williams, *Nation*, March 4, 1966.
37 'The British attitude ... is that if Trinidad is so upstart as to want Grenada [who

The only argument that made any sort of sense was the political one. Williams in fact told the convention that there was a 'solid political factor' that must be considered if the Party opted for Federation.

Could you be sure, Ladies and Gentlemen, that in a Federation, where the other places must get a number of seats ... that a Federation does not expose you to having a Federal Government constituted of an Opposition minority in Trinidad buying fluid votes in other territories and able to control the Trinidad economy through controlling the Federal Government? ... *You could be sure of it in a unitary state.* The question is not an academic issue at all ... the last Federal elections produced a government that has given the PNM more trouble than even the DLP.[38]

Williams felt that 'jealousy' and 'malice' towards the PNM and to him as its leader were so strong among Caribbean politicians that they would do anything to undermine its strength even if the interests of the West Indies were sacrificed in the process. They preferred to remain colonies and be 'tupenny' rulers in their own little bivouacs, rather than be led by the PNM, 'the undisputed intellectual leaders of the colonial nationalist movement in this part of the world'.[39] What Williams was in fact demanding, in his typically monopolistic 'zero-sum' approach to party politics, was 'one single state *ruled by one single party, the PNM, which lays down the blueprint for legislation and development*'.[40] The only way to save the eastern Caribbean was for Trinidad and Tobago to expand, absorb, and socialize its population into the norms which the PNM had defined for Trinidad. It was the very sort of missionary paternalism which the minorities in Trinidad were not prepared to accept, even though often it was the methods chosen to define and impose those norms, rather than the norms themselves, which were the main source of alienation.

There was a small element within the PNM which felt that the political dangers Williams cited were real but certainly not insurmountable. There was no reason why the Party could not expand within a federal system and undermine the old-line leadership in the eastern Caribbean just as easily as it assumed it could do in a unitary state. Was the PNM not confusing the people of these islands with their present leaders? PNM pro-federalists felt that a great deal of administrative rationality could be achieved within a strong federal

alone opted for the unitary state] to join it, Trinidad and Tobago must pay the cost.' *Ibid.*
38 *Speech on Independence*, pp. 38–9.
39 *Ibid.*, pp. 38–42.
40 *Ibid.*, p. 34 (italics supplied).

framework.[41] Williams was nevertheless right when he insisted that a unitary government would be less inhibited in its economic and social planning than would a federal government, though it was perhaps quite deceptive for him to suggest that a unitary government would be much better able to prevent inter-territorial migration.[42]

A large number of delegates at the convention accepted Williams' assurances but felt that the tone of the General Council resolution was harsh and an affront to the pride of the people of the eastern islands. Williams accepted this observation and agreed that 'particular attention would have to be paid to the sensibilities of a territory like Barbados, which has a long history of struggle for self-government, [and which was] the first place in the British Empire ... to demand self-government, 125 years before the mainland colonies in ... America'.[43] A few delegates also objected to what they believed was an attempt by the party leadership to force them to go along with the General Council's resolution. They objected to what they believed was the political leader's suggestion that if the Party wished to go into Federation, it would have to do so without him. Williams correctly noted that this remark had been made in the context of his discussion of the Lancaster House constitution. Even so the Party could not fail to notice that he had restated the principle that the 'political leader [of a democratic party] must go ... if [he] takes a particular stand on an issue on which he is not supported by his Party'.[44]

It should be noted that the convention did have a chance to consider an alternative motion:

41 Supporters of the federal proposal included Senators Wilfred Alexander and Hamilton Maurice, and the Hon Andrew Rose, Minister of Communication in the defunct Federation. Rose was suspected of having hopes of becoming the governor general of the Federation. It should also be noted that a sub-committee of the Party's policy committee which had been appointed to study the question of migration within the eastern Caribbean had come out in unanimous support of Federation. This document was not circulated at the convention. It is reported that the author of the report was discouraged from defending it at the General Council meeting. So far as can be discerned, Williams has never been defeated in the General Council, which he easily manipulates. Few General Council members could resist the dazzling round-the-world and historical analyses of Dr Williams. Top party and cabinet ministers have complained that Williams plays the General Council 'card' whenever he is having difficulty in the cabinet or executive.

42 'It is much easier for a unitary state to control the ... factors involved in migration than it is in a federal government, where you must have, if it is a proper federation, the right of freedom of movement, with the territory that is affected by the migrants having no effective economic power over the territories that supply the migrants.' *Speech on Independence*, p. 47.

43 *Ibid.*, p. 45.

44 *Ibid.*, p. 50.

That Trinidad and Tobago should agree to participate in a Federation of the Eastern Caribbean having the strongest possible central powers on condition

i   that adequate financial assistance will be forthcoming from the United Kingdom, the United States of America and Canada,

ii   that adequate representation for Trinidad and Tobago is assured in such a Federation, and

iii   that such participation will not delay the achievement of Independence for Trinidad and Tobago.[45]

The motion was withdrawn before it could be voted on, since it was quite obvious that there was little support for it on the floor of the convention. There was no doubt that majority sentiment in the Party was in favour of the General Council's proposal, which was eventually accepted with an amendment to the effect that a 'maximum degree of local government' be provided for those territories wishing to associate with Trinidad and Tobago.

Trinidadians might very well have chosen to stay with the eastern Caribbean in a new federation if the PNM had given them a lead in that direction. But it was quite obvious that the majority were not anxious to share their jobs and growing affluence with their 'have-not' neighbours. There was nothing to gain and everything to lose, at least in material terms, and the man in the street, and increasingly the middle class, had begun to renounce whatever little idealism they once had. With the Jamaican decision to 'go it alone', the appeal of federation had lost its magic. Trinidadians were no longer willing to be inhibited or restrained. The primary stream of insular egoism which had always been latent among the non-Indian population, and which Williams had whipped to a frenzy during the Chaguaramas 'crisis', was not at full tide. The remark of a delegate to the PNM convention – 'Mr Political Leader, to hell with Federation' – was one that would have found a responsive echo in many elements of the population for whom the difference between the federal and unitary proposals was scarcely intelligble. They wanted neither. Williams' dream of a 'wider Caribbean community' was lost on all but a few.

REACTION TO THE UNITARY STATE

The Indian community was very concerned about the possible racial significance of the PNM's decision to work for a unitary-state settlement. One could not really blame them for believing that it was just another immoral plot to

45   Andrew Rose took his political life in his hands to propose the motion. The political leader was known to be quite displeased, and it took a bit of persuading to have him agree to allow Rose to withdraw it after it was clear that it would have been decisively defeated on the floor. Many felt that Rose's political career in the PNM was finished.

swamp them. It seemed quite logical to them that it would be much easier for Negroes to neutralize them in a unitary than in a federal state. As one of their pamphleteers expressed it:

It is not so much the welfare of these little islands that the PNM is interested in, but the votes which they believe they will receive from them, and which they hope will abrogate the voting capacity of the Indians in Trinidad twenty or thirty years from now. The concept of a unitary state, therefore, is founded on racialism. We protest against any attempt to swamp Trinidad with Grenadians or any other people for no other reason but for vote-catching. ... We were in a Federation with these islands, and mainly through PNM connivance this Federation is now defunct. We are still prepared to consider the question of a Federation of the nine units, but we will not have any of them in any unitary state with Trinidad, it does not matter who says that we should.[46]

The argument was that, in a federation, the votes of the Negro population in the 'Little Eight' would not be of any assistance to the PNM in its aim to nullify Indian voting-strength twenty years hence.[47] In a unitary state, the Negro vote in these islands would provide the PNM with the voting strength they needed to establish a one-party racial dictatorship against the Indian community. But in view of the general agreement that any recreated federation would have had to be a strong and highly centralized one, it may be wondered whether it would really have been any less difficult for the PNM to manipulate the system against the Indians, if indeed this was its true aim.

One could not help speculating that the harsh terms which Williams proposed for such a union were meant to discourage anyone from taking them seriously. It seemed to be a new form of imperialism based on a new metropolitan centre, with the smaller units abandoning all hope of economic development based on industry. In fact, they would become tutelary wards of Trinidad, as was Tobago, a prospect which few eastern Caribbean politicians were likely to find attractive. Their response was almost predictable. The Chief Minister of Grenada, Eric Gairy, declared, 'The smaller units will not agree to any unitary state. They have their national aspirations and would not give in easily.'[48] R.A. Bradshaw, Chief Minister of St Kitts, was even more expressive: 'Federation has been brutally violated. It lies prostrate, frightfully dismembered and torn for all the world to see the destructive capabilities of some learned West Indians. ... The culprits are known, and the memory of what they've done will ever haunt them. They take a sadistic pride in their

---

46   H.P. Singh, *That Unitary State*, Port of Spain, 1962, pp. 11–12.
47   The birth rate of the Indian population was higher than that of any other group.
48   TG, Dec. 9, 1961.

destructive achievement. ... They have disgraced and made the West Indies the classic laughing-stock of the twentieth century.'[49]

The Premier of Barbados, Errol Barrow, who had offered to work closely with Williams in the new Federation, saw the PNM's offer as 'the most gratuitous insult that could ever have been extended to any group of people – an even more gratuitous insult than was offered by Vervoerd to native peoples in South Africa.'[50] Sir Grantley Adams, now an embittered man, simply urged that 'the feelings of the people of Trinidad should be tested'; Adams felt, quite mistakenly, that the average Trinidadian still wished to remain with the other units. 'Williams is fast becoming a little Castro', he complained.[51] Trinidad's premier calypsonian, the Mighty Sparrow, himself a native of Grenada, used the medium of the calypso to express his belief that 'this ain't no time to say we ain't federatin' no more'. Sir Arthur Lewis, a native of St Lucia, also lamented, 'To most West Indians, the disintegration of this group [of islands] into two independent states whose peoples would be foreigners to each other would come as an immeasurable personal tragedy, and the authors of such a break would have a sad niche in History.'[52]

West Indian intellectuals, especially those abroad, were deeply shamed and embittered by what seemed to be a cynical wrecking of the only real chance of Caribbean integration. Their hopes for a meaningful economic and political base for West Indian Independence were now dashed. The wave of disillusionment following Jamaica's decision to withdraw had merely served to make them even more determined to salvage what was left of the truncated union. They were convinced that the PNM leadership had quite irresponsibly allowed its partisanship and its animosity to the old-line leadership in the Caribbean to frustrate the long-held dream of a Caribbean Commonwealth. They were shocked to find that their intellectual leader had proven to be every whit as insular as those whom he had once chastised.

In Trinidad there were angry cries that the PNM had betrayed the solemn commitment it had made to take the issue to the public after the general elections.[53] Some were more opposed to the method by which the decision was

49 Debate in the Federal House, April 11, 1962.
50 TG, June 23, 1962.
51 *Ibid.*, April 27, 1962.
52 Report to Sir Grantley Adams on the prospect of an eastern Caribbean federation, cited in the *Statesman*, April 20, 1962. Lewis notes, 'The main economic reason for Trinidad's refusing to continue in Federation in 1962 or to start a new Federation was that the Trinidad blueprint [*The Economics of Nationhood*] was now generally acceptable.' Mordecai, *West Indies*, p. 460.
53 Williams had said on numerous occasions that his government would consult the people after the Party had made up its mind. At one election rally he declared, 'We

made than they were to the decision itself. A fairly typical comment came from
the President of the Southern Chamber of Commerce, who condemned what
he viewed as a serious breach of public faith:

Was the Party Convention the proper forum for the final consideration of a matter
which was obviously of national and not only Party importance? ... Why wasn't
the House of Representatives given an opportunity, at least similar to that given to
the Party, to decide whether Trinidad should 'go it alone', or continue in a Federation? What has become of the Party's promise to consult responsible organizations
in the Territory – political, economic, social, civic, cultural and fraternal, with
respect to 'going it alone'? Is the public correct in assuming that the Party's opinion
is all that must be taken into consideration? If so, is there any need for a House of
Representatives where opposing views are expressed?[54]

The basic complaint of a large section of the population was that no political
party, no matter how large its majority, had any right to take a decision of
such magnitude without consulting the people. The DLP was similarly an-
guished that its offer of a bipartisan approach to the questions of federation
and independence had been contemptuously refused.[55] There was in fact a
decided air of partisanship about the way the decision to reject federation was
arrived at. Williams himself told the Party that the government was not 'responsible to anybody except to [the] Party which put [them] in power and the
voters that voted for [them]. ... We [do not] have to answer to the DLP for
anything.'[56]

Williams was visibly annoyed by complaints that he should have sought a
broader consensus, and lashed out quite pugnaciously, and often contemptuously, at his critics. He declared in Woodford Square, 'We marched from here
... for Independence ... and whoever don't like it can go to hell. We educated
the people for Federation, we promoted Federation, ... we are not going to be
forced to stay in a truncated Federation. It is going to be legally dissolved as

will study Federation ... we will get all the necessary documents and put them
together, take them to the Party, let our Party decide, and when our Party has
decided on a particular line, we go to the population.' Williams to St George County
Council (undated tape). Whether this implied a referendum is difficult to say. It was
very unlikely, however, that after the Jamaican referendum Williams was anxious to
see the people, in all its 'virtue', make another 'mistake'.

54   TG, April 3, 1962.
55   The DLP affirmed that it had suggested to the PNM that the federal issue might be
taken out of the elections if it was agreed that a bipartisan parliamentary committee
would be appointed to work out an agreed approach to the political future of Trinidad and the West Indies.
56   *Speech on Independence*, pp. 34, 39.

it was politically broken by Jamaica's action.'[57] But, as critics counter-charged, the question was not whether Trinidad was under any legal obligation to continue in any form of Federation, but whether or not she *should* stay. The people and their representatives in Parliament had to decide this, and not the PNM. Many people, especially recent immigrants from the islands, had supported the PNM during the elections on the assumption that it would support Federation. Though Williams had given open hints during the campaign as to the line he would take, it cannot be said that he had any mandate from the country to 'go it alone', or to take any other course. The Premier had again proceeded in a very high-handed fashion to ignore political forces that were not associated with the PNM. Some top-ranking party members were known to have been quite embarrassed by the PNM's bad political manners, regardless of their own position on the substantive issue. By failing to establish truly national machinery for settling the federation issue, the PNM had needlessly plunged the community into bitter turmoil on the eve of Independence.

57   TG, April 17, 1962. The Federation was legally dissolved on June 1, 1962.

20

The constitutional imbroglio: the final phase

On May 9, 1962, one month after the PNM made its historic and revolutionary decision to take Trinidad to Independence alone, the cabinet published a 'draft independence constitution'. This initiative on the part of the government provoked the heaviest storm of public criticism the Party had yet sustained. Objection was taken both to the method of handling the constitutional issue and to the substantive provision of the draft; in some sinister way these things seemed integrally related. Organizations and individuals vociferously condemned the government's 'indecent haste' in putting the independence constitution on the political agenda with only six weeks allotted for comment, especially since nothing had as yet been done to consult the people on the unitary-state proposition. The substantial criticisms of the bill were directed mainly at the sections on civil liberties, the provisions for entrenchment, the composition of the Senate, the appointive power of the prime minister, and the machinery for the conduct of elections.

In a broadcast on April 10, 1962, the Premier had replied to some of the criticisms and announced that the government would establish consultative machinery to mobilize agreement on the constitution. Williams denied that the time given to the public was too short for proper study of the draft. He noted that 432 typewritten pages of comment had been received from eighty-four organizations and fifty-two private citizens. It was revealed that the government intended to collate and distribute the memoranda to those individuals and organizations who had submitted comments and that these parties would then be invited to a constitutional convention where the issues raised would be discussed. The compromises agreed upon would then be discussed by a select committee of the Legislature before the British government was approached. According to the Premier, this was being done in an honest and sincere attempt to achieve a democratic consensus on a matter of national concern. He boasted that 'No other country had adopted the course Trinidad and Tobago had decided upon in gathering response to constitutional proposals.'[1]

Observers could not help feeling that the Government had been forced into a constitutional conference, which Williams in fact termed a 'luxury' in the context of the extreme fluidity of discussions on the European Common Market. He seemed to be suggesting that the ideal of having popular participation on the constitution was less important than the need for an independent Trinidad to participate in negotiations which affected the future market of its basic products. As he declared later on:

It may surprise you to know that the greatest danger we had to face was not really the type of Constitution we should have. We can always let the citizens discuss and help us to change those parts of it that do not seem to meet requirements. The greatest trouble is how soon this tremendous dis-organization ... involving Britain's ... going into the European Economic Community [is going to take place]. We did not know in January when that would take place. We knew it was coming soon. You can see it a little more clearly in May. ... And, if we seem more prepared now, ... it is because of the action the Government took in January to prepare for the worst. The best Constitution in the world would be simply wasted paper if we were to disrupt and make unstable present trading arrangements with other territories, and we must move to protect the economic position of Trinidad and Tobago.[2]

Before the convention met, the Premier disclosed that his government was willing to accept many of the suggestions incorporated in the memoranda. But there were issues which he was reluctant to concede. Though admitting that hostility to the composition of the Senate was fairly widespread, he was unwilling to embarrass the individuals who had been asked to serve on that body: 'The Government refuses to associate itself with any suggestion that, within two months of the appointment of these citizens, ... after the issue had been debated for five years in the community, the system should be changed before anybody had had an opportunity to assess the value of what constituted an innovation on our part. ... If the community wishes to change it, that is another matter.'[3] This was an unmistakable hint that the government might give way on this point if pressed.

With respect to the proposal that provision should be made for a referendum to amend the constitution, he simply noted that the referendum was not a very British practice. The same type of observation was made to criticisms

1   TG, April 8, 1962.   2   *Ibid.*, May 19, 1962.   3   *Ibid.*, April 8, 1962.

that the Prime Minister was being given too much appointive power. This was quite normal in parliamentary democracies, he asserted. It was a rather strange reply coming from the head of an anti-colonial government which always insisted on its right to choose that which suited the particular needs of a cosmopolitan society.

Williams also turned his back quite resolutely on all proposals for proportional representation, which in fact meant racial or communal representation. He expressed himself as quite opposed to any suggestion that minority groups be given special constitutional standing:

There are those who would like the Trinidad and Tobago Independence Constitution to be patterned on that of Cyprus which means that the Constitution will emphasize, and in fact establish sharp lines of division between the various racial groups. ... I would far prefer to have a Government of Trinidad and Tobago accused of not dividing up the community into racial groups rather than have it accused of constitutional provisions which would establish a Negro President and an Indian Vice-President of a Republic, with a fixed proportion of seats or places to the various racial groups in the Cabinet, in Parliament, in the Judiciary, in the Police Service and in the Civil Service. As far as I am concerned, that way madness lies.[4]

While the concessions went a long way towards dispelling the suspicions of most critics, there were some who remained dissatisfied. It was observed that the number of memoranda submitted was not indicative of the adequacy of the time given for study of the draft. Most associations were only able to discuss those issues which concerned their clientele and were not as satisfied with other sections as the Premier had implied. Others noted that the fact that certain items in the draft were also found in other countries or in existing statutes was no particular recommendation for an independent Trinidad. 'The Government should use its good sense rather than its research abilities.' Objection was also taken to the Premier's reference to popular deliberations as a 'luxury'.

THE QUEEN'S HALL CONFERENCE

The constitutional conference held at Queen's Hall in April of 1962 was perhaps one of the finest democratic exercises that Trinidad had yet witnessed, despite its shaky beginning. Quite accidentally, the government had hit upon a method of obtaining popular participation in the constitution-making process. In his opening remarks to the delegates, the Premier remarked:

4   *Ibid.*

The presence of some 200 citizens from all walks of life, including representatives of religious, economic labour, civic, professional and political organizations as well as governmental agencies, constitutes a landmark in the history of our Territory. Today's meeting represents the closest approximation we have yet achieved towards the national community. ... All of you added together, with your collective views however divergent or contradictory, constitute a citizen's assembly the like of which has seldom been seen in the world. ... You are all here this morning ... the nation in conference, an educated democracy in deliberation, a Government seeking advice from its citizens.[5]

The utility of the conference as a consensus-building mechanism was, however, seriously impaired by the refusal of the leading representatives of the Hindu community to participate. The President General of the Maha Sabha, who claimed to speak for 250,000 Hindus, observed that since his organization had not been consulted before the constitution was drafted, and had in fact rejected it in its entirety, he could not possibly co-operate. The fact that there was no mutually agreed agenda for the conference also made it difficult for him to participate. Maraj still believed that it was the duty of the government to call a referendum on the question of Federation.

He strongly condemned the leadership of the DLP, who had agreed to participate: 'Where is the consistency, when the DLP refused to nominate their Senators, when the DLP has two serious matters before the Privy Council, and three others pending in the Supreme Court, all alleging mal-practice on the part of the Government, and all challenging the very life of the Government? Participation ... automatically vitiates all arguments as to who are the rightful government.'[6] He warned the DLP that by participating in the conference, it ran the risk of legitimating the PNM government and the decisions of that conference, which would very likely not be in accord with those which the Party was demanding. Maraj maintained that there was no question of his not being in favour of Independence, which he considered imperative. What he wanted was a constitution in which minorities would be given adequate safeguards. Until the government was 'prepared to sit down with minority groups for a full and frank discussion leading to a completely new draft constitution',[7] the Indian community would have to dissociate itself from the constitution-making process.

Whether or not the DLP agreed to participate merely to obstruct the proceedings and destroy its effectiveness is indeed difficult to determine. The

5   *Verbatim Notes of the Proceedings of the Meeting on the Draft Constitution,*
     April 25–7, 1962, Port of Spain, 1962, p. 3.
6   TG, April 25, 1962.
7   *Ibid.*

behaviour of its spokesmen and some of its supporters certainly created that impression. The Party took issue with the tight security arrangements surrounding the conference hall, the exclusion of the press and the members of the select committee, the five-minute speaking limitation, and the agenda imposed on the conference by the government.[8] The DLP delegates further objected to the ruling of the chairman that delegates would be permitted to speak only once, and then only on those issues which had been raised in their memoranda. This ruling was rejected on the grounds that it presumed acceptance of the general principles of the draft. It would also silence persons who did not make detailed criticisms, but who had in fact rejected the entire draft. The Hindu Youth Association and the African National Congress were in this predicament, and had no alternative but to accept the invitation of the chairman to leave the conference.[9] After some rather heated exchanges and threats the DLP also walked out of the conference, their behaviour doing much to destroy the sympathy which some delegates might have had for the Party's point of view. The walkout coloured much of the proceedings, especially those relating to the question of consultation with the leader of the opposition.

It would not be possible to analyse in detail the various points of view expressed during the conference. There were certain core issues, however, which dominated the proceedings and which must be reviewed. At the centre of every discussion there were two or three recurring premises or points of view. The debate, in fact, was essentially between the majoritarian democrats and the constitutional or qualitative democrats. The major areas of controversy were: (*a*) the nature of the constitution, (*b*) civil rights and liberties, (*c*) the composition of the Senate and the Boundaries Commission, and (*d*) the independence of the judiciary.

The nature of the constitution

The discussion about the relationship between the governor general and that prime minister posed a fundamental question about the basic ideological foundations of the constitution. Was Trinidad to be a republic like India or Ghana, or was it to be a constitutional monarchy like the older dominions? The

---

8   The Premier later advised that the government planned to make arrangements for broadcasting the full proceedings of the meeting. The opposition had feared that the public would have been given edited information releases. The government was probably hesitant at first to have an open meeting because of its uncertainty about the manner in which the conference would deal with the draft. It seemed unwilling to have it appear that it had been repudiated by the conference. It is also clear that the government did not trust the competence of the press.

9   The restrictions on speaking time and on the relevance of addresses to positions taken in memoranda were relaxed during the proceedings, which were brilliantly chaired.

author of the draft proposals, Sir Ellis Clarke, made it quite clear at the beginning of the conference that the government's preference was for the 'familiar constitutional monarchy based on the Westminster pattern'. Once the Westminster pattern was accepted, certain things inevitably followed. The Prime Minister must become the keystone of the constitution. The governor general, as the Queen's representative, must act only on the advice of the prime minister, as he in fact had been doing in the past, despite constitutional niceties. Clarke noted that the suggestions which gave certain appointive powers to the governor general went 'half way or three-quarters of the way towards a Republic'.[10] In the parliamentary system the governor general advises and warns, but never commands.

Only a minority at the conference openly expressed any preference for a republican constitution. One such spokesman declared that constitutional monarchy was a 'bad form of state headship' for the new nation. It gave the Queen too many residual opportunities for interfering in the life of the community. The question of where sovereignty rested was always in doubt. As far as he was concerned, 'Sovereignty must originate and reside here in Trinidad. ... You [do not become] completely sovereign as long as the Queen of England is also Queen of Trinidad and Tobago.'[11]

Other speakers were less sanguine about a republic, but wished nevertheless to vary the United Kingdom experiment to provide some of the checks and balances which in the United Kingdom were secured by convention and an alert and vocal public opinion. The Bar Council struck at the core of the issue when it declared: 'The absence of any confidence on the part of either political party in the other, and the division of the political parties on racial lines, make it imperative that for the time being anyway, the power vested in the ruling party should not be virtually absolute; that there should be some checks and balances; and that to such extent, the system obtaining in England should be modified.'[12] Mr G. Furness-Smith, who spoke for the Council, and at times for the creole European community of which he was a member, in fact wanted the governor general to have the right to appoint 'half a dozen or so vital officers of the State', including the Chief Justice, in the same way as he now appointed senators. He would of course consult with the leaders of both government and opposition, but the final discretion would be his. These ideas were not really undemocratic, he maintained: 'But let us assume that the idea does detract from some theoretical basis of democracy. Will it not be better to have a slight theoretical detraction from this idea of pure democracy, whatever pure democracy may be, and have practical safeguards and confidence of the people in the Constitution, than to have the most wonderfully democratic and

10   *Verbatim Notes*, p. 100.   11   *Ibid.*, p. 109.   12   *Ibid.*, p. 269.

theoretically perfect constitution the world has ever known, and find all sorts of minority or even majority communities in the country living in fear of political interference with their rights? Is it not better to sacrifice a little theory for a little practical safety and confidence?'[13]

The thesis was vigorously disputed by the majoritarians, who saw in it nothing but a denial of the rights of the majority. One PNM spokesman took the rather extreme position that 'In Independence there are no checks, there can be no checks, no safeguards, and no balance. ... The only checks and safe-guards and balances that can be in any independent country are the awareness and vigilance of the people themselves.'[14]

Another Party spokesman tried to pare to the core of the problem that was being posed by minority elements. 'Let's call a spade a spade', he snapped:

We have in our community certain groups who do not want to identify themselves politically, yet wish to retain certain political advantages and power. Now if you don't want to identify yourself politically, it means that you have in any democratic society to stand by the wishes of the majority. If you wish to change the majority, the only way to do it is to go into the majority and convince them. That is, get the shifting or the floating vote to move with you. This can only be done by political activity. So it is no use sitting on the fence like a pigeon and saying you want this, or you want that, without being prepared to come forward and accept political obligations and office. ... It is perhaps one of the greatest difficulties in our society, that you have certain intelligent thinking groups who do not attempt to propagate and give other groups the benefit of their thoughts publicly. It is no use drafting fancy documents if you are not prepared at the same time to get into the bodies that act politically and to influence them from *within* in order that you may have the sort of mosaic portrayed on the wall with your own views in them.[15]

It was a brilliant thrust, which considerably weakened the bargaining status of the qualitative democrats. Popular majoritarians also expressed the fear that in giving two people the power to appoint, one invited the risk of head-on collisions and public confusion.[16] As Clarke warned, 'By creating a system of dual control, you are setting up a President in the guise of a Governor General, and you are putting him as a rival to your Prime Minister.'[17] The conference seemed generally agreed that the governor generalship should be left as a symbolic office only.

---

13 *Ibid.*, pp. 106–7.   14   I.K. Merritt in *ibid.*, pp. 117–18.
15 K. Hudson Phillips, *ibid.*, pp. 116–17.
16 Demands had also been made that a discretionary right be given the governor general to dissolve the House if it was clear that the government had lost the confidence of the Legislature.
17 *Verbatim Notes*, p. 134.

The question of consultation between the prime minister and the leader of the opposition was less easy to dispose of. The Jamaican precedent which constitutionalized this provision seemed to have wide popularity, especially on account of the ethnic basis of the two-party system. The problem was somewhat complicated by the fact that the existing Leader of the Opposition had alienated large sections of the community, and many people were unwilling to force Dr Williams to work with him. But others, like Sir Hugh Wooding, were not sure that one should reject the principle of institutionalized consultation solely because it was difficult to conceive it in the context of the present state of party politics. The constitution was being constructed to last for a long time. Wooding, in fact, took the even more positive and sensible view that the opposition should be cultivated in spite of its systematic 'recalcitrance': 'It [is] better wisdom that we should try to encourage consultation even though it might be difficult, rather than hold up our hands in horror and say that because people choose the way of boycotts and walkouts, we will not give them an opportunity of mending their ways. ... We ought to teach them that this idea of boycotting is a regrettable and reprehensible idea.'[18] Wooding's own view was that it was highly necessary, especially in the condition of Trinidad, to make consultation a constitutional requirement. 'In supra-party matters, collective wisdom is better than the wisdom which reposes in a single party forming the Government.' He was prepared to concede, however, that in the event of any failure to agree, the view of the prime minister should prevail. Building the 'national community' would be a futile exercise without the co-operation of the leadership of the Indian community.

However, government forces were prepared to oppose to the limit any plan to write the principle of consultation into the constitution. It must grow up as a convention and not be made a compulsory requirement. Clarke took the view that consultation may not always be functional. It depended very much on the personalities of the leaders. If there is no natural co-operation between the men at the top, consultation can become farcical and ritualistic.[19] By making consultation a constitutional requirement, one could put road-blocks in the way of responsible decision-making. The provision would inhibit the function of government, as well as opposition, to say nothing of the embarrassment it would cause the governor general. Both parties could throw the blame for a wrong decision on the advice or agreement of the other.

Clarke disclosed that the Jamaican precedent was found in no other par-

18   *Ibid.*, p. 163.
19   As he told the conference, 'I hope you see with me the reasons why it cannot work *now*, but may well be encouraged and may well eventually become a feature of our Constitution.' *Ibid.*, p. 194 (italics in original).

liamentary democracy. It was born of special circumstances, 'obviously prepared by a Premier who fears that he will be Leader of the Opposition, and
accepted by a Leader of the Opposition who is not at all sure whether he will
be Premier'.[20]

While admitting the relevance of the arguments of Wooding and others,
one must agree with the popular majoritarians in their refusal to write consultation into the constitution. The office of the prime minister, it may be argued,
is not purely a party position. The prime minister is answerable to his cabinet,
to the Legislature, and to the country in a way in which the leader of the
opposition is not. The latter's office is a purely political one. Enforced consultation – especially when there is no way of agreeing just what is a 'supra-party'
matter – could make the positions of both sides intolerable. The whole argument presupposed the permanence of the two-party system. Given the tendency towards party instability in Trinidad and in other newly developing
areas, or for that matter in many older nations as well, a constitutional provision requiring consultation with *the* leader of the opposition was absurd.
Clarke was right in observing the 'contemporariness' of the Jamaican experiment.

It might be said, however, that the blame for the bitter battle over this
issue must rest squarely with the PNM – especially with Dr Williams and Dr
Solomon, who, despite their ideological commitment to the conventions of the
Westminster system, seemed temperamentally unable to inspire and sustain
confidence in an opposition which was growing more and more desperate because of its firm belief that the victory of the PNM, and the behaviour of its
rank and file, threatened to reduce it to the status of a marginal party.

Civil rights and liberties

On the question of civil rights and liberties, the position of the popular majoritarians was quite consistent. Clarke pointed out that the question of striking a
balance between the rights of the individual and minorities, and the rights of
the majority as represented by the government, had always posed a dilemma
for constitutional draughtsmen, but that, under the Westminster system with
which Trinidad was familiar, Parliament was supreme. The courts had no
power to declare an act of Parliament invalid because it violated the rights of
an individual. All the exceptions to those rights mentioned in the draft conferred no extra power on the Legislature in any way. Nor did the itemized
rights in any way deprive Parliament of the freedom to suspend them. It was
because of the need to recognize the right of the majority to act when need
arose that the draft had made such imprecise and comprehensive qualifications

20   *Ibid.*, p. 135.

to conceded rights.[21] Clarke again argued that the only real safeguard that individuals could rely on was an alert public opinion. If one attempted to describe in the constitution the precise conditions under which individual rights might be set aside, the product would become unusually long.

While acknowledging the legal correctness of Clarke's position, the representatives of the Bar Society were not satisfied that it could be applied to Trinidad: 'However troublesome it may be, and perhaps even though certain risks may have to be run in drawing certain clauses too tightly, which one might suppose might possibly embarrass a future Government, ... those risks should be taken.'[22] In the past, the liberties of the citizen were protected by the Governor, who was empowered to reserve legislation for the assent of the Crown. With Independence, the constitution must reinforce public opinion in providing that inhibiting function. With the experience of Ghana in mind, delegates felt that there was need for an entrenched bill of rights along the lines of the Canadian model, which could be set aside only under very special conditions. It was also felt that an effective system of judicial review should be instituted.

There was some demand that in the event of the government declaring an emergency while the Legislature was not in session, such a declaration, to remain valid, must be ratified within one month by a two-thirds or three-quarters majority of the Legislature. Only by such a procedure should fundamental rights like *habeas corpus* be set aside. This was a provision which strict majoritarians were unwilling to grant. The judgment of the government and its anticipation of public opinion were the only truly democratic safeguards that were needed in such situations. 'Your Executive and your Parliament [must be] in a position to ensure and guarantee that the individual has rights because it can restrain certain acts which might themselves deprive the individual of those rights. Anything that might happen in the future cuts two ways; Parliament must not be strait-jacketed.'[23]

It was also explained that the controversial provisions which permitted the Legislature to discriminate on the basis of race or creed were very necessary

---

21   It was noted (*ibid.*, p. 45) that the Canadian Bill of Rights specifically allowed Parliament to enact legislation which would override those rights. The provision referred to in the Canadian bill is as follows: 'Every law of Canada shall, unless it is expressly declared by an Act of Parliament of Canada that it shall operate notwithstanding the Canadian Bill of Rights, be so construed and applied as not to abrogate, abridge or infringe or to authorize the abrogation, abridgement or infringement of any of the rights or freedoms herein recognized and declared, and in particular no law of Canada should be construed or applied so as to authorize certain things ...'
22   G. Furness-Smith in *ibid.*, p. 57.
23   Ellis Clarke in *ibid.*, p. 91.

in a plural community in which some groups have customs which were not applicable to other communities.[24] The Legislature might also wish to discriminate between citizen and non-citizen in respect of certain privileges and responsibilities. It was not a sinister provision, but one designed to cover the government in matters of litigation. The unfortunate thing, however, was that it was there for possible misuse by anyone minded to take unfair action against target groups.

Demands were made for a strong and unequivocal provision against racial discrimination in any form, and these came from both Negro and Indian delegates. One trade unionist argued that an independent Trinidad must have no room for the type of discriminatory practices which were familiar in job recruitment. But while he as a Negro seemed especially concerned about discrimination against non-whites, Indian delegates were concerned with discrimination by Negroes against Indians. The representative of the Hindu Youth Association brought the following statistics to the notice of the conference: 'The Police Force of this country is a force of over 2,000 people, and there are 50 people of Indian origin in this Police Force. Secondly, the Civil Service; the Indian population is 301,946 and we have no more than 10 or 12 per cent of our people as civil servants. Scholarships: of every 100 scholarships awarded, 95 go to Negroes or people of African descent and others exclusive of Indians.'[25] The conference took no notice of these complaints; one delegate, a creole white, merely noted that these views were 'quite exceptional'.[26] But other voices in the country were already demanding 'parity or partition.'

The composition and role of the Senate
The debate on the Senate was quite low-keyed by comparison to some of the issues already discussed. Not everyone appeared to be convinced that there should be a Senate – only half of the memoranda submitted gave any support to the idea; but the sense of the conference was certainly that the opposition was inadequately represented. A number of variations were suggested, the aim of which was to give the governing party slightly less than a majority. Objections were also raised to the right given to the prime minister and the leader of the opposition to recall their nominees. It was felt that this would inhibit the impartiality of the proceedings of the Senate and its usefulness as a revisionary or delaying chamber, especially if the governing party were to be given a clear majority.

24   The case cited was the Moslem Marriage Ordinance, which permits differentiated standards for divorce.
25   *Ibid.*, p. 77.   26   *Ibid.*, p. 79.

There was also strong support for the view that entrenched proposals would need a two-thirds or three-quarters majority in the Senate as well. There was little controversy over these points, however, since government spokesmen indicated that they were quite willing to accept changes which would meet some of the objections raised. But no specific commitments were given as to what the precise changes would be, even though representatives of Hindu and Moslem groups had been making strong pleas for ethnic and creedal balance in the Senate.

The Boundaries Commission

The question of boundaries was somewhat more controversial, though government spokesmen were generally unwilling to comment. Strong views were expressed in favour of greater opposition participation in the deliberations of the commission. And implied in many of the statements was the feeling that the DLP had been unfairly treated in 1961. The draft had provided that reports of the commission were to be laid before the Legislature, and the government's view was that the opposition would have adequate opportunity to raise objections there. But what was objectionable was the provision that the Minister of Home Affairs could alter the decisions of the commission before its report was presented to the Legislature. It is true that the minister had to give explanations for his changes, but it was felt that it would be too easy for the government to use its majority to vary, to its own advantage, what the commission had thought to be a fair and equitable division. The new system, to which the government seemed committed, promised little improvement, if any, over the Select Committee procedure adopted in 1961.

The judiciary

There were many areas of disagreement relating to the judiciary. Here, however, attention is given mainly to the question of the relationship between the judicial and executive branches of the government. The core question concerned the appointment and dismissal of judges. The argument of the draft was that this power should be given mainly to the prime minister. It was feared, however, that judges would be influenced by political considerations because they owed their appointments, promotions, and extensions of term directly or indirectly to the prime minister. Fears were also expressed that, in making appointments to investigating tribunals, or to the Judicial and Legal Services Commission, the prime minister might be inclined to choose individuals who were partial to the administration's point of view. The members of the legal profession, especially those who were not affiliated with the PNM, were anxious that the power to appoint judges, other than the chief justice, be shared in some way with other legal bodies, or with the leader of the opposition.

It was argued that all the various commissions and tribunals which the prime minister had the power to appoint would be used as smoke-screens behind which influence and pressure would be peddled, influence which would be even more difficult to detect by an unsophisticated public opinion. The Bar Society noted that with the departure of the Colonial Office, more and more constitutional issues would be presented to the judiciary for settlement: 'Judges, more than before, will be the guardians of the law against political parties ... suspicion must be removed.'[27] Other legal spokesmen generally endorsed the view that English experience might have to be varied somewhat so that there might be a greater separation between the executive and the judiciary.

The position taken by the Government's constitutional advisor was that it was wrong to believe that judicial impartiality was impaired because a judge belonged to or supported a party. It was of prime importance that judges, regardless of how they were appointed, behaved in the best traditions of the profession. That was the only real check and balance that a mature people could ask for. He also drew attention to the fact that there was an additional safeguard for the security of the judiciary in that the Privy Council had the final authority as to whether a judge should be removed or not. What worried observers, however, was the provision that such appeals only went to the Privy Council if the three-judge tribunal appointed by the prime minister ruled that the case should be heard by that body. There was a possibility that a judge's career could be destroyed by the executive before the Privy Council ever had an opportunity to review the case. But the provision that a judge's suspension must cease if his case was not sent to the Privy Council was perhaps a strong enough inhibition against the possibility of his being suspended without just cause.

Although the conference did not settle all the controversial issues surrounding the constitution, it narrowed them down considerably. Before the conference came to a close, the Government had conceded, among other things, (a) a preamble which would include reference to God, (b) a bill of rights, (c) changes in the composition of the Senate, (d) tightening of the amendment procedure by requiring a 'satisfactory' majority in both Houses, (e) the right to appeal the decision of a judge granting or refusing leave to institute election petition proceedings, and (f) guarantees that the life of the present Legislature would not exceed five years. The government made further declarations which went even further to meet some of the criticisms aired at the conference. The cabinet conceded that proceedings for the removal of a puisne judge would be initiated by the Judicial and Legal Services Commis-

27   G. Furness-Smith, *ibid.*, p. 215.

sion and not by the prime minister. In regard to the chief justice, the prime minister was to act only after consultation with the Commission. The remaining issues were left for negotiation with the DLP on the Select Committee.

The conference had served a valuable purpose in that it had helped to dissolve much of the tension that the publication of the draft had created. Participants were extremely enthusiastic about the device which the Government had arranged to obtain the public's views. The spokesman of the Employers Consultative Association described the conference as being 'absolutely unique'. The representative of the Moslem Anjuman Sunnatul-Jamaat felt that the meeting was the 'most admirable step taken by a Government to satisfy all sections of the Territory. ... the greatest piece of democracy ever to be displayed by a Government of the Territory'.[28] Even His Grace the Archbishop of Port of Spain felt moved to invoke God's blessing 'upon the Government and its works'.[29]

Dr Williams himself was particularly proud of the 'novel' way which the community had found to create consensus on the constitution, though he had a mild rebuke for those who 'congratulated the Government' on the 'privilege' they had been afforded. Participation was a right and an obligation, not a favour, he reminded them. Williams also made the startling disclosure that the draft had been prepared in only three-and-a-half weeks. They were men in a hurry, he explained:

If there has appeared to be a certain amount of haste in this procedure, ladies and gentlemen, please understand that anybody who is a representative of the Government today, responsible for improving as rapidly as is humanly possible the material conditions under which our citizens live, [doesn't] have a great deal of time. We have to work to our time-tables. ... We are now in a twilight zone. ... We cannot afford to remain in this particular period for too long, where we have nobody to speak for us on this question of the European Common Market. So if there has appeared to be a certain element of haste, I give you the assurance that the sooner we could get this thing done, as far as the members of the Government are concerned, without in any way detracting from the participation of the widest possible number of the population in this exercise, then a lot of us would sleep a little more peacefully at night.[30]

He was also quite frank in admitting that the conference was 'accidental'. The Cabinet had intended to study the memoranda before agreeing upon a stand, but later agreed, on Williams' suggestion, that the citizenry should be made to do the homework. Williams declared himself extremely satisfied with the way

28 *Ibid.*, p. 280.   29 *Ibid.*, p. 275.   30 *Ibid.*, p. 284.

in which the conference had performed. Delegates had made it their business to study the constitutions of a number of countries, both new and old, in order that they might construct something worthy of admiration and respect. Williams asserted:

This meeting is a tribute to the citizens, not to the Government. It shows how you have done your homework, and I believe, at this moment of national pride, I may be pardoned the statement: that I doubt that there is any country in the world in which there has been such a demonstration of civic pride and civic responsibility on the part of citizens from all walks of life. It is your success and not ours. Our success, I take it, is in being able to stimulate response from the citizens. We as members of the Government have benefited from this meeting of the minds of the citizens.[31]

But there were other voices that were not as sanguine about the usefulness of the conference. C.L.R. James referred to it as a 'phony conference', which was not representative of all the people.[32] In the view of the DLP, the whole thing was a circus from start to finish. Opposition elements described it as a 'citizen's committee to cover a dirty dictatorship', a 'mahogany casket to hide a rotten corpse'. Others contended rather unfairly that it had been packed with PNM supporters. Critics also rejected the government's arguments that the country had to hurry to Independence, and thus could not allow the citizenry more time to debate the issue. One participant, noting the fawning attitude of some delegates, made the rather apt comment that the 'people of Trinidad and Tobago have been so accustomed to treat Colonial Governments with awe, that now that representative Government has been established, many of them regard the Premier as inviolable as they once regarded the Colonial Governor; any rebuff to the Premier's expressed will is regarded not by them as an assertion of the democratic right to protest ... but as an illustration of an unreasonable determination to be as unco-operative as possible.'[33] New premier was but old Governor writ large. It was a devastating and somewhat correct analysis, not only of the conference, but of many other aspects of the territory's political life as well.

THE SELECT COMMITTEE

The negotiations in the Select Committee of the Legislature did not go very far toward meeting the fundamental objections which the Indian National Association, the African National Congress, and the DLP raised to the govern-

---

31   *Ibid.,* pp. 282–3.
32   *Party Politics in the West Indies,* Port of Spain, 1962, p. 163.
33   Cyril Henry, 'The Rape of Democracy at Queen's Hall', TG, June 8, 1962.

ment's new draft proposals.[34] The DLP had in fact not abandoned its demand for an Eastern Caribbean Federation, though it now conceded that the federation might be considered after the achievement of Independence for Trinidad. The Party wanted, however, some firm agreement on the methods that might be chosen to consult the people on this issue. The government rejected this on the grounds that it was already committed to the idea of a unitary state.

Little purpose would be served by going into the details of the meetings and decisions of the Select Committee, since the points of disagreement between the DLP and the government remained substantially the same as before the Committee began its deliberations.[35] The Select Committee, which contained seven opposition, eleven government, and three independent representatives, disagreed on every major issue, the divisions being always fourteen to seven, with the DLP reserving its position for negotiations in 'another place'. The DLP seems to have felt that it had a much stronger chance of wringing concessions from the PNM at the forthcoming conference in England than it would have had in Trinidad, with all the attending pressures.

The only positive decisions worth noting at this juncture dealt with the Senate. The majority approved the government's proposal to increase the membership of the Senate to twenty-four, and to alter its composition so that thirteen senate places would go to the government, four to the opposition, and seven to vested interests who were now to be given responsibility for nominating their own candidates. The DLP's strong opposition to the retention of independent members in the upper house was rejected.

The failure of the two parties to settle their differences before going to the Colonial Office must in part be ascribed to the unfortunate procedure which the PNM chose to adopt in framing the constitution. As Dr Capildeo himself argued:

Wider measure of agreement would have been achieved if an attempt had been made to secure our co-operation from the outset. ... The Government, however, chose to ignore us and proceeded to prepare a draft on its own, so that when the joint select committee was belatedly appointed, the Government members of the committee had already closed their minds, and in committee they were not disposed to discuss issues but were determined to defend a draft to which they appeared to be irrevocably committed. The joint select committee, was, therefore, prejudiced from the beginning.[36]

34 The committee invited the INA and ANC to testify before it, but little was gained from these meetings.
35 *Report of the Joint Select Committee to Consider Proposals for an Independence Constitution for Trinidad and Tobago*, Senate Paper #1, 1962.
36 Capildeo at Lancaster House, TG, May 29, 1962.

But while it is clear that the PNM blundered in not consulting the opposition, it is to be wondered whether any co-operation was possible with the DLP in the climate that prevailed after the 1961 election. This, however, does not exonerate the PNM from the crassness of the methods it adopted to terminate the colonial period.

THE INDEPENDENCE CONFERENCE

At the opening of the Marlborough House Conference on May 29, 1962, the last of those frustrating pilgrimages to London, the leader of the DLP stated succinctly but emphatically what his delegation was after:

We want a judiciary which is independent, we want provisions which really guarantee effectively the rights and freedoms which ought to exist in a democratic society: we want Parliament democratically constituted, we want a procedure for the amendment of the Constitution which effectively protects us from the arbitrary exercises of the power to amend. We want the various commissions so constituted as to ensure that they function effectively and impartially.[37]

He was also insistent that elections be held before Independence to determine which of the parties would be the immediate beneficiaries of the transfer of power. This, he observed, was a vital precondition of harmony, unity, and confidence.

The demands of the Indian National Association went even further.[38] They wanted 'parity or partition'; they did not believe that the DLP, committed as it was to other ethnic groups, was in a position to make an effective case for the Indian population. As the President of the INA stated:

The Indian community must spear-head the demand for proportionate representation for all the ethnic groups in the councils of the nation. If, perchance the 'obscurantist' minorities are not interested in protecting themselves in this way against PNM racialism, then we, the Indians, must demand parity with the Negroes in government, in the Civil Service, in the Police and every aspect of government. If there are thirty seats in the House, we insist on having fifteen. If there are twelve Ministers, we demand six. We demand that 50 per cent of the jobs in the Civil

---

37 *Ibid.*
38 Apart from the three principals – the PNM, the DLP, and the Colonial Office – there were delegations from the Indian community made up of representatives of the Indian National Association, the All Indian Youth Association, and the Maha Sabha. The African National Congress was also present. None of these groups participated in plenary discussions, but they were permitted to state their cases to representatives of the Colonial Office.

Service be given Indians, and 50 per cent of the men in the Police Force be of our community, as well as 50 per cent of the officers.[39]

Singh believed that these stark alternatives could be avoided only if the 'dishonest machinery for election' was eliminated. The Trinidad Partition League also supported this claim in a cable to the Colonial Secretary.

None of the principals, including the DLP, endorsed the demands of what was considered an extremist minority of the Indian community.[40] The Colonial Secretary, Mr. Maudling, rejected partition quite firmly. As he advised, 'The last vestiges of external control, for better or worse, are about to be removed, and a heavy responsibility therefore lies upon those attending ... to ensure that the new Constitution they are devising will be one under which the peoples of a former dependency can emerge and govern themselves as a single nation.'[41] Since both the PNM and the DLP were in agreement that partition or proportional representation was undesirable and, in the case of partition, meaningless, no consideration was given to such proposals in the negotiations.

The proceedings of the conference were unduly long and frustrating. Neither side was anxious to concede, even though Maudling had made it clear that differences would have to be narrowed before Independence was granted. The DLP insisted on new elections first. The Maha Sabha even wanted the conference abandoned completely until such elections could be held. Those elections, moreover, would have to be held after an independent boundaries commission, consisting of representatives from either the United Kingdom or the United Nations, had redrafted the constituencies. Reintroduction of the ballot box was also demanded: Dr Capildeo admitted that both methods were open to fraud, but he felt that abuse of the machines could be more 'total'.

Williams angrily rejected these demands. The appointment of such a commission would be harmful to the reputation of the country. Moreover, the country could not afford the luxurious delays that these proposals would involve. He estimated that Independence would be delayed for at least four months.[42] The DLP felt this a small price to pay for social peace. Williams

39 H.P. Singh, *Hour of Decision*, Port of Spain, 1962, pp. 9–10.
40 The DLP strongly rebuked the INA for its extremism: 'The Indian Association is a many-sided thing. Cranks who have weird ideas of removing governments, communist sympathizers, frustrated people who would have liked to be candidates in the last elections. ... They are prepared to destroy left, right and centre if they do not get what they want. They conspire, intrigue and undermine. They, most of them, have chips on their shoulders.' 'The Indian Association Makes a Mess', *Statesman*, Nov. 30, 1962.
41 TG, May 24, 1962.
42 Before leaving for London, Williams warned about the disruption that would be caused by holding another election and swore that he would be ruthless with the Opposition if they should force another pre-Independence election on the country.

feared, however, that rather than promote harmony, new elections would only serve to disrupt even further the tattered fabric of the society.

On the question of entrenchment the DLP demanded a three-quarter majority in both Houses, and an entrenched right of appeal to the Privy Council on all issues relating to the interpretation of the constitution. Dr Capildeo declared that he had no faith in the integrity of Dr Williams, and could not accept his pledges or those of his Party. Williams had 'torn up' the federal constitution and the old Trinidad constitution and there was nothing to stop him from 'tearing up' the new constitution and making Trinidad a republic, as Nkrumah had done in Ghana. The DLP also wanted some sort of firm guarantee that the civil service, the police force, and the national guard would be more representative of the ethnic physiognomy of the community. Capildeo complained that at present, 'one section of the community was armed against the other'.

Deadlock in London only served to aggravate tensions in Trinidad. According to the President of the INA, extremists in the Indian community were already arming themselves in preparation for any emergency which might arise in case of an unfair imposition.[43] It was the INA, its President later asserted, which brought home to the Colonial Office the gravity of the crisis in Trinidad. The DLP organ in fact accused the *Guardian* of deliberately suppressing news of violence in the territory in the hope of strengthening Williams' hand. 'Dr Williams', the *Statesman* declared, 'could not afford to let the Colonial Office know that Trinidad was sitting on a volcano of racial hate ... a volcano which may violently blow up at any moment.' The PNM was warned that racialism would develop into a Frankenstein which it would not be able to control: the PNM 'have whipped racialism to such a pitch that it now threatens to become an inferno consuming everything. The schism between Negroes and other minorities, East Indians in particular, has become a yawning unbridgeable chasm. ... The white heat of anger is spreading.'[44]

The Marlborough House compromise

Whether at the instance of reports from Trinidad, or intuition that Trinidad might indeed witness a bloodbath, the PNM delegation finally agreed to compromise. The conference seemed on the verge of complete collapse when Williams decided that he would make a statement which he hoped would meet some of the objections of the DLP.[45] The concessions were:

---

43 Mr H.P. Singh informed the writer that he had to use his influence to restrain extremists who were in possession of concealed caches of arms.
44 *Statesman*, May 25, 1962.
45 Williams had first planned to have the Colonial Secretary serve as a liaison between

1 Special entrenchment of an increased number of provisions by a three-fourths majority of the members of the lower house and a two-thirds majority of the members of the upper house.[46]

2 An independent boundaries commission which would delineate new constituencies which would vary by no more than a margin of 20 per cent.

3 An elections commission which would be responsible for the conduct of elections and the registration of voters. The commission was also to be responsible for ensuring the accuracy and competence of voting machines and for seeing that these were fully tested and sealed in the presence of representatives of political parties. The commission was to be completely free of any direction or control from the executive or any other authority.

4 The widening of the right of appeal to the Privy Council in matters other than constitutional rights.

5 Limitation to six months of the period during which a proclamation of a state of emergency could remain in force without being extended by Parliament.

6 Strengthening of the provisions for the independence of the auditor general.

7 Entrenching of the provision that Trinidad remain a constitutional monarchy.

8 Entrenching of provisions relating to the independence of the judiciary from partisan political pressure.

9 Consultation with the Leader of the Opposition on important appointments including the chairmanship of the elections and boundaries commissions, and on all the important national issues.

This last concession was not promised as a part of a constitutional requirement. A promise was also given that a bipartisan committee of national integration would be appointed to examine the methods by which the community could be more satisfactorily integrated.

himself and Capildeo, but later decided to inform the opposition leader personally that he planned to make some new proposals. Capildeo made his reply contingent upon the content of the proposals. According to his version of the event, 'Dr Williams came to me and said, I intend to make a statement that we shall co-operate, that we shall meet and that we shall discuss our differences. I replied, that statement is very good to make under any circumstances. Go ahead and make it by all means. If you make that statement, I would underline it.' *Statesman*, Aug. 21, 1962.

46 These included clauses relating to the composition of Parliament, the amendment clause of the constitution, annual meetings of Parliament, dissolution of Parliament, general elections, the boundary and elections commissions, provisions for review of constituency boundaries, the Supreme Court, and tenure of judges, the right of appeal to the Privy Council, freedom of speech in Parliament, and the Independence Act of 1962.

Somewhat surprisingly, Williams argued that he had made no concessions. Even the 75 per cent provision, which he agreed was a 'stiff measure of entrenchment', he did not view as a concession. He noted that he would have nothing to do with a police state, and had no objections to any safeguards which would strengthen the independence of the judiciary. The DLP, for its part, accepted these promises and agreed to drop its demand for pre-Independence elections and for the constitutionalizing of the principle of consultation. It also agreed to the use of voting machines on the understanding that every machine would be fully examined before use and sealed in the presence of representatives of the political parties. Williams, who was extremely anxious to attend the Prime Ministers' Conference in September which would deal with the question of Britain's role in the Common Market and Commonwealth, declared that he was not surprised that DLP negotiators agreed to his proposals, and that there was a meeting of minds on the essential outstanding questions.[47] This was a rather curious statement, especially since Williams disclosed that 'one or two of the Colonial Secretary's proposals were a little hard to take, but we agreed to them.' It has never been made clear just what these proposals were.

In his post-conference broadcast to the people of Trinidad, Williams declared: 'We on the Government side approached the Conference from the point of view that ... if there was any particular safeguard that we could introduce for the benefit of the community as a whole, no matter what the origin of the proposal, we gave it the most serious consideration.'[48] This was an obvious attempt to conceal defeat, but a useful one in the circumstances. Williams quite rightly sought to convince the people of Trinidad and elsewhere that agreement was achieved on a 'happy note'. 'The Conference involved this question of inspiring confidence in the Community and removing tensions. So, at the end of the Conference, as the leader of the delegation, I made a clear statement indicating that we of the Government Party intended to extend an invitation to the Opposition to discuss all issues on our return to Trinidad which might retard or could retard the promotion and development of national unity.'[49]

It is worth noting that DLP spokesmen were quite convinced that Capildeo had triumphed over Williams. As one MLC exclaimed, 'You [Dr Capildeo] outfoxed Williams and he knows it. They are happy and so are we!' Another MLC, also a member of the DLP delegation, observed, 'The Constitution ... contains all the safeguards that it is possible to build into a constitution. If this

---

47   As early as May 30, 1962, he had said, 'We are not free to fix the date for Independence. The September 10 meeting of the Commonwealth Prime Ministers fixes the date.' TG May 31, 1962.

48   *Ibid.*, June 9, 1962.   49   *Ibid.*

Constitution fails to achieve the objective of safeguarding the democratic rights of the people, it will not be the fault of the Constitution, but of the men who have failed to exercise the eternal vigilance without which no constitution, however cleverly drafted, can prevail.'[50] The London press also seemed to feel that the Opposition had achieved most of its main aims. The *Trinidad Guardian*, however, observed in a rather puzzling headline that 'Williams' Team Wins All, Opposition Gets Nothing.'

Dr Capildeo was not as happy as some of his followers, but he was honest enough to admit that the DLP was as much to blame for its defeats as was the PNM. As he reflected:

The DLP could have achieved a great deal more, but had to struggle against the history of its own past leadership, with its internecine conflicts; but their defeat [especially on the elections issue] was also due to the fact that the assiduous propaganda of its opponents, that the country had no genuine alternative to the present Government, had been swallowed by the Colonial Office.[51]

Capildeo also argued that the PNM did not want to 'knock out' the opposition completely; it preferred to retain the mirage of a democratic two-party system while at the same time enjoying functional one-party control. He also ascribed his party's reverses to the fact that the communications media and the upper classes had turned their backs on the DLP, regardless of how they felt about the PNM:

Whatever purpose the Queen's Hall Constitution exercise may have served, it revealed one unpalatable fact, that the loudest well-to-do critics of the Government and those who criticized from what they fondly believed were well entrenched positions, did not want the DLP to form the Government. ... The sources of public information were also arrayed and marshalled against us. This is a grave defect in the body politic of Trinidad, and, in my opinion, constitutes a far greater danger, in that it creates the atmosphere conducive to a one-party state, and so encourages such results even if the direction of political leaders were otherwise oriented.[52]

He also disclosed that he, like Williams, was driven to compromise because of fear of the consequences for Trinidad, both internally and in terms of its reputation abroad, if racial war should break out.

At the start of the ... Conference, the decision confronting the leaders of the DLP was whether they should plunge the country into chaos with civil commotion and strife, or try to explore whatever reasonable avenues may be presented to us as

50 *Statesman*, June 19, 1962.   51 *Ibid.*, Aug. 12, 1962.
52 *Ibid.*, Aug. 24, 1962.

the Conference developed. ... It is easy to let slip the dogs of war; it is impossible to return to the positions before they were unleashed.[53]

Independent observers were quite surprised and pleased about the outcome of the deliberations. Maudling himself confessed that he was very pleasantly surprised by the developments after a day that had begun so unpromisingly. 'We have been very worried', he admitted. 'There were so many fears and suspicions, and the trouble with fears and suspicions is that they build on one another.' The *Times* was also very pleased with the constitutional settlement, and in fact, hailed it as a 'model of textbook perfection'. The constitution was 'as sound and water-tight a unitary constitution, safeguarding human rights, as yet has been put on paper'.[54] It was not overwritten, like Jamaica's, nor underwritten, like Ghana's or Tanzania's, both of which were too easy to change. According to the view of the *Times'* analyst, the fault of Jamaica's constitution was that it depended too much on a competent and co-operative opposition in order to function well. The weakness of underwritten constitutions like Tanzania's was that they 'presuppose the perpetual existence of a reliable governing body which will never be tempted to abuse freedom'. Trinidad's avoided these extremes. 'It ensures freedom of action of government within the framework of British democratic traditions.'[55] It contained a full guarantee of individual rights and at the same time permitted the executive to govern freely without possibly being hamstrung by a malintentioned opposition. It left the business of governing to the government, and not to both government and opposition, as the Jamaican constitution did.

Trinidadians were immensely relieved that what had begun on so ominous a note had at last been brought to a happy conclusion. Generally speaking, the majority of the population were pleased with the settlement. They were also proud that their leaders had been able to rise to levels of statesmanship of which they had already begun to despair. If there were persons who had reservations about Independence, they were quite mute in the months of July and August 1962, when the umbilical cord that had bound Trinidad and Tobago to the British Empire for 165 years was finally cut.

---

53   *Ibid.*, Aug. 19, 1962.   54   Cited in TG, June 17, 1962.
55   *Ibid.*

Part Four

The aim of these terminal chapters is to evaluate the extent to which the People's Nationalist Movement succeeded in achieving the goals which it set itself in 1956. Attention is given principally to its promises to decolonize the society integrally, to nurture an educated and participant democracy, to rationalize the economy and the administrative framework, and to create an ethnically integrated national community. The basic argument is that the PNM has failed in all of these areas *if it is judged by the standards which it set for itself.* If, however, a comparative focus is maintained, and if one takes into account the size of the society, the nature of its resources, and the strength of the legacies of the slave and colonial past, then it must be said the People's National Movement has turned in a creditable performance, one that compares favourably with performances in other newly independent nations.

Indeed, when one looks around at the wreckage to be found in most of Africa, Latin America, and Asia, Trinidad may very well seem a model nation. Serious problems exist, however – an economy that is losing its drive, persistent pluralism, a bureaucracy that is still struggling to cope with new demands, social inequality, widespread unemployment, alienation among the young and frustration among the old – and these have begun to exert serious strains on the political system. One can in fact say that the sixth stage of Trinidad's political development, the Williams era, is coming to a close, and that the Black Power demonstrations of February, March, and April of 1970, the army mutiny, the imposition of a state of emergency, the reintroduction of flogging, and the arrest and detention of radical black leaders are all signals of the birth of a new political order. Some predict that the PNM régime will manage to hold onto power and become a streamlined version of the Haiti régime, while others are optimistic that the new Trinidad will be a more wholesome and just society in which to live.

21
Integral decolonization

To the generation of Trinidadians who gained their political awareness during the election campaigns of 1956, one of the more puzzling features of the PNM has been its ambivalence about the problem of residual colonialism. Despite copious declarations of intention, no sustained and systematic attempt has yet been made to deal with this fundamental problem. It was expected, for example, that a radical anti-colonial regime would have established, as one of its top priorities, the rewriting of the history of the region so that the population, especially the young, would come to appreciate the significance of its past. Apart from Dr Williams' own efforts, very little has been done to encourage and subsidize the production of material for the proper teaching of Caribbean history, even though it has now been made a compulsory part of the school curriculum.[1] The readaptation of textbooks to relate instruction more closely to local needs and correct the ingrained tendency to disparage local culture, standards, and traditions is still in a rudimentary stage. The West Indian novel has not yet found a secure place in the teaching of literature, even at university level, nor has the bias of the curriculum shifted significantly to scientific and vocational education, though there has been a great deal of talk about the desirability of these policies. Not much has yet been done about the teaching of Indian and African culture, history, and politics. Indeed, the whole educational structure, including examinations, is still largely based on an inherited framework, one that is being radically changed in the metropolitan countries from which it was derived. A draft educational development plan

1 Eric Williams, *History of the People of Trinidad and Tobago*, New York, 1964; *idem, British Historians and the West Indies*, Port of Spain, 1964.

was published in 1968, but it has not yet been effectively translated into policy.[2] The plan is, however, more concerned with school places than with changing the basic nature of the educational system to make it more appropriate to the social and economic needs of the community.

The changes that have been made are largely administrative. Amid bitter Catholic opposition, the entire school system (with the exception of those schools that are financed completely by private funds), including the curriculum, was placed under closer Government control in 1965. The educational system is now a great deal more centralized than it was prior to Independence, with mixed results. Some of the grosser abuses in the recruitment of teachers and pupils have been eliminated, though complaints are still heard about persisting ascriptive recruitment at the level of secondary education and about the inability of the Ministry of Education to cope with the added responsibilities which it has assumed and those which it plans to absorb under the new plan.

Outside of the classroom, the PNM has done little to instil in the young the values and norms which would prepare them for their new roles as citizens. The same is true at the adult level. While the rhetoric of the Movement is still anti-colonial, the social and political behaviour of the élite contradicts their preachings. They have not yet managed to create in the popular mind concrete images of the new community to be developed. It was not until 1967, for example, that a decision was finally taken to alter the old imperial honour system.[3] The reluctance to provide adequate funds for the stimulation of his-

2 Among other things, the plan provides for the introduction of a 'shift' system, a system of senior and junior comprehensive secondary schools, curriculum modernization and standardization, reorganization of the library services, more emphasis on scientific and vocational training, and a greater awareness of the Caribbean setting. *Draft Plan for Educational Development in Trinidad and Tobago*, Port of Spain, 1968.

3 The Government admitted that since Independence 'more and more people have come to feel the need for a system of national awards' and invited all major groups to advance proposals for 'a truly national system of awards'. The people had in fact already moved ahead and created their own national awards. Curiously, the PNM agreed to create a new system but also to retain the old one except for those awards that related specifically to the Empire. To the consternation of many, Williams himself accepted a Companion of Honour from the Queen in 1969. As James Millette rather scornfully notes, Williams' case was tragicomic. 'No pressure was required from the colonial master to make him say his credo. His was a simple fulfillment of the ironic necessities of being a colonial protest leader who secretly yearns to return to the colonial cow pen, even when he has been complaining about the stench. ... Three cheers for decolonisation.' *Moko*, June 20, 1969. See also the cutting sarcasm of Adrian Espinet and Jacques Farmer: 'Lesser men covet colonial knighthoods.

torical research, for the establishment of a national archives and a national centre for cultural activities point up these contradictions.

Given the extent to which Trinidad and Tobago has been anglicized, given its geographic location in the Americas and the receptiveness of its economy to Anglo-American penetration, and given the virtual absence of any autochthonous traditions, cultural independence is not, of course, a realistic possibility; but just the same not enough has been done to impose some kind of 'cultural tariff' to insulate the population from the more baneful effects of the Anglo-American cultural impact. It is true that material resources are limited and that priorities must be established, but these investments have a valid claim upon the public purse, and have not yet been assigned the importance they deserve.[4]

Dr Williams himself acknowledges the failure of the PNM on the decolonization issue, and freely admits that the legacies of the past are still pervasive. As he lamented, 'It is one thing to get rid of colonialism on paper, but when it comes to removal of the entrenchments of colonialism, that is where the real problem lies.'[5] Williams attaches a great deal of blame to the foreign-owned communications media for the continuing colonial orientation of the society. The media, he says, debase the level of public life by pandering to the prejudices of the masses in the interest of profit. He complains of the low editorial and reporting standards and the penchant for salacity and muck. The Government has now committed itself to greater social ownership and control of the foreign-owned press and television station.[6]

But Williams has admitted that the media are only a reflection of the society in which they function. Trinidadian society, he notes, is no more than a 'factory', the prime concern of which is the acquisition of 'mass-produced imported rubbish'. 'Anybody who is trying to develop the normal attributes of a modern society ... comes up against this basic fact. ... We have not progressed

Williams' excellence claims nothing beneath the rare dignities of CH and Her Majesty's Privy Council – surely the final proofs of stature in this white man's world.' 'Pussonal Monarchy: The Paradox of Power in Trinidad', *Tapia*, Nov. 16, 1969.

4   In 1968 the Government announced plans to build a national archives and a cultural arts centre, but so far nothing has been done.

5   *Nation*, June 26, 1964.

6   Williams had only himself to blame for metropolitan ownership and control of the communications media, since it was he who encouraged the Thompson and King interests to move into Trinidad. In 1969, however, the government bought out the radio and television concerns owned by the Thompson chain. The *Trinidad Guardian* still remains under Thompson's control, however; The *Daily Mirror* (King) collapsed and has been replaced by a locally sponsored paper, the *Trinidad Express*. The *Express* has done a great deal to raise the level of public debate in the country.

much further than we were at the end of the eighteenth century. ... Intellectual decolonization has hardly begun.'[7] One occasionally detects in Williams' pronouncements a sense of frustration at the futility of his role and a willingness to write off the old generation and concentrate on the young. He once said, 'Suffer the little children to come unto me, for of such is the future independence of our democracy assured.'[8] But in practice, very little has been done to mobilize and resocialize the youth as has been done in Cuba. Educational opportunity has been widened and equalized to a considerable extent, but the content of the educational programme has remained essentially as it was prior to 1956.

Radical intellectuals are gravely concerned at this defiant persistence of colonialism not only in Trinidad but throughout Caribbean society. They complain that Independence has meant no more than a change of élites, a substitution of imitative 'Afro-Saxon' calibans for metropolitan carpetbaggers. George Lamming, dean of West Indian novelists, writes of the 'psychic shame' which continues to 'burn the hearts of men whose lives have been a history of genuflection'. Independence, he notes, has in no way altered the property or sociocultural relations of the society, and West Indians 'in their own home have to take not a middle, but a back seat, while other men ... give the ultimate directives about petroleum and sugar. Here is a humiliation that goes deep; a humiliation which no abstract independence can heal. No change of flag or anthem can stem this spiritual bleeding of men who have nothing to celebrate but a raise in salary. ... The vocabulary of politics has changed but the politics of their lives remains the same'.[9] The St Lucian poet Derek Walcott also laments:

> I cannot right new wrongs
> Waves tire of horizon and return
> I watch the best minds root like dogs
> For scraps of favour.[10]

---

7 *Nation*, May 21, 1956.
8 *Ibid.*, Feb. 4, 1966. Earlier he had observed, 'I am tired and sick of [snags in every aspect of the society]. I don't like this political life at all, I was not made for it, and every day I like it less. I don't know how long I propose to stay. ... Priority Number One in terms of my public responsibility is youth. I am going to forget as far as possible the ordinary day-to-day problems and work on children 13 to 18. ... I want your children, and the adults can go to hell where they belong. If I stay, it is to try and do one thing only, that is to try and improve the society. Otherwise you go your own way, and I go mine. ... All I want to do in my life now is to do some writing on the West Indies.' *Nation*, September 5, 1962. Williams laments, however, 'There is not much we can do to rewrite Caribbean history.' *Nation*, May 21, 1964.
9 *New World Quarterly*, vol. 2, no. 2, 1966, p. 68.
10 Cited in Lamming, *ibid.*, p. 68.

Lamming feels that 'shame is a revolutionary sentiment', and blames the West Indian political class for not pursuing initiatives that would articulate and harness the explosive and 'insane tensions – contained under that exterior of a leisurely and frivolous assurance' which envelop the West Indian bosom. He, like others who banded themselves together into a society called the New World Group, believe that there must and will be a confrontation with neo-colonialism and that the thrust would come from below as it did in the 1930s.* Lloyd Best, one of the more articulate spokesmen of the New World Group, claims that the struggle over Chaguaramas was the critical turning point of the anti-colonial struggle in the Caribbean. That struggle, he says, offered Trinidad and the English-speaking West Indies a golden opportunity to define institutions more appropriate to the specific needs of the area. A decision to expel the metropolitan military presence 'would have brought the conservative, creole, outward-looking culture of the dominant groups into more open conflict with the natural aspirations of the population at large'.[11] But by taking the line of least resistance, and bowing to American power, the PNM committed Trinidad to accepting an 'external definition of the national purpose' and made any further acceleration of the decolonization process impossible: 'The aim of the Agreement had been to trade submissiveness to imperial militarism for metropolitan economic assistance and more generally to maintain metropolitan confidence. By the same stroke, however, protection was offered to the plantation economy and to the metropolitan investors who controlled it. The further logic was to move into Independence as a Monarchy, and so to retain the symbols as well as the agents, instruments and relations of the old order.'[12]

Best argues that the 'ideological evasiveness' of the PNM and its refusal to destroy the plantation system or to restructure the property relations of the society force it to rely not on the human and physical resources of the 'people', but on North American capital and expertise. He bluntly accuses the PNM of 'zigzagging ... between a radical modernity in statement and a tame accommodation with traditionalism in fact'.[13] In his view, decolonization will be possible only if new economic strategies are based on the 'people' rather than on paid government servants who negotiate with foreign entrepreneurs. Decolonization in the context of an open economy is a will-o'-the-wisp. The tinkering of the PNM and the exhortations of Williams are weak reeds when compared to the ingrained habits of the past.[14]

---

*   The Trinidad unit of the New World Group ceased functioning in 1969. Its members have since joined other political groups.

11   'Chaguaramas to Slavery', *New World Quarterly*, vol. 2, no. 1, 1965, p. 44.

12   *Ibid.*, p. 61.   13   *Ibid.*, p. 62.

14   The advocations of the radical intellectuals are curiously reminiscent of the late Frantz Fanon, the French West Indian psychiatrist. Fanon argued, 'Decolonization

Best's argument is perhaps irrefutable, but a fundamental problem nevertheless remains. Can a small island society with limited and skewed natural resources and an immigrant population ever escape the thraldom of neo-colonialism in all its varieties and disguises? This question will be dealt with more fully later on but it is worth noting here that all the radicals admit that island societies are not permissive environments for the profound social change which is their goal. Full or even partial decolonization, they agree, is only possible in the context of a pan-Caribbean society. One may share the anguish and shame of the intellectuals, but one wonders whether the creation of some form of Caribbean unity will significantly improve the chances of cultural and economic autonomy, given the present domination of political and economic power by superstates, international corporations, and intercontinental communication systems. It would seem that, short of a total rebellion in the 'third world', the road of revolution is not open to societies in the Caribbean, and that change will have to fall short of total confrontation with the traditional order and American imperialism. This kind of prudence is less romantic and heroic than the strategy offered by the Cubans, but in the Caribbean there are well-defined limits to what even heroism can achieve. As the late Albert Camus once remarked, 'It requires basketsfull of blood and centuries of history to lead to an imperceptible modification in the human condition. ... For years heads fall like hail, terror reigns, revolution is touted, and one ends up by substituting constitutional monarchy for legitimate monarchy.'[15]

is always a violent phenomenon ... a program of complete disorder. ... The proof of success lies in a whole social structure being changed from bottom up ... in which the last shall be first and the first shall be last.' *The Wretched of the Earth*, New York, 1963, pp. 29–30.

15 For a good analysis of the strengths and weaknesses of mobilization systems in the modernization process, see David Apter, *Politics of Modernization*, Chicago, 1965, chaps. 10 and 11. See also Arthur Lewis, *Politics in West Africa*, Oxford, 1966, *passim.*

22
Rationalizing the administration

Within the administrative framework, the performance of the PNM in eliminating some of the *structural* manifestations of colonialism has been creditable. Over the course of the decade, the Party managed to destroy much of the old administrative framework, but it has had only partial success in getting the new structures to function in a manner equal to the tasks confronting the nation.

Getting the public and the civil service to accept the principle that ultimate responsibility for policy-making belonged to ministers of government, and not to civil servants, was one of the earliest problems that the new regime encountered.[1] During the colonial period the Governor was the chief decision-maker, subject only to Colonial Office supervision. He was assisted in the exercise of his responsibilities by a group of senior officers who were appointed by the Crown. During the transitional period of 1950–6, the responsibilities of Crown officials were shared with the five elected ministers, but it was not always clear whether ministers were constitutionally senior to the official group, or whether their authority was co-ordinate. Conflicts were frequent, and officials often appealed to the Governor over the heads of ministers.[2]

The nationalists were not prepared to tolerate this constitutional hybrid and insisted that all appointed officials be removed from the Governor's

---

1 According to the Prime Minister, reorganization of the civil service 'was the first major problem ... that we encountered as a Government'. *Hansard*, Nov. 20, 1959, p. 730.
2 Cf. *Report to the Honourable the Premier by the Honourable Ulric Lee on the Reorganization of the Public Service*, Port of Spain, 1959, p. 1.

Executive Council, which would then function like the Westminster cabinet with civil servants taking instructions from their ministers. Conflicts between the new ministers and senior officers arose not only over policy matters, but over matters of promotion, transfers, and responsibility for intra-departmental administration. The fact that some of these officers were whites with strong familial links to the upper class only served to exacerbate tensions. Charges that civil servants were sabotaging the government's plans, and counter-charges that the government was muzzling and victimizing civil servants, were heard quite frequently, and there is reason to believe that the promotion of native whites was suspended for some time as demands increased that senior jobs be given to those who had been excluded from them in the past. West Indianizing the service was taken by many to mean 'negrofying' it.

DECOLONIZING THE CIVIL SERVICE

It is interesting to note that Dr Williams at first took the view that it was unwise to West Indianize 'at a discount'. He expressed opposition to the view that West Indians should be appointed to senior positions simply because they were West Indians. 'The whole structure of self-government will be jeopardized if the principle is accepted that one only has to put a West Indian in a post because he is West Indian. The basis of the PNM Government's nationalism must be that the West Indian must be twice as good as the expatriate. If I must be condemned, let me be condemned for setting high standards.'[3] Over the period, however, the top levels of the administration were almost completely West Indianized with men who, though not twice as good, were nevertheless a fair match for the expatriates whom they replaced. The bulk of the appointees were mixed or fully Negro; very few were of Indian or European descent. For the most part the new appointees were people who had left the island in the forties and early fifties for English and Canadian universities, and were thus better equipped to move into the technical levels of the administration than were native whites who, hitherto, had had little need to acquire such skills to advance themselves in the public service. With the changing orientation of the service and the need for skilled technicians, especially economists, the white upper class found itself unable to compete with those who had been forced to go abroad because of blocked opportunities. Where whites were retained, they were either persons of admitted competence, or persons whom it would have

---

3   *Trinidad Guardian* (TG), Nov. 22, 1957. A former Governor, Sir John Shaw, had
    suggested in the 1940s that West Indians should be appointed to senior positions if
    they had 70 per cent of the ability of the expatriate. This policy was honoured more
    in the breach however.

been difficult to dismiss or replace without doing violence to the multiracial ideology of the Party. But few became dominant figures in the senior civil service[4]; for the most part, they were simply by-passed in the new system of relationships which developed. Today very few white creoles seek entry into the civil service.[5]

But nativization did not bring with it the desired transformation in the functioning of the bureaucratic apparatus. A recent team of investigators into its operations observed that 'the sort of concepts of administration that typified the colonial system' still persists.[6] Civil servants still see their role as assemblers of information in duly labelled files to be passed on to the top of the hierarchy. The report in fact warned that 'skill in paper passing is not enough to ensure that problems of financial policy ... or economic development are dealt with satisfactorily'.[7]

The achievement of economic modernization is, to a great degree, limited by the capacity and spirit of the bureaucratic structure.[8] Unless the public bureaucracy is capable of responding readily to new challenges and innovations, development is severely inhibited, especially in societies which, for a variety of circumstances, have to rely heavily on the state for the achievement of socio-economic transformation. But even where, as in Trinidad, the state does not intervene actively in the economy, the role of the public service is

4   Only one French creole (a rebel under the old régime) became a leading public servant in the new administration. He was retained by the Prime Minister as his Permanent Secretary and Head of the Civil Service. He was also one of the Prime Minister's principal aides, doing several key jobs which ministers claimed were really their responsibility.

5   The influence of whites in the civil service was also reduced by the abolition of the office of district warden, whose responsibilities were transferred to the Ministry of Finance and to the county councils. In the colonial period the wardens were de facto vice-regents of the Governor. Their officers evaluated properties, collected revenues, awarded contracts, and often adjudicated disputes in the districts under their control. The warden (who more frequently than not was of French ancestry), the expatriate clergyman, and the principal planters constituted a virtual power élite on the parish level. Few people were surprised when the nationalists moved quickly to abolish this 'survival from the donkey-cart age'. Hansard, Nov. 20, 1959, p. 750.

6   First Report of the Working Party on the Role and Status of the Civil Service in the Age of Independence, Port of Spain, September 1964, p. 4.

7   Ibid., p. 4.

8   Joseph La Palombara observes that, in the past, literature on the developmental process paid more attention to economics. 'Relatively little systematic attention ... [was] accorded the public sector – particularly the bureaucracy – as an important independent variable that greatly influences any kind of transformation in the developing countries.' Bureaucracy and Political Development, Princeton, 1963, p. 4. See also the highly significant work of Fred Riggs, Administration in Developing Countries, Boston, 1964.

still crucial. 'In a number of spheres, increased private activity is only possible because there is an appropriate increase in corresponding public activity.'[9]

One of the major weaknesses of the civil service in Trinidad is its lack of public spiritedness and national consciousness. There is an ingrained tendency to stand firm on regulations without too much concern for what is gained or lost by this lack of flexibility.[10] When flexibility is exercised, it is done mainly on ascriptive and particularistic grounds. Rule-breaking is more likely to take place if the individual thus accommodated looks important and conforms to the stereotype of the gentleman. Chances of prompt service increase if the individual is white, wears a coat and tie, or bears himself with starchy dignity. Civil servants, especially at the junior levels, have not yet come to relate their routines to the needs of the nation as an entity. The reality and the corresponding demands of nationhood have not become integrated with their roles as public servants. Despite the increased demands of Independence, life in the service goes on as it did in the past. The Working-Party report, in fact, observed that the administrative machinery has had great difficulty adjusting to the changes necessitated by the country's new status: 'In particular, the process of decision-making had evidently not yet become fully geared to cope with either the magnitude or the urgency of the problems which confronted the new nation. Examples were brought to our notice of the difficulty frequently experienced in securing prompt and clear-cut decisions. In many cases, it had not been possible to obtain even an acknowledgement, either of the original communication or of the several subsequent requests for an early reply.'[11]

But one cannot emphasize strongly enough that the attitude of public servants is a characteristic of large segments of the population.[12] Decoloniza-

---

9   *Working Party Report*, p. 1.

10   'It seemed to us that in far too many cases, the regulations were being used ... to penalize rather than to protect. Instead of being used as the servant of the administration, "the regulations" had too often been regarded as its master, to be obeyed to the letter, whatever the consequences in terms of human hardship and, sometimes, even of downright injustice.' *Ibid.*, p. 9.

11   *Ibid.*, p. 4. The Prime Minister himself complains of the bureaucratic octopus that is strangling the nation: 'In a new country like ours, you'll find that the top men are generally excellent, but the middle level, the junior officers, are frankly inadequate. It's not just a lack of ability. It's also often a lack of sympathy – a kind of indifference bred by the colonial system. TG, Nov. 30, 1965.

12   Cf. Riggs, *Administration*, and Robert Presthus 'Weberian vs. Welfare Bureaucracy in Traditional Society', *Administrative Science Quarterly*, vol. 6, June–March, 1961–2, pp. 1–24, for interesting discussions of the interrelationships between bureaucracy and political culture. As Presthus notes, 'the analysis of bureaucracy leads one quickly to the educational system which shaped the values and expertise of bureaucrats ... to questions of class, status and power. Bureaucratic conceptions of

tion of the civil service is integrally related to decolonization in the society as a whole. In essence, the failure of the ruling party to make much headway with bureaucratic reform has been due to its inability to come to grips with the persistence of colonial attitudes and institutions in the society at large. The education system is perhaps the most critical area where changes in orientation are necessary.

Trinidad was much more fortunate than many new states in its ability to recruit a sizable core of highly qualified and dedicated men who would have been a credit to any system which had the capacity to harness their skills. The Prime Minister admits that the problem is not essentially one of inadequate skills. He blames lack of 'sympathy' and 'colonialism'.[13] Perhaps a more correct explanation might be found in the organizational weaknesses of the system as a whole.

In the years following the nationalist triumph, zeal and enthusiasm compensated for lack of organization. Many of the young officers who were appointed to positions of authority were inspired by the challenges of moulding a new nation. They worked long and hard under the driving and inspiring leadership of Dr Williams, with glittering results. The sacrifices made by some of these men in terms of their private lives were enormous. Today it is the rare officer who is not jaded, 'fed up', disillusioned, and anxiously seeking job opportunities in the private sector, in state corporations, or abroad. So alarmed was the government by this flight of senior officers that it had to take steps to make it more difficult for officers to move at will.[14]

authority may usually be traced back to the family system and patterns of socialization begun there.' 'Comparing Bureaucracies', *Economic Development and Cultural Change*, vol. 13, no. 3, April 1965, p. 363.

13   There are some people who do not accept the thesis that colonialism can be made to bear the blame for all the ills of the civil service. According to one wag, the tendency to find the hand of colonialists behind every undesirable feature of the society is indeed 'the most comforting discovery of the age'. 'We cannot agree with the attempt to justify the slackness, inefficiency and general disorganization apparent in the service [by citing] the problems of colonial administration, now in the dim past. ... The simple fact is that some parts of the service have not provided the service that the public expects. If ... the public is critical of the civil service, it is because it is not prepared indefinitely to countenance the utter frustrations and annoyances that result from the lack of civility, the delay, indecision, and sometimes downright incompetence of some sections.' 'The Civil Service to the Forefront', *Enterprise* (official organ of the Trinidad Chamber of Commerce), Dec. 1964, p. 6.

14   The Minister of Finance noted that he 'had to intervene personally to prevent one of the Ministry's bright young technical officers from being spirited away by an oil company'. *Budget Speech*, 1965, Port of Spain, p. 33. The government has also begun to penalize officers who were trained abroad at public expense but who have elected to work with private employers.

The difficulties which the new officers faced were numerous. They found older public servants resenting their zeal and impatience with the established ways of doing things, their rapid mobility, and their easy access to the new political élite. The new recruits posed a clear threat to the pattern of relationships with which their seniors were familiar. The conflicts were particularly sharp between the new technical officers and the administrative cadres who were hold-overs from the old régime. Conflicts also arose between established technical officers and newly recruited permanent secretaries who were more acceptable to the new ministers, and between newly recruited technical officers and established administrative officers who were considered unsuited to the roles which they were assigned to play. There were frequent intra-departmental struggles to 'demonstrate beyond question exactly who was boss'.[15]

Blame for this development has been ascribed to the colonial inheritance. It has been suggested that when power is vested with expatriate officials, there is a tendency for the 'hierarchy of "local" officers' to become almost inflexible in its internal relationships. 'Any movement that appeared likely to disturb the basis of individual status and prestige was apt to be fiercely resisted, even at the expense of significant improvements in administrative efficiency. This is an understandable reaction to a situation of restricted mobility.'[16] As apt as this observation might be, the fact remains that conflict would have been inevitable in any situation where the rate of recruitment of élites was too rapid to permit ready socialization and domestication by the old system. The smallness of the society and the consequent absence of privacy and anonymity also tended to intensify jealousies and rivalries.[17]

There was a considerable amount of confusion over the juridical relationship between permanent secretaries and chief technical officers, and between ministries and the departments included under their portfolios. Permanent secretaries had little understanding of their roles vis-à-vis their ministers or technical officers. Some technical officers felt they should have direct access to ministers in order that the latter might have the benefit of first-hand professional advice. Some even insisted on their right to authorize the expenditure of money on behalf of the ministry on the grounds that certain projects were of technical rather than of administrative significance.[18]

---

15   *Working Party Report*, p. 6.   16   *Ibid.*

17   David Lowenthal has also drawn attention to the relation between size and interpersonal relationship in Caribbean society. The islanders display a 'narrow conservative outlook, and sometimes a pathological sensitivity to criticism, exacerbated by small-island feuds and a claustrophobic absence of privacy. Jealousies, rivalries, fears, and above all mutual ignorance tend to make each island a museum in which archaic distinctions are carefully preserved.' 'Variation of Caribbean Societies', *Annals of the New York Academy of Sciences*, vol. 83, no. 5, Jan. 1960, p. 789.

18   *Hansard*, Nov. 20, 1959, p. 781.

The government eventually fell back on British practice and ruled that permanent secretaries were to be the key men in their ministries, accountable only to ministers and the Public Accounts Committee. Chief technical officers were, however, to have access to ministers, provided meetings were arranged through the permanent secretary.[19] Given that many of the permanent secretaries were generalists and not particularly well equipped to cope with the demands of development administration, this was perhaps an unimaginative decision.

Despite this attempt to define roles and responsibilities within ministries, the administrative crisis continued. One of its more immediate consequences was the development of a system of personalized administration. More favoured officers began to bypass their colleagues and even their ministers (whose competence they suspected) to work directly with the Prime Minister. The élite corps of the service functioned virtually as personal aides of the charismatic leader. In the early years, this *ad hoc* system tended to raise both the quantity and quality of administrative output, but the long-term consequences were disastrous. It led to rivalries between the new technocracy and older civil servants, between the new officers and their ministers, and it generated a great deal of political opportunism.[20] The haphazard jumble of personal relationships frustrated the process of institutionalization and collapsed when the zeal and energy of the Prime Minister began to flag.

The system also tended to create difficulties for junior officers, who were harshly criticized for their lack of motivation and responsibility. It may be, however, that this deficiency was a direct result of the weaknesses of a system which failed to integrate and mobilize personnel to the fullest. There was a

19 *Cabinet Proposals regarding Reorganization of the Public Service*, Port of Spain, 1959, p. 8.
20 Because of the scarce supply of top-flight talent, some officers were called upon to perform a wide variety of roles, many of which were outside the civil service. They in fact became political rather than civil servants. This had certain dysfunctional influences which were not foreseen. As Dr James Millette of the University of the West Indies has observed, 'Such people [were] incorporated into the formal policy-making apparatus [and] carried with them the aura of power. [This] catapulted them into conflict with their colleagues. ... When such officials have walked in the corridors of power, they are no longer able, when the time comes, or when, tragically, they fall from grace, to go back to the bureaucracy. But go they must, unless they wish to forfeit the very considerable material advantages the Service holds for those who persevere.' 'Structure and Change in the Civil Service', *Civil Service Review*, July, 1965. The long-term consequences of free-style administration were also pointed out by a United Nations consultant to the Trinidad Government: 'To create a team requires a long-term relationship. It is not possible to have this development if the players are being changed constantly. The mobility of staff in some parts of the service is so great that it must be impossible to ... weld individuals into a productive group.' Cited in the 1965 *Budget Speech*, p. 32.

widespread feeling among junior officers that their presence was not in any way vital to the functioning of the machinery of government. This was indeed true in some cases where offices were clearly overstaffed, but junior officers were correct in their claim that they were not adequately briefed or given tasks for which they were competent.

Something of a vicious circle seems to have been generated. Senior officers, and indeed the Prime Minister himself, undertook many roles that should have been allocated to juniors because they did not have confidence in their probity, competence, or reliability. This in turn led junior officers to become less responsible, less involved, and more prone to paper-passing. The result was an increasing disparity in the workloads of junior and senior officers. Senior officers became tired and frustrated about their inability to cope with the serious policy matters that came before them. They found themselves buried under a never diminishing avalanche of purely operational decisions, while their junior colleagues, finding time heavy on their hands, sought refuge in clock-watching, absenteeism, gossiping, and 'freshening up'.[21]

The weaknesses of the civil service, then, are under-co-ordination, under-propulsion, and under-supervision. Poor co-ordination stems from the failure of the system to define adequately areas of responsibility and to generate team spirit not only within departments but among them as well. Under-propulsion is evident in the length of time that elapses between the initiation of discussion on policy and its satisfactory disposal. This is due in part to the unwillingness or fear on the part of junior officers to exercise initiative or to deal promptly with issues that come before them; but some blame must also be ascribed to senior officers, who often fail or refuse to impose sanctions on subordinates for dereliction of duty.[22] The PNM in fact recognizes that one of the prime weaknesses of the system is that there are not enough sanctions, either of a punitive or incentive-giving kind, to stimulate initiative and efficiency.[23]

Whatever the requisites of a 'law and order'-oriented bureaucracy, a modernizing state needs to create a bureaucracy which offers rewards to those

21   This situation is typical in most newly developing societies. What Robert Presthus says of 'time' in Turkey is also quite true of Trinidad: 'The ... general organization climate must also be seen in terms of prevailing conceptions of time in under-developed societies. ... Far from being viewed as a scarce resource, time is defined as a relatively abundant commodity.' Presthus, 'Weberian vs. Welfare Bureaucracy', p. 15.

22   Senior officers often lament that they 'can't get their subordinates to work'. Some have taken a rather nonchalant and cavalier attitude to the work performances of their staff, and bluntly admit that they do not care.

23   The Minister of Finance recently agreed: 'One great weakness has been the lack of sanctions for violations and disregard for official instructions.' '1966 Budget Speech', TG, Dec. 18, 1965.

who are competent and efficient. The Trinidad bureaucracy, and the Civil Service Association which speaks for it, stresses fringe benefits, security, tenure, and increments according to seniority regardless of performance, much more than it does development-oriented attributes. To use Presthus' term, it is 'welfare'-oriented rather than task-oriented. Recruitment is still based largely on formal academic qualifications and influence-peddling, rather than on any real test of administrative or technical competence.

The deficiencies of the service are, however, not all due to laziness, lack of sympathy on the part of officers, colonial inheritances, organizational or personality conflicts. The politicians must accept a large share of the blame for failing to deal with the problems expeditiously and definitively, even if it is admitted that administrative reform is not an easy problem.

Between 1956 and 1959, the PNM did make a genuine effort to rationalize the public service. In November of 1959 it came to the Legislature with what it proudly called 'the ultimate solution ... to the problem of the civil service'.[24] But the proposed reforms were bitterly opposed, especially those relating to emoluments and prerequisites. Civil servants objected strongly to curtailments of privileges formerly enjoyed by expatriates, especially paid-leave passages to the United Kingdom. Instead of providing an 'ultimate solution,' the government's proposals marked the beginning of a long and extremely bitter battle between the PNM and the Civil Service Association. Civil servants took to the streets in 1961, wore black mourning bands in 1965, and even threatened to strike if their grievances were not met. CSA officials claimed that the government planned to detain them in 1965, and that its aim was to destroy the Association's bargaining effectiveness by smearing its leaders with charges of subversion or communist-inspired sabotage. The Association also claimed, with some justification, that the Industrial Stabilization Bill of March 1965 was deliberately designed to forestall the threatened strike.[25]

Although several commissions and consulting teams were established after 1959 to try and settle the festering dispute, to civil servants and their supporters it appeared that the PNM was seeking out every ruse or device to postpone decisions which it knew had to be made. Civil servants are on good ground when they complain that, while the government demanded improved standards of employer-employee relationships in the private sector, it was treating its own servants in a cavalier and even disdainful manner.

Uncertainty, dissatisfaction, and organizational chaos tended to generate attitudes of cynicism and apathy in the service. The government's seeming insensitivity to its employees reinforced the insensitivity of officers both to

24   *Hansard*, Nov. 20, 1959, p. 730.
25   The bill, which curbed the right to strike freely, will be discussed below.

the public and to their employer, who in turn complained of sabotage and lack of sympathy.[26] The government appeared unwilling to accept demands for increased salaries because of pressure from private employers who feared that such a policy would start an inflationary cycle. The government also argued that, if salaries were increased, the public sector could not continue to absorb new recruits at the rate at which it had been doing before. Recurrent expenditure were already dangerously close to being in excess of recurrent revenues, a situation that was a source of grave concern, since it affected the Government's creditworthiness on the external loan market, and its own development programme.

Another area of controversy centred on the relationship between senior public servants and their ministers. Several senior officers complained that they did not enjoy the confidence of their ministers, or of the Prime Minister. Ministers, on the other hand, expressed dissatisfaction with the service and the quality of advice given them by their senior officers. Some officers believed that the officers themselves were to blame for much of this state of affairs. Officers, it was said, were timid and over-cautious, showed no drive or initiative, but instead hid behind the rules.[27] According to this point of view, senior officers could easily carry their ministers with them if they ceased being courtiers and carried out their professional obligations fearlessly. The low quality of ministerial timber put the trained officer at an advantage.

The working-party report (which was drawn up by senior officers) agreed that officers had not adjusted to the mode of operation expected of them in an independent nation. There still existed 'the mistaken belief that because the determination of policy is the constitutional responsibility of ministers, the formulation of policy is also their exclusive concern'.[28] Senior officers are said to have done no more than substitute the minister for the expatriate official.

---

26 Some officers claim that what the politicians calls 'administrative sabotage' is often the result of inadequate knowledge, inexperience, or simple carelessness on the part of officers. But some informants did admit that there were several occasions when aggrieved officers deliberately set out to create crises which would embarrass the government politically.

27 Everett Hagen argues that this type of bureaucratic behaviour is a characteristic of all traditional societies, 'Individuals in traditional bureaucracies "wear blinders"; they fail to see the presence of problems because by not doing so they avoid anxiety ... new solutions make them anxious. ... Anxiety is relieved by reliance on tradition ... or by referring ... upwards ... even the pettiest question for whose answer there is no clear precedent. ... This tendency [to refer upwards to the top official] is reinforced by his insistence on receiving them. ... The practice antedated colonial rule which only coincided with and confirmed it.' *On the Theory of Social Change*, Homewood, Ill., 1962, pp. 72–9.

28 *Working Party Report*, p. 4.

The authors of the report correctly noted that it was the duty of the officer to render expert advice even if it was not requested. Officers should not function as 'glorified amanuenses – merely recording instructions and ensuring that they are carried out'.[29]

There is no doubt, however, that many officers were genuinely afraid to render advice which they feared might be politically objectionable. In not a few cases the relationships between them and their ministers were not such as to stimulate a frank exchange of views. Those who were not in the good graces of the political élite tended to avoid making the decisions to which their rank entitled them. Fear of rebuke and victimization paralysed their willingness to act. Both the working-party report and the Civil Service Association gave expression to the malaise. The working party observed that 'There exists at present an undercurrent of fear among civil servants ... that unsought advice, or worse still, unsought and unfavourable advice, will not only be rejected, but ... used to justify ministerial displeasure.'[30] The president of the Civil Service Association expressed this view even more strongly:

It is my observation that the general mood among you is one of apathy and sheer disgust ... You have seen well tried and established procedures completely disregarded in favour of *ad hoc* solutions based on sheer expediency, and on worthless personal and political considerations; you are aware of many appointments in the civil service and in statutory boards which are based solely on political patronage, and you know of countless scholarships awarded on the same basis; you have witnessed officers of the highest rank among you sadly and seriously disturbed, sometimes to the point of distraction, as they are held in high favour one day and swiftly fall into disfavour on the next; you have seen your colleagues frowned upon and termed 'enemy' and 'subversive', or perhaps openly victimized for being manly enough to express independent opinions and to voice their honest dissent.[31]

There is good reason to believe that the fears of senior officers were not ill-founded.[32] Politicians in Trinidad, like politicians everywhere, can be very vindictive on occasion. In a society where there are a wide variety of career

29 *Ibid.*, p. 5.
30 *Ibid.*, p. 5.
31 *Civil Service Review*, July, 1965.
32 The *Working Party Report* is quite ambivalent on this point. On one occasion (p. 5) it denies that there is 'any real foundation for such fear'. Yet it also refers (p. 29) to 'the thinly veiled conflict of understanding and outlook between politician and civil servant which prevails', and calls upon the cabinet to do everything in its power to banish such fears by reaffirming 'the proper relationship which should exist between ministers and senior civil servants'.

outlets, officials can count on finding alternative opportunities; in a small and claustrophobic society with restricted outlets, the tendency to play the courtier in the interest of survival and advancement is considerably heightened. Perhaps, for this reason, officers have anticipated displeasure when none may have been forthcoming. But the fears are not unreal. One very senior officer revealed that fear paralyses ministers as well, who have also become courtiers of the Prime Minister. One minister even complained (in confidence) that many of his colleagues never quite knew where they stood with the Prime Minister.

Part of the explanation for this situation is the low level of competence and intellectual training of many ministers, and the great intellectual ability and energy of the Prime Minister himself. Williams has tended to monopolize the decision-making process. He does not trust the competence of many of his colleagues, and accordingly demands to settle personally many problems that in more institutionalized societies would be dealt with lower down the hierarchy.[33] While it is true that the Prime Minister in the Westminster system is now more than *primus inter pares*, and that the system is perhaps becoming more presidential in its functioning, there is still a significant willingness to delegate responsibility. Within the Trinidad cabinet there are numerous standing committees and *ad hoc* planning groups, but it is clear that the Prime Minister's office is overloaded with responsibilities which should be elsewhere. The Prime Minister has admitted this, but seems unable to do very much about it. In 1965, senior civil servants were advised to work through their ministers rather than with the Prime Minister, and ministers themselves were urged to assume greater responsibilities. But according to informants, ministers are still unwilling to make even operational decisions on their own authority for fear of encountering the displeasure of their colleagues and of the Prime Minister in particular. With the Prime Minister's responsibilities more and more broadly extended every day, the machinery has slowed down considerably. Ministers and civil servants have not proven capable of absorbing the slack.

One of the key blocks to efficiency has been the Ministry of Finance. Because of its lack of confidence in the judgment and reliability of civil servants, and even of other ministries, the Ministry of Finance maintains an extremely tight rein on operational expenditures of the entire public sector. This policy is obviously designed to ensure proper financial accountability and to reduce

---

33 'Practically every decision, no matter how simple, now seemed to involve the personal approval of the highest level of officers, and not infrequently of the highest authority itself.' *Working Party Report*, p. 8. More notes go to Cabinet in one month than go to the British Cabinet in an entire year.

public-sector costs, but, as necessary as this is, beyond a point it becomes dysfunctional. Ministries are hampered in their operations because of the 'restrictive and almost negative approach which characterised many of the decisions involving expenditure'.[34] As the working-party report noted, in a society where government spending was such a stimulant to economic activity, 'inverted Micawberism waiting for something to turn down' was a mistaken policy. It was recommended that ministries be given greater freedom and financial wherewithal to carry out promptly and effectively the policies authorized by the cabinet. It would be more prudent to sacrifice the virtue of strict accountability in the interest of greater overall productivity. The 1968 budget statement, however, reaffirmed the policy of holding the line on increases in the operating costs of the public sector, though it promised that 'justifiable increases in staff and other costs will be permitted ... in areas which have a direct bearing on revenue and on production, particularly in the fields of agriculture and customs'.[35]

Difficulties with the Ministry of Finance were not the only source of frustration. It has become increasingly clear that the promises of the ruling party to bring teamwork and coherence to the operations of government have not materialized. Misunderstandings and conflicts between ministries are rife. Co-ordination is often marginal. Some ministries refuse to reveal to other departments information which may be needed to carry out agreed policies. Civil servants have been told on occasion to withhold information and cabinet minutes from other officers and even ministers who, for one reason or another, are out of favour with their colleagues: 'In certain ministries, far too little is known by senior officers – even by permanent secretaries – about the policies which should direct their day-to-day activities. A shroud of secrecy often appears to envelop even the most trivial policy matters, and some who possess knowledge of policies in force tend to behave as though they were guardians of vital state secrets. Prudence in the disclosure of official policy is not a characteristic to be discouraged in public officers. Excessive secrecy ... is, however, not only contrary to the spirit of democracy, but also a contributor to administrative inefficiency.'[36]

---

34 *Ibid.*, p. 12.   35 *Budget Speech*, 1968, p. 63.
36 *Working Party Report*, p. 12. Dennis Solomon makes basically the same complaint. 'There is no standing inter-department committee on any matter whatever. The cabinet takes diametrically opposed decisions on the same question in successive weeks on the basis of separate submissions from separate ministries. There is hardly any machinery for devising, deciding among the projects for UN technical assistance that affects different ministeries. ... The records system is ... chaotic. ... The Organization and Methods branch is no more than a name.' 'The Machinery of Government', *Tapia*, Sept. 28, and Nov. 16, 1969.

THE BUREAUCRACY AND THE PRESSURE GROUPS

The inadequacies of the bureaucracy affect the operations not only of the public sector but of the private as well. Associational groups have been highly critical of the slow-moving operations of the administrative machine, and the criticisms have become more shrill since Independence. Not infrequently, one hears the comment that the old colonial service was more efficient. But there is no real evidence to indicate that standards have fallen in an absolute sense. Rather, the problem seems to be that the expanded range of governmental activity and the heightened level of public expectations have imposed demands on a bureaucracy which was not designed to cope with the new responsibilities.

The suggestion that the intensity of criticism is due to the release of a long-suppressed desire to 'reduce to size a section of society hitherto regarded as a pompous and prejudiced élite'[37] is not credible. Organized groups feel that the blame must rest squarely on the inadequacies of the service – understaffing at the senior level, lack of competence, civility, and a sense of urgency among many serving officers. Business organizations in particular are uniform in their basic criticisms: inefficient and slow port-clearing facilities, confusing and rapidly changing regulations, impossibility of obtaining prompt and definite rulings or replies or permission to act, difficulty of access to authoritative decision-makers, and the like.[38]

One Chamber of Commerce spokesman advanced the view that the government perhaps believed that groups did too much 'damn commenting' on policy issues, and for this reason often rushed through critical legislation before significant groups had time to make representations. The reluctance to consult with certain business groups, such as the Chamber of Commerce, was in part due to the fact that until recently they represented a white minority which was seeking to maintain the influence which it once had under the colonial system. At times the PNM élite treated big business with studied rudeness. The working party felt it necessary to urge the government to be more frank with business and to put an end to the 'scarcely-veiled mutual suspicions, resentments and antagonisms which so often make communication impossible'.[39]

Part of the difficulty is to be explained in terms of the temperament of the ruling élite, in the feelings of rectitude which they so often bring to solving

---

37 *Working Party Report*, p. 8.
38 One leading businessman has expressed the view that often the politicians themselves were not to be blamed, but rather the 'civil servant, who either misunderstands government policy, or who follows it so closely as to leave no room for some obviously special case'. 'The Relationship of the Businessman to Government in Our New Nation', *Enterprise*, Oct. 1963, p. 7.
39 *Ibid.*, p. 17.

problems.[40] As custodians of the public interest, they often go to extremes in their refusal to accommodate or even listen to the representations of organized groups. While it is agreed that final decision-making should remain at all times with elected officials, a great deal can be said for a system in which reasonable opportunities are given affected groups to scrutinize and comment upon public policy. The ruling party accepts this in theory, and openly proclaims that frankness between government and the public is highly desirable; but in practice it has often failed to be sufficiently permissive in its dealing with interest groups and even the public at large.

The interest groups themselves, especially business and labour organizations, contribute to this lack of openness in the administration. Too often they approach ministers and senior officers as individuals and spokesmen of splinter organizations, rather than with one coherent voice. More often than not, they are quite irresponsible and particularistic in their representations.[41] This lack of clarity and unity in their approach to public issues imposes a heavy strain on a system which is already ill-equipped to digest and assimilate even a normal level of information. The ruling party tried on more than one occasion to encourage unity among business and labour groups and, in 1963, established a National Economic Advisory Council which consisted of spokesmen of these groups as well as the public. The effort proved abortive, however, because of mutual suspicions and political in-fighting between politicians and the radical wing of the trade-union leadership. The Council was reactivated in 1967, and a number of tripartite conferences have since been held to discuss major economic problems such as retrenchment in public and private sector, oil legislation, the review of incentive legislation, and the future of the sugar industry.

Since April 1967, relationships between the government and business

40 During the 1959 debate on the reorganization of the civil service, the Premier reacted very strongly to the efforts of the Teachers' Union to lobby him. 'What I have had to go through ... comes close to *persecution*. ... I object in the strongest terms ... to persecution and lobbying when I have made a public statement on behalf of the Government. ... I do not make deals with anybody ... on any subject at all. The Government took a stand and I was satisfied that that stand was correct ... never have I exposed ... my employers to the sort of thing that has gone on here.' *Hansard*, Nov. 23, 1959, pp. 932–3. What the Premier did not recognize at the time was that he had become a prisoner of the very democratic forces which he had done so much to unleash.

41 Some businessmen agree that business has not always been frank with government, or sufficiently public-spirited. Instead, 'The aggrieved party mutters in his beard about what things are coming to in Trinidad, but is not prepared to do anything about it – he fancies that it is dangerous to make adverse comment in public about the course of events ... dangerous, that is, to his business.' 'The Relationship of the Businessman to Government', p. 7.

groups have improved considerably, so much so that radical elements now feel that workers and the national interests are being sacrificed to maintain investor confidence. But it is clear that the government is worried about shrinkages in private sector activity and is making a serious attempt to defuse the fears of local and foreign investors about the economic radicalism that seemed to be gaining ground in 1966.[42]

RECENT TRENDS

During the latter months of 1965 and throughout 1966 the PNM made a praiseworthy effort to cope with the problem of disorganization in the civil service. In co-operation with UN experts, it sponsored a number of in-training programmes designed to improve the technical and administrative competence of its officers. The programme included courses in data processing, systems analysis, and administrative decision-making. Spasmodic attempts have also been made to discipline officers for lateness, absenteeism, mishandling of documents, and unbecoming conduct.

In 1965 the government introduced a far-reaching bill to deal with the problems of reclassification, remuneration, and grievance machinery. All public servants have now been classified into categories depending on the nature of the job and the qualifications required for its performance. The bill also established the principle that merit and performance rather than seniority would be the criteria of advancement.[43] The new plan has gone a long way to meet many of the complaints of the civil service, though it has not by any means solved all the difficulties.[44] Apart from salary problems, which still cause considerable unhappiness and demoralization, three major sources of controversy remain: the right to appeal adjudications of the Public Services Commission on matters relating to appointment, promotions, dismissals and other matters of discipline; the composition of the Civil Service Tribunal, which was created to settle salary disputes; the fragmentation, as a result of the bill, of the Civil Service Association as a bargaining unit.[45]

42 Cf. chap. 25.
43 'All salary increases shall be granted on the basis of merit and are not to be considered automatic. ... The salary ranges ... applied to each kind of post or work reflect the levels of responsibility, the difficulty, academic qualifications required.' 'Policy Statement on the Reorganization of the Public Service', *Nation*, Nov. 19, 1965.
44 The CSA claimed in 1965 that there were more than a thousand matters still pending between itself and the Government.
45 Civil servants were given a $12 million (TT) increase in budgetary allocations in 1966. This has imposed severe strains on the already over-committed Treasury and

A great many proposals have been advanced for reforming the Trinidad civil service. These have included greater decentralization, a more rigorous procedure for the appointment, training, and promotion of civil servants, a pre-appointment period of national service, civil service internships for university and high school students, and the creation of a Caribbean School of Public Administration. There are some who argue that all these technical changes will be inadequate unless a basic change of policy orientation is made that will release new energies and enthusiasms. But administrative reform is never an easy task in any political system, and some of the most mature societies today are still wrestling with the problem. Even those which have revolutionary programmes such as Cuba and the Soviet Union are finding that the correct ideology may cure some ills but it also creates new ones. Administrative behaviour is very much influenced by the history and traditions of a society and often persists for centuries in spite of political change. In the case of Trinidad, it is clear that the political events that followed the victory of the PNM in 1956 have not altered the basic behaviour patterns of the civil service, though there have been sweeping structural and personnel changes. In the revolutionary euphoria of 1955–6, the difficulties of shaping a new administrative culture were grossly underestimated; indeed, many of the deficiencies for which the service is condemned are in fact reflections of the society from which its recruits come.

While the PNM can legitimately be accused of bungling the job of reform, it must be recognized that the job itself demanded more skills and technology than were available to the society and that it depended heavily on the very bureaucracy that was to be reformed. There is no doubt that the colonial heritage has been a contributing factor, and that more time is needed for the new system of relationships to crystallize.[46] The neglect of centuries cannot be remedied within the space of a decade. The checks and balances and other relationships which exist between ministers and civil servants, and between

has forced the government to retrench 8,000 daily paid workers. Monthly paid officers, however, feel that the increase was much less than they expected and that they are still at a disadvantage when wages in the private sector and in statutory corporations are compared. Instead of generating increased commitment and productivity, the wage settlement has had the reverse effect. It is worth noting that some government economists are of the view that an across-the-board wage cut in the public sector may be inevitable in the near future, though this will have the effect of speeding up the emigration of 'brains'.

46   As Sir Geoffrey King noted in his report of 1957, 'The political effects of introducing the Ministerial and Cabinet system were clearly foreseen and prepared for, but nothing like the same attention was given to preparing the administrative services for the new tasks which would fall upon it.' *Hansard*, Nov. 20, 1959, p. 740.

ministries in the Westminster system, on which Trinidad's system is patterned, took centuries to develop, and even here perfection is far from achieved.

Time and colonialism cannot, however, be made to absorb the entire burden of blame. The PNM failed in two crucial areas. After 1958 it was never able to win the confidence of its employees, or to convince them of its fairness and impartiality. To put it bluntly, the PNM has been more backward in treatment of its personnel than most private employers. Almost every settlement assumed the air of a 'take it or leave it' imposition, and on such a basis confidence and co-operation could never be achieved. The PNM also failed to retain the goodwill of its élite cadres and to harness the available talents effectively.

Initiative and zeal will be forthcoming only if senior officers are given maximum freedom of operation within agreed policy limits; reliable productivity is much more dependent upon individual desire to accomplish given tasks than upon the threat of punishment. Unless the administrative climate is made more permissive, the paralysis, the fear to go out on a limb, to exercise initiative, and the tendency to rely on the security of the rules will continue to be hallmarks of the civil service, structural reforms notwithstanding.

With all its limitations, however, the Trinidad civil service is still among the best in the newly developing areas. While petty corruption exists, this is not yet a cancerous problem. The basic structure is sound, and given tolerance and a willingness to co-operate on the part of both employer and employees, there is no reason why it should not within a generation or so become a more effective instrument for the execution of the manifold responsibilities that lie ahead. One must admit, nevertheless, that there is no certainty the future developments will represent progress. The level of frustration, disenchantment, and *ennui* is dangerously high, and a large number of skilled officers are leaving or planning to leave for positions in the private sector or abroad. Many who do not have skills that are easily marketable have resigned themselves to time-serving. Gone is the zeal and enthusiasm that drove men on in the early years after 1956. Unless a new type of participatory politics emerges soon, the prospect for genuine and meaningful administrative reform appears bleak, and the trend may be towards total disintegration, a sharp increase in corruption, and a scramble for short-term personal advantage.

23
Race and the national community

Progress towards the achievement of a genuinely multiracial community in Trinidad and Tobago after 1956 has been rather uneven. After a nearly disastrous beginning in the years immediately after the PNM came to power, a point was reached around 1962 where open racial conflict subsided considerably. While little advance was made in the direction of integration, there existed a growing willingness among many to recognize and tolerate continuing pluralism and to argue that economic and educational improvement rather than political mobilization would bring the ethnic groups closer together. After 1966, radical voices began to challenge this racial *détente* vigorously, seeing it as a hindrance to the goal of social equality to which they were committed.

THE STRUGGLE FOR BLACK POWER

After waging a bitter rearguard struggle against the PNM and the social forces which it represented, whites by-and-large retreated from active political life. For a while after Independence they continued to function politically through the DLP, but continuing leadership and policy rivalries brought this arrangement to an abrupt end in 1963. In the 1966 election, many of them gave their support to the Liberal Party which some of them had helped to form after the break with the DLP.[1]

---

1 The Liberal Party, which includes some of the members of the old POPPG, was badly beaten in the election, but picked up 41 per cent of the votes in Port of Spain North, the district of Port of Spain most heavily populated by whites and near whites.

Whites have, however, retained a great deal of the influence which they had in the colonial period. This influence is not as unquestioned as it once was, nor is it exercised in the same crude forms, but it is nevertheless abiding. Whites still enjoy most of their social and economic privileges, which have been reinforced by the increased incursion of Anglo-American capital and technological expertise. The government's fiscal initiatives, its restrictive policy towards the importation of managerial personnel, and its educational policies are constant sources of irritation, but they do not amount to any fundamental disruptions of the established socio-economic order.[2]

Outside of the public bureaucracy, colour, kinship, and other particularistic ties are still dominant considerations which affect vocational opportunities and primary social contacts. Improvements in recruitment policies have come about as business concerns feel the need for 'window-dressing', or as economic expansion and immigration policies dry up the available supply of white and fair-skinned personnel; but the pace of social change in this area has been painfully slow. Progress has been made in the oil and petro-chemical industries, and in some foreign-owned industrial and financial establishments, but in the native commercial sector, the older banks and the sugar industry, ascription is still widely prevalent as a basis of recruitment.[3]

The report of the recently appointed Commission of Inquiry into Racial and Colour Discrimination in the Private Sector agreed that there was racial and colour discrimination (as if one needed a commission to report on what was readily visible to all except the blind).[4] As the report notes, 'We are impressed generally in the case of the banks that a state of racial and colour imbalance does exist; that the imbalance exists because of the inheritance of

2 Legislation expanding government controls on denominational schools (1965) and increasing withholding and corporate taxes (1966) were bitterly opposed by white elements, as was the government's policy of granting work permits to aliens only when it could be shown that no native was available to perform the role. Businessmen claimed that the last two policies seriously undermined investors' confidence. They argued that unless a steady supply of competent experts was made available, investors would be reluctant to gamble their savings. The PNM was forced to withdraw many of the tough provisions of the tax legislation to which it had committed itself in 1966. Cf. chap. 25.

3 Though a few native firms have become public, most of them are still family concerns. Prior to 1956, whites normally went into the civil service. Now, most seek job opportunities in business or emigrate.

4 *Nation*, Nov. 13, 1970. The commission which was chaired by Professor Lloyd Braithwaithe, Vice-Chancellor of the University of the West Indies, was appointed following an incident at the Trinidad Country Club which refused two black visitors the use of its tennis facilities to which they were entitled as guests of the Hilton Hotel.

institutionalised forms of discrimination which have not been completely changed. ... Some banks have been more radical and progressive than others, but in general the older the bank, the more conservative its policy appeared. ... Even though active discrimination in new appointments may have ceased, the social effects of past discrimination still remain highly visible. ... This requires in the interest of social justice and public confidence that deliberate institutional measures be taken ... to see that this situation is brought to an end.'[5]

Radical elements are attempting to force the pace of change in this area as in others and have linked up the struggle for structural economic change with demands for the exercise of greater social and political power by 'oppressed' black people of Indian and African ancestry. They are struggling to stimulate greater racial pride and identification with Africa and the 'third world'. They campaign against tokenism, against the twisted values inherited from slavery and colonialism, against the ownership of the principal means of production and distribution by foreign whites and their native white and mulatto allies. The Guyanese historian Walter Rodney well expressed the mood of the radicals; when he proclaimed that the myth of a harmonious multiracial society must be blasted into nothingness. Georges Weekes also remarks, 'Our struggle for economic liberation must mean one thing, "Black Power". When we advise the Government to acquire British Petroleum holdings, what we are actually advocating is the transfer of power, white power, into the hands of black people, Africans and Indians.'[6]

The banning of Stokely Carmichael, Walter Rodney, and other Black Power militants, the prohibition placed on Black Power literature by West Indian governments, and the loud protests that have been forthcoming from whites, mulattos, and the black middle class about the growth of black narcissism ('black is beautiful') point to the fact that established elements are

---

5 *Ibid*. The *Guardian* has, however, correctly pointed out that there is racial imbalance in the public sector in favour of blacks and that racial minorities must also be given equal opportunities there as well. The *Guardian* welcomed the Prime Minister's warning to the private sector to set its houses in order 'or else', but warned against any policy which required proportional representation in every establishment. The *Guardian* felt that this kind of reasoning would lead to chaos. 'The primary criterion for employment must be capability ... irrespective of race and colour. ... For our part we think that the incidence of racial discrimination in employment is fast declining and that however useful legal persuasion might be in certain cases, it does not require heroic measures to resolve an issue which circumstances are causing to die a natural death.' TG, Oct. 12, 18, 1970. But the question that the *Guardian* does not address itself to is the urgency of the demand for equality and the fact that past recruitment policies tend to be cumulative in their effect.

6 *Vanguard*, Oct. 19, 1968.

becoming increasingly panicky about this threat to their social and economic power and the values which underpin it. While some dismiss the new surge of black consciousness as a passing fad or as insincere posturing, others are gravely concerned that a radical political movement based on a coalition of black radicals and black workers is a real possibility for the future.[7] The Jamaican government's brutal handling of Rodney is evidence enough that the threat is taken seriously. The Jamaican Minister of Home Affairs, in fact, remarked that Rodney was one of the most dangerous men who ever set foot on Jamaican soil, and it is obvious that Rodney's 'crime' in the eyes of the establishment was not that he wore African dress, visited Cuba, or called for guns, revolution, and the occupation or destruction of the University, but that he took his message to illiterate Rastafarians and workers. The response of the paria blacks to the banning of Rodney from Jamaica has helped to convince the establishment that an alliance of black brain and brawn is a real danger that had to be faced.[8]

To the surprise of most observers, it was in Trinidad and not Jamaica that the most serious confrontation between militant blacks and the establishment took place. While there was a general awareness that black pride and consciousness were growing, most Trinidadians were surprised at the massive support which the Black Power Movement gained between February and April of 1970. No one could have predicted in December 1970 that demonstrations and marches in support of Black Power would attract crowds in the vicinity of 20,000 people,[9] or that the substantial elements of the Trinidad and Tobago defence force would mutiny rather than obey orders to contain

7   Benedict Wight, a Trinidad journalist, feels that the university has failed in its task of educating the community about the irrelevance of race. 'It is a tragedy, because ... Trinidad ... more than America has been best placed to prove the uselessness and obsolescence of the concept of race. ... This sudden passion to identify with a slave past is made up of spite, not necessity or sincerity.' *Express*, Nov. 25, 1968.

8   Riots took place in October 1968 when Rodney was prohibited from re-entering Jamaica. During the course of the demonstrations in Kingston, fifty buses were burnt, several store-fronts were smashed, and numerous fires set. See *Weekly Gleaner*, Oct. 23, 1968. For a fuller analysis of this incident cf. *Moko*, No. 1–3, 1968.

9   A demonstrator who was shot to death by the police was given a 'state' funeral which by several accounts was the largest ever witnessed in Trinidad. One observer, Lloyd Best, describes the event in the following inimitable words:
'On the afternoon of April 9th, 1970, some 7-or-8,000 people were gathered in the People's Parliament, formerly the University of Woodford Square, to attend a political funeral. In the coffin was a faceless, unknown, strapling lad of twenty-four, from an obscure township to the east. The population was giving him a funeral in state.
We left the People's Parliament in the middle of the afternoon to march to the obscure cemetery up the Santa Cruz road. And there it was, at half-past five in the

and suppress the Movement when the Government declared a state of emergency on April 21, 1970.[10]

In those months shouts of 'power, power to the people' echoed throughout the length and breadth of the island. The clenched fist salute, 'Afro'-hair styles, and African dress had suddenly become the 'in' fashion (even among some government ministers) in a country where only a few years before an African student in traditional dress was derisively dismissed as a 'Congo man'. There is no doubt that a fundamental revolution had begun to take place among peoples of African descent and that it was beginning to have its impact on the social and political system. Politicians and businessmen suddenly found it expedient to make concessions to blackness. Most people who had written off the Movement as a passing fad or an unofficial extension of carnival conceded, sometimes grudgingly, that people did not march up and down the countryside in the blazing sun for nothing.[11] Something was fundamentally wrong with the system which more foreign investment could not eradicate. The yawning credibility gap which had gradually been developing between the black élite and the black masses on whose behalf they were supposed to be governing for the past fourteen years was dramatically revealed, and revolutionary change appeared imminent. As Mr Isaac Hyatali, Chief Judge of the Industrial Court noted:

In February of this year, the dynamic youth generation of our times descended upon the country in battle array, and began to articulate and demand radical reforms in every sector of the life of the nation.

The demanded reforms in political thought and actions, in religious dogmas and

afternoon – 15,000 people in the cemetery. It achieved the status of a test match, which tells something! In every tree around the ground, in the samaans which spread joy and cool all over the land, men were sitting on every branch; on every housetop there were people; on the walls around the cemetery, there were people; in every house down the valley – 10, 15, 20 people craning their necks and shouting "power to the people"; or at least, imagining that they were shouting it, because it was of course a funeral. ...

Shhh ... no noise! but there were the echoes of the days before, and of the week before, and of the weeks before that, when almost every day thousands of people were marching up and down the land and shouting "power to the people". And here was this funeral with 15,000 people in every manner of African raiment you can imagine – agbadas, kentes, dashikis – holding their heads high and marching behind this unknown warrior of the revolution. On the way, 15,000 other people had joined the march and left. So it was on that ordinary April afternoon in Trinidad; 30,000 people participated in a political funeral. And that, I want to assure you, was an act of major political significance!' *Tapia*, Dec. 20, 1970.

10   Cf. chap. 25 for a discussion of this event.
11   Carnival 1970 was a political carnival *par excellence* as bands of young people lampooned the absurdities of the social system.

adherences, in economic planning and doctrines, in attitudes to the poor and needy, in the methods pursued to eradicate the scourge of unemployment, in the efforts made to emancipate the black man from the shackles of economic servitude, in the system and objects of education, and in the pattern, structure and *modus operandi* of the public service.

The eyes of the whole nation turned towards them. Skilfully employing their fundamental democratic freedom of speech and of dissent, of organisation and of demonstration, they triggered a social revolution in the country, the like of which its people had never known, nor witnessed before.

And, *mirabile dictu,* they achieved this even though they had no control whatsoever of political machines, of the conventional instruments of power, or of the press, radio, or television.

Who is there amongst us who would reject the claim that they caused many hearts to change, many minds to turn, many attitudes to be transformed, many habits to be revised and many thoughts to stir?

Who is there amongst us who would not admit that they have catapulted the country to a new plateau, a new adventure and a new way of life?

And who is there amongst us who would deny that the reforms for which they pleaded are timely and that they are indispensable not only to the maintenance and enhancement of our dignity, our self-respect and our unique way of life, but also to our very survival and salvation as a nation?[12]

Unfortunately, extremists within the Black Power Movement overplayed their hand and gave the moderates and conservatives the opening which they were looking for to destroy the Movement. The looting, burning, and bombing of business establishments, the raping and indiscipline which attended some of the marches frightened many Trinidadians who never believed it could happen there. The attack of the militants on the Catholic Church, which was portrayed as a key element in the oppression of black people, also cost the Movement many friends, especially when demonstrators entered the Roman Catholic Cathedral in Port of Spain and painted a number of figurines black.[13]

The Black Power Movement has now been smashed (at least for the time being), but it has left deep scars. The population has become more racially polarized than it was, with most of the middle class hostile to the Movement to the point of demanding extreme punishment for the militants charged with treason and sedition against 'Her Majesty's Government'. Middle-class

---

12 *Express*, Nov. 7, 1970.
13 The incident inspired two Indian artists to do a mural in coloured clay called 'Christ in Majesty'. The mural, in which Christ appears in a *dashiki* and wearing an Afro-hair style, was commissioned by the Board of Governors of Bishop Anstey's High School, one of the leading Anglican secondary schools in the country.

elements accuse the Movement of being envious of their success, of wanting things for nothing, of being disrespectful towards age and authority, and of mindlessly aping styles and political techniques which have no relevance to Trinidad, where 'after all, power *is* black'.

Interestingly enough, Michael de Freitas, better known in radical black circles in Britain as Michael X, also argues that Black Power is irrelevant in the West Indies where, in his view, the situation is different from that existing in England or the United States. De Freitas believes that the tactics of the Trinidad Black Power Movement were wrong in a society which is predominantly black. He argues that the net effect of the strategy would be to make white capitalists uncomfortable about their investments. 'If I were a white man ... I would be damned uneasy about all that is going on here. I would think in terms of moving my capital out of this place, and naturally the only people who would suffer would be the poor black people.' De Freitas, who has resigned from the Black Power Movement in Britain and who now calls himself Michael Abdul Malik, believes that the emphasis should be on self-help and self-reliance. The Movement should encourage people to 'love and plant the land and love one another'.[14]

Unlike the Prime Minister of Jamaica, who also asserts that Black Power is completely irrelevant to the Caribbean, Dr Eric Williams has admitted that there are some aspects of the ideology which are indigenous to the region and consequently have authenticity. As he writes:

It is immediately obvious that the issue of the constitutional inequality of the blacks has no relevance for the West Indies. But it is absurd to expect black West Indians not to sympathize with and feel part of black American movements for the achievement of human rights by black Americans, or the emancipation of black Africans from white tyranny in Rhodesia, Portuguese Africa and South Africa, or pride in the historical and cultural past of the peoples of the African continent.

It is also absurd to expect younger people of one of the non-white historically dispossessed groups in the Caribbean not to become, as a result of this impact, more conscious of their cultural deprivations and of the economic and social disabilities still affecting many members of both groups in contemporary Trinidad and Tobago and other parts of the Caribbean.[15]

Williams, however, notes that Black Power cannot be accepted indiscriminately in a society which consists of other ethnic groups which have equal claims to being treated as full citizens. But he welcomes the new emphasis on Africa and pride in blackness:

14 Cf. The *Bomb*, Feb. 19, 1971. Malik is now being tried in a Trinidad court on charges of murder.
15 'PNM Perspectives in the World of the Seventies', *Nation*, Sept. 25, 1970.

Black people, culturally deprived and insulted for centuries, are now taking pride in origins that they dimly suspect and are happy to have confirmed. In the last few years there has been an enormous interest in African drumming. At this moment there is a growing revival of interest in African religion and religious practices, with particular emphasis on shango. There has been for some time a group whose special interest is in Yoruba culture.

It is very certain that the next few years will see a tremendous interest in the study and analysis of African survivals and influences in the entire Caribbean.

Thus all of us had better get used to the idea that African culture is here to stay. It is intellectually constructive and psychologically legitimate. It has its possible dangers if it is overplayed, if it seeks to impose the very apartheid of which it has been a victim in the past, and if it seeks to dominate and denigrate other cultures which have contributed to Trinidad and Tobago.[16]

While black militants do not question Williams' understanding of the historical roots of Black Power Movements in the Caribbean which he himself did a great deal to stimulate, they complain that he has not done enough during his long ministry to alleviate black oppression. And it is true that the PNM and the middle class which brought it to power have in a fundamental sense betrayed the black masses in whose name they govern.[17] The middle class adopted a style of life which was for the most part imitative of whites during the colonial era, a style which has had the effect, perhaps unintended, of excluding the bulk of the black masses from a meaningful share of the material wealth available in the society.

Novelist Earl Lovelace has drawn attention to the psychological fears which the brown and black middle class have about blackness: 'What Afro-Saxons are afraid of is not violence or Black Power. It is blackness. Their blackness frightens them, embarrasses them. Most of their lives have been

16   *Sunday Guardian*, Nov. 29, 1970.
17   The Prime Minister denies that this is the case. As he declared in a nationwide broadcast on March 23, 1970: 'We consciously sought to promote a multiracial society with emphasis on the economic and social upliftment of the two major disadvantaged groups. Our goal has always been Afro-Asian unity. We have consciously sought to promote Black economic power. We have in five years created 1,523 Black small farmers over the country; we have encouraged small businesses in manufacture and tourism; we have, without too much success, sought to promote fishing co-operatives. We have brought free secondary education within the reach of thousands of disadvantaged families who could not dream of it in 1956. We have sought to provide further training for the youths in youth camps, youth centres and trade centres. Our Public Service, at all levels, is staffed today almost entirely by nationals, mainly Black.' The militants concede all this, but insist it is not enough for a government that has been in power for fourteen years.

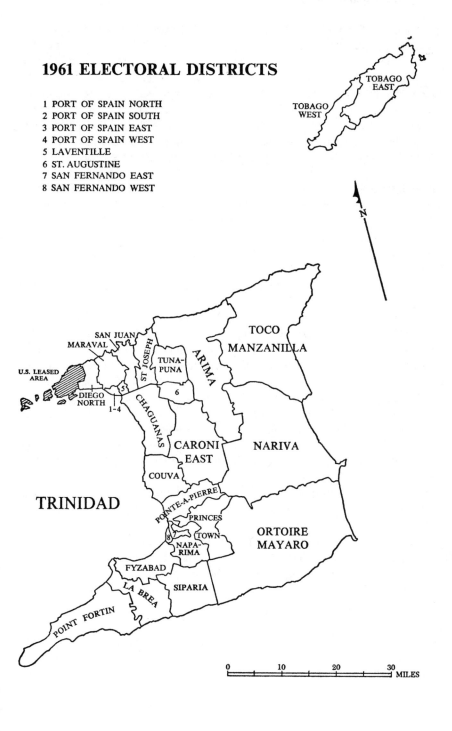

1961 ELECTORAL DISTRICTS

1 PORT OF SPAIN NORTH
2 PORT OF SPAIN SOUTH
3 PORT OF SPAIN EAST
4 PORT OF SPAIN WEST
5 LAVENTILLE
6 ST. AUGUSTINE
7 SAN FERNANDO EAST
8 SAN FERNANDO WEST

TOBAGO EAST

TOBAGO WEST

N

SAN JUAN

MARAVAL

U.S. LEASED AREA

ST JOSEPH

TUNA-PUNA

ARIMA

TOCO MANZANILLA

DIEGO NORTH

5

1-4

6

CHAGUANAS

CARONI EAST

NARIVA

COUVA

POINTE-A-PIERRE

TRINIDAD

PRINCES

TOWN

8

NAPA-RIMA

ORTOIRE MAYARO

FYZABAD

LA BREA

SIPARIA

POINT FORTIN

0   10   20   30
                                  MILES

spent atoning for their black skins. ... Black Power threatens to upset the psychological adjustment we have made to blackness.'[18] But while the psychological difficulties which Black Power presents are real, they are reinforced by powerful material considerations. In a society of scarcity, people discriminate, and connections ('contac' – to use a local expression) become important in resource allocation. Mixed bloods who claim that Black Power is irrelevant to Caribbean society realize that if it were to become the guiding philosophy, the privileges which they and their children now enjoy would have to find a new basis of legitimation and might in fact become untenable. For, as of now, access to scarce jobs, educational opportunities and a variety of services are still easier for those who are not obviously black. If significant numbers in the society come to accept the fact that 'black is beautiful', fundamental revisions will become necessary in the way in which social power is legitimized. Blacks who have managed to rise despite the restrictiveness of the system and who are anxious to preserve their gains also realize the revolutionary potential of the Black Power Movement.

It is a gross exaggeration to say that all those who have well-paying and status-defining jobs acquired them because of colour, race, or connection, but there is a pervasive feeling among many unemployed or lowly placed blacks that this is so and that their own deprivation is due to blackness rather than to laziness or lack of entrepreneurship.[19] The privileged are firmly convinced that what they enjoy has been legitimately acquired and are genuinely perplexed when they are accused of being 'racist' or exploiters of black people.

The majority are not racists in the conventional sense of the word, but it is true that the social system has certain built-in behavioural mechanisms that give a premium to lighter complexions. There is an unarticulated but generally held assumption that it is not tragic if the unemployed and the underfed, the poorly schooled and those with poor health and poor housing are blacks. It is assumed that blacks have a greater capacity to tolerate deprivation; either that, or their level of expectation is so low that they can safely be ignored, while the bulk of the resources are allocated to those who already have privilege.

Although the Black Power Movement in its organizational form is now in disarray and disrepute, its very being has helped to increase race and social consciousness in Trinidadian society. More than half the calypsos sung during the 1971 carnival were on the theme of Black Power (both for and

18   *Express*, Jan. 21, 1969.
19   Aldwin Primus, Chairman of the Black Panther Party (Trinidad), complains with anguish about the 'stench of a society that places us last among the composition of our multiracial nation', *Evening News*, Dec. 3, 1970.

against) and a significant proportion of the carnival bands portrayed African themes. The 1971 carnival queen was also unambiguously black, as was her runner-up, a circumstance that was unprecedented in the history of the competition.[20] The newspapers now give far more coverage to Africa and black struggles in the Americas than before. Beneath the joviality and cosmopolitanism that normally characterizes Trinidad society, one senses that decolonization has been taken a step further as a result of the 'February Revolution'.[21] The politicians have sensed it and are busily trying to cater to the new mood. No political party in the 1971 election sponsored white candidates, as in 1966 when four were returned to the Legislature. Policies have already begun to reflect the new emphasis on blackness in Trinidad society.

THE PNM AND THE INDIANS

In the pre-Independence period, it is clear that neither the PNM élite nor their followers understood the motivation of the Hindus in Trinidad. If they did, they would never have assumed that a few urban assimilationist Hindus could rally the Hindu masses behind the Movement. In the 1956 elections the PNM was never able to attract more than a few Hindus who had any legitimacy among their community, and those who were so attracted rapidly lost most of their supporters.[22] Many Hindus preferred to be *nimakharams* (ingrates) to

20 Reports are that militants had threatened to 'smash up' things if a black girl was not selected queen. There is some evidence that the competition was rigged to ensure this result.

21 The *Guardian*'s assessment of the consequences of the February-April events are fair and well balanced: 'These past months have shaken men, institutions, prejudices, and complacencies as they have never been shaken before in this multiracial community, where up till recently the populace pursued the even tenor of its way indifferent to rumblings that seemed to portend nothing of consequence, and perhaps even unaware of them.
The total effect of the disturbances followed by the seven months of emergency is as yet unfathomable, though looking around us we can clearly see many good as well as dubious and questionable elements coming to the front. We see in several directions a heightened conscience, a greater awareness of local potentialities for good, and efforts being made to bring out these potentialities; we see a revulsion against cant and hypocrisy, against the insensitivities and injustices of the social order, and a determination to initiate orderly adjustments.
We see, on the other hand, a heedless breakdown of moral standards, a disrespect for law and order, a reckless casting aside of some of mankind's oldest and safest moorings, and a denial of the rights of others in the midst of noisy assertions of one's own prerogatives. TG, Nov. 22, 1970.

22 A count of delegates at the seventh annual convention of the PNM in 1963 revealed that only 7 per cent were East Indians. A former PNM minister, Dr W. Mahabir,

leaders who had done them good service in the past but who had since joined the PNM rather than vote against the party of their 'chief', Bhadase Maraj, who had advanced the status of the entire ethnic group.[23]

Williams' attacks on the Hindi linguistic movement, the Hindu school-building programme, and the Maha Sabha in 1956 effectively destroyed whatever chances the PNM had of mobilizing the Hindus, who viewed the attacks, however justified some of them might have been, as gratuitous insults to the community as a whole. Some of the damage was rectified by Williams' success in getting Maraj to go to the federal conference in Jamaica in 1957, but the renewed attacks on Hindu nationalism in 1958 and his description of Hindus as a 'recalcitrant minority' was deeply resented. From 1958 onward they were in open and systematic revolt against the PNM. The events leading to Independence showed to what extent the community had become danger-ously polarized. The fact that the society was small, dense, claustrophobic, and without either privacy or viable cultural outlets only served to sharpen the inevitable confrontation between the groups.

agrees that the ruling party has made little inroads into the ranks of the Hindus from whom the opposition still gains its greatest support. 'Only a few stubborn urban dreamers delude themselves that all is well between all races and religions in the country. ... The Negro masses have tended in some instances to interpret the political success of Williams and the PNM in terms of Messianic deliverance from the threat of falling from the white frying-pan into the Indian fire. ... Both Dr Williams and Dr Capildeo by word and deed have appeared at times to indicate that their basic loyalties were to the Negro and Indian masses respectively.' Mahabir described the strategies of the two leaders as being 'completely damnable'. Speech to the Southern Chamber of Commerce, 1962, cited in the *Spectator*, Aug. 1963.

23 Klass's interesting account of the vote decision-making process in a cross-pressured village during the 1956 election bears repetition: 'For the Hon Bhadase Sagan Maraj, there is a strong sense of *praja* [obligation] on the part of the villagers. He is given full personal credit for having built the Hindu schools in Trinidad, and the weight that this carried for the average East Indian ... cannot possibly be overemphasized. He has a reputation for helping people in distress. ... He is admired for his wealth, respected as a Brahman, and hailed as the East Indian "chief" who has advanced the status of the entire ethnic group. On the other hand, the many villagers who had been personally assisted by Nandilal, and who were familiar with him felt closer to him than to the "chief", who was a distant, somewhat awesome figure. ... Since for most men to decide for either candidate was to be a *nimakharam* [ingrate] to the other, it was not an easy decision to make. That Nandilal did not in the end carry Amity can only be attributed to the fact that the really important men of the village threw their support behind the "chief". ... Once these men declared for the "chief", for many lesser men the problem of which way to vote became simplified immedi-ately; they voted according to the advice of the men to whom they "felt *praja*".' Morton Klass, *East Indians in Trinidad*, New York, 1961, pp. 223–4.

In their well-meaning attempt to create a programme of social action that would establish dominance over the divisive forces in the community, the nationalists did not realistically evaluate the extent to which the society was fractionalized. Urban dreamers as they were, they assumed that the charter was attractive enough to cut through the fear, hostility, and misunderstanding that had kept the groups socially distant for more than a century. They could not see that the withdrawal of the imperial power would activate latent conflicts, since it was their premise that the blame for such antagonisms rested solely on the ruthlessness of the imperial system. They simply presumed that once the imperial system was withdrawn, the divisive forces of the community would be harnessed by the effort to clear up the 'mess' which the imperialists had left behind. Theirs was the characteristic mistake of middle-class reformers who believe that the appeal of reason is powerful enough to dissolve prejudices.

In his proposals for constitutional reform in 1955, Williams did recognize that Trinidad was a plural rather than a homogeneous society. His proposals relating to the composition and powers of the upper chamber had been especially designed to accommodate the ethnic and creedal divisions in the society. He acknowledged that checks and balances were necessary in the context of Trinidadian society: 'In my effort to reconcile all conflicting interests and points of view, I have provided common ground for the widest possible measure of co-operation between all classes, races, colours and religions. ... A Second Chamber constituted along the lines I have recommended would provide all the checks and balances necessary in a democratic society. Such checks and balances are doubly necessary when, as is always possible, one party might sweep the polls and find itself without effective opposition in the elected House.'[24] But once in power, Williams became a strict and uncompromising majoritarian; any ethnic group which did not rally behind the PNM was either recalcitrant, treasonable, or obscurantist. Despite his genuine intellectual commitment to multiracialism, he refused to concede minority communities the right to elect their own kind, or to articulate their own version of the national community.[25] The majoritarian thesis implicitly promised a homogeneous society, a non-racial rather than a multiracial society.

Two hypotheses might be adduced to explain Williams' handling of the Indian problem. It may be that he recognized the composite nature of the

24 *Constitution Reform in Trinidad and Tobago*, Public Affairs Pamphlet no. 2, Port of Spain, 1955, pp. 35–6.
25 In a recently published letter, written to Dr Winston Mahabir in 1949, Dr Williams admits that he did not 'give a rambling damn about the whites. If they wish to come

society, but nevertheless deliberately ignored it on the grounds that the anti-colonial struggle and the social revolution had to be given priority, even if it meant a temporary postponement of the goal of establishing a loyal national community. It might be argued that Williams was driven to this position by his recognition that it was not going to be possible to bring the period of metropolitan tutelage to a quick end and achieve inter-ethnic consensus at the same time; one goal had to be temporarily sacrificed in a deliberate risk. It may also be that Williams believed that he had a responsibility to emancipate the Negro, to stimulate in him pride, dignity, and a feeling of independence, and that this goal necessitated an attack, however subtly concealed, on the European and Indian communities. The post-federal election and 'massa day done' speeches might be viewed in this light. If the Indian leadership was doing the same for the Hindus, and using the Europeans in their quest for power, why should he not alert the Negroes? Power considerations may have reinforced this line of thinking. A combination of Hindus and other minorities might again displace the PNM, as had happened in the federal elections of 1958.

The second hypothesis centres on the question of the accuracy with which Negroes and the coloured middle class had defined the problem. There is evidence that they took it for granted that the Indians had been assimilated into the society, and that the common experiences which they shared with Negroes on the plantation predisposed them to follow a national movement dedicated to an overthrow of the plantation system. The fact that they did not do so was perceived as the fault of their leaders, first in the PDP and then in the DLP, who in their quest for power deliberately exploited the residual differences that existed between Indians and Negroes.[26] It was not the masses, then, that were treasonable, subversive, anti-national, and recalcitrant, but the Indian élite. The PNM's stubborn refusal to co-operate with the DLP necessarily followed from this conclusion. Anyone who advocated co-operation with the opposition, or identified with it in any way, was disloyal and anti-national. The DLP

in well and good, but if coming in means the principle of white supremacy, then is hell with them. The Indians are an entirely different problem. ... The political line for the society ... must be economic and political equality and cultural autonomy for any minority that wishes it. ... The whole future of the West Indies hinges on the labour movement; that is a class, not a race issue. ... The Chinese will follow the Indians, and if they don't ... they don't.' *Vanguard*, April 1, 1966.

26 'We must not do the Indian people the gross injustice of believing or even pretending to believe that those Indians who claim to speak in their name are their genuine political leaders. The 1956 election showed that a large section of the population was waiting for people to come forward so that they could turn their backs on those who had led them for so many years.' *Perspectives for Our Party*, Port of Spain, 1958, p. 19.

was not a genuine or legitimate opposition.[27] The PNM would then have to appeal over the heads of the Hindu élite, as Williams in fact attempted to do during the 1961 election campaign.

There is an element of truth in both hypotheses, and taken together they go a long way towards explaining the failure of the PNM to domesticate the racial problem in the period up to 1962. At no time was the Party consistent in its handling of the problem. At times it seemed to appreciate the folly of its strategies and sought to co-operate with the DLP, but yet never with any degree of patience or determination.[28] While it is true that the DLP was a difficult group with which to work, the PNM élite never consistently accepted the view that the responsibility for bridging the abyssal gap which separated Negroes from Europeans and Hindus from Negroes was theirs, profuse declarations to the contrary notwithstanding. Instead, they either threw up their hands or sacrificed everything to narrow party advantage, forcing the Indians on the defensive.[29]

27   Dr Winston Mahabir has acknowledged the fact that ministers who advocated co-operation with the DLP were held in suspicion: 'It is no secret that at least two Cabinet Ministers of the last Government were under suspicion for disloyalty because they constantly advocated co-operation with the Opposition.' TG, July 17, 1962. Though Mahabir did not say it, it is well known that he and Mr K. Mohammed, and possibly Mr G. Montano, were the ones involved. Mahabir has recently complained of Dr Williams' ambivalence on racial and other social problems. 'I speak not of flexibility and compromise which are the core of the art of politics. I speak of observable, documentable, recurrent, mutually contradictory pronouncements and operations. I speak of ambivalence with respect to Indians and Whites, ambivalence towards the needs and aspirations of the labouring classes, ambivalence towards the trappings of colonialism, ambivalence towards West Indianism.' Speech at University of California, October 16, 1965. The *Vanguard*, April 15, 1966.

28   It is true that PDP and DLP politicians were extremely irresponsible during this period; but their behaviour cannot be ascribed entirely to spite, malice, or a lust for power. Their desperation was just as much a reciprocal product of hostile provocations of the PNM and its supporters. Prominent party members do not dispute this: 'The longer sections of the electorate believe they are unfairly and unjustly treated by reason of race, the easier it is to organize such resentment under the guise of a political party. I am far from satisfied that the PNM is entirely blameless for this unfortunate state of affairs. Living in harmony is, after all, a two-way process. And every member of the PNM has his part to play in ensuring that we here do in fact live in unity.' Lynn Beckles, *Nation*, Feb. 9, 1962.

29   C.L.R. James, once a leading activist in the PNM, now accuses the PNM leadership of fanaticism and gangsterism on the racial question. *West Indians of East Indian Descent*, Port of Spain, 1965, p. 7. James himself is not blameless on this issue, though he always took more of a class attitude to the pre-Independence crises than

The pre-Independence compromise worked out at Marlborough House in 1962 marked the introduction of a new chapter in race relations in the new nation. After Independence the Prime Minister showed great willingness to consult with the leader of the DLP and sought his co-operation on a large variety of projects. DLP supporters and parliamentarians in fact complained that Dr Capildeo worked too closely with the Prime Minister and that his freedom to criticize had been severely inhibited. By way of apology, Capildeo explained that if he had been an active opposition leader, Negro elements would have viewed his actions as being racially motivated. It would have been said that Indians were again 'harassing' the PNM, preventing it from getting on with the development programme. This, he felt, would have consolidated the PNM, which he believed would collapse on its own weight. The PNM also made efforts to recruit Indians to the police and defence forces, though these are still overwhelmingly Negro. The same is true of the senior ranks of the civil service. Hindus in particular are still a long way from achieving the type of representation in the public service to which they are entitled. Moslems, three of whom represent the PNM in the Legislature, seem to be improving their status more rapidly, and some of their spokesmen proudly refer to Williams as the 'Father of the Nation and Defender of All Faiths'.

Hindus feel that the promise of co-operation has not been adequately fulfilled. 'The Independence of the country itself was not celebrated together', complained the President of the Indian National Association. 'It was a PNM Independence Committee which made the preparations. ... The very national flag was not the result of our [working] together.'[30] Hindus complained that members of their community were not being appointed to ambassadorial and other important positions, most of which were being given to members of the PNM. In response to this accusation, the Government appointed a Christian Indian, the former Deputy Leader of the DLP, to the High Commissionership of India, a move that was highly acclaimed within the Indian community. The creation of a post in India was no doubt a belated signal to Indians that India was as important in the PNM's diplomatic pecking order as was Africa. Hindus also pressed successfully for the establishment of publicly supported Hindu secondary schools and official recognition of their religious festivals on the grounds that Christian religious groups were allowed similar privileges. One also hears claims that Indian sugar workers are treated as second-class citizens

did many others in the PNM. Cf. his appeal to the PNM, 'Why Abuse Him?', *Nation*, Feb. 28, 1959. James found it perfectly natural that a formerly oppressed group should want to raise its status by elevating one of its members to political leadership.
30   H.P. Singh, *That Unitary State*, Port of Spain, 1962, p. 12. Other Indian spokesmen made similar observations.

in housing and agricultural projects, that the cultural contributions of Indians are not given the same measure of support and public recognition as are those of Negroes, that secondary schools still discriminate against Indians, and that most of the public resources are allocated to areas that are predominantly Negro. The government denies these charges, but some have an element of truth. Demands have also been made for the teaching of Hindi in the schools, and complaints are often heard about the anti-Indian bias of the communications media and the European and Christian communities.[31] There is indeed a prevailing feeling among Indians that they are still discriminated against by creole society, and that the national motto 'Together We Aspire, Together We Achieve' has not yet become a reality. Until March 1970, however, there was general agreement that the fears of head-on confrontations between the two groups had receded considerably and that conflicts had returned to the state of latency which prevailed in the pre-1956 period.[32] Now there is a new concern that tensions between radical Black Power elements and established Indians who support the PNM may erupt into communal conflict even though radical elements are trying to present the issue as one involving class rather than race.

Radical blacks are still hoping to establish that historical link between Indian sugar-cane workers and the black proletariat which Cipriani, Butler, Williams, and others had attempted before, but prospects for a meaningful alliance look no more hopeful now than they have proven to be in the past. The Indians do not define themselves as blacks and do not share the anxieties and frustrations that people of African descent feel about their cultural identity. As Ramdath Jagessar notes:

Recently we have seen a new Negro consciousness of self arising, a racial and cultural upsurge. Some may be wrong in believing that we will see an equivalent

31 The media have begun to respond to these complaints and now give more attention to Indian culture. The national airline has also agreed to sponsor a national Indian orchestra to counterbalance the bias that favours the steel band.

32 The 'meet the people' tours of the Prime Minister, and the government's better village and community development programme did a great deal to reduce feelings of hostility and alienation among Indians, but it does not appear that this affected the voting behaviour of the Indians in any significant way. It is noteworthy, however, that Hindu groups have been garlanding Dr Williams, and that pundits have blessed him with 'water from the Ganges'. *Daily Mirror*, May 12, 1966. Dennis Mahabir regards this tendency to garland the Prime Minister as further evidence of his view that Indians no longer hanker after India and that they, in fact, have taken pride in their citizenship. 'While the social enclaves, the racial enclaves and political divisions exist, it must be recognized and accepted all Indians want to play an effective part in the country.' TG, Oct. 18, 1968.

consciousness growing among Indians; it may be wishful thinking. New World Negroes can talk at length of their growing consciousness because they never had any before. They lost it in the Middle Passage. Indians have had this for thousands of years – and they accept it. They do not have to argue, to shout aloud that Indians are beautiful. They do not have to justify their existence and claim equality. To them Indians are a superior people, and no question about it. Their definitive statement is 'I am an Indian, I am a Hindu'.

Philosophical problems such as their place in the universe and their value as a people have been solved ages ago. Historically they know the role they have played. Do you ever see them arguing about what the plantation system did to them, and how they should get freedom? Indians are already free. Their religion is a monument on which they can close their eyes and lean. It pervades them, is part of them.

It is the Western way to intellectualize and theorize on all problems. Such activity is strange to the East, whose way is acceptance rather than revolt and change. The lotus blooms in the West, but it is still a lotus.

If you talk of black people you cannot mean Indians. Physically they are not black; emotionally they do not feel the Negro stigma of blackness, or of colonialism. Indians are insulted at being considered black in the Negro sense of the word, and 'third-world peoples' means nothing to them. The average Indian knows little of his past, would be unable to argue well for his way of life or his religion, but he believes in it nonetheless.

The Indian does not hate Negroes and their way of life. Not caring for it, he ignores much of it. There is no active race hatred against Negroes. Indians are not that concerned. They remain separate because they have little in common with the urban Negro people. Indians do not identify with the flag or the tourist brochure idea of Trinidad. They go to their movies, listen to their music, eat their foods and perpetuate their living patterns. Most care little for calypso, carnival, steelband and other forms of Negro cultural life.

The solidity of the Indians is not as great as it was; but that does not mean Indianness is weak. Negroes cannot easily understand Indian unwillingness to accept anything else, for they do not know the power of such a tradition.

Those who delude themselves with facile hopes of early integration, assuming a growing unity of mind or body, may have before them the long empty road of frustration.[33]

Many radical Indians and blacks would not accept this analysis of the Indian community, but my own impressions suggest that what Jagessar has said is fundamentally correct for about 90 per cent of the Indian population. The

33　*Tapia*, Nov. 16, 1969.

Black Power radicals will have to take this into their political calculations if they are not to suffer the same fate which the PNM met in 1956–66.

One of the prime obstacles in the way of better relationships and greater social justice is the stubborn belief on the part of the majority that race relations are ideal, and that those Indians who protest are mischievous and misguided professional racialists. As C.L.R. James correctly observes, 'Everybody in public life pretends that [racialist practices] do not exist; they talk about them only to one another and in whispers. ... Let us face the fact; middle-class West Indians of African descent feel that this island ... is predominantly their field of operation.'[34] It has been suggested that a vast programme of rural reform based on a 'confrontation' with the sugar industry is needed if the Indian subculture is to be effectively integrated into the larger creole culture. But it is not clear that the possible gains to be achieved by this will compensate for the economic and political difficulties that such a programme must involve.[35] It is obvious, however, that unless a more determined effort is made to improve the performance of the agricultural sector of the economy at the expense of other urban-centred goals, genuine multiracialism based on a more egalitarian distribution of power, privilege, and well-being will not be achieved.

Multiracialism in Trinidad is still an essentially passive co-existence re-

34 *West Indians of East Indian Descent*, pp. 2 and 8. Vera Rubin has observed that opinions about the state of race relations in Trinidad vary among elements in the society. 'The racial world view of the student of mixed background tends to be rather benign. ... Rural East Indian students ... whether Moslem or Hindu have little ambivalence about any discrepancies between ... ideals ... and the ethno-political reality as they perceive it. They ... unhesitatingly attribute their feelings of minority deprivation to perceived prejudice in the ethno-political power structure. ... Christian East Indian students ... tend to be less embittered.' 'Culture, Politics and Race Relations', *Social and Economic Studies*, vol. 2, no. 4, Dec. 1962, pp. 446–8. This view reinforces my own observation that most of those who claim that Trinidad has no racial problem are members of the creole society into which few Indians are ever fully accepted, whatever their behavioural attributes.
The claim that Trinidad consists of 'fortunate multiracial isles with happy race relations' has been accepted by foreign opinion. Cf. The *Times Supplement on Trinidad and Tobago*, Jan. 25, 1966. See also the view of Arthur Krock that 'nowhere in the world has more progress been made in developing a non-racial society in which colour is not psychologically significant.' *New York Times*, April 27, 1961. Cited in Rubin, 'Culture', p. 436.

35 According to Lloyd Best, the situation 'required the PNM to transform itself into an efficient party ... and to forge an ideology which placed the cultural, social and economic interests of the rural people on a par with those of the urban and creole, and which effectively disavowed the colonial patterns of succession by which rural people – in Trinidad's case, mainly Indians – were automatically assigned the lowest status'. 'Chaguaramus to Slavery', *New World Quarterly*, vol. 2, no. 1, 1965, p. 46.

lationship with contacts between Indians and others being largely secondary rather than primary. Despite all the official proclamations about good race relations, creole elements on the whole do not consider the Indian subculture to be legitimate and worthy of promotion. They believe that the Indians are aggressive and 'pushy', and they do not take kindly to the prospect that in another decade or so – given present demographic projections which indicate that by 1975 Indians will constitute half the population – they might be ruled by a political coalition centred on the Hindus.

It is partly for this reason that a very hopeful alliance forged for the 1971 elections between one faction of the PNM led by A.N.R. Robinson and the less communal faction of the DLP led by Vernon Jamadar was rejected by many Negroes who felt that, should it win, Robinson would not last very long as leader of the coalition since he would be out-numbered and out-manoeuvred by the Indians. The experience of the DLP following the 1961 elections, when its three Negro members were isolated and later forced to leave the Party, is often cited by those who rejected the coalition as a viable alternative to the PNM. Indians also rejected the alliance for reasons which had to do with race. As the *Nation* noted, 'The kind of symbolism expressed by having Robinson and Jamadar shake hands in public and spout multiracialism does not eradicate from the recesses of the mind the bogey of race. ... Whoever believes this still has a lot to learn. ... Bhadase [Maraj] and Dr Capildeo fought with all their might [against] government being dominated by a Negro. ... One can confidently expect that [Maraj's] line ... would be that if ever the PNM and Dr Williams are defeated it would still be another Negro at the helm of the Government ... . [If the merger is victorious] Robinson cannot be expected to retain control over an organization which is primarily Indian and primarily Hindu.'[36]

In spite of this persistence of racialism, especially at election time, there are optimists within the younger generation of both ethnic groups who believe that the present situation is a temporary one, and that ethnically-based politics will disappear.[37] Such estimates, however, ignore the fact that the

---

36 *Nation*, Jan. 22, 1971.
37 Morton Klass argues that such optimism prevails only in 'West Indian' and not 'East Indian' circles. But among younger East Indians, one also detects some dissatisfaction with the present stalemate between the two groups. Klass' evaluation is as follows: 'West Indians see tension in politics as transitional. They see the development as a highly unfortunate one, but hope that the emergence of an East Indian party is a temporary phenomenon and that when East Indians have become West Indians, in time, and through education, ethnically oriented parties will have no reason to exist. East Indians, on the other hand, appear to see the emergence of such parties as natural and inevitable. They believe that in time they will elect their own

political identification of the mass-mind is based less on thought than on emotion. The results of the 1966 elections show convincingly that race is still a critical factor in Trinidad politics. The DLP won all of its twelve seats in areas which contained an Indian population of over 50 per cent of the total.[38] The small non-racial parties accused the PNM, the DLP, and the media of having conspired 'not only to maintain, but to strengthen the division and sense of rivalry between our citizens of African and East Indian descent'.[39] While there is no evidence of any conspiracy, it is clear that the electorate voted largely along ethnic lines in 1966, and that the DLP was the principal beneficiary. The Party had performed so miserably up to 1966 that no other explanation for its surprising survival is possible. It is clear that the leader of the DLP was supported as a communal hero rather than as a competent opposition leader.

Given the profoundly unstable character of Caribbean society today, it is difficult to predict the course that race relations will take. It is likely that we may see a fundamental escalation of racial tensions in the area as the struggles of black minorities in North America intensify. If this occurs and assumes a violent form, the consequences could be very serious. Conflicts in small societies such as the Caribbean islands often assume murderous proportions. As the Trinidadian writer Eric Roach remarks, 'On an island the feeling that danger is imminent in ... political or natural disaster is acute ... and people in power have always been driven to the harshest methods to combat them and to protect themselves. ... When disaster strikes an island, there is simply not enough room and so not enough time to manoeuvre and manipulate forces to contain it. In the limited space, one's back is immediately to the wall and one has either to annihilate or be annihilated.' The political development of the Caribbean well exemplifies this observation, and it is to be hoped that the peoples of the area will find ways to resolve the racial question without having to take the road to revolution.

leaders to office, and that the primary concern of a political leader is the well being of his particular ethnic group.' Klass, 'East Indian and West Indian,' *East Indians in Trinidad*, p. 860. Vera Rubin's study reinforces Klass's argument.

38 Cf. the findings of Dr Krisha Bahadoorsingh of the University of the West Indies, St Augustine, Trinidad, TG, Nov. 27, 1966. See also Krisha Bahadoorsingh, 'Trinidad Electoral Politics: The Persistence of the Race Factor', unpublished Ph.D. dissertation, University of Indiana, 1966.

39 Stephen Maharaj, *A New Domination*, San Fernando, Trinidad, 1966, p. 7.

24
Restructuring the economy

One of the principal stumbling blocks which retarded the development of the nationalist movement in the 1940s and early 1950s was the belief that the West Indies was fatalistically tied to the Anglo-American economic system. The meagreness of the territory's economic and human resources, its smallness, and its dependence on preferential markets had convinced many that self-reliant economic development was not a genuine possibility. It was in this context that a Puerto-Rican-style programme of 'industrialization by invitation' was begun by the quasi-ministerial régime of 1950–6. That programme resulted in the establishment of thirty-five industries, the creation of 2,195 jobs, and investment totalling $35 million (TT).[1] The 'Operation Jobs' programme of the PNM was only a promise to do better and more efficiently what had been begun by their predecessors.

The Party came to power during an upswing in the fortunes of the economy which began in 1954, and much of the economic growth that the country witnessed between 1954 and 1961 would doubtless have occurred without a change of régime.[2] This is not to deny the achievements of the PNM. Within the first years of its installation the Party made an exhaustive evaluation of the resources of the community and the economic problems with which it was faced, and its first five-year development programme (1958–62) was an am-

---

1 Frank Rampersad, *Growth and Structural Change in the Economy of Trinidad and Tobago 1951–1961*, Central Statistical Office Research Papers, Port of Spain, Dec. 1963. All dollar figures in this chapter are TT unless stated otherwise; $1.00 TT is worth $0.50 US approximately.
2 *Ibid.*, p. 94.

bitious attempt to come to grips with some of these. Properly speaking, it was not a systematic development plan, but a framework of priorities designed to provide the infrastructure for servicing the programme of privately financed industrialization on which its Operation Jobs was to be based. The emphasis was put on expanding the country's power and water supply, on improving road communications and health and education facilities, and on the preparation of industrial estates to attract capital. There was a calculated shift away from the plantation sector of the economy where 'old world' interests were more securely entrenched. Only 2.1 per cent of the $218.5 million development budget was spent *directly* on agriculture, and this mainly on small-scale farming operations.

The PNM was able to finance the programme almost entirely from public revenues and local borrowings, even though this was only achieved after its failure to raise loans and aid on the international market or to get money from the Colonial Development and Welfare Fund. Foreign loans and grants provided only 7 per cent of the development budget, an achievement that was later to prove embarrassing when attempts were made to find funds for the second development plan, more than half of which was expected to be financed by external borrowings or grants.

Despite the fact that the real average rate of growth of the gross domestic product over the period 1955–68 was in the vicinity of 8 per cent (real national income increased by 6.6 per cent per year), the largely capital-intensive industrialization programme failed to deliver the expectations of Operation Jobs. According to 1968 official figures, the seventy-four new industries which were granted 'pioneer' status (tax holidays, accelerated depreciation, duty-free imports) and the one hundred and eighty enterprises granted other concessions (free import of raw materials and equipment) gave jobs to only 7,959 persons.[3] In terms of industries not assisted by the Industrial Development Corporation, the performance was equally modest: By March 1966 the number of industries had increased from the December 1956 figure of ten to 178, only 120 of which had actually begun operations. If the 1950–6 industries and subsequent failures are taken into account, the entire seventeen-year industrialization programme had yielded around 350 industries, about 15,000 direct jobs, and about half as many indirect jobs. By comparison, Puerto Rico, with all its additional advantages, managed to attract over a thousand industries by 1966, and these were creating about 10,000 jobs each year.

The modern manufacturing sector, which in 1968 accounted for 17.5 per cent of the GDP, has clearly not produced the results which were confidently anticipated in 1956. In point of fact, it was the public sector which functioned

3   *Draft Third Five-Year Development Plan 1969–73*. Cited in TG, Dec. 28, 1968.

as the economy's principal absorbent sponge. While total employment increased by 7 per cent in 1963 and 5 per cent in 1964, employment in the public
sector increased by 10 per cent and 9 per cent respectively. Of the approximately 60,000 new jobs that had been created by the end of 1966, about 40
per cent were yielded by the public sector. As praiseworthy as some of the
PNM's efforts have been in the area of job creation, they are beggarly when
one considers that the birth rate has been growing by about 2.4 per cent per
year and the labour force by about 4 per cent per year. The problem is made
worse by the fact that women are seeking job opportunities more than previously and by increased life expectancy, which swells the labour force at both
ends of the age spectrum. Emigration has, however, begun to ease the problem
somewhat. In 1969 the population increased by only 0.9 per cent.

Ironically, the modest achievements in job creation have increased rather
than decreased manifest unemployment. The lure of higher wages has been
attracting people away from the rural areas into the con-urban complex (which
is growing at about 5 per cent per annum), with corresponding demands for
greater welfare services. Unemployment has increased from 6 per cent in
1956 to 15 per cent in 1966 according to official estimates, and most of this
(60 per cent) is among females and persons under 24 years of age. Disguised
unemployment is said to be in the vicinity of 7 per cent of the labour force.
Independent observers and radical critics claim that the true unemployment
figure is nearer 33 per cent. Government officials admit privately that the 15
per cent figure is conservative, but strongly deny that it is anywhere near 33.
The Prime Minister in fact claims that if a more restricted definition is used to
classify the unemployed (those without and looking for jobs up to one week
before the survey – instead of the three-month period which is used in Trinidad), the unemployment figure would be nearer 9 or 10 per cent. This formula, which is used in the United States, is not realistic in the context of
undeveloped societies.

Whatever the true figure, it is clear that the job crisis is getting worse rather
than better despite some further expansion of the manufacturing sector (7 per
cent between 1963 and 1968 compared to 9.7 per cent between 1951 and
1961). With the programme of 'easy' import substitution virtually completed
by 1962, the economy has been slowing down. Real GDP increased by only
3.5 per cent between 1962 and 1965. The growth rate improved between
1966 and 1968 (7 per cent), but this performance was largely due to the
buoyancy of the oil industry, which in 1966 grew by 12 per cent after virtual
stagnation in 1962–5. The general downturn of the economy since 1961 is
directly related to the completion of capital investments in the petroleum and
sugar industries, losses due to deterioration in the terms of trade – estimated to
be in the vicinity of 15 per cent between 1963 and 1968 – capital outflows,

shrinkages in capital inflows and tourist spending due to policies of economic nationalism in the US and UK, and poor performances of the local private sector. Until recently a large proportion of the profits earned by foreign capital was not being repatriated, especially in the petroleum and banking sectors.[4] This picture has now changed. Capital investment dropped from $295 million in 1962 to $255 million in 1967, or by 13 per cent.

Apart from the petro-chemicals industry, which accounted for 11 per cent of total exports, most of the new industrial establishments are operating below capacity owing to difficulties and prejudices encountered in both the export and home markets. The collapse of the Federation also narrowed export markets, and the lack of dynamism in the export promotion programme is well indicated by the fact that manufactures other than petro-chemicals accounted for only 2 per cent of total exports in 1968. With the establishment of the Caribbean Free Trade Association in 1969, however, there has been a dramatic increase in exports. Between 1968 and 1969, exports to the Commonwealth Caribbean increased by some 41 per cent.[5] A major weakness of the industrialization effort is its heavy reliance on imported raw and semi-processed materials. Exceptions to this tendency are to be found mainly in the petro-chemicals and food-processing industries.

Despite all the efforts that have been made to diversify output, the economy still remains a petroleum economy 'in the sense that its rhythm of development is determined by what happens to crude oil production'.[6] The oil industry (Trinidad produces less than 1 per cent of total world output) is responsible for 27 per cent of current government revenues, 28 per cent of GNP, 81 per cent of the value of total gross exports, but only 5 per cent of total employment (15,000 people). During the period 1956 to 1967, crude oil production soared from 29 million barrels to 65 million barrels per year, largely owing to secondary recovery techniques and successes in marine drilling. In 1969 and 1970 new and promising marine sources of oil were discovered which are expected to double local crude production. Until then, however, it was feared that time was running out on the industry and that it would soon have to rely on refining alone. One company, British Petroleum, ceased all drilling operations in 1968 on the ground that operations were not sufficiently profitable. Pre-1969 estimates of proven crude reserves – 500 million barrels – indicated that at present production rates only 50 million

4 'The commercial banks have within recent years increasingly employed their deposits in Trinidad and Tobago and on present performance can no longer be accused of being mere instruments for the siphoning off of our domestic savings abroad.' Minister of Finance, *Budget Speech, 1966*, Port of Spain, 1966, p. 7.
5 *Budget Speech, 1970*, Port of Spain, 1970.
6 *Draft Third Five-Year Plan 1969–73*, Port of Spain, 1968, p. 21.

barrels per year or ten years of additional production remained. Today the industry is in fact largely a refining one. Whereas only 5.7 per cent of crude throughputs was imported in 1931, about 60 per cent was being imported in 1969, mainly from Venezuela. As the 1963–4 *Report of the Commission of Enquiry into the Oil Industry of Trinidad and Tobago* noted, 'An elaborate refining industry has grown on the island and today presents the principal safeguard for the future of the oil industry in Trinidad. Trinidadian oil has remained competitive, in spite of its high cost of production, by virtue of the low cost of its refining operations.'[7] The report noted that due to a complex geology, the difficulty of interpreting geophysical data, and the small productive potential of wells, 'the cost of production is high compared with many producing areas in the world'.[8] Whereas wells average 41 barrels per day in Trinidad, an average of 4,000 is obtained in the Middle East. The oil companies claim that, to be economic, wells must yield at least 80,000 barrels compared to the average of 26,000 in Trinidad.

The crude reserves difficulty is compounded by the fact that oil prices have been under pressure since 1958, when the price stood at $3 US per barrel. Increased production in Africa, the Middle East, and the Soviet Union, coupled with discounting practices, created a buyer's market. An additional complication is the fact that the ECM and the Caribbean, to which much of Trinidad's oil was exported, are becoming self-sufficient. The ECM is now refining 90 per cent of its needs, and refineries have been established in Jamaica and Antigua. New sources of energy are also providing close competition and reducing demands for additional refining capacity.

Two serious consequences have been noticeable in the Trinidad economy because of the oil problem. The first is declining government revenues. The Treasury earns 2¼ times more on the refining of indigenous crude oil than it does on imported crude oil. Dependence on imported crude oil also affects balance of payments. Moreover, as local production declines, more and more workers are being retrenched despite an overall increase of about 63 per cent in refinery throughput between 1958 and 1965. Between 1956 and 1962 employment fell by about 2,300. In 1967 two companies announced that they intended to reduce their work force by a further 1,850 because of declining profits. Texaco, the largest of the companies operating in Trinidad, has not retrenched since 1962, but it has not been increasing its work force, which it claims is redundant to the extent of over 30 per cent. In the context of the growing unemployment crisis, these figures, seemingly small, assume critical proportions, especially since similar trends are to be found in other industries, especially sugar. There was a 15 per cent decrease in employment in the sugar

7   London, 1964, p. 11.   8   *Ibid.*

industry between 1956 and 1968. In industries employing fifty people and over, employment declined from 80,900 in 1957 to 78,500 in 1963.[9] The government is attempting to arrest this secular trend, and the oil industry is now required to obtain official permission before further reductions in its work force are made.

Reduced economic activity in the private sector has been forcing contractions in the public sector which is not absorbing graduates of secondary schools and universities as easily as it did in the past. Indeed, unemployment among secondary-school leavers is highest of all groups, and there are an increasing number of university graduates who are not being absorbed into remunerative and satisfying jobs.

The wisdom of continuing dependence on the Puerto Rican 'branch plant' model of economic development in the light of these alarming trends is being seriously questioned, especially since the experience of Puerto Rico itself is not heartening. In Puerto Rico, as in Jamaica and Trinidad, 'industrialization by invitation' has resulted only in the development of a small, relatively well-paid unionized working-class élite co-existing with a growing pool of unemployed people who are worse off because of the inflationary pressures on the economy. The PNM has refused, however, to countenance any departure from the Puerto Rican system and has deliberately turned its back on the Cuban model, which it believes has not yielded any solutions that are practicable in an 'orthodox' political system. Williams refers to the *Fidelistas* as 'middle class misfits directing guerilla bands ... and claiming to act in the name of the workers and farmers'.[10] Castro, he believes, has made a 'blooming mess' of the Cuban economy. Discussing the alternatives presented to Trinidad, Williams declared:

The Trinidad and Tobago Government and people have sought, and believe they have found, a middle way between outright nationalization and the old-fashioned capitalist organization backed by the marines and the dollars of the United States of America.

That middle way is an active partnership between Government and major foreign investors in both the formulation and the achievement of the Government's

9   It is also worth noting that asphalt, contrary to popular belief, is a wasting asset. The asphalt lake has fallen by 37 feet, and 27 acres have already been exhausted.

10   In the course of reviewing a recent study of Cuba, Williams remarked, 'The question ... is whether it needed the suppression of all opposition by Castro ... in order to achieve the very development objectives and techniques which the PNM is observing with parliamentary methods and with democratic freedoms which have no parallel anywhere else in the world. More important [it is to] explain whether the achievement of similar PNM objectives in Castro's Cuba necessitated ... a complete switch in Cuba's foreign trade ... to produce ... an intensification of the very monoculture pattern ... which Castroism began by castigating.' *Nation*, Nov. 26, 1965.

development targets and the Government's social objectives. The view of the Government of Trinidad and Tobago is that it is impossible to nationalize an economy which depends on foreign trade more than most countries do, and whose limited domestic market of 900,000 people could not possibly absorb the total production of large-scale industries such as petroleum and sugar, which, combined, contribute over ninety per cent of the total export trade. The inefficiency of much more modest efforts in the field of public ownership of public utilities is, in any case, an inauspicious beginning to public ownership of basic industries, the capital needs of which would seriously interfere with the requirements of Government financing of the public sector of the economy.[11]

Williams believes that the human, physical, and financial resources of Trinidad are not adequate for a full programme of nationalization.[12] He also believes that genuine neutralism is not possible in the Americas and that some measure of dependence, whether on the West or on the East, is inevitable. Until the events of 1970 forced him to reappraise his economic strategy, Williams quite unrealistically believed that with more financial and trade assistance from Western governments, Trinidad could diversify and expand its industrial and agricultural production sufficiently to ameliorate its unemployment problem by 1983. It was estimated that about $600 million would be needed to do the job.[13]

AGRICULTURE AND LAND REFORM

Since 1964 the government has been giving increased attention to the agricultural sector, which between 1951 and 1961 grew by 4.2 per cent per annum, and which contributed 12 per cent of the real total output in the latter year. In

11 'Trinidad and Tobago: International Perspectives', *Freedom Ways*, vol. 4, no. 3, summer 1964, p. 333.
12 As Williams told the eleventh party convention, independence and self-reliance do not necessarily involve any 'dramatic and irrational acts but ... a gradual strengthening of local initiative so that we can participate with some dignity and on more equal terms in the network of international economic relations.
      The more we develop our own local centres of economic decision-making, the more meaningfully can we participate in the economic interdependence which is the central feature of the contemporary world order. We must learn to do more things for ourselves, with outside help playing the vital role of contributing to this learning process. But we cannot change the pattern overnight.
      We shall still need external market support in the form of preferences; we shall still need external loans and aid for the public sector; we shall still need the presence of outside management; we shall still need inflows of capital from outside.' TG, Sept. 30, 1968.
13 Williams, 'Trinidad and Tobago', p. 30.

1968 this figure had dropped to 8 per cent, a performance which reflects the dominance of oil and the weakness of the domestic food-production sector rather than the structural transformation of the economy. Agriculture, which now employs about 22 per cent of the total work force, is being enthusiastically regarded by all as the critical hinge in the programme of job-creation and national community-building. The PNM's programme, one aspect of which involves the preparation and distribution of 20,000 acres of public land in varying sizes (five to fifteen acres depending on the kind of economic activity), is designed to absorb surplus manpower, slow down the drift to the towns, and cut down on the import food bill – $90 million in 1966 – which is a serious irritant to the balance of payments problem. The programme also has political and racial implications, since the DLP has represented the PNM's previous lack of interest in agriculture as an attempt to 'suppress one section of the community'.

The PNM claims that its programme is agro-technical rather than agrarian. The latter, which it imputes to its radical opponents, involves the mere distribution of appropriated land. The one is economic, the other is political. Agro-technical reform is costly and complex. It implies the creation of viable, stable, and contented farming communities, and it means, among other things, irrigation (only 10 per cent of the arable land in Trinidad is irrigated), housing, electricity, water, road and transportation facilities, co-operatives, mechanization, refrigeration and storage, pest controls and fertilizers, market intelligence, risk capital, subsidies, guaranteed prices, a rational land-tenure system, and skilled officers to disseminate and supervise new agricultural methods. Moreover, the farmer has to be systematically persuaded to begin using the scientific agricultural techniques that have lain at his doorstep on the plantations for so long. Links also have to be forged between agriculture and the growing manufacturing sector. All this takes time and a capable infrastructure. The PNM feels that the major bottleneck in its agricultural programme is not land, or even capital, but an insufficient number of entrepreneurial farmers, soil analysts, land surveyors, and dedicated agricultural officers.[14] Criticisms are frequently heard that agricultural officers are not doing enough to inform farmers of the new facilities that have been made available. Indeed, because of difficulties of one kind or another, only 6,500 acres of the planned 14,000 acres were distributed by the end of the 1963–8 plan period, and only $50 million of the $61 million planned budget was used.

The programme has been criticized by conservatives as well as by radicals. The former claim that most of the allocated plots are too small to permit

---

14 Recently a commercial bank could find no takers for its offer of loans for agricultural purposes. TG, Jan. 11, 1969.

economic and managerial viability. The PNM is said to be subsidizing inefficient and passive farmers rather than the proven entrepreneurs whose activities earn precious foreign exchange. Conservatives were also critical (unjustly) of the Agricultural Small Holdings Act, which was designed to give greater security of tenure to tenant farmers.[15] They feel that it was the landowner who needed protection against unproductive and destructive farmers. It is also felt that the resources ($58 million in the third development plan, 1969–73) and energy allocated to agriculture are much too small and that not enough is being done to improve agricultural education. The government's reply to these criticisms is that it cannot budget more than can be readily absorbed and that it is more concerned with raising low farm incomes, creating jobs, and producing domestic food than with the traditional export crops for which the future looks bleak. Very important too is the need to reduce the dualism between the plantation system and small peasant farming. As was noted in the second five-year development plan, 'On both economic and social grounds it is necessary to create a more broadly based pattern of agriculture ... where ... economic and human resources can be directed into certain non-traditional lines, with the small and medium-sized farming sector becoming increasingly more productive and the land becoming capable of sustaining an increasing number of people.'[16] It was also noted that the value of crops and livestock produced for local consumption is higher than that for exports. In 1960 the value of these amounted to $65 million, whereas the value of export crops was about $56 million, of which sugar contributed $38.5 million.

On the left, the programme is being criticized as being inadequate to meet the urgent needs of the rural workers and the unemployed. It is claimed, with justification, that the choice of farmers was often motivated by racial considerations and that lands were being allocated to party supporters and friends and relations of PNM politicians.[17] It is also claimed that the programme is too costly and that the farmers will never be able to repay the capital costs of the farms in the twenty-odd years allowed them. Radicals feel that a ceiling must be put on all private land holdings.

---

15   The act, passed in 1961 but only given effect in 1966, guarantees contracts for one to ten years, depending on the nature of the crop, and guarantees automatic renewals for up to twenty-five years, unless the owner can prove before a representative agricultural tribunal that the tennant is not husbanding properly, is endangering neighbouring estates, or has broken his contract.

16   *Draft Second Five-Year Plan 1964–68*, Port of Spain, 1963, p. 174.

17   Reports are that the selection process has now been improved and made more equitable. Thirty per cent of the farmers so far settled are said to be experiencing difficulties making their projects viable.

THE POLITICS OF SUGAR

One of the most controversial issues now being debated in Trinidad is the future role of the sugar industry. Radicals feel that the land being distributed by the PNM is not of the best and that the sugar lands are more arable, more accessible, and, equally important, already developed. These lands should be taken out of sugar and converted into cash crops and livestock for the domestic market. This policy, it is felt, would increase agricultural employment as well as agricultural incomes. Others who feel that sugar must be maintained but on a new basis assert that the lands should be divided among sugar workers and cane farmers, leaving processing to the companies as is done to a great extent in Puerto Rico. It is claimed that, properly supervised, the peasants will be even more productive than the estates are at present.[18]

Those who recommend the phasing out of the sugar do so on political, social, and economic grounds. The basic economic argument is that land use must not be determined purely in terms of private returns but from the standpoint of the social and economic returns to the country as a whole. If this were done, sugar cultivation would be seen to be inferior to other available alternatives. Concentration on new domestic crops, it is felt, would have more effective backward and forward linkages with the rest of the economy. Whereas most raw sugar is refined abroad, new crops could form the basis of a new industrial complex, especially if the incentives now given to foreign industrial capitalists are given to peasants and local entrepreneurs who wish to go into food processing, preferably on a co-operative basis. With the de-emphasis of sugar, local financial resources which are now channelled into the industry through the foreign banks would be available for other uses.

In response to the observation that foreign exchange earnings are an important consideration, as the experience of Cuba has shown, it is noted that the situation is somewhat different with respect to Trinidad, which has a major foreign-currency earner in its petroleum, petro-chemicals, and asphalt industries. Also, while sugar exports earn foreign exchange, there is also a foreign exchange leakage in terms of exported profits and imported materials. Moreover, diversification, by cutting down the food-import bill, would lead to savings of foreign exchange.

---

18 It is worth noting that Williams himself had endorsed this stand in 1961. 'Even if the cane farmer was not as efficient as the planter, the issue is not solely an economic one, and you may pay a certain price in terms of economic efficiency for the greater social stability and advantages that are associated with a widespread ownership and on a small scale.' *Hansard*, May 17, 1961, p. 21.

1966 ELECTORAL DISTRICTS

1 DIEGO MARTIN WEST
2 DIEGO MARTIN EAST
3 ST. JOSEPH
4 ST. AUGUSTINE
5 SAN JUAN EAST
6 SAN JUAN WEST
7 BARATARIA
8 LAVENTILLE
9 PORT OF SPAIN NORTHEAST
10 PORT OF SPAIN WEST
11 PORT OF SPAIN
12 SAN FERNANDO WEST
13 SAN FERNANDO EAST
14 NAPARIMA NORTH

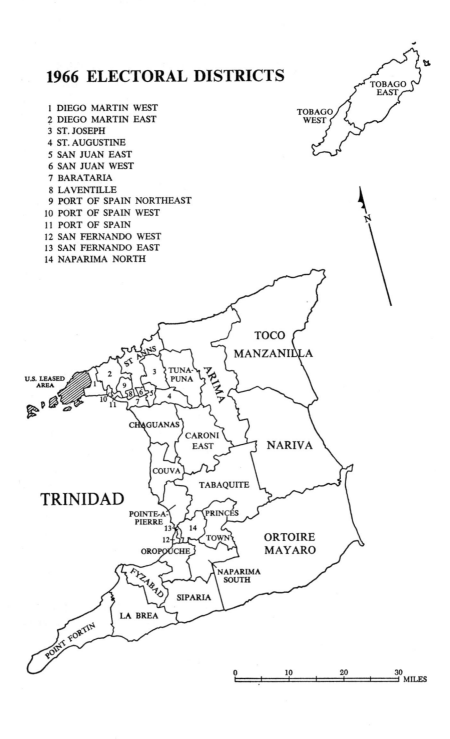

The social costs of maintaining the sugar industry are also said to be high. Sociologists like Orlando Patterson note that the shadow of the slave plantation still lingers over Caribbean society and that plantation life continues to nurture some of the effects that are associated only with the period of slavery. 'The sociological case against the sugar plantation is unanswerable. [It] destroys stable family life and in so doing destroys the whole fabric of our social order. It strangles community development. It induces the perpetuation of rigid class and status hierarchies. It is psychologically demoralizing and as such is an obstacle to progress, and last but not least, it is morally repugnant.'[19] Patterson notes that villages of independent farmers in Jamaica show a higher incidence of stable family life than villages on and around the plantation with its seasonal labour. In Trinidad, confronting sugar is seen as the only medium through which the malintegrated rural Indian population could be brought into the mainstream of the larger society. The bulk of these people are still employed on the estates or in cane farming, and it is felt that unless something radical is done to reorganize agriculture, there is no hope that they will ever become first-class citizens in a genuinely multiracial national community. Racial animosity between Indians and Negroes would continue to plague the island until sugar is destroyed and the rural population harnessed for agricultural reconstruction.

Relying on sugar also has significant political costs. In the first place, the need to secure favourable quotas and preferences contributes to the maintenance of that attitude of dependence which was a hallmark of colonial plantation society. It also perpetuates in a disguised form the old colonial political system in which planters and politicians worked closely together to maintain the hegemony of sugar while neglecting to exploit other alternatives fully. It is felt that a new and radical agricultural policy would lead to the involvement of the people in the achievement of national goals and would also help to break down the present polarization of the two major ethnic groups into racially based political parties, a division which now makes it difficult for the society to undertake the radical policies that are needed to repatriate and close the economy. As Lloyd Best observed in a critique of the PNM, 'It never built up the [sugar] issue in such a way as to secure the support of the large, rural, racially distinct subculture. ... This omission made the essentially urban creole party vulnerable by keeping the door open to another power grouping based on the rural subculture. Thus unless the sugar issue and all the attendant issues of rural reform to which it was central were brought into the arena ... the PNM could chance no programme involving the people without risking a defection of the élitist

19 Orlando Patterson, 'Social Aspects of the Sugar Industry', *New World*, vol. 5, nos. 1 and 2, 1969, p. 49.

wing of its own "nationalistic" support, uncompensated by converts from the countryside.'[20]

Some critics even go so far as to say that sugar should be destroyed at one fell swoop. According to Havelock Brewster, 'The logic of this approach is to create such extreme shock conditions [the only possibly effective stimulus to West Indian governments, in this view] that of necessity we would find, rather quickly, what the alternative activities are. In the course of finding these, a new type of social, economic and political organization would, by the very nature of the problem, become necessary.'[21] But as Brewster notes, this view has not 'gained widespread acceptance', and responsible critics urge a gradual phasing out of sugar while there is still time.

These policy recommendations have been strongly criticized by Caribbean governments and sugar interests, who concentrate most of their rebuttals on the economic arguments of the radicals. The government of Trinidad and Tate & Lyle (which is responsible for 90 per cent of the sugar produced in Trinidad) both deny that sugar is grown on the best available land. They argue that there is ample land in Trinidad for the cultivation of both sugar and new food crops without one displacing the other. They find reinforcement for this claim in the view expressed by an FAO study in 1957: 'The sugar estate area, although intensively cultivated, is naturally poorly endowed for agriculture; the soil is generally of low fertility and difficult to drain. In an uncultivated state it would appear far less suitable for agriculture than some presently uncultivated areas. ... It is probable that the ... uncultivated areas ... are generally less suitable for agriculture than those more intensely used. The difference in natural conditions should not, however, be exaggerated.'[22] According to Tate & Lyle, 'Reasonable yields are achieved only by the use of the resources of modern technology – from heavy agricultural machinery to fertilizers, herbicides and insecticides. The reason why this land is used is historical. In the absence of good roads, transport was a major factor in agricultural development. For this reason, sugar plantations were first established in the vicinity of Port of Spain and along the west coast. Produce and supplies were shipped across the Gulf of Paria to and from Port of Spain and Europe.'[23]

Spokesmen deny that the cultivation of sugar by the estates consumes local capital which could be deployed in other agricultural sectors. They also note that the chief food produced for domestic consumption is in fact sugar and

20   Unpublished manuscript, p. 10.
21   'The Sugar Industry, Our Life or Death,' New World pamphlet no. 4, 1967.
22   *The Role of Sugar in Trinidad and Tobago's Agriculture*, quarterly bulletin, Caroni Ltd., April 1966, Port of Spain, p. 3.
23   *Sugar and the Land*, quarterly bulletin, Caroni Ltd., April 1967, Port of Spain, p.5.

that sugar is used as a basic raw material for several domestic industries. The sugar company rejects the notion that it should only produce the quantity of sugar which can be disposed of on the UK-US premium market and release the remaining lands for market gardening. It notes that import quotas to these markets – especially the US market – are calculated on the basis of total output. Quotas fall as output falls. Moreover, sugar sold on the depressed world market helps to reduce the overhead costs of that produced for the premium market. The company also notes that there is more land devoted to cocoa (121,300 acres) than to sugar (90,000 acres) and sees no *economic* reason why lands should be taken out of sugar cultivation as opposed to other traditional crops. It maintains that its 72,000 acres (52,000 of which are in sugar) are fully utilized, and that no lands are available for release to independent farmers. Fragmentation, it believes, would destroy the industry:

It has been argued that the means of production should be in local hands so that all the benefits of a particular industry or industries may be distributed locally. On the face of it, this appears to be a reasonable argument and it is buttressed by its emotional appeal.

The fact is, however, that not only developing but also highly developed countries recognise that the scale of international trade in the 1960s required the resources of major international companies. The developed countries have had to accept the proposition that only massive injections of foreign investment can revitalize industries which otherwise would be unable to face up to the stresses and strains of international competition.

The less developed countries, whose international trade includes the export of primary agricultural products, are in an even more vulnerable position. Indeed at the present time the very survival of these industries would appear to depend on foreign ownership with all that this brings through capital investment, credit arrangements, the availability of management skills, scientific talent, entrepreneurial expertise and knowledge of international marketing arrangements.

It might be argued convincingly that the lack of such facilities is the main cause of the rapid decline of the other major export crops, especially cocoa.[24]

24 *Sugar and the Economy,* quarterly bulletin, Caroni Ltd., Dec. 1968, Port of Spain, p. 4–5. The number of cane farmers dropped from 26,425 in 1921 to about 4,000 in 1969. Ninety-five per cent of these produce on less than fifty acres. Cane farmers complain that their crop is accepted too late in the season after company canes are reaped and that part is often left unsold because of damage or the weather. They also complain about inadequate and unfair transportation and scale facilities, small daily quotas, and unilateral and discriminatory price-fixing. They would like an arrangement whereby they were allowed to produce at least 50 per cent of the canes. Farmers say they can produce more, but fear to take the risk without company guarantees. Whereas there were 101 factories in 1882, today only three are left.

Sugar cultivation in Trinidad has become an operation with small margins. The costs of production – $192 per ton – exceeded the 1968 world price by about $122 per ton, and it is only the premium prices which are paid for about 75 per cent of the crop in the British, American, and West Indian markets ($228, $220, and $225 respectively) that permitted the industry to survive. According to company claims, profits have been falling since 1959, and in the financial years 1965–6 and 1966–7 a loss was sustained on operations in Trinidad. A profit of $7 million was achieved in 1968, however, due to lower operating costs (higher sucrose content per ton of cane) and increased quota allocations from the US market.

The sugar industry, which for a long time was worried by the prospect of losing its preferences when Britain entered the ECM, is now cautiously optimistic and has in fact embarked on a limited expansion programme. This optimism has been generated by the 1968 Commonwealth Sugar Conference at which Britain agreed to extend the life of the Commonwealth Sugar Agreement indefinitely (the previous agreement was due to expire in 1974) and gave her commitment to try and maintain it intact even after entering the Common Market. The industry was also buoyed by the new International Sugar Agreement (1969–71), which set a floor price of $144 a ton for sugar sold on the open market, by Cuba's difficulties with its 1969 sugar crop, and by its willingness to abandon its earlier determination to destroy rival bourgeois producers.[25] The Caribbean Free Trade Agreement, which allows the industry to expand its markets in the eastern Caribbean, has also been welcomed.

But neither the government nor the sugar industry believes that the future of sugar is now secure. For one thing, Britain has not been able to obtain any firm guarantees about the agreement within the ECM beyond 1974, and as the third five year development plan (1969–73) notes, 'The new [International] Agreement does not eliminate the long-term precarious position of the industry, since under [it] all West Indian Sugar Association countries combined have been given a quota of 200,000 short tons – approximately the amount sold under preference by Trinidad alone in 1968.'[26] The industry is also concerned

---

25   It will be some time before the Cubans achieve their ten-million ton sugar target. In 1966 Castro declared that 'our sugar industry is in a position to compete with any capitalistic economy. Yes, we can even win them. We are not interested in sugar agreements because for many years we established prices which touched off sugar-cane cultivation in countries whose sugar cane producing factors were not good. ... Low sugar prices do not frighten us. We are not working for today but for the future. If you cannot stand these prices, withdraw from the market and produce for your domestic market, but do not ask us ... to reduce on sugar production.' *Nation*, Sept. 12, 1966.

26   *Draft Third Five-Year Plan 1969–73*, Port of Spain, 1968, p. 269.

about the growth of sugar substitutes (corn syrups, and artificial sweeteners) and feels that it must be permitted to mechanize or face the extinction met by the industries in St Vincent and St Lucia. The goals of maximum employment and the 'fulfilment of social obligations have to be balanced against economic necessity'. Plans are afoot to make greater use of automated pest- and weed-control devices and above all of mechanical harvesters and self-loading trailers which, when operated by two men, do the work of eighty-eight. Harvesters, it is claimed, would cut costs by about 50 per cent. The sugar company feels that its technology is as advanced as that in any country and that harvesting is the one area that remains to be rationalized.[27]

The sugar interests also demanded government backing for a wage-freeze in the industry. Average wages are said to have risen by over 84 per cent between 1958 and 1967, much faster than the 23 per cent rise in the retail prices. In an industrial dispute arbitration in 1966, the newly created Industrial Court (1965) gave the industry permission to proceed with its mechanization plan and to reduce its work force by attrition rather than by direct retrenchment. The company was also permitted to finance the wage increase and improved pension benefits ordered by the court by increasing the price of domestic sugar (which had not changed for sixteen years) and by drawing on the employers' share of the Price Stabilization and Sugar Rehabilitation Funds. In return, Tate & Lyle agreed to help settle redundant and seasonal labour on company lands and to assist the government's diversification and 'better village' programmes in whatever way it could. After waging a strong battle to prevent mechanization, the PNM conceded that the industry must be allowed to use the breathing spell offered by the present price arrangements to prepare for the world market competition which all see as inevitable. As the Prime Minister declared before a party convention in 1966, 'The best policy in the national interest is the production of sugar as efficiently as possible whilst redundant workers are settled on government lands to grow food crops.'[28] This policy

27   The sugar company notes that those who are 'retrenched' will be mainly part-time labourers, and that the remaining staff will be better paid, will work a longer year, and will enjoy more fringe benefits. It also claims that its field employees now work and average of 192 days a year compared to 137 days in 1958 and that while 50 per cent of Jamaican field hands are laid in the 'dead' season, 90 per cent of its workers are given some work at this time. Caroni News, Jan. 1969. The mechanization programme will be phased over twelve years, since planting patterns have to be reorganized for the use of the harvesters. Since wider planting will be required, a higher sucrose-yielding strain has to be found so that production levels can be maintained or increased on the same acreage. In 1968 only 7 per cent of the crop was harvested mechanically.

28   Nation, Sept. 14, 1966. It is worth noting that a policy of phased mechanization has been accepted reluctantly by the Jamaican government following the report of the Mordecai Commission into the sugar industry in Jamaica. The commission came out

was foreshadowed in the 1964–8 development plan, which announced that 'marginal producers will be encouraged to switch from cane-farming to some other form of agricultural undertaking'.[29]

Even if the seizure of the sugar estates was considered an economically worthwhile policy, the PNM would reject it on political grounds. As the Prime Minister once declared, 'We are not going to nationalize and take people's lands to have it owned by the state and then have people work for the state. Let them work and develop their own lands. The state is giving away land instead of taking it away as in communist countries.'[30] Williams accuses the radicals of being Castro-inspired and of pursuing a Bolshevik land-reform strategy, promising land to the peasants only to collectivize or nationalize it as Castro has done, with results that would be disastrous economically as well as politically. In his view the test of statesmanship in the new countries is 'to avoid the Charybdis of critical underdevelopment as well as the Scylla of chaotic rebellion or totalitarianism'.[31] The PNM, he boasts, has given Trinidad 'the finest agricultural programme in the West Indies'.[32]

Nationalization is said to be irrelevant in Trinidad, where the government owns about 35 per cent of the land and small farmers (owning under fifty acres) hold about 43 per cent of the remainder. Unlike Cuba and Brazil, says Williams, 'Trinidad is a paradise for the small farmer.' He notes that the sugar estates hold just over 16 per cent of the *private* lands, compared to Cuba where about 20 per cent of *all* lands were owned by absentee sugar interests. But while it is true that land-owning was more monopolistic in Cuba than it is in Trinidad, it is nevertheless true that 1.6 per cent of the holders of land own about 40 per cent of the total private acreage.[33] Just the same, the PNM is not convinced that fragmenting sugar-estate holdings among cane farmers will yield viable units for cane farming. 'To divide up the estate lands among tens of thousands of cane farmers is to destroy an industry which in 1965 earned us $42 million in foreign exchange out of a total of $673 million.'[34] Williams wrote as early as 1942: 'Haiti's ... revolution destroyed [her] wealth. Economic progress and political reform cannot be achieved by destructive means. Sugar is the curse, but it is also the staple of the Caribbean.'[35] Developing public

strongly against diversification of lands now in sugar for reasons similar to the ones outlined above. It also warned that mechanization was not the sole remedy for the industry's problems. There was a need to reorganize cultivation methods and routines, streamline overheads, supervision and operational costs. Two companies went out of production in Jamaica in 1969. It was the fear that this would become a trend that forced the acceptance of phased mechanization.

29 *Draft Third Five-Year Plan*, p. 192.   30 *Nation*, Jan. 14, 1966.
31 *Ibid.*, Nov. 11, 1965.   32 TG, July 20, 1966.
33 *Nation*, Sept. 14, 1966.   34 *Ibid.*
35 Eric Williams, *The Negro in the Caribbean*, Washington DC, 1942, p. 105.

lands represents the best and ultimately the least 'costly' line of attack on the employment and foreign exchange problems, everything else being considered. The key difficulty is to find enough money and skills to do the job properly.[36]

Many agricultural experts in Trinidad are pessimistic about the prospects of finding new long-term export crops to replace sugar and traditional tree crops; such crops would have to stand up to the hostile forces of nature in the Caribbean as well as to market forces. Breaking into new markets is tricky and requires high capital costs, high standards of grading and packaging, and general servicing of markets with sizable supplies. 'It is useless to tempt a market with a limited supply only to disappoint the would-be customer when he finds out that there is no more produce forthcoming.'[37] There are known instances when supply contracts were left unsigned because a large and continuous supply of fruits could not be guaranteed. It is also noted that the American market is already well served by Florida, Hawaii, Puerto Rico, Mexico, and the Philippines, and that many of Trinidad's fruits ripen when there is a glut of home-produced fruit on the European market. Moreover, several countries are trying to produce new fruit and vegetable crops, and this in turn forces down prices, leading to the ruin of producers.

The third five-year plan stresses the need to continue the emphasis on domestic food production and processing, with increased consideration being given to improving credit, marketing, irrigation, research and extension facilities, and the completion of the Crown lands project. The planners have expressed guarded satisfaction with the progress to date of the land settlement and other subsidized projects. Dramatic increases have been recorded in the production of fresh milk, eggs, poultry, and pork, and self-sufficiency has been achieved in these areas. Significant increases have also been recorded in the production of beef, tobacco, legumes, root crops, and fruits. The growth rate in the domestic food-producing sector has been in the vicinity of 4 per cent annually, and agricultural incomes have risen since 1964.

It is worth noting that after dropping slightly in 1967, food imports increased dramatically. In 1971 it was 19 per cent higher than it was in 1966. But food manufacturing is beginning to make a sizable contribution to GDP. Whereas in 1964 sugar production accounted for 63 per cent of the contribution of food production to GDP, it had dropped to 50 per cent in 1967.[38] Efforts at diversification have revealed certain basic problems, however, which will have to be overcome in the years ahead. Because of the small size of the

36 The allocation for agriculture in the third five year development plan has not been increased above the $41 million allocated in the second plan.

37 Trevor Chapman, 'New Crops and the Need for Better Farming,' J. Stollmeyer and P.N. Wilson (ed.), *Trinidad and Tobago's Agriculture*, Port of Spain, n.d., p. 39.

38 *Draft Third Five-Year Plan*, p. 269.

market, constraints develop quite quickly. Gluts have already appeared in poultry, pork, and certain kinds of vegetables. Production costs have also been high, largely because of over-capitalization of the stock-feeds producing industry and the high import content of raw materials used in the manufacture of feeds. Indeed, most of the foreign exchange that is saved as a result of reduced food imports is now lost on imported raw materials. Efforts are being made to develop local substitutes and to reduce feed and other production costs in the hope that this might lead to an expansion of the domestic and Caribbean markets.

Weaknesses have also been evident in the areas of agricultural planning, farm management, and general agricultural and livestock knowledge. As the plan notes, 'Government's efforts in the agricultural field over the past five years have revealed that agricultural administration is in fact a serious obstacle to the development and implementation of programmes and projects. ... The Ministry of Agriculture was unable, therefore, to bring into operation in a concentrated and consistent fashion the forms of agricultural technology which would have made an impact on the farmer.'[39] During the new plan period, energy will be directed mainly to improving agricultural methods on existing farm units, trying to break into foreign markets, and redirecting farmers out of glutted areas into the production of items which could be grown or raised locally, instead of being imported.

THE RADICAL CRITIQUE

The settlement in sugar drew stormy criticism from radicals and trade unionists in the country. The court and the PNM were accused of stabilizing and standardizing the age-old exploitation that has kept sugar workers poor. Like the oil companies, the sugar companies were accused of hiding profits, padding operating costs, and paying ridiculously low wages to native workers (despite increases in productivity of 40 per cent between 1956 and 1963), while paying astronomical salaries to expatriate staff and making as much profit as possible before 'the flood'. 'If sugar is uneconomic to produce it is so at least in part because the owners are taking too large a share of the wealth produced and the staff too large a share of wages.'[40]

---

39 *Ibid.*, p. 240–3.
40 'The accounts under senior staff and general administration ... amount to the startling figure of 25 per cent. One-quarter of the costs going to 400 men of whom 98 per cent are foreigners, while the other 75 per cent goes to 12,000 labourers.' It is also claimed that by issuing bonus shares the company has concealed the fact that it is paying 22.2 per cent on capital invested in 1952. 'The Case for the Sugar workers', *Vanguard*, Aug. 5, 1966. It is difficult to prove or disprove these rival claims in the absence of access to company documents.

It was noted that the whole question of the profitability of Tate & Lyle was difficult to determine because of the secrecy of its intra-corporate transactions. It is felt that Tate & Lyle does not lose anything on its international operations, though it may lose on its Trinidad or Jamaica operations. What it loses on the price of raw sugar, it makes up in shipping, rum distilling, and sugar refining, areas where a great deal of value is added. As Wilmot Perkins has observed, 'If the price of raw sugar is high, Tate & Lyle Jamaica shows gains and Tate & Lyle Canada shows losses. ... One might say that whatever happens to sugar Tate & Lyle will come out on top. But one certainly cannot say the same for Jamaica or any other of the Caribbean producers of sugar.'[41]

There is also growing evidence that mechanization does not necessarily cut costs. There has been a tendency for both wages and overhead to rise. Havelock Brewster believes that the work force might have to be trimmed by an unacceptable 50 per cent to effect a 10 per cent reduction in costs, a level he does not think to be effective in a competitive sense. Mechanization might be of advantage to Tate & Lyle, especially if it eliminates some kinds of industrial relations problems, but this need not be the case as far as the Caribbean is concerned.[42]

Radicals are convinced that the reformist strategy of the PNM will not solve the country's economic problems, and they are fundamentally correct in this belief. They observe that as a 'semi-developed' country with a fairly high per capita income – $815 US in 1970 – Trinidad does not receive any significant aid from the West, and when such aid is forthcoming the terms are unfavourable and burdensome. They feel that the attempt to transform the economy 'structurally' must begin now and that only a decade or so remains before the economy ceases to be viable. They feel that taxation rates are lower than purely domestic circumstances warrant – national revenues were about 19 per cent of the GDP in 1965 – and that there is really no need to rely so heavily on capital imports from abroad. This view is questioned by private capital which claims that tax rates are lower in other Caribbean countries with which Trinidad competes.[43] Uneasiness is also felt about the fact that the

41 'Viewpoint on Sugar', *New World*, vol. 5, nos. 1 and 2, 1969, p. 51.
42 'Sugar-Mechanizing: Our Life or Death', *ibid.*, p. 55.
43 Private companies have been demanding a reduction of company tax from 44 to 20 per cent and the right to earn profit margins of at least 25 per cent. The government, however, feels that its concessions are already too generous. As the Prime Minister noted, 'The relative unresponsiveness of revenue to increase in GDP is the result of the large concessions ... which Government has had to give in order to foster the industrialization of the country. ... The incidence of indirect taxation in this country is [also] much lower than it is in other developing countries.' Indirect taxes yield 50 per cent of government revenue compared to 62 per cent in Jamaica, 79 per cent in Ghana, and 87 per cent in Taiwan. *Budget Speech, 1968*, Port of Spain, 1968, p. 37.

economy is dominated by three foreign firms, that oil and sugar account for 90 per cent of the country's exports, and that as much as 83 per cent of the taxable company revenues are generated by foreign 'branch plant' firms in which local capital does not participate. It is also noted that between 75 and 80 per cent of all new manufacturing industry is dominated by foreigners.

The PNM's 'pioneer' industrial policy is also roundly condemned. It is felt that the tax concessions made to these 'fugitives from the law of diminishing returns on the mainland' are too generous and unnecessary, and the fear has been expressed that many of them will migrate again once the 'tax holiday' period is over, thus making the sacrifices in terms of revenue losses worthless. The number of jobs they generate is also inadequate and well below what they promised when making claims for exemptions. Moreover, the industries have not broken into export markets to any great degree, nor are the high-priced materials they offer on the domestic market in which they have protection of good quality.[44] In short, the radical left has strong doubts about the advisability of the programme, especially since it strengthens the dominance of Anglo-American economic and cultural influences and manipulative bureaucracy, and postpones efforts to create an ethnically integrated society based on popular participation, self-reliance, social equality, and cultural autonomy. Popular cynicism and unwillingness to make sacrifices for the future are said to be directly related to the failure of the PNM to define policies that have mass revolutionary appeal.

The radical opposition is also critical of the wide gap that exists between the 'eating and the starving' in Trinidad. According to official figures, the average monthly income of all paid employees in 1965 was $146.50 for males and $83.50 for females. While only 17 per cent of the working population received incomes of $300 or more per month and 4.3 per cent $500 or more, 24 per cent received incomes of less than $50 per month, these being mainly farmers, fishermen, and female service workers. Expatriate salaries are astronomical when compared with the local wage structure. Whereas males born in the United Kingdom, the United States, and Canada averaged $605, $597, and $449 respectively in 1960, males born in Trinidad averaged $92.50 in the same year.[45] According to another study, however, the concentration of incomes in Trinidad is much lower than it is in Jamaica and several other newly developing areas and is in fact much closer to that found in developed countries. Whereas the upper 10 per cent of Trinidad's income earners shared

44   Cf. 'Incentives – The Price Was too High,' special correspondent, TG, Jan. 5, 1969.
45   *Nation*, Feb. 17, 1967. Agricultural workers in 1967 were receiving about 58 cents per hour maximum and about 30 cents per hour minimum. Cf. also *Census Bulletin*, no. 20, Central Statistical Office. Cited in TG, Oct. 17, 1965.

33.3 per cent of the total national income, the comparable figures in Jamaica, the United States, and Mexico are 43.5, 30.3, and 46.7 respectively. For the upper 5 per cent, the figures are: Trinidad 22.5, Jamaica 30.2, United States 20.4, and Mexico 40 per cent.[46]

Whatever the comparative statistics may reveal, however, the feeling persists that income gaps are too wide and are being deliberately maintained by the 'black massa' in Whitehall who, it is said, pays greater attention to the representation of foreign investors and their domestic allies than to the needs of oppressed blacks.[47] The PNM is said to have become the client élite of a new form of indirect colonial rule more vicious and irresponsible than the old. This restorationist counter-revolution, it is claimed, became ascendant in 1960 with the Chaguaramas settlement, which alienated the masses and forced the PNM into the hands of the right-wing 'parasitic' elements of the coalition.[48] C.L.R. James, for example (until recently a leading figure in the WFP), argues that after 1960, Williams was confronted with a terrible dilemma: 'Williams was now face to face with the economics and the social relations of Trinidad and Tobago. I suspect that he now saw: "Either I go the whole way, organizing the party, getting a local daily paper, and tackling the economy, which means a fight even more merciless than all I have just gone through, and a mess of trouble with my Cabinet; either that, or I give all up." '[49] Williams, he said, chose to give it all up; he 'turned round, ran, and has been running ever since'. According to James, Williams' decision was a property of the colonial past and the existing class relations in the West Indies area. West Indian middle-class

46 E. Ahiram, 'Distribution of Income in Trinidad-Tobago and comparison with Distribution of Income in Jamaica', *Social and Economic Studies*, vol. 1, no. 2, June 1966, pp. 103–20.

47 In a remark that was clearly directed at his party colleagues, the Deputy Prime Minister, A.N.R. Robinson, told waterfront workers that demands were being made of them which were not being shared by those who made those demands. 'You must buy local when others have the opportunity of buying abroad by having the facility for frequent travel. You must educate your children locally when others can send their children wherever they will because they can afford it. You pay a higher proportion in taxes on the things that you buy and it is you whose children go into the Police Service and the Regiment to defend the country, if necessary, with their lives.' *Express*, Dec. 2, 1968.

48 Lloyd Best is the main exponent of this hypothesis. Cf. Best, 'Chaguaramas to Slavery', *New World Quarterly*, vol. 2, no. 1, 1965. I believe this is a false hypothesis. The economic strategy of the Party remained essentially as it was conceived in 1955–6. The difficulties which the PNM were encountering with the Colonial Office and the Americans made Williams *sound* more revolutionary than he ever anticipated. In 1960 the PNM merely returned to the orthodoxy which it had adopted in the charter.

49 *Party Politics in the West Indies*, Port of Spain, 1962, p. 160.

intellectuals, Manley, Adams, Jagan, all began as radical social reformers, but sooner or later were strangled by the West Indian environment. Williams' uniqueness was that he took such a short time to come full circle:

Little by little they were worn down until today they are busy building schools, building roads, West Indianizing, and begging for grants, loans, investments. ... Dr Williams ... was going to show the oil companies where to get off. He was the mortal enemy of the American State Department and the Colonial Office. But now he is finished with all that. He has followed the same course as Manley, Adams, Jagan. The question of political personality limited to personal characteristics sinks into total insignificance. The more highly placed a politician is, the more you can expect his personality to have historical attributes or express the pressure of social forces.[50]

James feels that what was needed was a genuinely national and properly organized mass party which would force the nation to be self-reliant and lift itself up by its own bootstraps. It is even claimed that such a solution would not 'imperatively and inescapably demand revolutionary measures as took place in Cuba in 1958'.[51] James, unlike some radicals, explicitly rejects demands for nationalizing the oil and sugar industries or the banks: 'Young West Indians ... talk of nationalization, even of revolution. They ... are either ignorant or crazy. Nationalize what? Oil? That is insanity. ... We should leave the sugar factories just where they are. ... To talk nationalization is to start a fight you are bound to lose: you thereby advertise your immaturity. Little countries ... must know their limitations, how and when to fight. We clarify the national purpose by discouraging any belief in nationalization as a panacea.'[52] He believes, however, that the West Indian masses, with their strange historical past – no native language, no native way of life, not even any native religion – must feel an organic link with the country. 'It is no use lecturing people on the plane of public morals and duty. You have to give the morals and the duty an objective base and a stimulating but realizable perspective. ... A government of national purpose can make demands on the population instead of continuous demands [being made] by the population on a government which cannot supply [them].'[53] James feels that native whites recognize that 'something must be done, and can be done' and that they can be persuaded to accept changes which would still allow them a strategic role in the system:

50   *Ibid.*, p. 162.
51   C.L.R. James, 'Parties, Politics and Economics in the Caribbean', *Freedom Ways*, vol. 4, no. 3, summer 1964, p. 318.
52   *Sunday Guardian*, Independence Supplement, Aug. 30, 1964, pp. 4 and 5.
53   *Ibid.*

The governments of these territories have got to sit down and plan and decide, in view of the general level of social life and economic life, in view of the special situation in the countryside, in view of the dangerous political pressures which the unemployment and other problems are bringing to bear upon the government, they will have to decide what industries it will be necessary to establish ... irrespective of the traditional profit motive. If we had 150 years ... there would be no need for this telescoping of economic developments. But I see no possibility of individual entrepreneurs, either inside the West Indies or from outside the West Indies, developing the economy to a pitch at which it will be possible for us to feel that the economy is now a going concern and sure to move forward, taking up the increases in population as time goes on. I cannot see it being done by private enterprise in the old sense of the term. There has to be a set plan, in which the State, taking all needs into consideration, not merely the ordinary economic demands but the social necessities of the population, will decide on a programme ... to satisfy the urgent needs of the people and, this is very important, because this is the political issue, to make an impatient people understand that some serious, tremendous, new and sustained effort is being made to satisfy the demands which are increasing every day.[54]

James claims that this sort of initiative would prove attractive to international financial organizations as well as Western governments, to whom it could be sold with the warning that the alternative is Cuba. He even feels that in the event that 'some misguided people' refuse to support the effort, 'We can fight them and we can win. There is irrefutable proof of this.' He has claimed in conversation with the author that the US will not dare to intervene since 'we licked them on Chaguaramas', a view that is hard to reconcile with his earlier analysis of that event.

Others who accept the need for a new economic strategy believe that it is not possible to implement it without social conflict, possibly involving violence. It is not a simple case of 'socializing the vacuum' or inviting people to join the national purpose. Lloyd Best, for example, contends:

Politically, either choice is messy. To opt for the continuance of old relations is to alienate the majority of the population. To re-structure the relations is to court the

54   *Federation: We Failed Miserably: How and Why*, Port of Spain, 1961, p. 21. James' 'non-antagonistic' solution is clearly too facile. As Albert Hirschman notes, 'Unrealistic expectation of universal cooperation with measures which in the mind of their sponsors had no antagonistic component has spelled the failure of many a technical assistance project. We tend to underestimate the difficulties of change in the case of (subjectively) non-antagonistic measures and are constantly surprised ... by the resistances which they encounter.' *Journeys toward Progress*, New York, 1965, p. 238.

disfavour of powerful entrenched interests at home and abroad, and to sacrifice material comforts in the short-run. But in the short-run there is no middle road. Entrenched interests are so powerful that a partial attack on the system must lead on and on to a total confrontation. ... A partial attack, which is not carried on and on to a total one, will fail, without doubt.[55]

Some sort of 'permanent revolution' is clearly involved which would necessitate a re-orientation of the present political system and a frontal encounter with US imperialism.

THE END OF ECONOMIC INNOCENCE

The PNM has acknowledged some of the criticisms that have been levelled at its policies, but is convinced that any strategy which might entail violent class confrontation and cold war is undesirable and that economic rationalization must stop short of this. Williams does not believe that people voluntarily renounce present consumption in favour of future generations, and he has no intention of coercing them by an authoritarian system of rule as Castro has done. He feels that 'unorthodox' economic strategies would sharpen rather than reduce racial conflict and would force the PNM to use dictatorial strategies to contain it. As he told a group of British MPs in 1962, 'We are particularly concerned with demonstrating the fallacy ... that despotism is normally associated with hot countries and that democracy is impossible in a multiracial society.'[56] As loud and as exuberant as was their nationalism, the Party élite always had an acute understanding of the limits of small state nationalism in the context of the revolution in warfare and in economic organization. They knew that the sovereign nation state was an atavism in the age of giant international corporations, capital markets, and big power politics, and though this had never been unambiguously articulated before the end of 1960, it was always implicit in the PNM's promise in 1956 to respect the Chaguaramas Agreement. Williams' political cautiousness was also evident in his consistent refusal to commit the Party to a socialist ideology, his refusal to buy into the oil industry when it was being sold to Texaco in 1955, and in his reluctance to take over the telephone and public transit companies.

Since 1965 the PNM has been showing greater boldness in devising new economic strategies, strategies that have alienated labour, capital, and other vested interests like the Catholic Church. The Party has gradually begun to

55 Unpublished manuscript. Best agreed that the smallness of scale of the society automatically rules out certain possibilities of development, namely the Stalinist model.
56 TG, June 15, 1962. See also the *Nation*, Sept. 12, 1966.

leave behind the era of economic innocence, though it has not departed very far from the fundamentals of the Puerto Rican model. The major new policy instruments have been an Industrial Stabilization Act, new finance, insurance and banking acts, and an officially endorsed birth-control programme.

Faced by growing labour militance – between 1960 and 1964 there were 230 strikes involving 74,574 workers and the loss of 803,899 man-days, mainly in the oil and sugar industries – the government embarked on a policy of disciplining the labour movement, which it had vowed it would never do. Acting under a pretext that there was a communist-inspired plot to create chaos in the country, the government declared a state of emergency in the sugar-belt in March 1965 under cover of which it steam-rollered a bill that has rigidly circumscribed the freedom to strike. The 'crisis' was clearly a manipulated one, and no hard evidence has been adduced to document it. The bill, which had obviously been in preparation for some time, was pushed through the Legislature in one day, with vested interests given almost no time to study it. The Trade Union Congress, which had marched in support of the PNM in 1961, was not consulted at all, though party-connected trade unionists may have been. Critics claim that the timing of the bill reflected the determination of the PNM to prevent the 'freedom fighters' in the sugar industry from seizing the leadership of the Sugar Workers Union from the accommodationist executive and linking up with the radical OWTU. It is claimed that a junction of these forces would have upset the political and ethnic balance and paved the way for a new, genuinely radical multiracial regime. The hypothesis is a plausible one, but there is no evidence that Indian sugar workers were ready to follow Negro political leaders, whatever they might do in the field of industrial relations. Negro workers have also consistently refused to return labour leaders to the Legislature.

The conditions under which strikes, go-slows, and lockouts could be initiated were circumscribed, and penalties for breaches were quite severe under the ISA; it also provided a formula for the recognition of trade unions by employers – a 51 per cent vote by the workers – and for an industrial court, the adjudications of which were to be binding on all parties subject only to appeals on points of law. The court was enjoined to ensure the workers a fair share of increases in productivity and to keep in mind the need to maintain and expand the level of employment, domestic capital formation, economic growth, and the competitiveness of Trinidad's industries in export markets. The court was also charged with the responsibility for ensuring the continued ability of the public sector to finance development projects and for maintaining a favourable balance of trade and payments. These were heavy responsibilities to impose on a quasi-judicial body, as the unions have consistently pointed out.

The PNM's position is that free and unrestrained collective bargaining is dysfunctional in the light of Trinidad's economic circumstances. According to official spokesmen, real national income increased by almost 41 per cent between 1956 and 1960, and real per capita income increased by 35 per cent between 1956 and 1961. While wages increased by 114 per cent between 1956 and 1966, productivity increased by about 66 per cent, and retail prices by about 27 per cent during the same period. The latter performance was due mainly to the fact that no restrictions were placed on imported supplies. It was also probably due to the narrowness of the selection of goods used to calculate the price index.

The PNM denies that it has sacrificed labour to capital. Rather, it wanted to change the 'old-fashioned loudmouthed' style of industrial bargaining by reducing the number of trade unions (there are now 165) and by helping to upgrade the bargaining skills of unionists through its newly created Labour College and the research facilities of the Industrial Court. It also hoped that the court would allow labour leaders to accept settlements in the national interest without running the risk of alienating their following. 'The days of agitation are over', declared Williams. The PNM claims that labour is now part of the establishment and has a responsibility to respect the needs of the national interest. The PNM in fact admits that the distribution of income in Trinidad is not as satisfactory as it might be, but it blames organized labour as much as business, if not more. The former Minister of Finance, A.N.R. Robinson complained that 'the increases in the proportion of income accruing to persons was at the expense of Government income and company savings'[57] (87.2 per cent in 1956 compared to 88.4 per cent in 1962).

The Industrial Stabilization Act was welcomed by employers and initially by the general population. But radical unionists and intellectuals bitterly condemned it and have vowed to have it repealed by constitutional means or, failing that, 'from below'. The unionists see the act as a return to the pre-1937 situation, which it clearly is not; as a restraint on free collective bargaining, which it is; and as the PNM's main instrument for maintaining stability and restraining the 'just' demands of labour for internationally comparable wages, in the interest of encouraging capital from outside. The unions and the OWTU in particular feel that they and not the PNM are the true guardians of the dignity of the worker and the national interest, since they are the ones leading the fight against mechanization and for the retention of profits in the country via increased wages for workers. The anti-ISA campaign was initially undercut by the performance of the court, which showed quite clearly that it was not partial to employers. Of the thirty-six rulings or conciliations made in its first year, only three were decidedly in favour of employers, while another three

57   TG, June 17, 1965.

were about evenly split. Even the *Vanguard*, the organ of the OWTU, grudgingly admitted that the 'court has done a fine job and has replaced the conference table as a place for negotiations'.[58] But the unions succeeded in forcing the government to amend the act on three occasions, and the court itself has had to warn the Government that its machinery was straining under the burden that it was expected to assume. Its crowded schedule has been exasperating and expensive for the unions. Delays allow employers to take advantage of leadership rivalries to divide the workers and to prolong negotiations in the hope of having the dispute referred to the court which has a long backlog of undelivered judgments. The result is growing frustration in the labour movement. As George Bowrin notes,

Frustration has bred an attitude of indifference which produces effects on industry which cannot be measured in loss of man-days, or in loss of millions of dollars, which Dr Williams is so fond of doing.

The Doctor is concerned with the appearance, the 'image' of stability. He does not give a damn about the reality which has resulted in a fall off in production, a worsening in industrial relations and a consequent increase in labour militancy. These cannot be measured in terms of 'strikes' or 'man-days lost,' or 'dollars and cents' lost, etc. But maybe that is the logical consequence of the doctor's pragmatism.[59]

It is worth noting that, despite the ISA, workers have been defying the Government by going on strike with increasing frequency. Officially, work stoppages for January 1971 have totalled fifteen as against fifty-five for all of 1970. Many of these have been in the public sector and the government is playing an opportunist game by prosecuting unions that are hostile to the PNM while ignoring strikes in politically sensitive industries like sugar, oil, and the docks. This state of affairs is worrying to business and to those concerned with law and order, but labour spokesmen welcome what they consider to be the unproclaimed demise of the ISA. As Bowrin notes, 'The workers have now taken over. They no longer ask Government to repeal the ISA. They have repealed it for themselves, nationally. They go slow, they go on strike, they call sympathy strikes with impunity. For them, whatever the Government may say, whatever the Industrial Court may do, the ISA, in so far as it hinders their freedom of action in "industrial matters", is REPEALED.'[60]

While the level of disenchantment with the ISA is high, there is general

---

58   *Vanguard*, April 20, 1966.   59   *Ibid.*, Oct. 24, 1970.
60   *Ibid.* The Attorney General agrees that strikes have been numerous, but notes that their effect on the business sector in terms of numbers of man-days lost was negligible compared to that during the period 1967–9. TG, Aug. 7, 1970.

agreement that a return to the pre-1965 pattern of industrial relations is undesirable, and efforts are being directed to create a labour code which would govern relationships between employers and employees. The Prime Minister's attitude to the ISA has softened considerably from those days when he insisted that not a comma of the act would be changed. In his June 30, 1970, speech on national reconstruction, he promised to change the act radically to relax the provisions relating to strikes and lockouts, to streamline the procedures for recognition and demarcation of jurisdictions between unions, greater government collaboration between the Labour Congress and a strengthened Ministry of Labour, and an improvement of the machinery and procedures of the Industrial Court which he insists must remain. The Prime Minister also gave encouragement and financial assistance to the recently created Workers' Bank and pledged the cabinet's support in enabling workers and unions to become shareholders in both the private and public sectors.

In 1971, the Government published for comment the draft of a new Industrial Relations Act which attempts to respond to some of the criticisms being made of the ISA. The IRA has, however, not received support from radical unions since it retains the principle of binding arbitration and limitations on the right to strike. The Council of Progressive Trade Unions – a break-away movement from the more pro-government Trinidad and Tobago Labour Congress – asserts that the IRA 'abrogates the rule of law for all workers by giving the Minister of Labour sweeping powers to intervene in all recognition claims, industrial disputes and collective bargaining agreements, as well as power to decide if workers may go on strike.'[61] It fears that the minister's power will be used whimsically and in a partisan manner. The CPTU would accept nothing less than a full restoration of the freedom to strike and the outlawing of attempts on the part of employers to found rival company unions by intrigue and bribery. More moderate unionists accept the need for some limitation on the right to strike, especially in critical industries – at least until all other alternatives are exhausted, and accuse the CPTU and the leadership of the OWTU in particular of misusing genuine industrial grievances as weapons to fight long drawn out political battles with the PNM. But indications are that the IRA would be as unpopular as was the ISA.

The president of the OWTU, George Weekes, and other members of the executive, have made no secret of their determination to drive the PNM from office, and the latter is equally determined to crush the OWTU which it sees as the major threat to its continued hold on the country. Weekes was detained during the 1970 emergency and the files of the OWTU offices were ransacked by security officers looking for evidence to link the OWTU to 'subversive'

61   TG, Sept. 8, 1971.

elements from Cuba and the Soviet bloc. Weekes and three other members of the Union's executive were arrested in September 1971 on charges of defrauding the Union and misusing funds for political ends. While there appears to be evidence to prove the charges, it is clear that the authorities have been very selective in choosing which would be investigated, and that this exercise is part of a well-orchestrated offensive by the PNM and the petroleum and other industries in which the OWTU has bargaining status, to cripple the OWTU.[62] It is worth noting that the militant activities of the OWTU, and reprisals by construction companies operating in the oil industry involving the dismissal of over two thousand workers, led to the declaration of another State of Emergency on October 20, 1971.

The Prime Minister explained that his action had become necessary because abuse of white supervisory staff had gone beyond tolerable limits and because strikes and go-slows were strangling the economy. Firms were closing down their operations with the result that there was a considerable loss of jobs and government revenue. Trinidad, he said, was again faced with a serious threat to law, order, and economic stability which seriously affected the peace of mind of the average law-abiding citizen. Twelve prominent activists, including George Weekes, were placed in protective custody. The Government also committed itself to a drastic reshaping of the country's labour laws.

The complementary aspect of the PNM's 1965 labour policy was an attempt at far-reaching fiscal reform. The reform programme, which began with the introduction of the pay-as-you-earn system of taxation in 1957, was expanded in 1963 when higher income and company taxes were levied and a comprehensive tariff reform was introduced to restrain (unsuccessfully) the consumption of unessential imports. In 1966, three major pieces of legislation

---

62 'Whether Mr. Weekes is found guilty or not of the charges alleged against him is almost immaterial. The act that committed him to stand trial was a political act. The President General of a large and powerful union does not find himself in court on fraud charges by accident, and certainly not in a society like this where fraud, peculation, malignant conversion and every species of public and private thievery have, by tradition, gone unchallenged and unpunished.

Indeed, one is almost tempted to say that if that is all that can be alleged against Weekes then he must be an honest man, more honest than his peers in this corruption-ridden society. Were the same vigilant standards now being applied to Weekes applied to the so-called government of this country, there is not a single Minister who would not be in the Royal Gaol in the morning. And the Prime Minister, the boss of four successive PNM administrations which have distinguished themselves by the wilful and wasteful expenditure of public funds, would be in for the longest stretch of all. Indeed, if justice were strictly applied, he would never be free again even if he lived to be a hundred.' *Moko*, Oct. 1, 1971.

were introduced in the fields of banking, insurance, and investment policy. The least controversial of these was the Central Bank Act, the aim of which was to provide the nation with instruments to regulate its money supply. The Central Bank has been given wide powers to regulate the commercial banks, hire-purchase credit, and interest rates in general, but the Bank has made it clear that its policies will be conservative. The governor of the Bank noted that the scope of monetary policy is limited by the fact that national interest rates cannot get far out of line with world interest rates.[63] The Bank was also charged with the responsibility of assisting in the organization of a develop-ment bank and a domestic capital market, institutions that are sorely needed in the Caribbean if indigenous share-holdings and public companies are to be stimulated. At present, capital market relationships are vertical (i.e., with metropolitan countries) rather than national or even regional. Of the 567 companies resident in Trinidad in 1966, only twenty were public companies.[64]

More controversial than the new banking legislation was the Insurance Act, passed in December 1966. The main aim of the act was to regulate the conditions under which insurance firms were to operate in Trinidad and above all to force them to invest more money domestically. It stipulated that 36 per cent of the assets of registered companies must be locally invested, and provided for annual increases of 6 per cent up to a maximum of 60 per cent. Companies are also required to make guarantee deposits of $250,000 in government issues. Three Canadian insurance companies found the terms of the long overdue act unacceptable and have stopped selling new policies in the country.

By far the most controversial of the acts was the Finance Act. The details of the act, adjudged esoteric and administratively indigestible by financial specialists, cannot be discussed here, but the main purposes are clear; it was an ambitious attempt to plug loopholes against tax evasion by both domestic and foreign businessmen, to discourage repatriation of profits, or alternatively to cream off some of these before they were sent abroad. It was argued that businessmen should pay some compensation for the 'benefits of the ISA'. The Minister of Finance complained that 75 per cent of the 640 companies operat-ing in Trinidad paid only $2 million in taxes. The act introduced the concept of the corporate tax for the first time. The old company tax system permitted shareholders to mix up their personal affairs with those of the company with the result that it was easy to obscure transactions that should have been sub-ject to taxation. Corporate taxes have now been set at 44 per cent, 1.5 per

---

63   TG, Aug. 27, 1966. It does not appear that the Central Bank has had much impact on economic life in Trinidad, certainly not enough to justify the costs of running it.
64   *Ibid.*, Aug. 8, 1966.

cent higher than the company tax rate set in 1963, and the act disallows the old practice of claiming company-paid taxes against personal income taxes. A wider range of transactions previously entered as costs, for example, fees for patents or management services of foreign head-office representatives, have also been brought within the tax net. The government's operating principle was that all income earned in Trinidad must be taxed in Trinidad; otherwise its forbearance would result in a straight gift to a foreign treasury. The act also provides incentives to domestic firms engaged in export creation.

Double taxation treaties have been negotiated with the US, UK, and Canadian governments, which in effect means that profits taxed in Trinidad will be exempt from taxation in these countries up to 5 per cent in the United States and 15 per cent in the United Kingdom and Canada. Many of the tough provisions of the act, such as a capital gains tax of 20 per cent and a withholding tax of as much as 30 per cent in addition to the corporate tax, were later withdrawn or modified because of strong pressure from business elements, the Liberal Party, labour organizations, and even PNM elements.[65] There was widespread fear that investment would dry up, and that the industrialization and job-creation programmes would be affected even further than they have been by 'normal' capital outflows and shrinking inflows. It is worth noting that the extremely consensualist approach pursued during the enacting of the Finance Act was vastly different from that followed in regard to the Industrial Stabilization Act, and labour elements did not hesitate to draw the logical conclusions.[66]

The government has also come out strongly in favour of state-subsidized family planning, and it is hoped that this will help to reduce the rate of population growth.

NEW ECONOMIC PERSPECTIVES

In September 1970, the PNM published a new policy statement, 'Perspectives for the New Society', which it claims will guide its activities in the seventies

65 A fiscal review committee, consisting of labour, business, and government representatives, recommended that withholding taxes should be lowered from 30 per cent to 15 in respect of remittances of dividends from subsidiary to parent companies, and from 30 per cent to 25 in respect of dividends to non-resident investors other than parent-subsidiary relationships. The capital gains provision was also dropped.

66 The PNM cabinet was openly split on the foreign capital issue. A.N.R. Robinson, who was the author of the Finance Act, strongly opposed the alterations which were made to it. As he told the Party, 'in politics as in business, the hard decisions must be taken if you are to deal with the underlying situation and not just postpone the problem until you create an unholy mess,' TG, Aug. 25, 1967. Robinson resigned from the PNM in 1970.

should it be given another mandate to govern. In a sense, the document is a fundamental revision of the 'People's Charter' which it issued in 1956 and which has been largely ignored. The new statement is deeply influenced by the black protest movement of the preceding months and is a calculated attempt by the party élite to appropriate what it considers to be the 'constructive' proposals of the Black Power militants. Neo-colonialism is now recognized as the great danger to be faced by Caribbean countries.'Too much dependence on metropolitan governments and metropolitan firms is incompatible with the economic sovereignty of the people of the Caribbean. Too much domination by the giant international corporations has the same effect in suppressing the potential of the West Indian people as did the mercantilist links of the plantation economy of the 17th and 18th centuries.'[67]

While admitting the need to strengthen popular participation in the economic life of the country and to localize decision-making over the key sectors of the economy, 'Perspectives' categorically rejects socialism either of the bureaucratic kind or of the totalitarian variety. 'We must definitely avoid the mistake made by many so-called "socialist" Third World countries in seeking state domination of the entire economy.' On the other hand, 'if we adopt the system of liberal capitalism ... the result will be increased prosperity for a relatively small group of people ... accompanied by increasing unemployment and the maldistribution of income and wealth.' Trinidad's past and present circumstances demand that a middle way be found between the Cuban and Puerto Rican models, a model in which the importance and legitimacy of four sectors of economic activity are recognized: the public sector, the national private sector, the people's sector, and the foreign sector.

The public sector

The emphasis now being given to the public sector is in a sense a belated attempt to rationalize and identify as a matter of chosen policy a number of unco-ordinated decisions which the government was forced to take under pressure from radicals. Even before the Black Power demonstrations of February-April 1970, there were strong demands that the banks should be nationalized and that Tate & Lyle and Texaco be brought under government ownership. The PNM strongly opposed this, pointing to the poor economic performance of concerns which it had already taken over, such as British West Indian Airways, the Public Transport Service Corporation, and the Trinidad Telephone Company. It had even sold 50 and 40 per cent of the

67 'Perspectives for the New Society', *Nation*, Sept. 25, 1970. 'Perspectives' has also been published in booklet form (Port of Spain, 1970) but the quotations given here and below have all been taken from the *Nation* and no page documentation is given.

state's equity in the telephone company and British West Indian Airways respectively,[68] and there were reports that plans were also being made to dispose of some of the state's holdings in the Hilton Hotel. The Prime Minister justified the buy-and-sell policy in terms of national economic need and ideological flexibility. Money, he said, was not just available to meet debt repayment schedules, operating costs of public utilities which were not paying their way, and the expansion programmes needed to create jobs. As Williams remarked, 'We must not be side-tracked into empty discussions on dogma regarding the respective roles and the lines of demarcation of the private and public sectors. A pragmatic view is necessary if we are to make a positive assault on the obstacles to our progress. Mixed forms of ownership and management ... appear to be particularly well suited to our needs and circumstances.'[69] The left, on the other hand, claimed that the birthright of the young was being sold for a mess of pottage. As A.N.R. Robinson complained, 'The Caribbean problem is fundamentally an economic one and the ability to run our economic services economically is the real test of independence. If we are unable to run our public enterprises ourselves, it is unlikely that we will be able to run anything else, and we might as well abandon all talk of nationhood and independence.'[70]

The government's vote of no confidence in the capacity of Trinidadians to run their economy was dramatically reversed as the chorus of criticism about foreign domination increased. In addition to the industries mentioned above, the public sector now includes:

The National Commercial Bank which was formed out of the assets purchased ($1.4 million) from the Banks of London and Montreal. The NCB confounded those who predicted failure by doubling its deposits and by making a profit of $208,567 (before tax) in its first year of operations;

The National Petroleum Company, which has been inactive so far but which is expected to be entrusted with the responsibility for running the chain of 24 petrol retails service stations which the government acquired from British Petroleum in May of 1971. The government is also trying to obtain other outlets from Shell, Texaco, and Esso and the ultimate aim is to gain control of at least one third of total retail outlets.

The National Sugar Company which was formed out of properties acquired from Orange Grove Sugar Estates. The small sugar company had problems

---

68 BWI, which had been bought from BOAC mainly to save jobs, is now managed by the Caribbean International Association, which has a 10 per cent interest. The airline's economic position has been improving, but it is still operating at a considerable loss.
69 TG, Oct. 5, 1968.
70 *Vanguard*, Aug. 5, 1967.

marketing its products but was nevertheless able to earn a profit after taxes of $580,000 and $68,000 in 1969 and 1970 respectively;

Radio Guardian and Trinidad and Tobago Television Company which were acquired from the Thompson Chain. The Columbia Broadcasting Service has a 10 per cent equity in TTT and the responsibilities of management;

The Port Landing Company in which the state has a 50 per cent equity;

Trinidad and Tobago External Communications in which the state also holds a 51 per cent equity.

Trinidad-Tesoro Oil Company: the state's 50.1 per cent share in this company was the assets which the PNM acquired from British Petroleum in 1969 for $44 million largely to save the jobs of 1,400 workers faced with retrenchment;

Tate & Lyle: 51 per cent of the shares which the government bought under pressure for $11 million in 1970. Tate & Lyle continues to manage the company, whose financial position is deteriorating rapidly. In 1970 and 1971, it reported a loss of $4.5 and $3.5 million respectively.

The government has also announced its intention to participate in Chaguaramas Terminals (a bauxite transhipment operation) to safeguard the interests of Guyana's bauxite industry the Canadian segment of which was recently nationalized. Guyana exports bauxite through the deep-water harbour in Chaguaramas.

The Prime Minister in fact now boasts that Trinidad has a larger public sector than any other Caribbean territory except Cuba. But, he warned, his government will keep in mind what happened in Ghana and Indonesia and will not 'sacrifice the welfare and well being of ... Trinidad and Tobago on the altar of some intellectual fetish which is now being considerably modified in the countries where it originated.'[71]

The PNM has also begun a policy of acquiring shares in newly established companies, some of which it promises to resell to individuals and organizations such as trade unions. It claims that this is one way in which it intends to ensure that the people participate in the economic development of the country. There have been complaints, however, that the government has not been keeping this pledge.[72] But there have already been complaints about the excessive secrecy that surrounds the negotiations for acquiring company shares and

---

71   TG, Oct. 2, 1971. Other English-speaking Caribbean governments like Jamaica have not done much nationalization. Rather, they have chosen to pressure foreign companies to incorporate locally and make shares available to indigenous investors. Guyana, which completely nationalized the Canadian segment of its bauxite industry, has announced that it has no plans to nationalize foreign commercial banks.

72   *Express*, Sept. 29, 1971, for complaints of the South Chamber of Commerce about the PNM's poor performance in terms of keeping its promises. It is worth noting that majority shares in one major company, the Trinidad Asphalt Company, have been bought out by local investors.

about the corruption that is rampant in some of the state-owned enterprises. Scandals have rocked the Transport Corporation which had a deficit in 1970 of about $5.2 million. As the *Guardian* notes, 'Government's activity here represents at one remove the economic power of the people and it is incumbent upon Government to submit periodic statements on how it administers that economic power. The Auditor General's report informs us that the Auditor General has precious little information on which to draw up a comprehensive report of Government's activities, particularly about Government's financial role in the acquisition of commercial ventures.'[73]

The national private sector

In the first and second development plan periods greater attention and assistance were given to foreign investors. Since 1969, however, attempts have been made to shift this emphasis by offering various inducements to the local investor. Unlike Tanzania and Cuba, the PNM has no reservations about the growth of a national bourgeoisie other than to insist that share-holding and ownership should not be concentrated in a few hands. Although this is not articulated as policy, one gets the distinct impression that the government now wishes to channel most of its financial and other support towards the creation of an unequivocally black bourgeoisie. But local businessmen – Indians and Chinese excepted – have not shown a great deal of self-reliance and aggressiveness and have, in the main, sought out areas where partnerships with foreign capital were available. As the new policy statement complains with a great deal of justification:

Regulatory policies designed to prevent complete economic penetration by highly efficient foreign enterprises well-endowed with capital, know-how and managerial and organizational skills, and to promote and develop a national economy are being resisted by some local businessmen. This is indeed strange, seeing that the very purpose of the policy is to protect and expand the area of decision-making (and profitable opportunity) for national enterprise – both public and private.

The only conceivable reason for this curious reaction, so different from that of the majority of Latin American and other Third-World businessmen, is the long strangulation of local initiative by our centuries-old colonial economy to the point where there is not a large enough number of national and nationally-oriented self-confident businessmen. Just as many among the dispossessed need to cast off their attitude of dependence on the Government, so do many of the business people have to cast off their inferiority complex vis-à-vis the large international corporation and come to realise that they are capable of doing much of the job of developing the country. They must make up their minds – do they belong to the Nation of Trinidad

73   TG, Oct. 16, 1970.

and Tobago or do they belong to the international enterprise? Do they belong to a country of the Third World or do they belong to the metropolis? It is in the last analysis a question of identity.[74]

The people's sector

The people's sector is the PNM's 'revolutionary' answer to the Black Power demands that the dispossessed sons of African slaves and Indian bonded-servants be encouraged and helped to own a piece of their patrimony. The sector will consist of small-scale agriculture, industry and transport and distribution activities, handicrafts, retail co-operatives, small guest houses, and the like. The people's sector differs from the national private sector in that its operations are labour-intensive, involve low capitalization, and emphasize self-reliance. At the peak of the Black Power Movement, a number of co-operative and other self-help schemes mushroomed, and to its credit the PNM has given them a measure of assistance with funds and technical assistance. According to the Prime Minister, through the people's sector 'we are giving the people ... a positive role in their economic development as Tanzania did in 1967 with its Arusha declaration of self-reliance.'[75]

The foreign sector

The basic economic policy of the PNM prior to 1970 was that the unemployment problem could only be solved by massive injections of foreign capital into urban infrastructure, tourism, and manufacturing industry. True, strong reservations had always been expressed about the unconscionable demands of foreign investors, but a great deal of the human and material resources of the state were mobilized to attract and retain their confidence. The new policy statement does not reject foreign capital, but insists it must now come in on a new basis: 'Aid and capital must become *adjuncts* to our internal efforts, not the centre page of our development strategy. Development ... can be achieved only by the people ... themselves.'[76]

Given the importance of the petroleum and petro-chemical industries which the PNM does not intend to nationalize but to regulate by legislative fiscal and administrative measures, the foreign sector will continue to be dominant, but the Party hopes that the native sectors will grow rapidly enough to overtake the non-petroleum foreign sector.

Unemployment and income distribution

The PNM now agrees that 1983 is no longer an appropriate target date for bringing the unemployment problem under control and that the events of

74 'Perspectives'.   75 *Ibid.*   76 *Ibid.*

February–April 1970 have made a solution more urgent. Hopes are being placed on the people's sector to generate a spirit of self-reliance and self-employment rather than of relying on the public and private sectors to provide wage-paying jobs. But the real solution to the problem is seen to be maximum utilization of land (about half the cultivable land is under-utilized or not used at all), the creation of agro-industries, and in greater exploitation of the media:

The real solution lies in a renewed commitment to rural development and the mo-bilisation of the people through an ideology which stresses the formation of indi-genous values and the rejection of metropolitan norms and through a change in the educational system and the mass media.

The educational system must now stress agriculture, rural development, and self-reliance. A reconstituted and revitalised radio and television service nationally oriented in the national interest has an important role to play in this regard. Rele-vant mass media services can have a profound effect in shaping values and per-ceptions and giving people confidence in themselves and the urge to 'do their own thing'.[77]

Reappraising Cuba

It is worth noting that Williams has abandoned his total hostility to Castro's Cuba, which he now views as the only Caribbean country which has a measure of real sovereignty over its economy; Cuba is also cited as the 'one bright spot' in the region where genuine racial integration is taking place. As Williams writes in his *From Columbus to Castro*:

Since the Revolution, Cuba has got rid of the traditional curse of the Caribbean – the sugar plantation – and she has got rid of the twentieth-century bane of the Third World – economic domination by metropolitan companies. She is also the first Caribbean country to have got rid of the legacy of slavery – the obsession with race and colour. Even in this respect she has been ahead of Haiti, where, ever since Independence, the mulatto élite has been in a privileged position vis-à-vis the black masses. In addition, she is the first Caribbean country (leaving aside the very small tourist economies) to have got rid of unemployment. Finally, whatever her econo-mic mistakes, she is the first Caribbean country to have mobilised the entire popu-lation in the task of national reconstruction.[78]

Williams also notes that Cuba has made significant breakthroughs in expanding the production of poultry, citrus, fish, vegetables, and stockfeeds, and acknowledges Cuba's achievements in educational development. Cuba's dependence on the Soviet Union is noted, but Williams agrees, that unlike its

77   *Ibid.*   78   London, 1970, pp. 508–9.

former involvement with the United States, it is a transitional phase through which Cuba has to go until it solves its foreign-exchange difficulties. Williams is not however anxious to import the Cuban model into Trinidad. 'The real tragedy of Cuba is that she has resorted to a totalitarian framework within which to ... transform her economy and society. ... The question arises as to whether there are alternative paths in the Caribbean to economic and social transformation ... [that are] less revolutionary and more gradualistic ... less totalitarian and more democratic than the Cuban path, but more autonomous and ultimately self-reliant than the Puerto Rican one.'[79] Williams believes that his blueprint provides that alternative.

'Perspectives' is, if anything, a confession of failure on the part of the PNM. Unsuspecting readers would be surprised to learn that it was the manifesto of a government which has been in power for fifteen years and not that of a party which was merely staking out its claims to power. The economic proposals in the document have been coolly received by the general population much to the chagrin of the PNM. There is a keen scepticism about the willingness and/or capacity of the Party to fulfil its numerous promises. The middle-class and business interests agree that there was a need to do something dramatic to defuse the politically explosive unemployment problem, and have grudgingly admitted that despite what they consider to be the economic unsoundness of the recent economic initiatives of the government, they have had the effect of making the PNM appear more purposeful and legitimate. But there has been a great deal of grumbling about Trinidad's tax structure which is said to be among the highest in the developing world, and about the 5 per cent unemployment surtax which was levied as of January 1, 1970, on the chargeable incomes of companies paying corporation tax and on individuals with chargeable incomes in excess of $10,000. As the *Guardian* complained, 'Our normally cautious local businessmen would be inclined to become over-cautious, not knowing when similar arbitrary demands may be made in the future. ... In its emphasis on making the small man a real man, the PNM runs the risk of alienating all other men in our society – men who have been hard-working and productive at a different level.'[80]

'PERSPECTIVES' AND ITS RADICAL CRITICS

'Perspectives' has been dismissed by the left with varying degrees of contempt. Some groups have accused the PNM of stealing their programme, of using the language of the left without any real understanding of what it in-

79   *Ibid.*, p. 510.   80   TG, June 7, 1970.

volves, of follow-fashioning and of making hasty concessions to the 'echoes of the People's Parliaments'. The Tapia Movement, of which Lloyd Best is the chief spokesman, accuses Williams of 'temporising and faltaying [faltering] on the vital question of our relations with metropolitan business ... for 13 ominous years'.[81] Best agrees that majority shareholding is an improvement on the old arrangements which involved total foreign ownership, but argues that:

Majority ownership is by no means the same thing as actual control. Real control comes from three things. The first is technological mastery of the intricacies of production, marketing and research. The second is the organisational capacity to translate paper plans into bricks and mortar. And the third is the moral authority to act in concert with the demands of the People's Parliament. The government does not have the technological command required to take hold of petroleum, sugar and banking. The talent and the skill do exist among Trinidadians and Tobagonians, but a climate of intrigue, favouritism and witch-hunting and chronic organisational disorder have completely frustrated the emergence of any solid corps of professional technocrats.

Many of our best minds just leave the country. Some stay and rot in the hope for better times. A favoured few become half-arsed politicians, accepting dozens of chairmanships and assignments in which they obviously can do no work save watch the political interest of the Doctor-Czar.

So after 14 years we do not even have a high-powered 'techretariat' for petroleum, our very line of life. If the bungling at the National Oil Company is anything like at BWIA and the Transport Corporation, we're in real trouble. At the Hilton and the Telephone Company we are still dependent on an anonymous who's who of alien experts. At Orange Grove, and now at Caroni, we have had to beg Tate & Lyle to continue management for us. This amounts to allowing them to take their cut even before the profits are computed. Technically incapable of using its legislative, administrative and diplomatic resources to advantage, the government is simply relieving London of putting up capital while we are now taking the risks ourselves.[82]

Best, who has emerged as the leading source of ideas for reforming the political and economic system, believes that what is needed is not simply the assumption of control, but an imaginative restructuring of the strategic institutions of the society to make them more relevant to the circumstances and needs of the common people. The emphasis in Tapia's programme has been put on localization. 'Localisation is not the same thing as nationalisation or expropriation. It may involve either or both or neither ... Economic control ... is to be achieved through a mixture of individual and co-operative ownership

81   *Tapia*, Aug. 9, 1970.   82   *Ibid.*

along with a certain amount of central and particularly local government participation in business ... The aim is to control not just to own ... government ownership has very little to do with popular control ... Ownership may of course be necessary for securing control. Where it is, localisation will demand ownership.'[83]

Tapia argues that the onus for economic transformation must rest on the private sector and on municipal bodies, and warns that nationalization by the central government would eventually lead to totalitarian control. What is really needed is that companies operating in Trinidad cease being mere branch plants, and take on a distinctly local personality; that decisions about pricing, investment, design, advertisement, income distribution, use of material, and technology be made locally; that majority shares be made available locally in forms and denominations that the common man can acquire; that accounts be kept in such a way as to facilitate scrutiny by a specialized secretariat; that certain key jobs be designated as national jobs to be held only by citizens; that bargaining and negotiation about the value of shares must be done openly; and that banking, insurance, and advertising services must be purchased locally.

With respect to banking, what is required, in addition to localization, is a reorganization of the system to encourage specialization into industrial, commercial, and household investment banking. Also needed are definitions of collateral which would allow ordinary people to raise loans against whatever valuables they are able to put up, and a system of personal references which would acknowledge the credit-worthiness of ordinary hard-working people of no special race, colour, education, occupation, or business connection. Tapia also advocates the introduction of a programme of banking services which would help ordinary people to make the link between household budgeting, saving, and investment in business. There also must be some integration of community sou-sous into the banking system through the use of mobile units and special saving schemes which use the sou-sous principle.[84]

Best believes that localization along the lines suggested would not destroy the confidence of investors who at the moment have to be 'playing games with

83   *Ibid.*, Aug. 9, 1970 (special Independence issue).
84   *Ibid.*, Sept. 28, 1970. Trinidad has to guard against creating a dual banking system in which the profitable operations are left to foreign banks while the various local banks undertake those that carry high risks and losses. The National Bank should be used as an instrument to force the private banks to become more relevant to the needs of the people as a whole. But in the long run there is no substitute for full control. The private banks are trying to stave off this by offering shares to the public and incorporating locally.

an administration that is itself playing possum and waiting to chop their heads off ... The ultimate aim of all these measures is to clear the field for a different kind of collaboration with the external world. Foreign investment and technology are sometimes useful. It is direct metropolitan investment which is anathema.'[85] What is needed are arrangements which would break the psychological and material barriers to the advance of Caribbean decision-makers.

It is worth noting that Tapia and the PNM are both agreed that rigid formulas of socialism and capitalism are irrelevant in Trinidad and Tobago and that slogans such as 'white power structure' and 'black power' are dangerous, misleading, and diversionary. There also seems to be agreement on the need to create a dynamic, self-confident, and socially responsible bourgeoisie as the major engine of growth and that nationalization for the sake of nationalization is not the proper response to feelings of black dispossession. Both share the belief that new investment opportunities must not lead to any further exaggeration of the dominant position presently enjoyed by local whites and 'high coloured', and that Africans and Indians must get a disproportionate share.[86] Tapia however believes that it is more competent to handle this transformation than the PNM, which, in its view, does no more than take over the slogans of the movement.

Unlike Tapia, which is a constructive as well as a destructive critic of Caribbean society, the National Joint Action Committee (NJAC) is still in its purely destructive phase. As the Committee notes in its publication, *Slavery to Slavery*:

We do not attempt to provide a blueprint for a new economic order. We do not believe in fostering the sense of helplessness nurtured in our people by colonialism which makes us feel that solutions for our problems can be handed down by a specially gifted élite. A New Society has to grow out of the conscious action of the people to change what exists. Our consciousness of what we want to create can only develop in relation to our understanding of what there is. What we attempt to do here is to assist the people to get a better understanding of one aspect of what there is – the economic dimension of our oppression.[87]

85 *Ibid.*, Aug. 9, 1971.
86 A recent study of the ethnic distribution of economic power in Trinidad and Tobago by Camejo shows that 53 per cent of the local business élite is white, 24 per cent 'off-white,' 10 per cent mixed, 9 per cent Indian, and 4 per cent African: 'The Indians have certainly not been moving like lightning. ... The impression that Indians are doing well is an African impression, but the Indians cannot be excited by their position in the whole picture.' 'Who Owns Trinidad and Tobago,' *ibid.*, Aug. 29, 1971.
87 Port of Spain, 1970, p. ii.

The NJAC, which now occupies the extreme left of the political spectrum, will accept nothing less than a complete take-over of the Caribbean economy by the Caribbean people. It wants a complete break with imperialism and the domination of white economic and political power. The NJAC catalogues in detail the extent to which the Trinidad economy is owned by foreign and local whites and complains that:

> There is not much left for us to scramble over. The Government under pressure from the people is engaging in some tokenism. They took a piece of Tate & Lyle on hire purchase, they bought a token bank and a token share of oil, they say. Nothing meaningful. And we can't even claim these things for Black People ...
> When the Government invests in oil and sugar they are going in to joint ventures with the foreigners; they are wasting our money to finance the pillars of a system which is anti-black. These companies operate as parts of large multi-national corporations. They base decisions on what is in the best interest of a whole international complex. So all this foolishness about setting up boards with local chairmen is game-playing, expensive game-playing, because we know none of the important decisions are made here anyway. What we want is ownership and control, not ownership in name. We are too much in need to be overpaying these people for company shares as political gimmicks.[88]

The NJAC rejects the PNM's attempts to promote black business as a trap. 'Black capitalism disguises white control just as Black government disguises colonialism. It is insulting to Black people to tell us that we should be contented with a little co-operative here, and a shop or store there on the fringes of the economy, when we know that this country is ours. Black business will have to operate within the rules of the system which means all our basic problems remain.'[89]

Offers of share-holding in foreign companies are also viewed as disguises that do nothing about the problem of control. 'There is no point in putting ready cash in the hands of people who will just use it to exploit us more effectively. Important decisions are not made by the local branches of foreign firms.' The 'game' of promoting 'black-faced management ... as buffers between the white controlling care and the Black dispossessed workers' is seen as further evidence of the contemptuousness of the white power structure:

> They like to put Black people as public relations officers and in other positions where they have to confront the workers and the public with decisions taken by their white bosses. This policy is for us to curse the Black stooge instead of the White exploiter.

88   *Ibid.*, pp. 1, 10.   89   *Ibid.*, p. 10.

Even when a Black man is made some manager or assistant manager, they empty the post of what little substance it had so the Black man carries the title without the responsibilities. This is the process we observe whenever an office formerly filled by a White expatriate is given over to a Black man.[90]

The NJAC is clearly not concerned with any minimum programme or with conventional politics. It wants the whole bread for the historically dispossessed and offers no blueprint for achieving this short of revolution. 'We need to destroy ... the system from its very foundations ... to get out of our economic mess (and) build a new society.'[91] In this new society, the people, educated by their revolutionary experience, will decide what will be produced and what technologies will be utilized. They will also understand that they will have to make sacrifices and give up acquired (imposed) habits. 'If we want the white man's goods, we have to use his technology and his capital ... and have his technicians running things for us. We remain slaves, unemployed, suffering.'[92]

Although NJAC does not wish to prescribe for the people, it does, however, have some idea of about 'what the people want'. These include: total ownership and control of land by the people; national ownership and control of the *entire* sugar industry including marketing and shipping; full utilization of lands in accordance with a national land-use plan; utilization of national resources by the people; industrialization linked to local agricultural production and the generation of local capital; diversification of trade links to reduce dependence; price controls and the transfer of the means of distribution to state and co-operative channels; abolition of unemployment in five years; free collective bargaining and unification of the Caribbean economy.[93]

There is no doubt that there is a powerful humanism running through the NJAC statement, and no one who understands the Caribbean dilemma can fail to have sympathy for its message or disagree with its analysis. It places great faith in the people's capacity to sacrifice and to be transformed by a revolutionary experience. Gone is the confidence in the charismatic saviours and bureaucratic élites that dominated the 1950s and early 1960s. But *Slavery to Slavery* is as pessimistic as it is Utopian: nothing will change unless everything is totally changed; nothing wholesome can be built in the Caribbean until the festering colonial edifice is completely pulled down. It was this revolutionary puritanism, this concern for the essentials of the colonial capitalist system, which did so much to unmask the hypocrisy and cant of Trinidadian society and its ruling élite and which brought Trinidad to the brink of revolution in April 1970. But it was this same romanticism which in the end fright-

90   *Ibid.*, p. 11.   91   *Ibid.*, p. 11.   92   *Ibid.*, p. 12.
93   *Policy Proposals for Liberation*, San Fernando, Dec. 1970.

ened the population, including many of the dispossessed who had marched behind NJAC, back into the tired arms of Dr Williams and the PNM.

Given the PNM's record of broken promises, there is no reason to believe that 'Perspectives for a New Society' will fare any better than the 'People's Charter'. What is needed now in Trinidad and the Caribbean are some firm decisions about what part of the economy will be allowed to remain in foreign hands, what will be reserved to nationals, and what will be completely or partially controlled by the state. At a minimum, there should be full control of sugar, the domestic distribution of petroleum products, and of banking and insurance institutions through which so much of the savings of the community is leaked abroad. Control should also involve the maximum use of local management, except where special types of technical skills are unavailable.

The various pioneer industry incentive schemes should also be drastically modified and made available only to firms using labour-intensive technology or firms that are locally owned and controlled. The type of tourist industry which has ruined the north coast of Jamaica and which threatens to turn the entire English-speaking Caribbean into a playground for North America must also be de-emphasized. Given the history of race relations in the Caribbean, a policy of touting for tourists is bound to have all kinds of latent sociological consequences which will exacerbate the race problem. Tourism in the Caribbean inevitably reinforces the old colonial tradition in which blacks catered to a white leisure class. The meagre economic returns (in real terms) of tourism simply do not justify the social costs.

All observers of the Trinidad scene agree that the answer to the job question must ultimately be found in optimum use of the land, and that given the urban bias of our society and the powerful influences exerted by the North-Atlantic culture zone, the restructuring of the educational system and the media must be given the highest priority. All energies and resources must now be focused onto these areas.

Trinidadians are a very inventive and highly trained people, but a great deal of this talent migrates in search of opportunity. Even more migrate mentally because of frustration and lack of purpose. Perhaps an opportunity to build a new society might mobilize some of this energy. Talent will no doubt migrate as sacrifices are demanded, but this will be more than compensated for by the return of those who, tired of the strain and humiliation of living in America and Britain, will grasp at an opportunity to help in building a community in which it can truly be said that Black Power (in its broadest and most tolerant sense) is enthroned. The whole history of Trinidad and the Caribbean demands that the enterprise of emancipation and decolonization begun over a century-and-a-half ago be brought to fruition before the end of the century.

25
Parties and the political process

In terms of the criteria which are usually associated with a pluralist democracy – a competitive party system, a neutral bureaucracy, free-wheeling interest groups, a free press, recognition of the rule of law, and an independent judiciary – it may be said that the political system of Trinidad and Tobago is a democratic one, more so than most political systems of the 'third world'. Western social scientists who specialize in the clever art of ranking countries in terms of their political development usually place Trinidad and Tobago and the other English-speaking Caribbean states in the democratic category. Scholars who know the area more intimately, however, are nevertheless very much aware that the democratic revolution in the West Indies is 'unfinished business'.[1] As Gordon Lewis notes, there is still little 'conception of Government in the national sense. Government, for most people, is something from which to extract special privileges denied to others. Authority is ... laughed at. ... There is little understanding of the idea of creative partnership between citizen and state.'[2]

That this state of affairs still remains more than a decade after the PNM launched its 'revolution of intelligence' is not altogether surprising. In the years that followed its electoral victory in 1956, the PNM did make a valiant attempt to create an educated and participant democracy. At public rallies throughout the country, at weekend schools, and at seminars, the Party tried to give the people a wider perspective on the problems that faced the com-

---

1 Wendell Bell (ed.), *The Democratic Revolution in the West Indies*, Cambridge, Mass., 1967, p. 225.
2 Gordon Lewis, *The Growth of the Modern West Indies*, New York, 1968, p. 393.

munity. A careful attempt was also made to work closely with the Party's Policy Advisory Committee, which in turn was fed by a number of sub-committees. But there is little evidence that the people, or even the member-ship of the Party, were ever allowed to decide anything. The Party very quickly became an electioneering machine, a sounding board, and a legitimat-ing agent for decisions taken by the élite or by the Leader himself.[3] The flow of traffic was almost always from the cabinet to the Party, and rarely the other way around.[4] The initiative came from the cabinet partly because the prestigious and talented leadership was concentrated in that body. The extra-govern-mental party lacked the competence and experience to function autonomously. The speed with which the Party came to power also prevented it from develop-ing a personality of its own independent of the government.[5]

Non-governmental members of the Party do not agree with these explana-tions, however. They feel that there was talent outside the government, but that there was a sort of tacit agreement that there should be no opposition to the political leader in the interest of unity. It is claimed that the first chairman of the Party, Sir Learie Constantine, had taken the position that Williams was a 'god-send' to the Party and the country, and that he should be allowed to 'soar' without constriction. Williams was to be warned and advised, but was not to be openly fought if he insisted on a particular course of action. He was also to be shielded from attacks from the rank and file lest the Party become enveloped in internecine strife. Party leaders are said to have gone along with the Constantine thesis, but now feel that it was a mistake to have allowed the Party to become little more than an extension of the personality of Williams.

3 The Party's election committee warned as early as 1958 that 'We are today ... in retrospect wondering whether in setting our plans to the capture of all the seats of Government – National and Local – we have not abdicated the role we assigned ourselves – "The Education of the People" – thus sowing the seeds of our destruc-tion. For while the primary purpose of the rank and file of a party may be the winning of elections, in this stage of our history, it is more important to associate the Political Party with the life of the community. The daily integration of the activities of the movement with community life should be the aim of the Party. The winning of elections should be subsidiary to that objective.' 'Files of the PNM's third annual convention', 1958. PNM Headquarters, Port of Spain.

4 As the public relations secretary of the Party noted, 'The Policy Advisory Committee is purely advisory to the Cabinet and is summoned at the instance of its Chairman, the Premier, on such matters as the Cabinet deems fit.' TG, Dec. 19, 1969.

5 Williams recognized this weakness: 'The difficulty with which the Party is faced has been its repeated successes and the speed with which it has been built up. In other countries, other parties have been built more slowly, and they have had time to build up their foundations more securely. The task that lies before us is to ensure that the gains are not dissipated by hasty action or complacency.' PNM *Weekly*, July 1, 1957.

A number of other factors also contributed to the ascendancy of the cabinet and governmental bureaucracy over the Party and the general public: the nature of the political system, the personality of the political leadership, the specialized nature of the political situation, and the deferential orientation of public opinion.

THE NATURE OF THE POLITICAL SYSTEM

Without really determining whether it was the system most suitable to the circumstances of Trinidadian society, the new régime took it for granted that it should operate according to the canons of the 'pattern state' at Westminster.[6] Inevitably this meant that the Party in the country had to take a secondary role in relation to the Party in government. It was easy for the cabinet to establish dominance over the Party, since it could always be argued that key decisions had to be made in cabinet and announced in the Legislature before they came before public and Party scrutiny. The requirements of official secrecy could also be invoked to exclude the Party from the crucial periods of the decision-making process.

It did not follow, of course, from the mere acceptance of the Westminster model that the Party would be pushed into the background. It was quite possible for the new élite to institutionalize methods for the communication of Party and public opinion to arenas of public policy-making before the cabinet itself had taken a stand on any issue. All that is being said here is that the adoption of the Westminster model made it easy for the new élite to slip, perhaps unconsciously, into the bureaucratic methods of the old colonial system. The output structures of the system quickly gained ascendancy over input structures in the nation and within the Party, which had created an elaborate network of safeguards to ensure against this very possibility.

Whereas the old ruling class had been able to use the authority of the imperial power to control, directly or indirectly, the entire system, including the structures of local government, statutory corporations, and other quasi-independent agencies, the new élite invoked the authority of the Party and the people to do the very same thing. In the name of administrative efficiency and financial rationalization, the system has in fact become even more centralized than it was before. But these developments cannot be properly understood without reference to the characteristics of the élite itself.

6   While it is agreed that the constitution under which the PNM took power made this somewhat inevitable, it was possible for them to devise arrangements for the public to participate more actively in the decision-making process.

PERSONALITY AND POLITICAL LEADERSHIP

Two forces have always been struggling for dominance within the PNM and very often within the minds of the same people – the one ultra-populistic, the other élitist. The first view held that the masses in Trinidad were, 'like the Athenians', highly sophisticated politically. Given the necessary stimulation and opportunity, they could make public policy for themselves. To quote Williams, 'I can say without fear of contradiction, except by those who stand to lose by it, that the political intelligence of the masses of the people is astonishingly high, their political instincts astonishingly sound, and that they are the best and most vital students I have encountered in any university in my experience.'[7]

The second view, and the one which gained dominance, held that the Trinidad masses were inert and politically uneducated. There was no public opinion in Trinidad. What was needed was a new intellectually oriented regime which would educate and organize public opinion through mass educational meetings, pamphlets, newspapers, and other media of propaganda. The élite would emancipate the masses. It was an essentially Marxist-Leninist image of the political party to which, according to C.L.R. James, Williams became exposed during his student days at London and Oxford during the 1930s.

But it is not necessary to go that far to explain Williams' political methods: his own intellectual gifts and his personality are more germane to the issue. Williams is a man driven by an overweening belief in his rectitude, wisdom, and historical mission. Because of his prodigious research talents, his amazing capacity for analyzing, organizing, and articulating information, and for manipulating people, he easily dominates the political stage. His essentially monopolistic personality also makes it difficult for him to share leadership readily. Williams has an inordinate capacity for inflicting deprivations upon himself, though he complains bitterly that it is the Party and public which mercilessly force him into playing so many roles. The personality dimension cannot be enlarged upon here;[8] it is mentioned only because it is one of the keys to an understanding of the decision-making apparatus.

Intellectually, Williams is firmly committed to the democratic ideal, and he goes to great lengths to conceal the fact that he is the chief decision-maker.

7 *The Case for Party Politics in Trinidad and Tobago*, Public Affairs Pamphlet no. 4, 1955, p. 12.
8 Colin Rickards has also drawn attention to Williams' personality structure, to his 'dogmatism, fanaticism and his intolerance. Williams is a man who needs an "oppressor". ... For the fire-eater of Woodford Square, a real or imagined "oppressor" upon whom to vent his wrath is not only a necessity, but a way of life.' *Caribbean Power*, London, 1963, p. 131.

His political methods are designed to keep everyone off guard by a seemingly deliberate confusion in the lines of authority. Persons and instrumentalities are manipulated as the situation demands; sometimes it is the cabinet, at other times the planning commission; sometimes the policy committee of the Party, at times the general council or the convention. In the process the masses are left out, except in so far as they are required to provide logistic support for the Party high command. Some Cabinet ministers have also complained bitterly about what one referred to as 'smokescreen government'.[9]

Every Cabinet member is aware that it is the political leader who commands the mass following, and no one interested in political survival or popular legitimacy really dares to push opposition too far. This is not to say that there is no opposition to Williams in the Cabinet or in the Party, but such opposition almost always functions within well-defined limits.[10] If the leader is known to feel strongly enough about a particular issue, the Party and Cabinet usually go along. The need for loyalty, sincerity, or discipline is readily invoked to silence 'recalcitrants' or 'individualists'. Williams also had a tendency in earlier years, not uncommon among leaders of movement régimes, to threaten resignation whenever he felt thwarted or harassed. The community or Party was reminded that he was performing an indispensable role which he was only too anxious to give up so that he might return to writing his delayed history of the West Indies.

Critics of Williams have accused him of instituting a personal monarchy and deliberately creating an image of an omnipotent superman, one who could keep all the levers of the system going effectively. In their view, however, it has been activity without purpose. Adrian Espinet and Jacques Farmer have put it aptly:

This paradox of energy turning pointlessly on itself is the crux of the problem about Williams' baffling exercise of statesmanship – an exercise that might precisely be described as one of controlled ineffectuality. The Prime Minister's hands

---

9   See the *cri de cœur* of Winston Mahabir, former Minister of Health. What Mahabir says of himself, that he was in a 'kind of political indentureship relationship', is true of many other ministers. 'The Real Eric Williams', *Express*, Jan. 5, 1969. Cf. the complaint of Benedict Wight about the PNM's tendency to govern 'by surprise'. *Ibid.*, Nov. 28, 1968.

10   David Nelson, a former Party colleague of Dr Williams, who was himself an early casualty, remarked that, 'Fear of the personal consequences of open disagreement with, or efforts to control, the political leader is today the only neutralizer of the poison which is slowly eating into the PNM system.' It is as true today as it was in 1959. Williams is a genius at alternating bluster and charm to hold cabinet and party members in line, and has often applied the knife to ministers who cross him. Exile to embassies or to less important cabinet or civil service positions have been an effective part of his armory. TG, Jan. 25, 1959.

are full of the buttons and the levers ... and he is visibly working them with a rare energy. Our problem is therefore to discover why all this apparatus is connected to nothing more creative than a treadmill.

The analysis must begin, then, with a look at the apparatus itself. The Prime Minister virtually exercises a 'pussonal' monarchy which in fact, if not in principle, comes closer to the republican presidential type than to the nominal Westminster cabinet model. No Commonwealth prime minister, not even Nkrumah at the height of his powers, has held so much personal control – direct and indirect – over the portfolios of his government. Finance Planning, Development, Local Government – all fall more or less directly within his competence. A number of them he manages, at one remove, through a cardboard Minister of State. By a variety of devices he succeeds in retaining the initiative in External Affairs, West Indian Affairs, and Labour. Internal Security, Defence and the Civil Service are his by virtue of their status as co-ordinating functions of government. Williams, in short, is the only begetter and we may fairly summarize his position by saying that no decision is too large for his single capacities, or too small to be beneath his notice.

The very scope of his omnipotence calls for enormous resources of energy and ability, and there can be no doubt that Williams brings them abundantly to the task. As a Prime Minister, he has varied the dubious formula of *primus inter pares* to a far more certain (though not always clear) one of the first among unequals – a patent fact which has led some observers to the view that every Member of the Cabinet is Williams' personal creation, his man to make or break by private fiat.

This view is almost certainly mistaken, and in fact the evidence for a counter-dependence of Williams on certain of his 'men' is as much there as the evidence for their dependence on him.

Williams, as we have seen, is certainly in charge; but in charge of what? There are strings on all those levers – the strings of sectional interests. Those strings cannot be broken not because they are strong ... but because the little king has failed to initiate the kind of political system that makes real control possible.[11]

Of the whole cabinet, only four ministers have had the ability to stand up to the Prime Minister. Two of them, Mr Gerald Montano and Mr John O'Halloran, have had a measure of indispensability because of their useful connections with the business community. Their resignation from the cabinet in May 1970 (probably forced by the Prime Minister) suggests that Williams has now become convinced that they and the groups they represented have become a liability to the Party. Mr Kamaluddin Mohammed, whose resignation has often been demanded, is of critical importance because he is the visible symbol of the PNM's alliance with the Moslem community.[12] Mr

11 *Tapia*, Nov. 16, 1969.
12 Mr Mohammed, a popular personality among the Moslem community, has survived numerous attempts to shunt him into political oblivion.

A.N.R. Robinson, the Deputy Prime Minister and Deputy Political Leader of the Party, was until 1970 considered sacrosanct, since he was generally identified as the leader of the left-of-centre members of the Party. Robinson's resignation in April 1970 means that the Party has now been deprived of the only remaining tenuous link which it had with the radical community.[13]

THE SPECIALIZED NATURE OF THE POLITICAL SITUATION

It must be noted that Williams and the Cabinet were virtually allowed to monopolize the political system. For the most part it was *not* a case of an élite seizing power from popular elements, as discontented intellectuals and some Party members like to claim. The documents of the Party are full of evidence to indicate that the rank and file deferred to the superior judgment of the leadership, and to the political leader in particular. Time and time again the Party simply abdicated its authoritative role with the declaration that the leader could be entrusted to make the best possible settlement on behalf of the nation and Party.[14] As one senior Party member wrote, 'The PNM rank and file have not yet reached the stage where the desire to participate in top level discussions is extremely pressing. Party members are satisfied so far with the conduct of Government business.'[15]

Generally speaking, annual conventions are not times of serious business, but occasions when the Party faithful from all parts of the country meet to exchange gossip and greeting. Even small bodies like the General Council invariably just listen to the political leader and other leading members of the Party and ratify what has already been decided in the 'corridors of power'. One cannot understand decision-making in the PNM without appreciating the strong moral influence which Williams has had over the membership.

13 Robinson began as a mainstream post-colonial politician, but by 1966 had moved towards the left of the Party. He authored the controversial Finance Act discussed in chapter 24 and never forgave the Prime Minister for giving in to the pressures of the business community. He has become identified with a policy of greater economic nationalism and gave moral support to the Black Power Movement.

14 A good example of this was the resolution on the Federation approved in September 1961: 'This Special Convention expresses its complete satisfaction with the handling of the question of a West Indian Federation by its Political Leader up to the present moment, and entrusts the future handling of this matter to its Political Leader in consultation with such units of the Party as he may see fit, and requires him to report to the Party on this matter as soon as it is politically proper and wise or in the best interest of the country to do so, and further that there should be no discussion on the topic of Federation until after the General elections.' Files of the PNM special convention, 1961.

15 *Nation*, May 19, 1961.

It should also be noted that the modernizing process involves the spread of achievement values, and inevitably brings to the fore the possessors of skills needed to manage the new society:

The establishment of a legal rational system is the end product of the process of modernization. As society becomes rationalized, a specialization of roles takes place. Specialization of roles requires the development of formal rules and a hierarchical structure for the enforcement of these rules and the settlement of conflicts. These pressures cluster together to dictate a bureaucratization of society with an increased power position for members of the formal bureaucracy. As this occurs, the nonrational (ideological) components of the political milieu tend to be dissipated. The political style tends to become pragmatic.[16]

Modernization demands the existence of a creative Faustian élite willing and able to bear the risks and strains of leadership.[17] Some such awareness predisposed the leadership and masses to de-emphasize the populist ingredients of the PNM ideology.

But while it is generally true that the rank-and-file willingly deferred to Party and government specialists, there was always a small element, usually 'out' members of the élite, who were very critical of the 'leave it to the Doc' attitude. They felt that such a development was destroying the vitality of Party organs and groups which were becoming atrophied for want of purpose; this was especially true in Party strongholds. They were also concerned about the leadership's cavalier treatment of party opinion. And there were occasions when Party abdication was not spontaneous, but came as a result of manipulative persuasion by the Party élite, who argued that some things needed to be done with dispatch and secrecy, and with room to manoeuvre. At such times the Party was treated as though it were a hindrance, especially when action involved the compromising of ideological goals. And frequently, when consultation was conceded, it was either ceremonial or made imperative because the leadership felt it was strategically necessary to obtain mass support for new policy departures.

There were frequent complaints about the dominance of ministerial

16   Carl Beck, 'Bureaucracy and Political Development in Eastern Europe', Joseph La Palombara (ed.), *Bureaucracy and Political Development*, Princeton, 1963, p. 270. Beck disagrees with this thesis as it applies to eastern Europe.

17   Radical intellectuals do not accept this thesis. They feel that the bureaucratic approach to modernization is inappropriate in the Caribbean context, considering the plantation legacies of the society. They argue that the situation requires an ideological solution which will allow the large majority of the West Indian people to become actively involved in the business of running the society and of creating a stable new order.

elements in the major policy-making organs of the Party, that the General Council was too large and unwieldy as a democratic instrument, too satellitic and pliable, and that those who disagreed with the leadership were not permitted to bring their differences out into the open. Rebels in the Party felt that its hierarchy, elected for five years, had become fossilized, self-satisfied, and timid.[18] They were accused of caring more for their own standing with the political leader than for the real problems of the mass Party. Members were also unhappy about the failure of the hierarchy, deliberate or otherwise, to provide the Party with important documents which were expected to form the basis of policy decisions in sufficient time to allow for proper study and thought. The writer has witnessed the extent to which this strategy makes it possible for the platform to seize the initiative from the floor of the convention, which is invariably forced to accept the manipulative interpretations of the political leader, without much chance of 'answering back'. The short time given to the consideration of policy issues, especially resolutions from the rank-and-file makes it difficult if not impossible for the Party to maintain a sufficient degree of self-direction. The same complaint has been made even of the proceedings of the General Council: 'So packed becomes the agenda, and so protracted the meetings, that intelligent group participation throughout an entire session is barely possible. General Council members are held responsible for decisions which they did not really make, and this leads to frustration.'[19]

Many members are also unhappy about the weakness of the Party's infor-

---

18 At the third annual convention, for example, the Party passed a motion to the effect that 'The Annual Convention is the supreme body of the Party, and as such its directives are to be complied with all due speed and attention.' In most cases opposition elements waged their struggles around constitutional issues or over the standing orders which were the ruling of the platform and not of the convention. Such provisions as the five-minute speaking rule at conventions and the finality of the chair's ruling were always opposed by this element on the floor. It was felt that the Chairman of the Party should not be a minister and that the General Council and the Policy Advisory Committee should be able to convene without ministerial initiative. There were also complaints that ministers were not attending General Council meetings or paying sufficient attention to the affairs of their constituency groups. One member warned, 'The strength of the Party lies in the thousands of little people who have laboured to build up, in the name of the PNM, small voluntary groups engaged in community activity. ... It is at this level one finds the hopes, aspirations, fears and frustrations of Trinidad and Tobago. ... In every sense it is a world in itself and it is not surprising that representatives who become PNM representatives without a period of work among groups, become bored with the trivialities of this level in contrast to "important" Government business [and] find themselves divorced from the hearts and minds of the people they represent.' Lynn Beckles, *Nation*, July 7, 1961.

19 Information supplied by a general council member to this writer.

mation services, about the fact that very often they learn of new policy from the public news media, and consequently have no superior information with which to combat distortions which might appear in such reports. Party groups, especially in the rural areas, remain inert from a similar lack of information and stimulation. This discontent can easily be detected in numerous resolutions submitted to conventions, one of which reads: 'Whereas it is found that too many important party matters, when discussed at hierarchy level, are kept secret, and whereas party members are never in a position to discuss these matters authoritatively, be it resolved that this Conference recommends to the Annual Convention that this Policy be abolished immediately, and plans made to familiarize party members with information before it is made public.'[20]

It is clear then that two tendencies are at work within the Party: the one deferential and satisfied; the other assertive and concerned about what members believe is the Party's real failure to improve on the performance of old-régime parties in the vital area of mass-level democracy. Williams himself has been a stern critic of the PNM. In an address to a Party convention in 1958 he admitted that the Party had been subordinated to the Movement and the government.[21] At other times he complained of the corruption, nepotism, factionalism, and individualism that strangles the Party as well as the 'lack of training ... political immaturity, complacency, and gross absenteeism of some of its principal representatives'.[22] 'The weakness of [its] organization weakens our efforts in every sphere of government and social life.'[23] The Party has to be made to loom larger in the life of the community so that 'legislators can introduce the boldest and most far-seeing legislation, confident that there can be no serious resistance because all reactionaries and disruptive elements will be aware of [its] strength in the population surrounding them'.[24]

To achieve this, the Party has to live a life of its own, to rely less on its legislative arm, and more on its own resources:

The Party must have its own 'Cabinet' and its own 'Ministers' ... who in calibre and in status must be on par with the legislative representatives of the Party. ... Building ... the Party cannot be carried out by legislators. If they attempt to do so, the only result will be that the scope and possibility of the Party will be cut down to the size which suits such time and energy and thought as the legislators can spare

20 Party Group no. 17, St George West, to the fourth annual convention, 1960.
21 *Perspective for Our Party*, Port of Spain, 1958, p. 7. This pamphlet clearly reflects the influence of C.L.R. James on Williams. It is very possible that James wrote the pamphlet. James in fact hinted as much to the author.
22 'Address to the Party Convention,' Sept. 24, 1960. Files of the PNM, p. 10.
23 *Ibid.*
24 *Ibid.*

for it, and you know how precious little time and energy and thought some legislators have spared for the Party.[25]

Williams also urged that greater effort be made to develop powerful press and propaganda machinery, and exhorted party members to function as leaders in all progressive causes and movements in the community.

In the pre-Independence era the Party was never able to summon the resources to reform itself, since most of its top officials were members of the governmental network and fully preoccupied with the anti-colonial struggle.[26] The lower political temperature that followed Independence made possible a serious attempt to restructure and re-invigorate the Party. In 1963 the constitution was revised substantially and a sizable core of new officers was returned to the Central Executive and Policy Committee. With Williams' encouragement this element made a praiseworthy attempt to inject some dynamism into the life of the organization and to make it an initiating agent. The Party organ which is under its control became somewhat more aggressive, and legislators began taking a greater interest in Party activity. Greater emphasis was also given to political education through lectures and seminars, and Williams found time to write informative book reviews and commentaries on national and international events for the benefit of readers of the Party weekly. Several important policy issues were also referred to the Party for study and recommendation, and some of the reports have been remarkably competent.

Despite all this activity, the PNM remained an essentially bureaucratic organization. In a comparative comment on politics in Cuba and Trinidad, Williams himself agreed that 'the capacity to enthuse thousands of people ... represent(s) one of the most decisive advantages which the Castro movement

25 *Ibid.*, pp. 9–10.
26 In an address to a party convention on September 5, 1962, Williams noted: 'You have all the confusion in Trinidad concentrated in the PNM. The PNM instead of being representative of the best in the country, instead of blazing the trail for the rest of the country, becomes nothing more than a gigantic conglomeration of all the vices in the country. You have too much in Trinidad concentrated in too few hands, too much responsibility placed on the too few shoulders.' Nine years later, the Political Leader was making similar criticisms to the Party's fifteenth convention. Williams complained about party feuds and intrigues, inefficiency, and irresponsibility. 'At too many levels of the party, a member is anxious to take on obligations of office, and then promptly proceeds to do no work at all or to do it in a slipshod and erratic manner. The selection of a party member for some national responsibility is no guarantee that the party policy will be carried out. It is the party member more than any other who is likely to go about the country saying that the Prime Minister wishes this done or wishes that not done, when the Prime Minister hasn't the faintest idea of the matter in hand and has had no discussions whatsoever with the party member.' TG, Sept. 26, 1971.

has had over the PNM', though he notes that the comparison is not quite fair, since 'Castro's procedures' and a 'one-party dictatorial state' give him decisive advantages in organizing the society.[27] The type of orthodox, pragmatic, and bureaucratic politics to which the PNM is wedded makes it difficult for it to appeal to the population for idealism and sacrifice. This indeed has been the major criticism of radical intellectuals who for the most part remain completely alienated from the Party.

During the latter months of 1964 Williams embarked on a dramatic 'meet the Party' tour in a determined attempt to reinvigorate languishing party groups. During the meetings, Party members complained that the leadership provided no incentives to encourage dynamism, that Party members got no special privileges, patronage, or information. Nothing was ever done to give them a distinctive role in the community. Williams admitted that liaison between Party and government left much room for improvement but noted that in many cases Party members themselves were to be blamed. Members, he noted, were not sufficiently vigilant, and, judging from their complaints, often seemed less informed than the general public on policy issues. They were urged to make a greater effort to follow the activities of their legislators through the medium of the daily and Party press, and through government announcements. If Party members felt that certain information was not being revealed to them, they should be alert enough to infer that political strategy or parliamentary protocol prevented disclosure. No government was completely free to reveal everything it had in mind at a particular time.

Williams also defended the record of members of government, noting that many of them were genuinely bogged down with affairs of state and were unable to make monthly oral reports to their constituency groups, as the Party's constitution prescribed. He suggested that a written report be acceptable when visits were not feasible, or that a Party senator be accepted as a substitute. It was also agreed that there was a pressing need for constituency offices on a non-partisan basis, through which citizens could make representations to the proper authorities.

Despite promises that greater efforts would be made to reinvigorate the Party, very little progress was made. A similar 'meet the Party' tour in 1968 revealed a more or less identical state of affairs. Williams confessed to the eleventh annual convention that he was 'deeply disturbed by the inactivity of many party groups and the unfinancial status of many party members. ... It is clear that many groups come to life only to select candidates for elections.' The Political Leader made the same promises he had made in 1964 – greater

27 There is no equivalent in Trinidad to Cuba's mass adult-education programme or to the mobilization of youth into distinctive groupings such as the Pioneers.

central scrutiny and stimulation of group activity, more training and involvement for youth and women members, and closer liaison between elected representatives and constituencies – and pledged to get 'very rough with those who do no more than use their positions for intrigue and self-aggrandisement'.[28]

In Williams' view, the fundamental difficulty affecting the Party was the passivity of the individual member, who, like the rest of the community, was more interested in what the Party could do for him than in what he could do for the Party or the community. The problem, he believes, stems from the laziness of the Trinidadian, his general lack of responsibility, his tendency to say 'man, I can't be bothered'.[29] Whereas in the pre-Independence period belief in the new world and the legitimacy of the PNM was enough to stimulate militancy, enthusiasm is now at an extremely low level. Attendance at unit meetings is scanty and the same holds true for public meetings. The 'University of Woodford Square' has in fact not heard from its once popular professor for many years. One of the complaints of the former Deputy Leader of the Party was that it had ceased to function meaningfully both in private and in public:

I could not be frank at a meeting of the central executive or the general council or the annual convention of the PNM. They have all been asphyxiated. I certainly cannot do so at the cocktail parties to which I am not invited even if I wished to go and which have become the substitute for the constitution of the PNM.

For almost four years since the General Election of 1966, the elected government and the ruling party held no public meetings except in the local government election of 1968 when they had to be suspended as they were a disaster. There were no press conferences by the head of government and hardly any radio broadcasts or television appearances. Even these, however, would be inadequate for a population that aspires to the closest possible identity between the voter and the elected government.[30]

After thirteen years in power and until it was badly shaken up by the Black Power crisis in 1970, the PNM remained an empirical, fairly efficient (in a bureaucratic sense) and disciplined organization, at least when compared to parties in the Caribbean and other developing areas. It avoided one of the weaknesses that bedevils the DLP, squabbling in public. Individuals who disagreed with the leadership, left, or were led out of the fold, but the general public remained largely unaware of the internal crises, which on occasion have been very serious. It is not an incorrupt organization, as Williams himself admits, but the level of corruption is much lower than one would expect from a

28 *Express*, Sept. 29, 1968.   29 *Nation*, July 24, 1964.
30 *Express*, Aug. 31, 1970.

party that has been in power for so long. Williams was on solid ground when he boasted that the PNM had managed to bring some decency, some order, some good sense, and some rational outlook to political activities in Trinidad. It is an achievement of which he, as its principal author, can be justly proud. Few dominant parties in the 'third world' can match its record.[31]

But the PNM has now lost a great deal of its former coherence and unity. Disagreement is open, and the deference typical of the earlier years has begun to evaporate. As Jacques Farmer notes, 'Within the Party, not only is there now an amount of "back-chat" and minor rebellion that was hitherto inconceivable, but the organization itself is in considerable disarray and "on the run". Grass-roots opinion, long frustrated by opinions and structures imposed from above, constantly erupts to make a mockery of the propagated view of a monolithic structure.'[32]

THE DEFERENTIAL ORIENTATION OF PUBLIC OPINION

The deference of Party members was a reflection of similar attitudes among the general population. Outside of the urban areas there is very little articulate public opinion in Trinidad and Tobago. In the countryside, the new citizen is not aware of the differences between the role he is now expected to fulfil and that which he performed in the past. The prevailing norm is still civic incompetence, a feeling of powerlessness to affect the direction of public policy. The old metropolitan bureaucracy which revolved around the Governor and the imperial civil service has simply been replaced by another local metropolitan bureaucracy. Except perhaps where public utilities and educational issues are concerned, few people organize themselves into pressure groups, write letters, or petition their members in the Legislature. They are more likely to go over the heads of their elected representatives to the Prime Minister, who to them is the real source of power; and when such efforts are made, there is on the whole, little continuity or follow-through. People sulk or withdraw support; hardly ever is discontent translated into continuous political activity.

That this should be true of the rural citizen is hardly surprising. But until recently the same type of civic inactivity was also widespread in the urban areas with their highly sophisticated middle-class population. Apart from the leadership of organized labour, which openly challenges the government, the organized political opposition, and the small radical group at the University, there

---

31   As one minister boasted, 'Only two organizations have the discipline of the PNM – the Catholic Church and the Communist party.' It is a discipline based not on physical violence or the threat of it, but on the persuasive and manipulative ability of Dr Williams as well as a widespread fear of incurring his displeasure.

32   *Tapia*, Dec. 21, 1969.

was little vocal political opinion on general issues. There were a substantial number of pressure groups which made their influence felt when the interests of their clientele were affected, but the middle class was extremely inarticulate in public. There were grumbles in private, but rarely did one hear voices raised in protest against violations of civil liberties, public immorality, or arrogance on the part of the bureaucracy or the political élite. The same passive attitude which was typical of the middle class in the colonial period continued to prevail in the era of self-government.

Part of this attitude can certainly be explained by the fact that many are civil servants, and as such cannot criticize the regime in public. There is also a widespread fear of incurring the anger or displeasure of the Prime Minister, who does not take kindly to 'disloyalty' or 'ill discipline'. C.L.R. James, who is at times unfairly harsh in his criticisms of the middle class, just the same understands their plight: 'One of the most precious heritages – the most precious – of the British connection is their ... instinctive, not merely legal, recognition of the right to differ without being penalized. Even before Independence, that is fast disappearing; you bend the knee, and keep it bent, or you are offered the choice, blows or a Government position.'[33]

Williams' 'if you don't like it, get to hell outa here' attitude terrified many into silence, especially those whose present economic existence and future well-being depended upon the grace of the political élite. The smallness of the community, which made authority close, and the number of job outlets in the private sector limited, only served to reinforce this timidity. It was an open secret that the ostensibly neutral Public Service Commission was manipulated by the politicians.

But fear and timidity, and the requirements of the civil service, do not entirely explain the attitude of many who did not really stand to lose much by voicing criticism. The fact is that among a large section of the Negro and mixed population there was an attitude of leave the Doctor alone. This was especially so in the pre-Independence period; in public as in private, criticism of the Premier was recognized not as the right of the citizen but as an expression of a fractious and unmannerly spirit.[34] The Premier was regarded essentially as

---

33 *Federation: We Failed Miserably*, Port of Spain, 1961, p. 3. Dr Winston Mahabir also complained about Williams' 'callousness' and his 'chronic need to make and break human beings' which, he notes, 'was always disquieting to those in orbit' around him. *Express*, Jan. 5, 1969.
34 Trinidad's proletarian poet laureate echoed the mood of the Negro masses to their beloved 'William the Conqueror' when he sang:
    'Leave the dam Doctor,
    He ain't trouble all you.
    Leave the dam Doctor;
    What he do, he well do.'

the old colonial governor, who was to be congratulated and flattered but not criticized[35]; those who did not share this point of view, the people of European or Chinese stock in particular, either stayed aloof and sullen or compromised the legitimacy of their contributions by open partisanship to the DLP. The absence until recently of a vibrant daily press and university community, and the almost total absence of any journals devoted to serious political analysis, only added to the general political blandness of the community.

Since 1965 more aggressive demands have been made for a fundamental democratization of the political system. University radicals and trade unionists have been in the vanguard of this movement, but public-spirited individuals and religious and professional groups are also becoming more concerned about the increasing tendency towards PNM authoritarianism. As Dennis Solomon has noted, the fear of being openly critical is beginning to subside:

Representative groups and their leaders, seeing the Government in open disarray, are snapping their fingers at Williams' powers of reprisal and are becoming more politicised day by day.

What we are witnessing, in short, is the death of the 'party' system as it has existed up to now – that is to say, as an extension of colonial authoritarianism disguised as Westminister parliamentary democracy. We are seeing the conversion of the population from their blind acceptance of this fiction, from their concession to Williams of the sole right to know what was or was not 'in the public interest', to an eager understanding of real issues and a determination to judge for themselves where the public interest lies.[36]

The establishment of a locally owned daily, the *Trinidad and Tobago Express*, and radical weeklies like the *People* (now defunct), the *Vanguard*, *Tapia*, and *Moko*, and the *New World Quarterly* have done a great deal to raise the level of public awareness and debate. The radical press has forced the PNM on the defensive and has given an outlet to currents of opinion which the foreign-owned press had hitherto neutralized. The *Vanguard*, which is the organ of the powerful Oilfield Workers Trade Union, has taken the line that the PNM has sold out to Anglo-American imperialism. The president of the union, George Weekes, insists that the real rulers of Trinidad are 'the big

---

35   Williams agrees that people behave towards him as they did to the old colonial governor. This is particularly manifested in the practice of seeking his intervention on every grievance or his 'grace' on every social occasion. As he wrote, 'In the colonial period, one wrote to the Governor for all manner of things. Today, in Independence you have the mentality unchanged, [people have] merely substituted the Prime Minister.' *Nation*, March 5, 1965. It appears, however, that many people seek his intervention only because their efforts to gain redress at lower levels have proven unrewarding.

36   *Tapia*, Sept. 28, 1970.

American and English oil and sugar companies who make loans to help the Government out in emergencies, advance income tax and ... offer inducements to politicians such as directorships that carry little work. They thereby get an altogether overwhelming political power which more than offsets that of the electorate.' Weekes argues that 'the goals which people hoped would follow Independence seem even further away than ever. People are disillusioned with democracy and are searching for other means to get what they want.'[37] Weekes raised the cry for Black Power and revolution, a call that has been endorsed by other radical elements in the society.

Radicals complain that Trinidad has become a police state. In support of this charge they cite a long list of grievances: the growing tendency of the PNM to regard all criticism as communist; the passage of the Industrial Stabilization Act which restricts the freedom to strike (1965); the appointment of a Commission of Inquiry into Subversive Activities (1965); the declaration of Stokely Carmichael as a prohibited immigrant (1968); the harassment of radical university lecturers and trade unionists; the house arrest of C.L.R. James (1965); the ban on all publications considered subversive (1967); the advice of the Minister of Home Affairs to the defence force to prepare to defend the country against Marxists who would sell out the country's independence for power (1968); the use of American-rigged voting machines to maintain the PNM in power; and most recently, the state of emergency which was declared in April 1970.[38] All these actions suggest to them a government which is beginning to panic and which can be expected to rely increasingly on repression to preserve the *status quo*. The Prime Minister has in fact declared open war on those who engage in treasonable and seditious activities against the lawfully elected government of the country,[39] and events in Jamaica, St Kitts and Dominica indicate that this is becoming a pattern throughout the Caribbean as dominant political parties begin to lose popular support.[40] (It is worth noting that Mr

37 *Vanguard*, Aug. 5, 1967.
38 See the *Report of the Commission of Inquiry into Subversive Activities in Trinidad and Tobago*, House Paper no. 2, GPO, Port of Spain, 1965. The Industrial Stabilization Act is discussed in chapter 24.
39 TG, Oct. 4, 1967.
40 Radical Black Power advocate Dr Walter Rodney, a Guyanese lecturer at the University of the West Indies, was summarily expelled from Jamaica. The government of Jamaica also ruthlessly supressed students who protested this arbitrariness and is increasingly harassing university lecturers who criticize its activities. The move to Jamaicanize the university is clearly related to a desire to silence criticism from this hotbed of radicalism. Similar repressive action has been evident in St Kitts, and Dominica has curbed the freedom of the press. The government of Barbados introduced a repressive Public Order Act in 1970 which imposes severe restrictions on freedom of assembly for which official permission now has to be obtained. Would-be speakers from other islands also have to get police permission.

Vere Bird, ruler of Antigua, was defeated in February 1971 by the Progressive Labour Movement of which young George Walter is the leader.)

ACTION COMMITTEE OF DEDICATED CITIZENS

The belief that authoritarian tendencies were gaining ground in the Party was also shared by elements within it. A.N.R. Robinson, who was generally regarded as the logical successor to Williams, complained publicly that 'there were definite signposts to danger' in the community. 'There are many people who know of wrongs being committed ... but are afraid of victimisation of one kind or another. In fact, there are many people who will not do their jobs for fear of losing their jobs.' Robinson lamented the 'epidemic of silence' which prevailed and warned, prophetically perhaps, that fear to speak has been one of the major causes of the breakdown of democratic regimes in the newly independent countries.[41]

Since his resignation from the cabinet in April 1970, Robinson has formed an Action Committee of Dedicated Citizens, the bulk of the membership being from disgruntled elements previously associated with the PNM. The ACDC claims that the PNM misunderstood and mishandled the events which led to the army mutiny and street demonstrations which took place in April 1970. It blames the crisis on a basic breakdown in communication and confidence between the government and the people in general and the labour movement in particular: 'The loss of confidence of the government in itself was evidenced by the numerous demonstrations and numerous complaints left unattended. The crisis grew while the action taken was always too weak, indecisive and late. It took a national disaster to move some ministers from the Cabinet. ... Those of us in the PNM who urged early and far-reaching action were dubbed alarmists. We were accused of creating a crisis where none existed.'[42]

Another factor contributing to the general malaise was the dramatic rise in the cost-of-living which followed devaluation and increased indirect taxation in 1968. The combined effect of the two measures was a 20 per cent increase in the cost-of-living in a single year. Also contributing to the deteriorating political situation were over-centralization in government machinery, discouragement of initiative, personal interference by the Prime Minister in all ministries, 'all of which have created a situation of uncertainty, insecurity and fear in the public service, and among ministers themselves'.[43] Corruption and the unwillingness or inability of the Prime Minister to do anything about it was also a serious problem, as was the PNM's tendency to zig-zag on basic policy issues. This was particularly evident in its handling of the economy. 'Today it

41 *Express*, Dec. 2, 1968.   42 *Ibid.*, Aug. 31, 1970.   43 *Ibid.*

is sell wholesale, tomorrow it is buy wholesale, and hardly anybody seems to know the full details of the transaction. All these causes have combined to produce a national crisis of the first dimension. They continue up to today, in most cases in even more exaggerated form. The gap between the government and people is wider than ever. Junior civil servants are catapulted into ministerial positions without any reference to party or people. The unemployment grows and the waste increases. While the population increases, the voters' list decreases.'[44]

Robinson also bitterly opposed the detention without charge of Black Power militants, and the repressive Public Order Bill which was introduced by the Government in August 1970. He described the bill as a 'series of prohibitions and penalties all of which give power to one man', the Minister of National Security:

It is a shameful declaration of no confidence in the people of Trinidad and Tobago, no confidence in the Independence of Trinidad and Tobago. If it goes through, Trinidad and Tobago will become the private family plantation of one man. The rest of us will be half slave and half free.

The Bill is worse than any colonial legislation, it is insulting, divisive and abominable. Nothing will entrench division and hatred in this community more than that Act. It must be withdrawn, destroyed and thrown into the waste-paper basket of history.[45]

Robinson argued that the only solution to the problem facing the country was for the government to resign and make arrangements for the formation of an interim government which would prepare the country for new elections. 'The electorate must be permitted to determine, in a free and fair election, at the earliest opportunity, whether one who has led us into the present situation can lead us out again. This has not been the experience in other countries, particularly newly independent countries. It is not likely to be the experience in Trinidad and Tobago. The Public Order Bill is testimony to this. ... No more substantial measures should be attempted by this Government.'[46]

Robinson believed that the PNM could be defeated in the 1971 elections,

44 *Ibid.* Robinson made the startling announcement that during the cabinet debate on the ISA, there was a proposal to bring in Canadian troops to quell unrest. He claims he fought successfully against this proposal.
45 The Minister of National Security at the time was also Prime Minister, Minister of Finance, Minister of Planning and Development, Minister of Local Government, Minister of Tobago Affairs, and Minister of External Affairs. On November 19, 1970, the Prime Minister gave up (on paper at least) three of his Ministries: National Security, Finance, and External Affairs.
46 *Express*, Aug. 31, 1970.

and that Williams himself would be beaten. He pointed out that Williams only received 5,478 votes out of a possible 13,800 in the 1966 elections and assumed that about 2,000 of Williams' supporters had either defected to other movements or did not bother to register. Indeed, according to figures released by the Elections and Boundaries Commission, Williams' constituency recorded the highest drop in electoral registration between 1966 and 1970 – from 12,801 to 7,728. 'That is why there has been tinkering about with the boundaries, why the boundaries [of Port of Spain South] had to be extended to include parts of Barataria.' Drawing attention to the fact that the PNM's share of the popular vote had also been falling dramatically since 1956, Robinson concluded that 'the PNM is not truly representative of the population'.[47]

Robinson was certainly correct in his assumption that the Trinidad voters, particularly the young and the urban-based, had lost interest in the electoral process and in the PNM. Whereas the number of registered electors was 459,839 in 1966, in 1968 it fell to 436,936 and in 1970 to 392,483, out of a possible 470,000. Migration and deaths are responsible for some of the 'missing' names, but many previous registrants and persons now entitled to vote simply did not bother to register. The number of eligible voters who went to the polls also declined sharply from 80.1 and 88.1 per cent in 1956 and 1961, respectively, to 66 per cent in 1966.[48]

47   TG, Feb. 12, 1971. Robinson has been bitterly attacked by PNM elements as well as by others. He has been called a 'rat who has deserted a ship which he thought was sinking'. Bomb, Dec. 4, 1970. The Bomb (Aug. 14, 1970) also accuses him of having made an abortive attempt to seize power on April 12 when the Prime Minister was expected to be out of the country. According to the Bomb's report, a mystery woman saved the Prime Minister from a coup d'etat: 'Two days before he was scheduled to fly out of the country she telephoned Dr Williams and told him, "Don't go, Bill. They want to treat you like Nkrumah. When you land in Jamaica, you won't be able to come back." The woman knew every inch of the plot and she pleaded with Dr Williams not to take any action against Mr Robinson. She also named certain top members of the People's National Movement and key members of the Opposition who had taken part in the proposed plot. She made it clear that Mr Robinson did not want a hair of Dr Williams touched, and that is why he wanted the PM out of the country.
She said Mr Robinson wanted no part of the Black Power Movement in his coup, although he conceded that they were the ones who had created the right climate for the take-over. But she said he would have no part of George Weekes and Clive Nunez, two leaders of the National Joint Action Committee.'
Robinson, who resigned the day after this incident is supposed to have taken place, denies involvement in any such plot and sued the Bomb for libel. Dr Williams has not commented publicly on the story, but did lead the public to believe that it had some substance. Many people seem to feel that Robinson would have been more credible if he had resigned on principle in 1966 when the Finance Bill (cf. chap. 24) was withdrawn, rather than four years later.

48   TG, Aug. 8, 1970. Low registration was heaviest in the urban areas, particularly in

The PNM's percentage of the total vote dropped from 57 per cent in 1961 to 52 per cent in 1966. Disaffection was even more evident during the local elections which were held in June 1968 after a lapse of nine years. Only 32 per cent of the registered electorate went to the polls, and in some urban areas the turnout was as low as 20 per cent![49] Although the PNM won sixty-nine of the one hundred seats (fourteen were uncontested), it got the support of only 49.9 per cent of these hard-core voters. It is also worth noting that for the first time a rebel PNM candidate was able to defeat a regular who had the active backing of the Party high-command.[50]

DEMOCRATIC LABOUR PARTY

The official opposition party, the DLP, had also been experiencing a significant loss of popular support. In the 1958 federal elections, the first the party contested, it won 47.4 per cent of the vote cast. In 1961, this figure dropped to 41.6 per cent, and in 1966 to 34 per cent. The Party also did poorly in the local council elections of 1968, winning the support of 14.2 per cent of the registered electorate and 40 per cent of the votes cast. Many observers expected the DLP to do much worse, however, since the Party continued to be ridden by the same leadership rivalries that plagued it from its inception. After his defeat in 1961, Dr Rudranath Capildeo returned to London University from where he attempted to lead the Party. For him politics became a vacation job. Absentee leadership created an intolerable situation, and defections produced the Liberal Party and the Workers and Farmers Party. Capildeo led the Party to defeat in 1966 and, despite firm promises that he would remain in Trinidad whether he won or lost, again attempted to lead it from London University. This precipitated another round of bitter squabbling and in July 1969 anti-Capildeo elements finally succeeded in having him removed at a convention of the Party. The leadership was given to a young lawyer, Vernon Jamadar, who had deputized for Capildeo during his absence from Parliament.

But this was not the end of the Party's difficulties. Bhadase Maraj claimed that, since he had handed over the leadership in 1960, he was the logical successor to Capildeo. Many traditional Hindus and Dr Capildeo himself sup-

Port of Spain and San Fernando. Constituencies in Tobago and in areas heavily populated by Indians recorded the highest rates of registration.

49 See TG, June 6, 1968. The 20 per cent poll was recorded in San Fernando.

50 Many PNM stalwarts supported the rebel candidate out of protest against the decision of the leadership to 'parachute' a favourite of the PNM into a constituency to which she did not belong. It was a triumph of localism over central dictation which badly shook the Party. See *Express*, June 26, 1968. Interestingly enough, the rebel candidate, Victor Marcano, joined the UNIP and was detained during the state of emergency.

ported this claim, and Maraj again became recognized as the leader of the communally-oriented Hindus. Maraj quarrelled in Parliament with the DLP and gave a great deal of unofficial political support to the PNM. Controversy about this and Maraj's 'boss-type' political style led to yet another split in the Party, and a majority of its MPs finally agreed to accept the leadership of Vernon Jamadar. Maraj and his supporters retaliated by forming a new party to contest the 1971 elections. Recognizing the symbolic importance of the initials DLP, Maraj called his new formation the Democratic Liberation Party.[51]

The 'new' Democratic Labour Party attracted a number of Indian professionals and a few Negroes like Dr E.C. Richardson, a founding member of the PNM.[52] Under Jamadar's leadership, they formed an electoral merger with the ACDC to challenge the PNM, a move that seemed to signal a major breakthrough for race relations in the country. Jamadar himself noted that racial unity was one of the prime objectives of the merger. There was a great need, he said, 'for the brothers of slavery and indenture' to close ranks.[53] While the merger seemed to have represented the most serious electoral threat to the PNM, the political history of Trinidad was full of evidence to generate scepticism about its long-term success. Rivalries over leadership were bound to take place if the leader of the largest bloc of support was not officially recognized as leader of the Party. Although many hoped that recent events had successfully destroyed racially based politics, the general assumption was that Jamadar would control the bulk of the voting support for the coalition and its parliamentary arm, and that Robinson, who was recognized as the merger's main standard-bearer, would be in serious difficulty. Negroes, for whom racial considerations were uppermost, withheld their support for this reason. Similarly, some communally oriented Indians vowed that they would give their support to Maraj who had decided that he would contest whatever constituency Jamadar chose. As it is, the merger collapsed before polling day, but many felt that rivalries between Maraj and Jamadar would have allowed the PNM to win a few seats in areas that had normally been considered DLP areas.

The ineffectiveness of the two-party system and the persistence of racial politics led many people, especially the young to abandon faith in conventional

51   See Augustus Ramrckersingh, 'DLP: The end of the Old Order', *Tapia*, Election Special No. 1, Jan. 31, 1971.

52   Richardson was made a Deputy Political Leader of theParty together with Dr Krishna Bahadoorsingh, a former lecturer in political science at the University of the West Indies. The reform faction almost splintered in November 1970 over the question of seats in the Senate. It is reported that the two sitting DLP senators refused to resign to make room for the new recruits, one of whom, Dr Richardson, reportedly threatened to resign over the issue. See the *Bomb*, Nov. 13, 1970.

53   TG, Feb. 12, 1971.

political processes. A large number of people did not believe that it would make any difference to their lives whether the PNM or the ACDC won the election. The policy positions of the two units were in fact not very different. The PNM's 'Perspectives for a New Society' and the ACDC's 'Road to Freedom' were both attempts to adopt what they considered to be the more 'acceptable' planks in the programme of the Black Power Movement.

'Perspectives' (also referred to as the Chaguaramas Declaration) accepted the need for 'revolutionary change', but insisted that this had to be guided by rational objectives and rational means rather than by 'romantic, anarchistic fantasies without programmes or objectives'.[54] Dissent must not mean sedition, mutiny or coup d'état. Also accepted was the need for 'drastic and fundamental reform of land tenure and other obsolete laws that are out of place in a politically independent country', greater economic power for the historically dispossessed groups, a more equitable distribution of the social product, greater popular participation in decisions affecting the community, and constitutional reform involving reconstitution of the Senate and the abandonment of the monarchy. 'Perspectives' also admitted that not enough had been done to restructure the educational system and stressed the need to concentrate more on vocational and technical education, especially business and agricultural management. 'We must make a clean break from metropolitan notions (more often outmoded in their countries of origin) in ... social norms and outlook. ... the PNM must seek to end the complete divorce between school and work which we ... inherited from the élitist system of 19th century Britain.'[55]

'The Road to Freedom' did not differ with 'Perspectives' on any fundamental issue. It also emphasized the need for educational reform, democratization of the political system, the cultivation of a spirit of self-reliance, full utilization of all productive resources, and domestication of the foreign sector. On the latter issue we were told that:

If we cannot control our resources, the level of unemployment will remain unresponsive to domestic decision and, to that extent, reflect the irresponsibility of the true decision-makers to the domestic population. Democracy will thereby be frustrated and become a farce. The basic approach of some countries has been wholesale nationalisation. However, nationalisation may not of itself resolve all the problems that must be resolved. In some cases it increases them. It does not necessarily resolve the problems of markets or of expertise.
Wholesale nationalisation can work in such economies as those of Russia and China. It will not work in small economies where the lines of production involve the

54 'Perspectives', *Nation*, Sept. 25, 1970.
55 *Ibid.*

country in a diversified foreign trading pattern. Such is the case of Trinidad and Tobago.

What is required of the foreign firm is not necessarily nationalisation but domestication. This means inducing it to undertake the obligations of a domestic owner to the society.

The level of domestication that can be achieved will often depend upon relative bargaining strengths. Bargaining strength can be maximised if, among other things, (i) conduct at the bargaining table is removed from corrupting influences; (ii) it is entrusted to competent negotiators committed to the national interest; (iii) the proportion of domestic to foreign investment is relatively high.

It cannot be over-emphasized that there is no substitute for expertise in the management of economic affairs.[56]

Like other organizations which were on the left of the PNM, the ACDC felt that the PNM had had fourteen unchallenged years to put a programme of decolonization into effect and that it had shown itself bankrupt of ideas and lacking in organizational competence. Robinson agreed that the PNM, which he described as an 'informal dictatorship', 'has done some good – the work towards Independence and schools ... . But the time has come when they are doing more harm than good ... . The PNM must not only cease to be in power, but must be disbanded as a political party.'[57]

---

56 TG, Oct. 16, 17, 1970.
57 *Express*, Nov. 22, 1970. For an interesting 'Trinidadianesque' commentary on Robinson, see Pete Simon, 'ANR, A victim of Political Tabanka', *Express*, October 25, 1970. As Simon writes: 'ANR was shifted from the very prestigeous position of Minister of Finance – the most all-embracing area of ministerial responsibility – to that of Minister of External Affairs. ...
Well, is from den dat de baccanal start! From that day was born a new ANR. His political role became most strange and out of character. He began doing things he never did before. To discerning folks, he was behaving like a man who had Tabanka! In the demonology of Trinidad and Tobago, he is the mischievously satanic instrument of lovers' quarrels. ...
'With the Tabanka complex dictating the pace to get even, he looked around for areas of irritation. Then the new ANR began to do his thing! Overnight ANR became the darling boy of the unions who were actually falling over one another, extending invitations to this protesting Cabinet Minister to grace their functions and deliver feature addresses.
'What really shocked most people, though, was the sudden transformation of ANR from the staid, formal, conservative dresser to the brash, pace-setting standard-bearer of the Mod Squad.
Afro-fat-head, big ornamental chains around the neck like a mayor, *dashikis*, Nehru jackets, hot shirts and all the external trappings of identity which are so dear to the hearts of the younger set, all became part and parcel of the new ANR image!'

UNITED NATIONAL INDEPENDENCE PARTY

Somewhat to the left of the PNM and ACDC-DLP was the United National Independence Party led by Dr James Millette. An offshoot from the New World Group, the UNIP believed that academics must accept political responsibility for their ideas by getting actively involved in politics. The Party, which was founded in 1970, has had a significant impact on political debate in the country, but its electoral potential was never great. It was the realization that the UNIP would not make any headway at the polls that led Dr Millette to join forces with the United Revolutionary Organization (URO) which has as its common denominator an agreement on the need for fundamental electoral reform. The URO, which also included the ACDC, the Tapia House Group, the WFP, the Transport and Industrial Workers Union, the National Freedom Organization, and a few other small groups, called for the lowering of the voting age to eighteen, a national referendum on the issue of the use of voting machines, equal access of all political groups to the media, an end to constituency gerrymandering, the complete registration of all eligible voters, and the establishment of an independent Elections and Boundaries Commission.[58] URO insisted that all these reforms had to take place *before* any election could be held, since 'this election can be the last'.

Millette's decision to take UNIP into URO led to a serious split in the Party and it became almost impossible for it to convince anyone that it was a serious alternative to the PNM. The anti-Millette group claimed that by joining the URO, Millette had given up hope of changing the PNM by conventional political processes. As George Dhanny, the leader of the 'conventional politics' faction complained, 'We joined the ... Party because we are interested in changing our present Government ... but Millette has shown no evidence he plans to fight an election this year or ever.'[59] Millette was accused of dictatorship, of being a classroom politician who had no capacity for conventional political leadership, and who therefore joined the URO out of desperation. Millette denied these

58 The Government mounted a massive campaign to ensure that all eligible voters were registered. It did not give in on the machines, but tried to allay suspicions of rigging by agreeing to have candidates draw for positions on the machine on the day of the poll. It also took belated steps to see that there were no massive breakdowns on election day as there were in 1966. It is worth noting that a poll conducted by the *Express* on the machines showed that as much as 47.9 per cent of the population opposed them. But there is no real evidence that the machines were ever rigged. The Government appointed a committee to study the voting age issue, but it was not very active. The Prime Minister expressed the view that the young had not shown that they were responsible enough to exercise the franchise. See *Express*, Feb. 14, 1971.

59 *Bomb*, Feb. 19, 1971; *Express*, Feb. 21, 1971.

charges, and insisted that the decision to join the URO was a majority decision, and that the division in the Party was 'between self-interest and national interest'.[60] But if Millette had found himself in a coalition which he believed stood a chance of defeating the PNM, it is certain that he would have contested the election.

UNCONVENTIONAL POLITICS

Two groups which have had an enormous influence on politics in Trinidad but which expressed no interest in contesting the 1971 or any other election under the present system are the National Joint Action Committee (NJAC) and the Tapia House Group. NJAC was formed in 1967 as a coalition of radical trade unions, student and youth groups, and several cultural and sporting organizations which were all concerned about the need for a more vigorous public opinion in national politics. The Movement gained prominence in 1969 when student elements physically confronted the Governor General of Canada while he was on a visit to the University of the West Indies in Trinidad over the question of the treatment of their 'black brothers' who were accused of smashing and burning the computer centre at Sir George Williams University in Montreal, Canada.[61] It was this involvement (in the movement to put pressure on the Trinidad government to intervene with Canadian authorities on behalf of the Trinidadian students who were on trial for that incident) which led the NJAC to begin questioning Canada's economic role in the Caribbean. Canadian banks, insurance companies, and industrial firms came in for strong condemnation, as did Canada's sugar-purchasing policy in the region.[62] Almost overnight, 'Canadian imperialism' became a formidable bogeyman. Canada was now seen not as a friendly neighbour to the north, but a country which had exploited its native Indians and blacks as well as those in the Caribbean with which it had been economically related for centuries.

Although the Trinidad government did provide legal, diplomatic, and financial help for the students in Canada, radical elements in the NJAC were

---

60 *Express*, Feb. 16, 1971.
61 The incident at Sir George Williams which took place in February 1969 grew out of a protest by West Indian students that they were being discriminated against by a biology professor. The students believed that the university authorities dealt with their case unfairly and treacherously and they reacted violently.
62 Canada buys West Indian sugar at world-market prices rather than at preferential prices paid in the UK and US. Canada had agreed in 1966 to pay a refund on West Indian sugar imports but terminated this arrangement unilaterally in 1970. A quota on shirts imported into Canada was also imposed unilaterally. Both measures caused bitterness in the Caribbean.

dissatisfied with the PNM's 'low-profile' stance during the controversy, and began to assert that the government was not only in collusion with Canadian authorities but that it had done nothing to break the control of Canadian economic imperialism. Protests in support of students soon escalated into demands for Black Power in Trinidad.

The street march in support of the students, which began in front of the Royal Bank of Canada on February 26, 1970, grew into demonstrations protesting Canadian racism and economic exploitation, and progressively became transformed into massive rallies protesting against the entire social and political system. The charismatic eloquence of Geddes Granger, who emerged as the major spokesman of the NJAC, attracted the attention of thousands of Trinidadians – the young, the unemployed, the people of the slums of Shanty Town – in a way that was curiously reminiscent of Williams in 1955–6.[63] The University of Woodford Square, having done its job of training a new generation of political activists, had now given way to the People's Parliament.[64]

The arrest without bail of the leaders of the demonstration (for unlawful assembly and behaviour calculated to cause disorder) helped to escalate the protest movement, and for sixty days the pounding feet of thousands of black marchers were heard all over Trinidad and Tobago. As Granger shouted, 'We shall walk without speaking, without shouting, without smiling, but we shall walk with anger.' Referring to the red, black, and green flags carried by the marchers, Granger declared that 'the red flags are a declaration of war, black is for victory and black unity, and green is for peace after we have achieved victory.'[65]

63 The NJAC took their protests into the slums of Shanty Town (which the government has at last started to rehabilitate) and sought to politicize the long-neglected grievances of the market vendors (which were also settled after they threatened to march). The march and demonstration technique was also used by workers in the Transport Corporation in a massive protest strike in April 1969. There were also constant marches protesting against the ISA as well as other forms of bureaucratic neglect. As the Express noted (Nov. 29, 1970): 'In Trinidad and Tobago today, everybody now knows that to get anything done, they have to attract attention: a human blockade for a pedestrian crossing; another for a garbage dump; a third for traffic lights. Protests for all of us has become a way of life; children demonstrating for toilet facilities, parents demonstrating for school places, the unemployed demonstrating for job opportunities, prisoners demonstrating for humane treatment, judges demonstrating (well, arguing anyway) for law reform. Where does it stop? Nowhere. It is the population's last weapon against bureaucracy, indifference or plain incompetence.'

64 Woodford Square, now the People's Parliament, was locked up by the PNM. It is as if one were to debar dissenters from using Hyde Park!

65 Cited, Frank McDonald, 'Trinidad, the February Revolution', mimeo in files of Institute of Current World Affairs, New York, 1970, p. 23.

As the NJAC saw it, white power and the collusion of 'white' Afro-Saxons was the root of the problem in the Caribbean:

Too many of us are blinded by the constitutional disguises which give the appearance of Black people being in control. This is the way the White power structure wants us to see it.

The economic control which white people have, gives them political control. Our politicians are turned into mere puppets. Once in every five years Black people get a little (very little in the set up) political bargaining status as election comes around. We are fed crash programmes and promises. Then the rest of the time is spent by the politicians bootlicking for the White Power Structure.

The White Imperialists used their control of the Economic System to divide Black people, African against African, African against Indian, Indian against Indian. In fact, divisions of race and class are embedded in the structure of the whole society.[66]

The PNM and its middle-class supporters soon began to panic, as did the police who reacted by using tear gas, horses, guns and night-sticks to disperse the demonstrations. Overnight, phrases such as 'pigs' and 'police brutality', long familiar in the black revolution in North America, became part of the radical vocabulary in Trinidad. During a court hearing, Dave Darbreau, one of the nine demonstrators arrested, urged black policemen to join the crusade. 'You police should be on our side. The army is on our side. All we need now is your help to seize power. We have suffered too long at the hands of those Canadian bastards.'[67]

The PNM was in a quandary about what steps it should take. Many people seemed to take it for granted that it was only a matter of time before it collapsed under the pressure of the crisis. The Minister of Commerce and Industry, Mr O'Halloran, reacted characteristically by declaring that 'the present black power demonstrations have been engineered by communist agents trained and paid by Fidel Castro'.[68] Williams, who knew better, built a wall around his house and waited for a full month before he finally spoke to the nation, a delay that angered middle-class elements, some of whom had begun to organize protective vigilante groups. There were strident demands that he crush the Black Power Movement as the government of Jamaica had done in

---

66 *Slavery to Slavery*, Port of Spain, 1970, p. ii.
67 McDonald, 'Trinidad, the February Revolution', p. 10.
68 *Ibid.*, p. 10. O'Halloran and Gerard Montano (Minister of Home Affairs) who had been the PNM symbols of accommodation with the whites and the business community were dropped from the cabinet and replaced by junior but unequivocally black civil servants who were given seats in the Senate. It was an attempt to give the government a new image.

October 1968. As one who had begun his career as a black militant, Williams must have been aware that he was in large part responsible for the events of those months. The NJAC was only trying to complete what the PNM had begun in 1956–60. Williams also understood the historical antecedents of the protest movement, as well as its relationship with the worldwide revolution of youth against authority, cant and hypocrisy:

The fundamental feature of the demonstrations was the insistence on Black dignity, the manifestation of Black consciousness, and the demand for Black economic power. The entire population must understand that these demands are perfectly legitimate and are entirely in the interest of the community as a whole. If this is Black Power, then I am for Black Power. ...

If anyone wishes to continue to march and demonstrate, by all means let him do so. Our Constitution guarantees this as a fundamental right. But I urge that this should be done without violence, without trespassing on the constitutional rights of others, without interference of any sort with the freedom of worship equally guaranteed by our Constitution. There must be no interference with the churches, no interference with the temples, no interference with the mosques, no interference with any place of worship.

Our young people are a part of the general world malaise, seeking something new and something better, and seeking it with a sense of urgency. They are restless, frustrated, possibly a little exuberant. But let there be no misunderstanding about this. It is a horse of a different colour if what is involved is arson and molotov cocktails. In that case the law will have to take its course.[69]

Williams was either hoping that the Black Power Movement would exhaust itself or that it would overreach itself and thereby provoke a 'backlash' to the benefit of the PNM. By mid-April the latter had begun to happen. There was growing restlessness in the labour movement and the Trinidad and Tobago Regiment, and it was well known that there was sympathy for the militants among enlisted men and elements in the junior officer corps. Robinson's resignation on April 13, taking with him a wing of the PNM, also led to wild speculation that he was closely tied up with the NJAC, and that he would be its choice

---

69 Nationwide broadcast, March 23, 1970. Although he endorsed Black Power, Williams warned about its divisive potential: 'There can be no Mother India for those whose ancestors came from India. There can be no Mother Africa for those of African origin and ... Trinidad and Tobago ... is heading for trouble if it seeks to create the impression or to allow others to act under the illusion that Trinidad and Tobago is an African society. There can be no Mother England and no dual loyalties. ... There can be no Mother China, even if one should agree as to which China is the Mother.' *Express*, June 17, 1970.

to replace Williams. There were also reports that Stokely Carmichael[70] was due to arrive in Trinidad; that mystery vessels had appeared in Trinidad territorial water; and that money was being channelled from outside to the marchers who were growing more daring and confident each day. On April 20, 1970, the NJAC made a dramatic and symbolic march into the sugar areas to attempt a link up with 'the brothers in indenture'.[71] There were also plans to have the sugar workers, who had struck over their own industrial grievances, march into Port of Spain on the following day; and rumours that a general strike was being planned for April 22. It was at this point that Williams concluded that the confrontation could no longer be avoided:

For some years now we have been aware of dissident elements in the society, especially among a minority of trade unions, seeking to displace the Government. At first they tried to do so by the electoral process; no one can have any quarrel with that. When that failed, however, they turned increasingly to unconstitutional means and armed revolution. ...

The first date selected for the contemplated overthrow of the Government was foiled by developments which I do not wish to discuss tonight. The alternative date selected was ruled out by the declaration of the State of Emergency.

During the weekend before the declaration of the State of Emergency, after weeks and weeks of demonstrations, a new factor was introduced into the situation. This was the total repudiation by certain workers in one of the statutory boards of all recognised trade-union practices and procedures. In the process all the agreements reached by the Government as employer with the union involved in respect of classification and compensation were thrown out of the window. This had enormous implications for the entire Public Service. This was in the context of public statements by the dissident element in the society that the sugar workers and the

---

70   The airlines were prohibited from even allowing Carmichael to pass through Trinidad.

71   The march into Caroni was not as successful as the NJAC claims. Indians were curious and courteous but did not embrace the marchers with open arms. They were willing, as they always have been, to allow urban Negro leaders to use whatever leverage they had to help them with their industrial grievances. This bothered both the government and Bhadase Maraj, president of the All Trinidad Sugar Workers Union. As James Millette notes, 'Mr Maraj was one of several straw-men erected by the Government in the arena of trade unionism and other group representation; but he was possibly the most important of them. His role in the sugar areas possessed not only trade union but political significance as well. Crucially, therefore, successful Black Power infiltration in the sugar areas threatened to promote, at one and the same time, the break-up of unrepresentative trade unionism and of the antiquated racial politics in which Maraj as well as Williams had a heavy personal stake.' 'The Politics of Succession', *Express*, June 9, 1970.

workers in water were to march on April 21 to link up with transport workers, to be followed on Wednesday, April 22, by some action in the oil industry.

Both at home and abroad the question has been raised as to why the Government waited so long to act. There was one principal consideration. The Black Power Movement enlisted the sympathy of a number of people, especially young people, who bitterly resented discrimination against Black people at home and abroad. This is a legitimate grievance, and I would have been no party to any attempt to repress this. I knew that much more was involved. But these young idealists had to see for themselves the ulterior motives of those who were seeking to use slogans of Black dignity and Black economic power as the basis of enlisting mass support. They had to see for themselves how the Black Power slogan degenerated into race and hatred and even to attacks on Black business in Tobago and Point Fortin. Moreover, if I had told the general population of the larger plan I have indicated to you tonight, 75 per cent of you would have been sceptical and would not have believed it. You had to be made to put your finger in the wound in order to believe. It was only when the total breakdown of the trade-union movement was imminent that I decided to act.[72]

As in 1965 when a similar coming together of sugar and oil appeared imminent, Williams declared a state of emergency on the night of April 20. In a pre-dawn raid, security forces, casting a very wide net, arrested the leaders of the Movement. The move had been expected and the NJAC had even called upon its followers to defy it. As Granger had declared on the night of April 14:

From the time the Emergency is declared, come to town to demonstrate. By God we will fight fire with fire. If you bow to the State of Emergency, mark my word here tonight, your children will curse the day you were born. Your children will not respect you, your wives will turn against you. ... We will not retreat one single inch. This is war. We are going to show them that the will of God is the will of the people. Come to town. If they want to lock you up, let them lock up all 'ah we' ... . No rum drinking. From tonight do not buy anything except food. Do not pay your bills ... . This is war.[73]

The stealth with which most of the leaders of the Movement were picked up did not prevent the anticipated confrontation with the police. But in the short run, at least, it was a futile confrontation. In the words of Lloyd Best,

72 Nationwide broadcast, May 3, 1970. The population is divided on whether the state of emergency was justified. Some think it was long overdue, while others saw it as an attempt by the PNM to use the power of the state to save itself from political collapse. A good case can be made for both views and it all depends on what brief one holds.

73 McDonald, 'Trinidad, the February Revolution,' p. 23.

'On the morning of the 21st, the population assemble[d] in the public square, smash[ed] up all the store fronts in Port of Spain, every one ... a final grand romantic gesture, finish[ed] and go [went] home. No leadership left. All the terror in the system is police terror, official terror.'[74]

An important dimension of the decision to declare a state of emergency was revealed in a heated public exchange between the Prime Minister and Mr Clive Spencer, a former senator and president of the Trinidad and Tobago Labour Congress. According to Dr Williams, on the morning of April 20, the President of the Labour Congress issued an 'ultimatum' to the government:

If immediate action was not taken by the Government to bring the whole situation under control, then the Labour Congress, which controlled what he called the responsible unions, would bring the whole community to a standstill by calling out the workers in the Port, the Airport, external and internal communications, the Civil Service, and the daily paid workers.

It was clear to the Ministers present and particularly to the Prime Minister that the time had come for decisive action; it was no longer a problem of aimless marches and wild public statements; the whole Labour Movement was threatened.

An emergency Cabinet session was summoned three hours later and the decision taken that a State of Emergency should be declared at such time as the Prime Minister thought it fit.[75]

Williams also added that Spencer thanked him for declaring the state of emergency and requested the Prime Minister to intervene to get the police authorities 'to issue arms to a vigilante group that he had set up for the protection of one of the most important public utilities'.[76] Stung by Williams' disclosures, which in his view were designed to make him an object of hate and disaffection, Spencer gave his version of the story. Spencer agreed that he gave the Prime Minister an ultimatum, and that he agreed to help mobilize volunteers 'twice the number of the Army if it becomes necessary' to contain the army rebellion and the militants in Port of Spain. Spencer said he was forced to do this because NJAC elements were poaching on union affiliates, had called workers from the Water and Sewerage Authority off their jobs, and were making violent threats to union leaders:

I told him further that whoever survived after that will rule as it appeared that although he was reigning he was afraid to rule and that the Congress was not prepared to tolerate the Government's 'wait and see' attitude anymore.

74 'The February Revolution: its causes and meaning', *Tapia*, Dec. 20, 1970. Thirty-seven store and bank show-windows were smashed.
75 TG, Sept. 25, 1971.   76 *Ibid.*

The Prime Minister replied that he had heard me 'loud and clear' and that his Government was watching the situation and will not allow it to deteriorate any further, but that he was not aware that it was as serious as I had indicated.[77]

Spencer said that he was concerned about what might happen during the massive demonstrations which the militants had planned for April 21. 'With all these workers on the streets and with WASA pump attendants having been told to lock off all supplies of water, ... the smallest spark could burn the city, and what may have to be done then could result in serious bloodshed and loss of lives and property.'[78]

Spencer also revealed that the cabinet was divided as to whether an emergency should be declared, that the Americans had responded to the Prime Minister's call for help by telling him that they were not prepared to interfere in the internal affairs of Trinidad until and except American lives and property were in danger, and that he warned the Prime Minister that three officers of the Army and about sixty dissident soldiers might obstruct the Army from coming to the assistance of the government and that he ought to recheck the loyalty of the Army before taking any action. The Prime Minister, who had been assured by his ministers that there were just 'a few dissatisfied soldiers whom there could be no trouble in controlling', was 'on the verge of tears' when he later learnt that the Army had revolted.[79] There are also other reports that other cabinet members were in a state of panic and hysteria and that helicopters and BWIA planes had been ordered to stand by to fly members of the government to Tobago or further afield if necessary.

Information now coming to light indicates that the Prime Minister went 'soft' during the crisis and that he had to be pressured into acting by Party members, business elements, and the unions. It is also evident that Venezuelan army authorities were more eager to intervene to contain the militants than were the Americans, who were better informed about what was taking place in Trinidad. The Venezuelan military thought the militants Cuban-inspired and were unwilling to stand by and allow Trinidad to become a jumping-off ground for subversives or a sanctuary for Venezuelan terrorists. The Venezuelans, who flew reconnaissance planes over Trinidad during the crisis, had their naval vessels turned back by the Trinidad Coast Guard after strong protests had been lodged by loyalist elements about their involvement. Radicals, who had once thought that their greatest enemy was the US marines, have now to take the aggressive Venezuelan military into account in their future plans for revolution.

77 *Express*, Sept. 28, 1971.   78 *Ibid.*
79 *Ibid.*

MUTINY OR TREASON?

The crisis in the armed forces created a dramatic complication which seriously hurt the protest movement. The army had been in a state of severe unrest for several months and morale was extremely low. No one had given much thought to what the role of an army in Trinidad ought to be and there was a great deal of purposelessness and boredom among enlisted men. Mental health problems were also serious. Senior officers were being accused of nepotism and corruption, of professional inefficiency, of condoning the perpetuation of racially discriminatory practices in the use of beaches and mess facilities, of misusing the army band and personnel for private purposes, and of stifling creative junior officers. Senior officers, many of whom were not professionally trained, were also accused of being party hacks who encouraged spying on officers suspected of being hostile to the PNM and sympathetic to Black Power.[80]

Whatever the facts, and the charges appear to have some foundation, junior officers of the Regiment, which on that morning was for some curious reason without its senior commanding officers,[81] seized the opportunity either to try and force the authorities to deal with their own internal grievances or to attempt a take-over of the government. The soldiers claim that they mutinied for sound reasons. Lt. Raffique Shah, one of the key officers involved, declared that 'We acted because of corruption and inefficiency at the Regimental level.'[82] Shah and his colleagues also claim that they felt it unwise to take a restless army which had no confidence in its senior officers into a crisis situation when there was no telling what the officers might do. They deny the accusation that they were leading soldiers into Port of Spain bent on arson, rape, and looting, or that they ever had any plans to seize the government, either independently or in collusion with the NJAC or any other organization. Also denied are reports that they were going into 'town to help their black brothers', or that one of

---

80 For the accused soldiers' account of these problems, see Lt Raffique Shah's plea, Tapia Pamphlet no. 3, Jan. 1971. Shah's counsel, Mr Desmond Allum, told the court martial that his client found the army to be in shambles; 'discipline eroded to the bone, favouritism and injustice rampant, profiteering, theft and the conversions of government property openly practised. Night-clubbing, gambling and all manner of dissolution were not only condoned but encouraged as a way of life by their senior officers. They found a total lack of professional concern on the part of the amateurs who held the authority for reform and who not only refused to exercise it but actively resented and visited with victimization anyone who was unwilling to acquiesce in their manner of discharging their sinecures.' Moko, March 26, 1971.

81 Most of the senior officers, fearing a rebellion in the Regiment, either fled to the Coast Guard which was officered by a white expatriate or to the police. Many of them were not professional soldiers and have since been removed.

82 Tapia Pamphlet no. 3.

Shah's demands during negotiations with the Government was for the formation of a national government. Shah, in fact, argues that the court martial was a
PNM 'political play [designed] to win the people's confidence at election time.
They have used the charge of treason against us so that they may appear to be
the messiahs and the saviours of this country.'[83]

Although the authorities never attempted to prove, or succeeded in proving, that there was any collusion between Black Power sympathizers in the
Regiment and those in the NJAC, PNM politicians claim that there was indeed
a conspiracy, and that a political-military coup was only narrowly averted by
the intervention of the Coast Guard which shelled and blocked the only road
linking the base with the city of Port of Spain. It was not mere coincidence that
dissident elements chose an hour of national crisis to try and settle internal
grievances. Whether or not there was any collusion is difficult to say. No one
who was involved has made any such claim, and the PNM has not published the
findings of the committee which investigated the Regiment. But the PNM has
succeeded in convincing enough people that there was a link, and this helped to
strengthen the government in its dealings with the dissidents.

PNM propaganda notwithstanding, many independent observers are con-

---

83   *Ibid.* The sentences imposed on the three officers were heavy. Shah was given twenty
      years, Lt Rex Lassalle was given fifteen years and Lt Bazie seven years. Shah and
      Lassalle had their sentences reduced by five and three years respectively. Some of the
      accused soldiers wanted the state to press the charge of treason rather than mutiny.
      A strong 'Free our Black Soldiers' campaign was mounted by the ACDC-DLP, the
      NJAC, and various student bodies, but despite public compassion for the soldiers,
      the campaign did not gain popular support. It was noted by counsel for the accused
      that thirty-one soldiers had been committed to stand trial at the next assizes for
      treason, and that justice required that they be heard in a civil court before they be
      heard by the court martial. See the *Nation*, Nov. 6, 1970. Either the PNM did not
      want to have to impose the death penalty or they felt they could not ensure con-
      viction. Opposition elements believe the latter to be more likely, especially since a
      magistrate's court had acquitted eighteen soldiers at a preliminary hearing. The
      stunning defeat on the Public Order Bill may well have been a decisive factor since
      some of its strongest opponents were lawyers and jurists. The mutiny charge was
      easier for the prosecution to press since the evidence was more convincing. It is
      worth noting that the court that tried the soldiers consisted of military officers from
      the black Commonwealth, and that one of them, a Ugandan, was recalled to become
      a minister in the government of General Idi Amin who had staged a successful coup
      against Milton Obote. Two years after the crisis, the treason and sedition charges
      have neither been pressed nor dropped. There is a strong but unheeded demand for
      the Government to either bring the 31 detained soldiers to court or to release them.
      The Appeal Court freed Lts. Shah and Lassalle in February 1971 on the ground
      that their misdemeanours had been condoned during the negotiations that followed
      the mutiny. But the State has appealed the decision to the Privy Council which has
      not yet disposed of the matter.

vinced that Lts. Shah, Bazie, and Lassalle did have treasonable political ambitions, and that they had established links with radical elements in the city. It was known even before the crisis (though the reports were denied by commanding officers) that arms were being taken out of the ammunition dump. There are even reports (unverified) that ministers had been earmarked for assassination and that, unable to agree on who was to take charge after the coup, the country had been divided into military zones by Shah and Lassalle. It appears that the soldiers were told by the officers that the police were 'beating up black people in town' and that they had to go to the help of 'their black brothers'. The unexpected intervention of the Coast Guard threw the soldiers into a state of panic and forced them to retreat. Promises of negotiations and hints of amnesty gave the authorities the breathing space they needed to deploy American and Venezuelan arms to the police. The soldiers were able to hold out for five tension-filled days, but were completely outmanoeuvred by the government.

Between the months of April and November 1970, Trinidad's jails were crowded for the first time with political prisoners. Eighty-seven soldiers and fifty-four militants were arrested and charged variously with treason, sedition, and mutiny.[84] The arrested included trade-union leaders, university students, graduates, and lecturers, not all of whom were centrally involved in the demonstrations. The police, who unlike the soldiers remained loyal to the government,[85] were hastily equipped with arms which, ironically, Williams had requested from the Americans on April 22, ten years to the day after he had threatened to force them out of the Chaguaramas peninsula which the Regiment now occupies.[86]

84 The charge against the soldiers reads like something out of the sixteenth century: 'Between the 21st and 25th days of April, 1970 ... being persons owing allegiance to Our Sovereign Lady the Queen, maliciously and traitorously by themselves and together with divers others levied war against Our Sovereign Lady the Queen to subvert and destroy her Legislature and Government then established, and in order to fulfil, perfect and bring to effect this most evil and wicked treason, maliciously and treasonably did ... seize and armed themselves and others with large quantities of arms, ammunition, hand-grenades, explosives and other weapons of war ... [and did] tumultuously march and parade on and towards the City of Port of Spain in hostile, warlike military order by themselves and with others under the cover of divers civilian persons.' TG, June 30, 1970.

85 The reasons for the loyalty of the police force despite the similarity of their social origins are difficult to determine, but it may have been due to: (1) better leadership, discipline, and professionalism; (2) traditional rivalries between the police and the Regiment; (3) the fact that the police had borne the brunt of the verbal attacks of the militants; (4) greater politicization in the army because of low morale and greater evidence of racial and rank discrimination.

86 Williams said he tried to obtain arms because the 'rebel' soldiers controlled the

During those tension-filled months there were dramatic manhunts, seizures of documents, reports of hidden weapons being found, charges of harassment in the prisons, and clashes between soldiers and prison officials. Four persons were killed in skirmishes with the police who, feeling threatened, began making demands that guns be made a regular part of their uniform. A dusk-to-dawn curfew was also imposed, though subsequently relaxed on May 1.

The intensity of the crisis was heightened considerably on August 7 when the Government introduced the draft National Security Act 1970 (Public Order Bill) which it had been threatening since 1965. The bill was a Draconian piece of legislation. It was a compilation of some of the most repressive colonial laws and a few new ones tailored to suit the contemporary situation in Trinidad. The following are excerpts from the explanatory notes which prefaced the bill:

This Bill seeks to make provisions with respect to the public safety, public order and defence of Trinidad and Tobago ... .

Part I would regulate public meetings and marches. In the case of the holding of a public meeting, persons desiring to do so are required to notify the Commissioner at least seventy-two hours before, but not more than fourteen days before, the holding of a meeting. The Commissioner may prohibit the meeting or impose conditions and he is required so to do within forty-eight hours of receipt of the notification. In the case of a public march a permit must be obtained.

The Bill provides for the special case of a political meeting held between the day of publication of the notice of election and the day preceding polling day. The Commissioner may not refuse permission to hold a political meeting and there will be no restrictions on the use of loudspeakers for the purpose of advertising or conducting the election campaign beyond 11 pm.

Part II of the Bill would penalize any person inciting others to racial hatred or to violence. Prohibit the publication or communication of unlawful statements calculated to incite persons to subvert established authority.

Part III of the Bill would prohibit the organization or training of quasi-military organizations, and unlawful oathtaking. There would be established a specific offence relating to looting in times of public disorder or other emergency.

Part IV would give power of entry to the Police for the purpose of search of any premises or place as well as the power to seize any firearms. ...

Part V would enable the Minister to make detention orders and orders restricting

armoury and the police were ill-equipped. He said he tried to obtain arms from Africa, Jamaica, and Guyana but in the end had to buy a supply from the US and Venezuela. Williams was obviously embarrassed about this dependence on the US as he was by the American and Venezuelan naval presence just outside Trinidad's territorial waters.

the movement of suspected persons as well as power to give directions and impose restrictions on the right of citizens to leave the country, where the Minister is satisfied that it is necessary in the interest of public order, public safety or defence.

All such orders and directions would be subject to review by a Tribunal. In the case of a detention order, the detainee may not be detained thereunder for a longer period than three months, unless the Tribunal has reported that there is sufficient cause for his detention. If the Tribunal determines that there is insufficient cause, the detainee must be released. Qualification for membership of the Tribunal would be the holding of the office of a Judge of the Supreme Court or not less than ten years standing as a barrister-at-law. There would be provision for *ex-gratia* payments for the maintenance of a detainee's dependents if the Minister is satisfied that the detainee is unable so to do by reason of his detention. This Part would remain in force for a period of twelve months only, but may be continued in force from time to time by resolution of the House of Representatives passed by a simple majority. Where, however, the provisions of this Part cease to be in force by failure to pass the necessary resolution, they may be revived by a Proclamation of the Governor General for a period of three months. Thereafter the provisions may similarly be renewed by resolution of the House.[87]

The basic weakness of the bill is that it left undefined such nebulous concepts as 'subversion', 'established authority', 'incite', 'necessary and expedient', and relied on the judgment and partiality of politicians and law men. Judging by the experience of countries with similar laws, the criterion for their utilization has more often than not been whim, grudge, or political expediency. One section of the bill which drew almost unanimous hostility was that which dealt with meetings. For a meeting to be held, one not only had to inform the police,

---

87   *An Act to Make Provision respecting the Public Safety, Public Order and Defence of Trinidad and Tobago*, Government Printery, Port of Spain, 1970, pp. 2–3. For another view, see the *Nation*, Sept. 4, 1970. The *Nation* argued that several countries, including India and England, had public order acts, and that most of what the bill contained was updated and in some cases improved versions of what was already on the books – inherited from the colonial period. The opposition to the bill was dismissed as lies, political propaganda, and opportunism. It was pointed out that the draft act actually improved on the constitution in providing justice for those detained preventively, and that old colonial laws which allowed a judge to ban a newspaper for a year were not incorporated into the new act. The *Nation* felt the Public Order Act was necessary because militants were: (1) stirring up racial hatred; (2) abusing rights of minorities, especially whites who were spat upon and slapped; (3) abusing the freedom of women to dress as they chose by pulling off wigs; (4) using language calculated to incite violence ('burn, baby burn', 'take now, pay later', i.e. loot); (5) concealing weapons and dynamite. But the real question is not whether such laws are necessary, but how they are framed, how they are used, and by whom. The 'state' needs to be respected by citizens, but citizens also require defence from overzealous representatives of the 'state'.

but also to give the date, the time, the organizers, and the names of speakers who were not citizens of Trinidad. Moreover, even when permission was obtained, the meeting could be dispersed by an officer above the rank of inspector if he felt that public safety was endangered.

Many commentators felt that this power, if misused (and the political climate led many to suspect it would be) would allow the government in power to control all political activity except at election time. As the Medical Association, which felt that the PNM was reacting like a 'blind man with a pistol', commented:

This is so repressive that it is likely to have the effect of immediately creating an illegitimate and violent opposition and of driving it underground, to explode spasmodically in acts of violence and sabotage.

Far from protecting the ordinary citizen, this would add to the dangers attending his daily life and increase further his sense of insecurity. This section is thus both unjustified and unintelligent and we reject it entirely.[88]

The outcry against the bill was vehement and overwhelming with criticisms coming not only from radical militants, but establishment lawyers, doctors, the unions, the official opposition, university students, and the established press. The only major body to endorse the bill openly was the Catholic Church which spoke through an editorial in the *Catholic News*. A great deal of the support which the PNM had rallied after April evaporated, and on September 13 it withdrew the bill much to the chagrin of the Attorney General. He offered his resignation to the Prime Minister, but it was not accepted.

Once again the PNM had shown that it lacked all sense of public relations. The bill should never have been introduced in the form in which it appeared, let alone during the last months of the life of the government. Even assuming that the government wished to take precautionary measures to prevent a recurrence of the February-April crisis when the state of emergency was lifted, it did not take the trouble to explain to a frightened public why it was resurrecting old colonial laws, or why it felt it necessary to set aside basic constitutional freedoms that Trinidadians had assumed they would never be deprived of. The fact that such laws existed in England or had been used in colonial days was no justification for making them the cornerstone of the Trinidad nation-state. Many people feared that Trinidad was on its way to becoming a typical repressive dictatorship.

Despite the fact that it was able to attract a large crowd at the first public meeting which it held after the emergency was lifted on November 19, the NJAC became somewhat isolated on the extreme radical fringe of Trinidad

88   TG, Sept. 9, 1970.

politics. It has become associated in the public mind with violence, arson, and looting, and the PNM is doing all it can to reinforce that image. As the *Nation* commented, 'As an organization, the stereotype of the NJAC in the minds of the average law-abiding citizen (and most people are such) is that it is an organization associated with destruction of property, arson, rape, even murder, and very few people, except the leftist extremists, want to identify with such an organization. ... People found ... NJAC had nothing to offer but revolution and keep-fit but tiring marches in a para-military exercise.'[89]

The real problem with the NJAC, as with so many other radical groups in the Caribbean, is that its skills are essentially destructive. Its strength is in its ability to define problems, to lay bare contradictions in society and to mobilize the frustrations that are so widespread at all levels of society. The NJAC lacks the organization to channel into constructive outlets the consciousness and the energies which it has roused so dramatically. Intoxicated by its spectacular but unexpected success, it sought a premature confrontation with the establishment hoping to bring it to its knees. As Lloyd Best notes, the NJAC was trying to win by 'knockout' instead of on points when it lacked the capacity to do so. But you 'can't provoke a revolutionary situation unless you have the resources to take the power – and we did not have them'.[90] Best argues that unconventional politics is not necessarily the politics of violence. It could be a politics of participation and involvement. The NJAC, in pursuit of its maximalist strategy, failed to realize that only a few of its supporters were ready for revolution, and that the bulk of its support came from people who wanted jobs, better economic and social opportunities for the dispossessed and black dignity, but wanted this to be achieved short of total revolution. Thus, when the demonstrations began to turn into 'Molotov cocktail parties', and began to have the effect of driving away investment and destroying existing plants, many abandoned them. The NJAC might have been correct in pointing out that certain kinds of investments should not be encouraged to remain in Trinidad at all, but this is an intellectual viewpoint not shared by those who want a job at any cost. As the *Nation* noted, 'The NJAC refused to recognise the basic facts ... when they appealed to the masses not to take up the "bribes" of the Government by accepting jobs on the Special Works Programme. The isolation of the hard-core NJAC elements began when the unemployed registered heavily at the various registration centres.'[91]

---

89 *Nation*, Jan. 29, 1971. Some irresponsible persons talked about 'national rape and arson week'.
90 The defeat of the Public Order Act is the sort of 'points' victory Best has in mind. *Tapia*, Dec. 20, 1970.
91 The *Nation*, Jan. 29, 1971.

The NJAC refused to contest the 1971 election, since it associated Parliament, elections, parties, and other conventional political institutions and processes with 'the frequent frustrations felt by our people'. It believes that what is now needed are new institutions and processes that genuinely involve the people. They are not bothered by the rising tide of reaction among the middle class and the middle aged since their strategy is based on the fact that the bulk of its hard-core support comes from the young who have shown a marked contempt for 'conventional' politics.[92]

If the NJAC expects to have any influence in the future, it must turn to the task of building up a grass-roots following by becoming involved in community action. It must also abandon its romantic 'all or none' strategy and begin the painstaking task of working towards creative but intermediate solutions. Lloyd Best is right when he accuses the NJAC of simplifying the issues and of refusing to do their intellectual homework:

The weakness of the Black Solidarity movement here is its tendency to over-simplify the issues and to see things in terms of black and white, we vs. they, capitalists vs. workers, intellectual discussion vs. direct action. ... It is crucial that in the ranks of the dispossessed there are no white, but the real war is still between the dispossessed and the over-privileged. ... To define the issue this way is not to underplay the significance of blackness but to guard against the danger of racism in reverse. ... Blowing up Kirpalanis and slapping up white people out of a sense of outrage and resentment will never destroy tyranny.[93]

Best also warns that demonstrations and protest are not enough:

We cannot risk destroying more than we create. We cannot even risk threatening to do so because that would be playing into the hands of reaction ... . We [must] seek to avoid the kind of 'revolution' which by taking a 'leap in the dark' succeeds only in replacing one tyranny by another.[94]

92 The *Express* in an editorial (Nov. 22, 1970) commented on crowd reaction to the first political meeting sponsored by the NJAC, ACDC-DLP, and other groups after the ending of the emergency. 'The striking difference of course is that the crowd is now against the PNM. ... There is not ... the simple preoccupation with voting a Government or Dr Eric Williams, out of power. It is wider in scope. It embraces the feeling that the time has come to straighten out the mess the country is in. The people want their politics to mean more than Cabinet reshuffles ... and rhetoric about law and order and about a new society. And this is where NJAC is right and wrong at the same time. The people do not want "conventional politics" if it means the kind of politics they now have. They want people politics – which is the basis on which our conventional politics started out.'
93 'National Crisis', *Tapia*, Special 1, n.d.
94 *Ibid.*

Tapia House was founded in 1969 by Lloyd Best to symbolize his belief that genuine reconstruction must begin from the bottom up using material and procedures that the folk are familiar with.[95] It was also regarded as a gesture of protest against Best's colleagues in the New World Group who had opted for conventional political activity. Best expressed disdain for what he referred to as 'doctor politics'. He argued that all the movements that have appeared in the Caribbean so far have failed because they were essentially charismatic movements based on devotion to a single leader. In Trinidad, Cipriani, Butler, Solomon, Williams, Capildeo, Millette, and even Granger failed because they did not organize genuine grass-roots movements, because they assumed that all that was needed to transform Caribbean society was to capture and manipulate existing institutions of the state. Best felt that 'We have to stop being duped by personalities into forming now-for-now political parties. We have to discard the Westminster parliamentary model and design a form of government appropriate to our needs.'[96]

Best asserted that the present system of government in Trinidad was established from outside, and that it had no roots in the people. But there is no evidence that the existing constitution was imposed by the Colonial Office. It is far more accurate to say that the political élite borrowed metropolitan institutions uncritically, and that the bulk of the population simply assumed that these were the only acceptable alternatives since they knew about nothing else. But it is true that the party system does not work well in Trinidad, that no one takes Parliament seriously, and that the Westminster framework merely disguises what is in fact a modernization of the authoritarian colonial system.

Best and the Tapia Group are scornful of Williams and the PNM as the following quotations from their highly influential newspaper indicate:

Perspectives For a New Society – fourteen years too late. ... Instant confidence in the people! Instant morality! ... Williams has been taking over the language of this movement, but he cannot copy the way of living and relating. He does not have the moral authority to adopt our programmes because the implementation requires dedication and sacrifice on a scale he could never command.[97]

The Little King cannot even organise a dance. He has promised at least six reorganisations of the civil service and countless reorganisations of the PNM. But his

---

95 The thatched roof tapia hut in which the group meets and carries on its cultural activities is situated at the rear of Best's home.
96 *Tapia*, Nov. 29, 1970.
97 *Ibid.*, Sept. 28, 1970.

overriding need for sycophants, flatterers and news-carriers and his insistence on perpetually demonstrating who is head-boy have made any serious improvement impossible. ... No Afro-Saxon King can afford any real decentralisation of power.[98]

Best accuses Williams of having become a traditional Caribbean *caudillo*, a 'Papa Doc' who now relies on bribes, intimidation, and terror to maintain control now that he has lost the 'mandate of heaven'. But he does not see this as a personal failing on the part of Williams. 'The Williams failure is a failure not of motive or of skill, it is a failure of messianic method.'[99]

Like Williams and other radicals before him, Best is contemptuous of the established churches in Trinidad, particularly the Catholic Church which he accuses of aiding and abetting reaction, and of being an 'evil incubus on society'. He condones the Black Power demonstration which took place in the Roman Catholic Cathedral in Port of Spain and says, 'We have no apologies; we have no respect for Church or State. One cannot have respect simply because a Primate or a Prime Minister demands it. Respect is the ... spontaneous recognition of integrity. ... His Disgrace the Archbishop lives in a "Palace", and talks mealy-mouthed about "wanting to help". If he wants to help, let him take off his absurd medieval trappings and discard the phony glamour of his office. ... Let him stand up minus his green beret and be counted for a genuine commitment to the cause of social justice.'[100]

The courts and the army high command were also ridiculed, as were the new movements and mergers of old formations that were being arranged for the 1971 elections. The ACDC-DLP was dismissed as a '*jamette* (prostitute) association'. 'Rats from old movements cannot conjure up brand new movements from a hat.'[101] Robinson was accused of trying to straddle the old world and the new, of tailoring an image that would make him appear safe to businessmen and hip to radicals.

Best also chided his former colleagues in the New World Group who formed the UNIP. That decision he believed was a premature attempt to replace one doctor with another who may well turn out to be 'Dr Worse'. 'We must discard the conventional politics of exchanging messiahs in the square ... of looking for a man with a plan for disciples to follow ... on to the promised land. ... From the frying-pan into the frying-pan.'[102]

Referring to the question that was being so frequently asked in Trinidad by those who felt the need for change – 'but who we go put?' – Best warned that the issue was not 'whom we put, but how we change the system'. The time had come to 'lift our politics above the manoeuvrings and posturings of the

98 *Ibid.*, Aug. 9, 1970.
100 'National Crisis', *Tapia*, Special 1. n.d.
102 *Ibid.*

99 *Ibid.*, Jan. 31, 1971.
101 *Tapia*, Jan. 31, 1971.

kingmakers and would-be kings. To the extent that we succeed, it will be a matter of "the king is dead, long live the people".'[103] The Tapia Group feels that what Trinidad needs most now is a radically new and popularly based constitution. To forge this, a constituent assembly consisting of representatives of all recognized groups and institutions must be summoned. The assembly, which would be an informal government, would not only work out a new constitutional settlement, but would also define the *basic* policy alternatives that the country would pursue in the years ahead. As Augustus Ramrekersingh noted:

Open discussion will go beyond the constitutional issue. It will embrace all other fundamental issues affecting the nation. Of course, there will be some confusion in the initial stages; then, too, there are likely to be conflicts and some horse-trading. But at the end of a free and open discussion, a basic consensus will be reached – a consensus about the type of constitutional arrangements and about the type of economy and society we need.

New political alignments, based on clearly defined interests and issues, will almost certainly be formed. For the first time in this country constitutional change will be initiated from below and not by colonial officials, party conventions, cabinet meetings and rigged Queen's Hall discussions. Who will summon this Constituent Assembly? Not the Government and not Williams. Only the people can do it. When the state breaks down, only the people have the moral authority to set it up again.[104]

Tapia's proposals for constitutional change are far-reaching but highly imaginative:

1   Abandon the Monarchy. ... Establish a Participatory Republic with a Governor General as Ceremonial Head of State and a Prime Minister as Head of Government.
2   Establish an island-wide system of Local Councils in Trinidad. Give them real power. The PNM has almost completely eroded the functions of local councils.
3   Establish a specially powerful Local Authority in Tobago.
4   Change the basis for selecting the Senate and increase the size of that Assembly. Enhance its power over appointments and strengthen its influence on State opinion. Representatives of Senate must be chosen by community interests

---

103 *Ibid.*, Sept. 28, 1970. 'Leadership is continuously providing for its own obsolescence. To the extent that his leadership is successful, the leader expects to be superseded, precisely because he understands that the basic condition of his success is the active participation of those whom he leads. Without this participation leadership turns to messianic prophecy, in which case its utmost destiny is to preside over eternal crisis.' *Ibid.*, Nov. 10, 1969.
104 *Ibid.*

rather than by the government. It would select the President of the Republic from among its own members, the Auditor General, the Electoral and Boundaries Commissions and Commissions of Enquiry. It could also initiate legislation and supervise the operation of the state-owned media.

5   Establish a National Panchaiyat [Congress] of both Houses and give it influence on appointments and on legislation.

6   Entrench Congressional power of Constitutional Review every two generations (30 years). Maintain flexibility.

7   Give Congress power to review representation in the Senate every five years. Members can be included or excluded by simple majority. The Senate will keep up with the times. While Congress and the Senate will thus be important, the elected Legislature will however have final authority in all matters not specifically assigned to these other bodies.

8   Abandon the Privy Council and establish a Local Court, preferably a West Indian Court. Reform the rules of the Civil Service to grant more freedom. Reform the rules of the Teaching Service to grant more freedom.

9   Establish National Service to help community spirit.

10   Shift the Capital out of Port of Spain to help decentralization.[105]

Only after the assembly had met and done its work would there be elections. But it is not clear whether the Tapia House Group would be willing to contest even these elections. The Group appears to have a real fear of being contaminated by the exercise of power. Despite its Rousseauist concern for popular involvement and the futility of imposing ideas from outside, it seems that the Group would be content if there was a government in power to which it would have access and influence.

Tapia members feel that a great deal of work still needs to be done *before* the group formally becomes or joins a political party. For the time being, they are content to work at the community level in active co-operation with people. Out of this collaborative effort a new political culture and new policy alternatives might well begin to emerge. In his recommendations for a participatory democracy, Best indeed comes very close to what Williams was preaching in the early days of his ministry:

The time will certainly come when we will need a political party. But if it is to be an authentic political party and not just the electoral apparatus of another Doctor or set of Doctors, it needs to be based on confident, competent membership, well organised in the constituencies. Since we are beginning from a position where people have had little experience of community collaboration and political participation, where the Central Government dominates the lives of the population, and

105 'Constitutional reform, Tapia's Proposals', Tapia Pamphlets no. 4, 5, June 13, 1971.

where local leadership is systematically suppressed by social and economic processes, the strategy must be to undertake schemes which will promote grass-roots development.

The innovation we can make is to encourage more local and private initiatives and to promote wider mobilization of local and private resources. We must ... reject Doctor politics and assume the fullest responsibility for solving specific day-to-day problems of living.

In this way, the confidence and the commitment which have been lacking will soon begin to show themselves. There will be a movement among the people. Out of this, new politics and a new party will in due course arise. It will be change from below. And that is the only real change.

Those who are most concerned with politics and the early transfer of power may believe that this transition should be escaped. But this is possible only at a very high price. A political party by its nature will have to insist on discipline and organisation of a kind that risks frustrating the emergence of the community leaders which we so badly need. Pressures will be brought to bear on the party by the Press and the public to take positions on issues which are yet to be sorted out by party members. This can only mean *ex cathedra* declarations by the Doctor leaders. The dissatisfaction which this will cause among independent thinkers in the organization will force these Doctors, in the legitimate interest of maintaining a solid party front, to excommunicate all dissenters. We have to guard against it happening again.[106]

The February-April events and the massive public outcry which forced the Government to withdraw the Public Order Bill helped to convince Tapia and many other sceptics that a significant number of people were ready for a new kind of politics and were feeling towards other strategies of economic organization. As *Tapia* itself comments, 'We are certain that the ingredients of serious politics are available now to the country and that we have only to bring them together in public. We think that the time has [been] reached to found a national political system based on realistic alignments and compromises; we can feel such a system coming with radical unity as one result. But all this lies a little way ahead – beyond confrontation No. 3.'[107]

Despite this growing confidence and feeling of imminence, *Tapia* conceded that Williams and the PNM would win the next election. Its strategy, however, was to try and make that victory as Pyrrhic as possible by inducing the electorate to boycott the election and by harassing the PNM after its 'victory'. As Best noted, 'There is no sense in which we can "lose" the election. We will be getting stronger every day and we will be calling the tune for the government.'[108] The PNM may reign, but it would not be allowed to rule. The alternatives are not PNM or chaos, but PNM *and* chaos.

106 *Tapia*, Oct. 19, 1969.   107 *Ibid.*, Nov. 29, 1970.   108 *Ibid.*, Oct. 19, 1969.

THE 1971 ELECTION

The 1971 election was full of political surprises, the most dramatic being that the PNM won all thirty-six seats in a poll that was the lowest in the nation's history. One of the most significant political events of the election was the fact that the ACDC-DLP withdrew from the contest. The group had spent a great deal of money advertising its programme, and appeared to many to be gearing itself for a close and bitter contest. Three days before nomination day and two weeks before election day, its leader, A.N.R. Robinson, declared to a stunned nation that he would neither contest the elections, nor support any party or candidate who did. Some of his party colleagues who were on the rostrum with him and who had in their speeches talked about going to the polls were dumbfounded. Jamadar complained bitterly and angrily about Robinson's autocratic behaviour. Williams dismissed Robinson as a 'half-wit' and ridiculed the ACDC-DLP with the remark that its 'marriage' of December had ended in 'divorce' by May.[109]

There are a number of possible explanations for Robinson's decision. He himself justified his behaviour in terms of principle. He argued that a successful election boycott would indicate clearly that the existing political system was no longer legitimate, and that the ensuing crisis would generate new social demands for a redefinition of Trinidad's political economy. Anything short of a fundamental reappraisal of the political and economic system would constitute a 'mockery'. Some of Robinson's critics, on the other hand, felt that an equally powerful explanation was his awareness that the alliance could not win the election and that he himself might not be re-elected. Robinson might indeed have calculated that he stood a better chance of victory at a subsequent election, and that it was not prudent for him to acquire the stigma of being a 'loser'. Like most opposition leaders, he did not relish being on the opposition benches, especially since he had himself enjoyed power for fourteen years. He would have Williams' 'crown' or nothing at all. Robinson must also have been aware that if the alliance was not victorious, Jamadar would have a stronger claim to leadership since Indians would dominate the opposition benches.

DLP leaders were certain, however, that they would retain the twelve seats which they held previously, and felt that there was a good chance that the ACDC could win the extra seats needed to defeat the PNM. They were constantly puzzled by Robinson's campaign strategy of concentrating on 'sure' DLP constituencies and there was speculation that having failed to break up the PNM, he was hell-bent on smashing the DLP. Others even believed that there was a racially motivated plot between Robinson and the PNM to destroy the DLP! As the Democratic Liberation Party 'Organ', the *Bomb*, put it: 'There were

109 *Newsweek*, June 7, 1971, p. 11.

several unsavoury features about the campaign ... [one being] the plot between Williams and Robinson to bamboozle Jamadar and company and deprive the Opposition from serving in Parliament. ... Every move made by Robinson since he quit the PNM and ... became leader of the DLP nailed him as the man sent to block the Opposition from going to Parliament.'[110] The DLP leadership does not accept the collusion thesis, but they strongly believe that Robinson's aim was to 'emasculate' the DLP as an organization. As the Party declared after the election,

Mr A.N.R. Robinson broke with the PNM and formed the ACDC. After a few private discussions with Mr Robinson and members of his team, the DLP cabinet appointed a negotiating team led by Dr Elton Richardson to discuss a merger with the ACDC. Early in the talks it appeared that the ACDC wanted a unitary Party in which youth and new faces would be the dominating characteristic. With patience we explained that our Party, the DLP, had roots deeply embedded in a slowly changing world and that partnership and equality was our concept of unity. After some difficulties, agreement was reached. The agreement and its supplementary decisions weighed heavily in favour of the ACDC. They insisted on control of the treasury, organization and the leadership.

We conceded in the interest of unity and the deep felt need to answer the PNM challenge. Despite our over generous concessions, we were assured that 'partnership and equality' which were the cornerstones of our agreement, will be scrupulously respected. This has proven not to be so. Despite pious pronouncements, it is now clear to everyone that the objective of the ACDC and its leadership was the emasculation of the DLP, the capture of its support and the discreditation of its leadership. Mr Robinson appears convinced that all politicians and political parties except the ACDC are irrelevant and should be disbanded totally.[111]

But it is also clear that Jamadar was hoping to use Robinson not only to unseat Williams, but also to maintain leadership of the DLP in the face of challenges from Bhadase Maraj (whose electoral threat to contest whatever constituency he chose, he took very seriously). Although there was strong pressure on Jamadar by Indian communalists to desist from the merger which could lead to the creation of another Negro prime minister, Jamadar felt that this was the best opportunity ever presented to the Indians to break out of the role of opposition into which the racial structure of the society had confined them. Robinson needed a popular base in the rural areas if he was to unseat the PNM and thought he found this in the DLP. But he was fully aware that unless the DLP appeared in a new guise, urban blacks would not give the merger their support.

110 May 28, 1971.   111 TG, June 19, 1971.

It is difficult to disentangle the facts from the myths surrounding the crisis of the ACDC-DLP, but it is known that the strategy committee of coalition was badly split over the issue of whether to contest the election or not. A vote taken to determine the policy to be adopted indicated that a narrow majority was in favour of doing so. Robinson, who was in the minority, was not only concerned about the possibility of losing the election, but was also under strong pressure by the URO to co-operate with its no-vote campaign. Robinson's strategy (perhaps it was sheer indecision) was to recommend that the decision ought not to be made public until the people had been consulted. A voters' rally was called on May 9, and Robinson, after engaging in a dialogue with the crowd felt that he had been given a mandate to boycott the 'mock' election. The crowd, he felt, had confirmed what his own political conscience had pre-disposed him to do.

Robinson's colleagues in the merger accused him of treachery, undemocratic behaviour, and political cowardice. A crowd at a party rally was not the electorate, they argued. It was also felt that Robinson had cleverly manipulated a section of the crowd into opting for the no-vote strategy without giving those who disagreed a fair opportunity to be heard. The executive of the strategy committee believed that the decision ought to have been taken collegially and not by Robinson alone.

Those who felt that the election should be contested (and they included elements of the ACDC) opted to continue without Robinson. It was argued that staying out of the election was an irresponsible tactic, given the political climate in the country. The preservation of the system of conventional politics had to take priority over the legitimate demands for electoral reform: 'A decision not to vote means defeat for the constitutional system of government and an unsettling period in which the constitutional and the unconventional forces will sooner or later have to resolve which of the two will handle the running of the country, and whether constitutional progress will be replaced by another system of government.'[112]

But despite the fact that some elements in the business community were bank-rolling the coalition, the demoralization caused by Robinson's decision proved too difficult to overcome, especially since he had control of the purse-strings. Jamadar was not certain that he could defeat Maraj, and attendance at rallies had made it clear that no major breach could be made in PNM strongholds. In spite of its previously expressed concern with constitutionl propriety, the DLP decided to join the boycott campaign.

Radical groups were elated by the collapse of the merger. The PNM, which was certain it would be returned, was dismayed, and invited the DLP to change

112 *Ibid.*, May 11, 1971.

places with the jackasses in the canefields.[113] The *Guardian*, although agreeing on the validity of some of the demands of the opposition, spoke for moderate elements when it declared that 'boycotting the election would open the door for the extremist and totalitarian elements to exploit the situation – indulge in violence, confuse the masses and disrupt the social and economic progress of the country. This would be an ideal situation for those who wish to obstruct the political and economic progress of Trinidad and Tobago.'[114]

Only two parties challenged the PNM electorally. The more important was Bhadase Maraj's Democratic Liberation Party, which offered no manifesto or programme. The Party sponsored twenty candidates, many of whom were political has-beens from the pre-Independence era. The African National Congress, of which few people knew very much, presented seven candidates. The PNM was unopposed in eight constituencies. The election campaign was marked by sporadic incidents of violence, including the throwing of home-made bombs into the headquarters of the ruling party and into the homes of the Commander in Chief of the Defence Forces and a PNM minister. Attempts were also made to assassinate the commander in chief of the Coast Guard and the chief state prosecutor in one of the courts martial. Both were seriously injured.

The Democratic Liberation Party made little impact on the electorate and was supported by only 14,921 voters or 4.22 per cent of those registered.[115] The Party did poorly even in areas which are heavily populated by Indians. It gained the support of no more than 4.88 per cent of the votes cast in areas previously held by the Labour Party, a performance that may well have brought to an end the political careers of Bhadase Maraj and persons like Lionel Seukeran, Surujpat Mathura, Stephen Maharaj, and other old political notables of the Indian community. Much to everyone's surprise, Maraj himself lost to a virtually unknown Negro in an area which was over 90 per cent Hindu.[116] The same pattern held for other DLP areas even though PNM support actually declined in nine of these constituencies. Although PNM supporters claim that the capture of DLP seats represented a triumph for their Party, a

---

113 *Newsweek*, June 7, 1971, p. 11.   114 TG, May 11, 1971.
115 Cf. Table x. Cf. also TG, May 28, 1971 for figures issued by the Electoral Commission.
116 For Maraj, the president of the powerful Hindu Maha Sabha, the defeat in a Hindu stronghold was so galling that he threatened to retire from public life. As he complained. 'The people are not interested in me politically, union-wise, religiously or in any other form. It is clear they wanted a dictatorship and a one party state.' *Moko*, May 28, 1971. Maraj however clung tenaciously to the leadership of the Sugar Workers Union and was re-elected in June 1971 to the presidency of the Maha Sabha for the nineteenth consecutive term. Maraj died shortly after in October 1971.

TABLE X

Performance of the parties 1971:
28 contested constituencies

Constituency	PNM	DLP	ANC	Ind.
Port of Spain East	4,651		694	
Port of Spain South	4,352		810	
Port of Spain Central	4,761	289		
Port of Spain North East	4,430		551	
Port of Spain West	4,211	150	50	
Diego Martin East	4,877		536	
Diego Martin West	4,005			752
San Juan West	3,928		129	
San Juan East	4,356	385		
St Joseph	4,424	519		
Tunapuna	4,594	114	91	
Fyzabad	3,346	509		
La Brea	4,473	284		
Point Fortin	4,310	483		
Toco-Manzanilla	4,499	524		
Tobago West	2,425			245
FORMER DLP CONSTITUENCES				
St Augustine	2,439	2,104		
Caroni East	3,019	363		
Chaguanas	2,052	911		
Couva	3,542	1,380		
Pointe-a-Pierre	3,366	534		
Naparima North	3,242	1,167		
Naparima South	1,169	871		
Princes Town	3,606	831		
Oropouche	1,691	1,467		
Tabaquite	2,456	284		
Nariva	2,995	1,351		
Siparia	2,551	341		

SOURCE: Trinidad and Tobago Electoral Commission

more likely explanation is that the hard-core of PNM supporters who came out to vote were actively assisted by the Democratic Labour Party which was less concerned about a PNM victory than about the prospect that the Democratic Liberation Party would become the official opposition. Despite the fact that the Labour Party endorsed the no-vote campaign, they surreptitiously campaigned *for* the PNM in Maraj's constituency.[117]

It is worth noting that despite their late conversion to the principle of boycotting the election, the Labour Party was very effective in keeping its supporters away from the polls. The highest incidence of non-voting was in the DLP areas, a fact which urban-based opponents of Williams conveniently ignore when they characterize the results of the polls in these areas as a vote

117 Reported to the author by a member of the Labour Party's executive.

TABLE XI
Performance of the electorate 1966 and 1971
(28 constituencies)

Constituency		Electorate	Votes Cast	Percentage	Non-voters	Percentage
Port of Spain East	1966	13,638	7,707	56.51	5,931	43.49
	1971	12,027	5,345	44.44	6,682	55.56
Port of Spain South	1966	12,801	6,656	52.00	6,145	48.00
	1971	12,543	5,162	41.15	7,381	58.85
Port of Spain Central	1966	12,941	7,332	56.70	5,609	43.30
	1971	12,272	5,050	41.15	7,222	58.15
Port of Spain North East	1966	13,336	7,500	56.20	5,836	43.80
	1971	12,484	4,981	39.90	7,503	60.10
Port of Spain West	1966	12,016	6,583	54.80	5,433	45.20
	1971	11,968	4,411	59.75	7,557	60.25
Diego Martin East	1966	13,989	8,235	58.90	5,754	41.10
	1971	13,188	5,412	41.04	7,775	58.96
Diego Martin West	1966	14,020	7,935	56.60	6,985	43.40
	1971	12,379	4,757	38.43	7,622	61.57
San Juan West	1966	13,360	7,144	53.50	6,216	46.50
	1971	12,596	4,057	32.21	8,439	67.79
San Juan East	1966	13,373	8,226	59.70	5,150	40.30
	1971	12,357	4,741	38.37	7,616	61.63
St Joseph	1966	13,055	8,232	63.10	4,823	36.90
	1971	13,114	4,943	37.69	4,171	62.31
Tunapuna	1966	14,111	9,540	67.61	4,571	32.39
	1971	13,079	4,829	36.92	9,387	63.08
Fyzabad	1966	12,944	9,778	75.50	3,166	24.50
	1971	12,056	3,855	31.98	8,201	68.02
La Brea	1966	12,162	7,934	65.20	4,128	34.80
	1971	12,589	4,757	37.79	7,832	62.21
Point Fortin	1966	13,359	8,950	67.00	5,409	33.00
	1971	12,461	4,793	38.46	7,668	61.54
Toco-Manzanilla	1966	12,299	8,553	69.50	3,746	30.50
	1971	12,178	5,023	41.25	7,155	58.75
Tobago West	1966	8,528	5,889	69.10	2,639	30.90
	1971	8,308	2,670	32.14	5,638	67.86
FORMER DLP CONSTITUENCIES						
St Augustine	1966	14,206	9,422	66.30	4,784	33.70
	1971	12,541	4,543	36.22	7,998	63.78

TABLE XI continued

Constituency		Electorate	Votes Cast	Percentage	Non-voters	Percentage
Caroni East	1966	12,635	8,587	68.00	4,048	32.00
	1971	12,239	3,382	27.63	8,857	72.37
Chaguanas	1966	13,373	9,768	73.00	3,605	27.00
	1971	12,548	2,963	23.61	9,585	76.39
Couva	1966	11,699	9,195	78.60	2,504	21.40
	1971	12,033	4,922	40.90	7,111	59.10
Pointe-a-Pierre	1966	12,119	9,500	78.40	2,613	22.60
	1971	13,117	3,900	29.73	9,217	70.27
Naparima North	1966	13,017	9,704	74.50	3,213	25.50
	1971	14,320	4,409	30.79	9,911	69.21
Naparima South	1966	11,200	9,133	81.50	2,057	18.50
	1971	13,760	2,040	14.82	11,720	85.18
Princes Town	1966	11,883	9,527	80.20	2,356	19.80
	1971	14,180	4,437	31.29	9,743	68.71
Oropouche	1966	13,685	10,534	77.00	3,151	23.00
	1971	14,069	3,158	22.45	10,918	77.55
Tabaquite	1966	12,532	9,352	74.60	3,180	25.40
	1971	13,147	2,740	20.84	10,407	79.16
Nariva	1966	13,761	9,441	68.60	4,320	31.40
	1971	12,735	4,376	34.36	8,359	65.64
Siparia	1966	13,426	10,015	74.60	3,411	25.40
	1971	12,514	2,892	23.11	9,622	76.89

Source: *Express*, June 8, 1971, compiled by Hiralal Bajnath.

of no confidence in Williams and an endorsement of their own programme. The fact that in seven DLP constituencies as much as 70 per cent of the electorate stayed away was more a gesture of deference to the DLP leadership than it was a vote of non-confidence in Williams and conventional politics. As Hiralal Bajnath notes, 'The entire voting pattern was reversed in ... DLP areas, that is, the percentages of voters almost equated themselves as non-voters in 1971. The magnitude of non-voters in the traditional opposition areas was chiefly responsible for the record low poll.'[118]

The DLP has now dissociated itself from the ACDC, which it claims has been taken over by extremists and subversives 'intent on revolutionary activities and confrontation with the Government'.[119] The Party has again opted for

118 *Express*, June 8, 1971.   119 TG, June 19, 1971.

conventional politics and is anxious to convince the electorate that it is still the only reasonable alternative to the PNM. It nevertheless refused to contest the local government elections which were held in October 1971.

The African National Congress, which had challenged what it considered to be the PNM's betrayal of Black Power, did even worse than the Democratic Liberation Party, winning only 2,861 votes or less than 1 per cent of the electorate. The two independents who contested attracted only 997 voters.

The PNM lived up to its claim of being the 'premier organized party in Trinidad and Tobago'.[120] Despite strong pressures to resign, or at least to introduce pre-electoral reforms, Williams, sensing the political confusion of the opposition, called an election which the opposition claims caught it by surprise.[121] Using a campaign style that resembled that of the 'old world' which it had come to bury in 1956, Williams tried hard to look less 'Afro-Saxon' by abandoning the proverbial coat and tie in favour of an open shirt and neckkerchief. During the carnival season he visited a large number of steelband yards and calypso tents and generally tried to project an image that was 'blacker' culturally than had been the case since Independence. The popular view was that Williams was 'playing mas' (i.e. masquerading) for the benefit of the electorate. Similar visits were made to Muslim festivals. In spite of this new 'mod' and 'Afro'-image, the power base of the Party had come to rest more and more on the old, the fair-skinned, and the established.[122] This silent minority made a special effort to turn out to vote for the PNM which they saw as the last defendable fortress against chaos and subversion.

To the great surprise of everyone in Trinidad and the Caribbean, and much to Williams' embarrassment, the elections gave the PNM complete control of Parliament, making Trinidad a de facto one-party state. But the PNM victory was not as unequivocal as appeared initially. As the opposition had hoped, there was massive non-voting: of the 352,802 persons who were

120 'PNM Perspective in the Seventies,' ibid., Nov. 29, 1970.
121 The Opposition complained that there were only four weeks notice of the election, but Williams had announced in late January that the elections would come like a thief in the night. The PNM had started to organize in January. The opposition on the other hand seemed completely paralysed.
122 The PNM claims that between June 1969 and June 1971 its membership rose by 6,610 to approximately 60,000. Membership is said to have increased dramatically after April 1970. 'Many a citizen who had formerly been on the sidelines felt he must record his support for a Party which had governed democratically for 15 years.' But of the 6,610 new members, 5,787 were adults and 923 were youths. New membership was heaviest in the middle-class constituency of St Anns. New recruits were difficult to come by in the inner city – in central Port of Spain there were 52 new recruits of whom only one was a youth – and in the rural areas. TG, Sept. 29, 1971.

registered, only 118,549 or 33.6 per cent voted. Of these, 99,770 or 28.28 per cent voted for the PNM. If all 36 seats had been contested, however, and if the average turnout in the 28 constituencies were to be taken as a guide, the PNM might well have increased its share of the voting electorate to somewhere in the vicinity of 43 per cent. This, however, is still the lowest turnout in Trinidad's postwar history. Intimidation and fear of what might happen on polling day discouraged many from turning up at the polls. The absence of meaningful competition also had the same effect, even though the issue of voting *per se* was the central theme in the election. Many would-be PNM supporters assumed that there was no threat, and that there was therefore no need to be inconvenienced by going to the voting-booth.[123]

The details of the election results indicate quite clearly that the PNM would have retained all the seats it won in 1966 except the one held by Robinson if the ACDC-DLP had contested the election. Surprisingly, the Party *increased* its support in six constituencies, and in all but three others its loss of support was below 10 per cent. The decrease of support over the 28 constituencies was 19,120, while the gain was 2,865, giving a net loss of 16,225 votes. In the Prime Minister's constituency, the decrease was 1,126 or 8.09 per cent and in no constituency did more than 45 per cent of the electorate vote. Sixteen constituencies, including all those formerly controlled by the DLP, were won by less than one-third of the eligible votes, and in ten cases by less than one-quarter. In two cases, seats were won by less than one-eighth of the eligible votes.

While it is true that the erosion of support for the PNM was not as dramatic as expected – only 4.8 per cent over the 28 constituencies contested, if one takes into account the fact that the eligible electorate in 1971 was lower than it was in 1969 by over 100,000 – it is hard to avoid the conclusion that the PNM's victory was a hollow one, and that the issue of who will rule Trinidad authoritatively for the next five years had not been settled. Williams is, however, certain that he is still the source of power and authority. As he declared on the eve of polling day (in language reminiscent of Albert Gomes' 1955 statement that 'I am the Government of Trinidad and Tobago'), 'I'm the one who has the power here. When I say "come", you "cometh", and when I say "go", you "goeth".'[124] Williams did not seem to be unduly bothered by the fact that there is no 'legal opposition' in Parliament, but he did feel it neces-

123 The opposition denies this and insists that the election was *the* issue and that the PNM campaigned heavily on it using all the administrative and financial resources of the state. For a good reply to the PNM's assertion that its performance at the polls compared favourably with that of other minority regimes that were nevertheless conceded legitimacy, see 'Damned Lies and Statistics', *Moko*, June 11, 1971.

124 See *Newsweek*, June 7, 1971, p. 11, and *Express*, June 28, 1971.

sary to promise that democratic procedures would be scrupulously respected, and that there would be dialogue with the nation on all major issues. As the Government declared in its Throne speech:

In the face of the reality of the political alignment in Parliament, [this] Government will adopt four types of measures to ensure that alternative views are heard and respected. It will seek to elicit the widest possible comment on its proposed legislation before the legislation is passed. Government proposals will be circulated as widely as possible, and will allow for the longest possible period of consultation with the people without interfering with the efficiency of government. ...

Wherever possible, legislation will first be introduced into the Senate, to the extent that this can be done constitutionally, and without departing too radically from the established Parliamentary tradition of the paramountcy of the elected Chamber. [This] Government will further enlist the assistance of the Senate in respect of Joint Committees of both Houses of Parliament. The first such Committee, to be immediately appointed, will consider the question of the reduction of the voting age and the age of the legal majority.

To ensure the strictest possible control over Government expenditures by Parliament, [the] Government will immediately make provision for the appointment of a Member from the Senate to head the Public Accounts Committee. This will follow the precedent established in the Parliament of 1961 when two Senators, one of whom became Chairman, were appointed to the Public Accounts Committee.[125]

But despite Williams' bland assertion that there was no political or constitutional crisis and that the PNM had won the election, there is a large body of opinion in the country which feels that the PNM is neither a legal nor legitimate government. The *Express* spoke for many when it declared: 'The results of the 1971 General Elections [do] not amount to a victory for the Government. The unprecedented winning by the PNM of all the seats in Parliament simply [makes] obvious the serious crisis which the country has been staring in the eye for a long time now.'[126] The UNIP (Millette faction) wrote in its official organ, *Moko*: 'There is no government existing in Trinidad and Tobago. There is no Prime Minister; there are no ministers ... no cabinet ... no parliament. In fact there is nothing. ... Any attempt to impose a PNM government will be an attempt to impose an illegal government in this country. The PNM must be toppled. The people have made an ass of the PNM. The PNM cannot now be permitted to make an ass of the people.'[127]

Robinson, who lost a great deal of credibility during and after the campaign, also claimed that the PNM had no moral authority or mandate to govern, and warned that anyone who accepted a position in the régime should

---

125 TG, June 19, 1971.   126 *Express*, May 26, 1971.   127 *Ibid.*, May 28, 1971.

expect no respect from the country. 'To accept a senatorship would be to sell the country for a mess of pottage. Let us see how the privileged section of the community will behave.'[128] He further noted that few people of any political significance contested the election.

Robinson argued that a situation in which a party that had the support of only 28 per cent of the electorate had won all the seats was 'subversive' of the constitution. He accused the 'grave-yard' government of the PNM of using illegal devices to get around the 1962 constitution which provided for a leader of the opposition who had the responsibility for nominating four persons to the Senate. The reference here is to Williams' gauche and unsuccessful attempt to get the leader of the opposition in the former parliament to nominate four senators on the pretext that until the new parliament met he still held that post![129]

Robinson criticized the Governor General for asking the PNM to form the government, and felt that the latter should have declared a state of emergency and appoint an interim government which would arrange for electoral reform including voting by ballot box, and the proper conduct of elections within a month.[130] This proposal was clearly unrealistic, and received support from no other group.

The PNM ridiculed Robinson's proposals, especially the question of having the Governor General declare a state of emergency. As Williams told the PNM, 'Imagine last year this same man opposed the creation of the State of Emergency and now he wants the Governor General to declare a State of Emergency.'[131] Williams also declared that he could not be expected to resign because the opposition did not contest the election. 'We got our vote. What do you want us to do? Stop a race because one horse did not go?' The fact that there was no opposition in Parliament was not new, Williams stressed, since 'for 18 months they [the DLP] said nothing and on occasions walked out to leave us to carry on.'[132]

Despite opposition, Williams named his cabinet and advised the Governor General to name thirteen party and seven independent senators whose names were proposed by some of the major corporate bodies in the society. The four opposition senatorships were simply left vacant, a device that in no way

128 TG, June 6, 1971. It is worth noting that the Roman Catholic Church declined the invitation to nominate a Senator. The Archbishop has been busily trying to change the image of the Church. He had even agreed to march with the Black Power militants but changed his mind in the face of strong opposition.

129 Jamadar told the Governor General that it would be unconstitutional, illegal, immoral, unethical, and wrong in every possible way for him to appoint senators. TG, June 2, 1971.

130 *Ibid.*, June 6, 1971.   131 *Express,* May 31, 1971.   132 *Ibid.*

violated the letter of the constitution which in section 39(2) states that: 'Each House may act notwithstanding any vacancy in its membership (including any vacancy not filled when the House first meets after the commencement of this Constitution or after any dissolution of Parliament) and the presence or participation of any person not entitled to be present at or to participate in the proceedings of the House shall not invalidate those proceedings.'[133]

Even though Parliament was legally constituted, the spirit of the constitution and its conventions which require consultation between the prime minister and the leader of the opposition was not fulfilled. But constitutions cannot provide for every political 'accident', and it is not clear what opposition voices would have said if a party or a coalition with great moral and popular authority had emerged and had won all the seats. The legal problem would have been the same even though the moral circumstances would have been different. There is really no way to avoid the conclusion that the crisis in Trinidad and Tobago in 1971 was political rather than constitutional and that the opposition was guilty, perhaps deliberately, of formalism. The real opposition to the PNM after 1962 had always been outside of Parliament – the trade unions, the newspapers, elements in the university community, and in the Chamber of Commerce – and this is where it will continue to be until the PNM is removed by constitutional or revolutionary methods.

Despite Williams' political bravado, he conceded the strength of the opposition's campaign by appointing an independent high-powered commission to hear testimony and prepare a draft for a new constitution.[134] The radical opposition has, however, questioned the legitimacy of a constitutional commission appointed by the PNM. As *Tapia* asserted,

The government's decision to establish a constitutional commission ... represents the height of executive impertinence. The decision could not be more strictly in the logic of Crown colony government. It maintains the tradition of government from above and therefore misses the whole point of the February Revolution. ... If Williams had called a constitutional commission ... between October 1968 and April 1970 ... it would have been quite feasible for the Commission to initiate meaningful reforms acceptable to the entire population. Now it is too late because

---

133 The Trinidad and Tobago Independence Act, Port of Spain, 1962 (10 and 11 Elizabeth 2c 54), page 25–6.
134 The Commission is chaired by the former Chief Justice, Sir Hugh Wooding. The Vice-Chairman is Mr P.T. Georges, former Chief Justice of Tanzania, now a member of the Appeal Court of Trinidad and Tobago. Other members are Mr Mitra Sinanan, Mr Hamilton Maurice, Mr Gaston Benjamin, Mr Solomon Lutchman, Mr Reginald Dumas, Dr Anthony Maingot, Mr Michael de Labastide, and Dr Selwyn Ryan.

it is the *bona-fides* of the executive which is the issue of the day ... If there is to be a constitutional commission, only a constituent assembly or some kind of citizens' conference can have the right to appoint it.[135]

The UNIP said more or less the same thing:

The Party repudiates the establishment of the constitutional commission to write a new constitution for Trinidad and Tobago. With very few exceptions the persons chosen have no qualification except a legal and some other spurious or assumed association with the pulse of the country and its people. ... A body of men such as that now established has no hope of providing a new constitution worthy of the name for this country at this point in its history, and they are foolish even to think of trying.[136]

The UNIP, however, expressed sharp disagreement with *Tapia*'s emphasis on the constituent assembly. According to Millette, 'A constituent assembly has never been on any real politician's agenda.'[137] Millette accused Best and his colleagues of running away from the crisis and of inadvertently playing into the hands of the PNM: 'By calling the constituent assembly, which is what Williams has done by establishing the constitutional commission, Williams has virtually torpedoed Tapia ... The constituent assembly is important to [Tapia]. But it is not important to the people ... at this stage ... To topple Williams remains the number one priority.'[138]

But majority opinion appeared willing to accept Williams' guarantee of an independent commission as an acceptable compromise to Tapia's proposal for a constituent assembly of citizens, provided that the PNM did not insist on having the final say. The DLP agreed to co-operate, and both leading daily newspapers endorsed the idea. As the *Express* noted:

The commission is to 'operate in complete independence of the government and the Parliament, except insofar as finances and staff'. And it is the commission which will determine its own procedures for consultation with organizations and individuals wishing to express their views. The commission, in short, can operate as a kind of constituent assembly if it chooses.

135 *Tapia*, June 27, 1971. In its statement on the throne speech, (*Express*, June 28, 1971) the Tapia Group noted that its stand was not based on a lack of trust in the *bona fides* of the commission: 'We are not totally happy with that commission, it is true, even though there are men on it who certainly reflect the temper and spirit of Tapia and the New World Movement.' The Democratic Action Congress, the new name of the ACDC, has described the appointment of the Constitutional Commission as a 'trap' and vows to bring down the 'unconstitutional' regime by April 1972 using whatever sanctions are available. *Express*, Oct. 4, 1971.

136 *Moko*, June 25, 1971.   137 *Ibid.*   138 *Ibid.*

Nothing has been said, of course, of the government having the final say in the commission's recommendations. It is here that the crunch may come, as commissions in the past have discovered. But for the moment let us be optimistic. Let us see how the commission decides to carry out its work and let us not suffer anxieties about its success.[139]

Tapia's notion of a citizen's conference calling a constituent assembly was considered vague and unrealistic, and it was widely conceded that the government had to be allowed to exercise the initiative provided it did not insist on being the final authority on what was acceptable. As a party it is, however, free to urge its views on the commission. It is worth noting that the government would have gone a long way towards disarming its critics if it had made it clear from the beginning that it did not intend to act unilaterally on the draft once the commission completed its work. It might be recalled that during the 1962 constitutional debate, the PNM had to be forced by public outcry to call a constitutional conference. That sort of crisis must be avoided if the new constitution is to have any legitimacy amongst a broad cross-section of the population.

A NOTE ON THE OPPOSITION

If it could be argued that the PNM and Williams have lost the 'mandate of heaven', it is clear that the opposition has failed to win it. Although Best, Millette, the NJAC, and others in the URO have articulated a number of brilliant ideas, many of them have not been carefully thought out or related to the contemporary realities of Trinidadian society. It was unreasonable of the opposition to expect Williams to resign after the election when it was quite clear to everyone in the country, including Williams' strongest critics, that the alternatives offered by the opposition were fragmentation and political irresponsibility. The country was looking for an alternative to Williams and the opposition allowed itself to be misled into believing that the best strategy for defeating Williams was to boycott the election.

The difficulty with the leaders of opposition movements is that they all want to be the new king. Each believes he is brighter than the other, and no one is willing to defer in the interest of unity. Best and Tapia talked about 'new politics' and refused alliances just as the PNM did at the inception of its career. But the PNM learned that politics involve compromise and alliances and managed to outwit all its rivals. During the last few years the electorate

139 June 19, 1971.

has been treated to a parade of new parties all of which had the same goal – overthrowing Williams. But none could muster much popular following simply because they lacked organizational credibility. There were splits in the New World Group, in the UNIP, in the DLP, in the ACDC-DLP, in the NJAC, and in URO, and the opposition deluded itself when it assumed that those who stayed away from the polls would support them in a new election. As Syl Lowhar of the Tapia Group rightly noted, 'A.N.R. Robinson and the ACDC-DLP combined neither appreciate the dynamics of politics nor the nature of the constitutional crisis. ... They see a crack in the wall ... and assume that those who abstained from voting would vote for them in an election. But they have not got the message. For they too would have been rejected.'[140]

When it was pointed out that Tapia itself did not have much of a popular following, Lowhar noted that Tapia will grow 'as the biblical mustard seed'. After all, 'Christ started with twelve in his crusade.'[141] The opposition was, of course, on firm ground when it tried, as a political strategy, to embarrass the PNM by complaining of rigged elections and voting machines. But if the machines were indeed rigged, one wonders why they were not programmed to increase the poll or to provide a semblance of an opposition. Maraj had worked closely with the PNM, and the government would have been happy to have him as leader of the opposition. It is also strange that the opposition used the figures released by the much criticised electoral commission without any reservations to prove that it 'won' the election. Although many Trinidadians believe that the machines were rigged, there is no available evidence to prove that machine-rigging rather than race has been the critical variable that explains the pattern of *electoral* politics in Trinidad and Tobago. The mechanical performance of the machines has, however, been extremely unsatisfactory, and a majority of voters lack confidence in them.

The opposition is feverishly trying to provoke a cataclysmic confrontation with the PNM. It insists that the country's main problem is Williams who must be bridled. Trade-union militancy is an important part of the strategy of action, and the aim is to force the Government to a point where it would have to act repressively and further undermine its legitimacy. The government also appears to be willing to confront the unions and the radicals and is being heavily backed by the business community and a large section of the middle class. There is a widespread feeling of unease in Trinidad and a general assumption that another social upheaval is not far off. Radicals openly shouted that the PNM would be toppled before 1971 was out, though not much was done to organize a serious movement that could take over without

140 TG, June 9, 1971.   141 *Ibid.*

confusion.[142] Indeed, it is this fear of confusion and extremism that leads many, even the business community, to remain with the PNM when they would be happier with an alternative. The PNM has cleverly exploited the weaknesses of the opposition, and is quite convinced that the worst is over and that it can hold onto power for another term if not longer.

The Prime Minister, however, appears to have recognized that he and the 'class of 1956' must give way to younger élites. As he explained when announcing the composition of the new government, 'If ... the Government appears to be unduly large, ... put the cost down to expenditure on training.'[143] Williams appointed a cabinet with five new faces and unburdened himself of a great deal of his vast ministerial responsibilities. He declared that he would concern himself with national awards and public holidays, constitutional matters, information, public relations, training, supervision, co-ordination, and nation-building. This is still a large portfolio, but considerably smaller than that held previously. It is also worth noting that there are few men in the new cabinet powerful and independent enough to stand up to Williams who is, in any event, congenitally incapable of any real decentralization of power.

The best that can be hoped is that Williams will phase himself out of Trinidad politics before he is forced out rudely, as were Butler, Solomon, Gomes, Maraj, and others. A former political colleague of his, Dennis Mahabir, in fact urged this course upon him. As Mahabir wrote: 'The explosive years arrived. The gap between Eric Williams and the country is not a cliché. Our National heroes are too few. Those we have we do not cherish. Let us then hope that the country will have the co-operation of Eric Williams and that he will go out with grace and dignity. Let him lay down his troubled crown now and write some more history. The nation will forgive him for his blunders of recent years, his ambivalence and failures. But it will remember him for his courage in 1956. And in the years to come people may even worship his memory as a national hero.'[144]

At the fifteenth annual convention of PNM in September 1971, Williams, who was then sixty years old, hinted that he was thinking of retiring soon. 'The time approaches,' he said, 'when, in the words of your popular song, like a bridge over troubled waters, I will lay me down.'[145] Stung by the behaviour of

---

142 There was even talk of forming a guerrilla movement, and frequent suggestions that it is legitimate to use illegal means to overthrow an illegal government. Cf. *Moko*, May 28, and June 11, 1971. Millette, however, admitted that the opposition was now lethargic and unable to capitalize on its gains during the election. This might have been due in part to fear of police action, but it might also have been due to fear of the social consequences of revolutionary action.

143 *Express*, May 28, 1971.   144 *Ibid.*, May 19, 1970.

145 *Ibid.*, Sept. 25, 1971.

his 'traitorous deputy' (A.N.R. Robinson), Williams appointed three deputy political leaders without indicating which of the three, if any, was being groomed as his successor.[146] Many of Williams' critics were sceptical about his announced intention which they viewed as a clever strategy to take the steam out of the campaign against him. It was also claimed that by appointing a *troika* deputy leadership, he was generating the sort of party intrigue that would provide him with the excuse to hang onto office. One can, however, be more charitable and argue that Williams wants to phase himself out of active politics before the next election, provided there is evidence that the Party could agree on a successor who would hold it together and lead it to victory. The radical opposition is, however, determined to destroy both Williams and the PNM, and should they succeed in provoking another major confrontation without having the resources to overthrow the regime, one could be certain that Williams will be on the political scene for several more years to come, perhaps as the first President of the Republic of Trinidad and Tobago!

The enterprise of decolonization, begun so hopefully in 1955, has now reached a major impasse. Government and opposition now accuse each other of ruling or attempting to rule by the gun and by declarations of states of emergency. The PNM believes that there exists in Trinidad 'an extremist, anarchist element dedicated to murder, mayhem, kidnaps and violent revolution'.[147] The opposition on the other hand claims that guns, force, and official violence have become the order of the day and that the corrupt holy alliance which brutalizes the people – the civil service, the Church, the police, and the white power structure – must be completely destroyed before a new edifice can be built. One can only hope that some way will be found to break through the present impasse without having the community destroy itself in the process.

146 The three deputies were Mr Kamaluddin Mohammed, Mr Errol Mahabir, and Mr George Chambers. They were made responsible for legislative, party matters, and policy matters respectively. Of the three, Mohammed is senior, having been with the Party from the very beginning. Tough, durable and resourceful, Mohammed however has many detractors who believe that he has used his office to amass a huge fortune. Many Negroes will also oppose him and Mr Mahabir on racial grounds. It is possible that the man most likely to succeed Williams is the present Attorney General, Karl Hudson-Phillips who for some reason was not named as a deputy. Hudson-Phillips is a strong advocate of law and order and provokes more antagonism within the opposition than Williams himself. He might be the best person to hold the PNM together, but may well be disastrous for the country.
147 *Express*, Sept. 27, 1971.

26
Conclusions

The main aim of this study has been to describe the political and constitutional evolution of Trinidad and Tobago and to identify and analyse the factors which have impeded the development of a disciplined and united nationalist movement with a socially relevant development programme. The obstacles which the early nationalist movement had to overcome were numerous. Among them were the small size of the territory and the limited nature of its physical resources, which made any confident belief in its economic viability difficult. Extensive metropolitan economic, cultural, and ideological penetration also resulted in the creation of an élite that was extremely British and dependent in its orientation and unwilling to sever the links of Empire. Of importance too was the existence of a strategically dominant European community which successfully monopolized the political and economic system, using constitutional and other time-tested devices, and a large number of partially mobilized and unassimilated Indians, who made important contributions to the economic development of the area, but who played a crucial role in slowing down its rate of constitutional advancement. Together with loyalist Europeans and a large number of status-minded mixed middle-class elements, they formed one of the main stumbling blocks to the struggle of the black working class for political reform. The attitude of the Indian was largely one of fear of domination by an assimilationist creole majority, a fear that was by no means unjustified. The creole majority, committed as it was to a universalistic majoritarian ideology, neglected to recognize and gratify the special and legitimate needs of the Indian minority.

Attention has also been drawn to the efforts of Captain Arthur Cipriani, Adrian Cola Rienzi, and Tubal Uriah Butler to forge a Negro-Indian coalition based on class rather than on racial issues, and to the reasons for their failure. 'Butlerism' was one of the fundamental obstacles to unity among left-wing forces in the colony. Butler was also partly responsible for driving middle-class elements into the conservative coalition, and it may be that, had he been a more competent leader gifted in organization, the nationalist movement might have crystallized a decade earlier. One conclusion of this study is that the major cause for the frustrations of the nationalist movement was not specifically the Crown colony constitution or metropolitan misrule and division of the races, as had been argued by Dr Williams and other anti-colonialist radicals. The latter causes were of course important, but more of the blame must be borne by Trinidadians themselves, especially in the years after the visit of Lord Moyne in 1938–9.

Dr Williams, whose contributions to the historiography of the Caribbean has been seminal, passionately believes that metropolitan exploitation is mainly responsible for the backwardness of the Caribbean. In his 'Introduction' to *History of the People of Trinidad and Tobago* he states:

This book tells the story of the travails and tribulations of a British Colony ...
It is the story of the misrule of metropolitan bureaucracy and the indifference of metropolitan scholarship. Trinidad and Tobago attracted metropolitan attention only in periods of riot and disorder (1903 and 1937), only when the discovery of oil made it an object of interest to the British Navy and British capitalism, only when its invaluable natural harbour, Chaguaramas, made it a useful pawn to be traded by Britain against American aid in the Second World War.
These developments apart, Trinidad and Tobago was merely a crown colony, forgotten and forlorn.[1]

Backwardness and disunity were due to 'the deliberate metropolitan policy ... [of excluding] the West Indies from the metropolitan political system and ideas', and to the ingrained tendency of European and American bureaucrats to view the Caribbean islands 'as nothing more than pawns on the international chessboard on which empires contested for supremacy'. Metropolitan interests found intellectual justification in British universities, which in turn produced the 'expatriate bureaucrats who maintained the Empire overseas'.[2]

One may be fully sympathetic to Williams' passionate hostility to colonialism in all its masquerades, but the historian has a responsibility to the past as well as to the future which he is trying to influence. He should try to prevent the poison in his system from interfering with his objectivity.[3] Misrule, indif-

---

1 New York, 1964, p. vii.
2 *The Approach of Independence*, Port of Spain, 1960, pp. 2–4.
3 Williams notes that writing West Indian history is not a mere hobby. It also helps to

ference, racism, economic distortion, and exploitation there certainly were, and British colonial reports document this very well. But the fundamental question to be answered is whether or not this was the only face of British colonialism. If British colonialism was merely harsh and malevolent, as Williams suggests, why then did the English-speaking Caribbean never produce a passionate nationalist movement similar to that of India? Williams is not unmindful of the importance of this question, as the following statement indicates:

Four and a half centuries of metropolitan control would weigh like an alp, in the political sense, on the head of any country. They weighed equally, however, on Ireland, so that the time factor must not be exaggerated. But it must not be minimized. The other colonial areas of the world have been somewhat more fortunate than the West Indies. One hundred years ... of British hegemony in the Gold Coast, sixty years of British control of Nigeria, a century and a quarter of French rule in Algeria, made it impossible for imperialist attitudes to harden and crystallize to a similar extent as in the West Indies. From another angle, the vast size of India or Indonesia reduced metropolitan overlordship to a control at the top hardly touching directly or visible to the millions of peasants at the bottom; the West Indies, by contrast, are so small that colonialism was something you touched, saw, heard and felt every day everywhere. All these other victims of imperialism have had decisive advantages over the West Indies. They had a language of their own, a culture of their own, a religion of their own, a philosophy of their own as in India, a family structure of their own as in Ghana, a sense of values of their own which they could oppose to Western Imperialism. We in the West Indies have nothing of our own – a few artifacts and place names are all that remain of the aboriginal civilization. We are a people transplanted into slavery to a transplanted crop, and we have remained political satellites of the metropolitan economy whose economic interests we were intended to serve. We have become in the Martiniquan saying 'peau noir, masque blanc', a black skin, a white mask, a European culture in an Afro-Asian environment. ... That is our history. That is our heritage. That is our dilemma.[4]

This is a more plausible explanation for the lack of national fervour in the English-speaking Caribbean, but it does not necessarily suggest a harsh colonial experience nor that of a people excluded from the metropolitan system of ideas. The West Indies, as Williams agrees, is an immigrant society, the creation of colonialism. If that colonialism was not always enlightened, if its

'get out of his system some of the poison which is perhaps unnecessarily imbibed in political activity in countries which have learned only too well the lessons of colonialism.' *History*, p. x.

4   *The Approach of Independence*, pp. 4–5.

main characteristics were negligence and racial exclusivism, the explanation is not at all hard to find. The attitude which the metropolitan ruling class had to colonials was not fundamentally different from that which it had to its own proletariat up to the end of the Second World War, though race did add a unique dimension. One could not reasonably expect welfare colonialism to antedate welfare nationalism. It is rather puzzling to find hard-headed intellectuals talking imperialist propaganda about 'trusteeship responsibility' more seriously than it was ever intended. It is also irritating to find them complaining at one and the same time that too little and too much was done in the name of Empire. As a political strategy designed to sharpen national consciousness, a crude anti-colonialist interpretation of West Indian history is a useful approach. But it would not do for serious scholarship.

It is true that British political institutions were withheld from Trinidad and Tobago when they were being demanded, but there is good reason to believe that in the early nineteenth century the Crown was genuinely reluctant to hand over control because of the feeling that blacks would be savagely exploited by white settlers.[5] The fact that expatriate officials were not always solicitous of the interests of the general population does not necessarily mean that the latter would have been better off without their presence. The expatriate bureaucrats were far more liberal and humane than white settlers, and many well-meaning metropolitan initiatives were frustrated by the political representatives of the latter. It is for this reason that the main thrust of the nationalist movement was directed at the local ruling class and not the Colonial Office. Butler and Cipriani, for example, always remained loyal to the Crown and were believers in British justice.

It is possible, of course, to blame the Colonial Office for its abdication of responsibility. The Colonial Secretary was the final arbiter in the colonial equation. But as Hewan Craig notes, until the Second World War the Colonial Office 'was not ideologically or technically equipped to combat the more subtle forms of exploitation which ... occur in a modern economy'.[6] To some extent the explosions of the 1930s generated new concern about the forgotten trusteeship responsibility:

The need for this new interpretation of the role of the imperial government had no doubt existed for some time before the disturbances. ... It lay, as it were, in the womb of the future and could not perhaps have been brought forth without the travail of the disturbances. Whatever blame may attach to the imperial government for the conditions which gave rise to the disturbances, it was not slow to grasp their

5   The Colonial Office agreed with Williams that 'popular franchises in the hands of slave-owners were the worst instruments of tyranny ever forged for the oppression of mankind.' Williams, *The Negro in the Caribbean*, Washington, DC, 1942, p. 15.
6   *The Legislative Council of Trinidad and Tobago*, London, 1951, p. 138.

implications and to adapt its policy to meet the changed circumstances of West Indian society which they revealed.[7]

It could be argued that if Britain had conceded a fuller measure of self-government when it was being demanded in the years just before and following the Second World War, Trinidad and Tobago would be further along the road towards developing a more viable economy and a more mature social system. This may be so, though from what is known about the political élite of the time, scepticism is justifiable.[8] In any event, the Colonial Office was less responsible for this delay than were the divisions of Trinidadian society. Very often the Colonial Office proposed more liberal constitutional arrangements than did the local committees which were appointed to draft them. As Williams himself notes, 'It was not necessary for [Britain] to divide the West Indian territories in order to rule. The West Indian territories were divided, and so Britain ruled easily.'[9]

It is worth observing that some West Indian scholars disagree with the view that colonial rule in the West Indies was harsh.[10] Whereas Williams argues that 'the national character ... of the people of Trinidad and Tobago

7 *Ibid.*, p. 141. See also B.C. Roberts, *Labour in the Tropical Territories of the Commonwealth*, Durham, NC, 1964, pp. 182 ff.

8 We have argued that the 1950–6 regime was not as bankrupt as Williams argued in 1956, and that there is much more continuity between it and the 1956–66 period than PNM propaganda would have one believe. This is especially true in the economic sector, as will be indicated below.

9 'Reflections on the Caribbean Economic Community', *Nation*, Oct. 15, 1965. Williams agrees that minority fears were a main obstacle to constitutional advance, but blames colonialism for this. 'The last apology or excuse for colonization will have been removed when *Caribbean democracy can prove that minority rights are quite safe in its hands,* and that the imperialist policy of divide and rule, of holding the balance between conflicting interests, was the root cause of racial tension, which only a nationalist movement transcending race can contain and ultimately eliminate.' 'Race Relations in a Caribbean Society', in *Caribbean Studies: A Symposium*, Vera Rubin (ed.), Kingston, Jamaica, 1957, p. 60 (italics supplied).

10 This argument is not to be taken to mean that colonialism in the West Indies was never harsh or brutal. What is being argued here is that on the whole it was not. By selecting certain specific historical incidents where British officials blundered badly, it is possible to give a totally false picture of the British in the West Indies. See Williams, *British Historians and the West Indies*, London, 1965, for an example of this approach. For a critique of Williams' approach to British colonialism cf. Gordon Lewis, 'British Colonialism in the West Indies: The Colonial Legacy', *Caribbean Studies*, vol. 7, no. 1, April 1967. Lewis writes (p. 21), 'Williams ... considerably underestimates the contribution, however minor, of the best British spirit to West Indian life. ... The British, in all conscience, were colonialists. But it is at once historically inaccurate and psychologically unconvincing to write about them as if they were devils in human form.'

[was in part] developed ... by [the] harsh pressures, political, economic and social, to which they have been subjected by metropolitan domination', H.W. Springer of Barbados sees the reverse as being true. Springer argues that once Britain 'sensed the direction of the winds of change in the Caribbean, it gave its ready co-operation to the nationalist movement'.[11] It was for this reason that

West Indian nationalism was taken for granted ... and [was] rarely felt or pursued with passion ... never took on the quality of a crusade. ... Rabid nationalism arises in response to long felt and long resented oppression by an alien power, or in situations where there is legal discrimination based on racial or cultural differences, where the persistent occurrence of affronts to personal dignity ... engendered strong feelings of corporate resentment against the dominant power. This is not the situation in the West Indies where, during the century and a quarter since the abolition of slavery, equality before the law has been effectively provided for all, and where such expressions of prejudice as do occur are attributed not to external but to local origins. Nor does there exist the motive of defending or promoting an indigenous culture in the face of the encroachment of an alien one. There is in fact no indigenous culture. ... Far from being alien, the metropolitan culture was there first, and was the only culture recognized and fostered. ... Inevitably the Colonial Office was included among the targets for attack by the agitators for constitutional reform, since the British government was the ultimate source of power, and it was of course the one target that was common to them all. If the Colonial Office had shown intransigence in the face of local demands, strong and passionate feelings would certainly have been aroused against it. But it did not. On the contrary, the Crown was traditionally regarded as the protector of the weak, especially since the days of Queen Victoria, and the Colonial Office had come to be generally regarded as more liberal in its attitude to the welfare and dignity of the common people than those in power locally. Strong feelings were therefore reserved for the immediate targets for attack – the local government and legislatures, and the interest groups they represented. In any case Britain soon appeared in the role of counsellor and friend, or perhaps 'uncle' is the appropriate word.
In this rarefied atmosphere of benevolent co-operation, the flame of West Indian nationalism was bound to flicker and burn low. ... There was no cause to keep [it] fresh, and it quietly withered.[12]

Nationalism in the West Indies was driven more by hostility to the racial exclusivism of the settler community than it was by anti-imperialism, and it was

11   *Reflections on the Failure of the First West Indian Federation*, Cambridge, Mass., 1962, pp. 39–40.
12   *Ibid.*

for this reason that Indians in Trinidad were never ardent 'nationalists'. They were much more distrustful of the Negro than they were of creole whites and the Colonial Office, which the majority of them viewed as a form of political insurance. The anti-imperialist theme only became dominant in West Indian politics when metropolitan bungling on Chaguaramas provided Williams with an opening which he used to advantage to earn his place among the ranks of the heroes of the anti-colonialist movement. And it was reluctance to forfeit metropolitan 'benevolence' that led other West Indian public figures to stay on the sidelines or to oppose the strategy of the PNM.

Williams is in part correct when he blames the 'picaroon' individualism and the status-climbing that is characteristic of Trinidad society on the colonial political and social system. But two qualifications need to be made. In an economy of scarcity that is at the same time widely open to the influence of 'bourgeois' metropolitan life, such characteristics are bound to be exaggerated. As Williams himself noted, 'It is the economy that strangles the West Indies and not the flag that floats over it.'[13] Moreover, it can be argued that it was the benevolence of colonial rule that was to some extent responsible for the lack of cohesiveness in Trinidadian society. National consciousness and cohesiveness might have been more fully developed if it had had an opportunity to mould itself in the white heat of a crusade against a harsh colonial dictatorship.

Another basic conclusion that has emerged from this study is that colonial attitudes and structures have remained firmly entrenched even though a nationalist government has been in power for fifteen years. These values and patterns of behaviour continue to bedevil the administrative system, influence educational and economic policy, and circumscribe achievement in the area of race relations. Indeed, what Governor Harris said following the emancipation of the slaves – a race has been freed, but a society has yet to be formed – still remains true of contemporary Trinidad.

A new generation of radicals has emerged to challenge their elders and radical precursors. They are unwilling to accept the view that decolonization in the Caribbean has run its course and are urgently probing new frontiers in their quest for a society that is socially equal and authentic. They are uneasy about the continued domination of sugar and oil, the pervasiveness of foreign economic power, the continued social entrenchment of the white and near-white minority, and the exclusion of the majority of the black population from the returns on the economic programmes of the past two decades. While it is not denied that some blacks have done well, the feeling is that too many are unemployed, underemployed, and underpaid.

The new movement has expressed itself in terms of Black Power, with a

13   *The Negro in the Carribean*, p. 45.

strong anti-white bias and a marked contempt for the 'Afro-Saxons' now in power, and for the obsequious postures that they have taken in their dealings with the former colonial power and the forces of neo-colonialism. As Lloyd Best puts it:

The crisis has arisen because of the kind of contribution [the PNM has made]. They have raised levels of material welfare for the Negro as for everybody else; yes, they have wrought all manner of changes across the face of the land. But the one thing that the PNM has not done is to redress the historical balance and to give the Negro a sense of being master in the castle of his skin.

In the final analysis, the PNM did not know how to use the political control which it won in 1956 and we must see that this failure falls strictly in the logic of the Afro-Saxon strategy which we adopted in the nineteenth century. Accustomed to advancing by denying our own worth, we have found it easier to rely on outside help in our quest for change. We have found it easier to rely on a Doctor than to take up our own beds and walk.

Instead of dealing with sugar, petroleum and the banks, instead of breaking the metropolitan stranglehold on the economy which had kept the West Indian people in chains from the start, Williams and the PNM adopted the Lewis prescription of industrialization by invitation. We hoped for economic transformation by borrowing capital, by borrowing management, by borrowing that, and by kowtowing before every manner of alien expert we could find.

We failed to see that this kind of dependence in our territorial context amounted to nothing but obsequiousness, servility, and in the last resort, to a shattering vote of no-confidence in the population of Trinidad and Tobago.[14]

It is not difficult to discern that, though their language and style are different, the contemporary radicals are saying much the same thing that Williams and his colleagues were saying in 1955-6. The charge against Williams is that he betrayed the blacks and the dispossessed and that he had feet of clay; and among the young and alienated there is a strong feeling, indeed a strident demand, that he must move on into history with Alfred Richards, Arthur Cipriani, Uriah Butler, Patrick Solomon, Adrian Rienzi, and others. Even some who still think kindly of Williams have been urging him to retire with dignity rather than be humiliated as were Butler and Cipriani. Dennis Mahabir suggests that the alternative is 'a solitary figure standing on the rocks of West Indian politics gazing over the Caribbean Sea and the setting sun. Behind him – the far off murmur of the Woodford Square crowd where he was once the hero and of which he claimed to be the boss – lost to him forever.'[15]

14 *Black Power and National Reconstruction*, Port of Spain, 1970, p. 4.
15 *Express*, April 2, 1970.

Though it is clear that the PNM is at the end of its 'legitimate' reign, it must be admitted that the Party has in a way been a victim of some of its successes. It was the PNM which stimulated the political consciousness of the people and which laid down the infrastructure upon which successor élites are hoping to build. No one could deny that the PNM has had a significant impact on the political life of Trinidad and Tobago and that it has brought the community a long way from its condition in 1956. Generally speaking, it has been a force for progress, given the material with which it had to work and the legacies of the plantation. Nation-building is a long and arduous process, and the young may be guilty of concentrating on the pathologies of the community rather than on features which represent health.

On the credit side there is much to cite: the introduction and maintenance of disciplined party government, the widespread prevalence of achievement and instrumental values, the phenomenal extension of facilities for technical communication, the stimulation of the political consciousness of a sizable stratum of the population, the creation of a political system that was until recently stable and coherent, with the capacity to innovate without disintegration despite continuing gaps in the framework of social communication. Also worthy of note is the significant widening of opportunities in primary and secondary education for persons of all social and racial origins (93 per cent of the population is literate) and the considerable measure of occupational re-stratification that has taken place. Moderate success has also been achieved in improving the system's capacity to mobilize and allocate resources for development goals. Indeed, notwithstanding the claims that Trinidad is not yet 'structurally transformed' and that it is a misdeveloped 'enclave' or 'dual' society (what society is not?) highly dependent on import-export relationships rather than on interrelated domestic transactions, or the claim that the high standards achieved in social overhead investments are artificial and ephemeral, the fact remains that, comparatively speaking, Trinidad is not a typical under-developed country.[16] As Dr Werner Gatz observed in a report prepared for the German government, 'The already achieved standards of the educational system, of the public utilities and of the social services ... must be considered truly remarkable. There can be no justification for continuing to grant Trinidad the status of an underdeveloped country. Trinidad is an emergent country in the best sense of the word.'[17]

Given the limits of traditional democratic politics, the size and location of

---

16   For a good analysis of Trinidad's 'underdevelopment' see William Demas, *The Economics of Development in Small Countries*, Montreal, 1965, *passim*.

17   *Economic Conditions and Development Potentials in Trinidad and Tobago*, Port of Spain, 1962, pp. 6, 18.

the country, the nature of its resource base, and the sociological origins of the PNM leadership, the Party has perhaps succeeded as well as anyone could realistically expect. What Trinidad needs now is a new kind of decentralized and participatory political movement that can harness the frustrations of the people and direct them into constructive social and economic action, concerned not merely with fulfilling the statistical demands for economic growth but with the needs of the bottom levels of the society, the mass of dispossessed Indians and blacks. In short, what is now needed is a movement that can find new ways to implement the People's Charter which was launched with such optimism and hope in 1956.

Index